NW15763   SAAPKB £23·99·

KU-712-103

WITHDRAWN

Term time opening hou

READINGS IN COGNITIVE PSYCHOLOGY

N 0113408 6

READINGS IN
COGNITIVE PSYCHOLOGY

Robert J. Sternberg
Yale University

Richard K. Wagner
Florida State University

Editors

NEWMAN COLLEGE
BARTLEY GREEN
BIRMINGHAM B32 3NT

CLASS 153.4
BARCODE 0134086
AUTHOR REA

WADSWORTH

THOMSON LEARNING

Australia • Canada • Mexico • Singapore • Spain • United Kingdom • United States

Publisher	Earl McPeek
Executive Editor	Carol Wada
Associate Acquisitions Editor	Lisa D. Hensley
Product Manager	Kathleen Sharp
Developmental Editor	Susan Petty
Project Editor	Louise Slominsky
Production Manager	Andrea A. Johnson
Art Director	David A. Day

Cover image: "Black/White Faces Sectioned" copyright © Wiktor Sadowski/Stock Illustration Source, Inc.

ISBN: 0-15-504105-3
Library of Congress Catalog Card Number: 98-72573

COPYRIGHT © 1999 Wadsworth,
a division of Thomson Learning, Inc.
Thomson Learning ™ is a trademark
used herein under license.

ALL RIGHTS RESERVED. No part of this work covered by the
copyright hereon may be reproduced or used in any form or by any
means — graphic, electronic, or mechanical, including photocopying,
recording, taping, Web distribution, or information storage or retrieval
systems — without the written permission of the publisher.

Wadsworth Group/Thomson Learning
10 Davis Drive
Belmont CA 94002-3098
USA

For information about our products, contact us:
Thomson Learning Academic Resource Center
1-800-423-0563
http://www.wadsworth.com

For permission to use material from this text, contact us by
Web: http://www.thomsonrights.com
Fax: 1-800-730-2215
Phone: 1-800-730-2214

Printed in the United States of America
10 9 8 7 6 5 4

PREFACE

Cognitive psychology texts do a remarkable job of summarizing and integrating an ever-growing body of research that defines the field. Yet no text, however good it is, can substitute for reading original articles. We think that students must begin learning how to read the scientific literature in a field as undergraduates. After teaching cognitive psychology for a long time, we are convinced that a book of readings is a great way to begin this learning process. Why assign a book of readings? We see three advantages.

First, students cannot learn how to read original articles with high levels of comprehension without considerable assistance. A book of readings can provide an introduction to each reading that alerts readers to pay special attention to key ideas and findings, placing the reading in the broader context of cognitive psychology. We have prefaced each reading with such an introduction and followed each reading with five questions that are designed to help students monitor their comprehension, think critically about what they have just read, and reinforce and extend the main lessons to be taken away.

Second, the readings contained in this book are acknowledged to be part of the core of the field. Rather than relying exclusively on our own judgment, we solicited nominations for key articles from a nationwide sample of faculty who teach cognitive psychology. A prime consideration for including a reading was that it received multiple nominations from our nationwide sample. We then edited the list of nominated readings for balance in covering the major areas of cognitive psychology.

A third reason for assigning a book of readings is that obtaining permission to reproduce articles complicates the process of assembling readings. By adopting a book of readings, you transfer the work of obtaining permissions to the book's authors!

The set of selected readings reveals a dynamic and rapidly expanding field. The readings are divided into 11 sections. The reading in *general issues* addresses capacity limitations in information processing. Readings in *cognitive neuroscience* address the localization of cognitive operations to specific brain regions and implications of neuropsychological evidence for understanding the nature of visual images. Readings in *perception and attention* address relationships between attention and memory, features of visual processing, and the span of information available to the eye when reading. Readings in *memory* address topics ranging from classics, such as levels of processing and control of short-term memory, to such contemporary topics as implicit memory and repressed memories. Readings in *concepts and categories* address the principles of categorization and conceptual structure. Readings in *knowledge representation and expertise* address mental rotation and the structure and acquisition of expertise. Readings in *language* address text comprehension and context effects in sentence comprehension. Readings in *problem solving* address solving insight problems and word arithmetic problems from the classroom and from the everyday world. Readings in *reasoning, judgment, and decision making* address choices, values, frames, and natural logic reasoning. Readings in *cognitive development* address issues ranging from network representations of children's knowledge about dinosaurs to development of word meaning. Finally, the reading in *intelligence* provides a contemporary perspective on these topics.

This book would not have been possible without the assistance of many individuals. We would like to thank the authors and publishers who granted permission for use of their articles. We also would like to thank Harcourt Brace, particularly Lisa Hensley, Christopher Klein, and Susan R. Petty. We would also like to thank our many colleagues who nominated the readings. They are:

Jeanette Altarriba
State University of New York, Albany

Michael Birnbaum
California State University, Fullerton

Stephen Buggie
University of New Mexico, Gallup

Linda Buyer
Governors State University, University Park, IL

Rich Carlson
Pennsylvania State University

Sandra Carpenter
University of Alabama

David Carroll
University of Wisconsin, Superior

Stephen Chew
Samford University, Birmingham, AL

William L. Chovan
Western Carolina University, Cullowhee, NC

John Colombo
University of Kansas, Lawrence

Leda Cosmides
University of California, Santa Barbara

Nelson Cowan
University of Missouri, Columbia

Brian C. Cronk
Missouri Western State College

Paul F. Cunningham
Rivier College, Nashua, NH

R. Dale Dick
University of Wisconsin, Eau Claire

Dara Dunn
Moravian College, Bethlehem, PA

Delbert W. Ellsworth
Elizabethtown College

Ronald P. Fisher
Florida International University, North Miami

Michael Gaynor
Bloomsburg University, PA

Gary Gillund
College of Wooster, OH

Art Glenberg
Madison, WI

Jonathan M. Golding
University of Kentucky, Lexington

Jolene Scully Gordon
William Paterson College, Wayne, NJ

Robert Greene
Case Western Reserve University, Cleveland, OH

Lowell Groninger
Baltimore, MD

David E. Grover
Clark Hall, IUP, Indiana, PA

Karl Haberlandt
Trinity College, Hartford, CT

Douglas A. Hershey
Oklahoma State University, Stillwater

Dianne Horgan
University of Memphis, TN

Nancy E. Jackson
University of Iowa

Robert T. Keegan
Pace University, Pleasantville, NY

Julian Keith
University of North Carolina,
Wilmington

Andrew Konick
Hiram College, OH

David H. Krantz
Columbia University

Robert G. Kunzendorf
University of Lowell, MA

Michelle Leichtman
Harvard University

David MacEwen
Mary Washington College,
Fredericksburg, VA

R. P. Markley
Fort Hays State, Hays, KS

Michael Maratsos
University of Minnesota

Donnie W. Massaro
University of California, Santa Cruz

Margaret W. Matlin
State University of New York, Geneseo

John D. Murray
Georgia Southern University, Statesboro

Jerome L. Myers
University of Massachusetts

Keith Nelson
Pennsylvania State University

Lisa Onorato
Hartwick College, Oneonta, NY

Elizabeth Weiss Ozorak
Allegheny College, Meadville, PA

Donald T. Payne
Hopewell, NJ

David J. Pittenger
Marietta College, OH

Dennie Proffitt
University of Virginia, Charlottesville

G. A. Radvansky
University of Notre Dame

Lynne Reder
Carnegie-Mellon University,
Pittsburgh, PA

Lauretta Reeves
Rowan College, Glassboro, NJ

A. Rene Schmauder
University of South Carolina

Johnna K. Shapiro
Illinois Wesleyan University,
Bloomington

Paul Shulman
State University of New York, Institute
of Technology, Utica

R. Solso
University of Nevada, Reno

Padmanabhan Sudevan
University of Wisconsin, Stevens Point

Catherine Tamis-LeMonda
New York University

Holly Taylor
Tufts University

Charles Thompson
Manhattan, KS

X. T. Wang
University of South Dakota

Charles A. Weaver, III
Baylor University, Waco, TX

Thomas L. Wilson
Bellarmine College, Louisville, KY

Lynn A. Winters
Purchase College, NY

Steven Yantis
Johns Hopkins University

Carole Young
Bethel College, St. Paul, MN

We would like especially to thank those colleagues who reviewed portions of the manuscript: James I. Chumbley, University of Massachusetts, Amherst; Kenneth D. Kallio, State University of New York, Geneseo; John Mavromatis, St. John Fisher College, Rochester; Greg B. Simpson, University of Kansas, Lawrence; and James R. Stein, Southern Illinois University.

Contents

READINGS IN COGNITIVE PSYCHOLOGY

1

WHAT IS COGNITIVE PSYCHOLOGY? GENERAL ISSUES

THE MAGICAL NUMBER SEVEN, PLUS OR MINUS TWO: SOME LIMITS ON OUR CAPACITY FOR PROCESSING INFORMATION

George Miller

The Magical Number Seven, Plus or Minus Two: Some Limits on Our Capacity for Processing Information

George Miller

INTRODUCTION

If any field recognizes a single "most classical" paper, George Miller's article "The Magical Number Seven, Plus or Minus Two" might enjoy that distinction in the field of cognitive psychology. In this article, Miller points out how the number 7, plus or minus 2, keeps popping up in studies of capacity limits of the human information-processing system.

Although this article was undertaken as an inquiry into the mysterious appearance and reappearance of the number 7, its true value to cognitive psychology far exceeded that goal. First, the article showed the usefulness of cognitive theories and methods in studying diverse aspects of human cognition. The varied appearances of the number 7 were only detected by applying techniques, quite sophisticated for the time, to explore the workings of the human mind.

Second, the article showed that applications of these sophisticated techniques could uncover surprising consistencies in human behavior. Often, phenomena that appeared to be a disorderly mess really had an underlying order, which cognitive psychology would help to uncover. Underlying the disorder and diversity was an orderly and principled system of human cognition.

Third, the article introduced a broad range of readers to the newly emerging field of cognitive psychology. At the time, the field was a mere fledgling; behaviorism, with its claims of having discovered laws of human behavior, was in full force. Miller showed, in an article published in a journal for all psychologists, that cognitive psychology held promise for revealing the laws not just of human behavior, but of the human mind.

———

M y problem is that I have been persecuted by an integer. For 7 years this number has followed me around, has intruded in my most private data, and has assaulted me from the pages of our most public journals. This number assumes a variety of disguises, being sometimes a little larger and sometimes a little smaller than usual, but never changing so much as to be unrecognizable. The persistence with

Source: From *The Psychological Review, 63* (2), pp. 81-97. "The magical number seven, plus or minus two: Some limits on our capacity for processing information." Miller, G. (1956).

which this number plagues me is far more than a random accident. There is, to quote a famous senator, a design behind it, some pattern governing its appearances. Either there really is something unusual about the number or else I am suffering from delusions of persecution.

I shall begin my case history by telling you about some experiments that tested how accurately people can assign numbers to the magnitudes of various aspects of a stimulus. In the traditional language of psychology these would be called experiments in absolute judgment. Historical accident, however, has decreed that they should have another name. We now call them experiments on the capacity of people to transmit information. Since these experiments would not have been done without the appearance of information theory on the psychological scene, and since the results are analyzed in terms of the concepts of information theory, I shall have to preface my discussion with a few remarks about this theory.

INFORMATION MEASUREMENT

The "amount of information" is exactly the same concept that we have talked about for years under the name of "variance." The equations are different, but if we hold tight to the idea that anything that increases the variance also increases the amount of information we cannot go far astray.

The advantages of this new way of talking about variance are simple enough. Variance is always stated in terms of the unit of measurement—inches, pounds, volts, etc.—whereas the amount of information is a dimensionless quantity. Since the information in a discrete statistical distribution does not depend upon the unit of measurement, we can extend the concept to situations where we have no metric and we would not ordinarily think of using the variance. And it also enables us to compare results obtained in quite different experimental situations where it would be meaningless to compare variances based on different metrics. So there are some good reasons for adopting the newer concept.

The similarity of variance and amount of information might be explained this way: When we have a large variance, we are very ignorant about what is going to happen. If we are very ignorant, then when we make the observation it gives us a lot of information. On the other hand, if the variance is very small, we know in advance how our observation must come out, so we get little information from making the observation.

If you will now imagine a communication system, you will realize that there is a great deal of variability about what goes into the system and also a great deal of variability about what comes out. The input and the output can therefore be described in terms of their variance (or their information). If it is a good communication system, however, there must be some systematic relation between what goes in and what comes out. That is to say, the output will depend upon the input, or will be correlated with the input. If we measure this correlation, then we can say how much of the output variance is attributable to the input and how much is due to random fluctuations or "noise" introduced by the system during transmission. So we see that the measure of transmitted information is simply a measure of the input–output correlation.

There are two simple rules to follow. Whenever I refer to "amount of information," you will understand "variance." And whenever I refer to "amount of transmitted information," you will understand "covariance" or "correlation."

The situation can be described graphically by two partially overlapping circles. Then the left circle can be taken to represent the variance of the input, the right circle the variance of the output, and the overlap the covariance of input and output. I shall speak of the left circle as the amount of input information, the right circle as the amount of output information, and the overlap as the amount of transmitted information.

In the experiments on absolute judgment, the observer is considered to be a communication channel. Then the left circle would represent the amount of information in the stimuli, the right circle the amount of information in his responses, and the overlap the stimulus–response correlation as measured by the amount of transmitted information. The experimental problem is to increase the amount of input information and to measure the amount of transmitted information. If the observer's absolute judgments are quite accurate, then nearly all of the input information will be transmitted and will be recoverable from his responses. If he makes errors, then the transmitted information may be considerably less than the input. We expect that, as we increase the amount of input information, the observer will begin to make more and more errors; we can test the limits of accuracy of his absolute judgments. If the human observer is a reasonable kind of communication system, then when we increase the amount of input information the transmitted information will increase at first and will eventually level off at some asymptotic value. This asymptotic value we take to be the *channel capacity* of the observer: It represents the greatest amount of information that he can give us about the stimulus on the basis of an absolute judgment. The channel capacity is the upper limit on the extent to which the observer can match his responses to the stimuli we give him.

Now just a brief word about the *bit* and we can begin to look at some data. One bit of information is the amount of information that we need to make a decision between two equally likely alternatives. If we must decide whether a man is less than 6 feet tall or more than 6 feet tall and if we know that the chances are 50–50, then we need one bit of information. Notice that this unit of information does not refer in any way to the unit of length that we use—feet, inches, centimeters, etc. However you measure the man's height, we still need just one bit of information.

Two bits of information enable us to decide among four equally likely alternatives. Three bits of information enable us to decide among eight equally likely alternatives. Four bits of information decide among 16 alternatives, five among 32, and so on. That is to say, if there are 32 equally likely alternatives, we must make five successive binary decisions, worth one bit each, before we know which alternative is correct. So the general rule is simple: Every time the number of alternatives is increased by a factor of two, one bit of information is added.

There are two ways we might increase the amount of input information. We could increase the rate at which we give information to the observer, so that the amount of information per unit time would increase, or we could ignore the time variable completely and increase the amount of input information by increasing the number of alternative stimuli. In the absolute judgment experiment we are interested in the second alternative. We give the observer as much time as he wants to make his response; we simply increase the number of alternative stimuli among which he must discriminate and look to see where confusions begin to occur. Confusions will appear near the point that we are calling his "channel capacity."

ABSOLUTE JUDGMENTS OF UNIDIMENSIONAL STIMULI

Now let us consider what happens when we make absolute judgments of tones. Pollack (1952) asked listeners to identify tones by assigning numerals to them. The tones were different with respect to frequency, and covered the range from 100 to 8,000 cps. in equal logarithmic steps. A tone was sounded and the listener responded by giving a numeral. After the listener had made his response he was told the correct identification of the tone.

When only 2 or 3 tones were used the listeners never confused them. With 4 different tones confusions were quite rare, but with 5 or more tones confusions were frequent. With 14 different tones the listeners made many mistakes.

These data are plotted in Figure 1. Along the bottom is the amount of input information in bits per stimulus. As the number of alternative tones was increased

FIGURE 1   Data from Pollack (1952, 1953a) on the amount of information that is transmitted by listeners who make absolute judgments of auditory pitch. As the amount of input information is increased by increasing from 2 to 14 the number of different pitches to be judged, the amount of transmitted information approaches as its upper limit a channel capacity of about 2.5 bits per judgment.

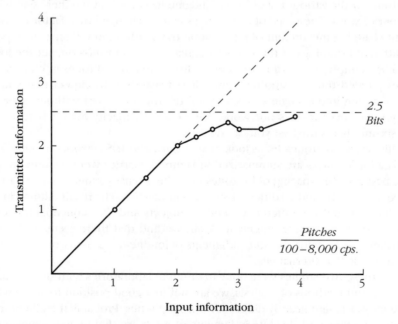

to 14, the input information increased from 1 to 3.8 bits. On the ordinate is plotted the amount of transmitted information. The amount of transmitted information behaves in much the way we would expect a communication channel to behave; the transmitted information increases linearly up to about 2 bits and then bends off toward an asymptote at about 2.5 bits. This value, 2.5 bits, therefore, is what we are calling the channel capacity of the listener for absolute judgments of pitch.

So now we have the number 2.5 bits. What does it mean? First, note that 2.5 bits corresponds to about six equally likely alternatives. The result means that we cannot pick more than six different pitches that the listener will never confuse. Stated slightly differently, no matter how many alternative tones we ask him to judge, the best we can expect him to do is to assign them to about six different classes without error. Again, if we know that there were N alternative stimuli, then his judgment enables us to narrow down the particular stimulus to one out of $N/6$.

Most people are surprised that the number is as small as six. Of course, there is evidence that a musically sophisticated person with absolute pitch can identify accurately any one of 50 or 60 different pitches. Fortunately, I do not have time to discuss these remarkable exceptions. I say it is fortunate because I do not know how to explain their superior performance. So I shall stick to the more pedestrian fact that most of us can identify about one out of only five or six pitches before we begin to get confused.

It is interesting to consider that psychologists have been using seven-point rating scales for a long time, on the intuitive basis that trying to rate into finer categories does not really add much to the usefulness of the ratings. Pollack's results indicate that, at least for pitches, this intuition is fairly sound.

Next you can ask how reproducible this result is. Does it depend on the spacing of the tones or the various conditions of judgment? Pollack varied these conditions in a number of ways. The range of frequencies can be changed by a factor of about 20 without changing the amount of information transmitted more than a small percentage. Different groupings of the pitches decreased the transmission, but the loss was small. For example, if you can discriminate five high-pitched tones in one series and five low-pitched tones in another series, it is reasonable to expect that you could combine all ten into a single series and still tell them all apart without error. When you try it, however, it does not work. The channel capacity for pitch seems to be about six and that is the best you can do.

While we are on tones, let us look next at Garner's (1953) work on loudness. Garner's data for loudness are summarized in Figure 2. Garner went to some trouble to get the best possible spacing of his tones over the intensity range from 15 to 110 db. He used 4, 5, 6, 7, 10, and 20 different stimulus intensities. The results shown in Figure 2 take into account the differences among subjects and the sequential influence of the immediately preceding judgment. Again we find that there seems to be a limit. The channel capacity for absolute judgments of loudness is 2.3 bits, or about five perfectly discriminable alternatives.

Since these two studies were done in different laboratories with slightly different techniques and methods of analysis, we are not in a good position to argue whether five loudnesses is significantly different from six pitches. Probably the difference is in the right direction, and absolute judgments of pitch are slightly more accurate than

Data from Garner (1953) on the channel capacity for absolute judgments of auditory loudness.

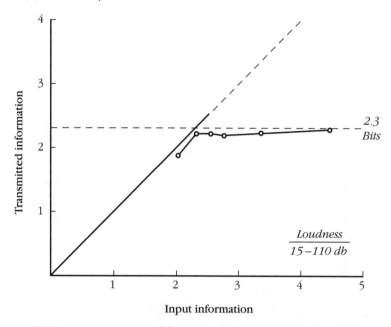

absolute judgments of loudness. The important point, however, is that the two answers are of the same order of magnitude.

The experiment has also been done for taste intensities. In Figure 3 are the results obtained by Beebe-Center, Rogers, and O'Connell (1955) for absolute judgments of the concentration of salt solutions. The concentrations ranged from 0.3 to 34.7 gm. NaCl per 100 cc. tap water in equal subjective steps. They used 3, 5, 9, and 17 different concentrations. The channel capacity is 1.9 bits, which is about four distinct concentrations. Thus taste intensities seem a little less distinctive than auditory stimuli, but again the order of magnitude is not far off.

On the other hand, the channel capacity for judgments of visual position seems to be significantly larger. Hake and Garner (1951) asked observers to interpolate visually between two scale markers. Their results are shown in Figure 4. They did the experiment in two ways. In one version, they let the observer use any number between zero and 100 to describe the position, although they presented stimuli at only 5, 10, 20, or 50 different positions. The results with this unlimited response technique are shown by the filled circles on the graph. In the other version, the observers were limited in their responses to reporting just those stimulus values that were possible. That is to say, in the second version the number of different responses that the observer could make was exactly the same as the number of different stimuli that the experimenter might present. The results with this limited response technique are shown by the open circles on the graph. The two functions are so similar that it

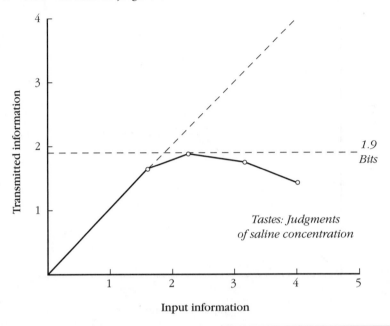

FIGURE 3   Data from Beebe-Center, Rogers, and O'Connell (1955) on the channel capacity for absolute judgments of saltiness.

seems fair to conclude that the number of responses available to the observer had nothing to do with the channel capacity of 3.25 bits.

The Hake–Garner experiment has been repeated by Coonan and Klemmer. Although they have not yet published their results, they have given me permission to say that they obtained channel capacities ranging from 3.2 bits for very short exposures of the pointer position to 3.9 bits for longer exposures. These values are slightly higher than Hake and Garner's, so we must conclude that there are between 10 and 15 distinct positions along a linear interval. This is the largest channel capacity that has been measured for any unidimensional variable.

At the present time, these four experiments on absolute judgments of simple, unidimensional stimuli are all that have appeared in the psychological journals. However, a great deal of work on other stimulus variables has not yet appeared in the journals. For example, Eriksen and Hake (1955) have found that the channel capacity for judging the sizes of squares is 2.2 bits, or about five categories, under a wide range of experimental conditions. In a separate experiment Eriksen (1954) found 2.8 bits for size, 3.1 bits for hue, and 2.3 bits for brightness. Geldard has measured the channel capacity for the skin by placing vibrators on the chest region. A good observer can identify about four intensities, about five durations, and about seven locations.

One of the most active groups in this area has been the Air Force Operational Applications Laboratory. Pollack has been kind enough to furnish me with the results of their measurements for several aspects of visual displays. They made measure-

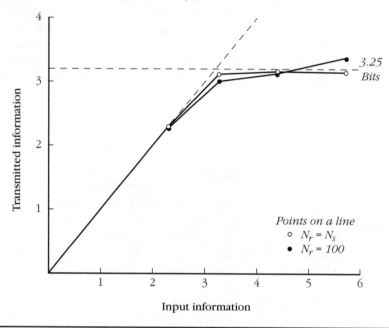

FIGURE 4   Data from Hake and Garner (1951) on the channel capacity for absolute judgments of the position of a pointer in a linear interval.

ments for area and for the curvature, length, and direction of lines. In one set of experiments they used a very short exposure of the stimulus—1/40 second—and then they repeated the measurements with a 5-second exposure. For area, they got 2.6 bits with the short exposure and 2.7 bits with the long exposure. For the length of a line, they got about 2.6 bits with the short exposure and about 3.0 bits with the long exposure. Direction, or angle of inclination, gave 2.8 bits for the short exposure and 3.3 bits for the long exposure. Curvature was apparently harder to judge. When the length of the arc was constant, the result at the short exposure duration was 2.2 bits, but when the length of the chord was constant, the result was only 1.6 bits. This last value is the lowest that anyone has measured to date. I should add, however, that these values are apt to be slightly too low because the data from all subjects were pooled before the transmitted information was computed.

Now let us see where we are. First, the channel capacity does seem to be a valid notion for describing human observers. Second, the channel capacities measured for these unidimensional variables range from 1.6 bits for curvature to 3.9 bits for positions in an interval. Although there is no question that the differences among the variables are real and meaningful, the more impressive fact to me is their considerable similarity. If I take the best estimates I can get of the channel capacities for all the stimulus variables I have mentioned, the mean is 2.6 bits and the standard deviation is only 0.6 bit. In terms of distinguishable alternatives, this mean corresponds to about 6.5 categories, one standard deviation includes from 4 to 10 categories, and the total range is from 3 to 15 categories. Considering the wide variety of different variables that have been studied, I find this to be a remarkably narrow range.

There seems to be some limitation built into us either by learning or by the design of our nervous systems, a limit that keeps our channel capacities in this general range. On the basis of the present evidence it seems safe to say that we possess a finite and rather small capacity for making such unidimensional judgments and that this capacity does not vary a great deal from one simple sensory attribute to another.

•   •   •

SUBITIZING

I cannot leave this general area without mentioning, however briefly, the experiments conducted at Mount Holyoke College on the discrimination of number. In experiments by Kaufman, Lord, Reese, and Volkmann (1949), random patterns of dots were flashed on a screen for ⅕ of a second. Anywhere from 1 to more than 200 dots could appear in the pattern. The subject's task was to report how many dots there were.

The first point to note is that on patterns containing up to five or six dots the subjects simply did not make errors. The performance on these small numbers of dots was so different from the performance with more dots that it was given a special name. Below seven the subjects were said to *subitize;* above seven they were said to *estimate.* This is, as you will recognize, what we once optimistically called "the span of attention."

This discontinuity at seven is, of course, suggestive. Is this the same basic process that limits our unidimensional judgments to about seven categories? The generalization is tempting, but not sound in my opinion. The data on number estimates have not been analyzed in informational terms; but on the basis of the published data I would guess that the subjects transmitted something more than four bits of information about the number of dots. Using the same arguments as before, we would conclude that there are about 20 or 30 distinguishable categories of numerousness. This is considerably more information than we would expect to get from a unidimensional display. It is, as a matter of fact, very much like a two-dimensional display. Although the dimensionality of the random dot patterns is not entirely clear, these results are in the same range as Klemmer and Frick's for their two-dimensional display of dots in a square. Perhaps the two dimensions of numerousness are area and density. When the subject can subitize, area and density may not be the significant variables, but when the subject must estimate perhaps they are significant. In any event, the comparison is not so simple as it might seem at first thought.

This is one of the ways in which the magical number seven has persecuted me. Here we have two closely related kinds of experiments, both of which point to the significance of the number seven as a limit on our capacities. And yet when we examine the matter more closely, there seems to be a reasonable suspicion that it is nothing more than a coincidence.

THE SPAN OF IMMEDIATE MEMORY

Let me summarize the situation in this way. There is a clear and definite limit to the accuracy with which we can identify absolutely the magnitude of a unidimensional stimulus variable. I would propose to call this limit the *span of absolute judgment,* and I maintain that for unidimensional judgments, this span is usually somewhere in the neighborhood of seven. We are not completely at the mercy of this limited span, however, because we have a variety of techniques for getting around it and increasing the accuracy of our judgments. The three most important of these devices are (*a*) to make relative rather than absolute judgments; or, if that is not possible, (*b*) to increase the number of dimensions along which the stimuli can differ; or (*c*) to arrange the task in such a way that we make a sequence of several absolute judgments in a row.

The study of relative judgments is one of the oldest topics in experimental psychology, and I will not pause to review it now. The second device, increasing the dimensionality, we have just considered. It seems that by adding more dimensions and requiring crude, binary, yes–no judgments on each attribute we can extend the span of absolute judgment from 7 to at least 150. Judging from our everyday behavior, the limit is probably in the thousands, if indeed there is a limit. In my opinion, we cannot go on compounding dimensions indefinitely. I suspect that there is also a *span of perceptual dimensionality* and that this span is somewhere in the neighborhood of ten, but I must add at once that there is no objective evidence to support this suspicion. This is a question sadly needing experimental exploration.

Concerning the third device, the use of successive judgments, I have quite a bit to say because this device introduces memory as the handmaiden of discrimination. And, since mnemonic processes are at least as complex as are perceptual processes, we can anticipate that their interactions will not be easily disentangled.

Suppose that we start by simply extending slightly the experimental procedure that we have been using. Up to this point we have presented a single stimulus and asked the observer to name it immediately thereafter. We can extend this procedure by requiring the observer to withhold his response until we have given him several stimuli in succession. At the end of the sequence of stimuli he then makes his response. We still have the same sort of input-output situation that is required for the measurement of transmitted information. But now we have passed from an experiment on absolute judgment to what is traditionally called an experiment on immediate memory.

Before we look at any data on this topic I feel I must give you a word of warning to help you avoid some obvious associations that can be confusing. Everybody knows that there is a finite span of immediate memory and that for a lot of different kinds of test materials this span is about seven items in length. I have just shown you that there is a span of absolute judgment that can distinguish about seven categories and that there is a span of attention that will encompass about six objects at a glance. What is more natural than to think that all three of these spans are different aspects of a single underlying process? And that is a fundamental mistake, as I shall be at some pains to demonstrate. This mistake is one of the malicious persecutions that the magical number seven has subjected me to.

My mistake went something like this. We have seen that the invariant feature in the span of absolute judgment is the amount of information that the observer can

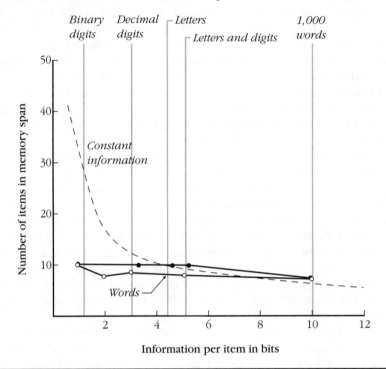

FIGURE 5   Data from Hayes (1952) on the span of immediate memory plotted as a function of the amount of information per item in the test materials.

transmit. There is a real operational similarity between the absolute judgment experiment and the immediate memory experiment. If immediate memory is like absolute judgment, then it should follow that the invariant feature in the span of immediate memory is also the amount of information that an observer can retain. If the amount of information in the span of immediate memory is a constant, then the span should be short when the individual items contain a lot of information and the span should be long when the items contain little information. For example, decimal digits are worth 3.3 bits apiece. We can recall about seven of them, for a total of 23 bits of information. Isolated English words are worth about 10 bits apiece. If the total amount of information is to remain constant at 23 bits, then we should be able to remember only two or three words chosen at random. In this way I generated a theory about how the span of immediate memory should vary as a function of the amount of information per item in the test materials.

The measurements of memory span in the literature are suggestive on this question, but not definitive. And so it was necessary to do the experiment to see. Hayes (1952) tried it out with five different kinds of test materials: binary digits, decimal digits, letters of the alphabet, letters plus decimal digits, and 1,000 monosyllabic words. The lists were read aloud at the rate of one item per second and the subjects had as much time as they needed to give their responses. A procedure described by Woodworth (1938) was used to score the responses.

The results are shown by the filled circles in Figure 5. Here the dotted line indicates what the span should have been if the amount of information in the span were constant. The solid curves represent the data. Hayes repeated the experiment using test vocabularies of different sizes but all containing only English monosyllables (open circles in Figure 5). This more homogeneous test material did not change the picture significantly. With binary items the span is about nine and, although it drops to about five with monosyllabic English words, the difference is far less than the hypothesis of constant information would require.

There is nothing wrong with Hayes's experiment, because Pollack (1953b) repeated it much more elaborately and got essentially the same result. Pollack took pains to measure the amount of information transmitted and did not rely on the traditional procedure for scoring the responses. His results are plotted in Figure 6. Here it is clear that the amount of information transmitted is not a constant, but increases almost linearly as the amount of information per item in the input is increased.

And so the outcome is perfectly clear. In spite of the coincidence that the magical number seven appears in both places, the span of absolute judgment and the span of immediate memory are quite different kinds of limitations that are imposed on our ability to process information. Absolute judgment is limited by the amount of information. Immediate memory is limited by the number of items. In order to capture this distinction in somewhat picturesque terms, I have fallen into the custom of distinguishing between *bits* of information and *chunks* of information. Then I can say

FIGURE 6 Data from Pollack (1953b) on the amount of information retained after one presentation plotted as a function of the amount of information per item in the test materials.

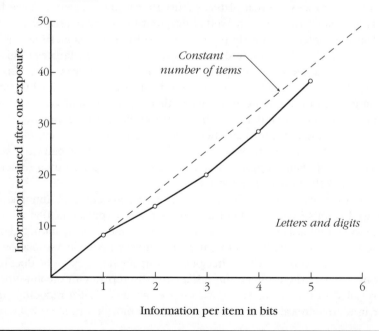

that the number of bits of information is constant for absolute judgment and the number of chunks of information is constant for immediate memory. The span of immediate memory seems to be almost independent of the number of bits per chunk, at least over the range that has been examined to date.

The contrast of the terms *bit* and *chunk* also serves to highlight the fact that we are not very definite about what constitutes a chunk of information. For example, the memory span of five words that Hayes obtained when each word was drawn at random from a set of 1,000 English monosyllables might just as appropriately have been called a memory span of 15 phonemes, since each word had about three phonemes in it. Intuitively, it is clear that the subjects were recalling five words, not 15 phonemes, but the logical distinction is not immediately apparent. We are dealing here with a process of organizing or grouping the input into familiar units or chunks, and a great deal of learning has gone into the formation of these familiar units.

RECODING

In order to speak more precisely, therefore, we must recognize the importance of grouping or organizing the input sequence into units or chunks. Since the memory span is a fixed number of chunks, we can increase the number of bits of information that it contains simply by building larger and larger chunks, each chunk containing more information than before.

A man just beginning to learn radio-telegraphic code hears each *dit* and *dah* as a separate chunk. Soon he is able to organize these sounds into letters and then he can deal with the letters as chunks. Then the letters organize themselves as words, which are still larger chunks, and he begins to hear whole phrases. I do not mean that each step is a discrete process, or that plateaus must appear in his learning curve, for surely the levels of organization are achieved at different rates and overlap each other during the learning process. I am simply pointing to the obvious fact that the dits and dahs are organized by learning into patterns and that as these larger chunks emerge the amount of message that the operator can remember increases correspondingly. In the terms I am proposing to use, the operator learns to increase the bits per chunk.

In the jargon of communication theory, this process would be called *recoding*. The input is given in a code that contains many chunks with few bits per chunk. The operator recodes the input into another code that contains fewer chunks with more bits per chunk. There are many ways to do this recoding, but probably the simplest is to group the input events, apply a new name to the group, and then remember the new name rather than the original input events.

Since I am convinced that this process is a very general and important one for psychology, I want to tell you about a demonstration experiment that should make perfectly explicit what I am talking about. This experiment was conducted by Sidney Smith and was reported by him before the Eastern Psychological Association in 1954.

Begin with the observed fact that people can repeat back eight decimal digits, but only nine binary digits. Since there is a large discrepancy in the amount of information recalled in these two cases, we suspect at once that a recoding procedure could be used to increase the span of immediate memory for binary digits. In Table 1

| **TABLE 1** | Ways of Recoding Sequences of Binary Digits |

BINARY DIGITS (BITS)	1	0	1	0	0	0	1	0	0	1	1	1	0	0	1	1	1	0
2 : 1 Chunks	10		10		00		10		01		11		00		11		10	
Recoding	2		2		0		2		1		3		0		3		2	
3 : 1 Chunks	101			000			100			111			001			110		
Recoding	5			0			4			7			1			6		
4 : 1 Chunks	1010				0010				0111				0011				10	
Recoding	10				2				7				3				2	
5 : 1 Chunks	10100					01001					11001					110		
Recoding	20					9					25					6		

a method for grouping and renaming is illustrated. Along the top is a sequence of 18 binary digits, far more than any subject was able to recall after a single presentation. In the next line these same binary digits are grouped by pairs. Four possible pairs can occur: 00 is renamed 0, 01 is renamed 1, 10 is renamed 2, and 11 is renamed 3. That is to say, we recode from a base-two arithmetic to a base-four arithmetic. In the recoded sequence there are now just nine digits to remember, and this is almost within the span of immediate memory. In the next line the same sequence of binary digits is regrouped into chunks of three. There are eight possible sequences of three, so we give each sequence a new name between 0 and 7. Now we have recoded from a sequence of 18 binary digits into a sequence of 6 octal digits, and this is well within the span of immediate memory. In the last two lines the binary digits are grouped by fours and by fives and are given decimal-digit names from 0 to 15 and from 0 to 31.

It is reasonably obvious that this kind of recoding increases the bits per chunk, and packages the binary sequence into a form that can be retained within the span of immediate memory. So Smith assembled 20 subjects and measured their spans for binary and octal digits. The spans were 9 for binaries and 7 for octals. Then he gave each recoding scheme to five of the subjects. They studied the recoding until they said they understood it—for about 5 or 10 minutes. Then he tested their span for binary digits again while they tried to use the recoding schemes they had studied.

The recoding schemes increased their span for binary digits in every case. But the increase was not as large as we had expected on the basis of their span for octal digits. Since the discrepancy increased as the recoding ratio increased, we reasoned that the few minutes the subjects had spent learning the recoding schemes had not been sufficient. Apparently the translation from one code to the other must be almost automatic or the subject will lose part of the next group while he is trying to remember the translation of the last group.

Since the 4 : 1 and 5 : 1 ratios require considerable study, Smith decided to imitate Ebbinghaus and do the experiment on himself. With Germanic patience he drilled himself on each recoding successively, and obtained the results shown in Figure 7. Here the data follow along rather nicely with the results you would predict on the basis of his span for octal digits. He could remember 12 octal digits. With the 2 : 1 recoding, these

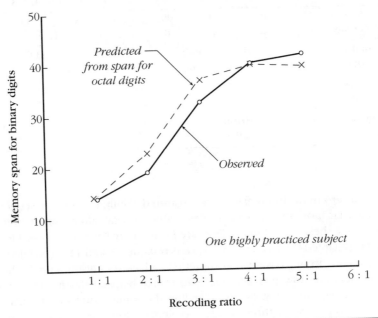

| FIGURE 7 | The span of immediate memory for binary digits is plotted as a function of the recoding procedure used. The predicted function is obtained by multiplying the |

span for octals by 2, 3, and 3.3 for recoding into base 4, base 8, and base 10, respectively.

12 chunks were worth 24 binary digits. With the 3 : 1 recoding they were worth 36 binary digits. With the 4 : 1 and 5 : 1 recodings, they were worth about 40 binary digits.

It is a little dramatic to watch a person get 40 binary digits in a row and then repeat them back without error. However, if you think of this merely as a mnemonic trick for extending the memory span, you will miss the more important point that is implicit in nearly all such mnemonic devices. The point is that recoding is an extremely powerful weapon for increasing the amount of information that we can deal with. In one form or another we use recoding constantly in our daily behavior.

In my opinion the most customary kind of recoding that we do all the time is to translate into a verbal code. When there is a story or an argument or an idea that we want to remember, we usually try to rephrase it "in our own words." When we witness some event we want to remember, we make a verbal description of the event and then remember our verbalization. Upon recall we recreate by secondary elaboration the details that seem consistent with the particular verbal recoding we happen to have made. The well-known experiment by Carmichael, Hogan, and Walter (1932) on the influence that names have on the recall of visual figures is one demonstration of the process.

The inaccuracy of the testimony of eyewitnesses is well known in legal psychology, but the distortions of testimony are not random—they follow naturally from the particular recoding that the witness used, and the particular recoding he used depends upon his whole life history. Our language is tremendously useful for repackaging material into a few chunks rich in information. I suspect that imagery is a form of recoding, too, but images seem much harder to get at operationally and to study experimentally than the more symbolic kinds of recoding.

It seems probable that even memorization can be studied in these terms. The process of memorizing may be simply the formation of chunks, or groups of items that go together, until there are few enough chunks so that we can recall all the items. The work by Bousfield and Cohen (1955) on the occurrence of clustering in the recall of words is especially interesting in this respect.

SUMMARY

I have come to the end of the data that I wanted to present, so I would like now to make some summarizing remarks.

First, the span of absolute judgment and the span of immediate memory impose severe limitations on the amount of information that we are able to receive, process, and remember. By organizing the stimulus input simultaneously into several dimensions and successively into a sequence of chunks, we manage to break (or at least stretch) this informational bottleneck.

Second, the process of recoding is a very important one in human psychology and deserves much more explicit attention than it has received. In particular, the kind of linguistic recoding that people do seems to me to be the very lifeblood of the thought processes. Recoding procedures are a constant concern to clinicians, social psychologists, linguists, and anthropologists and yet, probably because recoding is less accessible to experimental manipulation than nonsense syllables or T mazes, the traditional experimental psychologist has contributed little or nothing to their analysis. Nevertheless, experimental techniques can be used, methods of recoding can be specified, behavioral indicants can be found. And I anticipate that we will find a very orderly set of relations describing what now seems an uncharted wilderness of individual differences.

Third, the concepts and measures provided by the theory of information provide a quantitative way of getting at some of these questions. The theory provides us with a yardstick for calibrating our stimulus materials and for measuring the performance of our subjects. In the interests of communication, I have suppressed the technical details of information measurement and have tried to express the ideas in more familiar terms; I hope this paraphrase will not lead you to think they are not useful in research. Informational concepts have already proved valuable in the study of discrimination and of language; they promise a great deal in the study of learning and memory; and it has even been proposed that they can be useful in the study of concept formation. A lot of questions that seemed fruitless 20 or 30 years ago may now be worth another look. In fact, I feel that my story here must stop just as it begins to get really interesting.

And finally, what about the magical number seven? What about the seven wonders of the world, the seven seas, the seven deadly sins, the seven daughters of Atlas in the Pleiades, the seven ages of man, the seven levels of hell, the seven primary colors, the seven notes of the musical scale, and the seven days of the week? What about the seven-point rating scale, the seven categories for absolute judgment, the seven objects in the span of attention, and the seven digits in the span of immediate memory? For the present I propose to withhold judgment. Perhaps there is something deep and profound behind all these sevens, something just calling out for us to discover it. But I suspect that it is only a pernicious, Pythagorean coincidence.

REFERENCES

Beebe-Center, J. G., Rogers, M. S., & O'Connell, D. N. (1955). Transmission of information about sucrose and saline solutions through the sense of taste. *J. Psychol., 39,* 157-160.

Bousfield, W. A., & Cohen, B. H. (1955). The occurrence of clustering in the recall of randomly arranged words of different frequencies-of-usage. *J. Gen. Psychol., 52,* 83-95.

Carmichael, L., Hogan, H. P., & Walter, A. A. (1932). An experimental study of the effect of language on the reproduction of visually perceived form. *J. Exp. Psychol., 15,* 73-86.

Eriksen, C. W. (1954). Multidimensional stimulus differences and accuracy of discrimination. *USAF, WADC Tech. Rep.* No. 54-165.

Eriksen, C. W., & Hake, H. W. (1955). Absolute judgments as a function of the stimulus range and the number of stimulus and response categories. *J. Exp. Psychol., 49,* 323-332.

Garner, W. R. (1953). An informational analysis of absolute judgments of loudness. *J. Exp. Psychol., 46,* 373-380.

Hake, H. W., & Garner, W. R. (1951). The effect of presenting various numbers of discrete steps on scale reading accuracy. *J. Exp. Psychol., 42,* 358-366.

Hayes, J. R. M. (1952). Memory span for general vocabularies as a function of vocabulary size. In *Quarterly Progress Report.* Cambridge, Mass.: Acoustics Laboratory, Massachusetts Institute of Technology, Jan.-June.

Kaufman, E. L., Lord, M. W., Reese, T. W., & Volkmann, J. (1949). The discrimination of visual number. *Amer. J. Psychol., 62,* 498-525.

Pollack, I. (1952). The information of elementary auditory displays. *J. Acoust. Soc. Amer., 24,* 745-749.

Pollack, I. (1953a). The information of elementary auditory displays. II. *J. Acoust. Soc. Amer., 25,* 765-769.

Pollack, I. (1953b). The assimilation of sequentially encoded information. *Amer. J. Psychol., 66,* 421-435.

Woodworth, R. S. (1938). *Experimental psychology.* New York: Holt.

QUESTIONS FOR FURTHER THOUGHT

1. What plausible explanation might explain the prevalence of the number seven as a limit in human information processing?

2. What is channel capacity, and why is it important to human information processing?

3. What is a bit of information, and how is it related to channel capacity?

4. What is responsible for the information bottleneck that chunking helps to break through?

5. How does chunking enable human information processors to expand the amount of information they can remember?

2

COGNITIVE NEUROSCIENCE

LOCALIZATION OF COGNITIVE OPERATIONS IN THE HUMAN BRAIN

Michael Posner, Steven Petersen, Peter Fox, and Marcus Raichle

IS VISUAL IMAGERY REALLY VISUAL? OVERLOOKED EVIDENCE FROM NEUROPSYCHOLOGY

Martha Farah

LOCALIZATION OF COGNITIVE OPERATIONS IN THE HUMAN BRAIN

Michael Posner, Steven Petersen, Peter Fox,
and Marcus Raichle

INTRODUCTION

Michael Posner is a world leader in the field of cognitive psychology and also is a key figure in the field of cognitive neuroscience. Posner established his reputation as an experimental cognitive psychologist studying attention, perception, and related processes. Through this work, Posner became one of the most widely cited cognitive psychologists in the world. In midcareer, he switched his emphasis, however, and started studying the relationship of cognition to brain function. Many other cognitive psychologists followed and continue to follow his lead. Today, the field of cognitive neuroscience is closely integrated with the field of cognitive psychology, in part due to Posner's leadership.

How do mental operations like those addressed in cognitive theories relate to the functioning of the human brain? In a seminal article, Michael Posner and his colleagues have argued that cognitive operations can be mapped fairly precisely onto the functioning of the brain. In particular, the elementary cognitive operations are strictly localized in the brain, but because many cognitive operations combine to perform a particular task, this performance typically involves multiple and even diffuse areas of the brain. This article represents a major contribution to the field of cognitive psychology as one of the earliest demonstrations of specific mappings between brain functions and cognitive processes.

For example, Posner and his colleagues used positron emission tomography (PET) scanning, which traces the flow of blood to different regions of the brain, to identify the brain processes activated during the reading of single words. The investigators employed a model of serial (sequential) information processing in order to assess the correlation between the brain processes and cognitive processes. They found that visual processing of word forms could be linked to five distinct areas of the occipital lobe, which is normally associated with visual functioning. Semantic processing of words in reading, however, was localized in the left frontal lobe, which is normally associated with complex verbal functioning.

In short, the work of Posner and his colleagues opened the way for studies that would challenge the view of cognitive psychology and neuropsychology as

Source: From Posner, M. I., Petersen, S. E., Fox, P. T., and Raichle, M. E. (1988). Localization of cognitive operations in the human brain. *Science, 240,* 1627–1630. Copyright © (1988) American Association for the Advancement of Science. Reprinted with permission.

distinct fields, instead allowing their integration into a single field, sometimes called *cognitive neuropsychology*.

———

The human brain localizes mental operations of the kind posited by cognitive theories. These local computations are integrated in the performance of cognitive tasks such as reading. To support this general hypothesis, new data from neural imaging studies of word reading are related to results of studies on normal subjects and patients with lesions. Further support comes from studies in mental imagery, timing, and memory.[1] ∎

The question of localization of cognition in the human brain is an old and difficult one (Churchland, 1986). However, current analyses of the operations involved in cognition (Anderson, 1980) and new techniques for the imaging of brain function during cognitive tasks (Raichle, 1983) have combined to provide support for a new hypothesis. The hypothesis is that elementary operations forming the basis of cognitive analyses of human tasks are strictly localized. Many such local operations are involved in any cognitive task. A set of distributed brain areas must be orchestrated in the performance of even simple cognitive tasks. The task itself is not performed by any single area of the brain, but the operations that underlie the performance are strictly localized. This idea fits generally with many network theories in neuroscience and cognition. However, most neuroscience network theories of higher processes (Mesolam, 1981; Goldman-Rakic, 1988) provide little information on the specific computations performed at the nodes of the network, and most cognitive network models provide little or no information on the anatomy involved (McClelland & Rumelhart, 1986). Our approach relates specific mental operations as developed from cognitive models to neural anatomical areas.

The study of reading and listening has been one of the most active areas in cognitive science for the study of internal codes involved in information processing (Posner, 1986). In this article we review results of studies on cognitive tasks that suggest several separate codes for processing individual words. These codes can be accessed from input or from attention. We also review studies of alert monkeys and brain-lesioned patients that provide evidence on the localization of an attention system for visual spatial information. This system is apparently unnecessary for processing single, foveally centered words. Next, we introduce data from positron emission tomography (PET) concerning the neural systems underlying the coding of individual visual (printed) words. These studies support the findings in cognition and also give new evidence for an anterior attention system involved in language processing. Finally, we survey other areas of cognition for which recent findings support the localization of component mental operations.

INTERNAL CODES

The most advanced efforts to develop cognitive models of information processing have been in the area of the coding of individual words through reading and listening

(Posner, 1986; Marshall & Newcombe, 1973; LaBerge & Samuels, 1974; Carr & Pollatsek, 1985; Coltheart, 1985). These efforts have distinguished between a number of internal codes related to the visual, phonological, articulatory, and semantic analysis of a word. Operations at all these levels appear to be involved in understanding a word.

This view began with efforts to develop detailed measurements of the time it takes to execute operations on codes thought to be involved in reading. Figure 1 shows the amount of time needed to determine if two simultaneously shown visual letters or words belong to the same category (Posner, Lewis, & Conrad, 1972). The reaction time to match pairs of items that are physically identical (for example, AA) is faster than reaction time for matches of the same letters or words in the opposite case (Aa), which are in turn faster than matches that have only a common category (Ae). These studies have been interpreted as involving a mental operation of matching based on different codes. In the case of visual identity the code is thought to be the visual form, whereas in cross-case matching it is thought to be the letter or word name. The idea that a word consists of separable physical, phonological, and semantic codes and that operations may be performed on them separately has been basic to many theories of reading and listening (Marshall & Newcombe, 1973; LaBerge & Samuels, 1974; Carr & Pollatsek, 1985; Coltheart, 1985). Thus the operation of rotating

FIGURE 1   Results of reaction time studies in which subjects were asked to classify whether pairs of letters were either both vowels or both consonants (A) or whether pairs of words were both animals or both plants (B). Reaction times are in milliseconds. Each study involved 10 to 12 normal subjects. Standard deviations are typically 20% of the mean value. Data argue in favor of these matches being made on different internal codes (Posner, 1986; Marshall & Newcombe, 1973; LaBerge & Samuels, 1974; Carr & Pollatsek, 1985; Coltheart, 1985). Abbreviations: PI, physical identity; NI, name identity; and RI, rule identity. [Reprinted from Posner, Lewis, & Conrad (1972) with permission of MIT Press.]

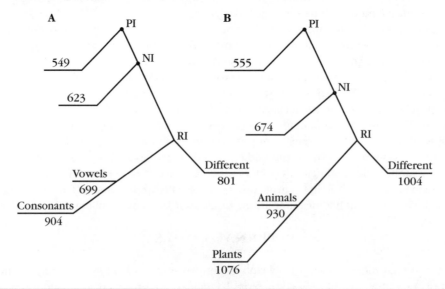

a letter to the upright position is thought to be performed on the visual code (Cooper, 1976), whereas matching to determine if two words rhyme is said to be performed on a phonological representation of the words (Kleiman, 1975). These theories suggest that mental operations take place on the basis of codes related to separate neural systems.

It is not easy to determine if any operation is elementary or whether it is based on only a single code. Even a simple task such as matching identical items can involve parallel operations on both physical and name codes. Indeed, there has been controversy over the theoretical implications of these matching experiments (Boles & Everland, 1981). Some results have suggested that both within- and cross-case matches are performed on physical (visual) codes, whereas others have suggested that they are both performed on name codes (Boles & Everland, 1981). A basic question is to determine whether operations performed on different codes involve different brain areas. This question cannot be resolved by performance studies, since they provide only indirect evidence about localization of the operations performed on different codes.

It has been widely accepted that there can be multiple routes by which codes interact. For example, a visual word may be sounded out to produce a phonological code and then the phonology is used to develop a meaning (Posner, 1986; Marshall & Newcombe, 1973; LaBerge & Samuels, 1974; Carr & Pollatsek, 1985; Coltheart, 1985). Alternately, the visual code may have direct access to a semantic interpretation without any need for developing a phonological code (Posner, 1986; Marshall & Newcombe, 1973; LaBerge & Samuels, 1974; Carr & Pollatsek, 1985; Coltheart, 1985). These routes are thought to be somewhat separate because patients with one form of reading difficulty have great trouble in sounding out nonsense material (for example, the nonword "caik"), indicating they may have a poor ability to use phonics; but they have no problems with familiar words even when the words have irregular pronunciation (for example, pint). Other patients have no trouble with reading nonwords but have difficulty with highly familiar irregular words. Although there is also reason to doubt that these routes are entirely separate, it is often thought that the visual to semantic route is dominant in skilled readers (Marshall & Newcombe, 1973; LaBerge & Samuels, 1974; Carr & Pollatsek, 1985; Coltheart, 1985).

VISUAL SPATIAL ATTENTION

Another distinction in cognitive psychology is between automatic activation of these codes and controlled processing by means of attention (Posner, 1986; Marshall & Newcombe, 1973; LaBerge & Samuels, 1974; Carr & Pollatsek, 1985; Coltheart, 1985). Evidence indicates that a word may activate its internal visual, phonological, and even semantic codes without the person having to pay attention to the word. The evidence for activation of the internally stored visual code of a word is particularly good. Normal subjects show evidence that the stimulus duration necessary for perceiving individual letters within words is shorter than for perceiving the same letter when it is presented in isolation (Reicher, 1969; McClelland & Rumelhart, 1981).

What is known about the localization of attention? Cognitive, brain lesion, and animal studies have identified a posterior neural system involved in visual spatial attention. Patients with lesions of many areas of the brain show neglect of stimuli from the side of space opposite the lesion (DeRenzi, 1982). These findings have led to network views of the neural system underlying visual spatial attention (Mesulam, 1984). However, studies performed with single-cell recording from alert monkeys have been more specific in showing three brain areas in which individual cells show selective enhancement due to the requirement that the monkey attend to a visual location (Mountcastle, 1978; Wurtz, Goldberg, & Robinson, 1980; Petersen & Robinson, 1985). These areas are the posterior parietal lobe of the cerebral cortex, a portion of the thalamus (part of the pulvinar), and areas of the midbrain related to eye movements—all areas in which clinical studies of lesioned patients find neglect of the environment opposite the lesion.

Recent studies of normal (control) and patient populations have used cues to direct attention covertly to areas of the visual field without eye movements (Posner, Walker, Friedrich, & Rafal, 1984). Attention is measured by changes in the efficiency of processing targets at the cued location in comparison with other uncued locations in the visual field. These studies have found systematic deficits in shifting of covert visual attention in patients with injury of the same three brain areas suggested by the monkey studies. When the efficiency of processing is measured precisely by a reaction time test, the nature of the deficits in the three areas differs. Patients with lesions in the parietal lobe show very long reaction times to targets on the side opposite the lesion only when their attention has first been drawn to a different location in the direction of the lesion (Posner, Walker, Friedrich, & Rafal, 1984). This increase in reaction time for uncued but not cued contralesional targets is consistent with a specific deficit in the patient's ability to disengage attention from a cued location when the target is in the contralesional direction. In contrast, damage to the midbrain not only greatly lengthens overall reaction time but increases the time needed to establish an advantage in reaction time at the cued location in comparison to the uncued location (Posner, Cohen, & Rafal, 1982). This finding in consistent with the idea that the lesion causes a slowing of attention movements. Damage to the thalamus (Rafal & Posner, 1987) produces a pattern of slowed reaction to both cued and uncued targets on the side opposite the lesion. This pattern suggests difficulty in being able to use attention to speed processing of targets irrespective of the time allowed to do so (engage deficit). A similar deficit has been found in monkeys performing this task when chemical injections disrupt the performance of the lateral pulvinar (Petersen, Robinson, & Reys, 1985). Thus the simple act of shifting attention to the cued location appears to involve a number of distinct computations (Figure 2) that must be orchestrated to allow the cognitive performance to occur. We now have an idea of the anatomy of several of these computations.

Damage to the visual spatial attention system also produces deficits in recognition of visual stimuli. Patients with lesions of the right parietal lobe frequently neglect (fail to report) the first few letters of a nonword. However, when shown an actual word that occupied the same visual angle, they report it correctly (Sieroff, Palatsek, & Posner, in press). Cognitive studies have often shown a superiority of words over nonwords (Reicher, 1969; McClelland & Rumelhart, 1984). Our results fit with the idea that words do not require scanning by a covert visual spatial attention system.

| **FIGURE 2** | Top of figure illustrates an experimental situation in which attention is summoned from fixation (center) to righthand box by a brightening of the box. This is followed by a target at the cued location or on the opposite side. The boxes below indicate mental operations thought to begin by presentation of the cue. The last four operations involve the posterior visual–spatial attention system; specific deficits have been found in patients with lesions in the parietal (disengage), midbrain (move), and thalamic (engage) areas (Posner, Walker, Friedrich, & Rafal, 1984; Posner, Cohen, & Rafal, 1982; Rafal & Posner, 1987). [Reprinted from Posner, Inhoff, Friedrich, & Cohen (1987) with permission of the Psychonomics Society.] |

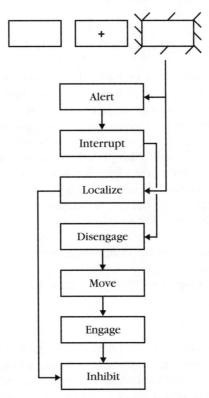

ATTENTION FOR ACTION

In cognitive studies it is often suggested that attention to stimuli occurs only after they have been processed to a very high degree (Allport, 1980; Duncan, 1980). In this view, attention is designed mainly to limit the conflicting actions taken toward stimuli. This form of attention is often called "attention for action." Our studies of patients with parietal lesions suggest that the posterior visual spatial attention system is connected to a more general attention system that is also involved in the processing of language stimuli (Posner, Inhoff, Friedrich, & Cohen, 1987). When normal subjects and patients had to pay close attention to auditory, or spoken, words, the ability of a visual cue to draw their visual spatial attention was retarded. Cognitive studies have been unclear on whether access to meaning requires attention. Although semantic information may be activated without attention being drawn to the specific lexical unit (Marcel, 1983), attention strongly interacts with semantic activation (Henik, Friedrich, & Kellogg, 1983; Hoffman & Macmillan, 1985). Considerable evidence shows that attention to semantic information limits the range of concepts activated. When a person attends to one meaning of a word, activation of alternative meanings of the same item tends to be suppressed (Neely, 1977).

PET IMAGING OF WORDS

How do the operations suggested by cognitive theories of lexical access relate to brain systems? Recently, in a study with normal persons, we used PET to observe brain processes that are active during single word reading (Petersen, Fox, Posner, Mintun, & Raichle, 1988). This method allows examination of averaged changes in cerebral blood flow in localized brain areas during 40 seconds of cognitive activity (Fox, Mintun, Reiman, & Raichle, in press). During this period we presented words at a rate of one per second. Previous PET studies have suggested that a difference of a few millimeters in the location of activations will be sufficient to separate them (Fox et al., 1986).

To isolate component mental operations we used a set of conditions shown in Table 1. By subtracting the control state from the stimulus state, we attempted to isolate areas of activation related to those mental operations present in the stimulus state but not in the control state. For example, subtraction of looking at the fixation point, without any stimuli, from the presentation of passive visual words allowed us to examine the brain areas automatically activated by the word stimuli.[2]

VISUAL WORD FORMS

We examined changes in cerebral blood flow during passive looking at foveally presented nouns. This task produced five areas of significantly greater activation than found in the fixation condition. They all lie within the occipital lobe: two along the calcarine fissure in left and right primary visual cortex and three in left and right lateral regions (Figure 3). As one moves to more complex naming and semantic activation tasks, no new posterior areas are active. Thus the entire visually specific coding takes place within the occipital lobe. Activated areas are found as far anterior as the

TABLE 1	Conditions for PET Subtractive Studies of Words	
CONTROL STATE	**STIMULUS STATE**	**COMPUTATIONS**
Fixation	Passive words	Passive word processing
Repeat words	Generate word use	Semantic association, attention
Passive words	Monitor category	Semantic association, attention (many targets)[a]

[a]The extent of attentional activation increases with the number of targets.

FIGURE 3 Areas activated in visual word reading on the lateral aspect of the cortex (A) and on the medial aspect (B). Triangles refer to the passive visual task minus fixation (black triangle, left hemisphere; white triangle, right hemisphere). Only occipital areas are active. Squares refer to generate minus repeat task. Circles refer to monitor minus passive words task. Solid circles and squares in (A) denote left hemisphere activation; however, in (B), on the midline it is not possible to determine if activation is left or right. The lateral area is thought to involve a semantic network while the midline areas appear to involve attention (Petersen, Fox, Posner, Mintun, & Raichle, 1988).

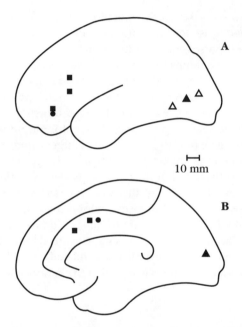

occipital temporal boundary. Are these activations specific to visual words? The presentation of auditory words does not produce any activation in this area. Visual stimuli known to activate striate cortex (for example, checkerboards or dot patterns) do not activate the prestriate areas used in word reading (Fox et al., 1986; Fox, Miezin, Allman, Van Essen, & Raichle, 1987). All other cortical areas active during word reading are anterior. Thus it seems reasonable to conclude that visual word forms are developed in the occipital lobe.

It might seem that occipital areas are too early in the system to support the development of visual word forms. However, the early development of the visual word form is supported by our evidence that patients with right parietal lesions do not neglect the left side of foveally centered words even though they do neglect the initial letters of nonword strings (Sieroff, Pollatsek, & Posner, in press). The presence of pure alexia from lesions of the occipital temporal boundary (Damasio & Damasio, 1983) also supports the development of the visual word form in the occipital area.

Precise computational models of how visual word forms are developed (McClelland & Rumelhart, 1986; Reicher, 1969; McClelland & Rumelhart, 1981) involve parallel computations from feature, letter, and word levels and precise feedback among these levels. The prestriate visual system would provide an attractive anatomy for models relying on such abundant feedback. However, presently we can only tentatively identify the general occipital areas that underlie the visual processing of words.

SEMANTIC OPERATIONS

We used two tasks to study semantic operations. One task required the subject to generate and say aloud a use for each of 40 concrete nouns (for example, a subject may say "pound" when presented with the noun "hammer"). We subtracted the activations from repeating the nouns to eliminate strictly sensory and motor activations. Only two general areas of the cortex were found to be active (Figure 3, square symbols). A second semantic task required subjects to note the presence of dangerous animals in a list of 40 visually presented words. We subtracted passive presentation of the word list to eliminate sensory processing. No motor output was required and subjects were asked to estimate only the frequency of targets after the list was presented. The same two areas of cortex were activated (Figure 3, circles).

One of the areas activated in both semantic tasks was in the anterior left frontal lobe. Figure 4 shows an illustration of this area from averaged scans in auditory and visual generate (minus repeat) and in visual monitoring (minus passive words). This area is strictly left lateralized and appears to be specific to semantic language tasks. Moreover, lesions of this area produce deficits in word fluency tests (Benton, 1968). Thus we have concluded that this general area is related to the semantic network supporting the type of word associations involved in the generate and monitoring tasks.

FIGURE 4

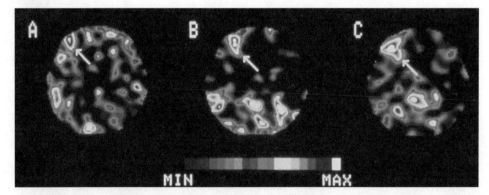

Sample data from the PET activation studies. The arrows indicate areas of activation in the left inferior prefrontal cortex found active in all three semantic processing conditions. (Left) Monitoring visual words for dangerous animals (minus passive visual words). (Middle) Generating uses (minus repeat) for visual stimuli. (Right) Generating uses (minus repeat) for auditory stimuli. In each condition an area of cortical activation was found in the anterior cingulate gyrus on a higher slice (Figure 3). The color scale indicates the relative strength of activation (black indicates the minimum and white, the maximum, for that condition; Petersen, Fox, Posner, Mintun, & Raichle, 1988).

PHONOLOGICAL CODING

When words are presented in auditory form, the primary auditory cortex and an area of the left temporoparietal cortex that has been related to language tasks are activated (Geschwind, 1965). This temporoparietal left-lateralized area seemed to be a good candidate for phonological processing. It was surprising from some perspectives that no visual word reading task activated this area. However, all of our visual tasks involved single common nouns read by highly skilled readers. According to cognitive theories of reading (Marshall & Newcombe, 1973; LaBerge & Samuels, 1974; Carr & Pollatsek, 1985; Coltheart, 1985), these tasks should involve the visual to semantic route. One way of requiring a phonological activation would be to force subjects to tell whether two simultaneous words (for example, pint-lint or row-though) rhymed. This method has been used in cognitive studies to activate phonological codes (Kleiman, 1975). Recent data from our laboratory (Petersen, Fox, Posner, & Raichle, unpub.) show that this task does produce activation near the supramarginal gyrus. We also assume that word reading that involves difficult words or requires storage in short-term memory or is performed by unskilled readers would also activate phonological operations.

ANTERIOR ATTENTION

There is no evidence of activation of any parts of the posterior visual spatial attention system (for example, parietal lobe) in any of our PET language studies. However, it is possible to show that simple tasks that require close monitoring of visual input or that use visual imagery (Petersen, Fox, Miezin, & Raichle, 1988) do activate this parietal system. We conclude, in agreement with the results of our lesion work (Sieroff, Pollatsek, & Posner, in press), that visual word reading is automatic in that it does not require activation of the visual spatial attention system.

In recent cognitive theories the term *attention for action* is used to summarize the idea that attention seems to be involved in selecting those operations that will gain control of output systems (Allport, 1980). This kind of attention system does not appear to be related to any particular sensory or cognitive content and is distinct from the more strictly visual functions assigned to the visual-spatial attention system. Although attention for action seems to imply motor acts, internal selections involved in detecting or noting an event may be sufficient to involve attention in this sense (Duncan, 1980). Whenever subjects are active in this way, we see an increase in blood flow in areas of the medial frontal lobe (Figure 3B, square symbols). When motor output is involved (for example, naming words), these areas tend to be more superior and posterior (supplementary motor area); but when motor activity is subtracted away or when none is required, they appear to be more anterior and inferior (anterior cingulate gyrus). The anterior cingulate has long been thought to be related to attention (Mesulam, 1988) in the sense of generating actions, since lesions of this area produce akinetic mutism (Damasio & Van Hoesen, 1983).

We tested the identification of the anterior cingulate with attention and the left lateral frontal area with a word association network. This was done by applying a cognitive theory that attention would not be much involved in the semantic decision of whether a word belonged to a category (for example, dangerous animal) but would be involved in noting the targets even though no specific action was required. The special involvement of attention with target detection has been widely argued by cognitive studies (Duncan, 1980). These studies have suggested that monitoring produces relatively little evidence of heavy attentional involvement, but when a target is actually detected there is evidence of strong interference so that the likelihood of detecting a simultaneous target is reduced. Thus we varied the number of dangerous animals in our list from one (few targets) to 25 (many targets). We found that blood flow in the anterior cingulate showed much greater change with many targets than with few targets. The left frontal area showed little change in blood flow between these conditions. Additional work with other low-target vigilance tasks not involving semantics also failed to activate the anterior cingulate area.[3] Thus the identification of the anterior cingulate with some part of an anterior attention system that selects for action receives some support from these results.

CONCLUSIONS

The PET data provide strong support for localization of operations performed on visual, phonological, and semantic codes. The ability to localize these operations in studies of average blood flow suggests considerable homogeneity in the neural systems involved, at least among the right-handed subjects with good reading skills who were used in our study.

The PET data on lexical access complement the lesion data cited here in showing that mental operations of the type that form the basis of cognitive analysis are localized in the human brain. This form of localization of function differs from the idea that cognitive tasks are performed by a particular brain area. Visual imagery, word reading, and even shifting visual attention from one location to another are not performed by any single brain area. Each of them involves a large number of component computations that must be orchestrated to perform the cognitive task.

Our data suggest that operations involved both in activation of internal codes and in selective attention obey the general rule of localization of component operations. However, selective attention appears to use neural systems separate from those involved in passively collecting information about a stimulus. In the posterior part of the brain, the ventral occipital lobe appears to develop the visual word form. If active selection or visual search is required, this is done by a spatial system that is deficient in patients with lesions of the parietal lobe (Friedrich, Walker, & Posner, 1985; Riddoch & Humphreys, 1987). Similarly, in the anterior brain the lateral left frontal lobe is involved in the semantic network for coding word associations. Local areas within the anterior cingulate become increasingly involved when the output of the computations within the semantic network is to be selected as a relevant target. Thus the anterior cingulate is involved in the computations in selecting language or other forms of information for action. This separation of anterior and posterior attention systems helps clarify how attention can be involved both in early visual processing and in the selection of information for output.

Several other research areas also support our general hypothesis. In the study of visual imagery, models distinguish between a set of operations involved in the generation of an image and those involved in scanning the image once it is generated (Kosslyn, 1980). Mechanisms involved in image scanning share components with those in visual spatial attention. Patients with lesions of the right parietal lobe have deficits both in scanning the left side of an image and in responding to visual input to their left (Bisiach & Luzzatti, 1978). Although the right hemisphere plays an important role in visual scanning, it apparently is deficient in operations needed to generate an image. Studies of patients whose cerebral hemispheres have been split during surgery show that the isolated left hemisphere can generate complex visual images whereas the isolated right hemisphere cannot (Kosslyn, Holtzman, Farah, & Gazzaniga, 1985).

Patients with lesions of the lateral cerebellum have a deficit in timing motor output and in their threshold for recognition of small temporal differences in sensory input (Ivry, Keele, & Diener, in press). These results indicate that this area of the cerebellum performs a critical computation for timing both motor and sensory tasks. Similarly, studies of memory have indicated that the hippocampus performs a computation needed for storage in a manner that will allow conscious retrieval of the item once it has left current attention. The same item can be used as part of a skill even though damage to the hippocampus makes it unavailable to conscious recollection (Squire, 1986).

The joint anatomical and cognitive approach discussed in this article should open the way to a more detailed understanding of the deficits found in the many disorders involving cognitive or attentional operations in which the anatomy is poorly understood. For example, we have attempted to apply the new knowledge of the anatomy of selective attention to study deficits in patients with schizophrenia (Early, Posner, & Reiman, in preparation).

REFERENCES

Allport, D. A. (1980). In G. Claxton (Ed.), *Cognitive psychology: New directions* (pp. 112–153). Boston: Routledge & Kegan Paul.

Anderson, J. R. (1980). *Cognitive psychology and its implications.* San Francisco: Freeman.

Benton, A. L. (1968). *Neuropsychologia 18,* 53.

Bisiach, E., & Luzzatti, C. (1978). *Cortex 14,* 129.

Boles, D. B., & Eveland, D. C. (1983). *J. Exp. Psychol. Hum. Percept. Perform. 9,* 657; Proctor, R. W. (1981). *Psychol. Rev. 88,* 291.

Churchland, P. S. (1986). *Neurophilosophy.* Cambridge, MA: MIT Press.

Cooper, L. A. (1976). *Percept. Psychophys. 7,* 20.

Damasio, A. R., & Damasio, H. (1983). *Neurology 33,* 1573.

Damasio, A. R., & Van Hoesen, G. W. (1983). In K. M. Heilman and P. Satz (Eds.), *Neuropsychology of Human Emotion* (pp. 85–110). New York: Guilford.

DeRenzi, E. (1982). *Disorders of space exploration and cognition.* New York: Wiley.

Duncan, J. (1980). *Psychol. Rev. 87,* 272.

Early, T. S., Posner, M. I., & Reiman, E. M. (in preparation).

Fox, P. T. et al. (1986). *Nature 323,* 806.

Fox, P. T., Miezin, F. M., Allman, J. M., Van Essen, D. C., & Raichle, M. E. (1987). *J. Neurosci. 7,* 913.

Fox, P. T., Mintun, M., Reiman, E. M., & Raichle, M. E. (in press). *J. Cereb. Blood Flow Metab.*

Friedrich, F. J., Walker, J. A., & Posner, M. I. (1985). *Cog. Neuropsychol. 2,* 250; Riddoch, J. M., & Humphreys, G. W. (1980). In M. Jeannerod (Ed.), *Neurophysiological and neuropsychological aspects of spatial neglect* (pp. 151–181). New York: Elsevier.

Geschwind, N. (1965). *Brain 88,* 227.

Henik, A., Friedrich, F. J., & Kellogg, W. A. (1983). *Mem. Cognit. 11,* 363; Hoffman, J. E., & Macmillan, F. W. In M. I. Posner and O. S. M. Marin (Eds.), *Attention and performance XI* (pp. 585–599). Hillsdale, NJ: Erlbaum.

Ivry, R. I., Keele, S. W., & Diener, H. C. (in press). *Exp. Brain Res.*

Kleiman, G. M. (1975). *J. Verb. Learn. Verb. Behav. 24,* 323.

Kosslyn, S. W. (1980). *Image and mind.* Cambridge, MA: Harvard Univ. Press.

Kosslyn, S. W., Holtzman, J. D., Farah, M. J., & Gazzaniga, M. S. (1985). *J. Exp. Psychol. Gen. 114,* 311.

Marcel, A. (1983). *Cog. Psychol. 15,* 197.

Marshall, J. C., & Newcombe, F. J. (1973). *J. Psychol. Res. 2,* 175; LaBerge, D., & Samuels, J. (1974). *Cog. Psychol. 10,* 293; Carr, T. H., & Pollatsek, A. (1985). In D. Besner, D. Waller, & G. E. Mackinnon (Eds.), *Reading research,* vol. 5. New York: Academic Press, pp. 1–82; Coltheart, M. (1985). In M. I. Posner & O. S. M. Marin (Eds.), *Attention and performance XI,* Hillsdale, NJ: Erlbaum, pp. 3–37.

McClelland, J. L., & Rumelhart, D. E. (1986). *Parallel distributed processing,* vol. 2. Cambridge, MA: MIT Press, pp. 170–215.

Mesulam, M. M. (1981). *Ann. Neurol. 10,* 309; Goldman-Rakic, P. S. (1988). *Annu. Rev. Neurosci. 11,* 156.

Mountcastle, V. B. (1978). *J. R. Soc. Med. 71,* 14; Wurtz, R. H., Goldberg, M. E., & Robinson, D. L. (1980). *Prog. Psychobiol. Physiol. Psychol. 9,* 43; Petersen, S. E., Robinson, D. L., & Keys, W. (1985). *J. Neurophysiol. 54,* 367.

Neely, J. (1977). *J. Exp. Psychol. Gen. 3,* 226.

Petersen, S. E., Fox, P. T., Miezin, F. M., & Raichle, M. E. (1988). *Invest. Ophthalmol. Vis. Sci. 29,* 22 (abstr.).

Petersen, S. E., Fox, P. T., Posner, M. I., Mintun, M., & Raichle, M. E. (1988). *Nature 331,* 585.

Petersen, S. E., Fox, P. T., Posner, M. I., & Raichle, M. E., unpublished data.

Petersen, S. E., Robinson, D. L., & Keys, W. J. (1985). *Neurophysiology. 54,* 207.

Posner, M. I. (1986). *Chronometric explorations of mind.* Oxford: Oxford Univ. Press.

Posner, M. I., Cohen, Y., & Rafal, R. D. (1982). *Proc. R. Soc. London Ser. B 298,* 187; Posner, M. L., Choate, L., Rafal, R. D., & Vaughan, J. (1985). *Cog. Neuropsychol. 2,* 250.

Posner, M. I., Inhoff, W. R., Friedrich, F. J., & Cohen, A. (1987). *Psychobiology 15,* 107.

Posner, M. I., Lewis, J., & Conrad, C., (1972). In J. F. Kavanaugh & I. G. Mattingly (Eds.), *Language by ear and by eye.* Cambridge, MA: MIT Press, pp. 159–192.

Posner, M. I., Walker, J., Friedrich, F. J., & Rafal, R. D. (1984). *J. Neurosci. 4,* 1863.

Rafal, R. D., & Posner, M. I. (1987). *Proc. Natl. Acad. Sci. U.S.A. 84,* 7349.

Raichle, M. E. (1983). *Annu. Rev. Neurosci. 6,* 243.

Reicher, G. M. (1969). *J. Exp. Psychol. 81,* 274; McClelland, J. L., & Rumelhart, D. E. (1981). *Psychol. Rev. 88,* 375.

Sieroff, E., Pollatsek, A., & Posner, M. I. (in press). *Cog. Neuropsychol.;* Sieroff, E., & Posner, M. I. (in press). *Cog. Neuropsychol.*

Squire, L. R. (1986). *Science 232,* 1612.

NOTES

1. Supported by the Office of Naval Research contract N00014-86-K-0289 and by the McDonnell Center for Higher Brain Studies. The imaging studies were performed at the

Malinckrodt Institute of Radiology of Washington University with the support of NIH grants NS 06833, HL 13851, NS 14834, and AG 03991. We thank M. K. Rothbart and G. L. Shulman for helpful comments.

2. Subtraction was used to infer mental processes by F. C. Donders in 1868 for reaction time data. The method has been disputed because it is possible that subjects use different strategies as the task is made more complex. By using PET, we can study this issue. For example, when subtracting the fixation control from the generate condition, one should obtain only those active areas found in passive (minus fixation) plus repeat (minus passive) plus generate (minus repeat). Our preliminary analyses of these conditions generally support the method.

3. The studies of the visual monitoring task were conducted by S. E. Petersen, P. T. Fox, M. I. Posner, and M. E. Raichle. Unpublished studies on vigilance were conducted by J. Pardo, P. T. Fox, M. I. Posner, and M. E. Raichle, using somatosensory and visual tasks.

QUESTIONS FOR FURTHER THOUGHT

1. What kinds of techniques do Posner and his colleagues use to localize cognitive functions?

2. How is PET scanning used to study cognitive processes? What kinds of assumptions does PET scanning make?

3. What is the reason for subtracting activations recorded in a control state from those recorded during presentation of a target stimulus?

4. What is the joint approach that Posner believes to be the key to understanding many cognitive disorders?

5. To what extent should researchers generalize the results of studies of patients with brain lesions to people in general? Support your position.

Is Visual Imagery Really Visual?
Overlooked Evidence From
Neuropsychology

Martha Farah

INTRODUCTION

Create an image in your mind of the following scene: You are sitting on a beach looking out at the ocean as a sailboat slowly moves across the horizon. This visual image you have created must involve some kind of representations in your mind. Are these representations the same ones you would have created had you actually been sitting on a beach and viewing the scene, as opposed to merely imagining it?

One view, traceable at least to the writings of Hume (1739/1969), holds that a person creates the visual images that make up a scene, like the beach scene you imagined, by activating the same perceptual representations activated by input from the eyes and other sensory organs. Relevant to this argument is the Shepard and Metzler reading in this volume on mental rotation of three-dimensional objects. Shepard and colleagues showed that visual images can only be reoriented by a continuous mental rotation akin to physically rotating a real object (Shepard, 1984).

An alternative view, attributable to Pylyshyn (1973), holds that visual images do not involve the perceptual representations activated by sensory input. Rather, visual images are the products of general cognitive processes and individuals' tacit (i.e., unconscious) knowledge about how their visual systems operate. Studies of people with congenital blindness provide evidence that visual images may not necessarily involve perceptual representations activated by sensory input. Despite being blind from birth, these subjects show essentially normal performance on tasks such as image rotation.

As is often the case, evidence from psychological studies does not weigh in with sufficient strength on one side or the other to uproot either position. Farah attempts to resolve this impasse by incorporating evidence from neuropsychological studies, including studies of brain activity that occurs while subjects are creating visual images and studies of subjects with damage to the part of the brain used for seeing. Both vision and visual imagery appear to activate similar areas of the brain.

Source: From Farah, M. J. (1988). Is visual imagery really visual? Overlooked evidence from neuropsychology. *Psychological Review, 95,* 307–317. Copyright © 1988 by the American Psychological Association. Adapted with permission.

Is Visual Imagery Really Visual? Overlooked Evidence From Neuropsychology

35

It is difficult to understate the importance of this result. The result suggests that visual imagery not only achieves a kind of subjective reality to those who experience, but it achieves a kind of objective, brain-based reality as well. Moreover, the result suggests why visual imagery can seem so real: People experience it in roughly the same parts of the brain as they experience actual visual sensations. Those who doubt the reality of visual imagery would have a difficult time accounting for Farah's results.

———

Does visual imagery engage some of the same representations used in visual perception? . . . This article reviews previously overlooked neuropsychological evidence on the relation between imagery and perception. . . . This evidence includes electrophysiological and cerebral blood flow studies localizing brain activity during imagery to cortical visual areas, and parallels between the selective effects of brain damage on visual perception and imagery. ■

The question of whether visual imagery is really visual, that is, whether it involves some of the same representations of stimuli normally engaged by the perception of those stimuli, has been the subject of a long-standing debate in cognitive psychology. This article reviews a set of empirical findings from neuropsychology that are directly relevant to this debate. I will argue that this generally overlooked source of data can play an important role in determining the relation between imagery and perception, because it is immune to many of the criticisms and alternative explanations that have plagued the cognitive psychology approach to this topic.

One side of the debate maintains that imaging consists of the top-down activation of perceptual representations, that is, representations that are also activated automatically by an external stimulus during perception. This idea dates back at least as far as the philosophical writings of Hume (1739/1969) and has been put forth more recently by Hebb (1968), Shepard (1978, 1984) and Finke (1980). In contrast, the other side of the debate maintains that the representations used in imagery are not the representations used in perception, and that the recall of visual information, even when accompanied by the phenomenology of "seeing with the mind's eye," is carried out using representations that are distinct from those used in veridical seeing (Pylyshyn, 1973, 1978, 1984, chap. 8).

What is at stake in this debate, that it should continue to be a focus of research and discussion on mental imagery? To begin with, it is a basic question about the representations underlying mental imagery, and on these grounds alone it warrants focused attention from cognitive psychologists. In an early and influential critique of imagery research, Pylyshyn (1973) concurred with imagery researchers that this issue is central: "Atwood (1971) is quite right when he states, 'The most elementary question that can be asked about mnemonic visualization is the following: Does the mnemonic image actually involve the visual system?'" A decade and a half of active research on this issue has ensued. (See Finke, 1985, for a recent review.) The resolution of this controversy would also have broader implications beyond our understanding of mental imagery per se: For example, if visual imagery does engage visual perceptual representations, then at least some perceptual representations are not "informationally encapsulated" (see Fodor, 1983) insofar as they may take input from higher cognitive processes (i.e., imagery) as well as from bottom-up perceptual processes triggered by external stimuli. Furthermore, such a conclusion would imply that thinking in images involves representations (in the perceptual system) that are distinct from the representations used in nonimagistic thought, in turn implying a modular structure for the representations underlying thought (cf. Anderson, 1983; Fodor, 1983).

In discussing the theoretical implications of the relation between imagery and perception, it is worth noting explicitly an issue for which this relation has no direct implications, namely, the issue of the format of mental images. Claims that images are pictorial or descriptive, array-like or propositional, analog or symbolic, are all claims about the format of images. As Block (1983) has pointed out, the relation of imagery to perception and the format of mental imagery are issues which are often conflated but are in principle independent. The finding that imagery shares representations with perception would not imply that imagery is pictorial; both imagery and perception might be descriptive. Furthermore, perceptual representations and mental images could have the same format (pictorial or descriptive) and yet be distinct representations.

• • •

EVIDENCE FROM NEUROPSYCHOLOGY

A considerable number of findings from neuropsychology are relevant to the relation between imagery and perception, although even within neuropsychology there seems to be little awareness of the quantity and coherence of these many separate findings. The importance of this evidence is that it expands qualitatively, as well as quantitatively, the support for visual perceptual mechanisms in visual mental imagery. The relevant findings in neuropsychology can be roughly grouped into two categories: those that implicate the use of visual processing areas of the brain in visual imagery, and those that implicate shared functional mechanisms for visual imagery and visual perception, above and beyond the fact that they share common brain regions.

COMMON NEURAL SUBSTRATES FOR IMAGERY AND PERCEPTION

Cortical visual processing begins in the occipital lobes, which contain primary and secondary visual cortex, and continues in the posterior parietal and temporal lobes, which contain modality-specific visual representations as well as multimodal representations. The earliest suggestion that imagery might involve the use of the visual areas of the brain came from case reports of cortically blind patients. Cortical blindness is loss of vision due to destruction of the occipital cortex. Many of these patients appear unable to use mental imagery, despite the relative preservation of other cognitive abilities (Brown, 1972; Symonds & Mackenzie, 1957). A systematic assessment of

Is Visual Imagery Really Visual? Overlooked Evidence From Neuropsychology

37

imagery ability in cortically blind patients with well-localized lesions could in principle provide strong evidence on the relation between the neural substates of visual imagery and visual perception; in practice, however, the documented cases do not provide sufficiently detailed information about the patients' impaired and intact cognitive abilities to be more than suggestive.

Stronger evidence that parts of the visual cortex participate in visual imagery comes from the use of regional cerebral blood flow and electrophysiological techniques for measuring and localizing brain activity in normal subjects. Regional cerebral blood flow provides a spatially precise method of measuring regional brain activity in normal humans, with increased blood flow indexing increased activity. Roland and Friberg (1985) examined regional cerebral blood flow while subjects rested and during three cognitive tasks: mental arithmetic (subtracting 3s starting at 50), memory scanning of an auditory stimulus (mentally jumping every second word in a well-known musical jingle), and visual imagery (visualizing a walk through one's neighborhood making alternating right and left turns starting at one's front door). Subjects were periodically queried as to their current answer (i.e., the number they were on in the mental arithmetic task, the word they were on the auditory rehearsal task, and the location they were at in the imagery task). This procedure yielded error rates, from which the authors concluded that the three tasks were equally difficult. In each of the 11 normal subjects tested, the pattern of blood flow in the visual imagery task showed massive activation of the posterior regions of the brain compared to the resting state, including the occipital lobe (the visual cortex proper) and posterior superior parietal and posterior inferior temporal areas important for higher visual processing. These are the same areas that normally show increased blood flow during visual-perceptual tasks (Mazziotta, Phelps, & Halgren, 1983; Roland, 1982; Roland & Skinhoj, 1981). Furthermore, these areas did not show increases in blood flow compared with the resting state in the other two cognitive tasks.

Roland and Friberg's (1985) results demonstrate visual cortical involvement in a fairly complex imagery task that includes both visualizing scenes from memory and transforming them (at each turn in the imaginary walk). Goldenberg, Podreka, Steiner, and Willmes (1987) devised a simpler imagery task, along with a control task differing from the imagery task only in the absence of imagery. Different groups of normal subjects were given the same auditorily presented lists of concrete words to learn under different instructional conditions: One group was told to just listen to the words and try to remember them, and the other group was told to visualize the referents of the words as a mnemonic strategy. Some subjects in the no-imagery group reported spontaneously imaging the words when questioned after the experiment, and they were reclassified as imagery condition subjects. Recall was higher overall for the imagery group, as would be expected if these subjects did indeed differ from the no-imagery group in their use of imagery. The patterns of blood flow recorded during the two conditions also differed, by two distinct measures. First, there was relatively more blood flow to the occipital lobes, particularly the left inferior occipital region, in the imagery condition. Second, the pattern of covariation of blood flow among brain areas (calculated by a Smallest Space Analysis; Lingoes, 1979), which provides another index of regional brain activity, was also greater in the occipital and posterior temporal areas of the brain bilaterally in the imagery condition compared to the nonimagery condition.

Goldenberg, Podreka, Steiner, Suess, Deeke, & Willmes (in press) compared the patterns of regional blood flow while subjects tried to answer several types of questions, among which were questions that require visual imagery to answer (e.g., "Is the green of pine trees darker than the green of grass?") and questions that do not require imagery to answer (e.g., "Is the categorical imperative an ancient grammatical form?"). Despite the superficial similarity of the two types of task, answering yes–no general-knowledge questions, they differed significantly in the patterns of regional cerebral blood flow they evoked: The imagery questions caused greater occipital blood flow than did the nonimagery questions. The results of the Smallest Space Analysis also implicated occipital activity in the imagery condition, as well as revealing activity in the posterior temporal and posterior parietal visual processing areas. In contrast, the nonimagery condition did not reveal visual area activation.

Might the increased visual area activity in Goldenberg et al.'s (in press) imagery tasks merely index greater effort by subjects in those tasks than in the nonimagery control tasks? This is unlikely for three reasons. First, task effortfulness is generally reflected in blood flow changes to the frontal lobes, and has not been observed to produce occipital changes (Ingvar & Risberg, 1967; Lassen, Ingvar, & Skinhoj, 1978). Second, subjects in the first experiment who were given the more effortful task of memorizing lists of abstract words, rather than concrete words, under the same task conditions with no imagery instructions, did not show increased blood flow. Third, whereas the imagery condition of Goldenberg et al.'s (1987) first experiment involved more effortful processing than the nonimagery condition, the imagery condition of Goldenberg et al.'s (in press) experiment was easier than the nonimagery condition (as evidenced by the lower error rates).

In three very different experimental paradigms, one a rather open-ended request to visualize a walk through familiar territory, another a verbal list-learning task in which imagery use was manipulated by explicit instructions, and the third a question-answering task in which imagery use was manipulated by implicit differences in the nature of the questions, convergent findings emerged: In each case, the imagery induced blood flow to the visual areas of the brain. Furthermore, in the two latter studies, the imagery conditions differed minimally from the comparison conditions, which did not show these increases.

Further evidence that the visual cortex participates in visual imagery comes from electrophysiological techniques: electroencephalography (EEG) and event-related potentials (ERP). In EEG techniques, suppression of alpha rhythm (EEG activity in a certain range of frequencies) is associated with increased brain activity. Many authors have found that visual imagery is accompanied by alpha rhythm attenuation over the visual areas of the brain (Barratt, 1956; Brown, 1966; Davidson & Schwartz, 1977; Golla, Hutton, & Gray Walter, 1943; Short, 1953; Slatter, 1960). Unfortunately, a methodological flaw in most of these studies is the lack of control for the degree of overall mental effort involved in the visual imagery and comparison conditions. However, the study of Davidson and Schwartz (1977) does contain the appropriate control measures and provides a clear and elegant demonstration of the modality-specific nature of the brain activity underlying imagery: Davidson and Schwartz measured the EEG alpha rhythm simultaneously over the visual (occipital) and tactile (parietal) areas of the brain, during visual imagery (imagining a flashing light), tactile imagery (imagining one's forearm being tapped), and combined visual and tactile imagery (imagining the flashes and taps together). Whereas there was no difference in total alpha attenuation between the visual and tactile imagery conditions (i.e., the overall effects of tactile and visual imagery on general effort and arousal were the same), the site of maximum alpha attenuation in the visual imagery condition was over the visual areas and the site of maximum alpha attenuation in the tactile imagery condition was over the tactile areas. Alpha attenuation in the combined visual and tactile imagery condition showed a more balanced pattern of distribution across both visual and tactile areas.

Recent work using ERP techniques offers another electrophysiological window on the areas of the brain engaged during imagery. Event-related potentials differ from EEG in that they measure only the electrical activity of the brain that is synchronized with (and thus presumably "related" to) the processing of a stimulus. Farah, Peronnet, Weisberg, and Perrin (1988) measured the ERP to visually presented words under two different instructional conditions: simply reading the words, and reading the words and imaging their referents (e.g., if the word is *cat,* imaging a cat). The words were presented for 200 ms each. The ERPs were recorded from 16 standard sites on the scalp, including occipital, parietal, temporal, and frontal locations. The first 450 ms of the ERPs in both conditions were indistinguishable, reflecting their common visual and lexical processing stages. However, later components of the two conditions differed from one another: In the imagery condition there was a highly localized increase in positivity of the ERP, relative to the reading-only condition, at the occipital electrodes, implicating occipital activity during the process of imaging. Scalp current density analyses of the ERP data, which provide enhanced localization (Perrin, Bertrand, & Pernier, 1986) revealed a central occipital current source and lateral occipital current sinks, consistent with ERP generators in occipital cortex; and two occipito-temporal current sources and lateral fronto-temporal current sinks, consistent with an ERP generator in each temporal lobe.

Is it possible that this occipital ERP reflects general effects of cognitive load and is not specifically related to imagery? To test this possibility, subjects were presented with a new task, the misspelling detection task, which involved the same stimuli presented under the same conditions as the previous experiment. This experiment compared the reading-only of correctly spelled words to the detection of occasional misspellings, an effortful visual task using the same stimuli as the imagery task (except that about one in eight words was misspelled). The difference between the ERPs from reading and misspelling detection showed a different polarity as well as a different temporal and spatial distribution compared with the imagery effect observed earlier: This effect consisted of increased negativity rather than positivity, affecting a broader region of the posterior scalp (extending to the anterior temporal electrodes), and peaking about 200 ms earlier. Therefore, the focal occipital positivity observed when subjects form images is not merely a manifestation of a general "visual effort" effect on the evoked potential, but is tied more specifically to the processes taking place in the imagery condition of the experiment. Furthermore, when the imagery condition was changed in a subsequent experiment from one in which the subject images a different object from memory on each trial, to the repeated imaging of a small set of line drawings that subjects memorized just before ERP recording, the same focal occipital positivity ensued.

Farah, Peronnet, Gonon, and Giard (in press) took a different approach to localizing mental imagery in the brain using event-related potential techniques, by examining the effect of imagery on the ERP to visual stimuli. Subjects were instructed to image stimuli while being presented with real stimuli, so that we could observe the effect of imagery on the ERP to stimuli. We reasoned that if imagery has a systematic effect on the ERP to stimuli, then there must be some common brain locus at which imagery and perceptual processing interact. More important, if the interaction between imagery and perception is content specific—that is, for example, if imaging an *H* affects the ERP to *H*s more than the ERP to *T*s, and imaging a *T* affects the ERP to *T*s more than the ERP to *H*s—then that interaction must be taking place at some locus where information about the differences between *H*s and *T*s is preserved, that is, at a representational locus. In this experiment, subjects imaged *H*s and *T*s while performing a detection task in which an *H*, a *T*, or no stimulus was presented on each trial. The image that the subject was instructed to form on a given trial was nonpredictive of the upcoming stimulus. The ERPs to *H*s and *T*s while subjects imaged the same letter were compared with the ERPs to *H*s and *T*s while subjects imaged the other letter. In this way, we could observe the content-specific effect of imagery on the visual ERP while holding constant the actual stimuli to which the ERPs were recorded (equal numbers of *H*s and *T*s in both conditions) and the effort of forming and holding an image (equal numbers of *H* and *T* images in each condition). If there is a content-specific effect of imagery on the visual ERP, then by localizing it we can put constraints on the location of representations accessed by both imagery and perception.

Imagery had a content-specific effect on the evoked potential within the first 200 ms of stimulus processing, and this effect was localized at the occipital recording sites. Furthermore, the inference that the underlying brain location of the image-percept interaction is occipital is strengthened by the fact that the time course of the effect of imagery on the ERP was the same as that of the first negative peak of the visual ERP waveform, which is believed to originate in occipital cortex (Lesevre & Joseph, 1980; Maier, Dagnelie, Spekreijse, & Van Dijk, 1987). The finding that an effect is maximal just when an ERP component is maximal implies that the neural locus of the effect is one or more of the generators of the ERP component.

To sum up the relevant electrophysiological literature, two measures, EEG and ERP, have been used in a variety of experiments involving imagery. In all cases, imagery activity was localized to the occipital regions. Furthermore, in a subset of this body of experiments (Davidson & Schwartz, 1977; Farah, Peronnet, Weisberg, & Perrin, 1988; Farah, Peronnet, Gonon, & Giard, in press), control conditions were included which allow us to assess the cognitive specificity of these electrophysiological effects, and in each case they were associated with visual imagery activity per se. The electrophysiological evidence is thus in agreement with results from a very different methodology, regional cerebral blood flow, in implicating occipital activity during imagery. Across a variety of tasks, it has been found that imagery engages visual cortex, whereas other tasks, many of which are highly similar save for the absence of visual imagery, do not.

The most straightforward and parsimonious conclusion from this pattern of results is that mental images are visual representations, that is, they consist at least in part of some of the same representations used in vision. However, there does exist a logically correct alternative explanation according to which mental images are not visual representations, but are merely accompanied by activation in visual brain areas. On this account, the visual area activation is epiphenomenal with respect to the functions of imagery. To distinguish between these alternatives, we must find out whether destruction of visual brain areas results in imagery impairments as well as visual impairments. Parallel impairments in imagery and perception after brain damage imply that the visual areas implicated in the localization studies reviewed earlier do play a functional role in imagery, whereas the finding that imagery is unimpaired in patients with visual disorders following brain damage implies that activation of visual areas during imagery is epiphenomenal. The data reviewed in the next section allow us to distinguish between a functional and an epiphenomenal role for the visual system in imagery by reporting the effects of damage to the visual system on imagery ability. In addition, these data add quantitatively to the accumulating evidence for the involvement of the visual system in mental imagery.

FUNCTIONAL PARALLELS BETWEEN IMAGERY AND PERCEPTION AFTER BRAIN DAMAGE

The existence of highly selective deficits in visual abilities has contributed to our understanding of the functional architecture of visual perception by demonstrating which perceptual abilities are independent of which other abilities. If visual imagery uses the same representational machinery as visual perception, then one should expect selective deficits in the imagery abilities of patients that parallel their selective perceptual deficits. In fact, for all of the types of selective visual deficits due to cortical lesions in which imagery has been examined, parallel imagery deficits have been observed.

At early stages of cortical visual processing, color is represented separately from other visual stimulus dimensions, and brain damage affecting the cortical visual areas can therefore result in relatively isolated color vision deficits (see Cowey, 1982; Meadows, 1974). A long history of the case-by-case study of patients with acquired cerebral color blindness has documented an association between loss of color perception and loss of color imagery (e.g., Beauvois & Saillant, 1985, Case 2; Heidenhain, 1927; Jossman, 1929; Lewandowsky, 1908; Pick, 1908; Riddoch & Humphreys, 1987; Sacks & Wasserman, 1987; Stengel, 1948). In addition to being unable to identify or discriminate among colors, these patients cannot report the colors of common objects from memory (e.g., the color of a football, cactus, or German Shepard's back), a task that most people find requires imaging the object in color. These patients are not generally impaired in their cognitive functioning. In fact, Sacks and Wasserman (1987) and Riddoch and Humphreys (1987) have documented good general imagery ability in their patients with acquired cerebral color blindness, as assessed by drawings and descriptions of objects from memory; the only aspect of imagery that was impaired was imagery for color. The implication of this association between the perception of color and imagery for color is that the two abilities depend upon the same neural substrates of color representation.

DeRenzi and Spinnler (1967) pointed out the need for a more systematic study of color-related impairments after brain damage, and undertook a large group study of unilaterally brain-damaged patients in which they assessed color vision and color imagery. Color vision was tested in two ways: having the patient sort a set of colored paper squares into pairs having the same color, and having the patient name or trace out the digit embedded in random dots that are segregated into digit and background only by color (the "Ishihara" test of color blindness). Color recall was also tested in two ways: having the patient respond verbally to questions of the form "What color is a tangerine?" and "What color is cement?" and having the patients color black and white line drawings of objects with their characteristic color chosen from a set of colored crayons. DeRenzi and Spinnler found that patients who had impaired color vision also had impaired color imagery. Perhaps it is not surprising that a patient with a color vision deficit would perform poorly on the coloring task, in which color vision is needed to select the appropriate crayon, or that patients with language or memory impairments would do poorly on a verbal task of color memory. However, the relation between color vision impairment and color imagery impairment held high statistical significance even when patients who were neither language impaired nor memory impaired were considered on just the verbal test of color imagery.

Another source of evidence that color is represented by the same neural structures in imagery and perception comes from an intriguing case study by Beauvois and Saillant (1985, Case 1) of a patient whose visual areas had been neuroanatomically disconnected from her language areas by a stroke. The patient was able to perform color tasks that were purely visual, such as sorting objects on the basis of color and identifying the embedded characters in the Ishihara test of color blindness, because her visual areas had not been damaged. Her general verbal ability was also quite intact, as evidenced by a verbal IQ score of 123, because her language areas had not been damaged. However, if the task involved coordinating a visual and verbal representation, for example, naming a visually presented color or pointing to a named color, her performance was extremely poor, owing to the neuroanatomical disconnection between her language and vision areas. The patient was tested on various color memory tasks, including two similar to those of DeRenzi and Spinnler (1967): viewing correctly and incorrectly colored drawings of objects and distinguishing between them, and answering verbally posed questions about the color of common objects of the form "What color is a—?" The patient was able to perform the purely visual color memory task, implying that her mental images of colored objects were not disconnected from the visual areas used in recognizing and discriminating among the colored pictures. Her performance on the verbally posed color questions depended upon the nature of the question: For questions that made use of verbal associations between objects and colors (e.g., "What color is Paris ham?" where "Paris ham" is also called "white ham"; or "What color is envy?") the patient performed normally. In contrast, for questions that appear to require mental imagery (e.g., "What color is a gherkin?"), she performed poorly. Again, this implies that whereas verbal memory associations for colors were not disconnected from the language areas of this patient with visual–verbal disconnection, imagistic representations of color were. Finally, Beauvois and Saillant directly manipulated whether the patient used imagery or nonimagistic memory representations for retrieving the same information. In one condition, they asked questions such as "You have learnt what color snow is. It is often said. What do people say when they are asked what color snow is?" or "It is winter. Imagine a beautiful snowy landscape . . . Can you see it? Well, now tell me what color the snow is." The patient performed normally when biased toward a verbal recall strategy, and her performance dropped significantly when biased toward an imagery recall strategy. This is again what one would expect to find if the color of mental images is represented in the same neural substrate as the color of visual percepts.

In sum, three types of evidence support the hypothesis that imaging an object in color requires some of the same neural representations necessary for color vision: Individual cases of acquired central color blindness are reported to have lost their color imagery, in a group of patients with varying degrees of color vision impairment color imagery is correlated with color vision, and in a case of visual–verbal disconnection, images were equivalent to visual representations in terms of their interactions with other visual and verbal task components.

Patients with bilateral parieto-occipital disease often have trouble knowing where an object is in the visual field, without any difficulty identifying what the object is (DeRenzi, 1982). The impairment in the localization of stimuli in space may be quite selective to the visual modality, so that these patients can orient to tactile and auditory stimuli. At the same time, these patients are unimpaired in their ability to recognize visual stimuli. Thus, such a patient may quickly identify an object such as a postage stamp held somewhere in his or her visual field, but may be unable to indicate its position either verbally or by pointing. Other patients, with bilateral temporo-occipital disease, may show the opposite pattern of visual abilities (Bauer & Rubens, 1985). These "agnosic" patients are impaired in their ability to recognize visually presented stimuli, despite adequate elementary visual capabilities (e.g., size of visual field, acuity), and their failure of recognition is modality specific: They are able to recognize objects by touch or by characteristic sounds. Furthermore, their ability to localize visually presented objects is unimpaired. Thus, such a patient might fail to recognize a postage stamp by sight but could accurately point to its location. This dissociation is evidence for a rather counterintuitive division of labor in the visual system between the localization of stimuli and their identification, an idea which is also supported by animal experimentation (Ungerleider & Mishkin, 1982). Levine, Warach, and Farah (1985) studied the imagery abilities of a pair of patients, one with visual localization impairment after bilateral parieto-occipital damage and one with visual object identification impairment after bilateral temporo-occipital damage, with special attention to the distinction between spatial location information and single object appearance information in visual images. We found that the preserved and impaired aspects of vision in each patient were similarly preserved or impaired in imagery: The patient with object identification difficulties was unable to draw or describe the appearances of familiar objects, animals, and faces from memory, despite being able to draw and describe in great detail the relative locations of cities and states on a map, furniture in his house, and landmarks in his city. The patient with object localization difficulties was unable to describe the relative locations of landmarks in his neighborhood, cities in the United States, or, when blindfolded, to point to furniture in his hospital room. He was, however, able to give detailed descriptions of the appearance of a variety of objects, animals, and faces. In a review of the literature for similar cases, we found that for a majority of the published cases of selective visual "what" or "where" deficit, when the appropriate imagery abilities were tested they showed parallel patterns of imagery deficit, and in no case was there a well-documented violation of this parallelism: Of 28 cases of object identification difficulties in the literature, 14 were reported to have parallel imagery impairments, 6 were not examined regarding imagery, and 3 were reported to have intact imagery. For all 3 of this last group of patients, the authors of the case reports relied exclusively on the patients' own introspective assessments of their imagery ability. Of 26 cases of visual disorientation, imagery for spatial relations was tested in only 12. In 9 of these cases it was found to be defective. Of the remaining 3, the information concerning their imagery consisted of in one case having "good memory for paths in the city" with no other details given, in another case being able to "describe a geographic map" and in a third being able to describe the ward plan accurately. This third patient was unusual for a case of visual disorientation in that she was able to find her way about.

Dissociations between object recognition abilities within the temporo-occipital "what" system also exist. One form of dissociation that has been observed corresponds roughly to an impairment in recognizing living things (people, animals, and plants) with relatively better recognition of nonliving things. Farah, Hammond, Mehta, and Ratcliff (in press) studied a patient with this constellation of recognition abilities, comparing his ability to image the appearances of living and nonliving things. Imagery was tested by yes–no questions, such as "Are the hind legs of a kangaroo shorter than the front legs?" and "Does a guitar have a round-shaped hole in it?" The patient was significantly more impaired at recalling the appearances of living things than nonliving things, relative to the performance of age and education-matched normal subjects. His general knowledge about living and nonliving things was tested by similar yes–no questions, such as "Is peacock served in French restaurants?" and "Were wheelbarrows invented before 1920?" In contrast to his ability to recall appearances, his ability to recall nonvisual information was normal for both living and nonliving things.

Beyn and Knyazeva (1962) compared the visual recognition and visual imagery abilities of an agnosic patient on an item-by-item basis for a small set of items. They found a close association between the particular visual stimuli that could be recognized and imaged: The patient recognized 3 out of 16 items that he was unable to image (as assessed by drawings from memory) and 13 out of 16 objects that he could image.

The most selective deficit of visual object recognition consists of profoundly impaired face recognition with roughly intact recognition of other classes of visual stimuli as well as intact general intellectual and memory functioning. Shuttleworth, Syring, and Allen (1982) examined the relation between face recognition and face imagery in a patient with a selective face recognition deficit (their Case 2) and in the published literature on face recognition deficits. Their patient was reported to have "no voluntary visual recall (revisualization) of faces but was able to revisualize more general items such as buildings and places" (p. 313). Shuttleworth et al. found that approximately 40% of 74 cases of face recognition deficit in the neurology literature reported impairments in face imagery. They went on to caution that in many of the cases in which face imagery was not noted to be impaired, "the accuracy of the image could not be ascertained and was seriously questioned in a number of cases" (p. 313).

Patients with right-parietal-lobe damage often fail to detect stimuli presented in the left half of the visual field, even though their elementary sensory processes for stimuli on the affected side of space are intact (Heilman, Watson, & Valentstein, 1985;

Is Visual Imagery Really Visual? Overlooked Evidence From Neuropsychology

45

Posner, Walker, Friedrich, & Rafal, 1984). This deficit is known as "visual neglect," and also appears to manifest itself in visual imagery. Bisiach and his colleagues (Bisiach & Luzzatti, 1978; Bisiach, Luzzatti, & Perani, 1979) have shown that right-parietal patients with visual neglect also fail to access the left sides of imagined objects and scenes. In Bisiach and Luzzatti's initial report, two right-parietal-lobe-damaged neglect patients were asked to imagine viewing a famous square in Milan (the Piazza del Duomo, with which the patients had been familiar before their brain damage) from a particular vantage point, and to describe the view. Both patients omitted from their descriptions the landmarks that would have fallen on the left side of that scene. The patients were then asked to repeat the task, this time from the opposite vantage point, from which the buildings, statues, and other landmarks that fell on the left side of the previous view were visible on the right, and vice versa. The patients' descriptions of their images now included the items that had previously been omitted, and omitted the items on the left side of their current image (which had before been reported).

Bisiach et al. (1979) followed up these case studies with a group study of neglect for visual images. Right-parietal-lobe-damaged patients with left-sided neglect and a control group of patients without neglect were shown abstract cloud-like shapes passing behind a screen with a narrow vertical slit in the center. Because all of the stimulus input in this task is presented centrally in the visual field, any effect of left-sided neglect in this task cannot be attributed to perceptual neglect. After viewing pairs of such shapes, the patients were to decide whether the two members of the pair were identical or different. This presumably requires mentally reconstructing images of the stimuli from the successive narrow vertical views. Patients who neglected the left halves of visual stimuli also neglected the left halves of their images, as evidenced by a greater number of errors when pairs of shapes differed on their left sides than when they differed on their right sides in the task.

• • •

REFERENCES

Anderson, J. R. (1983). *The architecture of cognition.* Cambridge, MA: Harvard University Press.

Atwood, G. E. (1971). An experimental study of visual imagination and memory. *Cognitive Psychology, 2,* 290–299.

Barratt, P. E. (1956). Use of the EEG in the study of imagery. *British Journal of Psychology, 47,* 101–114.

Bauer, R. M., & Rubens, A. B. (1985). Agnosia. In K. M. Heilman & E. Valenstein (Eds.), *Clinical neuropsychology* (2nd ed.) (pp. 187–241). New York: Oxford University Press.

Beauvois, M. F., & Saillant, B. (1985). Optic aphasia for colours and colour agnosia: A distinction between visual and visuo-verbal impairments in the processing of colours. *Cognitive Neuropsychology, 2* (1), 1–48.

Beyn, E. S., & Knyazeva, G. R. (1962). The problem of prosopagnosia. *Journal of Neurology, Neurosurgery and Psychiatry, 25,* 154–158.

Bisiach, E., & Luzzatti, C. (1978). Unilateral neglect of representational space. *Cortex, 14,* 129–133.

Bisiach, E., Luzzatti, C., & Perani, D. (1979). Unilateral neglect, representational schema and consciousness. *Brain, 102,* 609-618.

Brown, B. B. (1966). Specificity of EEG phoptic flicker responses to color as related to visual imagery ability. *Psychophysiology, 2* (3), 197-207.

Brown, J. W. (1972). *Aphasia, apraxia and agnosia: Clinical and theoretical aspects.* Springfield, IL: Charles C. Thomas.

Carpenter, P. A., & Eisenberg, P. (1978). Mental rotation and the frame of reference in blind and sighted individuals. *Perception & Psychophysics, 23,* 117-124.

Davidson, R. J., & Schwartz, G. E. (1977). Brain mechanisms subserving self-generated imagery: Electrophysiological specificity and patterning. *Psychophysiology, 14,* 598-601.

DeRenzi, E. (1982). *Disorders of space exploration and cognition.* New York: John Wiley & Sons.

DeRenzi, E., & Spinnler, H. (1967). Impaired performance on color tasks in patients with hemispheric lesions. *Cortex, 3,* 194-217.

Farah, M. J., Hammond, K. H., Mehta, Z., & Ratcliff, G. (in press). Category specificity and modality specificity in semantic memory. *Neuropsychologia.*

Farah, M. J., Peronnet, F., Gonon, M. A., & Giard, M. H. (in press). Electrophysiological evidence for a shared representational medium for visual images and percepts. *Journal of Experimental Psychology: General.*

Farah, M. J., Peronnet, F., Weisberg, L. L., & Perrin, F. (1988). *Brain activity underlying mental imagery: An ERP study.* Manuscript submitted for publication.

Finke, R. A. (1980). Levels of equivalence in imagery and perception. *Psychological Review, 87,* 113-132.

Finke, R. A. (1985). Theories relating mental imagery to perception. *Psychological Bulletin, 98,* 236-259.

Finke, R. A., & Schmidt, M. J. (1977). Orientation-specific color aftereffects following imagination. *Journal of Experimental Psychology: Human Perception and Performance, 3,* 599-606.

Finke, R. A., & Schmidt, M. J. (1978). The quantitative measure of pattern representation in images using orientation-specific color aftereffects. *Perception & Psychophysics, 23,* 515-520.

Fodor, J. A. (1983). *The modularity of mind.* Cambridge, MA: MIT Press.

Goldenberg, G., Podreka, I., Steiner, M., Suess, E., Deeke, L., & Willmes, K. (in press). Regional cerebral blood flow patterns in imagery tasks–results of single photon emission computer tomography. In M. Denis, J. Engelkamp, & J. T. E. Richardson (Eds.), *Cognitive and neuropsychological approaches to mental imagery.* Dodrecht, The Netherlands: Martinus Nijhoff.

Goldenberg, G., Podreka, I., Steiner, M., & Willmes, K. (1987). Patterns of regional cerebral blood flow related to memorizing of high and low imagery words: An emission computer tomography study. *Neuropsychologia, 25,* 473-486.

Golla, F. L., Hutton, E. L., & Gray Walter, W. G. (1943). The objective study of mental imagery. I. Physiological concomitants. *Journal of Mental Science, 75,* 216-223.

Hebb, D. O. (1968). Concerning imagery. *Psychological Review, 75,* 466-479.

Heidenhain, A. (1927). Beitrag zur kenntnis der seelenblindheit [contribution to the knowledge of mindblindness]. *Monatsschrift fur Psychiatric und Neurologie, 65,* 61-116.

Heilman, K. M., Watson, R. T., & Valenstein, E. (1985). Neglect and related disorders. In K. M. Heilman & E. Valenstein (Eds.), *Clinical neuropsychology* (2nd ed.)(pp. 243-293). New York: Oxford University Press.

Hume, D. (1969). *A treatise in human nature.* Baltimore: Pelican Books. (Original work published 1739)

Ingvar, D. H., & Risberg, J. (1967). Increase of regional cerebral blood flow during mental effort in normals and in patients with local brain disorders. *Experimental Brain Research, 3,* 195-211.

Jossman, P. (1929). Zur psychopathologie des optisch-agnostichen storungen [on the psychopathology of optical agnosic disturbances]. *Monatsschrift fur Psychiatric und Neurologie, 72,* 81-149.

Lassen, N. A., Ingvar, D. H., & Skinhoj, E. (1978). Brain function and blood flow. *Scientific American, 239,* 62-71.

Lesevre, N., & Joseph, J. P. (1980). Hypotheses concerning the most probable origins of the various components of the pattern evoked potential. In C. Barber (Ed.), *Evoked potentials* (pp. 159-166). MTP Press.

Levine, D. N., Warach, J., & Farah, M. J. (1985). Two visual systems in mental imagery: Dissociation of 'what' and 'where' in imagery disorders due to bilateral posterior cerebral lesions. *Neurology, 35,* 1010-1018.

Lewandowsky, M. (1908). Ueber abspaltung des farbensinnes [about divisions of color sense]. *Monatsschrift fur Psychiatric and Neurologie, 23,* 488-510.

Lingoes, J. C. (1979). *The Guttman-Lingoes nonmetric program series.* Ann Arbor, MI: Mathesis Press.

Mazziotta, J. C., Phelps, M. E., & Halgren, E. (1983). Local cerebral glucose metabolic response to audiovisual stimulation and deprivation: Studies in human subjects with positron CT. *Human Neurobiology, 2,* 11-23.

Perrin, F., Bertrand, O., & Pernier, J. (1986). Scalp current density mapping: Value estimation from potential data. *IEEE: Biomedical Engineering, 34,* 283-288.

Pick, A. (1908). *Arbeiten aus den deutschen psychiatrischen Universitaetsklinik in Prag* [Reports from the German Psychiatric Clinic in Prague]. Berlin: Krager.

Posner, M. I., Walker, J. A., Friedrich, F. J., & Rafal, R. D. (1984). Effects of parietal lobe injury on covert orienting of visual attention. *Journal of Neuroscience, 4,* 1863-1874.

Pylyshyn, Z. W. (1973). What the mind's eye tells the mind's brain: A critique of mental imagery. *Psychological Bulletin, 80,* 1-24.

Pylyshyn, Z. W. (1978). Imagery and artificial intelligence. In C. W. Savage (Ed.), *Perception and cognition: Minnesota studies in the philosophy of science* (pp. 19-55). Minneapolis: University of Minnesota Press.

Pylyshyn, Z. W. (1984). *Computation and cognition.* Cambridge, MA: MIT Press.

Riddoch, M. J., & Humphreys, G. W. (1987). A case of integrative visual agnosia. *Brain, 110,* 1431-1462.

Roland, P. E. (1982). Cortical regulation of selective attention in man. *Journal of Neurophysiology, 48,* 1059-1078.

Roland, P. E., & Friberg, L. (1985). Localization of cortical areas activated by thinking. *Journal of Neurophysiology, 53,* 1219-1243.

Roland, P. E., & Skinhoj, E. (1981). Focal activation of the cerebral cortex during visual discrimination in man. *Brain Research, 222,* 166-171.

Sacks, O., & Wasserman, R. (1987, November 19). The case of the colorblind painter. *New York Review of Books,* 25-34.

Shepard, R. N. (1978). The mental image. *American Psychologist, 33,* 125-137.

Shepard, R. N. (1984). Kinematics of perceiving, imagining, thinking, and dreaming. *Psychological Review, 91,* 417-447.

Short, P. L. (1953). The objective study of mental imagery. *British Journal of Psychology, 44,* 38-51.

Shuttleworth, E. C., Syring, V., & Allen, N. (1982). Further observations on the nature of prosopagnosia. *Brain and Cognition, 1,* 302-332.

Slatter, K. H. (1960). Alpha rhythm and mental imagery. *Electroencephalography and Clinical Neurophysiology, 12,* 851–859.

Stengel, E. (1948). The syndrome of visual alexia with colour agnosia. *Journal of Mental Science, 94,* 46-58.

Symonds, C., & Mackenzie, I. (1957). Bilateral loss of vision from cerebral infarction. *Brain, 80,* 415–455.

Ungerleider, L. G., & Mishkin, M. (1982). Two cortical visual systems. In D. J. Ingle, M. A. Goodale, & R. J. W. Mansfield (Eds.), *Analysis of visual behavior* (pp. 549-586). Cambridge, MA: MIT Press.

QUESTIONS FOR FURTHER THOUGHT

1. What kinds of evidence does Farah present to support her claim that visual imagery engages some of the same mental representations as does visual perception?

2. What is an example of tacit knowledge that individuals might have about their visual systems?

3. What is the ERP technique, and how does it differ from the EEG technique?

4. How might a critic of the concept of mental imagery respond to Farah's arguments?

5. Are you persuaded by Farah's argument that understanding the nature of visual imagery has implications for areas of cognitive psychology beyond visual imagery? Why or why not?

3

PERCEPTION AND ATTENTION

THE SPAN OF THE EFFECTIVE STIMULUS DURING A FIXATION IN READING
George McConkie and Keith Rayner

FEATURES AND OBJECTS IN VISUAL PROCESSING
Anne Treisman

ACTIVATION, ATTENTION, AND SHORT-TERM MEMORY
Nelson Cowan

The Span of the Effective Stimulus During a Fixation in Reading

George McConkie and Keith Rayner

INTRODUCTION

Literate individuals may read many millions of words during their lifetimes, but what, exactly, do they do when they read? What do they see at a given time, and how do they progress from seeing one thing to another? This article by George McConkie and Keith Rayner has become a classic because it applied sophisticated measurement techniques to examine eye movements and figure out just what people do when they read. Moreover, the results were somewhat surprising, adding to the article's impact on the field of cognitive psychology.

Your eyes may seem to you to move smoothly across this page as you read, but they do not. Rather, your eyes shoot from point to point in jerks called *saccades*. In the periods of time between the saccades, your eyes stop for short periods of time called *fixations*. (If you have never done so, witness this phenomenon for yourself by watching a friend's eyes from close up when reading. The best way is to face the person from a distance of a couple of feet and peer over the book he or she is holding.) A reader acquires information from a page only during fixations. During the saccades, everything appears as a blur.

How wide is the window of information available to your eyes during any given fixation? McConkie and Rayner used sophisticated equipment called an *eye-tracker* to answer this question. While subjects read text displayed on a computer screen, their eye movements were tracked by means of a beam of infrared light bounced off their eyeballs. The computer gave the researchers the remarkable ability even to change the text surrounding the point of fixation as the subject's eyes moved across a page.

In a series of experiments, McConkie and Rayner varied the size of the window of text available to their readers. They also manipulated the text outside the window in varying ways to determine what kinds of information the reader uses. For example, word-length information remained when researchers replaced the letters of words outside the window with a string of *x*s but maintained the spaces between words, as compared to a condition in which even the spaces contained *x*s.

Their results indicated a relatively narrow window of information available to a reader's eyes during a single fixation. You can make out letters and words only

Source: From McConkie, G. W., & Rayner, K. (1975). The span of the effective stimulus during a fixation in reading. *Perception and Psychophysics, 17,* 578–586. Reprinted by permission of Psychonomic Society, Inc.

for about 10 letter positions to the right of the point of fixation—a distance of a couple of words. Information about word length is available from up to about 15 letter positions to the right. The window of useful information is not symmetric. Readers of English primarily obtain information from the right of the point of fixation. However, this preference merely reflects practice at reading print from left to right. Readers of Hebrew view a window that extends to the left, consistent with the fact that Hebrew writing is read from right to left.

———

A computer-based eye-movement-controlled display system was developed for the study of perceptual processes in reading. A study was conducted to identify the region from which skilled readers pick up various types of visual information during a fixation while reading. This study involved making display changes, based on eye position, in the text pattern as the subject was in the act of reading from it, and then examining the effects these changes produced on eye behavior. The results indicated that the subjects acquired word-length pattern information at least 12 to 15 character positions to the right of the fixation point, and that this information primarily influenced saccade lengths. Specific letter- and word-shape information were acquired no further than 10 character positions to the right of the fixation point. ∎

Psychologists have long been interested in the question posed by Woodworth (1938) in his review of research on reading: "How much can be read in a single fixation?" The investigation of this question has a long history, dating back to some of the earliest research on reading. Cattell, in 1885 (summarized by Huey, 1908), provided data on the number of letters that could be reported following a tachistoscopic presentation of letter strings of different types. Since then, a number of studies have been conducted to investigate this question. If a person fixates a letter on a page of text, he often finds that he can recognize words two or even three lines above and below the one being fixated, as well as words some distance to the left and right. Beyond that, punctuation marks, capital letters, and the beginnings and ends of paragraphs are visible. On the other hand, if a string of random letters is presented visually by means of a tachistoscope, a person is likely to be able to identify only four to six letters. The answer to the question then depends on the type of materials used and the presentation and task conditions.

While the studies that have been conducted on this question have yielded information about how much it is possible to see and to report from a single fixation, and how far into the periphery of the retina visual information can be identified, they fail to resolve the original concern about reading. A better statement of the original question, as it relates to reading, would probably be, "How far into the periphery are specific aspects of the visual stimulus typically acquired and used during fixations in reading?" This restatement differs from the original question in several respects. First, it recognizes that different types of visual information might be available and used by the reader in different retinal areas. Thus, there probably is not a single perceptual span, but a family of spans depending on the aspects of the visual stimulus that are being studied. Second, it notes that there may be a difference between what information is available to the subject during a particular fixation and what he actually acquires and uses for a particular task. Thus, the perceptual span estimates that one obtains from subjects involved in different tasks are likely to differ. This leads to the third point, that in order to answer the perceptual span question about reading, it is necessary to study subjects who are engaged in the act of reading. The major concern for a theory of reading is not what people are capable of seeing during a fixation, but what information they typically acquire and use as they read.

Previous studies of the perceptual span cannot be taken as providing a definite answer to our restated question for either of two reasons. Most of these studies have involved subjects in a task quite different from normal reading, typically using single tachistoscopic presentations from which the subject is asked to identify the letters, numbers, or words presented (Bouma, 1973; Mackworth, 1965). Those studies that have involved the reading of passages, on the other hand, have still used tasks which interfere greatly with normal reading behavior (Bouma & de Voogd, 1974; Newman, 1966; Poulton, 1962).

The research to be reported here was an attempt to develop a method for obtaining information about the size of the region from which specific types of visual information are obtained during fixations while the subjects are involved in reading a passage, with as few constraints on their reading behavior as possible. An eye-movement-controlled display system was developed which permitted a computer to frequently sample the reader's eye position as he read from a computer-generated text display on a cathode-ray tube (CRT). With this system, it was possible to modify the text display on the basis of the reader's eye position. The research involved displaying an unreadable pattern on the CRT, with every letter of the original text replaced by another letter. Then, when the subject fixated the first line of text, the display was modified by replacing letters within a certain region to the left and right of the fixation point on that line with the corresponding letters from the original text. This created a "window" of normal text for the reader on that fixation. When the reader made a saccade, the text in the window returned to its modified form, and a window of normal text was created at the next fixation location. Thus, wherever the reader looked, there was normal text for him to see, allowing him to read quite normally. However, the experimenter could determine the size of the region of normal text, as well as the nature of the pattern beyond this window region.

The experiment involved having subjects read with different-size windows and different peripheral text patterns. The text patterns appearing in peripheral vision (outside the window) maintained or destroyed certain visual characteristics of the original text. It was assumed that if the window were large enough for the reader to obtain all useful visual information within that region, the presence or absence of certain visual characteristics in the region beyond the window would make no difference; that is, data on eye movements and test performance would not be affected. However, if the window were made smaller, a point would be reached where the deletion of those visual characteristics outside the window would interfere with reading; that is, visual information normally obtained and used in reading had been destroyed. Thus, the research strategy was to maintain or destroy certain visual characteristics of the original text in the peripheral text pattern, and then to determine how small the window must be made before a difference in reading was produced by the nature of the peripheral text pattern used. This would indicate how far into the periphery that visual aspect of the text was obtained and used in reading.

METHOD

SUBJECTS

Six high school students participated as subjects in the study. All were seniors or juniors and were identified as being among the best readers in their school. They were paid for participation, receiving a base rate plus a bonus based on their performance on test questions. All had participated in an earlier study and were familiar with the equipment and procedures used.

MATERIALS

Sixteen 500-word passages were selected from a high school psychology text. None of the subjects had taken a course in psychology. Each passage was divided into six approximately equal-size pages, which were displayed one at a time, double-spaced, during the experiment.

Six algorithms were used to substitute letters for characters in the original text to produce modified versions of the text, called *peripheral text patterns.* Six peripheral text patterns were prepared for each passage, conforming to a 2 by 3 design: XS, XF, CS, CF, NCS, and NCF. In the *X* versions, each letter in the original text was replaced by an *X*. In the C versions, each letter was replaced by a letter visually similar (confusable) with it. The substitutions were taken from confusability matrices developed by Bouma (1971) and Hodge (1962). In the NC versions, each letter was replaced by a letter visually different (nonconfusable) from it, with ascending letters replaced by letters that did not extend above or below the line or by descenders, and with descenders replaced by ascenders or letters that did not extend beyond the line of print. In addition, the S (spaces) form of each of these maintained spaces and punctuation, whereas in the F (filled) form each space and punctuation mark was replaced by an appropriate letter, an *x* in the XF version and other letters in the CF and NCF versions. In addition, in the XF version all replacement was done using capital *X*s, thus eliminating capitalization characteristics. Figure 1 shows a line of normal text and the corresponding line after having letters substituted to produce each of the peripheral text versions.

Two multiple-choice test questions were prepared for each page of text, thus yielding 12 questions for each passage. These questions tested retention of information clearly stated in individual sentences in the passage. Each question had four alternatives from which the subject was to choose.

DESIGN

Forty-eight display conditions were used in this study, produced by factorially combining eight window sizes with six peripheral text patterns. The six peripheral text

FIGURE 1	An example of a line of text and the various peripheral text patterns derived from it.

```
       Graphology means personality diagnosis from hand writing. This is a

XS     Xxxxxxxxxx xxxxx xxxxonality diagnosis xxxx xxxx xxxxxxx. Xxxx xx x

XF     XXXXXXXXXXXXXXXXXXXXonality diagnosisXXXXXXXXXXXXXXXXXXXXXXXXXXXXXXXX

CS     Cnojkaiazp wsorc jsnconality diagnosis tnaw kori mnlflrz.  Ykle le o

CF     Cnojkaiaqpewsorcejsnconality diagnosisetnawekoriemnlflrqeecYkleeleco

NCS    Hbfxwysyvo tifdl xiblonality diagnosis abyt wfdn hbemedv. Awcl el f

NCF    Hbfxwysyvoctifdlcxiblonality diagnosiscabytewfdnehbemedveecAwclcclcf
```

Note: On each line, a window of size 17 is shown, assuming the reader is fixating the letter *d* in *diagnosis.*

---

patterns have already been described: window sizes used were: 13, 17, 21, 25, 31, 37, 45, and 100 character positions. Thus, for the smaller windows, each successively larger window size extended the window by two character positions at each end. As can be seen in Figure 1, with a window size of 17, the character being fixated and eight character positions to the left and right of the fixated character comprise the window.

Each subject read all 16 passages (96 pages), with two of the passages being read under each of the 48 presentation conditions. All subjects read the passages in the same order, but the condition order was unique for each subject. An attempt was made to balance presentation conditions over passage and page sequence order as far as possible. Each presentation condition occurred once in the first eight passages, and again in the last eight, for each subject.

PROCEDURE

When a subject arrived for the experiment, a bite bar was prepared for him which served to reduce head movement during the experiment. Then the eye-tracking sensors, mounted on glasses frames and held more securely with a headband, were placed on him and adjusted. He then had the opportunity to warm up by reading two or three passages under conditions of various window sizes and peripheral text patterns.

Prior to reading each passage, the subject was engaged in a calibration task. A target spot appeared on the display, and the subject was instructed to look directly at it and press a lever located next to his right hand. When the lever was pressed, the computer stored the signals being received from the eye-tracking equipment, and moved the target to a new location. This sequence occurred 25 times, giving the computer the values needed for identifying from the eye-position signal where the subject's gaze was directed. An additional push of the lever brought the first page of text onto the CRT, and later pages of a passage were also called by depressing the lever. As the subject read each page, the computer kept a complete record of the position and duration of each fixation and of the time required for each saccade. All times were recorded in 60ths of a second and later converted to milliseconds. After reading all six pages of a passage, the subject came off the equipment and took a test for that passage. Prior to reading the next passage, the test was scored and he was informed of his score. In order to encourage subjects to put their emphasis on understanding and remembering the content of the passages, they were given 1 cent for each correct answer on the test.

Each subject participated in the study for two 2-hour sessions, reading the first eight passages during the first session and the last eight during the second session.

APPARATUS

The equipment used for this research has been described in detail elsewhere (McConkie & Rayner, 1974), and is similar to a system described by Reder (1973). It consisted of a Biometrics Model SG eye-movement monitor interfaced with a Digital Equipment Corporation (DEC) PDP-6 computer, permitting on-line recording of eye movements. The computer also controlled a DEC Model 340 display, which had a character generator for upper- and lowercase letters. The PDP-6 was also interfaced to a PDP-10 time-sharing system. The experiment was conducted using the PDP-6, while the PDP-10 did all file handling.

The CRT had a displayable area of 20.96 × 18.42 cm, capable of displaying 40 lines of 80 characters each. Only 8 to 10 lines of text were displayed at once, double spaced. The subject was 53.34 cm from the CRT, so a full line of text (72 characters) occupied about 18 degrees of visual angle, or about four letters per degree. The CRT had a P-7 phosphor, which is actually composed of two phosphors, one blue-white and of short persistence, the other yellow and of long persistence. A dark-blue theater gel was used to filter out the yellow image, leaving a rapid-decaying image having characteristics similar to those of a P-11 phosphor. There was no noticeable flicker.

The Biometrics eye-movement monitor uses a corneal reflection method of monitoring eye position. There were two problems with its use. First, although it is relatively accurate in identifying eye position on the horizontal dimension, it is quite inaccurate on the vertical dimension, where it monitors position of the eyelid rather than of the eye itself. When a subject is asked to fixate a target, the computer indicates the eye as being directed to a letter no more than three characters from the target, and almost always within two character positions (½ degree of visual angle), on the horizontal dimension. The vertical signal was so inaccurate that it was decided to ignore it and to use a heuristic to identify the line being read. It was assumed that the reader began on the top line, and that a long vertical movement, or series of movements totaling at least 45 character positions, indicated that he was progressing to the next line. The subjects were instructed to read line by line and not to try to return to an earlier line. They were given practice with the equipment and encouraged to try violating these requests, to observe the conditions under which the window would not follow their eye positions. They experienced no difficulty on confirming to these requests, though the number of regressions they typically made was likely reduced.

The second problem with the eye-movement monitoring equipment concerned the great amount of noise in the signal. To reduce this, a filter built into the equipment was left engaged and another added. Following the research, it was learned that the first filter delayed the signal substantially. Presenting one of the photodiodes in the sensors with a fast-rising infrared signal caused the analogue output from the equipment to begin rising almost immediately, reaching a maximum level in 4 to 5 msec. With the filter engaged, however, although the output signal began rising almost immediately, it reached maximum level only after 25 msec or more. The second filter delayed the signal less than ½ msec.

The computer was programmed to sample the signal from the eye-movement monitor 60 times per second. On each sample, it was determined whether the eye was moving or still by comparing the change in the signal since the last sample with a threshold value. If the change was greater than the threshold value, the eye was declared to be in a saccade, if less, to be fixated. When the eye was first found to be fixated after a saccade, the CRT was turned off and the display instructions were changed to create a window at the appropriate location in the text. The CRT was then turned back on. The time the display was off, with a window size of 17 characters, was 6 msec, short enough for no blink to be detected. For each 20-character increase in the window size, the CRT off time was increased by 5 msec. The largest window size, 100 character positions, required the CRT to be off for 30 msec and produced very noticeable blinking of the display.

Since the display was changed each time a fixation was made, the question of lag between the time the eye stopped and the detection of the eye being stopped is particularly important. Two features of the system used made this lag substantially greater than was realized at the time the study was conducted. First, the filter in the eye-movement equipment already mentioned increased the lag substantially. Second, a relatively slow sampling rate of (60 sec or once every 16 msec) further increased the lag. With this sampling rate, it would be quite possible for the eye to be stopped for 18 msec prior to detecting the fixation, even with a fast-responding eye-movement signal. If the fixation occurred at just the right time, it might be detected after only a few milliseconds. These two factors, the filter and sampling rate, resulted in a variable lag which is difficult to assess exactly, but which could have been as much as 40 msec at times. Identification of the onset of a saccade was probably faster. Subjects did not have an experience of seeing one pattern change to another during a fixation, however, probably due to a combined effect of visual suppression during and after saccades and of visual masking (Haber & Hershenson, 1973).

RESULTS AND DISCUSSION

THE DATA

For each page of text read by each subject, summary statistics were obtained for a number of aspects of eye-movement behavior, in addition to scores on the retention test. Each fixation and saccade in the eye-behavior data was categorized as one of four types: a forward movement and fixation, a regressive movement and fixation, a forward movement and fixation in a regression (if a regression had previously been made and this forward movement failed to bring the eye back to the point from which the regression was originally made), or as a return sweep. On the movement or series of movements which advanced the eye to the next line, all movements were categorized as return sweep movements, and fixations bounded on both sides by return sweep movements were identified as return sweep fixations. The fixation occurring at the end of a return sweep, which was then followed by a forward movement, was identified as a forward fixation.

Three types of eye-movement data were analyzed. The first was time data. The reading time per 100 characters was computed for the page, and then this was broken down in two ways. First, it was broken into time spent in movement (movement time) versus time spent in fixations (fixation time). Time spent in forward movements and in forward fixations was also obtained. Second, time was broken down by the categories of movements and fixations, yielding total time per 100 characters for forward movements and fixations, regressions, forward movements and fixations in regressions, and return sweeps.

The second type of data consisted of simple counts of the number of fixations and movements per 100 characters, both total for the entire page and broken down into forward, regression, forward in regression, and return sweep, in order to have the number of each of these types of movements and saccades that occurred.

The third type of data was measures of saccade lengths, saccade durations, and fixation durations. Saccade lengths were measured in number of character positions. First, second, and third quartiles were obtained from the distributions of all fixation durations and forward-fixation durations for each page. Second quartiles (medians) were obtained for the distributions of fixation durations for regressions, forward movements in regressions, and return sweeps. The same statistics were obtained for the distributions of saccade lengths and saccade durations, except that no statistics were included for distributions of total saccade lengths and durations. Thus, there were 34 dependent variables for which one score was obtained per page for each subject.

Effects of Peripheral Text Patterns. For each of these variables, eight three-way analyses of variance were carried out, one for each window size. The purpose of each analysis was to determine whether at that window size the peripheral text pattern had any effect on the dependent variable. The three factors in each analysis of variance were subjects (six), letter-replacement algorithm used in producing the peripheral text pattern (called *letter replacement,* with three levels for C, NC, and X versions), and whether the peripheral text pattern had spaces and punctuation remaining or removed (called *space versus filled,* with two levels for S and F versions). This led to a large number of analyses, a total of 272, being carried out. Since this was bound to lead to a number of significant effects on the basis of chance alone, the following strategy was used to identify differences that were likely to be reliable. A difference was considered to be reliable if it occurred at two successive window sizes, with a significance level less than .10 at each window size, and with the data pattern at both window sizes being similar.

For most dependent variables, there was a significant main effect for subjects, and for some, subjects interacted with other variables. These effects will not be explored here, but attention will be given to main effects for letter replacement and for space

For window sizes of 31 and greater, there were no reliable effects using the above definition of reliability. Where significant effects were found at one window size, the data pattern observed at adjacent window sizes was not the same. Thus these effects were assumed to be due to chance factors. It is concluded that with a window size of 31, there is no evidence that the readers were acquiring either word-shape or word-length pattern information from the region beyond the window. Thus, there is no evidence that this information was acquired more than 15 character positions from the point of central vision by the subjects of this experiment. One possible exception to this conclusion will be noted later.

A number of reliable main effects and interactions were found at the smaller window sizes. These are listed in Table 1. These could be broken down into four categories: variables that influenced saccade lengths, those that influenced the duration of fixations, those that influenced the number of regressions, and those that were more gross measures of eye behavior and hence were affected by the three categories already mentioned.

Saccade lengths were affected only by the presence or absence of spaces in the peripheral text pattern. Figure 2 presents the average first, second, and third quartiles for the distributions of saccade lengths for the S and F peripheral text patterns, together with an indication of the significant effects. As can be seen, when word-length

FIGURE 2   The length of forward saccades as a function of window size and of the presence or absence of word-length information in the peripheral text pattern; first, second, and third quartiles.

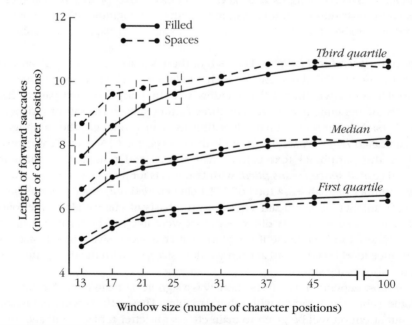

| TABLE 1 | A List of Reliable Effects Not Involving the Subject Factor |

VARIABLE	WINDOW SIZE	EFFECT[a]	F VALUE	df	SIGNIFICANCE LEVEL
Forward fixation time per 100 characters	17	S	31.60	1,5	.003
	21	S	4.14	1,5	.10
Forward movement and forward fixation time per 100 characters	17	S	30.33	1,5	.004
	21	S	4.47	1,5	.09
Number of fixations per 100 characters	13	S	5.91	1,5	.06
	17	S	11.49	1,5	.02
	13	SL	3.29	2,10	.08
	17	SL	3.41	2,10	.07
Number of forward fixations per 100 characters	13	S	19.06	1,5	.008
	17	S	41.53	1,5	.002
	21	S	4.60	1,5	.08
Number of regressive fixations per 100 characters	13	L	5.67	2,10	.02
	17	L	3.87	2,10	.06
	25	L	5.60	2,10	.02
Saccade length–second quartile	13	S	3.94	1,5	.10
	17	S	13.36	1,5	.02
Saccade length–third quartile	13	S	21.87	1,5	.006
	17	S	24.79	1,5	.005
	21	S	18.65	1,5	.008
	25	S	6.27	1,5	.06
Saccade length of regressions–second quartile	13	SL	8.48	2,10	.007
	17	SL	8.01	2,10	.009
Duration of forward movements–second quartile	13	S	5.91	1,5	.06
	17	S	9.35	1,5	.03
Duration of forward fixations–first quartile	21	SL	7.81	2,10	.009
	25	SL	8.00	2,10	.009
Duration of forward fixations–second quartile	17	L	3.51	1,5	.07
	21	L	4.47	1,5	.04
Duration of regressive fixations–second quartile	21	L	5.58	1,5	.02
	25	L	4.20	1,5	.05

[a]S indicates significant effect for spaces versus filled, L indicates significant effect for letter replacement, SL indicates a significant interaction.

patterns were eliminated from the peripheral text pattern by filling the spaces, the saccades tended to be shorter. This effect is most noticeable at the third quartile, indicating that it tended primarily to reduce the number of long saccades, thus constricting the distribution of saccade lengths at the high end, rather than simply shifting the entire distribution down. The difference between S and F versions is present at least up to a window size of 25, and may be present even further, though the difference there is not significant. It appears, then, that word-length pattern information is acquired at least as far as 12 character positions (3 degrees) from the center of vision, and perhaps even farther, and may be used in guiding the eye during reading.

A significant main effect for spaces versus filled was also found for saccade duration data at the three smallest window sizes. With word-length pattern eliminated from the peripheral text pattern, saccades were of shorter duration, which of course simply reflects the fact that saccades were of shorter distance under these conditions, as already noted.

The average length of regressive saccades also tended to be less when word-length information was eliminated from the peripheral text pattern, though the difference was significant only at window size 17. The spaces versus filled by letter replacement interaction was significant at the .01 level for regression saccade length data at the two smallest window sizes, but the data pattern changed greatly between the two window sizes, so these interactions will not be considered reliable or explored further. There was a tendency for the XS condition to produce particularly short regressive saccades at the 17, 21, and 25 window sizes, with saccade lengths for that condition being more like those of the filled conditions than the other spaces conditions.

While lengths of saccades were influenced primarily by the presence or absence of word-length pattern in the peripheral visual areas, the duration of fixations was influenced largely by letter replacement. Significant main effects for letter replacement were found for the second and third quartiles of the distributions of forward-fixation durations and for the third quartile for total fixation durations at window sizes 17 and 21. The forward fixation-duration data are presented in Figure 3. Total fixation-duration data are almost identical. From this figure, it can be seen that there tends to be a small difference in the duration of fixations between the C and NC letter-replacement conditions at the two smallest window sizes, but that this difference disappears at window size 21. At the smaller sizes, having improper word-shape patterns in the peripheral text pattern inflates the fixation durations slightly. With window size 21, however, it seems to make no difference whether the peripheral text pattern presents accurate or inaccurate word-shape information, suggesting that general word-shape information is not acquired by these readers as much as 10 character positions from the point of central vision.

At the three smallest window sizes, the X letter-replacement condition leads to the lowest fixation durations. The X condition has the characteristic that the boundaries of the windows are well marked; the contrast between the normal text in the window region and the homogeneous X pattern in the peripheral area is very noticeable. Thus, it would seldom happen that a reader would make the error of attempting to integrate letters from outside the window into the text pattern within the window itself. On the other hand, with the C and NC letter-replacement conditions, the boundaries of the window are not at all obvious, and the reader undoubtedly quite

| **FIGURE 3** | The duration of forward fixations as a function of window size and of the presence or absence of word-shape information in the peripheral text pattern: first, second, and third quartiles. |

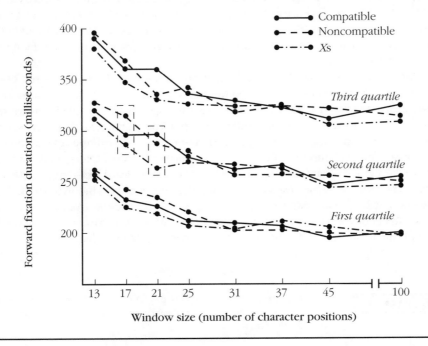

frequently picks up letters from outside the window area and attempts to integrate these with the normal text in the window, thus producing some disruption. This disruption likely leads to the longer durations for the C and NC conditions as compared to the X conditions. If this is so, then the fact that there is a difference in fixation durations between the X and the C and NC conditions at window size 21 suggests that the reader is picking up specific letter information under the C and NC conditions as much as 10 character positions from his point of central vision. These differences disappear at window size 25, suggesting that this type of visual information is not being acquired by the readers at 12 character positions from the point of central vision.

The first quartile forward fixation duration data showed a spaces versus filled by letter replacement interaction at window sizes 21 and 25. However, the data pattern was not consistent from one window size to the next, so these interactions will not be considered reliable.

This consideration of the fixation duration data leads to two conclusions: First, the subjects acquired specific letter information no more than 10 or 11 character positions (2½ degrees) from the point of central vision; second, general word-shape information was not acquired any further into the periphery than this either. Thus, word-shape patterns, other than word-length characteristics, appear to be acquired no further into the periphery than is specific visual information needed to identify letters.

The number of regressions made by subjects per 100 characters was reliably affected by the letter-replacement pattern. Significant main effects are shown in Figure 4. Here it is seen that the C condition produced the most regressions, whereas the X condition produced the least. The reason for this difference is not known, though it may have something to do with the naturalness of the appearance of the peripheral text pattern. The least natural-appearing pattern was the one which led to the fewest regressions.

The differences in saccade length, fixation duration, and number of regressions produced by the variables resulted in differences in other more gross measures of eye behavior in reading. A significant main effect for spaces versus filled was found at window sizes 13 and 17 for total reading time per 100 characters, total time spent in forward movements and fixations per 100 characters, total number of fixations per 100 characters, total number of forward fixations per 100 characters, total time spent in fixations per 100 characters, and total time spent in forward fixations per 100 characters. The latter variable also showed a significant effect at window size 21. These data will not be presented in detail, since they simply resulted from the previously noted effects of the variables on specific eye-behavior measures and by themselves add nothing to the understanding of the reading processes involved.

FIGURE 4   The number of regressive movements per 100 characters as a function of window size and of the presence or absence of word-shape information in the peripheral text pattern.

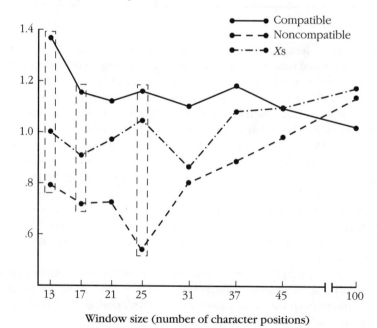

Window size (number of character positions)

General Effects of Window Size. Figure 5 shows the effect of window size on the time required to read the text. The dependent variable is time required to read 100 characters. Reducing the window size caused this time to rise from 4.33 to 6.92 sec, a 60% increase. This increase resulted primarily from an increase in the amount of time the eye was fixated; total time in movement rose 10%, while total time spent in fixations rose 76%. As seen in earlier figures, this increase was a result of the subjects' making both more fixations (a 33% increase from 12.82 fixations per 100 characters to 16.98) and fixations of longer durations (a 31% increase from 245 msec median forward fixation duration to 320 msec). The larger number of fixations was entirely the result of readers making shorter forward saccades, with median saccade length dropping from 8.76 to 6.43 character positions. There was no increase in the number of regressive movements as the window size was reduced. The median number of regressive movements per 100 characters ranged from 1.1 to 0.9 for the different window sizes. Thus, the increase in reading time with smaller window sizes was not due to a change in the number of regressions, but was the result of changes in the normal forward saccade and fixation pattern.

As seen in Figure 5, reading time continued to drop as window sizes became larger, and reached asymptote only at the largest sizes. Median saccade lengths and fixation durations showed the same pattern. This change may be due to either of two

FIGURE 5   Effect of window size on time to read 100 characters of text.

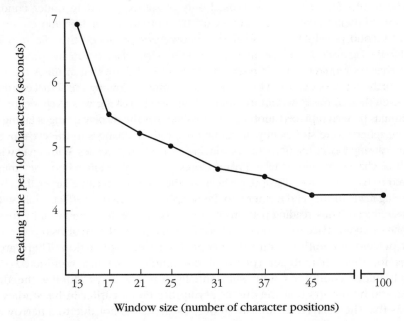

types of influence: (1) Either subjects were obtaining some useful visual information from the normal text regions as wide as 45 character positions, which was not available in the peripheral text patterns, or (2) reducing the window size itself changed the reader's behavior or produced artifacts which were reflected in his eye-movement behavior. The first of these possibilities does not seem likely in view of the earlier-reported results from this experiment. The evidence seemed to indicate that the readers were not obtaining word-shape or specific letter information from a region extending more than about 10 or 11 character positions from the point of central vision, and that they were not acquiring word-length pattern information more than about 15 character positions into the periphery. If this is so, it is difficult to imagine what other visual characteristics of the text might be acquired further into the periphery which were not present in the peripheral text patterns. Therefore, it will be assumed that the continued drop in the reading time and other curves with increased window size has some other basis.

Among the many possible reasons why reducing the window size might produce the effects noted, two seem particularly likely. One possibility is that subjects have the ability to control the size and location of the general area from which they acquire visual information on each fixation during reading. Thus, as the window became smaller, they may have tended to constrict their field of visual attention to a narrower region. This may also have caused them to make shorter saccades and perhaps even longer fixations as the window became smaller, but at the same time would not have led to differences in reading behavior as a function of type of peripheral text pattern. If this explanation were in fact correct, it would invalidate the previous conclusions about the size of the region from which the subjects tended to pick up visual information: The results found would be typical only of subjects reading under conditions which forced them to narrow their range of attention during each fixation.

The second possibility why smaller window sizes produced the effects noted is related to the lag discussed earlier in identifying the onset of a fixation and producing the display changes required for this research. It was noted there that at times the display change might not have occurred for as much as 40 msec following the actual eye-fixation onset. Even though this is within the time when visual masking was likely occurring as one stimulus pattern replaced another, it is possible that the display changes taking place in the periphery were sufficiently distracting to produce changes in the eye-movement patterns, causing longer fixations and producing more short saccades. With small window sizes, these changes would be taking place closest to central vision, where they might be expected to have the most disrupting effect. As the window became larger, the changes were being made further and further into the periphery, where their effect, while still present, was reduced. Thus, reading patterns may have been affected somewhat by these display changes taking place even some distance from the point of central vision.

At present, the authors tend to accept this latter explanation. There are two reasons for this. First, Reder (personal communication) has conducted similar research under conditions with substantially less lag in producing the display change, and he reports that the curves asymptote much earlier in his studies. This suggests that the delayed asymptote in our research was not due to a narrowing of the field of attention, since if it were, the same phenomenon would be expected to be present in Reder's data. Rather, it is probably due to the relative slowness with which our display changes were taking place. Second, Rayner (1975) has reported a study which did not involve the type of display changes used in the present study, and which would not tend to induce the reader to narrow his field of attention. He reported results concerning the size of the perceptual span in reading which are quite compatible with the estimates from the present study. Thus, it is concluded that the window-size effects were probably due to artifacts produced by the display change itself rather than to changes in the width of the field of attention.

Retention Test Performance. The retention tests were constructed to have two questions taken from the information on each page of text. This made it possible to carry out a four-way analysis of variance on retention test scores to determine whether the variables influenced the subjects' retention of information from the passages. The only significant effect was the window size by subjects interaction ($F = 1.553, p < .03$, 35 and 288 df). Window size did not have an effect on test performance ($F = 1.371, p < .25$, 7 and 35 df). The significant interaction was plotted to determine whether there was a tendency for some subjects, but not for others, to perform more poorly with smaller window sizes. No such tendency could be found. The interaction seemed to arise primarily from lack of complete counterbalancing in the experiment due to the small number of subjects in relation to the large number of passages. Curves for individual subjects were very irregular across window sizes, with no observable trends.

GENERAL DISCUSSION

This experiment has provided data which begin to answer the question about the size of the perceptual span during a fixation in reading. Although it may be possible in tasks other than reading for subjects to identify letters, word shapes, and word-length patterns some distance into the peripheral areas, in fluent reading this information appears to be obtained and used from a relatively narrow region. Thus, a theory of fluent reading need not suppose that word-shape and specific letter information is obtained from a region occupied by more than about three or four words during a fixation, and perhaps not that large if the span is not symmetrical around the point of central vision, a question not tested in the present study. Thus, it does not appear to be true that entire sentences are seen during a fixation; in fact, for most fixations, not even a complete phrase will lie within this area.

It has often been suggested that poor comprehension in reading can be the result of a narrow perceptual span. Smith (1971), for instance, suggests that having a narrow span, thus perceiving smaller groups of words at a time, results in the cognitive processing system having to deal with more "chunks" of information. This is said to produce a heavier load on the processing system, which reduces the reader's ability to see relationships in the text, thus reducing comprehension of the text. It is of interest, then, that reducing the perceptual span of the readers in this study by reducing the size of the window, although it slowed their reading considerably, did not reduce their comprehension test scores. Thus, no evidence was found for the notion that a reduced perceptual span produces reduced comprehension.

The fact that word-length patterns are acquired somewhat further into the periphery than the more specific letter and word-shape information, and that the presence or absence of this aspect of the visual pattern in the periphery is related to saccade length, is harmonious with the position that the eye is guided during reading on the basis of characteristics of the peripheral visual pattern (Hochberg, 1970). The nature of this guidance is presently unknown, but it is of interest that we have found informally that people can mark phrase boundaries in text fairly reliably when all letters have been replaced by *x*s. Thus word-length patterns are related to syntactic structure to some degree.

For the subjects studied here, saccades of median length carry the eye to a location just short of the furthest point where letter- and word-shape information tend to be acquired. This means that a large proportion of the saccades carry the eye beyond that point. Further studies need to explore whether the span for features of the text on which interpretation can be based is symmetrical or asymmetrical, which will indicate the degree to which this span overlaps from fixation to fixation. Finally, further study is also needed to investigate whether useful visual information is acquired from other lines than the one being directly fixated in reading.

Although many questions about the nature of the perceptual spans during reading remain unanswered, the present study suggests that a technique involving manipulating the display on the basis of eye-position information may have the power to provide answers to these questions.

REFERENCES

Bouma, H. (1971). Visual recognition of isolated lower-case letters. *Vision Research, 11,* 459–474.

Bouma, H. (1973). Visual interference in the parafoveal recognition of initial and final letters of words. *Vision Research, 13,* 767–782.

Bouma, H., & deVoogd, A. H. (1974). On the control of eye saccades in reading. *Vision Research, 14,* 273–284.

Haber, R. N., & Hershenson, M. (1973). *The psychology of visual perception.* New York: Holt, Rinehart & Winston.

Hochberg, J. (1970). Components of literacy: Speculations and exploratory research. In H. Levin and J. P. Williams (Eds.), *Basic studies on reading.* New York: Basic Books.

Hodge, D. C. (1962). Legibility of a uniform-stroke width alphabet: 1. Relative legibility of upper and lower-case letters. *Journal of Engineering Psychology, 1,* 34–46.

Huey, E. B. (1908). *The psychology and pedagogy of reading.* New York: Macmillan.

Mackworth, H. H. (1965). Visual noise causes tunnel vision. *Psychonomic Science, 3,* 67–68.

McConkie, G. W., & Rayner, K. (1974). Identifying the span of the effective stimulus in reading. Final Report OEG2-71-0531, U.S. Office of Education. This report is available from ERIC Document Reproduction Service.

Newman, E. B. (1966). Speed of reading when the span of letters is restricted. *American Journal of Psychology, 79,* 272–278.

Poulton, E. C. (1962). Peripheral vision, refractoriness and eye movements in fast oral reading. *British Journal of Psychology, 53,* 409–419.

Rayner, K. (1975). The perceptual span and peripheral cues in reading. *Cognitive Psychology, 7,* 65–81.

Reder, S. M. (1973). On-line monitoring of eye position signals in contingent and noncontingent paradigms. *Behavior Research Methods & Instrumentation, 5,* 218–228.

Smith, F. (1971). *Understanding reading.* New York: Holt, Rinehart & Winston.

Woodworth, R. S. (1938). *Experimental psychology.* New York: Holt.

QUESTIONS FOR FURTHER THOUGHT

1. What is the approximate span of the effective stimulus during reading?

2. How do McConkie and Rayner determine the approximate span of the effective stimulus during reading?

3. According to McConkie and Rayner, what is the relationship between reduced perceptual span in reading and reduced reading comprehension?

4. What might be a disadvantage using a sample of only six subjects, all of whom had participated in prior eye-tracker studies?

5. Does the replacement of words outside the window with various perceptual patterns create questions about whether the study's results apply to normal reading?

FEATURES AND OBJECTS IN VISUAL PROCESSING

Anne Treisman

INTRODUCTION

Look around the area where you are now located. If you are inside, you are likely to see furniture, windows, walls, and a floor; if you are outside, you are likely to see plants, the sky, and perhaps a road or a sidewalk. Of course, you do not really directly see these objects. You actually detect details like edges, movement, and spatial clues about distances, then these features and properties somehow combine into meaningful wholes. How does simple feature detection become perception of multidimensional, complete objects? This perceptual task, which humans do effortlessly, has turned out to be remarkably difficult for computers to accomplish, much more so than complex tasks such as chess or solving mathematical problems.

Treisman has described some general conclusions about visual perception that are emerging from research done in her lab and elsewhere. The visual perception of an object appears to involve three steps. The first step is coding simple features with reference to maps that preserve spatial (i.e., location) information. The second step requires focused attention (i.e., paying attention to the object being perceived) and results in a temporary representation of the object. The third step is to compare the temporary representation with descriptions of objects stored in memory. If a match is found between the temporary representation and a stored description, the object has been recognized, completing the process of visual perception.

Why should an article on vision written for a general scientific magazine be included in a book of readings in cognitive psychology? For one consideration, its author is one of the foremost contributors in the world to the field of vision. This article gives readers a chance to learn about her work in a forum that is more accessible than some of the original journal articles that have published the work. For another, this article gives a broader account of vision than would many individual journal articles. In this article, Treisman displays an important skill that many cognitive psychologists lack: the ability to describe complicated concepts and findings from their work and that of others in a way that is accessible to the general reader. Such a task, easy as it sounds, in fact is quite a difficult challenge. One has to make sure that the ideas and findings are presented correctly and

Source: From Treisman, A. (1986). Features and objects in visual processing. *Scientific American, 255* (5), 114-125. Reprinted with permission. Copyright (1986) by Scientific American, Inc. All rights reserved.

clearly and in a way that general readers can understand. One has to know not only what details to include, but what details to omit. Also, one has to know how to relate one's own work to that of others in a way that is informative and not self-serving. Treisman is among the best writers of such articles.

———

The seemingly effortless ability to perceive meaningful wholes in the visual world depends on complex processes. The features automatically extracted from a scene are assembled into objects. ∎

If you were magically deposited in an unknown city, your first impression would be of recognizable objects organized coherently in a meaningful framework. You would see buildings, people, cars, and trees. You would not be aware of detecting colors, edges, movements, and distances, and of assembling them into multidimensional wholes for which you could retrieve identities and labels from memory. In short, meaningful wholes seem to precede parts and properties, as the Gestalt psychologists emphasized many years ago.

This apparently effortless achievement, which you repeat innumerable times throughout your waking hours, is proving very difficult to understand or to simulate on a computer—much more difficult, in fact, than the understanding and simulation of tasks that most people find quite challenging, such as playing chess or solving problems in logic. The perception of meaningful wholes in the visual world apparently depends on complex operations to which a person has no conscious access, operations that can be inferred only on the basis of indirect evidence.

Nevertheless, some simple generalizations about visual information processing are beginning to emerge. One of them is a distinction between two levels of processing. Certain aspects of visual processing seem to be accomplished simultaneously (that is, for the entire visual field at once) and automatically (that is, without attention being focused on any one part of the visual field). Other aspects of visual processing seem to depend on focused attention and are done serially, or one at a time, as if a mental spotlight were being moved from one location to another.

In 1967, Ulric Neisser, then at the University of Pennsylvania, suggested that a "preattentive" level of visual processing segregates regions of a scene into figures and ground so that subsequent, attentive level can identify particular objects. More recently, David C. Marr, investigating computer simulation of vision at the Massachusetts Institute of Technology, found it necessary to establish a "primal sketch": a first stage of processing, in which the pattern of light reaching an array of receptors is converted into a coded description of lines, spots, or edges and their locations, orientations, and colors. The representation of surfaces and volumes and finally the identification of objects could begin only after this initial coding.

In brief, a model with two or more stages is gaining acceptance among psychologists, physiologists, and computer scientists working in artificial intelligence. Its first stage might be described as the extraction of features from patterns of light; later stages are concerned with the identification of objects and their settings. The phrase "features and objects" is therefore a three-word characterization of the emerging hypothesis about the early stages of vision.

I think there are many reasons to agree that vision indeed applies specialized analyzers to decompose stimuli into parts and properties, and that extra operations are needed to specify their recombination into the correct wholes. In part the evidence is physiological and anatomical. In particular, the effort to trace what happens to sensory data suggests that the data are processed in different areas of considerable specialization. One area concerns itself mainly with the orientation of lines and edges, another with color, still another with directions of movement. Only after processing in these areas do data reach areas that appear to discriminate between complex natural objects.

Some further evidence is behavioral. For example, it seems that visual adaptation (the visual system's tendency to become unresponsive to a sustained stimulus) occurs separately for different properties of a scene. If you stare at a waterfall for a few minutes and then look at the bank of the river, the bank will appear to flow in the opposite direction. It is as if the visual detectors had selectively adapted to a particular direction of motion independent of *what* is moving. The bank looks very different from the water, but it nonetheless shows the aftereffects of the adaptation process.

How can the preattentive aspect of visual processing be further subjected to laboratory examination? One strategy is suggested by the obvious fact that in the real world parts that belong to the same object tend to share properties: they have the same color and texture, their boundaries show a continuity of lines or curves, they move together, they are at roughly the same distance from the eye. Accordingly the investigator can ask subjects to locate the boundaries between regions in various visual displays and thus can learn what properties make a boundary immediately salient—make it "pop out" of a scene. These properties are likely to be the ones the visual system normally employs in its initial task of segregating figure from ground.

It turns out that boundaries are salient between elements that differ in simple properties such as color, brightness, and line orientation but not between elements that differ in how their properties are combined or arranged (Figure 1). For example, a region of *T*s segregates well from a region of tilted *T*s but not from a region of *L*s made of the same components as the *T*s (a horizontal line and a vertical line). By the same token, a mixture of blue *V*s and red *O*s does not segregate from a mixture of red *V*s and blue *O*s. It seems that the early "parsing" of the visual field is mediated by separate properties, not by particular combinations of properties. That is, analysis of properties and parts precedes their synthesis. And if parts or properties are identified before they are conjoined with objects, they must have some independent psychological existence.

This leads to a strong prediction, which is that errors of synthesis should sometimes take place. In other words, subjects should sometimes see illusory conjunctions of parts or properties drawn from different areas of the visual field. In certain conditions such illusions take place frequently. In one experiment my colleagues and I flashed three colored letters, say a blue *X*, a green *T*, and a red *O*, for a brief period (200 milliseconds, or a fifth of a second) and diverted our subjects' attention by asking them to report first a digit shown at each side of the display and only then the colored letters. In about one trial in three, the subjects reported the wrong combinations—perhaps a red *X*, a green *O*, or a blue *T*.

FIGURE 1 Boundaries that "pop out" of a scene are likely to reveal the simple properties, or features, of the visual world that are seized on by the initial stage of visual processing. For example, a boundary between Ts and tilted Ts pops out, whereas a boundary between Ts and Ls does not (a). The implication is that line orientations are important features in early visual processing but that particular arrangements of conjunctions of lines are not. A boundary between Os and Vs pops out (b). The implication is that simple shape properties (such as line curvature) are important.

a

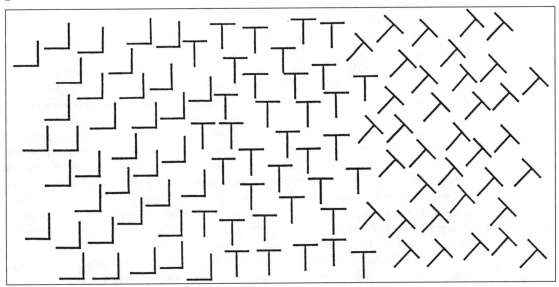

b

The subjects made these conjunction errors much more often than they reported a color or shape that was not present in the display, which suggests that the errors reflect genuine exchanges of properties rather than simply misperceptions of a single object. Many of these errors appear to be real illusions, so convincing that subjects demand to see the display again to convince themselves that the errors were indeed mistakes.

We have looked for constraints on the occurrence of such illusory conjunctions. For example, we have asked whether objects must be similar for their properties to be exchanged. It seems they do not: Subjects exchanged colors between a small, red outline of a triangle and a large, solid blue circle just as readily as they exchanged colors between two small outline triangles. It is as if the red color of the triangle were represented by an abstract code for red rather than being incorporated into a kind of analogue of the triangle that also encodes the object's size and shape.

We also asked if it would be harder to create illusory conjunctions by detaching a part from a simple unitary shape, such as a triangle, than by moving a loose line. The answer again was no. Our subjects saw illusory dollar signs in a display of Ss and lines. They also saw the illusory signs in a display of Ss and triangles in which each triangle incorporated the line the illusion required (Figure 2). In conscious experience the triangle looks like a cohesive whole. Nevertheless, at the preattentive level, its component lines seem to be detected independently.

To be sure, the triangle may have an additional feature, namely the fact that its constituent lines enclose an area, and this property of closure might be detected preattentively. If so, the perception of a triangle might require the detection of its three component lines in the correct orientations and also the detection of closure. We should then find that subjects do not see illusory triangles when they are given only the triangles' separate lines in the proper orientations (Figure 3). They may need a further stimulus, a different closed shape (perhaps a circle), in order to assemble illusory triangles. That is indeed what we found.

Another way to make the early, preattentive level of visual processing the subject of laboratory investigation is to assign visual-search tasks. That is, we ask subjects to find a target item in the midst of other, "distractor" items. The assumption is that if the preattentive processing occurs automatically and across the visual field, a target that

FIGURE 2   Illusory dollar signs are an instance of false conjunctions of features. Subjects were asked to look for dollar signs in the midst of Ss and line segments (a). They often reported seeing the signs when the displays to which they were briefly exposed contained none (b). They had the same experience about as often when the line segment needed to complete a sign was embedded in a triangle (c). The experiment suggests that early visual processing can detect the presence of features independent of location.

a

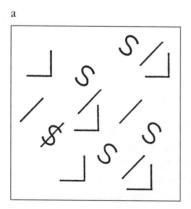

b

c

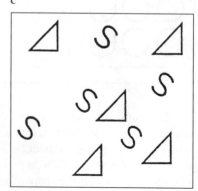

FIGURE 3 Illusory triangles constitute a test of what features must be available to support the perception of triangles. Subjects seldom reported seeing a triangle when they were briefly exposed to displays consisting of the line segments that make up a triangle (a). They saw triangles far more often when the displays also included closed stimuli, that is, shapes that enclose a space, in this case *O*s (b). Evidently, closure is a feature analyzed in early visual processing. This conclusion was supported by showing displays that lack the diagonal line to make a triangle (c, d). Subjects seldom saw triangles in such displays.

is distinct from its neighbors in its preattentive representation in the brain should "pop out" of the display. The proverbial needle in a haystack is hard to find because it shares properties of length, thickness and orientation with the hay in which it is hidden. A red poppy in a haystack is a much easier target; its unique color and shape are detected automatically.

We find that if a target differs from the distractors in some simple property, such as orientation or color or curvature, the target is detected about equally fast in an array of 30 items and in an array of three items. Such targets pop out of the display, so that the time it takes to find them is independent of the number of distractors. This independence holds true even when subjects are not told what the unique property of the target will be. The subjects take slightly longer overall, but the number of distractors still has little or no effect.

On the other hand, we find that if a target is characterized only by a conjunction of properties (for example, a red *O* among red *N*s and green *O*s), or if it is defined only by its particular combination of components (for example, an *R* among *P*s and *Q*s that together incorporate all the parts of the *R*), the time taken to find the target or to decide that the target is not present increases linearly with the number of distractors. It is as if the subjects who are placed in these circumstances are forced to focus attention in turn on each item in the display in order to determine how the item's properties or parts are conjoined. In a positive trial (a trial in which a target is present) the search ends when the target is found; on the average, therefore, it ends after half of the distractors have been examined. In a negative trial (in which no target is present) all the distractors have to be checked. As distractors are added to the displays, the search time in positive trials therefore increases at half the rate of the search time in negative trials.

The difference between a search for simple features and a search for conjunctions of features could have implications in industrial settings. Quality-control inspectors might, for example, take more time to check manufactured items if the possible errors in manufacture are characterized by faulty combinations of properties than they do if the errors always result in a salient change in a single property. Similarly, each of the symbols representing, say, the destinations for baggage handled at airline terminals should be characterized by a unique combination of properties.

In a further series of experiments on visual-search tasks, we explored the effect of exchanging the target and the distractors. That is, we required subjects to find a target distinguished by the fact that it *lacks* a feature present in all the distractors. For example, we employed displays consisting of *O*s and *Q*s, so that the difference between the target and the distractors is that one is simply a circle whereas the other is a circle intersected by a line segment (Figure 4). We found a remarkable difference in the search time depending on whether the target was the *Q* and had the line or was the *O* and lacked the line. When the target had the line, the search time was independent of the number of distractors. Evidently, the target popped out of the display. When the target lacked the line, the search time increased linearly with the number of distractors. Evidently, the items in the display were being subjected to a serial search.

The result goes against one's intuitions. After all, each case involves the same discrimination between the same two stimuli: *O*s and *Q*s. The result is consistent, however, with the idea that a pooled neural signal early in visual processing conveys the presence but not the absence of a distinctive feature. In other words, early vision extracts simple properties, and each type of property triggers activity in populations of specialized detectors. A target with a unique property is detected in the midst of distractor items simply by a check on whether the relevant detectors are active. Conversely, a target lacking a property that is present in the distractors arouses only slightly less activity than a display consisting exclusively of distractors. We propose, therefore, that early vision sets up a number of what might be called *feature maps*. They are not necessarily to be equated with the specialized visual areas that are mapped by physiologists, although the correspondence is suggestive.

We have exploited visual-search tasks to test a wide range of candidate features we thought might pop out of displays and so reveal themselves as primitives: basic elements in the language of early vision. The candidates fell into a number of categories: quantitative properties such as length or number; properties of single lines such as orientation or curvature; properties of line arrangements; topological and relational properties such as the connectedness of lines, the presence of the free ends of lines or the ratio of the height to the width of a shape.

Among the quantitative candidates, my colleagues and I found that some targets popped out when their discriminability was great. In particular, the more extreme targets—the longer lines, the darker grays, the pairs of lines (when the distractors were single lines)—were easier to detect. This suggests that the visual system responds positively to "more" in these quantitative properties and that "less" is coded by default. For example, the neural activity signaling line length might increase with increasing length (up to some maximum), so that a longer target is detected against the lower level of background activity produced by short distractors. In contrast, a shorter target, with its concomitant lower rate of firing, is likely to be swamped by the greater activity produced by the longer distractors. Psychophysicists have known for more than a century that the ability to distinguish differences in intensity grows more acute with decreasing background intensity. We suggest that the same phenomenon, which is known as Weber's law, could account for our findings concerning the quantitative features.

Our tests of two simple properties of lines, orientation and curvature, yielded some surprises. In both cases we found pop-out for one target, a tilted line among vertical distractors and a curved line among straight lines, but not for the converse target, a vertical line among tilted distractors and a straight line among curves. These findings suggest that early vision encodes tilt and curvature but not verticality or straightness. That is, the vertical targets and the straight targets appear to lack a feature the distractors possess, as if they represent null values on their respective dimensions. If our interpretation is correct, it implies that in early vision, tilt and curvature are represented relationally, as deviations from a standard or norm that itself is not positively signaled.

A similar conclusion emerged for the property of closure. We asked subjects to search for complete circles in the midst of circles with gaps and for circles with gaps among complete circles. Again we found a striking asymmetry, this time suggesting that the gap is preattentively detectable but that closure is not—or rather that it becomes preattentively detectable only when the distractors have very large gaps (that is, when they are quite open shapes like semicircles). In other words, closure is preattentively detectable, but only when the distractors do not share it to any significant degree. On the other hand, gaps (or the line ends that gaps create) are found equally easily whatever their size (unless they are too small for a subject, employing peripheral vision, to see).

Finally, we found no evidence that any property of line arrangements is preattentively detectable. We tested intersections, junctions, convergent lines and parallel lines. In every case we found that search time increases with an increasing number of distractors. The targets become salient and obvious only when the subject's attention is directed to them; they do not emerge automatically when that attention is disseminated throughout the display.

In sum, it seems that only a small number of features are extracted early in visual processing. They include color, size, contrast, tilt, curvature, and line ends. Research by other investigators shows that movement and differences in stereoscopic depth are also extracted automatically in early vision. In general the building blocks of vision appear to be simple properties that characterize local elements, such as points or lines, but not the relations among them. Closure appears to be the most complex property that pops out preattentively. Finally, our findings suggest that several preattentive properties are coded as values of deviation from a null, or reference, value.

FIGURE 4   Presence or absence of a feature can have remarkably different effects on the time it takes to find a target in the midst of distractors. In one experiment (a) the target was a circle intersected by a vertical line segment or a circle without that feature. The search time for the intersected circle (solid) proved to be largely independent of the number of items in the display, suggesting that the feature popped out. The search time for the plain circle (dashed) increased steeply as distractors were added, suggesting that a serial search of the display was being made. A second experiment (b) required subjects to search for a vertical line (dashed) or a tilted line (solid). The tilted line could be found much faster; evidently only the tilted line popped out of the displays. A third experiment (c) tested an isolated line segment (dashed) or intersecting lines in the form of a plus sign (solid). Evidently neither popped out.

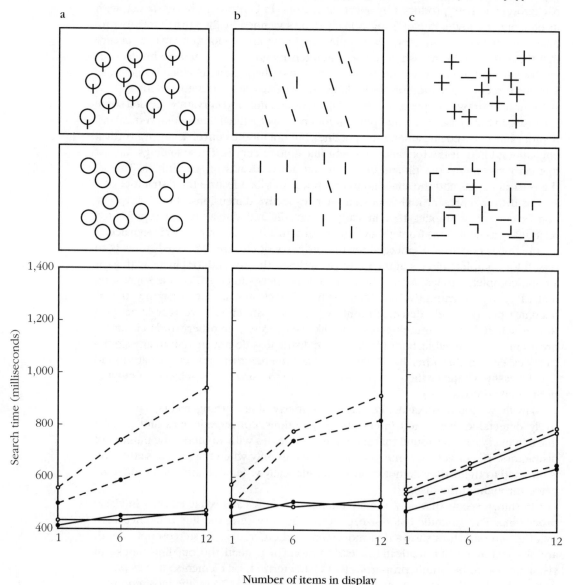

Number of items in display

(Continued)

FIGURE 4 A fourth experiment (d) tested parallel lines (dashed) or converging lines (solid). Again neither popped out. A fifth experiment (e) tested closure with complete circles (dashed) or circles with a gap of a fourth of their circumference (solid). A sixth experiment (f), again testing closure, had complete circles (dashed) or circles with smaller gaps (solid). The size of the gap seemed to make no difference: The incomplete circle popped out. On the other hand, a complete circle became harder to find as the size of the gaps in distractors was reduced. Open dots represent data from trials in which the display included only distractors.

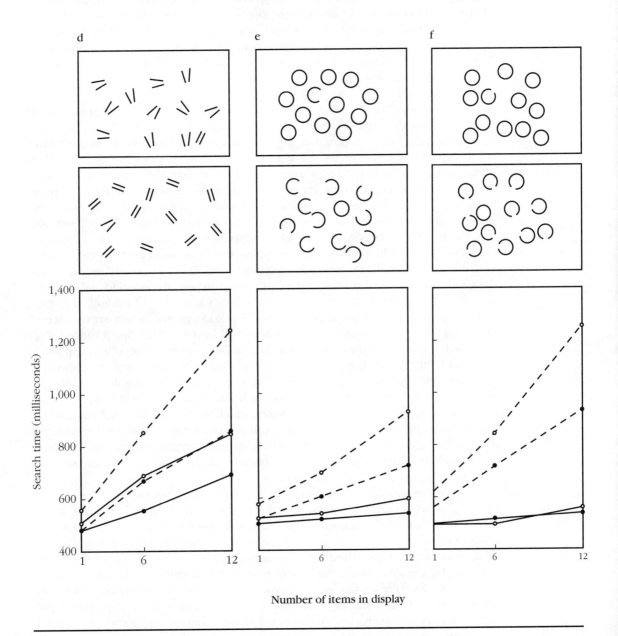

Up to this point I have concentrated on the initial, preattentive stages of vision. I turn now to the later stages. In particular I turn to the evidence that focused attention is required for conjoining the features at a given location in a scene and for establishing structured representations of objects and their relations.

One line of evidence suggesting that conjunctions require attention emerges from experiments in which we asked subjects to identify a target in a display and say where it was positioned. In one type of display only a simple feature distinguished the target from the distractors. For example, the target was a red *H* in the midst of red *O*s and blue *X*s or an orange *X* among red *O*s and blue *X*s. In other displays, the target differed only in the way its features were conjoined. For example, it was a blue *O* or a red *X* among red *O*s and blue *X*s.

We were particularly interested in the cases in which a subject identified the target correctly but gave it the wrong location. As we expected, the subjects could sometimes identify a simple target, say a target distinguished merely by its color, but get its location wrong. Conjunction targets were different: The correct identification was completely dependent on the correct localization. It does indeed seem that attention must be focused on a location in order to combine the features it contains.

In a natural scene, of course, many conjunctions of features are ruled out by prior knowledge. You seldom come across blue bananas or furry eggs. Preattentive visual processing might be called "bottom up," in that it happens automatically, without any recourse to such knowledge. Specifically, it happens without recourse to "top down" constraints. One might hypothesize that conjunction illusions in everyday life are prevented when they conflict with top-down expectations. There are many demonstrations that we do use our knowledge of the world to speed up perception and to make it more accurate. For example, Irving Biederman of the State University of New York at Buffalo asked subjects to find a target object such as a bicycle in a photograph of a natural scene or in a jumbled image in which different areas had been randomly interchanged. The subjects did better when the bicycle could be found in a natural context (see the photo).

In order to explore the role of prior knowledge in the conjoining of properties. Deborah Butler and I did a further study of illusory conjunctions. We showed subjects a set of three colored objects flanked on each side by a digit. Then, some 200 milliseconds later, we showed them a pointer, which was accompanied by a random checkerboard in order to wipe out any visual persistence from the initial display. We asked the subjects to attend to the two digits and report them, and then to say which object the pointer had designated. The sequence was too brief to allow the subjects to focus their attention on all three objects.

The crucial aspect of the experiment lay in the labels we gave the objects. We told one group of subjects that the display would consist of "an orange carrot, a blue lake, and a black tire." Occasional objects (one in four) were shown in the wrong color to ensure that the subjects could not just name the color they would know in advance ought to be associated with a given shape. For another group of subjects the same display was described as "an orange triangle, a blue ellipse, and a black ring."

The results were significant. The group given arbitrary pairings of colors and shapes reported many illusory conjunctions: 29 percent of their responses represented illusory recombinations of colors and shapes from the display, whereas 13 percent were reports of colors or shapes not present in the display. In contrast, the

Prior knowledge as a guide in visual perception is tested by asking subjects to search for a familiar object in a photograph of an unexceptional scene (top) and in a jumbled photograph of the scene (bottom). Here, the task is simply to find the bicycle. It tends to take longer in the jumbled image. The implication is that knowledge of the world (in this case, expectations about the characteristic locations of bicycles in urban landscapes) speeds up perception and makes it less subject to error. Certain early aspects of the information processing that underlies visual perception nonetheless seem to happen automatically: without the influence of prior knowledge. The illustration was modeled after experiments done by Irving Biederman of the State University of New York at Buffalo.

group expecting familiar objects saw rather few illusory conjunctions: They wrongly recombined colors and shapes only 5 percent more often than they reported colors and shapes not present in the display.

We occasionally gave a third group of subjects the wrong combinations when they were expecting most objects to be in their natural colors. To our surprise we found no evidence that subjects generated illusory conjunctions to fit their expectations. For example, they were no more likely to see the triangle (the "carrot") as orange when another object in the display was orange than they were when no orange was present. There seem to be two implications: Prior knowledge and expectations do indeed help one to use attention efficiently in conjoining features, but prior knowledge and expectations seem not to induce illusory exchanges of features to make abnormal objects normal again. Thus illusory conjunctions seem to arise at a stage of visual processing that precedes semantic access to knowledge of familiar objects. The conjunctions seem to be generated preattentively from the sensory data, bottom-up, and not to be influenced by top-down constraints.

How are objects perceived once attention has been focused on them and the correct set of properties has been selected from those present in the scene? In particular, how does one generate and maintain an object's perceptual unity even when objects move and change? Imagine a bird perched on a branch, seen from a particular angle and in a particular illumination. Now watch its shape, its size, and its color all change as it preens itself, opens its wings, and flies away. In spite of these major transformations in virtually all its properties, the bird retains its perceptual integrity: It remains the same single object.

Daniel Kahneman of the University of California at Berkeley and I have suggested that object perception is mediated not only by recognition, or matching to a stored label or description, but also by the construction of a temporary representation that is specific to the object's current appearance and is constantly updated as the object changes. We have drawn an analogy to a file in which all the perceptual information about a particular object is entered, just as the police might open a file on a particular crime, in which they collect all the information about the crime as the information accrues. The perceptual continuity of an object would then depend on its current manifestation being allocated to the same file as its earlier appearances. Such allocation is possible if the object remains stationary or if it changes location within constraints that allow the perceptual system to keep track of which file it should belong to.

In order to test this idea we joined with Brian Gibbs in devising a letter-naming task (Figure 5). Two letters were briefly flashed in the centers of two frames. The empty frames then moved to new locations. Next, another letter appeared in one of the two frames. We devised the display so that the temporal and spatial separations between the priming letter and the final letter were always the same; the only thing that differed was the motion of the frames. The subjects' task was to name the final letter as quickly as possible.

We knew that the prior exposure to a given letter should normally lessen the time it takes to identify the same letter on a subsequent appearance; the effect is known as *priming*. The question that interested us was whether priming would occur only in particular circumstances. We argued that if the final letter is the same as the priming letter and appears in the same frame as the priming letter, the two should be seen as belonging to the same object; in this case, we could think of the perceptual task as simply re-viewing the original object in its shifted position. If, on the other

FIGURE 5 Integration of sensory information into what amounts to a file on each perceptual object was tested by the motion of frames. In each trial, two frames appeared, then two letters were briefly flashed in the frames (a). The frames moved to new locations, and a letter appeared in one of the two (b). The subject's task was to name the final letter as quickly as possible. If the final letter matched the initial letter and appeared in the same frame, the naming was faster than if the letter had appeared in the other frame or differed from the initial letter. The implication is that it takes more time to create or update a file on an object than it does simply to perceive the same object a second time.

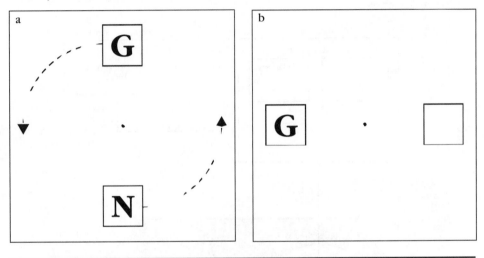

hand, a new letter appears in the same frame, the object file should have to be updated, perhaps increasing the time it takes for subjects to become aware of the letter and name it.

Actually the priming was found to be object-specific: Subjects named the final letter some 30 milliseconds faster if the same letter had appeared previously in the same frame. They showed no such benefit if the same letter had appeared previously in the other frame. The result is consistent with the hypothesis that the later stages of visual perception integrate information from the early, feature-sensitive stages in temporary object-specific representations.

The overall scheme I propose for visual processing can be put in the form of a model (Figure 6). The visual system begins by coding a certain number of simple and useful properties in what can be considered a stack of maps. In the brain such maps ordinarily preserve the spatial relations of the visual world itself. Nevertheless, the spatial information they contain may not be directly available to the subsequent stages of visual processing. Instead the presence of each feature may be signaled without a specification of *where* it is.

In the subsequent stages, focused attention acts. In particular, focused attention is taken to operate by means of a master map of locations, in which the presence of discontinuities in intensity or color is registered without specification of what the discontinuities are. Attention makes use of this master map, simultaneously selecting, by

FIGURE 6   Hypothetical model of the early stages in visual perception emerges from the author's experiments. The model proposes that early vision encodes some simple and useful properties of a scene in a number of feature maps, which may preserve the spatial relations of the visual world but do not themselves make spatial information available to subsequent processing stages. Instead, focused attention (employing a master map of locations) selects and integrates the features present at particular locations. At later stages, the integrated information serves to create and update files on perceptual objects. In turn, the file contents are compared with descriptions stored in a recognition network. The network incorporates the attributes, behavior, names, and significance of familiar objects.

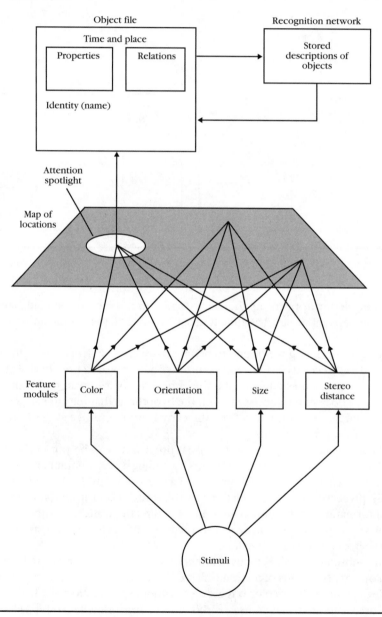

means of links to the separate feature maps, all the features that currently are present in a selected location. These are entered into a temporary object representation, or file.

Finally, the model posits that the integrated information about the properties and structural relations in each object file is compared with stored descriptions in a "recognition network." The network specifies the critical attributes of cats, trees, bacon and eggs, one's grandmothers, and all other familiar perceptual objects, allowing access to their names, their likely behavior, and their current significance. I assume that conscious awareness depends on the object files and on the information they contain. It depends, in other words, on representations that collect information about particular objects, both from the analyses of sensory features and from the recognition network, and continually update the information. If a significant discontinuity in space or time occurs, the original file on an object may be canceled: it ceases to be a source of perceptual experience. As for the object, it disappears and is replaced by a new object with its own new temporary file, ready to begin a new perceptual history.

QUESTIONS FOR FURTHER THOUGHT

1. What are the two main levels of processing in visual perception, and how do they differ?
2. Describe the kinds of visual-search tasks Treisman has used in her research.
3. What is pop-out?
4. Why did Treisman conclude that a serial search was conducted for a plain circle as distractors were added?
5. What is the role of attention in visual processing?

ACTIVATION, ATTENTION, AND SHORT-TERM MEMORY

Nelson Cowan

INTRODUCTION

Consider what you are thinking at this very moment—you currently are attending to and aware of certain phenomena. Now consider what you were thinking about just before reading this selection, perhaps a minute or two ago. Now think of something you can recollect thinking about sometime last week. How are these three kinds of information different and how are they like one another?

Cowan provides a way to answer these questions with a model of attention and memory (Cowan, 1988). His model distinguishes three kinds of information.

Information that is the focus of attention refers to what you are thinking about now. The memory representations of this information are at their maximum levels of activation. Information that is in active memory refers to what you were thinking about previously, up to a minute or two ago. The memory representations of this information are not as highly activated as those that are the focus of attention, but nevertheless these representations remain sufficiently active to allow you easily to bring them back into the focus of attention. Finally, information that is in long-term memory includes what you were thinking about a while ago, for example, last week. The memory representations of this information are at their baseline (inactive) levels.

A major contribution of this paper comes from its attempt to show that the short-term memory concept is not dead, but it needs revision. Cowan identifies three kinds of hierarchically related information corresponding to the focus of attention, active memory, and long-term memory. The term *focus of attention* refers to that part of active memory that is maximally active because it is involved in current information-processing operations. *Active memory,* in turn, refers to the part of long-term memory above baseline levels of activation because it was involved in recent processing.

The premise of this paper is that the popular term "short-term memory" (STM) is vague because it is used to refer to either (1) the set of representations from long-term memory currently in a state of heightened activation or (2) the focus of attention or content of awareness. A more coherent conception of STM

Source: From Cowan, N. (1993). Activation, attention, and short-term memory. *Memory & Cognition, 21* (2), 162–167, reprinted by permission of Psychonomic Society, Inc.

is hierarchical, with the focus of attention depicted as a subset of the activated portion of long-term memory. Research issues are discussed to illustrate that this simple conception of STM leads to testable predictions and useful lines of inquiry. ■

There is a simple, subjective description of one's short-term memory (STM) and awareness with which few would disagree. A small set of ideas, objects, events, and so forth, fill one's current attention and awareness. A somewhat larger set is outside of this focus but nevertheless remains especially available should one want to shift attention to it. An example is something that was said about a minute ago. The present paper examines empirical evidence for this description and its relation to research on STM.

What are the most basic characteristics of STM, and how can they be examined? STM often seems needlessly confusing because two definitions have been used in the literature. First, some have considered it to be the set of elements from long-term memory that currently are in an activated state (e.g., the reverberatory circuits of Hebb, 1949). Second, others have considered it to be the items that are in the current focus of attention (e.g., the primary memory of James, 1890). At times, I even have seen these two definitions used as if they were interchangeable.

The two definitions cannot logically be interchangeable, if there is such a thing as the activation of memory outside of awareness. Such activation has been demonstrated by many recent studies, for example, those on the effects of masked primes on lexical access (for reviews, see Holender, 1986, and Merikle & Reingold, 1990). Even if one does not believe the recent research on automatic semantic activation, the ubiquitous finding of priming effects for recently presented items suggests that at least previously *attended* items stay active in memory for a while after they leave awareness.

Here, then, is a maximally simple theoretical depiction of STM (see Figure 1), which has been distilled from Cowan (1988). STM is represented as a nested subset of long-term memory. Specifically, the currently activated features comprise a subset of long-term memory, and the current focus of attention is in turn a subset of this activated memory.

Two immediate qualifications are in order. First, the boundaries shown in the figure could be fuzzy rather than discrete. Second, given the present limitations of the field of neurophysiology, the term "activation" does not refer to neural activity directly; indeed, for all we know, greater activation could correspond to more neural inhibition. Activation is better defined for our purposes more behaviorally (e.g., as the temporary state of memory representations that would allow these representations to have a priming effect on subsequent stimuli; cf. Cowan, 1988). In neural terms, the only expectation at present is that this activation would be represented as some particular spatiotemporal pattern of activity.

The model shown in Figure 1 obviously is very simple. One might wonder why many interesting distinctions were omitted, such as sensory versus abstract versus motor memory, verbal versus spatial memory, and so on. This omission is important and has to do with the intent of the model. The intent was not to develop a detailed,

FIGURE 1 | A schematic diagram of the memory system as discussed by Cowan (1988). STM has been defined either as the currently active portion of memory or as the current focus of attention.

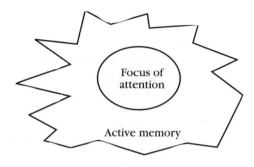

explicit model of how the processing system *might* work. The model is aimed instead at the *necessary* instead of the possible: the most basic memory faculties that must exist according to all available evidence. As far as we know at present, the various domains of STM such as sensory, abstract, and motor memory can be grouped together on the basis that they all may operate on the same dynamic principles. For example, representations of any one type may be susceptible to interference from subsequent stimuli with similar features. Stimuli with sensory features similar to the prior input would interfere with its sensory memory representations, stimuli evoking similar motor responses would interfere with its motor memory representations, and so on. The various types of activated memory also may have similar properties of memory decay. The key distinction, however, would be between activated memory features that are in the current focus of attention versus features outside of that focus (Cowan, 1988).

This theoretical conception of STM is similar in some ways to the working-memory model of Baddeley (1986). It differs from his model, though, in the present assumption that transient, activated memory of various types (sensory, phonological, semantic, and motor) may be instances of a common, general storage medium with many dynamic properties and principles that are common across features types, instead of separate, distinct modules such as Baddeley's visuospatial scratch pad and articulatory loop. It also differs because a wider variety of strategic mechanisms is considered. For example, although Baddeley's process of "covert rehearsal," which serves to reactivate items in memory, also can be described within the present conception (e.g., as a type of activated memory scheme that must be initiated within the focus of attention, although it might then carry on automatically), there also might be other memory reactivation mechanisms. We will see below that some of the work that Baddeley has attributed to covert rehearsal may be accomplished instead by high-speed search processes (Cowan, 1992).

The research that I will discuss begins to address three basic questions about the present, hierarchical view of STM. First, how long can stimuli be retained for immediate recollection when attention is directed toward as opposed to away from them? Second, what roles do activation and attention play in STM tasks? Third, how can we tell if the activated information in STM truly is based on information from long-term memory? These questions will be addressed in turn.

EFFECTS OF ATTENTION ON SHORT-TERM RETENTION

Cowan, Lichty, and Grove (1990) investigated the relation between selective attention and memory retention in a task in which subjects had to read a novel, silently or by whispering, and were instructed to ignore syllables of speech presented through headphones. Occasionally, the subjects received a visual cue to stop reading and to identify the last syllable presented through headphones. This study was modeled after a previous one by Eriksen and Johnson (1964), except that we were looking at the delayed recognition of speech syllables rather than the delayed detection of tones. The subjects first received familiarization and practice with a set of spoken syllables presented through headphones. Then, in the test phase, they read a novel while the syllables were presented. Although syllables were presented at irregular intervals ranging from 1 to 13 sec, test trials occurred much less frequently, only nine times per hour. In each test trial, the subject was to put down the novel and identify the last syllable presented by circling the correct choice out of nine possible syllables depicted on an answer sheet. This last syllable occurred 1, 5, or 10 sec before the test cue, so memory decay functions could be plotted from the data. The delay period always was quiet because there were no intervening syllables, and subjects either read silently or whispered the reading.

After identifying the last spoken syllable, the subject was to write a sentence about what was going on most recently within the reading. Finally, at the end of the session, there was a reading comprehension test. To keep subjects honest, they were told about the final reading test at the beginning of the experimental session. There were several control experiments that demonstrated that the auditory stimuli did not detract from the subjects' reading ability.

The nine test syllables were [bi], [bI], [bE], [di], [dI], [dE], [gi], [gI], and [gE]. Because they consist of the three consonant phones [b], [d], and [g] crossed with the three vowel phones [i], [I], and [E] (as in *bean, bin,* and *Ben,* respectively), we could score performance on consonants and vowels separately. This is of some value because the three vowels are more discriminable than the three consonants; therefore, performance can be viewed at two levels of difficulty. The response sheet looked like a 3×3 matrix.

In the most informative experiment in the set (Cowan et al., 1990, Experiment 4), the subjects whispered the reading. In the practice session in which subjects listened to the syllables and did not read, identification was over 90% correct for both consonants and vowels. However, memory for syllables that were to be ignored at the time of presentation dropped off dramatically as the postsyllabic delay increased from 1 to 10 sec. Similar decay functions were obtained for consonants and vowels, although at a much higher overall level for the vowels.

In this experiment, we also were able to test for subtle shifts of attention away from the reading inasmuch as the subjects had whispered the reading instead of reading silently. We recorded the whispering and were able to examine it for pauses. If a subject did not whisper at all for either 1 sec before or 1 sec after the onset of the target syllable, we reasoned that a shift of attention away from the reading and toward the headphone channel could have occurred. Measured in this way, possible attention shifts occurred on about 20% of the trials. On those trials, there was not much difference from the previous result for memory of the easier, vowel phonemes, but there was a dramatic difference for the more difficult, consonant phonemes. In fact, for the shorter delay intervals, this subtle shift of attention improved performance by about 20%. The benefit of attention diminished at longer delays, as the subjects usually turned their attention back to the reading.

What happens when attention is more consistently divided between the two channels? To examine this in another experiment (Cowan et al., 1990, Experiment 3), subjects not only read the novel, they also were to press a button every time that a [dI] occurred through headphones. The syllabic-recognition test trials used in the previous experiment also were administered in this one. The subjects were able to detect about 60% of the [dI] syllables while reading, with a very low false-alarm rate. However, the memory performance under these divided attention circumstances was very different. There was very little forgetting of the target syllable, even at the 10-sec delay.

The results of these experiments suggest, first, that there is considerable memory for spoken stimuli that are not fully attended at the time of presentation, although this memory decays rapidly. Second, subtle shifts of attention toward particular stimuli can be shown to markedly improve memory for these stimuli.

ACTIVATION AND ATTENTION IN STM TASKS

The second research question concerns the role that activation and attention play in more typical STM tasks. The kind of task that I have examined, to begin to look at this question, is the common one in which a list of words is presented and the subject is simply to repeat the list immediately after its presentation. One possible role of activation can be inferred from the assumption (Baddeley, 1986; Cowan, 1988) that the items in a verbal list are represented in the form of a temporarily activated sequence of units. These units decay after activation unless there is some process that reactivates them.

One prediction from this conception of short-term recall is as follows. While a subject is receiving a list of items and is not currently responding to the list, rehearsal processes may reactivate items. However, whenever the subject is busy verbally repeating an item, it presumably is impossible to rehearse the other items at the same time. For this reason, activated memory should decay, at least at certain times, within the response period.

This prediction was examined by Cowan et al. (1992). The stimulus words were inspired by some that Baddeley, Thomson, and Buchanan (1975) used. The two word sets had identical numbers of phonemes and syllables. However, with such stimuli, it still takes subjects longer to pronounce words in the set marked "long" than in the set marked "short." Therefore, the processing of words in the long set should allow more memory decay to occur. Baddeley et al. found that memory performance was better for short sets than for longer sets, and we replicated this finding.

Baddeley et al.'s (1975) word-length effect could occur for at least two different reasons, however, corresponding to the two paths of articulation in the STM model: covert rehearsal and overt pronunciation. The reason favored by Baddeley et al. was that the longer words slow down the rehearsal process. This may be true, but we were interested in the effects of word length on the decay of memory during the subject's overt verbal response to the list.

To examine the effects of word length on overt recall processes, we used mixed lists. The length of words in the first and second halves of each list was varied independently. Therefore, there were four types of lists: short–short, short–long, long–short, and long–long, according to the length of words in each half-list. (Stated more precisely, inasmuch as five-word lists were used, the length of the middle word was counterbalanced across trials in each of the length combinations.) This procedure was similar to an experiment conducted by Watkins (1977), except that he manipulated word frequency rather than word length and used a span task, which could not yield the serial position information that we found to be especially informative. Subjects received a printed list at the rate of 2 sec/word. In the most informative experiment, there was a printed cue following the last word in the list that told the subjects to recall the words in either forward or backward order.

We reasoned that, if there were an effect of word length during the repetition of the list, the specific effects of word length would depend on the order of recall. The words that are repeated first delay the output of the remaining words in the list, and the lengths of those words repeated first should have a large effect on recall. In contrast, the words that are repeated last do not delay the output of any other words, and they therefore should have much less effect.

The results were very clearly as predicted. When words were to be recalled in the forward order, there was a significant effect of the length of words in the first half of the list, and this effect extended across the list. However, there was no effect of word length in the second half of the list. In the backward recall order, though, the results were just the opposite. There, it was the length of words in the second half of the list that made a difference for recall throughout the list, not the length of words in the first half of the list. In other words, it was always the length of just the words in the part of the list to be repeated first that made a significant difference. This pattern of results is reproduced in Figure 2. It supports the idea that during the time when a subject repeats any one word in the list, the memory for the other words in the list can decay from activation.

This finding is only a start toward answering the question of what roles activation and attention play in STM tasks. There are two alternative, slightly more detailed descriptions of what might happen as subjects repeat words in such tasks. The first possibility is that memory activation decays steadily while the subject repeats words. According to this account, the subject would have to finish his or her recall before too much memory decay takes place. Across many memory span studies with a variety of subject groups and stimulus conditions, it has been observed that people can remember about as much as they can say in about 2 sec (for a review, see Baddeley, 1986). Therefore, some researchers (Schweickert & Boruff, 1986; Stigler, Lee, & Stevenson, 1986) simply have assumed that a version of this first mechanism is correct, with an effective memory decay period of about 2 sec. Their hypothesis is that the period of repetition of a span-length list is limited to little more than 2 sec.

FIGURE 2   Results of Experiment 3 of Cowan et al. (1992). Top panel: Forward recall as a function of serial position for lists with a short versus long first half (collapsed across the second-half word length, which was not significant). Bottom panel: Backward recall as a function of serial position for lists with a short versus long second half (collapsed across the first-half word length, which was not significant). Notice that it was always the length of words to be pronounced first that made a difference for recall. Reprinted from Cowan et al. (1992) with the permission of Academic Press.

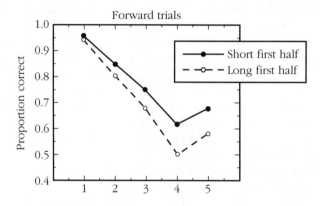

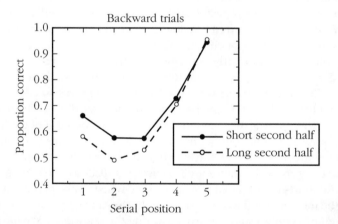

Most of the studies on the relation of speech rate to memory span have based their findings on the rate of speeded pronunciation in special tasks in which the subject is to repeat just a few words as quickly as possible. They have not focused on the actual duration of the subject's repetition of the lists to be recalled. However, the 2-sec-recall-period hypothesis mentioned above would seem to require that type of data. Stigler et al. (1986) did examine the duration of spoken recall responses and found a mean for adults' overt pronunciation of span-length word lists of under 3 sec, both in English- and in Chinese-speaking subjects, even though there was a higher span length in the latter.

Despite the finding of Stigler et al. (1986), an alternative, more complex account of processing during the recall phase cannot be ruled out. While a subject devotes attention to speaking a particular word, there would indeed be some decay of the activation of other words, but during pauses between words, some reactivation of memory would take place as the subject scans, rehearses, or in some other way processes some of the items that are still to be recalled. This scanning might or might not be conducted for the specific purpose of reactivating items; all that is necessary is the assumption that items processed during interword pauses are in fact reactivated in memory. This account could be correct, despite the findings of Stigler et al., because it might be that the reactivation periods in their adult subjects were rapid enough so that the recall period was not extended much beyond the expected 2-sec limit.

Even without making a commitment about exactly what process takes place during the pauses between words during recall, the hypothesis of a decay-and-reactivation cycle, with decay during word pronunciations and reactivation of some words during interword pauses, leads to a distinct prediction. The duration of span-length spoken recall need not correlate with memory span. Subjects who can remember more might do so by extending the total duration of memory activation, and they might achieve that by engaging in more rapid or efficient covert processing in the pauses between words.

To distinguish between the two accounts of STM recall (monotonic decay versus decay-and-reactivation cycles), Cowan (1992) examined some tape-recorded protocols for memory span in forty-four 4-year-old children by using an acoustic waveform editor (MacRecorder Soundedit) to measure the timing of recall. The hope was that processes causing reactivation would take place more slowly, and thus be more easily detectable, in these subjects than in adults. The subjects' memory spans varied from two to five items. The duration of recall was measured in a number of slightly different ways, but the result was the same for each method. The *duration* of recall certainly was not limited to 2 sec or to any other fixed period. Instead, there was a linear relation between an individual's memory span and the duration of that individual's recall for span-length lists. In fact, the children with the highest spans produced responses that lasted for almost 5 sec. Also, in contrast to the finding in the literature (e.g., Baddeley et al., 1975) of a strong correlation between memory *span* and the rate of pronunciation in speeded pronunciation tasks, no relation between an individual's memory span and speech rate in spoken recall was observed.

One way to explain the strong relation between span and the duration of recall in span-length lists while defending the monotonic decay theory would be to assume that the duration of decay varies markedly among subjects (e.g., from about 2 to 5 sec in the 4-year-old subjects). However, that type of account could not explain why people can recall about as much as they can say in a speeded task in about 2 sec, regardless of memory level. A better account of all of the data is the decay-and-reactivation account. It would suggest that individual differences in span result from differences in the speed and/or efficiency with which subjects can retrieve and reactivate items in the pauses between words in the response.

Additional findings of Cowan (1992) yield further information about what may be going on in recall. Although children of different spans pronounced their recall at comparable rates within their respective span-length lists (about 1.2 words/sec), they pronounced lists of length span −1 at a faster rate (about 1.4 words/sec), and lists of length span −2 at a still faster rate (about 1.6 words/sec). Moreover, this effect of list length relative to span on pronunciation rate was localized entirely in the pauses between words, with no effect of list length on the duration of words in the response. These findings are entirely parallel to what has been obtained previously by Sternberg and his colleagues (Sternberg, Monsell, Knoll, & Wright, 1978; Sternberg, Wright, Knoll, & Monsell, 1980) in a different procedure, in which subjects received a ready signal on each trial and then pronounced a subspan-length list as quickly as possible. Sternberg and his colleagues have argued on the basis of many types of converging evidence for a model in which subjects rapidly scan the list during pauses in the response, in search of the item with the correct serial position marker to be pronounced next. It seems likely that this scanning process, or whatever search process actually accounts for the timing of speech in Sternberg and his colleagues' procedure, will end up accounting for the timing of spoken recall in span tasks as well. This is encouraging, given that there is a known relationship between memory search rate and memory span (Cavanagh, 1972). It strengthens the hypothesis that individual differences in memory span might be accounted for by differences in the efficiency of memory search taking place during pauses in the response.

In one way, this result is reminiscent of the finding of Cowan et al. (1990) regarding memory for ignored syllables of speech. In both cases, it appears that there is a decay of memory activation over time but that there are subtle but frequent shifts of attention that initiate processes resulting in reactivation. In ordinary STM tasks, it often may be difficult to observe the decay of activation precisely because subjects are frequently shifting attention between items in order to postpone memory decay, even within a single response sequence. This activation–attention interaction should be a key topic for additional investigation.

CONCEPT OF SHORT-TERM ACTIVATION OF LONG-TERM MEMORY

The third general research question posed at the beginning of this paper was whether activated memory necessarily is drawn from long-term memory, as was proposed. (An alternative possibility is that STM is a completely separate resource or structure, as proposed for example by Broadbent, 1984, and Shallice & Warrington, 1970.) A number of recent studies of other investigators are relevant here. First, Charles Hulme and his colleagues (Hulme, Maughan, & Brown, 1991) did a study of speeded pronunciation and memory span in adults, using both English words and nonsense words as stimuli. The usual linear relation between speech rate and memory span was obtained, but with a much higher intercept for words than for nonwords. This illustrates that one's long-term lexical familiarity with the material to be activated makes a big difference in STM tasks.

Second, some new research by Cantor and Engle (1992) shows a clear inverse relation between an individual's working memory span and the magnitude of his or her propositional fan effect. Of course, fan effects (in which the mean time to recognize that two items have appeared together in an experiment is positively related to how many other items have been paired with either of the two items in question) have been used to demonstrate limitations in the spread of semantic activation through the propositional network in long-term memory (Anderson, 1974). The implication of Cantor and Engle's study is that working memory span also may depend on the extent of network activation.

Nairne's (1992) research on the long-term serial recall of verbal lists also is relevant. Previous studies on immediate recall (e.g., Lee & Estes, 1981) show a very systematic set of order errors. Nairne's findings are similar but concern delayed recall over minutes or even hours. One explanation of this finding is that STM sets up a pattern of activation that becomes etched into long-term memory also, in a Hebbian (see Hebb, 1949) manner.

Across all of these recent studies, it seems fair to say that long-term memory is both the source and the beneficiary of the activation pattern in STM.

CONCLUDING REMARKS

Theoretically, STM serves as the interface between everything we know and everything we perceive or do. Yet, there is quite a gap between this central theoretical role of STM and the much more confined scope revealed by the conventional procedures for examining STM (e.g., digit span). One way to bridge this gap is to expand the arsenal of procedures, but another way is to work harder to obtain a better understanding of the role of theoretical mechanisms in the conventional tasks. However, it is my belief that there has been considerable confusion in the use of terms and that this has at times gotten in the way of a theoretical understanding of the mechanisms operating in STM tasks.

A simple suggestion of Cowan (1988) is that STM is a hierarchical construct, with one component being the currently activated portion of the memory system and another component being the subset of this activated memory that currently is in the focus of attention. However, this conception of STM serves only as a beginning, not an ending, point. I believe that it is a good beginning because it permits a search for general principles and deliberately avoids making further subdivisions of STM for which the processes have not been proved to operate in fundamentally different ways. Even when differences are observed, it is important to consider if they arise specifically from different STM modules or from differences in contributing perceptual processes. For example, the well-known auditory modality superiority in list recall tasks does not imply that the decay period is longer in audition than in vision, since various data suggest that it probably results instead from the basically more temporal organization of audition as opposed to the more spatial organization of vision (Cowan, 1988; Penney, 1989).

From this beginning, it was shown that various lines of research can make progress by focusing on the details of specific mechanisms of activation and attention in STM tasks. Many fundamental questions remain to be addressed. For example, how can the amount of activation and attention be measured? Are the boundaries between these subsets of memory discrete or continuous? Is the focus of attention simply the subset of memory with the highest level of activation, or does it differ in a qualitative manner from memory outside of the focus? Although the present theoretical approach is simple and perhaps intuitively obvious, it still can lead to interesting empirical ramifications that are not so obvious and that clearly warrant further research.

REFERENCES

Anderson, J. R. (1974). Retrieval of propositional information from long-term memory. *Cognitive Psychology, 6,* 451–474.

Baddeley, A. D. (1986). *Working memory.* Oxford, UK: Clarendon.

Baddeley, A. D., Thomson, N., & Buchanan, M. (1975). Word length and the structure of short-term memory. *Journal of Verbal Learning & Verbal Behavior, 14,* 575–589.

Broadbent, D. E. (1984). The Maltese cross: A new simplistic model for memory. *Behavioral & Brain Science, 7,* 55–94.

Cantor, J., & Engle, R. (1992, November). *A test of an activation notion of working memory.* Paper presented at the annual meeting of the Psychonomic Society, St. Louis.

Cavanagh, J. P. (1972). Relation between the immediate memory span and the memory search rate. *Psychological Review, 79,* 525–530.

Cowan, N. (1988). Evolving conceptions of memory storage, selective attention, and their mutual constraints within the human information-processing system. *Psychological Bulletin, 104,* 163–191.

Cowan, N. (1992). Verbal memory span and the timing of spoken recall. *Journal of Memory & Language, 31,* 668–684.

Cowan, N., Day, L., Saults, J. S., Keller, T. A., Johnson, T., & Flores, L. (1992). The role of verbal output time in the effects of word length on immediate memory. *Journal of Memory & Language, 31,* 1–17.

Cowan, N., Lichty, W., & Grove, T. R. (1990). Properties of memory for unattended spoken syllables. *Journal of Experimental Psychology: Learning, Memory, & Cognition, 16,* 258–269.

Eriksen, C. W., & Johnson, H. J. (1964). Storage and decay characteristics of nonattended auditory stimuli. *Journal of Experimental Psychology, 68,* 28–36.

Hebb, D. O. (1949). *The organization of behavior: A neuropsychological theory.* New York: Wiley.

Holender, D. (1986). Semantic activation without conscious identification in dichotic listening, parafoveal vision, and visual masking: A survey and appraisal. *Behavioral & Brain Sciences, 9,* 1–66.

Hulme, C., Maughan, S., & Brown, G. D. A. (1991). Memory for familiar and unfamiliar words: Evidence for a long-term memory contribution to short-term memory span. *Journal of Memory & Language, 30,* 685–701.

James, W. (1890). *The principles of psychology.* New York: Henry Holt.

Lee, C. L., & Estes, W. K. (1981). Item and order information in short-term memory: Evidence for multilevel perturbation processes. *Journal of Experimental Psychology: Human Learning & Memory, 7,* 149–169.

Merikle, P. M., & Reingold, E. M. (1990). Recognition and lexical decision without detection: Unconscious perception? *Journal of Experimental Psychology: Human Perception & Performance, 16,* 574–583.

Nairne, J. S. (1992). The loss of positional certainty in long-term memory. *Psychological Science, 3,* 199–202.

Penney, C. G. (1989). Modality effects and the structure of short-term verbal memory. *Memory & Cognition, 17,* 398–422.

Schweickert, R., & Boruff, B. (1986). Short-term memory capacity: Magic number or magic spell? *Journal of Experimental Psychology: Learning, Memory, & Cognition, 12,* 419–425.

Shallice, T., & Warrington, E. K. (1970). Independent functioning of verbal memory stores: A neuropsychological study. *Quarterly Journal of Experimental Psychology, 22,* 261–273.

Sternberg, S., Monsell, S., Knoll, R. L., & Wright, C. E. (1978). The latency and duration of rapid movement sequences: Comparisons of speech and typewriting. In G. E. Stelmach (Ed.), *Information processing in motor control and learning* (pp. 117–152). New York: Academic Press.

Sternberg, S., Wright, C. E., Knoll, R. L., & Monsell, S. (1980). Motor programs in rapid speech: Additional evidence. In R. A. Cole (Ed.), *Perception and production of fluent speech* (pp. 507–534). Hillsdale, NJ: Erlbaum.

Stigler, J. W., Lee, S.-Y., & Stevenson, H. W. (1986). Digit memory in Chinese and English: Evidence for a temporally limited store. *Cognition, 23,* 1–20.

Watkins, M. J. (1977). The intricacy of memory span. *Memory & Cognition, 5,* 529–534.

QUESTIONS FOR FURTHER THOUGHT

1. How does Cowan's conception of short-term memory differ from the conventional conception?

2. How does Cowan test his conception of short-term memory?

3. What is the relationship between attention and memory in Cowan's framework?

4. What, in Cowan's view, is the relationship of short-term memory to long-term memory? How does his view differ from the conventional view?

5. Is Cowan's view necessarily incompatible with the conventional view? Why or why not?

4

MEMORY

THE CONTROL OF SHORT-TERM MEMORY

Richard Atkinson and Richard Shiffrin

INTRODUCTION

How does information make its way from the environment to memory? How do people remember information, and why do they sometimes forget it?

Richard Atkinson and Richard Shiffrin proposed what has come to be called the "standard model" for the encoding, storing, and retrieving information for memory. Although many alternative models have since been proposed, the staying power of the Atkinson–Shiffrin model is shown by its continuing status as the standard against which other models are compared. This durability of the model has earned the article introducing it a place in the history of psychology. Even today, the model dominates thinking about memory.

The standard model proposes three stores through which memories potentially can pass. The limited-capacity sensory registers hold information only for very brief periods of time, on the order of a half-second to a second or so. Atkinson and Shiffrin suggested that a distinct sensory register may correspond to each sense, for example, one for the visual sense, one for the auditory sense, and so on.

Some information is lost in the sensory registers, but other information makes its way to the limited-capacity short-term store, where it lasts from several seconds to several minutes if strategies are used to retain it. One such strategy is rehearsal, repetition, usually silent, to oneself. Information is lost from the short-term store largely through a process of interference, in which new information knocks out old information unless the old information is rehearsed. Finally, some of the information from the short-term store may reach the long-term store, where it may remain for extremely long, perhaps indefinite periods of time.

The long-term store differs from the other two stores in its almost unlimited capacity, according to the model. To the extent that there are limits, they have yet to be discovered.

———

Memory has two components: short-term and long-term. Control processes such as "rehearsal" are essential to the transfer of information from the short-term store to the long-term one. ■

Source: From Atkinson, R. C., & Shiffrin, R. M. (1971). The control of short-term memory. *Scientific American, 225,* 82–90. Reprinted with permission.

The notion that the system by which information is stored in memory and retrieved from it can be divided into two components dates back to the 19th century. Theories distinguishing between two different kinds of memory were proposed by the English associationists James Mill and John Stuart Mill and by such early experimental psychologists as Wilhelm Wundt and Ernst Meumann in Germany and William James in the United States. Reflecting on their own mental processes, they discerned a clear difference between thoughts currently in consciousness and thoughts that could be brought to consciousness only after a search of memory that was often laborious. (For example, the sentence you are reading is in your current awareness; the name of the baseball team that won the 1968 World Series may be in your memory, but to retrieve it takes some effort, and you may not be able to retrieve it at all.)

The two-component concept of memory was intuitively attractive, and yet it was largely discarded when psychology turned to behaviorism, which emphasized research on animals rather than humans. The distinction between short-term memory and long-term memory received little further consideration until the 1950s, when such psychologists as Donald E. Broadbent in England, D. O. Hebb in Canada, and George A. Miller in the United States reintroduced it [see "Information and Memory," by George A. Miller, *Scientific American*, August, 1956]. The concurrent development of computer models of behavior and of mathematical psychology accelerated the growth of interest in the two-process viewpoint, which is now undergoing considerable theoretical development and is the subject of a large research effort. In particular, the short-term memory system, or short-term store (STS), has been given a position of pivotal importance. That is because the processes carried out in the short-term store are under the immediate control of the subject and govern the flow of information in the memory system; they can be called into play at the subject's discretion, with enormous consequences for performance.

Some control processes are used in many situations by everyone and others are used only in special circumstances. "Rehearsal" is an overt or covert repetition of information—as in remembering a telephone number until it can be written down, remembering the names of a group of people to whom one has just been introduced or copying a passage from a book. "Coding" refers to a class of control processes in which the information to be remembered is put in a context of additional, easily retrievable information, such as a mnemonic phrase or sentence. "Imaging" is a control process in which verbal information is remembered through visual images; for example, Cicero suggested learning long lists (or speeches) by placing each member of the list in a visual representation of successive rooms of a well-known building. There are other control processes, including decision rules, organizational schemes, retrieval strategies and problem-solving techniques; some of them will be encountered in this article. The point to keep in mind is the optional nature of control processes. In contrast to permanent structural components of the memory system, the control processes are selected at the subject's discretion; they may vary not only with different tasks but also from one encounter with the same task to the next.

We believe that the overall memory system is best described in terms of the flow of information into and out of short-term storage and the subject's control of that flow, and this conception has been central to our experimental and theoretical investigation of memory. All phases of memory are assumed to consist of small units of information that are associatively related. A set of closely interrelated information units is termed an image or a trace. Note that "image" does not necessarily imply a visual representation; if the letter-number pair *TKM-4* is presented for memory, the image that is stored might include the size of the card on which the pair is printed, the type of print, the sound of the various symbols, the semantic codes, and numerous other units of information.

Information from the environment is accepted and processed by the various sensory systems and is entered into the short-term store, where it remains for a period of time that is usually under the control of the subject. By rehearsing one or more items, the subject can keep them in the short-term store, but the number that can be maintained in this way is strictly limited; most people can maintain seven to nine digits, for example. Once an image is lost from the short-term store it cannot thereafter be recovered from it. While information resides in short-term storage it may be copied into the long-term store (LTS), which is assumed to be a relatively permanent memory from which information is not lost. While an image is in short-term storage, closely related information in the long-term store is activated and entered in the short-term store, too. Information entering the short-term store from the sensory systems comes from a specific modality—visual, auditory or whatever—but associations from the long-term store in all modalities are activated to join it. For instance, an item may be presented visually, but immediately after input its verbal "name" and associated meanings will be activated from the long-term store and placed in the short-term one (Figure 1).

Our account of short-term and long-term storage does not require that the two stores necessarily be in different parts of the brain or involve different physiological structures. One might consider the short-term store simply as being a temporary activation of some portion of the long-term store. In our thinking we tend to equate the

FIGURE 1   Information flow through the memory system is conceived of as beginning with the processing of environmental inputs in sensory registers (receptors plus internal elements) and entry into the short-term store (STS). While it remains there, the information may be copied into the long-term store (LTS), and associated information that is in the long-term store may be activated and entered into the short-term store. If a triangle is seen, for example, the name *triangle* may be called up. Control processes in the short-term store affect these transfers into and out of the long-term store and govern learning retrieval of information and forgetting.

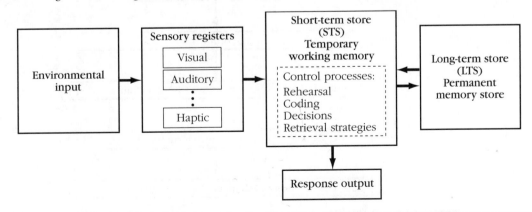

short-term store with "consciousness," that is, the thoughts and information of which we are currently aware can be considered part of the contents of the short-term store. (Such a statement lies in the realm of phenomenology and cannot be verified scientifically, but thinking of the short-term store in this way may help the reader to conceptualize the system.) Because consciousness is equated with the short-term store and because control processes are centered in and act through it, the short-term store is considered a working memory: a system in which decisions are made, problems are solved and information flow is directed. Retrieval of information from short-term storage is quite fast and accurate. Experiments by Saul Sternberg of the Bell Telephone Laboratories and by others have shown that the retrieval time for information in short-term storage such as letters and numbers ranges from 10 to 30 milliseconds per character.

The retrieval of information from long-term storage is considerably more complicated. So much information is contained in the long-term store that the major problem is finding access to some small subset of the information that contains the desired image, just as one must find a particular book in a library before it can be scanned for the desired information. We propose that the subject activates a likely subset of information, places it in the short-term store and then scans that store for the desired image. The image may not be present in the current subset, and so the retrieval process becomes a search in which various subsets are successively acti-

FIGURE 2   Retrieval from the long-term store requires a choice of strategy and selection of certain information as a "probe" that is placed in the short-term store. The probe activates a "search set" of information in the long-term store. The search set is placed in the short-term store and examined for the desired information. If it is not found, search is halted or recycled with a new probe.

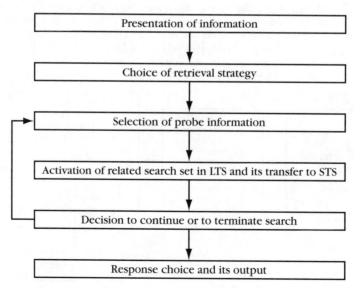

the subject selects the appropriate "probe information" and places it in the short-term store. A "search set," or subset of information in the long-term store closely associated with the probe, is then activated and put in the short-term store. The subject selects from the search set some image, which is then examined. The information extracted from the selected image is utilized for a decision: Has the desired information been found? If so, the search is terminated.

If the information has not been found, the subject may decide that continuation is unlikely to be productive or he may decide to continue. If he does, he begins the next cycle of the search by again selecting a probe, which may or may not be the same probe used in the preceding cycle depending on the subject's strategy. For example, a subject asked to search for U.S. states starting with the letter M may do so by generating states at random and checking their first letter (in which case the same probe information can be used in each search cycle), or he may generate successive states in a regular geographic order (in which case the probe information is systematically changed from one cycle to the next). It can be shown that strategies in which the probe information is systematically changed will result more often in successful retrieval but will take longer than alternative "random" strategies. (Note that the Freudian concept of repressed memories can be considered as being an inability of the subject to generate an appropriate probe.)

This portrayal of the memory system almost entirely in terms of the operations of the short-term store is quite intentional. In our view, information storage and retrieval are best described in terms of the flow of information through the short-term store and in terms of the subject's control of the flow. One of the most important of these control processes is rehearsal. Through overt or covert repetition of information, rehearsal either increases the momentary strength of information in the short-term store or otherwise delays its loss. Rehearsal can be shown not only to maintain information in short-term storage but also to control transfer from the short-term store to the long-term one. We shall present several experiments concerned with an analysis of the rehearsal process.

The research in question involves a memory paradigm known as "free recall," which is similar to the task you face when you are asked to name the people present at the last large party you went to. In the typical experimental procedure a list of random items, usually common English words, is presented to the subject one at a time. Later, the subject attempts to recall as many words as possible in any order. Many psychologists have worked on free recall, with major research efforts carried out by Bennet Murdock of the University of Toronto, Endel Tulving of Yale University, and Murray Glanzer of New York University. The result of principal interest is the probability of recalling each item in a list as a function of its place in the list, or "serial-presentation position." Plotting this function yields a U-shaped curve (see panel a in Figure 3). The increased probability of recall for the first few words in the list is called the *primacy effect;* the large increase for the last 8 to 12 words is called the *recency effect.* There is considerable evidence that the recency effect is due to retrieval from short-term storage and that the earlier portions of the serial-position curve reflect retrieval from long-term storage only. In one experimental procedure the subject is required to carry out a difficult arithmetic task for 30 seconds immediately following presentation of the list and then is asked to recall. One can assume that the

FIGURE 3   Probability of recall in free-recall experiments varies in a characteristic way with an item's serial position in a list: A "primacy effect" and a "recency effect" are apparent (a). If an arithmetic task is interpolated between presentation and recall, the recency effect disappears (b). Words in long lists are recalled less well than words in short lists (c). Slower presentation also results in better recall (d). The curves are idealized ones based on experiments by James W. Deese, Bennet Murdock, Leo Postman, and Murray Glanzer.

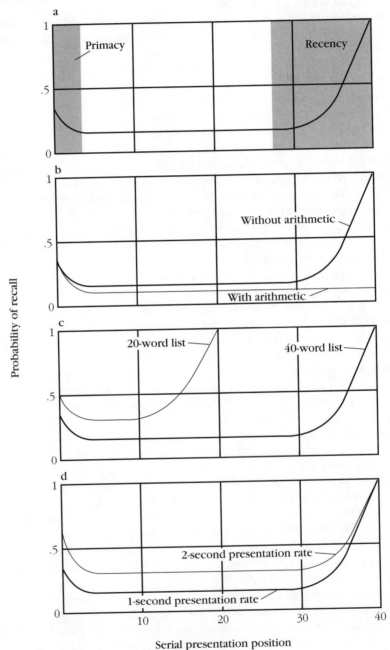

Probability of recall

Serial presentation position

arithmetic task causes the loss of all the words in short-term storage, so that recall reflects retrieval from long-term storage only. The recency effect is eliminated when this experiment is performed; the earlier portions of the serial-position curve are unaffected (panel b in Figure 3). If variables that influence the long-term store but not the short-term one are manipulated, the recency portion of the serial-position curve should be relatively unaffected, whereas the earlier portions of the curve should show changes. One such variable is the number of words in the presented list. A word in a longer list is less likely to be recalled, but the recency effect is quite unaffected by list length (panel c). Similarly, increases in the rate of presentation decrease the likelihood of recalling words preceding the recency region but leave the recency effect largely unchanged (panel d).

In free-recall experiments, many lists are usually presented in a session. If the subject is asked at the end of the session to recall all the words presented during the session, we would expect his recall to reflect retrieval from long-term storage only. The probability of recalling words as a function of their serial position within each list can be plotted for end-of-session recall and compared with the serial-position curve for recall immediately following presentation (see Figure 4). For the delayed-recall curve, the primacy effect remains, but the recency effect is eliminated, as predicted. In summary, the recency region appears to reflect retrieval from both short-term and long-term storage, whereas the serial-position curve preceding the recency region reflects retrieval from long-term storage only.

FIGURE 4 Effect of delay is tested by asking subjects to recall at the end of a session all words from the entire session and then plotting probability of recall against serial position within each list. An experiment by Fergus Craik compares immediate recall (solid line) with delayed recall (dashed line). The delayed-recall curve emphasizes the transitory nature of the recency effect.

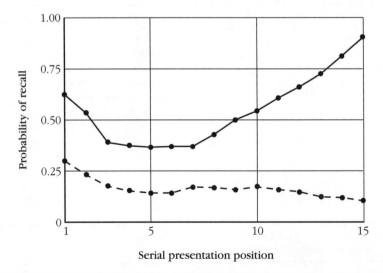

In 1965, at a conference sponsored by the New York Academy of Sciences, we put forward a mathematical model explaining these and other effects in terms of a rehearsal process. The model assumed that in a free-recall task, the subject sets up a rehearsal buffer in the short-term store that can hold only a fixed number of items. At the start of the presentation of a list the buffer is empty; successive items are entered until the buffer is filled. Thereafter, as each new item enters the rehearsal buffer, it replaces one of the items already there. (Which item is replaced depends on a number of psychological factors, but in the model the decision is approximated by a random process.) The items that are still being rehearsed in the short-term store when the last item is presented are the ones that are immediately recalled by the subject, giving rise to the recency effect. The transfer of information from the short-term to the long-term store is postulated to be a function of the length of time an item resides in the rehearsal buffer; the longer the time period, the more rehearsal the item receives and therefore the greater the transfer of information to long-term storage. Since items presented first in a list enter an empty or partly empty rehearsal buffer, they remain longer than later items and consequently receive additional rehearsal. This extra rehearsal causes more transfer of information to long-term storage for the first items, giving rise to the primacy effect.

This rehearsal model was given a formal mathematical statement and was fitted to a wide array of experiments, and it provided an excellent quantitative account of a great many results in free recall, including those discussed in this article. A more direct confirmation of the model has recently been provided by Dewey Rundus of Stanford University. He carried out free-recall experiments in which subjects rehearsed aloud during list presentation. This overt rehearsal was tape-recorded and was compared with the recall results. The number of different words contained in the "rehearsal set" (the items overtly rehearsed between successive presentations) was one after the first

TABLE 1 Overt-Rehearsal	
ITEM PRESENTED	**ITEMS REHEARSED (REHEARSAL SET)**
1. REACTION	Reaction, reaction, reaction, reaction
2. HOOF	Hoof, reaction, hoof, reaction
3. BLESSING	Blessing, hoof, reaction
4. RESEARCH	Research, reaction, hoof, research
5. CANDY	Candy, hoof, research, reaction
6. HARDSHIP	Hardship, hoof, hardship, hoof
7. KINDNESS	Kindness, candy, hardship, hoof
8. NONSENSE	Nonsense, kindness, candy, hardship
•	•
•	•
•	•
20. CELLAR	Cellar, alcohol, misery, cellar

An experiment by Dewey Rundus shows the effect of rehearsal on transfer into long-term storage. The subject rehearses aloud. A partial listing of items rehearsed in one instance shows typical result: early items receive more rehearsals than later items.

word was presented and then rose until the fourth word; from the fourth word on, the number of different words in the rehearsal set remained fairly constant (averaging about 3.3) until the end of the list. The subjects almost always reported the members of the most recent rehearsal set when the list ended and recall began. A close correspondence is evident between the number of rehearsals and the recall probability for words preceding the recency effect; in the recency region, however, a sharp disparity occurs (see Table 1 and Figure 5). The hypothesis that long-term storage is a function of the number of rehearsals can be checked in other ways. The recall probability for a word preceding the recency region was plotted as a function of the number of rehearsals received by that word; the result was an almost linear, sharply increasing function. And words presented in the middle of the list given the same number of rehearsals as the first item presented had the same recall probability as that first item.

With efficacy of rehearsal established both for storing information in the long-term store and for maintaining information in the short-term store, we did an experiment in which the subjects' rehearsal was manipulated directly. Our subjects were trained to engage in one of two types of rehearsal. In the first (a one-item rehearsal set) the most recently presented item was rehearsed exactly three times before presentation of the next item; no other items were rehearsed. In the second (a three-item rehearsal set) the subject rehearsed the three most recently presented items once each before presentation of the next item, so that the first rehearsal set contained three rehearsals of the first word, the second rehearsal set contained two rehearsals of the second word and one rehearsal of the first word, and all subsequent sets contained one rehearsal of each of the three most recent items (see Table 2 and Figure 6).

FIGURE 5   Effect of rehearsal is demonstrated by comparison of an item's probability of recall (solid line) with the total number of rehearsals the item receives (dashed line). The two are related in regions reflecting retrieval from long-term storage (preceding recency region). That is, long-term storage efficacy depends on the number of rehearsals and is reflected in retrieval.

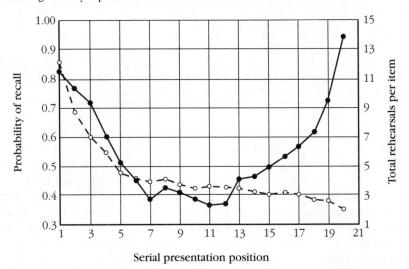

| TABLE 2 | One-Item Rehearsal Scheme | | |

SERIAL POSITION	ITEM PRESENTED	ITEMS REHEARSED	TOTAL REHEARSALS PER ITEM
1	A	AAA	3
2	B	BBB	3
3	C	CCC	3
4	D	DDD	3
5	E	EEE	3
6	F	FFF	3
•	•	•	•
•	•	•	•
•	•	•	•
14	N	NNN	3
15	O	OOO	3
16	P	PPP	3

Three-Item Rehearsal Scheme

SERIAL POSITION	ITEM PRESENTED	ITEMS REHEARSED	TOTAL REHEARSALS PER ITEM
1	A	AAA	5
2	B	BBA	4
3	C	CBA	3
4	D	DCB	3
5	E	EDC	3
6	F	FED	3
•	•	•	•
•	•	•	•
•	•	•	•
14	N	NML	3
15	O	ONM	2
16	P	PON	1

The number of rehearsals is controlled with two schemes. In one (top table) only the current item is rehearsed and all items have three rehearsals. In the other (bottom table) the latest three items are rehearsed; early ones have extra rehearsals. (Letters represent words.)

When only one item is rehearsed at a time, each item receives an identical number of rehearsals and the primacy effect disappears, as predicted. Note that the recency effect appears for items preceding the last item even though the last item is the only one in the last rehearsal set. This indicates that even when items are dropped from rehearsal, it takes an additional period of time for them to be completely lost from short-term storage. The curve for the three-item rehearsal condition shows the effect also. The last rehearsal set contains the last three items presented and these are recalled perfectly, but a recency effect is still seen for items preceding these three. It should also be noted that a primacy effect occurs in the three-rehearsal

FIGURE 6	Primacy effect disappears with one-item rehearsal (thin line), in which all items have equal rehearsal, but remains with three-item rehearsal (thick line). The recency effect is pronounced for both schemes in immediate recall (solid lines). The curves for delayed recall (broken lines), which reflect only retrieval from long-term storage, parallel the number of rehearsals.

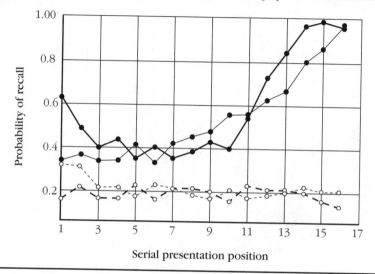

condition. This was predicted because the first item received a total of five rehearsals rather than three. A delayed-recall test for all words was given at the end of the experimental session. The data confirmed that long-term-store retrieval closely parallels the number of rehearsals given an item during presentation, for both rehearsal schemes.

These results strongly implicate rehearsal in the maintenance of information in the short-term store and the transfer of that information to the long-term system. The question then arises: What are the forgetting and transfer characteristics of the short-term store in the absence of rehearsal? One can control rehearsal experimentally by blocking it with a difficult verbal task such as arithmetic. For example, Lloyd R. Peterson and Margaret Peterson of Indiana University [see "Short-Term Memory," by Lloyd R. Peterson; *Scientific American,* July, 1966] presented a set of three letters (a trigram) to be remembered; the subject next engaged in a period of arithmetic and then was asked to recall as many letters of the trigram as possible. When the probability of recall is plotted as a function of the duration of the arithmetic task, the loss observed over time is similar to that of the recency effect in free recall (see Figure 7). Short-term store loss caused by an arithmetic task, then, is similar to loss from short-term storage caused by a series of intervening words to be remembered. The flat portion of the curve reflects the retrieval of the trigram from long-term storage alone and the earlier portions of the curve represent retrieval from both short-term and long-term storage; the loss of the trigram from short-term storage is represented by the decreasing probability of recall prior to the asymptote.

Does the forgetting observed during arithmetic reflect an automatic decay of short-term storage that occurs inevitably in the absence of rehearsal or is the intervening

FIGURE 7 An arithmetic task before recall reduces the probability of recall. Lloyd R. Peterson and Margaret Peterson charted recall probability against duration of an arithmetic task. The probability falls off with duration, until it levels off when recall reflects retrieval from long-term storage alone. Does the curve reflect only a lack of rehearsal or also the nature of the intervening task?

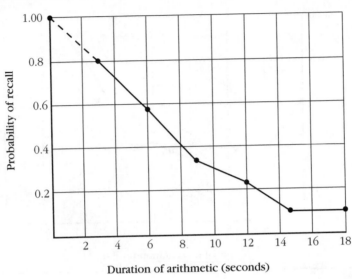

activity the cause of the loss? There is evidence that the amount of new material introduced between presentation and test is a much more important determinant of loss from short-term storage than simply the elapsed time between presentation and test. This finding is subject to at least two explanations. The first holds that the activity intervening between presentation and test is the *direct* cause of an item's loss from short-term storage. The second explanation proposes that the rate of intervening activity merely affects the number of rehearsals that can be given the item to be remembered and thus *indirectly* determines the rate of loss.

It has recently become possible to choose between these two explanations of loss from the short-term store. Judith Reitman of the University of Michigan substituted a signal-detection task for the arithmetic task in the Petersons' procedure. The task consisted in responding whenever a weak tone was heard against a continuous background of "white" noise. Surprisingly, no loss from short-term storage was observed after 15 sec of the task, even though subjects reported no rehearsal during the signal detection. This suggests that loss from the short-term store is due to the type of interference during the intervening interval: Signal detection does not cause loss but verbal arithmetic does. Another important issue that could potentially be resolved with the Reitman procedure concerns the transfer of information from the short-term to the long-term store: Does transfer occur only at initial presentation and at subsequent rehearsals, or does it occur throughout the period during which the information resides in the short-term store, regardless of rehearsals?

To answer these questions, the following experiment was carried out. A consonant pentagram (a set of five consonants, such as *QJXFK*) was presented for 2.5 sec for the subject to memorize. This was followed by a signal-detection task in which pure tones were presented at random intervals against a continuous background of white noise. The subjects pressed a key whenever they thought they detected a tone. (The task proved to be difficult; only about three-fourths of the tones presented were correctly detected.) The signal-detection period lasted for either 1 sec, 8 sec, or 40 sec, with tones sounded on the average every 2.5 sec. In conditions 1, 2, and 3, the subjects were tested on the consonant pentagram immediately after the signal detection; in conditions 4, 5, and 6, however, they were required to carry out 30 sec of difficult arithmetic following the signal detection before being tested (see Figure 8). In order to increase the likelihood that rehearsal would not occur, we paid the subjects for performing well on signal detection and for doing their arithmetic accurately but not for their success in remembering letters. In addition, they were instructed not to rehearse letters during signal detection or arithmetic. They reported afterward that they were not consciously aware of rehearsing. Because the question of rehearsal is quite important, we nevertheless went on to do an additional control experiment in which all the same conditions applied but the subjects were told to rehearse the pentagram aloud following each detection of a tone.

The results indicate that arithmetic causes the pentagram information to be lost from the short-term store but that in the absence of the arithmetic, the signal-detection task alone causes no loss (see Figure 9). What then does produce forgetting from the short-term store? It is not just the analysis of any information input, since signal detection is a difficult information-processing task but causes no forgetting. And time alone causes no noticeable forgetting. Yet verbal information (arithmetic) does cause a large loss. Mrs. Reitman's conclusion appears to be correct: forgetting is caused by the entry into the short-term store of other, similar information.

What about the effect of rehearsal? In the arithmetic situation, performance improves if subjects rehearse overtly during the signal-detection period. Presumably the rehearsal transfers information about the pentagram to the long-term store; the

FIGURE 8   Two tasks were combined in an experiment with these six conditions. Five consonants were presented for 2.5 sec (black), followed by a signal-detection task for 1 sec, 8 sec, or 40 sec (white), followed in three cases by arithmetic (hatched). Then came the test (arrows). Rehearsal during detection was included in a control version.

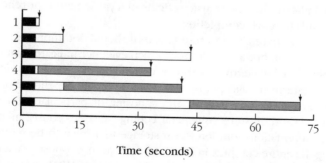

Time (seconds)

| FIGURE 9 | Nature of tasks is seen to have an effect. In the absence of arithmetic, signal detection leaves the short-term store virtually unaffected, with rehearsal (broken thin curve) or without (solid thin line). Arithmetic, however, causes loss from the short-term store (thick); the decreased recall shown reflects retrieval from long-term store only. Retrieval improves with duration of signal detection with rehearsal, which increases transfer to the long-term store (broken thick curve) but not in the absence of rehearsal (solid thick). |

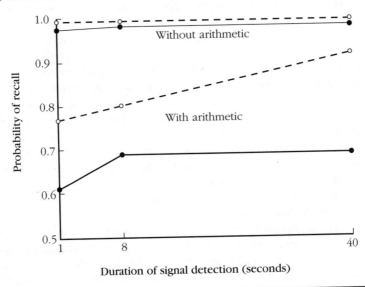

additional transfer during the long signal-detection period is reflected in the retrieval scores, and the rehearsal curve rises. The no-rehearsal curve is horizontal over the last 32 seconds of signal detection, however, confirming that no rehearsal was occurring during that period. The fact that the lowest curve is flat over the last 32 seconds has important implications for transfer from the short-term store to the long-term. It indicates that essentially no transfer occurred during this period even though, as the results in the absence of arithmetic show, the trace remained in the short-term store. Hence, the presence of a trace in the short-term store is alone not enough to result in transfer to the long-term store. Apparently, transfer to the long-term system occurs primarily during or shortly after rehearsals. (The rise in the lowest curve over the first 8 sec may indicate that the transfer effects of a presentation or rehearsal take at least a few seconds to reach completion.)

The emphasis we have given to rote rehearsal should not imply that other control processes are of lesser importance. Although much evidence indicates that transfer from short-term storage to long-term is strongly dependent on rehearsals, effective later retrieval from long-term storage can be shown to be highly dependent on the type of information rehearsed. Coding is really the choosing of particular information to be rehearsed in the short-term store. In general, coding strategies consist in adding appropriately chosen information from long-term storage to a trace to be remembered and then rehearsing the entire complex in the short-term store. Suppose you are given (as is typical in memory experiments) the stimulus-response pair *HRM–4;* later *HRM* will be presented alone and you will be expected to respond "*4.*" If you simply rehearse *HRM–4* several times, your ability to respond correctly later will probably not be high. Suppose, however, *HRM* reminds you of "homeroom" and you think of various aspects of your fourth-grade classroom. Your retrieval performance will be greatly enhanced. Why? First of all, the amount and range of information stored appears to be greater with coding than with rote rehearsal. Moreover, the coding operation provides a straightforward means by which you can gain access to an appropriate and small region of memory during retrieval. In the above example, when *HRM* is presented at the moment of test, you are likely to notice, just as during the initial presentation, that *HRM* is similar to "homeroom." You can then use "homeroom" (and the current temporal context) as a further probe and would almost certainly access "fourth grade" and so generate the correct response.

As the discussion of coding suggests, the key to retrieval is the selection of probe information that will activate an appropriate search set from the long-term store. Since in our view the long-term store is a relatively permanent repository, forgetting is assumed to result from an inadequate selection of probe information and a consequent failure of the retrieval process. There are two basic ways in which the probe selection may prove inadequate. First, the wrong probe may be selected. For instance, you might be asked to name the star of a particular motion picture. The name actually begins with *T* but you decide that it begins with *A* and include *A* in the probe information used to access the long-term store. As a result the correct name may not be included in the search set that is drawn into the short-term store, and retrieval will not succeed.

Second, if the probe is such that an extremely large region of memory is accessed, then retrieval may fail even though the desired trace is included in the search set. For example, if you are asked to name a fruit that sounds like a word meaning "to look at," you might say "pear." If you are asked to name a living thing that sounds like a word meaning "to look at," the probability of your coming up with "pear" will be greatly reduced. Again, you are more likely to remember a "John Smith" if you met him at a party with five other people than if there had been 20 people at the party. This effect can be explained on grounds other than a failure of memory search, however. It could be argued that more attention was given to "John Smith" at the smaller party. Or if the permanence of long-term storage is not accepted, it could be argued that the names of the many other people met at the larger party erode or destroy the memory trace for "John Smith." Are these objections reasonable? The John Smith example is analogous to the situation in free recall where words in long lists are less well recalled from long-term storage than words in short lists.

The problem, then, is to show that the list-length effect in free recall is dependent on the choice of probe information rather than on either the number of words intervening between presentation and recall or the differential storage given words in lists of different size. The second issue is disposed of rather easily: In many free-recall experiments that vary list length, the subjects do not know at the beginning of the list what the length of the list will be. It is therefore unlikely that they store different amounts of information for the first several words in lists of differing length. Nevertheless, as we pointed out, the first several words are recalled at different levels.

To dispose of the "interference" explanation, which implicates the number of words between presentation and recall, is more difficult. Until fairly recently, as a matter of fact, interference theories of forgetting have been predominant [see "Forgetting," by

Benton J. Underwood, *Scientific American,* March, 1964, and "The Interference Theory of Forgetting," by John Ceraso, October, 1967]. In these theories, forgetting has often been seen as a matter of erosion of the memory trace, usually by items presented following the item to be remembered but also by items preceding the item to be remembered. (The list-length effect might be explained in these terms, since the average item in a long list is preceded and followed by more items than the average item in a short list.) On the other hand, the retrieval model presented in this article assumes long-term storage to be permanent; it maintains that the strength of long-term traces is independent of list length and that forgetting results from the fact that the temporal-contextual probe cues used to access any given list tend to elicit a larger search set for longer lists, thereby producing less efficient retrieval.

In order to distinguish between the retrieval and the interference explanations, we presented lists of varying lengths and had the subject attempt to recall not the list just studied (as in the typical free-recall procedure) but the list before the last. This procedure makes it possible to separate the effect of the size of the list being recalled from the effect of the number of words intervening between presentation and recall. A large or a small list to be recalled can be followed by either a large or a small intervening list. The retrieval model predicts that recall probability will be dependent on the size of the list being recalled. The interference model predicts that performance will be largely determined by the number of words in the intervening list.

We used lists of 5 and of 20 words and presented them in four combinations: 5–5, 5–20, 20–5, 20–20; the first number gives the size of the list being recalled and the second number the size of the intervening list. One result is that there is no recency effect (see Figure 10). This would be expected since there is another list and another recall

FIGURE 10   Length of list rather than amount of "interference" governs recall probability. Subjects were asked to recall the list before the one just studied. Five-word lists (top) were recalled better than 20-word lists (bottom) whether they were followed by intervening lists of 5 words (solid) or of 20 words (dashed). The data are averages from three experiments.

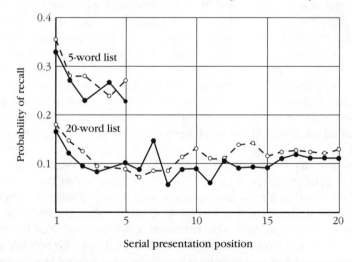

intervening between presentation and recall; the intervening activity causes the words in the tested list to be lost from short-term storage, and so the curves represent retrieval from long-term storage only. The significant finding is that words in lists 5 words long are recalled much better than words in lists 20 words long, and the length of the intervening list has little, if any, effect. The retrieval model can predict these results only if a probe is available to access the requested list. It seems likely in this experiment that the subject has available at test appropriate cues (probably temporal in nature) to enable him to select probe information pertaining to the desired list. If the experimental procedure were changed so that the subject was asked to recall the 10th preceding list, then selection of an adequate probe would no longer be possible. The results demonstrate the importance of probe selection, a control process of the short-term store.

The model of memory we have described, which integrates the system around the operations of the short-term store, is not in any sense a final theory. As experimental techniques and mathematical models have become increasingly sophisticated, memory theory has undergone progressive changes, and there is no doubt that this trend will continue. We nevertheless think it is likely that the short-term store and its control processes will be found to be central.

QUESTIONS FOR FURTHER THOUGHT

1. Briefly describe the Atkinson–Shiffrin model of human memory.
2. What is the role of rehearsal?
3. What is the relative duration of stimuli in each of the memory stores in the Atkinson–Shiffrin model?
4. Is a memory store a discrete location in the brain? If so, where is each store? If not, what is a memory store?
5. How is information retrieved from permanent memory?

LEVELS OF PROCESSING: A FRAMEWORK FOR MEMORY RESEARCH

Fergus Craik and Robert Lockhart

INTRODUCTION

The three-store model (sensory registers for immediate storage, followed by the short-term store for brief storage, and the long-term store for permanent or nearly permanent storage of memories) has dominated memory research for many years, and it continues in wide use. Important alternatives have been proposed, however.

One such alternative is the levels-of-processing view proposed by Fergus Craik and Robert Lockhart. Although the theory is generally not accepted today in the form it was originally proposed, the notion of levels of processing continues to exert a powerful influence upon the field of cognitive psychology.

A basic idea underlies this theory: When people first encode new information, they can encode it to various depths. The more deeply the information is encoded, and hence processed by the cognitive system, the more likely the information is to be retained, especially over the long term. Thus, memory does not consist of a countable number of discrete stores (such as the three stores of the Atkinson–Shiffrin model); rather it represents a potentially infinite number of levels, ranging from very shallow to very deep, to which information can be encoded and hence processed.

Suppose, for example, that you need to learn a list of nouns, such as *dog, fruit, boy, arm,* and so on. You could be encouraged to process the information to varying levels by the kinds of tasks you do while learning the words. For example, you might be asked whether each word is presented in upper or lower case, or to generate a rhyme for each word, or to generate a synonym for each word. Each of these questions is presumed to require encoding of information to a successively deeper level of processing (although independent confirmation that these questions actually lead to successively deeper levels of processing was never forthcoming). In fact, memory tends to improve for words encoded to the hypothesized greater depths of processing over words encoded at the hypothesized shallower levels of processing.

The Craik and Lockhart study became one of the most widely cited papers of the 1970s, probably because it turned memory research on its head. Prior to Craik and Lockhart's work, memory researchers had simply assumed that memory can be divided into discrete stores with largely distinct and separable functions. Craik

Source: From Craik, F. I. M., & Lockhart, R. S. (1972). Levels of processing: A framework for memory research. *Journal of Verbal Learning & Verbal Behavior, 11,* 671–684. Reprinted with permission of Academic Press, Inc.

and Lockhart questioned this assumption. Researchers who question assumptions that virtually everyone takes for granted, and who provide evidence that these assumptions may be wrong, often become the best remembered people in their fields. These investigators show that truly creative scientists take little for granted and willingly question the assumptions that others take to be correct without even thinking about them.

———

This paper briefly reviews the evidence for multistore theories of memory and points out some difficulties with the approach. An alternative framework for human memory research is then outlined in terms of depth or levels of processing. Some current data and arguments are reexamined in the light of this alternative framework and implications for further research considered. ■

Over the past decade, models of human memory have been dominated by the concept of stores and the transfer of information among them. One major criterion for distinguishing between stores has been their different retention characteristics. The temporal properties of stored information have, thus, played a dual role: Besides constituting the basic phenomenon to be explained, they have also been used to generate the theoretical constructs in terms of which the explanation is formulated. The apparent circularity has been avoided by the specification of additional properties of the stores (such as their capacity and coding characteristics) thereby characterizing them independently of the phenomena to be explained. The constructs, thus formulated, have been used to account for data across a variety of paradigms and experimental conditions. The essential concept underlying such explanations is that of information being transferred from one store to another, and the store-to-store transfer models may be distinguished, at least in terms of emphasis, from explanations which associate different retention characteristics with qualitative changes in the memory code.

In the present paper we will do three things: (*a*) examine the reasons for proposing multistore models, (*b*) question their adequacy, and (*c*) propose an alternative framework in terms of levels of processing. We will argue that the memory trace can be understood as a by-product of perceptual analysis and that trace persistence is a positive function of the depth to which the stimulus has been analyzed. Stimuli may also be retained over short intervals by continued processing at a constant depth. These views offer a new way to interpret existing data and provide a heuristic framework for further research.

MULTISTORE MODELS

THE CASE IN FAVOR

When man is viewed as a processor of information (Miller, 1956; Broadbent, 1958), it seems necessary to postulate holding mechanisms or memory stores at various points in the system. For example, on the basis of his dichotic listening studies, Broadbent (1958) proposed that information must be held transiently before entering the limited-capacity processing channel. Items could be held over the short term by recycling them, after perception, through the same transient storage system. From there, information could be transferred into and retained in a more permanent long-term store. Broadbent's ideas have been developed and extended by Waugh and Norman (1965), Peterson (1966), and Atkinson and Shiffrin (1968). According to the modal model (Murdock, 1967), it is now widely accepted that memory can be classified into three levels of storage: sensory stores, short-term memory (STM), and long-term memory (LTM). Since there has been some ambiguity in the usage of terms in this area, we shall follow the convention of using STM and LTM to refer to experimental situations, and the terms "short-term store" (STS) and "long-term store" (LTS) to refer to the two relevant storage systems.

Stimuli can be entered into the sensory stores regardless of whether or not the subject is paying attention to that source: That is, sensory stores are "preattentive" (Neisser, 1967). The input is represented in a rather literal form and can be overwritten by further inputs in the same modality (Neisser, 1967; Crowder & Morton, 1969). Further features which distinguish the sensory registers from later stores are the modality-specific nature and moderately large capacity of sensory stores and the transience of their contents.

Attention to the material in a sensory register is equivalent to reading it out and transferring it to STS. Here, verbal items are coded in some phonemic fashion (Shulman, 1971) or in auditory–verbal–linguistic terms (Atkinson & Shiffrin, 1968). The STS is further distinguished from sensory memories by virtue of its limited capacity (Miller, 1956; Broadbent, 1958), by the finding that information is lost principally by a process of displacement (Waugh & Norman, 1965), and by the slower rate of forgetting from STS: 5–20 seconds as opposed to the ½ second estimates for sensory storage. While most research has concentrated on verbal STS, there is evidence that more literal "representational" information may also be held over the short term (Posner, 1967), although the relationship between such modality-specific stores and the verbal STS has not been made clear.

The distinctions between STS and LTS are well-documented. Whereas STS has a limited capacity, LTS has no known limit; verbal items are usually coded phonemically in STS but largely in terms of their semantic features in LTS (Baddeley, 1966); forgetting from STS is complete within 30 seconds or less while forgetting from LTS is either very slow or the material is not forgotten at all (Shiffrin & Atkinson, 1967). In the free-recall paradigm, it is generally believed that the last few items are retrieved from STS and prior items are retrieved from LTS; it is now known that several variables affect one of these retrieval components without affecting the other (Glanzer, 1972). Further persuasive evidence for the STS/LTS dichotomy comes from clinical studies (Milner, 1970; Warrington, 1971). The distinguishing features of the three storage levels are summarized in Table 1.

The attractiveness of the "box" approach is not difficult to understand. Such multistore models are apparently specific and concrete; information flows in well-regulated paths between stores whose characteristics have intuitive appeal; their properties may be elicited by experiment and described either behaviorally or mathematically. All that remains, it seems, is to specify the properties of each component more precisely and to work out the transfer functions more accurately.

TABLE 1	Commonly Accepted Differences Between the Three Stages of Verbal Memory (See Text for Sources)		
FEATURE	**SENSORY REGISTERS**	**SHORT-TERM STORE**	**LONG-TERM STORE**
Entry of information	Preattentive	Requires attention	Rehearsal
Maintenance of information	Not possible	Continued attention Rehearsal	Repetition Organization
Format of information	Literal copy of input	Phonemic Probably visual Possibly semantic	Largely semantic Some auditory and visual
Capacity	Large	Small	No known limit
Information loss	Decay	Displacement Possibly decay	Possibly no loss Loss of accessibility or discriminability by interference
Trace duration	¼–2 sec	Up to 30 sec	Minutes to years
Retrieval	Readout	Probably automatic Items in consciousness Temporal/phonemic cues	Retrieval cues Possibly search process

Despite all these points in their favor, when the evidence for multistore models is examined in greater detail, the stores become less tangible. One warning sign is the progressively greater part played by "control processes" in more recent formulations (for example, Atkinson & Shiffrin, 1971). In the next section, we consider the adequacy of multistore notions more critically.

THE CASE AGAINST

The multistore approach has not been without its general critics (Melton, 1963; Murdock, 1972). Other workers have objected to certain aspects of the formulation. For example, Tulving and Patterson (1968) argued against the notion of information being transferred from one store to another. Similarly, Shallice and Warrington (1970) presented evidence against the idea that information must necessarily "pass through" STS to enter LTS.

In our view, the criteria listed in the previous section do not provide satisfactory grounds for distinguishing between separate stores. The adequacy of the evidence will be considered with reference to the concepts of capacity, coding, and finally, the retention function itself.

CAPACITY

Although limited capacity has been a major feature of the information flow approach, and especially a feature of STS in multistore models, the exact nature of the capacity limitation is somewhat obscure. In particular, it has been unclear whether the limitation is one of processing capacity, storage capacity, or is meant to apply to some interaction between the two. In terms of the computer analogy on which information flow models are based, the issue is whether the limitation refers to the storage capacity of a memory register or to the rate at which the processor can perform certain operations. The notion of a limited-capacity channel (Broadbent, 1958) appears to emphasize the second interpretation while later models of memory, such as that of Waugh and Norman (1965), appear to favor the storage interpretation. Both interpretations are present in Miller (1956) but the relationship between the two is not explicitly worked out.

Attempts to measure the capacity of STS have leant towards the storage interpretation, and considered number of items to be the appropriate scale of measurement. Such attempts have provided quite a range of values. For example, recent estimates of primary memory size (Baddeley, 1970; Murdock, 1972) have yielded values between two and four words. However, measures of memory span (which have been said to reflect the limited capacity of the STM box) are typically between five and nine items, depending on whether the items in question are words, letters or digits (Crannell & Parrish, 1957). Finally, if the words in a span test form a sentence, young subjects can accurately reproduce strings of up to 20 words (Craik & Masani, 1969). Thus, if capacity is a critical feature of STM operation, a box model has to account for this very wide range of capacity estimates.

The most widely accepted explanation of this variation is that capacity is limited in terms of chunks, and that few or many items can be recoded into a chunk depending on the meaningfulness of the material. Apart from the difficulty of defining a chunk independently from its memorial consequences, this view entails a rather flexible notion of STS as a storage compartment which can accept a variety of codes from simple physical features to complex semantic ones.

From the standpoint of the present paper, the concept of capacity is to be understood in terms of a limitation on processing; limitations of storage are held to be a direct consequence of this more fundamental limitation.

CODING

Working with verbal material, Conrad (1964) and Baddeley (1966) provided one plausible basis for distinguishing STS and LTS. They concluded that information in STS was coded acoustically and that coding was predominantly semantic in LTS. Further research has blurred this distinction, however. First, it has been shown that STS coding can be either acoustic or articulatory (Levy, 1971; Peterson & Johnson, 1971). Second, recent papers by Kroll and his colleagues (Kroll et al., 1970) have demonstrated that even with verbal material, STS can sometimes be visual. Apparently STS can accept a variety of physical codes.

Can STS also hold semantic information? The persistence of contradictory evidence suggests either that the question has been inappropriately formulated or that the answer depends on the paradigm used. When traditional STM paradigms are considered, the answer seems to be "no" (Kintsch & Buschke, 1969; Craik & Levy, 1970), although Shulman (1970, 1972) has recently presented persuasive evidence in favor of a semantic STS. While type of coding may originally have seemed a good basis for the distinction between short-term and long-term memory, the distinction no longer appears satisfactory. A defender of the multistore notion might argue that STS coding is flexible, but this position removes an important characteristic by which one store is distinguished from another.

We will argue that the coding question is more appropriately formulated in terms of the processing demands imposed by the experimental paradigm and the material to be remembered. In some paradigms and with certain material, acoustic coding may be either adequate or all that is possible. In other circumstances processing to a semantic level may be both possible and advantageous.

FORGETTING CHARACTERISTICS

If memory stores are to be distinguished in terms of their forgetting characteristics, a minimal requirement would seem to be that the retention function should be variant across different paradigms and experimental conditions. While this invariance has not been rigorously tested, there are cases where it clearly breaks down. We will give two examples. First, in the finite-state models of paired-associate learning, the state commonly identified as STS shows forgetting characteristics which are different from those established for STS in other paradigms (Kintsch, 1970, p. 206). In the former case, STS retention extends over as many as 20 intervening items, while in the free-recall and probe paradigms (Waugh & Norman, 1965), STS information is lost much more rapidly. As a second example, the durability of the memory trace for visual stimuli appears to depend on the material and the paradigm. According to Neisser (1967), the icon lasts 1 sec or less; Posner (1969) and his colleagues have found evidence for visual persistence of up to 1.5 sec, while other recent studies by Murdock (1971), Phillips and Baddeley (1971) and Kroll et al. (1970) have yielded estimates of 6, 10, and 25 sec, respectively. Estimates are even longer in recognition memory for pictures (Shepard, 1967; Haber, 1970). Given that we recognize pictures, faces, tunes, and voices after long periods of time, it is clear that we have long-term memory for relatively literal nonverbal information. Thus, it is difficult to draw a line between "sensory memory" and "representational" or "pictorial" memory.

We will argue that retention depends upon such aspects of the paradigm as study time, amount of material presented and mode of test; also upon the extent to which the subject has developed systems to analyze and enrich particular types of stimuli; that is, the familiarity, compatibility, and meaningfulness of the material.

Although we believe that the multistore formulation is unsatisfactory in terms of its capacity, coding, and forgetting characteristics, obviously there are some basic findings which any model must accommodate. It seems certain that stimuli are encoded in different ways within the memory system: A word may be encoded at various times in terms of its visual, phonemic, or semantic features, its verbal associates, or an image. Differently encoded representations apparently persist for different lengths of time. The phenomenon of limited capacity at some points in the system seems real enough and, thus, should also be taken into consideration. Finally, the roles of perceptual, attentional, and rehearsal processes should also be noted.

One way of coping with the kinds of inconsistencies we have described is to postulate additional stores (see, Morton, 1970; Sperling, 1970). However, we think it is more useful to focus on the encoding operations themselves and to consider the proposal that rates of forgetting are a function of the type and depth of encoding. This view is developed in the next section.

LEVELS OF PROCESSING

Many theorists now agree that perception involves the rapid analysis of stimuli at a number of levels or stages (Selfridge & Neisser, 1960; Treisman, 1964; Sutherland, 1968). Preliminary stages are concerned with the analysis of such physical or sensory features as lines, angles, brightness, pitch, and loudness, while later stages are more concerned with matching the input against stored abstractions from past learning; that is, later stages are concerned with pattern recognition and the extraction of meaning. This conception of a series or hierarchy of processing stages is often referred to as "depth of processing" where greater "depth" implies a greater degree of semantic or cognitive analysis. After the stimulus has been recognized, it may undergo further processing by enrichment or elaboration. For example, after a word is recognized, it may trigger associations, images, or stories on the basis of the subject's past experience with the word. Such "elaboration coding" (Tulving & Madigan, 1970) is not restricted to verbal material. We would argue that similar levels of processing exist in the perceptual analysis of sounds, sights, smells and so on. Analysis proceeds through a series of sensory stages to levels associated with matching or pattern recognition and finally to semantic–associative stages of stimulus enrichment.

One of the results of this perceptual analysis is the memory trace. Such features of the trace as its coding characteristics and its persistence thus arise essentially as by-products of perceptual processing (Morton, 1970). Specifically, we suggest that trace persistence is a function of depth of analysis, with deeper levels of analysis associated with more elaborate, longer lasting, and stronger traces. Since the organism is normally concerned only with the extraction of meaning from the stimuli, it is advantageous to store the products of such deep analyses, but there is usually no need to store the products of preliminary analyses. It is perfectly possible to draw a box around early analyses and call it *sensory memory* and a box around intermediate analyses called *short-term memory,* but that procedure both oversimplifies matters and evades the more significant issues.

Although certain analytic operations must precede others, much recent evidence suggests that we perceive at meaningful, deeper levels before we perceive the results of logically prior analyses (Macnamara, 1972; Savin & Bever, 1970). Further elaborative coding does not exist in a hierarchy of necessary steps and this seems especially true of later processing stages. In this sense, "spread" of encoding might be a more accurate description, but the term "depth" will be retained as it conveys the flavor of our argument.

Highly familiar, meaningful stimuli are compatible, by definition, with existing cognitive structures. Such stimuli (for example, pictures and sentences) will be processed to a deep level more rapidly than less meaningful stimuli and will be well-retained. Thus, speed of analysis does not necessarily predict retention. Retention is a function of depth, and various factors, such as the amount of attention devoted to a stimulus, its compatibility with the analyzing structures, and the processing time available, will determine the depth to which it is processed.

Thus, we prefer to think of memory tied to levels of perceptual processing. Although these levels may be grouped into stages (sensory analyses, pattern recognition, and stimulus elaboration, for example) processing levels may be more usefully envisaged as a continuum of analysis. Thus, memory, too, is viewed as a continuum from the transient products of sensory analyses to the highly durable products of semantic–associative operations. However, superimposed on this basic memory system there is a second way in which stimuli can be retained—by recirculating information at one level of processing. In our view, such descriptions as "continued attention to certain aspects of the stimulus," "keeping the items in consciousness," "holding the items in the rehearsal buffer," and "retention of the items in primary memory" all refer to the same concept of maintaining information at one level of processing. To preserve some measure of continuity with existing terminology, we will use the term *primary memory (PM)* to refer to this operation, although it should be noted that our usage is more restricted than the usual one.

We endorse Moray's (1967) notion of a limited-capacity central processor which may be deployed in a number of different ways. If this processing capacity is used to maintain information at one level, the phenomena of short-term memory will appear. The processor itself is neutral with regard to coding characteristics: The observed PM code will depend on the processing modality within which the processor is operating. Further, while limited capacity is a function of the processor itself, the number of items held will depend upon the level at which the processor is operating. At deeper levels the subject can make greater use of learned rules and past knowledge; thus, material can be more efficiently handled and more can be retained. There is apparently great variability in the ease with which information at different levels can be maintained in PM. Some types of information (for example, phonemic features of words) are particularly easy to maintain while the maintenance of others (such as early visual analyses—the "icon") is apparently impossible.

The essential feature of PM retention is that aspects of the material are still being processed or attended to. Our notion of PM is, thus, synonymous with that of James (1890) in that PM items are still in consciousness. When attention is diverted from the item, information will be lost at the rate appropriate to its level of processing—slower rates for deeper levels. While PM retention is, thus, equivalent to continued processing, this type of processing merely prolongs an item's high accessibility without leading to formation of a more permanent memory trace. This Type I processing, that is, repetition of analyses which have already been carried out, may be contrasted with Type II processing, which involves deeper analysis of the stimulus. Only this second type of rehearsal should lead to improved memory performance. To the extent that the subject utilizes Type II processing, memory will improve with total study time, but when he engages in Type I processing, the "total time hypothesis" (see Cooper & Pantle, 1967) will break down. Stoff and Eagle (1971) have reported findings in line with this suggestion.

To summarize, it is suggested that the memory trace is better described in terms of depth of processing or degree of stimulus elaboration. Deeper analysis leads to a more persistent trace. While information may be held in PM, such maintenance will not in itself improve subsequent retention; when attention is diverted, information is lost at a rate which depends essentially on the level of analysis.

Existing Data Reexamined

Incidental Learning

When memory traces are viewed as the product of a particular form of processing, much of the incidental learning literature acquires a new significance. There are several reviews of this literature (Postman, 1964; McLaughlin, 1965), and we will make no attempt to be comprehensive. An important characteristic of the incidental learning paradigm is that the subject processes the material in a way compatible with or determined by the orienting task. The comparison of retention across different orienting tasks, therefore, provides a relatively pure measure of the memorial consequences of different processing activities. According to the view of the present paper, and in agreement with Postman (1964), the instruction to learn facilitates performance only insofar as it leads the subject to process the material in a manner which is more effective than the processing induced by the orienting task in the incidental condition. Thus, it is possible, that with an appropriate orienting task and an inappropriate intentional strategy, learning under incidental conditions could be superior to that under intentional conditions.

From the point of view of this paper, then, the interesting thing to do is to systematically study retention following different orienting tasks within the incidental condition, rather than to compare incidental with intentional learning. Under incidental conditions, the experimenter has a control over the processing the subject applies to the material that he does not have when the subject is merely instructed to learn and uses an unknown coding strategy.

We will consider several examples which illustrate this point. Tresselt and Mayzner (1960) tested free recall after incidental learning under three different orienting tasks: crossing out vowels, copying the words, and judging the degree to which the word was an instance of the concept "economic." Under the last condition, the number of words recalled was four times higher than that of the first and twice that of the second condition. Similar results using the free-recall paradigm have been obtained by Hyde and Jenkins (1969) and Johnston and Jenkins (1971). The experiments by Jenkins and his colleagues showed that with lists of highly associated word pairs, free recall and organization resulting from an orienting task which required the use of the word as a semantic unit, was equivalent to that of an intentional control group with no incidental task, but both were substantially superior to an incidental group whose task involved treating the word structurally (checking for certain letters or estimating the number of letters in the word). These results are consistent with those of Mandler (1967) who showed that incidental learning during categorization of words yielded a similar recall level to that of a group who performed the same activity but who knew that their recall would be tested.

Experiments involving the incidental learning of sentences (Bobrow & Bower, 1969; Rosenberg & Schiller, 1971) have shown that recall after an orienting task that required processing the sentence to a semantic level was substantially superior to recall of words from equivalently exposed sentences which were processed non-semantically.

Schulman (1971) had subjects scan a list of words for targets defined either structurally (such as words containing the letter *A*) or semantically (such as words denoting living things). After the scanning task, subjects were given an unexpected test of recognition memory. Performance in the semantically defined target conditions was significantly better than that in the structurally defined conditions, although scanning time per word was approximately the same in most cases.

These results support the general conclusion that memory performance is a positive function of the level of processing required by the orienting task. However, beyond a certain stage, the form of processing which will prove optimal depends on the retrieval or trace utilization requirements of the subsequent memory test. There is clear evidence in the incidental learning literature that the relative value of different orienting tasks is not the same for all tests of memory.

This conclusion is supported by comparisons of the differential effects of orienting tasks on recognition and recall. Eagle and Leiter (1964) found that, whereas free recall in an unhindered intentional condition was superior to that of an incidental group and to a second intentional group who had also to perform the orienting task, these latter two conditions showed superior recognition performance. Such a result poses no difficulty provided it is assumed that optimal processing does not take the same form for both memory tests. In the Eagle and Leiter (1964) experiment, the orienting task, while almost certainly involving some degree of semantic analysis, might have served to prevent the kind of elaborative processing necessary for later access to the stored information. On the other hand, such elaborative coding might hinder subsequent discrimination between target words and the associatively related distractors used in this experiment. Results consistent with this kind of analysis have also been reported by Dornbush and Winnick (1967) and Estes and DaPolito (1967).

While the orienting tasks used by Wicker and Bernstein (1969) in their study of incidental paired-associate learning all required analysis to a semantic level, they did not facilitate subsequent performance to the same degree. When the orienting task involved the production of mediating responses, performance was equal to that of unhindered intentional learning and superior to when the orienting task was rating words for pleasantness. In single-trial free recall, this latter orienting task produces performance equal to that of intentional learning (Hyde & Jenkins, 1969). Identical orienting tasks do not seem to have equivalent effects across different paradigms. The interaction between initial encoding and subsequent retrieval operations is worth emphasizing. Although the distinction between availability and accessibility (Tulving & Pearlstone, 1966) is a useful one, the effectiveness of a retrieval cue depends on its compatibility with the item's initial encoding or, more generally, the extent to which the retrieval situation reinstates the learning context.

SELECTIVE ATTENTION AND SENSORY STORAGE

Moray (1959) showed that words presented to the nonattended channel in a dichotic listening test were not recognized in a later memory test. Similarly, Neisser (1964) has shown that nontarget items in a visual search task left no recognizable trace. Thus, if stimuli are only partially analyzed, or processed only to peripheral levels, their record in memory is extremely fleeting. This point was neatly demonstrated by Treisman

(1964). When the same prose passage was played to both ears dichotically, but staggered in time with the unattended ear leading, the lag between messages had to be reduced to 1.5 sec before the subject realized that the messages were identical. When the attended (shadowed) ear was leading, however, subjects noticed the similarity at a mean lag of 4.5 sec. Thus, although the subjects were not trying to remember the material in either case, the further processing necessitated by shadowing was sufficient to treble the durability of the memory trace. Treisman also found that meaningfulness of the material (reversed speech versus normal speech, and random words versus prose) affected the lag necessary for recognition, but only when the attended channel was leading. If the message was rejected after early analyses, meaningfulness played no part; but when the message was attended, more meaningful material could be processed further and was, thus, retained longer. The three estimates of memory persistence in these experiments (1.5 sec for all nonattended material, 3 sec for attended reversed speech and attended strings of random words, and 5 sec for attended prose) can be attributed to the functioning of different stores, but it is more reasonable, in our view, to postulate that persistence is a function of processing level.

While further studies will not be reviewed in such detail, it may be noted that the findings and conclusions of many other workers in the area of sensory memory can also be accommodated in the present framework. Neisser (1967, p. 33) concluded that "longer exposures lead to longer-lasting icons." Studies by Norman (1969), Glucksberg and Cowen (1970), and Peterson and Kroener (1964) may all be interpreted as showing that nonattended verbal material is lost within a few seconds.

Massaro (1970) suggested that memory for an item is directly related to the amount of perceptual processing of the item, a statement which is obviously in line with the present proposals, although his later arguments (Massaro, 1972), that echoic memory inevitably lasts only 250 msec are probably overgeneralizations. Shaffer and Shiffrin concluded from an experiment on picture recognition that "it might prove more fruitful to consider the more parsimonious view that there is just a single short-term visual memory. This short-term visual memory would decay quickly when the information content of the visual field was high and more slowly when the information content was greatly reduced" (Shaffer & Shiffrin, 1972, p. 295). Plainly this view is similar to our own, although we would argue that the continuum extends to long-term retention as well. We would also suggest that it is processing level, rather than information content, which determines the rate of decay.

THE STS/LTS DISTINCTION

The phenomenon of a limited-capacity holding mechanism in memory (Miller, 1956; Broadbent, 1958) is handled in the present framework by assuming that a flexible central processor can be deployed to one of several levels in one of several encoding dimensions, and that this central processor can only deal with a limited number of items at a given time. That is, items are kept in consciousness or in primary memory by continuing to rehearse them at a fixed level of processing. The nature of the items will depend upon the encoding dimension and the level within that dimension. At deeper levels, the subject can make more use of learned cognitive structures so that the item will become more complex and semantic. The depth at which primary memory operates will depend both upon the usefulness to the subject of continuing to process at that level and also upon the amenability of the material to deeper processing. Thus, if the subject's task is merely to reproduce a few words seconds after hearing them, he need not hold them at a level deeper than phonemic analysis. If the words form a meaningful sentence, however, they are compatible with deeper learned structures and larger units may be dealt with. It seems that primary memory deals at any level with units or "chunks" rather than with information (see Kintsch, 1970, pp. 175–181). That is, we rehearse a sound, a letter, a word, an idea, or an image in the same way that we perceive objects and not constellations of attributes.

As pointed out earlier, a common distinction between memory stores is their different coding characteristics; STS is said to be predominantly acoustic (or articulatory) while LTS is largely semantic. According to the present argument, acoustic errors will predominate only insofar as analysis has not proceeded to a semantic level. There are at least three sources of the failure of processing to reach this level; the nature of the material, limited available processing capacity, and task demands. Much of the data on acoustic confusions in short-term memory is based on material such as letters and digits which have relatively little semantic content. The nature of this material itself tends to constrain processing to a structural level of analysis, and it should be no surprise, therefore, that errors of a structural nature result. Such errors can also occur with meaningful material if processing capacity is diverted to an irrelevant task (Eagle & Ortoff, 1967).

A further set of results relevant to the STS/LTS distinction are those that show that in free recall, variables such as presentation rate and word frequency affect long-term but not short-term retention (Glanzer, 1972). Our interpretation of these findings is that increasing presentation rate, or using unfamiliar words, inhibits or prevents processing to those levels necessary to support long-term retention, but does not affect coding operations of the kind that are adequate for short-term retention. It follows from this interpretation that diverting processing capacity as in the Eagle and Ortoff (1967) experiments should result in a greater decrement in long-term than in short-term retention and, indeed, there is good evidence that such is the case (Murdock, 1965; Silverstein & Glanzer, 1971).

Conversely, manipulations that influence processing at a structural level should have transitory, but no long-term, effects. Modality differences (Murdock, 1966) provide a clear example. Finally, long-term recall should be facilitated by manipulations which induce deeper or more elaborative processing. We suggest that the encoding variability hypothesis as it has been used to account for the spacing effect in free recall (Madigan, 1969; Melton, 1970) is to be understood in these terms.

The Serial Position Curve

Serial-position effects have been a major source of evidence for the STS/LTS distinction (see Broadbent, 1971, pp. 354–361; Kintsch, 1970, pp. 153–162). In free recall, the recency effect is held to reflect output from STS while previous items are retrieved from LTS (Glanzer & Cunitz, 1966). Several theoretical accounts of the primacy effect have been given, but perhaps the most plausible is that initial items receive more rehearsals and are, thus, better registered in LTS (Atkinson & Shiffrin, 1968; Bruce & Papay, 1970). We agree with these conclusions. Since the subject knows he must stop attending to initial items in order to perceive and rehearse subsequent items, he subjects these first items to Type II processing; that is, deeper semantic processing. Final list items can survive on phonemic encoding, however, which gives rise to excellent immediate recall (since they are still being processed in primary memory) but is wiped out by the necessity to process interpolated material. In fact, if terminal items have been less deeply processed than initial items, the levels of processing formulation would predict that in a subsequent recall attempt, final items should be recalled least well of all list items. The finding of negative recency (Craik, 1970) supports this prediction. An alternative explanation of negative recency could be that recency items were rehearsed fewer times than earlier items (Rundus, 1971). However, recent studies by Jacoby and Bartz (1972), Watkins (1972), and Craik (1972) have shown that it is the type rather than the amount of processing which determines the subsequent recall of the last few items in a list.

In serial recall, subjects must retain the first few items so that they can at least commence their recall correctly. The greatly enhanced primacy effect is thus probably attributable, in part at least, to primary-memory retention. The degree to which subjects also encode initial items at a deeper level is likely to depend on the material and the task. Using a relatively slow (2.5 sec) presentation rate and words as visually presented stimuli, Palmer and Ornstein (1971) found that an interpolated task only partially eliminated the primacy effect. However, Baddeley (1968) presented digits auditorily at a 1-sec rate and found that primacy was entirely eliminated by the necessity to perform a further task.

REPETITION AND REHEARSAL EFFECTS

One suggestion in the present formulation is that Type I processing does nothing to enhance memory for the stimulus; once attention is diverted, the trace is lost at the rate appropriate to its deepest analyzed level. Thus, the concept of processing has been split into Type I or same-level processing and Type II processing which involves further, deeper analysis of the stimulus and leads to a more durable trace. Similarly, the effects of repeated presentation depend on whether the repeated stimulus is merely processed to the same level or encoded differently on its further presentations. There is evidence, both in audition (Moray, 1959; Norman, 1969), and in vision (Turvey, 1967), that repetition of an item encoded only at a sensory level does not lead to an improvement in memory performance.

Tulving (1966) has also shown that repetition without intention to learn does not facilitate learning. Tulving's explanation of the absence of learning in terms of interitem organization cannot easily be distinguished from an explanation in terms of levels of processing. Similarly, Glanzer and Meinzer (1967) have shown that overt repetition of items in free recall is a less effective strategy than that normally used by subjects. Although both Waugh and Norman (1965), and Atkinson and Shiffrin (1968) have suggested that rehearsal has the dual function of maintaining information in primary memory and transferring it to secondary memory, the experiments by Tulving (1966) and by Glanzer and Meinzer (1967) show that this is not necessarily so. Thus, whether rehearsal strengthens the trace or merely postpones forgetting depends on what the subject is doing with his rehearsal. Only deeper processing will lead to an improvement in memory.

CONCLUDING COMMENTS

Our account of memory in terms of levels of processing has much in common with a number of other recent formulations. Cermak (1972), for example, has outlined a theoretical framework very similar to our own. Perceptually oriented attribute-encoding theories such as those of Bower (1967) and Norman and Rumelhart (1970) have a close affinity with the present approach, as does that of Posner (1969), who advocates stages of processing with different characteristics associated with each stage.

If the memory trace is viewed as the by-product of perceptual analysis, an important goal of future research will be to specify the memorial consequences of various types of perceptual operations. We have suggested the comparison of orienting tasks within the incidental learning paradigm as one method by which the experimenter can have more direct control over the encoding operations that subjects perform. Since deeper analysis will usually involve longer processing time, it will be extremely important to disentangle such variables as study time and amount of effort from depth as such. For example, time may be a correlate of memory to the extent that time is necessary for processing to some level, but it is possible that further time spent in merely recycling the information after this optimal level will not predict trace durability.

Our approach does not constitute a theory of memory. Rather, it provides a conceptual framework—a set of orienting attitudes—within which memory research might proceed. While multistore models have played a useful role, we suggest that they are often taken too literally and that more fruitful questions are generated by the present formulation. Our position is obviously speculative and far from complete. We have looked at memory purely from the input or encoding end; no attempt has been made to specify either how items are differentiated from one another, are grouped together and organized, or how they are retrieved from the system. While our position does not imply any specific view of these processes, it does provide an appropriate framework within which they can be understood.

REFERENCES

Atkinson, R. C., & Shiffrin, R. M. (1968). Human memory: A proposed system and its control processes. In K. W. Spence and J. T. Spence (Eds.), *The psychology of learning and motivation: Advances in research and theory*, Vol. II (pp. 89–195). New York: Academic Press.

Atkinson, R. C., & Shiffrin, R. M. (1971). The control of short-term memory. *Scientific American, 224*, 82–89.

Baddeley, A. D. (1966) Short-term memory for word sequences as a function of acoustic, semantic, and formal similarity. *Quarterly Journal of Experimental Psychology, 18,* 362–365.

Baddeley, A. D. (1968). How does acoustic similarity influence short-term memory? *Quarterly Journal of Experimental Psychology, 20,* 249–264.

Baddeley, A. D. (1970). Estimating the short-term component in free recall. *British Journal of Psychology, 61,* 13–15.

Bobrow, S. A., & Bower, G. H. (1969). Comprehension and recall of sentences. *Journal of Experimental Psychology, 80,* 455–461.

Bower, G. H. (1967). A multicomponent theory of the memory trace. In K. W. Spence and J. T. Spence (Eds.), *The psychology of learning and motivation: Advances in research and theory*, Vol. 1 (pp. 230–325). New York: Academic Press.

Broadbent, D. E. (1958). *Perception and communication.* New York: Pergamon Press.

Broadbent, D. E. (1971). *Decision and stress.* New York: Academic Press.

Bruce, D., & Papay, J. P. (1970). Primacy effect in single-trial free recall. *Journal of Verbal Learning and Verbal Behavior, 9,* 473–486.

Cermak, L. S. (1972). *Human memory: Research and theory.* New York: Ronald.

Conrad, R. (1964). Acoustic confusions in immediate memory. *British Journal of Psychology, 55,* 75–84.

Cooper, E. H., & Pantle, A. J. (1967). The total-time hypothesis in verbal learning. *Psychological Bulletin, 68,* 221–234.

Craik, F. I. M. (1970). The fate of primary memory items in free recall. *Journal of Verbal Learning and Verbal Behavior, 9,* 143–148.

Craik, F. I. M. (1972, March). A 'levels of analysis' view of memory. Paper presented at the 2nd Erindale Symposium on Communication and Affect.

Craik, F. I. M., & Levy, B. A. (1970). Semantic and acoustic information in primary memory. *Journal of Experimental Psychology, 86,* 77–82.

Craik, F. I. M., & Masani, P. A. (1969). Age and intelligence differences in coding and retrieval of word lists. *British Journal of Psychology, 60,* 315–319.

Crannell, C. W., & Parrish, J. M. (1957). A comparison of immediate memory span for digits, letters, and words. *Journal of Psychology, 44,* 319–327.

Crowder, R. G., & Morton, J. (1969). Precategorical acoustic storage. *Perception and Psychophysics, 5,* 365–373.

Dornbush, R. L., & Winnick, W. A. (1967). Short-term intentional and incidental learning. *Journal of Experimental Psychology, 73,* 608–611.

Eagle, M., & Leiter, E. (1964). Recall and recognition in intentional and incidental learning. *Journal of Experimental Psychology, 68,* 58–63.

Eagle, M., & Ortoff, E. (1967). The effect of level of attention upon "phonetic" recognition errors. *Journal of Verbal Learning and Verbal Behavior, 6,* 226–231.

Estes, W. K., & DaPolito, F. (1967). Independent variation of information storage and retrieval processes in paired-associate learning. *Journal of Experimental Psychology, 75,* 18–26.

Glanzer, M. (1972). Storage mechanisms in recall. In G. H. Bower (Ed.), *The psychology of learning and motivation: Advances in research and theory,* Vol. 5, (pp. 129–193). New York: Academic Press.

Glanzer, M., & Cunitz, A. R. (1966). Two storage mechanisms in free recall. *Journal of Verbal Learning and Verbal Behavior, 5,* 351–360.

Glanzer, M., & Meinzer, A. (1967). The effects of intralist activity on free recall. *Journal of Verbal Learning and Verbal Behavior, 6,* 928–935.

Glucksberg, S., & Cowen, G. N. (1970). Memory for nonattended auditory material. *Cognitive Psychology, 1,* 149–156.

Haber, R. N. (1970). How we remember what we see. *Scientific American, 222,* 104–112.

Hyde, T. S., & Jenkins, J. J. (1969). The differential effects of incidental tasks on the organization of recall of a list of highly associated words. *Journal of Experimental Psychology, 82,* 472–481.

Jacoby, L. L., & Bartz, W. H. (1972). Encoding processes and the negative recency effect. *Journal of Verbal Learning and Verbal Behavior, 11,* 561–565.

James, W. (1890). *Principles of psychology.* New York: Holt.

Johnston, C. D., & Jenkins, J. J. (1971). Two more incidental tasks that differentially affect associative clustering in recall. *Journal of Experimental Psychology, 89,* 92–95.

Kintsch, W. (1970). *Learning, memory, and conceptual processes.* New York: Wiley.

Kintsch, W., & Buschke, H. (1969). Homophones and synonyms in short-term memory. *Journal of Experimental Psychology, 80,* 403–407.

Kroll, N. E. A., Parks, T., Parkinson, S. R., Bieber, S. L., & Johnson, A. L. (1970). Short-term memory while shadowing. Recall of visually and aurally presented letters. *Journal of Experimental Psychology, 85,* 220–224.

Levy, B. A. (1971). Role of articulation in auditory and visual short-term memory. *Journal of Verbal Learning and Verbal Behavior, 10,* 123–132.

Macnamara, J. (1972). Cognitive basis of language learning in infants. *Psychological Review, 79,* 1–13.

Madigan, S. A. (1969). Intraserial repetition and coding processes in free recall. *Journal of Verbal Learning and Verbal Behavior, 8,* 828–835.

Mandler, G. (1967). Organization and memory. In K. W. Spence and J. T. Spence (Eds.), *The psychology of learning and motivation: Advances in research and theory,* Vol. 1 (pp. 328–372). New York: Academic Press.

Massaro, D. W. (1970). Perceptual processes and forgetting in memory tasks. *Psychological Review, 77,* 557–567.

Massaro, D. W. (1972). Preperceptual images, processing time, and perceptual units in auditory perception. *Psychological Review, 79,* 124–145.

McLaughlin, B. (1965). "Intentional" and "incidental" learning in human subjects: The role of instructions to learn and motivation. *Psychological Bulletin, 63,* 359–376.

Melton, A. W. (1963). Implications of short-term memory for a general theory of memory. *Journal of Verbal Learning and Verbal Behavior, 2,* 1–21.

Melton, A. W. (1970). The situation with respect to the spacing of repetitions and memory. *Journal of Verbal Learning and Verbal Behavior, 9,* 596–606.

Miller, G. A. (1956). The magical number seven, plus or minus two: Some limits on our capacity for processing information. *Psychological Review, 63,* 81–97.

Milner, B. (1970). Memory and the medial temporal regions of the brain. In K. H. Pribram and D. E. Broadbent (Eds.), *Biology of memory* (pp. 29–50). New York: Academic Press.

Moray, N. (1959). Attention in dichotic listening: Affective cues and the influence of instructions. *Quarterly Journal of Experimental Psychology, 9,* 56–60.

Moray, N. (1967). Where is capacity limited? A survey and a model. In A. Sanders (Ed.), *Attention and performance.* Amsterdam: North-Holland.

Morton, J. (1970). A functional model of memory. In D. A. Norman (Ed.), *Models of human memory* (pp. 203–254). New York: Academic Press.

Murdock, B. B., Jr. (1965). Effects of a subsidiary task on short-term memory. *British Journal of Psychology, 56,* 413–419.

Murdock, B. B., Jr. (1966). Visual and auditory stores in short-term memory. *Quarterly Journal of Experimental Psychology, 18,* 206–211.

Murdock, B. B., Jr. (1967). Recent developments in short-term memory. *British Journal of Psychology, 58,* 421–433.

Murdock, B. B., Jr. (1971). Four channel effects in short-term memory. *Psychonomic Science, 24,* 197–198.

Murdock, B. B., Jr. (1972). Short-term memory. In G. H. Bower (Ed.), *Psychology of learning and motivation,* Vol. 5 (pp. 67–127). New York: Academic Press.

Neisser, U. (1964). Visual search. *Scientific American, 210,* 94–102.

Neisser, U. (1967). *Cognitive psychology.* New York: Appleton-Century-Crofts.

Norman, D. A. (1969). Memory while shadowing. *Quarterly Journal of Experimental Psychology, 21,* 85–93.

Norman, D. A., & Rumelhart, D. E. (1970). A system for perception and memory. In D. A. Norman (Ed.), *Models of human memory* (pp. 21–64). New York: Academic Press.

Palmer, S. E., & Ornstein, P. A. (1971). Role of rehearsal strategy in serial probed recall. *Journal of Experimental Psychology, 88,* 60–66.

Peterson, L. R. (1966). Short-term verbal memory and learning. *Psychological Review, 73,* 193–207.

Peterson, L. R., & Johnson, S. T. (1971). Some effects of minimizing articulation on short-term retention. *Journal of Verbal Learning and Verbal Behavior, 10,* 346–354.

Peterson, L. R., & Kroener, S. (1964). Dichotic stimulation and retention. *Journal of Experimental Psychology, 68,* 125–130.

Phillips, W. A., & Baddeley, A. D. (1971). Reaction time and short-term visual memory. *Psychonomic Science, 22,* 73–74.

Posner, M. I. (1967). Short-term memory systems in human information processing. *Acta Psychologica, 27,* 267–284.

Posner, M. I. (1969). Abstraction and the process of recognition. In G. H. Bower and J. T. Spence (Eds.), *The psychology of learning and motivation: Advances in research and theory,* Vol. III (pp. 152–179). New York: McGraw–Hill.

Postman, L. (1964). Short-term memory and incidental learning. In A. W. Melton (Ed.), *Categories of human learning* (pp. 145–201). New York: Academic Press.

Rosenberg, S., & Schiller, W. J. (1971). Semantic coding and incidental sentence recall. *Journal of Experimental Psychology, 90,* 345–346.

Rundus, D. (1971). Analysis of rehearsal processes in free recall. *Journal of Experimental Psychology, 89,* 63–77.

Savin, H. B., & Bever, T. G. (1970). The nonperceptual reality of the phoneme. *Journal of Verbal Learning and Verbal Behavior, 9,* 295–302.

Schulman, A. I. (1971). Recognition memory for targets from a scanned word list. *British Journal of Psychology, 62,* 335–346.

Selfridge, O. G., & Neisser, U. (1960). Pattern recognition by machine. *Scientific American, 203,* 60–68.

Shaffer, W. O., & Shiffrin, R. M. (1972). Rehearsal and storage of visual information. *Journal of Experimental Psychology, 92,* 292–296.

Shallice, T., & Warrington, E. K. (1970). Independent functioning of verbal memory stores: A neuropsychological study. *Quarterly Journal of Experimental Psychology, 22,* 261–273.

Shepard, R. N. (1967). Recognition memory for words, sentences, and pictures. *Journal of Verbal Learning and Verbal Behavior, 6,* 156–163.

Shiffrin, R. M., & Atkinson, R. C. (1967). Storage and retrieval processes in long-term memory. *Psychological Review, 76,* 179–193.

Shulman, H. G. (1970). Encoding and retention of semantic and phonemic information in short-term memory. *Journal of Verbal Learning and Verbal Behavior, 9,* 499–508.

Shulman, H. G. (1971). Similarity effects in short-term memory. *Psychological Bulletin, 75,* 399–415.

Shulman, H. G. (1972). Semantic confusion errors in short-term memory. *Journal of Verbal Learning and Verbal Behavior, 11,* 221–227.

Silverstein, C., & Glanzer, M. (1971). Concurrent task in free recall: Differential effects of LTS and STS. *Psychonomic Science, 22,* 367–368.

Sperling, G. (1970). Short-term memory, long-term memory, and scanning in the processing of visual information. In A. Young and D. B. Lindsley (Eds.), *Early experience and visual information processing in perceptual and reading disorders* (pp. 198–215). Washington: National Academy of Sciences.

Stoff, M., & Eagle, M. N. (1971). The relationship among reported strategies, presentation rate, and verbal ability and their effects on free recall learning. *Journal of Experimental Psychology, 87,* 423–428.

Sutherland, N. S. (1968). Outlines of a theory of visual pattern recognition in animals and man. *Proceedings of the Royal Society. Series B, 171,* 297–317.

Treisman, A. (1964). Monitoring and storage of irrelevant messages in selective attention. *Journal of Verbal Learning and Verbal Behavior, 3,* 449–459.

Tresselt, M. E., & Mayzner, M. S. (1960). A study of incidental learning. *Journal of Psychology, 50,* 339–347.

Tulving, E. (1966). Subjective organization and effects of repetition in multi-trial free-recall learning. *Journal of Verbal Learning and Verbal Behavior, 5,* 193–197.

Tulving, E., & Madigan, S. A. (1970). Memory and verbal learning. *Annual Review of Psychology, 21,* 437–484.

Tulving, E., & Patterson, R. D. (1968). Functional units and retrieval processes in free recall. *Journal of Experimental Psychology, 77,* 239–248.

Tulving, E., & Pearlstone, Z. (1966). Availability versus accessibility of information in memory for words. *Journal of Verbal Learning and Verbal Behavior. 5,* 381–391.

Turvey, M. T. (1967). Repetition and the preperceptual information store. *Journal of Experimental Psychology, 74,* 289–293.

Warrington, E. K. (1971). Neurological disorders of memory. *British Medical Bulletin, 27,* 243–247.

Watkins, M. J. (1972). The characteristics and functions of primary memory. Unpublished Ph.D. thesis. University of London.

Waugh, N. C., & Norman, D. A. (1965). Primary memory. *Psychological Review, 72,* 89–104.

Wicker, F. W., & Bernstein, A. L. (1969). Association value and orienting task in incidental and intentional paired-associate learning. *Journal of Experimental Psychology, 81,* 308–311.

QUESTIONS FOR FURTHER THOUGHT

1. How does the Craik–Lockhart model differ from the modal (Atkinson–Shiffrin) model of memory?

2. What is depth of processing, and how is it measured?

3. How might an advocate of the Atkinson–Shiffrin model account for findings that appear to challenge it?

4. Can you think of a current example of a model that is nearly universally accepted without questioning its assumptions, and therefore possibly ripe for the dramatic kind of challenge that the levels-of-processing framework represented to the Atkinson–Shiffrin model?

5. What are the implications of the Craik–Lockhart research for improving one's learning in academic subject matter?

HIGH-SPEED SCANNING IN HUMAN MEMORY

Saul Sternberg

INTRODUCTION

How do people scan information that they are holding in their short-term memory? For example, if you read the digits 6–0–1–9–7, and commit them to memory, how would you than go about identifying whether the number 1, or the number 5 for that matter, was among the set of numbers you committed to memory?

In a paradigm-setting series of studies, Saul Sternberg compared alternative models of how people might scan such information. The models differed in serial or parallel, and self-terminating or exhaustive, methods.

According to a serial model, people would scan each of the successive digits in turn, one after another. According to a parallel model, however, people would scan the digits simultaneously—all at once. A serial model would predict, Sternberg believed, a variable scanning time—scanning more digits would take longer to scan. A parallel model would predict a constant scanning time regardless of the number of symbols in the string. For example, a parallel model would expect the same amount of time to scan three digits (8–2–4) or six (8–2–4–1–6–3).

According to a self-terminating information-scanning model, someone will scan until encountering the desired digit and respond "yes" as soon as it appears. A person scans to the end of the list only if the digit is the last one or is not in the set to be remembered. According to an exhaustive model, in contrast, someone always scans to the end of the list, regardless of the number of items to be scanned. The self-terminating model predicts faster responses for items early in the stimulus set (such as the 8 in 8–2–4), and slower responses for items later in the stimulus set (such as the 4 in 8–2–4).

Sternberg found that the number of items in the stimulus set affected response time, but serial position did not. He therefore concluded that people were using a serial, exhaustive scanning process. Scanning can take anywhere from 10 to 30 milliseconds per stimulus item.

The Sternberg studies are among the most famous in cognitive psychology for several reasons. First, they were exceedingly elegant, showing in a way that seemed compelling at the time that individuals use a serial, exhaustive scan when searching for items in short-term memory. Later study revealed that the demonstration was nowhere nearly as compelling as it had first appeared, thus reinforcing the impossibility of so-called "critical" experiments that decide something once and for all, at least in psychology. Second, the work introduced a task

Source: Reprinted with permission from Sternberg, S. (1966). High-speed scanning in human memory. *Science, 153,* 652–654. Copyright © (1966) American Association for the Advancement of Science.

to psychology, short-term memory scanning, that became widely used and is still fairly widely used today, three decades later. Third, the work introduced a method, called the *additive-factor method,* for isolating stages of processing in cognition. Sternberg argued that one could infer independent stages of processing by showing that variables that affect one stage of processing have no effect on other stages. For all these reasons, Saul Sternberg's work became a classic in the study of cognition.

———

When subjects judge whether a test symbol is contained in a short memorized sequence of symbols, their mean reaction-time increases linearly with the length of the sequence. The linearity and slope of the function imply the existence of an internal serial-comparison process whose average rate is between 25 and 30 symbols per sec. ■

How is symbolic information retrieved from recent memory? The study of short-term memory (*1*) has revealed some of the determinants of failures to remember, but has provided little insight into error-free performance and the retrieval processes that underlie it. One reason for the neglect of retrieval mechanisms may be the implicit assumption that a short time after several items have been memorized, they can be immediately and simultaneously available for expression in recall or in other responses, rather than having to be retrieved first. In another vocabulary (*2*), this is to assume the equivalence of the "span of immediate memory" (the number of items that can be recalled without error) and the "momentary capacity of consciousness" (the number of items immediately available). The experiments reported here (*3*) show that the assumption is unwarranted.

Underlying the paradigm of these experiments is the supposition that if the selection of a response requires the use of information that is in memory, the latency of the response will reveal something about the process by which the information is retrieved. Of particular interest in the study of retrieval is the effect of the number of elements in memory on the response latency. The subject first memorizes a short series of symbols. He is then shown a test stimulus, and is required to decide whether or not it is one of the symbols in memory. If the subject decides affirmatively, he pulls one lever, making a positive response; otherwise he makes a negative response by pulling the other lever. In this paradigm, it is the identity of the symbols in the series, but not their order, that is relevant to the binary response. The response latency is defined as the time from the onset of the test stimulus to the occurrence of the response.

Because they are well learned and highly discriminable, the ten digits were used as stimuli. On each trial of experiment 1, the subject (*4*) saw a random series of from one to six different digits displayed singly at a fixed locus for 1.2 seconds each. The length, *s,* of the series varied at random from trial to trial. There followed a 2.0-second delay, a warning signal, and then the test digit. As soon as one of the levers was pulled, a feedback light informed the subject whether his response had been correct.

The trial ended with his attempt to recall the series in order. For every value of s, positive and negative responses were required with equal frequency. Each digit in the series occurred as a test stimulus with probability $(2s)^{-1}$, and each of the remaining digits occurred with probability $[2(10 - s)]^{-1}$.

Each subject had 24 practice trials and 144 test trials. Feedback and payoffs were designed to encourage subjects to respond as rapidly as possible, while maintaining a low error rate. The eight subjects whose data are presented pulled the wrong lever on 1.3 percent of the test trials (5). Recall was imperfect on 1.4 percent of the trials. The low error-rates justify the assumption that on a typical trial the series of symbols in memory was the same as the series of symbols presented.

Results are shown in Figure 1. Linear regression accounts for 99.4 percent of the variance of the overall mean response-latencies (6). The slope of the fitted line is 37.9 ± 3.8 msec per symbol (7); its zero intercept is 397.2 ± 19.3 msec. Lines fitted separately to the mean latencies of positive and negative responses differ in slope by 9.6 ± 2.3 msec per symbol. The difference is attributable primarily to the fact that for $s = 1$, positive responses were 50.0 ± 20.1 msec faster than negative responses. Lines fitted to the data for $2 \le s \le 6$ differ in slope by an insignificant 3.1 ± 3.2 msec per symbol.

FIGURE 1   Relation between response latency and the number of symbols in memory, s, in experiment 1. Mean latencies, over eight subjects, of positive responses (filled circles) and negative responses (open circles). About 95 observations per point. For each s, overall mean (heavy bar) and estimates of $\pm\sigma$ are indicated (6). Solid line was fitted by least squares to overall means. Upper bound for parallel process (broken curve).

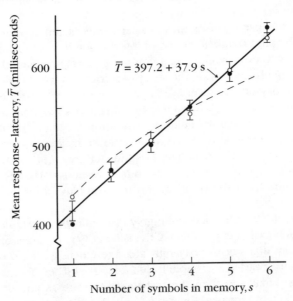

The latency of a response depends in part, on the relative frequency with which it is required (8). For this reason the frequencies of positive and negative responses and, more generally, the response entropy (8), were held constant for all values of s in experiment 1. However, the test-stimulus entropy (predictability) was permitted to co-vary with s.

Both response and test-stimulus entropies were controlled in experiment 2, in which the retrieval process was studied by an alternative method similar to that used in more conventional experiments on choice-reaction time. In experiment 1, the set of symbols associated with the positive response changed from trial to trial. In contrast to this varied-set procedure, a fixed-set procedure was used in experiment 2. In each of three parts of a session, a set of digits for which a positive response was required (the positive set) was announced to the subject (4); there followed 60 practice trials and 120 test trials based on this set.

The subject knew that on each trial, any of the ten digits could appear as the test stimulus, and that for all the digits not in the positive set (the negative set) the negative response was required. Each subject worked with nonintersecting positive sets of size s = 1, 2, and 4, whose composition was varied from subject to subject.

Stimulus and response entropies were both held constant while s was varied, by means of specially constructed populations of test stimuli. Let x_1, y_1, y_2, z_1, . . . , z_4 and w_1, . . . , w_3 represent the ten digits. Their relative frequencies in the population were x_1, 4/15; each y, 2/15; each z, 1/15; and each w, 1/15. The three sequences of test stimuli presented to a subject were obtained by random permutation of the fixed population and assignment of x_1, the y_1, or the z_1 to the positive response. Thus, the population of test stimuli, their sequential properties, and the relative frequency of positive responses (4/15) were the same in all conditions (9).

A trial consisted of a warning signal, the test digit, the subject's response, and a feedback light. Between a response and the next test digit, 3.7 seconds elapsed. As in experiment 1, feedback and payoffs were designed to encourage speed without sacrifice of accuracy. The six subjects whose data are presented pulled the wrong lever on 1.0 percent of the test trials (5).

The results, shown in Figure 2, closely resemble those of experiment 1. A positive set in experiment 2 apparently played the same role as a series of symbols presented in experiment 1, both corresponding to a set of symbols stored in memory and used in the selection of a response. As in experiment 1, linear regression accounts for 99.4 percent of the variance of the overall mean response-latencies (6). The slope of 38.3 ± 6.1 msec per symbol is indistinguishable from that in experiment 1; the zero intercept is 369.4 ± 10.1 msec. In experiment 2, the relation between latencies of positive and negative responses when s = 1 is not exceptional. Lines fitted separately to latencies of the two kinds of response differ in slope by an insignificant 1.6 ± 3.0 msec per symbol.

The linearity of the latency functions suggests that the time between test stimulus and response is occupied, in part, by a serial-comparison (scanning) process. An internal representation of the test stimulus is compared successively to the symbols in memory, each comparison resulting in either a match or a mismatch. The time from the beginning of one comparison to the beginning of the next (the comparison time) has the same mean value for successive comparisons. A positive response is made if there has been a match, and a negative response otherwise.

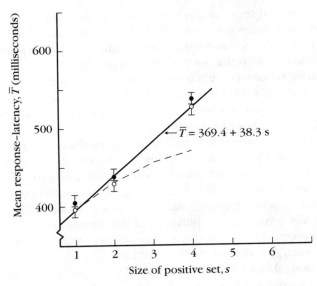

FIGURE 2   Relation between response latency and the size of the positive set, *s*, in experiment 2. Mean latencies, over six subjects, of positive responses (filled circles) and negative responses (open circles). About 200 (positive) or 500 (negative) observations per point. For each *s*, overall mean (heavy bar) and estimates of ±σ are indicated (6). Solid line was fitted by least squares to overall means. Upper bound for parallel process (broken curve).

On trials requiring negative responses, *s* comparisons must be made. If positive responses were initiated as soon as a match had occurred (as in a self-terminating search), the mean number of comparisons on positive trials would be (*s* + 1)/2 rather than *s*. The latency function for positive responses would then have half the slope of the function for negative responses. The equality of the observed slopes shows, instead, that the scanning process is exhaustive: even when a match has occurred, scanning continues through the entire series. This may appear surprising, as it suggests nonoptimality. One can, however, conceive of systems in which a self-terminating search would be inefficient. For example, if the determination of whether or not a match had occurred were a slow operation that could not occur concurrently with scanning, self-termination would entail a long interruption in the scan after each comparison.

On the basis of the exhaustive-scanning theory, the zero intercept of the latency function is interpreted as the sum of the times taken by motor response, formation of the test-stimulus representation, and other unknown processes whose durations are independent of the number of symbols in memory. The slope of the latency function represents the mean comparison-time. The two experiments, then, provide a measure of the speed of purely internal events, independent of the times taken by sensory and motor operations. The average rate of between 25 and 30 symbols per second is about four times as high as the maximum rate of "subvocal speech" when the words are the names of digits (*11*). This difference suggests that the silent rehearsal (*12*) reported by subjects in both experiments should probably not be identified with high-speed scanning, but should be thought of as a separate process whose function is to maintain the memory that is to be scanned.

In view of the substantial agreement in results of the two experiments, one difference in procedure merits particular emphasis. A response in experiment 1 was the first and only response based on a particular series, made about 3 sec after the series had been presented. In contrast, the positive set on which a response was based in experiment 2 had been used on an average of 120 previous trials. Evidently, neither practice in scanning a particular series nor lengthening of the time it has been stored in memory need increase the rate at which it is scanned.

In accounting for human performance in other tasks that appear to involve multiple comparisons, theorists have occasionally proposed that the comparisons are carried out in parallel rather than serially (13, 14). This perhaps corresponds to the assumption mentioned earlier that the momentary capacity of consciousness is several items rather than only one. Are the present data inconsistent with such a proposal? Parallel comparisons that begin and also end simultaneously (14) are excluded because the mean latency has been shown to increase with s. A process in which multiple comparisons begin simultaneously is more difficult to exclude if the comparison times are independent, their distribution has nonzero variance, and the response is initiated when the slowest comparison ends. A linear increase in mean latency cannot alone be taken as conclusive evidence against such a process. The magnitude of the latency increase that would result from a parallel process is bounded above, however (15); it is possible to apply the bound to these data (16). This was done for the negative responses in both experiments, with the results shown by the broken curves in Figures 1 and 2. Evidently, the increase in response latency with s is too great to be attributed to a parallel process with independent comparison times (17).

Other experiments provide added support for the scanning theory (16). Two of the findings are noted here: (i) variation in the size, n, of the negative set ($n \geq s$) had no effect on the mean latency, indicating that stimulus confusability (10, 18) cannot account for the results of experiments 1 and 2; (ii) variation in the size of a response-irrelevant memory load had no effect on the latency function, implying that the increase in latency reflects the duration of retrieval and not merely the exigencies of retention.

The generality of the high-speed scanning process has yet to be determined, but there are several features of experiments 1 and 2 that should be taken into account in any comparison with other binary classification tasks (14, 19): (i) at least one of the classes is small; (ii) class members are assigned arbitrarily; (iii) relatively little practice is provided; (iv) high accuracy is required and errors cannot be corrected; and (v) until the response to one stimulus is completed the next stimulus cannot be viewed.

REFERENCES AND NOTES

1. A. W. Melton, *J. Verbal Learning Verbal Behavior 2*, 1 (1963).
2. G. A. Miller, *Psychology, the science of mental life* (Harper and Row, New York, 1962), p. 47.

3. These experiments were first reported by S. Sternberg, "Retrieval from recent memory: Some reaction-time experiments and a search theory," paper presented at a meeting of the Psychonomic Society, Bryn Mawr, August 1963.

4. Subjects were undergraduates at the University of Pennsylvania.

5. These trials were excluded from the analysis. Three other subjects in experiment 1 (two in experiment 2) were rejected because they exceeded an error criterion. Their latency data, which are not presented, resembled those of the other subjects.

6. For both experiments the data subjected to analysis of variance were, for each subject, the mean latency for each value of s. So that inferences might be drawn about the population of subjects, individual differences in mean and in linear-regression slope were treated as "random effects." Where quantities are stated in the form $a \pm b$, b is an estimate of the standard error of a. Such estimates were usually calculated by using variance components derived from the analysis of variance.

7. The analyses of variance for both experiments provided a means of testing the significance of differences among individual slopes. Significance levels are .07 (experiment 1) and .09 (experiment 2), suggesting true intersubject differences in slope; the population distribution of slopes has an estimated standard deviation of 8.0 msec per symbol.

8. W. R. Garner, *Uncertainty and structure as psychological concepts* (Wiley, New York 1962).

9. A result of this procedure is that other factors in choice-reaction time were also controlled: stimulus discriminability (*10*); information transmitted (*8*); and information reduced, M. I. Posner, *Psychol. Rev. 71*, 49 (1964); P. M. Fitts and I. Biederman, *J. Exp. Psychol. 69*, 408 (1965).

10. R. N. Shepard and J. J. Chang, *J. Exp. Psychol. 65*, 94 (1963); M. Stone, *Psychometrika 25*, 251 (1960).

11. T. K. Landauer, *Percept. Mot. Skills 15*, 64 (1962).

12. D. E. Broadbent, *Perception and communication* (Pergamon, New York, 1958), p. 225.

13. L. S. Christie and R. D. Luce, *Bull. Math. Biophys. 18*, 89 (1956); A. Rapoport, *Behavioral Sci. 4*, 299 (1959).

14. U. Neisser, *Amer. J. Psychol. 76*, 376 (1963); *Sci. Amer. 210*, 94 (1964).

15. H. O. Hartley and H. A. David, *Ann. Math. Stat. 25*, 85 (1954).

16. S. Sternberg, in preparation.

17. Exponentially distributed parallel comparison (*13*) and other interesting theories of multiple comparisons (*18*) lead to a latency function that is approximately linear in log. Deviations of the overall means from such function are significant ($p < .03$) in both experiments.

18. A. T. Welford, *Ergonomics 3*, 189 (1960).

19. I. Pollack, *J. Verbal Learning Verbal Behavior 2*, 159 (1963); D. E. Broadbent and M. Gregory, *Nature 193*, 1315 (1962).

QUESTIONS FOR FURTHER THOUGHT

1. On what basis did Sternberg conclude that scanning of short-term memory is a serial, exhaustive process?

2. Approximately how long does it take to scan one digit in short-term memory?

3. What is the logic of the additive-factor method?

4. Why is there less interest today in what would seem to be a fundamental and general issue, namely, the choice between serial or parallel processing?

5. Might some alternative interpretation explain Sternberg's data? If not, why not? If so, what?

WORKING MEMORY

Alan Baddeley

INTRODUCTION

A model of memory has gained increasing favor during recent years with the suggestion that temporary storage and manipulation of memory may occur through a far more active and complex system than was originally proposed by Richard Atkinson and Richard Shiffrin as the short-term store. According to Alan Baddeley's model, temporary storage and manipulation of information occur in a temporarily activated portion of long-term memory called *working memory*. According to Baddeley, with whom the notion is most strongly associated, working memory comprises three main systems, which work together.

Baddeley calls the first system the *central executive.* This system controls and monitors a person's attention according to needs current at a given time. This central executive is particularly important in activities that require one to attend to and manipulate large amounts of information in brief periods of time, as when one plays chess or mentally solves a difficult arithmetic problem.

Two *slave systems* also operate under the control of the central executive. A *visuospatial sketch pad* manipulates visual images, and a *phonological loop* stores and rehearses speech-based information.

The popularity of the working-memory model stems from its theoretical elegance, its empirical support, and its usefulness not only in the study of memory but in the study of other aspects of cognition, as well. For example, recent research suggests that differences in working-memory abilities may largely account for individual differences in complex processes as diverse as reading comprehension and inductive reasoning (as when one completes a series of numbers such as 3,8,13,?). Today, Baddeley's model is probably the one that most strongly competes with the early Atkinson–Shiffrin model. Its widespread usage in cognitive research has earned it a place as one of the key seminal contributions to the study, not only of memory, but of cognition in general.

———

The term working memory *refers to a brain system that provides temporary storage and manipulation of the information necessary for such complex cognitive tasks as language comprehension, learning, and reasoning. This definition has evolved from the concept of a unitary short-term memory system.*

Source: Reprinted with permission from Baddeley, A. (1992). Working memory. *Science, 255,* 556–559. Copyright © 1992 American Association for the Advancement of Science.

Working memory has been found to require the simultaneous storage and processing of information. It can be divided into the following three subcomponents: (i) the central executive, which is assumed to be an attentional-controlling system, is important in skills such as chess playing, and is particularly susceptible to the effects of Alzheimer's disease; and two slave systems, namely (ii) the visuospatial sketch pad, which manipulates visual images, and (iii) the phonological loop, which stores and rehearses speech-based information and is necessary for the acquisition of both native and second-language vocabulary. ■

The question of whether memory should be regarded as a single unitary system or whether it should be fractionated into two or more subsystems formed one of the major controversies within cognitive psychology during the mid-1960s. During that time, evidence began to accumulate in favor of a dichotomy (*1*). Some of the most convincing evidence came from the study of brain-damaged patients; those suffering from the classic amnesic syndrome appeared to have gross disruption of the capacity to form new lasting memories but showed preserved performance on a range of tasks that were assumed to test short-term memory (*2*). Conversely, a second type of patient was identified who appeared to show normal long-term learning but had a short-term memory span limited to one or two items (*3*). It was suggested that such patients had a deficit in short-term storage, in contrast to the long-term storage deficit that occurs in the amnesic syndrome. This finding, together with considerable evidence from the study of normal subjects, appeared by the late 1960s to argue for a dichotomous view of memory, such as that proposed by Atkinson and Shiffrin (*4*).

By the early 1970s, it was becoming clear that the two-component model was running into difficulties. One of its problems was inherent in the neuropsychological evidence that initially appeared to support it so strongly. Atkinson and Shiffrin (*4*) suggested that the short-term store within their model acted as a working memory, being necessary for learning, for the retrieval of old material, and for the performance of many other cognitive tasks. If that were the case, one would expect patients with a grossly defective short-term store to show many other cognitive problems, including impaired long-term learning. In fact, such patients appeared to have a normal long-term learning capacity and surprisingly few cognitive handicaps.

Pursuing this issue was difficult because patients with a pure short-term memory deficit are rare. We therefore attempted to simulate this condition in unimpaired subjects by using a dual-task technique (*5*). We argued as follows: If the digit-span procedure depends on the short-term store, with the number of digits retained determined by the capacity of the store, then it should be possible to interfere systematically with the operation of the working memory system by requiring the subject to remember digits while performing other cognitive tasks. As the concurrent digit load is increased, the remaining short-term capacity would decrease and the interference would increase, with performance presumably breaking down as the digit load reached the capacity of the system.

Reasoning, comprehension, and learning tasks all showed a similar pattern. As concurrent digit load increased, performance declined, but the degree of disruption fell far short of that predicted. Subjects whose digit memory was at full capacity could reason and learn quite effectively.

These results, together with others, encouraged the abandonment of the idea of a single, unitary short-term store that also functions as a working memory. Instead, we proposed the tripartite system shown in Figure 1, which comprises an attentional controller and the central executive, supplemented by two subsidiary slave systems. The articulatory or phonological loop was assumed to be responsible for maintaining speech-based information, including digits in the digit-span test, whereas the visuospatial sketch pad was assumed to perform a similar function in setting up and manipulating visuospatial imagery.

The concept of working memory has increasingly replaced the older concept of short-term memory (6). Research has subsequently tended to concentrate on one of two complementary but somewhat different approaches. One of these defines working memory as the system that is necessary for the concurrent storage and manipulation of information; tasks are devised that combine processing and storage, and the capacity of such tasks to predict a range of other cognitive skills, such as reading, comprehension, and reasoning, is tested. This psychometric approach, which has flourished most strongly in North America, frequently focuses on the extent to which performance on working memory tasks can predict individual differences in the relevant cognitive skills.

An alternative approach, which has been more favored in Europe, uses both dual-task methodology and the study of neuropsychological cases in an attempt to analyze the structure of the working memory system. Most effort has been devoted to the two slave systems, on the grounds that these offer more tractable problems than the more complex central-executive system.

The two approaches are complementary, and both have strengths and weaknesses; the psychometric correlational approach has the advantage that it can tackle what is probably the most crucial component of the system, the central executive, and can furthermore work directly on problems of practical significance, such as reading comprehension or the reasoning tasks used in tests of intelligence. The weakness of this approach lies in the reliance on complex working memory tasks that have a somewhat

FIGURE 1   A simplified representation of the Baddeley and Hitch working memory model (5).

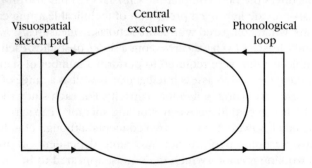

arbitrary construction and that do not readily lend themselves to a more detailed analysis of the component processes. The dual-task and neuropsychological approach can be utilized to successfully analyze the constituent processes of the slave systems but has made less headway in teasing apart the complexities of the executive controller.

INDIVIDUAL DIFFERENCES IN WORKING MEMORY

The essence of the psychometric approach is to develop tasks that require the combined storage and manipulation of information and to correlate performance on these tasks with the performance of practically and theoretically important cognitive skills. One influential study in this area was carried out by Daneman and Carpenter (7), who examined the processes involved in reading comprehension. They devised a series of working memory tasks, one of which required subjects to read aloud or listen to a series of short sentences while retaining the last word from each sentence for subsequent immediate recall. Hence, subjects might read or hear: "The sailor sold the parrot. The vicar opened the book." They should then respond "parrot, book." The test typically starts with two sentences and increases to a point at which subjects are no longer able to recall all the terminal words. This point is designated the subject's working memory span.

Daneman and Carpenter, and others using similar techniques, typically found a correlation coefficient of about 0.5 or 0.6 between working memory span and reading comprehension, as measured by standardized tests (8). The span task does not have to involve language processing because similar correlations are found when simple arithmetic, combined with word recall, is substituted for sentence processing (9).

Subsequent studies have indicated that students with high working memory span were better at coping with "garden path sentences," which contain misleading context, and that they are better at drawing inferences from text, suggesting that they have a better grasp of its meaning (10).

A second area in which the individual differences approach has been applied to the analysis of working memory is concerned with the study of reasoning and concentrates particularly on tasks that have traditionally been used to measure intelligence. One example of this is the working memory analysis by Carpenter, Just, and Shell (11) of performance on the Raven's matrices task, a test in which one sector is missing from a complex pattern and the subject is required to choose which of six possible options offers the best completion. Christal (12) has also shown that working memory tests provide improved prediction of technical learning capacity in U.S. Air Force recruits, when compared with more scholastic measures.

Kyllonen and Christal (13) have carried out a series of studies, each involving several hundred subjects who were required to perform a number of standardized tests of reasoning of the type used to assess intelligence as well as a range of tasks that had been devised to estimate working memory capacity. For each study, their results suggested a very high correlation between working memory capacity and reasoning skill. They concluded, however, that the two concepts, although closely related, were not synonymous; reasoning performance was more dependent on previous knowledge than was working memory, which in contrast appeared to be more dependent on sheer speed of processing.

COMPONENTS OF WORKING MEMORY

Although concurrent storage and processing may be one aspect of working memory, it is almost certainly not the only feature; indeed, Baddeley, Barnard, and Schneider and Detweiler (*14*) all suggest that the coordination of resources is the prime function of working memory, with memory storage being only one of many potential demands that are likely to be made on the system.

One proposed role for the central executive is that of coordinating information from two or more slave systems. This feature of the central executive was used in an attempt to test the proposal that Alzheimer's disease is associated with a particularly marked deficit in central executive functioning (*15*). Patients with Alzheimer's disease, and both young and elderly normal subjects, were required to perform two tasks concurrently, one visual and one verbal. The difficulty of each task was adjusted so that the Alzheimer patients were making the same proportion of errors as the control subjects, and subjects were then required to perform both tasks at the same time. Normal elderly subjects were no more impaired than young controls by this requirement to coordinate, whereas the Alzheimer patients showed a marked impairment in performance on both the memory and tracking tasks when required to combine them (*16*). As the disease progressed, performance on the individual tracking and memory span tasks held up very well (Figure 2), whereas performance on the combined tasks deteriorated markedly, as would be predicted by the hypothesis of a central executive deficit in Alzheimer's disease (*17*).

FIGURE 2 Dual-task performance of patients with Alzheimer's disease in a series of three sequential tests (1, 2, and 3) 6 months apart. *T*, tracking task; *MS*, memory span task. Normal subjects did not show a difference between single and dual-task conditions. Data from Baddeley et al. (*17*).

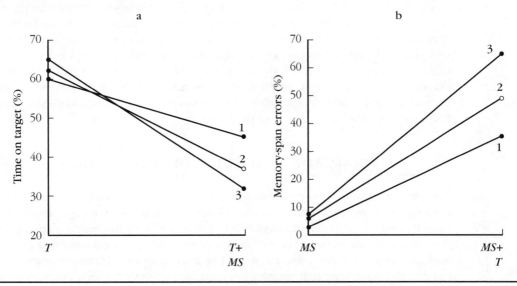

THE SLAVE SYSTEMS OF WORKING MEMORY

Although an analytic approach to the central executive is beginning to bear fruit, there is no doubt that considerably more progress has been made with the simpler task of understanding the peripheral slave systems of working memory. The dual-task paradigm has been used to demonstrate the separability of the memory systems responsible for learning by means of visuospatial imagery and of learning by rote repetition. Imagery is disrupted by the requirement of performing a visuospatial task, such as tracking a spot of light moving on a screen, by certain types of eye movement, or by the presentation of irrelevant visual material during learning (*18*).

There are separable spatial and visual components, with different tasks differentially recruiting the two. Farah (*19*) distinguishes one imagery component that is principally concerned with the representation of pattern information and that involves the occipital lobes from a second more spatial component that seems to be dependent on parietal lobe functioning. Neuropsychological evidence supports this dichotomy, with some patients having great difficulty in imaging and recalling such visual features as the shape of the ears of a spaniel dog or the color of a pumpkin but having no difficulty in spatial tasks such as describing routes or locating towns on maps; other patients show exactly the reverse pattern of deficits (*20*).

Having found ways of separately disrupting spatial and verbal processing, one can explore the relative contribution of different subsystems to complex tasks. One example of this application concerns the nature of the cognitive processes involved in playing chess. The literature reviewed by Holding [in (*21*)] indicates that both visual and verbal coding have been claimed to be crucial by different studies that principally rely on subjective report. We have sought more objective evidence through a series of experiments that utilize the secondary-task technique to disrupt either the phonological loop, the sketch pad system, or the central executive. Our first study involved memory for complex chess positions and tested subjects ranging from the modest club player to the international grand master. As expected, expertise correlated highly with memory performance, but all subjects showed the same basic pattern: no disruption from the concurrent verbal task but clear impairment from the tasks occupying the visuospatial sketch pad or the central executive. A second study required subjects to choose the optimum next move from a complex middle-game position and found exactly the same pattern. Disruption of verbal activity had no effect, whereas visuospatial disruption was clear, and this problem-solving task was even more susceptible to central executive disruption than the task in the first study (*22*).

ANALYZING THE PHONOLOGICAL LOOP

The phonological loop is probably the simplest and most extensively investigated component of working memory. It lies closest to the earlier concept of short-term memory and has been investigated most extensively with the memory-span procedure. It is assumed to comprise two components, a phonological store that can hold acoustic or speech-based information for 1 to 2 sec, coupled with an articulatory control process, somewhat analogous to inner speech. This system serves two functions;

it can maintain material within the phonological store by subvocal repetition, and it can take visually presented material such as words or nameable pictures and register them in the phonological store by subvocalization.

This simple model is able to give a good account of a rich range of laboratory-based findings. These include the following:

1. *The acoustic similarity effect.* This is the observation that the immediate ordered recall of items is poorer when they are similar rather than dissimilar in sound (*23*). Hence, hearing and repeating dissimilar words such as "pit, day, cow, pen, rig," is easier than a phonologically similar sequence such as "man, cap, can, map, mad." This phenomenon is assumed to occur because the basic code involved in the store is phonological; similar items have fewer distinguishing cues than dissimilar items and are therefore more susceptible to being forgotten. Similarity of meaning does not have this effect, suggesting that this subsystem does not reflect semantic coding.

2. *The irrelevant speech effect.* This refers to a reduction in recall of lists of visually presented items brought about by the presence of irrelevant spoken material (*24*). Once again, the semantic characteristics of the material are not important, with a language that is unfamiliar to the subject being just as disruptive as words in his or her native tongue and nonsense syllables being as disruptive as meaningful words. The effect is not due to simple distraction, because loud bursts of noise have little or no effect (*25*). These results are interpreted under the assumption that disruptive spoken material gains obligatory access to the phonological memory store.

3. *The word-length effect.* This provides evidence on the nature of the subvocal rehearsal process. Memory span for words is inversely related to spoken duration of the words. Subjects can generally remember about as many words as they can say in 2 sec (*26*). This phenomenon accounts for differences in digit span when subjects are tested in different languages; languages in which digits tend to have long vowel sounds or more than one syllable take longer to rehearse and lead to shorter memory spans (*27*). The model can also explain the marked tendency for digit span in children to increase with age; as children get older, they are able to rehearse faster (*28*).

4. *Articulatory suppression.* It is possible to disrupt the use of subvocal rehearsal by requiring subjects to utter some repeated irrelevant sound, such as the word "the." This process, known as articulatory suppression prevents the subjects from rehearsing the material they are trying to remember and thus removes the effect of word length. Suppression also prevents subjects from registering visually presented material in the phonological store. Recall of such visual material is reduced, and the acoustic similarity effect is abolished (*29*).

The performance of neuropsychological patients with impaired short-term memory can also be explained as a deficit in the phonological store. They typically show no evidence of phonological coding in memory tasks when presentation is visual, no word length effect, and no influence of articulatory suppression, suggesting that these patients make little or no use of their defective phonological short-term store (*30*).

THE FUNCTION OF THE PHONOLOGICAL LOOP

Patients with a specific phonological loop deficit seem to have remarkably few signs of general cognitive impairment. Although they typically have difficulty in comprehending certain types of complex sentences, interpretation of results in this area remains controversial (31). The most commonly held view is that the phonological store serves as a backup system for comprehension of speech under taxing conditions but may be less important with simple, clearly presented material.

In recent years, we have been exploring another possible function of this system, namely, its role in long-term phonological learning, such as acquiring the vocabulary of one's native, or even a foreign, language. In one study, we asked a patient with a very specific short-term phonological memory deficit to learn eight items of Russian vocabulary, a language with which the patient was unfamiliar; we compared the results with the patient's capacity to learn to associate arbitrary pairs of words in the patient's native language (32). People tend to learn pairs of familiar words in terms of their meaning, and, as expected, the patient's performance on this task was entirely normal. In contrast, the patient failed to learn the Russian words with auditory presentation and was severely impaired relative to control subjects even when presentation was visual. This result suggests that short-term phonological storage is important for new long-term phonological learning. Subsequent studies with normal adults have shown that factors that influence the phonological loop, such as articulatory suppression, word length, and phonological similarity, strongly influence foreign vocabulary acquisition yet show no effect on learning to associate pairs of familiar words (33).

Evidence for the importance of the phonological loop in native-language learning comes from a number of sources. Gathercole and Baddeley (34) studied a group of children with a specific language disorder and found that their most striking cognitive deficits occurred in a task involving hearing and repeating back unfamiliar nonwords; on this nonword repetition task, 8-year-old children with the language development of 6-year-olds functioned like 4-year-olds. Further investigation suggested that this was due neither to perceptual difficulties nor to difficulties in speech production but probably resided in the operation of the phonological short-term store.

A subsequent study assessed the role of the phonological short-term store in the development of vocabulary across the normal range (35). A sample of 118 children was tested after starting school between the ages of 4 and 5 years. Their capacity for nonword repetition was measured, as was their nonverbal intelligence and their vocabulary, which was tested by speaking a series of words to the children and requiring them to point to appropriate pictures. Nonword repetition proved to be highly correlated with vocabulary and to be a powerful predictor of vocabulary 1 year later.

In an experimental simulation of new word learning (36), we taught children new names for toy monsters. Two groups were tested that were matched for nonverbal intelligence but that differed in nonword repetition capacity. Those with low capacity showed poor learning, particularly in the case of unfamiliar invented names.

Service (37) has studied the acquisition of English as a second language by young Finnish children. Service took a number of measures of cognitive skill before the course began, including measures of nonverbal intelligence and of nonword repetition capacity. Two years later, the children's performances on a range of tests of English language were correlated with these earlier measures. Once again, nonword repetition capacity, which is assumed to depend on short-term phonological storage, was clearly the best predictor of subsequent success. Thus, the evidence supports the view that short-term phonological memory is crucial in the acquisition of vocabulary.

CONCLUSION

The concept of a working memory system that temporarily stores information as part of the performance of complex cognitive tasks is proving to be productive. Studies that have utilized the individual difference approach have linked working memory to performance on a range of important tasks, including language comprehension and reasoning. The more analytic approach has shown that the concept forms a useful conceptual tool in understanding a range of neuropsychological deficits, which in turn have thrown light on normal cognitive functioning.

Working memory stands at the crossroads between memory, attention, and perception. In the case of the slave systems, the phonological loop, for example, probably represents an evolution of the basic speech perception and production systems to the point at which they can be used for active memory. Any adequate model of the phonological loop is thus likely to overlap substantially with an adequate model of speech perception and speech production. The visuospatial sketch pad is probably intimately related to the processes of visual perception and action. The central executive clearly reflects a system concerned with the attentional control of behavior, with subsequent developments almost certainly depending on parallel developments in the study of attention and of the control of action. If these links can be sustained and developed, the concept of working memory is likely to continue to be a fruitful one.

REFERENCES

1. See A. D. Baddeley [*Human memory: Theory and practice* (Allyn and Bacon, Needham Heights, MA, 1990), pp. 39–66] for a review.
2. _____ and E. K. Warrington, *J. Verb. Learn. Verb. Behav. 9,* 176 (1970); B. Milner, in *Amnesia,* C. W. M. Whitty and O. L. Zangwill, Eds. (Butterworths, London, 1966), pp. 109–133.
3. T. Shallice and E. K. Warrington, *Q. J. Exp. Psychol. 22,* 261 (1970); A. Basso, H. Spinnler, G. Vallar, E. Zanobio, *Neuropsychologia 20,* 263 (1982); G. Vallar and T. Shallice, *Neuropsychological impairments of short-term memory* (Cambridge Univ. Press, Cambridge, 1990).
4. R. C. Atkinson and R. M. Shiffrin, in *The psychology of learning and motivation: Advances in research and theory,* K. W. Spence, Ed. (Academic Press, New York, 1968), vol. 2, pp. 89–195.
5. A. D. Baddeley and G. J. Hitch, in *The psychology of learning and motivation,* G. A. Bower, Ed. (Academic Press, New York, 1974), vol. 8, pp. 47–89.

6. R. G. Crowder, *Acta. Psychol. 50,* 291 (1982).

7. M. Daneman and P. A. Carpenter, *J. Verb. Learn. Verb. Behav. 19,* 450 (1980).

8. A. D. Baddeley, R. Logie, I. Nimmo-Smith, N. Brereton, *J. Mem. Lang. 24,* 119 (1985); M. E. J. Masson and G. A. Miller, *J. Educ. Psychol. 75,* 314 (1983).

9. J. V. Oakhill, N. Yuill, A. J. Parkin, *J. Res. Read. 9,* 80 (1986); M. L. Turner and R. W. Engle, *J. Mem. Lang. 28,* 127 (1989).

10. M. Daneman and P. A. Carpenter, *J. Exp. Psychol. Learn. Mem. Cogn. 9,* 561 (1983); J. V. Oakhill, *Br. J. Educ. Psychol. 54,* 31 (1984).

11. P. A. Carpenter, M. A. Just, P. Shell, *Psychol. Rev. 97,* 404 (1990).

12. R. E. Christal, *Armstrong Laboratory Human Resources Directorate Technical Report AL-TP-1991-0031* (Brooks Air Force Base, TX, 1991).

13. P. C. Kyllonen and R. E. Christal, *Intelligence 14,* 389 (1990).

14. A. D. Baddeley, *Working memory* (Oxford Univ. Press, Oxford, 1986); P. Barnard, in *Progress in the psychology of language,* A. Ellis, Ed. (Erlbaum, London, 1985), vol. 2, pp. 197-258; W. Schneider and M. Detweiler, in *The psychology of learning and motivation,* G. H. Bower, Ed. (Academic Press, New York, 1987), vol. 21, pp. 54-119.

15. J. T. Becker, in *Alzheimer's disease: Advances in basic research and therapies,* R. J. Wurtman, S. H. Corkin, J. H. Growdon, Eds. (Center for Brain Sciences and Metabolism Charitable Trust, Cambridge, 1987), pp. 343-348; H. Spinnler, S. Della Sala, R. Bandera, A. D. Baddeley, *Cogn. Neuropsychol. 5,* 193 (1988).

16. A. D. Baddeley, R. Logie, S. Bressi, S. Della Sala, H. Spinnler, *Q. J. Exp. Psychol. 38A,* 603 (1986).

17. A. D. Baddeley, S. Bressi, S. Della Sala, R. Logie, H. Spinnler, *Brain,* in press.

18. L. R. Brooks, *Q. J. Exp. Psychol. 19,* 289 (1967); A. D. Baddeley, S. Grant, E. Wight, N. Thomson, in *Attention and performance,* P. M. A. Rabbitt and S. Dornic, Eds. (Academic Press, London, 1973), vol. 5, pp. 205-217 {see R. H. Logie and A. D. Baddeley in *Imagery: Current developments,* J. Richardson, D. Marks, P. Hampson, Eds. (Routledge and Kegan Paul, London, 1990), pp. 103-128 for a review}; A. D. Baddeley and K. Lieberman, in *Attention and performance,* R. S. Nickerson, Ed. (Erlbaum, Hillsdale, NJ, 1980), vol. 8, pp. 521-539.

19. M. J. Farah, *Psychol. Rev. 95,* 307 (1988).

20. _____, K. M. Hammond, D. N. Levine, R. Calvanio, *Cogn. Psychol. 20,* 439 (1988).

21. D. H. Holding, *The psychology of chess skill* (Erlbaum, Hillsdale, NJ, 1985); A. D. Baddeley, in *Attention: Selection, awareness, and control,* A. D. Baddeley and L. Weiskrantz, Eds. (Oxford Univ. Press, Oxford, in press).

22. T. W. Robbins *et al.,* in preparation.

23. R. Conrad, *Br. J. Psychol. 55,* 75 (1964); A. D. Baddeley, *Q. J. Exp. Psychol. 18,* 302 (1966).

24. H. A. Colle and A. Welsh, *J. Verb. Learn. Verb. Behav. 15,* 17 (1976); P. Salamé and A. D. Baddeley, *ibid. 21,* 150 (1982).

25. H. A. Colle, *ibid. 19,* 722 (1980); P. Salamé and A. D. Baddeley, *Ergonomics 30,* 1185 (1987).

26. A. D. Baddeley *et al., J. Verb. Learn. Verb. Behav. 14,* 575 (1975).

27. N. C. Ellis and R. A. Hennelley, *Br. J. Psychol. 71,* 43 (1980); M. Naveh-Benjamin and T. J. Ayres, *Q. J. Exp. Psychol. 38,* 739 (1986).

28. R. Nicolson, in *Intelligence and learning,* M. P. Friedman, J. P. Das, N. O'Connor, Eds. (Plenum, London, 1981), pp. 179-184; G. J. Hitch and M. S. Halliday, *Philos. Trans. R. Soc. London B 302,* 325 (1983); C. Hulme, N. Thomson, C. Muir, A. Lawrence, *J. Exp. Child Psychol. 38,* 241 (1984).

29. A. D. Baddeley, V. J. Lewis, G. Vallar, *Q. J. Exp. Psychol. 36,* 233 (1984); D. J. Murray, *J. Exp. Psychol. 78,* 679 (1968).

30. G. Vallar and A. D. Baddeley, *J. Verb. Learn. Verb. Behav. 23,* 151 (1984).

31. G. Vallar and T. Shallice, Eds., *Neuropsychological impairments of short-term memory* (Cambridge Univ. Press, Cambridge, 1990).
32. A. D. Baddeley, C. Papagno, G. Vallar, *J. Mem. Lang. 27,* 586 (1988).
33. C. Papagno, T. Valentine, A. D. Baddeley, *ibid.,* in press; C. Papagno and G. Vallar, *Q. J. Exp. Psychol. 44A,* 47 (1992).
34. S. Gathercole and A. D. Baddeley, *J. Mem. Lang. 29,* 336 (1990).
35. _____, *ibid. 28,* 200 (1989).
36. _____, *Br. J. Psychol. 81,* 439 (1990).
37. E. Service, *University of Helsinki general psychology monograph* (Univ. of Helsinki Press, Helsinki, Finland, 1989), no. B9.

QUESTIONS FOR FURTHER THOUGHT

1. What is working memory?

2. What are the main parts of working memory, and how do they work together?

3. How does the model of working memory differ from the modal (Atkinson–Shiffrin) model of memory?

4. Which part of the working-memory model affects learning the pronunciations of words in a foreign language?

5. How compelling do you find the neuropsychological evidence that supports Baddeley's model?

IMPLICIT MEMORY: HISTORY AND CURRENT STATUS

Daniel Schacter

INTRODUCTION

Although studies of memory can take and have taken many forms, almost all have asked participants to remember certain information, assuming that they would be aware of what they were doing at the time of test. Whether recalling a list of words, recognizing whether a particular digit was part of a memorized list, or deciding whether a canary is a bird, the individual is consciously aware that retrieval of information is, so to speak, the name of the game.

Yet, in many, if not most studies that ask subjects to retrieve information, they are not consciously aware that they are engaged in retrieval. For example, when people talk or write spontaneously, the words typically seem just "to come." They make no conscious effort to retrieve the words and may not even be aware that they are doing so until a word just does not come to mind. Then they may engage in a very deliberate retrieval process, which in turn may reveal the full importance of retrieval all along.

Implicit memory is retrieval without awareness of the retrieval process. It can be contrasted with *explicit memory*, which implies awareness of retrieval. Daniel Schacter, a leader in implicit memory research, reviews the field in this classic article on the topic. Schacter shows that implicit and explicit memory have different properties, and that the differences are probably rooted in differences in the functioning of the brain. For example, although explicit memory may be severely compromised in various forms of amnesia, the disorder may leave largely intact implicit memory. Studying both kinds of memory is therefore important for a full understanding of how the memory system operates.

Despite Schacter's youth, his work on implicit memory is among the most widely cited bodies of work in cognitive psychology. For one thing, Schacter has elaborated the construct more than have others. For another thing, Schacter has used ingenious techniques of several kinds, including cognitive and neuropsychological ones, to show the existence and importance of implicit memory. Finally, he has demonstrated the difficulty of constructing a complete theory of memory without taking implicit memory into account. For example, his work illustrates that amnesia typically results not from overall loss of memory, as had

Source: From Schacter, D. L. (1987). Implicit memory: History and current status. *Journal of Experimental Psychology, 13,* 501–518. Copyright © 1987 by the American Psychological Association. Reprinted with permission.

once been thought, but rather from loss of explicit rather than implicit memory. Schacter's interest in memory, it turns out, goes beyond academic motives. He is the owner of an impressive "memory art" collection that contains fine works of art dealing with topics in memory.

———

Memory for a recent event can be expressed explicitly, *as conscious recollection, or* implicitly, *as a facilitation of test performance without conscious recollection. A growing number of recent studies have been concerned with implicit memory and its relation to explicit memory. This article presents an historical survey of observations concerning implicit memory, reviews the findings of contemporary experimental research, and delineates the strengths and weaknesses of alternative theoretical accounts of implicit memory. It is argued that dissociations between implicit and explicit memory have been documented across numerous tasks and subject populations, represent an important challenge for research and theory, and should be viewed in the context of other dissociations between implicit and explicit expressions of knowledge that have been documented in recent cognitive and neuropsychological research.* ∎

Psychological studies of memory have traditionally relied on tests such as free recall, cued recall, and recognition. A prominent feature of these tests is that they make explicit reference to, and require conscious recollection of, a specific learning episode. During the past several years, however, increasing attention has been paid to experimental situations in which information that was encoded during a particular episode is subsequently expressed without conscious or deliberate recollection. Instead of being asked to try to remember recently presented information, subjects are simply required to perform a task, such as completing a graphemic fragment of a word, indicating a preference for one of several stimuli, or reading mirror-inverted script; memory is revealed by a facilitation or change in task performance that is attributable to information acquired during a previous study episode. Graf and Schacter (1985, 1987; Schacter & Graf, 1986a, 1986b) have labeled this type of memory *implicit memory*, and have used the term *explicit memory* to refer to conscious recollection of recently presented information, as expressed on traditional tests of free recall, cued recall, and recognition.

Recent cognitive and neuropsychological research has demonstrated a variety of striking dissociations between implicit and explicit memory and has shown that under certain conditions, implicit and explicit memory can be entirely independent of one another. These observations have raised fundamental questions concerning the nature and composition of memory, questions that will have to be addressed by any satisfactory theory of memory. The purposes of this article are to present an historical survey of observations concerning implicit memory, to review modern experimental studies and theoretical analyses, with particular emphasis on recent work in cognitive psychology and neuropsychology, and to suggest directions for future research.

Before the historical survey is initiated, two points regarding the terms *implicit* and *explicit memory* should be clarified. First, I use these terms in the manner suggested by Graf and Schacter (1985). Implicit memory is revealed when previous experiences facilitate performance on a task that does not require conscious or intentional recollection of those experiences; explicit memory is revealed when performance on a task requires conscious recollection of previous experiences. Note that these are *descriptive* concepts that are primarily concerned with a person's psychological experience at the time of retrieval. Accordingly, the concepts of implicit and explicit memory neither refer to, nor imply the existence of, two independent or separate memory-systems. The question of whether implicit and explicit memory depend on a single underlying system or on multiple underlying systems is not yet resolved, as will be discussed later in this article. Second, the term *implicit memory* resembles two more familiar terms from the psychological literature: *unconscious memory* (e.g., Freud & Breuer, 1966; Prince, 1914) and *unaware memory* or *memory without awareness* (e.g., Eriksen, 1960; Jacoby & Witherspoon, 1982). These two terms have been used to describe phenomena that will be referred to here with the term *implicit memory*. The main reason for adopting *implicit memory* in favor of either *unconscious memory* or *unaware memory* has to do with the conceptual ambiguity of the latter two terms. The terms *unconscious* and *unaware* have a large number of psychological meanings and implications (e.g., Bowers, 1984; Ellenberger, 1970; Eriksen, 1960), many of which do not apply to the phenomena of interest here. Although the term *implicit* is not entirely free of conceptual ambiguity, it is less saturated with multiple and possibly misleading meanings than are *unconscious* or *unaware*.

IMPLICIT MEMORY: AN HISTORICAL SURVEY

This section considers ideas and observations concerning implicit memory contributed by philosophers, psychologists, neurologists, psychiatrists, and others from the 17th century until the middle of the 20th century. Unless otherwise stated, these investigators did not actually use the term *implicit memory* in their writings. They did, however, describe and discuss situations in which memory for recent experiences was expressed in the absence of conscious recollection. I sometimes use the phrase *implicit memory phenomena* in reference to these observations. This is done purely for purposes of expositional clarity and should not be seen as an attempt to put present concepts in the minds of past observers.

PHILOSOPHICAL ANALYSES: DESCARTES, LEIBNIZ, AND MAINE DE BIRAN

It is widely recognized that both Plato and Aristotle commented extensively about the nature of memory, but both appear to have been concerned exclusively with explicit memory. During the Middle Ages, St. Augustine and St. Thomas Aquinas had a great deal to say about explicit retrieval and search processes, but I have not found any discussion of implicit memory in their writings.

The first clear reference to an implicit memory phenomenon appears to have been made by Descartes in his 1649 *The Passions of the Soul* (cited by Perry & Laurence, 1984), in which he observed that a frightening or aversive childhood experience may "remain imprinted on his [the child's] brain to the end of his life" without "any memory remaining of it afterwards" (Haldane & Ross, 1967, p. 391). Descartes did not, however, elaborate on the philosophical consequences of this phenomenon. In 1704, Gottfried Wilhelm Leibniz developed a systematic doctrine that both allowed for and made reference to implicit memory (Leibniz, 1916). He emphasized the importance of "insensible" or "unconscious" perceptions: ideas of which we are not consciously aware, but which do influence behavior. Leibniz explicitly claimed that people may have "remaining effects of former impressions without remembering them," and that ". . . often we have an extraordinary facility for conceiving certain things, because we formerly conceived them, without remembering them" (1916, p. 106). Although Leibniz's ideas concerning unconscious perceptions were later championed by several students and followers, they constituted a minority view during the 18th century, owing largely to the predominance of the British associationists. Locke, Hume, Mill, Brown, Hartley, and others discussed memory at considerable length, but their analysis was restricted entirely to the domain of explicit memory; they had virtually nothing to say about implicit memory. Darwin (1794, p. 12) distinguished between *involuntary* and *voluntary* recollection, but both of these concepts were used in reference to explicit memory phenomena.

The first philosopher after Leibniz to systematically discuss phenomena of implicit memory was a French philosopher known by the surname Maine de Biran. Though virtually unknown today, he published an important treatise in 1804 entitled *The Influence of Habit on the Faculty of Thinking* (Maine de Biran, 1929). Like others before him, Maine de Biran believed that the analysis of habit was central to an understanding of human thought and behavior. Unlike others, however, Maine de Biran elucidated a feature of habit that had not been discussed previously in philosophical or scientific analyses: After sufficient repetition, a habit can eventually be executed *automatically* and *unconsciously* without awareness of the act itself or of the previous episodes in which the habit was learned. Thus, he observed that repeated actions are eventually executed with "such promptitude and facility that we no longer perceive the voluntary action which directs them and we are absolutely unaware of the source that they have" (p. 73). The most striking feature of Maine de Biran's system, however, was his delineation and detailed discussion of three different types of memory: mechanical, sensitive, and representative. The first two types are driven by habit and are involved in the largely unconscious or implicit expression of repeated movements (mechanical) and feelings (sensitive); the third type (representative) is involved in conscious recollection of ideas and events (pp. 156–157). Thus, according to Maine de Biran,

> If signs [in Maine de Biran's system, a *sign* is a motor response code] are absolutely empty of ideas or separated from every representative effect, from whatever cause this isolation may arise, recall is only a simple repetition of movements. I shall call this faculty for it *mechanical* memory. When the . . . recall of the sign is accompanied or immediately followed by the clear appearance of a well circumscribed idea, I shall

attribute to it *representative memory.* If the sign expresses an affective modification, a feeling or even a fantastic image whatsoever, a vague, uncertain concept, which cannot be brought back to sense impressions . . . the recall of the sign . . . will belong to *sensitive memory.* (p. 156)

Maine de Biran's scheme represents the first clear articulation of what we might now call a *multiple memory system* interpretation of differences between implicit and explicit memory. Although it is alleged that Maine de Biran influenced the thinking of both Pierre Janet and Henri Bergson (Ellenberger, 1970), his ideas went almost entirely unrecognized outside of France. Most subsequent 19th-century philosophers did not systematically discuss the implicit expressions of memory that were so central to Maine de Biran's view. One exception was Johann Friedrich Herbart, who in 1816 introduced the notion that "suppressed ideas," which are unable to exceed the threshold of conscious awareness, can nevertheless influence conscious thinking (Herbart, 1896). The next systematic contributions were made by 19th-century scientists who approached the issue from the standpoint of biology and physiology.

MIDDLE 19TH CENTURY: UNCONSCIOUS CEREBRATION AND ORGANIC MEMORY

It is now widely recognized that various 19th-century thinkers were concerned with the general problem of unconscious mental processing (cf. Ellenberger, 1970; Perry & Laurence, 1984). One of the most prolific of them was the British physiologist William Carpenter, who invoked the term *unconscious cerebration* to refer to mental activity that occurs outside of awareness (Carpenter, 1874). To support this idea, Carpenter marshalled clinical and anecdotal observations which demonstrated that the effects of recent experiences could be expressed without conscious awareness of those experiences. For example, drawing on observations of automatic writing (writing that appears to occur involuntarily while a subject is in a hypnotic or similar state), he claimed that "It is a most remarkable confirmation of this view [unconscious cerebration], that ideas which have passed out of the *conscious* memory, sometimes express themselves in *involuntary muscular movements,* to the great surprise of the individuals executing them . . ." (1874, pp. 524–525). To Carpenter, the striking lack of autobiographical recognition or awareness that characterized implicit memory phenomena highlighted the critical role of such awareness in normal memory:

Without this recognition, we should live in the present alone; for the reproduction of past states of consciousness would affect us only like the succession of fantasies presented to us in the play of the imagination . . . I am satisfied that I am the person to whom such and such experiences happened yesterday or a month, or a year, or twenty years ago; because I am not only conscious at the moment of the ideas which represent those experiences, but because I recognize them as the revived representations of my past experiences. (1874, p. 455)

Carpenter's concept of unconscious cerebration and consequent interest in implicit memory derived from a more general attempt to relate physiology and psychology. A similar integrative effort was made by the Viennese physiologist Ewald Hering, who in 1870 introduced the idea of *organic* or *unconscious* memory (Hering, 1920). Hering criticized earlier writers for restricting their analyses to conscious or explicit memory: "The word 'memory' is often understood as though it meant nothing more than our faculty of intentionally reproducing ideas or series of ideas" (1920, p. 68). Hering argued that it is necessary to consider unconscious memory, which is involved in involuntary recall, the development of automatic and unconscious habitual actions, and even in the processes of ontogenetic development and heredity. Although this latter aspect of Hering's analysis clearly lies outside the domain of the present concerns, his psychological analyses of involuntary recall and the development of automaticity shared much in common with the earlier ideas of Maine de Biran. Following Hering's lead, a large number of psychologists, biologists, and others developed ideas concerning organic memory and its relation to what they referred to as conscious memory (see Schacter, 1982, chap. 7).

LATE 19TH AND EARLY 20TH CENTURY: SYSTEMATIC EMPIRICAL AND THEORETICAL DEVELOPMENTS

Toward the end of the 19th century, systematic empirical and theoretical analyses of implicit memory emerged in five different areas: "psychical" research, neurology, psychiatry, philosophy, and experimental psychology.

Psychical Research. Although modern practitioners might be reluctant to admit it, a good case can be made that 19th-century psychical researchers were the first to document implicit memory phenomena on the basis of controlled empirical observation. Two major "implicit memory tests" were used: crystal ball gazing and automatic writing. Both procedures were characterized by the main feature of an implicit memory test: When performing these tasks, subjects made no explicit reference to a specific past event; they either reported what they "saw" in the crystal or wrote whatever came to mind. Although the purpose of these procedures was to document phenomena such as telepathy and clairvoyance, several investigators reported that fragmentary representations of past experiences, devoid of any familiarity or autobiographical reference, frequently appeared during crystal gazing and automatic writing.

In an anonymously authored article in the *Journal of the Society for Psychical Research* (Miss X, 1889), it was reported that information that had been registered unconsciously (i.e., without attention) during the recent past often surfaced as an unfamiliar "vision" during crystal gazing. On the basis of this observation, the author questioned "spiritual" interpretations of crystal visions: "It is easy to see how visions of this kind, occurring in the age of superstition, almost irresistibly suggested the theory of spirit-visitation. The percipient, receiving information which he did not recognize as already in his own mind, would inevitably suppose it to be derived from some invisible and unknown source external to himself" (p. 513). In studies of automatic writing, several investigators described the emergence of knowledge acquired during past episodes which subjects were not aware that they possessed and that seemed foreign to their conscious personalities (Binet, 1890; Prince, 1914). On the basis of his own experiments with automatic writing, Barkworth (1891) concluded that "nothing is every really forgotten, though the bygone memories evoked by pencil, or crystal, may appear so new and strange that we fail to recognize them as ever having been included in our experience" (p. 29).

Neurology. In 1845, the British physician Robert Dunn described the case of a woman who became amnesic after a near drowning and a long period of unconsciousness. During her amnesic state, the woman learned how to make dresses, even though she apparently did not explicitly remember that she had made any dresses: "She applied herself closely to her new occupation and abandoned altogether the old one. Still she had no recollection from day to day what she had done, and every morning began something new unless her unfinished work was placed before her" (1845, p. 588). Dunn did not discuss the theoretical implications of his observations.

Perhaps the first investigator to document implicit memory phenomena in neurological cases of amnesia and to delineate their theoretical implications was Sergei Korsakoff (1889). In one of his two classic papers describing the amnesic syndrome that now bears his name, Korsakoff observed that ". . . although the patient was not aware that he preserved traces of impressions that he received, those traces however probably existed and had an influence in one way or another on the course of ideas, at least in unconscious intellectual activity" (1889, p. 512). Korsakoff provided several insightful observations to support this notion. For example, he described a patient whom he had given an electrical shock. Though this patient did not explicitly remember being given any shocks, when Korsakoff showed him a case that contained the shock apparatus, "he told me that I probably came to electrify him, and meanwhile I knew well that he had only learned to know that machine during his illness" (p. 512). Korsakoff went on to argue that amnesic patients retained "weak" memory traces that could affect behavior unconsciously, but were not "strong" enough to enter conscious memory. He emphasized that his observations had important implications for psychologists:

> We notice that a whole series of traces which could in no way be restored to consciousness, neither actively nor passively, continue to exist in unconscious life, continue to direct the course of ideas of the patients, suggesting to him some or other inferences and decisions. That seems to me to be one of the most interesting peculiarities of the disturbance about which we are speaking. (p. 518)

Over 20 years later, Claparède (1911/1951) reported observations that were similar to Korsakoff's although they are somewhat better known today. Claparède described the now famous example of an amnesic woman who refused to shake hands with him after he pricked her with a pin, even though she did not explicitly remember that Claparède had done so. Claparède interpreted this implicit expression of memory in terms of a disconnection between the ego and the memory trace. At about the same time, Schneider (1912, cited in Parkin, 1982) reported experiments in which he demonstrated that amnesic patients required progressively less information across learning trials to identify fragmented pictures, even though patients did not explicitly remember having seen the pictures before.

Psychiatry. Seminal observations concerning implicit memory were reported in the late 1880s and early 1890s by Pierre Janet and by Sigmund Freud, partly in collaboration with Josef Breuer. For both Janet and Freud, the critical phenomena were observed in patients suffering hysterical amnesia as a result of emotional trauma. Although these patients could not explicitly remember the traumatic events, their memories of them were expressed indirectly (implicitly) in various ways. Janet (1893), for example, described a case in which a woman became amnesic after being mistakenly informed by a man who appeared suddenly in her doorway that her husband had died. Even though she subsequently could not consciously remember this incident, she "froze with terror" whenever she passed the door that the man had entered. In a later article, Janet (1904) described a woman who had become amnesic following the death of her mother. Though she could not consciously remember any of the events surrounding her mother's death, she experienced "hallucinations" that preserved the contents of those events. After describing numerous other cases of implicit memory in hysteric patients, Janet concluded that hysterical amnesia consists of two key factors: "1. the inability of the subject to evoke memories consciously and voluntarily, and 2. the automatic, compelling, and untimely activation of these same memories" (1904, p. 24). He theorized that hysteria was attributable to a pathological process of dissociation that interfered with the ability to synthesize memories into the "personal consciousness."

Freud's observations on hysteria were similar to Janet's insofar as he emphasized that traumatic memories, inaccessible to consciousness, were expressed unconsciously by the patient as hysterical symptoms (see Freud & Breuer, 1966, for relevant cases). Although Freud later changed this view (Ellenberger, 1970), he never abandoned the idea that unconscious memories exert powerful influences on behavior.

Both Janet and Freud emphasized the role of unconscious or implicit memory in psychopathology. The American psychiatrist Morton Prince clearly delineated the importance of implicit memory for normal cognitive function. In *The Unconscious* (1914), Prince drew together numerous observations of implicit memory from work with hysterical patients, hypnosis, dreams, and automatic writing, in which ". . . memories of the forgotten experiences [are expressed] without awareness therefore on the part of the personal consciousness" (p. 13). Noting that ". . . memories may be made to reveal themselves, without inducing recollection, at the very moment when the subject cannot voluntarily recall them" (p. 63), Prince concluded that ". . . a conscious experience that has passed out of mind may not only recur again as conscious memory, but may recur subconsciously below the threshold of awareness" (p. 8). These observations, Prince argued, demonstrate that experiences that are not available to conscious or voluntary recall nevertheless influence cognition and behavior in everyday life:

> In normal life ideas of buried experiences of which we have no recollection intrude themselves from time to time and shape our judgments and the current of our thoughts without our realizing what has determined our mental processes. We have forgotten the source of our judgments, but this forgetfulness does not affect the mechanism of the process. (p. 68)

Philosophy. The major philosophical contribution to the analysis of implicit memory was made by Henri Bergson. In *Matter and Memory* (1911), he argued that *"The past survives under two distinct forms: first, in motor mechanisms; secondly, in independent recollections"* (p. 87). The first form of memory involves gradual learning of habits and skills and does not entail explicit reference to any specific past events; a learned habit ". . . bears upon it no mark which betrays its origin and classes it in the past; it is part of my present . . ." (p. 91). Bergson's second form of memory, recollection, entails explicit remembering of "memory-images" that represent specific events from one's past. Although this view is clearly reminiscent of Maine de Biran, Bergson did not actually discuss or even reference Maine de Biran's views anywhere in *Matter and Memory.*

Experimental Psychology. Experimental psychologists paid relatively little attention to implicit memory phenomena in the late 19th and early 20th centuries. Even though there was a large and thriving field in this post-Ebbinghausian era (cf. Schacter, 1982, chap. 8), most practitioners did not distinguish between explicit and implicit memory. Several exceptions, however, can be identified. Ebbinghaus (1885) himself acknowledged that not all effects of memory are expressed in conscious awareness (1885, p. 2). He also made a relevant empirical contribution, noting that savings was observed over a 24-hr retention interval for items that he did not consciously remember having studied before (pp. 58–59; see Slamecka, 1985a, 1985b; Tulving, 1985b). This intriguing observation was not systematically followed up by Ebbinghaus or others. Ebbinghaus' savings paradigm, in which memory is tested by relearning previously studied lists, can be viewed more generally as an implicit memory test: Explicit recollection of a prior episode or list is not called for during relearning (Slamecka, 1985b). Indeed, Ebbinghaus noted that one advantage of the savings method was that it could provide evidence for the existence in memory of information that could not be recollected consciously (1885, p. 8). Of course, numerous subsequent investigators used the savings method to analyze learning and transfer of training. Although there is a sense in which "the entire literature on transfer of training may be perceived as the study of implicit memory" (Slamecka, 1985b, p. 499), researchers did not view it as such and did not elaborate any distinctions like the one between implicit and explicit memory.

After Ebbinghaus, three lines of experimental investigation were concerned with certain aspects of implicit memory. First, Thorndike conducted a large number of experiments that, he claimed, demonstrated that subjects could learn various rules without conscious awareness of them or explicit memory for them (Thorndike & Rock, 1934; see Irwin, Kauffman, Prior, & Weaver, 1934, for methodological criticisms). Second, Poetzl reported in 1917 that unreported features of subliminally exposed pictures appeared in subjects' subsequent imagery and dreams, even though they did not remember these features and were allegedly unaware of them at the time of stimulus exposure (see Poetzl, 1960). Poetzl's experiments, however, were characterized by serious methodological deficiencies (Dixon, 1981; Erdelyi, 1970). Third, studies of hypnotic phenomena by Clark Hull (1933) and his students provided numerous demonstrations of implicit memory for skills, conditioned responses, and facts acquired during hypnosis. Hull's description of the quality of recall by hypnotic subjects resembled Claparède's and Korsakoff's earlier observations of organic amnesia: "In such cases they stated that the name seemed to come from 'nowhere' and was not accompanied by any recollection that the character or syllable had ever been encountered before" (1933, p. 134).

One further contribution from experimental psychology ought to be noted. In *Outline of Psychology* (1924), William McDougall became the first investigator to use the terms *implicit* and *explicit* with reference to the different ways in which memory can be expressed. He distinguished between explicit recognition, which involves conscious recollection of a past event, and implicit recognition, which involves a change in behavior that is attributable to a recent event yet contains no conscious recollection of it or explicit reference to it (1924, pp. 308–309).

SUMMARY OF HISTORICAL SURVEY

Four general points can be made regarding the historical survey. First, observations of implicit memory were reported across a broad range of tasks, subjects, and conditions. Perhaps the richest sources of implicit memory phenomena were the clinical observations made by Claparède, Freud, Janet, Korsakoff, Prince, and others. With the exception of Prince, these clinicians did not set out with the specific aim of distinguishing between forms of memory. Nevertheless, they were insightful observers who recognized clearly that the phenomena they described had important implications for theories of normal and abnormal mental function. Indeed, there were relatively few investigators who explicitly raised the issue of whether different forms of memory could be distinguished and then went on to report original empirical observations; Ebbinghaus and Prince should be counted prominently among them. A second, related point is that most empirical observations either were anecdotal, were made under relatively uncontrolled clinical conditions, or were reported in experiments that lacked methodological rigor. Thus, even though the early observers reported phenomena that are broadly similar to those of interest today, methodological inadequacies limit the degree to which they bear directly on contemporary theoretical concerns. Third, there were only a few attempts to develop theoretical accounts of the dissociations that had been observed. The most popular idea was that implicit memory phenomena were produced by memory traces that are too "weak" to exceed the threshold of strength or activation needed for explicit memory (Herbart, 1896; Leibniz, 1916; Korsakoff, 1889; Prince, 1914). As will be shown later, recent experimental work has provided grounds for rejecting this view. However, several other ideas were advanced, including the multiple-memories view of Maine de Biran and Bergson, and the notion of a dissociation between memory traces and the "self" articulated by Claparède and Janet. Fourth, the various investigators who were concerned with implicit memory phenomena exhibited little or no knowledge of each other's work. This circumstance is perhaps not surprising, because observations of implicit memory were made in disparate fields of study.

MODERN RESEARCH ON IMPLICIT MEMORY

Let us now consider research concerning implicit memory from the 1950s to the present. Data from five different though partly overlapping research areas will first be reviewed: savings during relearning, effects of subliminally encoded stimuli, learning and conditioning without awareness, repetition priming, and preserved learning in amnesic patients. This review is followed by a consideration of contemporary theoretical approaches to implicit memory.

SAVINGS DURING RELEARNING

As noted earlier, it is possible to view the phenomenon of savings during relearning as an index of implicit memory, in the sense that relearning a previously studied list does not require explicit reference to a prior learning episode, although the influence of the prior episode is revealed by savings (cf. Slamecka, 1985b). However, little of the voluminous research on savings has addressed the question of whether subjects do indeed rely on explicit memory for prior learning episodes when relearning a list, so it is not entirely clear what savings studies tell us about implicit memory. The most directly pertinent evidence has been provided by Nelson (1978), who has shown savings for items that are neither recalled nor recognized, which thereby suggests that savings can occur in an entirely implicit manner.

EFFECTS OF SUBLIMINALLY ENCODED STIMULI

The controversy concerning subliminal perception is well known to experimental psychologists (Dixon, 1971). Although early experiments purporting to demonstrate subliminal perception were severely criticized (Eriksen, 1960), recent studies using a variety of new experimental techniques have supplied more convincing evidence that stimuli that are not represented in subjective awareness (Cheesman & Merikle, 1986) are nevertheless processed to high levels by the perceptual system (e.g., Cheesman & Merikle, 1986; Dixon, 1981; Fowler, Wolford, Slade, & Tassinary, 1981; Marcel, 1983; see Holender, 1986, for a methodological critique). More relevant to the present concerns, several studies have purported to show that stimuli that are not consciously perceived, and hence cannot be explicitly remembered, influence subsequent behavior and performance on tasks that do not require conscious recollection of the subliminal stimulus, such as free association (Haber & Erdelyi, 1967; Shevrin & Fritzler, 1968) and imaginative story and fantasy productions (Giddan, 1967; Pine, 1960). However, questions regarding interpretation of these results have been raised (Dixon, 1981; Erdelyi, 1970).

The foregoing experiments did not systematically examine the relation between implicit and explicit memory for subliminally exposed stimuli. However, recent studies have demonstrated implicit memory for subliminal or briefly exposed stimuli under conditions in which subjects exhibit little or no explicit memory. Kunst-Wilson and Zajonc (1980) showed subjects geometric shapes at exposure durations that they contended were too brief (1 msec) to permit conscious perception. Explicit memory for the shapes, as indexed by forced-choice recognition performance, was at chance. However, subjects demonstrated implicit memory by showing a reliable preference for the previously exposed shapes on a test in which they rated which of two shapes—one old, one new—they liked better. Similar results have been reported by Seamon, Brody, and Kauff (1983) and Wilson (1979). Mandler, Nakamura, and Van Zandt (in press) showed that brief stimulus exposures that yield chance levels of recognition memory can influence nonaffective stimulus judgments (i.e., brightness).

Bargh and Pietromonaco (1982) examined the effects of subliminal exposures to "hostile" words (e.g., unkind, thoughtless) on a subsequent impression formation task. Subjects who had been given subliminal exposures to hostile words later rated a target person more negatively than did those who had not received such prior exposure, even though explicit recognition of the hostile words was at the chance level. Bargh, Bond, Lombardi, and Tota (1986) observed similar implicit effects following subliminal exposure to various other types of words. Lewicki (1985) found that after subliminal exposure to adjective-noun pairs (e.g., *old–tree*) subjects tended to choose the previously exposed adjective in response to questions concerning how they "felt" about the noun (e.g., *Is a tree big or old?*).

A recent study by Eich (1984) that used a different method to attenuate conscious perception of target materials yielded data consistent with the foregoing results. Eich used an auditory divided attention task in which homophones were presented on the unattended channel together with words intended to bias the low frequency interpretation of the homophone (e.g., *taxi–FARE*). Subjects subsequently showed no explicit memory for the homophones on a *yes/no* recognition test. However, when required to spell the target words, subjects provided the low frequency spelling of the homophones more often than in baseline conditions, thereby demonstrating implicit memory for the unattended information.

LEARNING AND CONDITIONING WITHOUT AWARENESS

In learning-without-awareness studies, subjects allegedly learn rules or contingencies without awareness of learning them and, hence, without explicit memory for them (cf. Greenspoon, 1955; Thorndike & Rock, 1934). The phenomenon was studied extensively during the 1950s in multitrial learning experiments in which subjects were reinforced for making specific responses or types of responses. Several investigators reported that subjects who were unaware of the reinforcement-response contingency provided the reinforced response with increasing frequency across trials, but others pointed to the lack of appropriate methods for determining subjects' awareness of the reinforcement-response contingency (for review, see Eriksen, 1960). Studies that used more rigorous methods for assessing awareness reported some positive evidence of learning without awareness (Giddan & Eriksen, 1959; Krieckhaus & Eriksen, 1960), as did research in which the reinforcement-response contingency was thoroughly disguised (Rosenfeld & Baer, 1969; see also Nisbett & Wilson, 1977). However, many negative observations were also reported (Brewer, 1974).

In related research, several investigators presented evidence that subjects could acquire various types of classically conditioned responses without awareness of conditioning contingencies (cf. Adams, 1957; Lacey & Smith, 1954), but assessment of awareness was often insufficient (Brewer, 1974). Along these same lines, research concerning the phenomenon of subception (Lazarus & McCleary, 1951) indicated that an experimentally acquired conditioned response, revealed by the galvanic skin response to nonsense syllables that had been accompanied by shock, could be subsequently elicited by brief exposures to the nonsense syllables, even though subjects did not detect the presence of the syllables. Although some questions and criticisms were raised about interpretations of the subception phenomenon, the finding that a conditioned response could sometimes be elicited by an unreported stimulus was not challenged (Eriksen, 1960, pp. 287–288).

Recent evidence concerning rule or contingency learning without awareness has been reported in a series of experiments by Reber and his colleagues concerning a phenomenon that they call *implicit learning* (e.g., Reber, 1976; Reber, Allen, & Regan, 1985; see also Brooks, 1978; Gordon & Holyoak, 1983; McAndrews & Moscovitch, 1985). In these studies, subjects were presented with letter strings that were organized according to various rules of a synthetic grammar. Reber and his associates reported that subjects learned to identify grammatically correct strings even when they were not consciously or explicitly aware of the appropriate rules (for critique and discussion, see Dulany, Carlson, & Dewey, 1984, 1985; Reber et al., 1985). Using a somewhat different procedure, Lewicki (1986) showed that contingencies between different features of stimulus information influenced latencies to respond to questions regarding the contingent features, even though none of the subjects could explicitly state the nature of the contingency.

REPETITION PRIMING EFFECTS

Most of the recent work in cognitive psychology that can be characterized as implicit memory research has been concerned with the phenomenon of direct or repetition priming (cf. Cofer, 1967): facilitation in the processing of a stimulus as a function of a recent encounter with the same stimulus. Repetition priming has been observed on a variety of tests that do not make explicit reference to a prior study episode. The tests most commonly used in priming research are *lexical decision, word identification,* and *word stem* or *fragment completion.* On the lexical decision test (e.g., Forbach, Stanners, & Hochhaus, 1974; Scarborough, Gerard, & Cortese, 1979), subjects are required to state whether or not a particular letter string constitutes a legal word; priming is reflected by a decreased latency in the making of a lexical decision on the second presentation of a letter string relative to the first. On the word identification test (also referred to as *tachistoscopic identification* or *perceptual identification;* e.g., Feustel, Shiffrin, & Salasoo, 1983; Jacoby & Dallas, 1981; Neisser, 1954), subjects are given a brief exposure (e.g., 30 msec) to a stimulus and then attempt to identify it. Priming on this task is indicated by an increase in the accuracy of identifying recently exposed items relative to new items or by a decrease in the amount of exposure time necessary to identify recently exposed items. On word completion tests (e.g., Graf, Mandler, & Haden, 1982; Tulving, Schacter, & Stark, 1982; Warrington & Weiskrantz, 1974), subjects are either given a word *stem* (e.g., tab_____ for table) or *fragment* (e.g., __ss__ss__ __ for assassin) and are instructed to complete it with the first appropriate word that comes to mind. Here, priming is reflected by an enhanced tendency to complete test stems or fragments with words exposed on a prior study list. Other priming tests include reading of transformed script (Kolers, 1975, 1976; Masson, 1984), face identification (Bruce & Valentine, 1985; Young, McWeeny, Hay, & Ellis, 1986), and free association (Storms, 1958; Williamsen, Johnson, & Eriksen, 1965).

The current interest in repetition priming derives from two distinct and at times independent areas of investigation. The first area grew out of research on word recognition and lexical organization. The general purpose of these studies was to use the pattern of priming effects observed on tasks such as word identification and lexical decision as a basis for making inferences about the nature of lexical access and representation (cf. Morton, 1979; Murrell & Morton, 1974; Scarborough et al., 1979). This line of research has yielded a number of useful findings about performance on implicit memory tests. Several investigators who attempted to distinguish between modality-specific and modality-nonspecific components of lexical organization by examining the effect of auditory–visual modality shifts on the magnitude of repetition priming reported little or no priming of tachistosopic identification (e.g., Kirsner & Smith, 1974; Kirsner, Milech, & Standen, 1983) and lexical decision performance (e.g., Kirsner et al., 1983; Scarborough et al., 1979) following an auditory study presentation. A number of studies have compared repetition priming of real words and nonwords, and have generally found that nonwords show either no priming or smaller amounts of priming than real words (Forbach et al., 1974; Forster & Davis, 1984; Kirsner & Smith, 1974; Scarborough, Cortese, & Scarborough, 1977), although robust priming of nonwords has been observed under some experimental conditions (Feustel et al., 1983; Salasoo, Shiffrin, & Feustel, 1985).

Several studies have demonstrated that priming of word identification performance occurs for morphologically similar words (e.g., exposure to *seen* facilitates identification of *sees;* Murrell & Morton, 1974), but not for visually similar words (*seen* does not facilitate *seed;* Murrell & Morton, 1974; see also Osgood & Hoosain, 1974) or phonologically similar words (*frays* does not facilitate *phrase;* Neisser, 1954). In an important study, Winnick and Daniel (1970) examined word identification performance following three types of study conditions: reading a familiar word from a visual presentation of it, generation of the word from a picture of it, or generation of the word from its definition. They observed significant priming on the word identification task following visual presentation but observed no priming in either of the generation conditions. By contrast, they found that free recall of words in both generation conditions was considerably higher than in the read condition. Although Winnick and Daniel did not set out to compare implicit and explicit memory, their results revealed a sharp dissociation between these two forms of memory (for similar results, see Jacoby, 1983b).

The second line of investigation concerned with priming effects was initiated in the context of research on episodic memory. It was stimulated largely by Warrington and Weiskrantz's (1968, 1974) work on amneisa, which will be reviewed in the next section. Their experiments demonstrated that amnesic patients showed excellent retention when required to complete three-letter stems of recently presented words, despite their inability to remember the prior occurrence of the words on a *yes/no* recognition test. Several investigators examined whether similar dissociations could be produced in normal subjects by manipulation of appropriate experimental variables (e.g., Graf et al., 1982; Jacoby & Dallas, 1981; Tulving et al., 1982), and thereby initiated systematic comparison of performance on implicit and explicit memory tests. Data generated by this line of investigation indicate that repetition priming effects on implicit memory tests can be experimentally dissociated from explicit recall and recognition in a number of ways.

First, several studies have demonstrated that variations in level or type of study processing have differential effects on priming and remembering, in conformity with the finding first reported by Winnick and Daniel (1970). For instance, Jacoby and Dallas

(1981) showed subjects a list of familiar words and had them perform a study task that required elaborative processing (e.g., answering questions about the meaning of target words) or did not require elaborative processing (e.g., deciding whether or not a word contains a particular letter). Memory for the words was subsequently assessed with *yes/no* recognition and word identification tests. As expected on the basis of many previous experiments (cf. Craik & Tulving, 1975), explicit memory was influenced by type of study processing: Recognition performance was higher following elaborative study tasks than nonelaborative study tasks. Implicit memory, however, was unaffected by the study task manipulation; priming effects on word identification performance were about the same following the elaborative and nonelaborative processing tasks. Graf et al. (1982) reported a similar pattern of results by using free recall as an index of explicit memory and stem completion as an index of implicit memory. More recently, Graf and Mandler (1984) found dissociable effects of a study-task manipulation on implicit and explicit memory when test cues were identical (i.e., three-letter word stems) and only instructions were varied. When subjects were told to use the stems to try to remember study-list words (explicit memory instructions), more items were recalled following elaborative study processing than following nonelaborative study processing. However, when subjects were instructed to write down the first word that came to mind in response to a test stem (implicit memory instructions), type of study task did not affect the amount of priming observed. Schacter and McGlynn (1987) assessed implicit memory for common idioms (e.g., SOUR–GRAPES) with a free-association test (e.g., SOUR–?), in which subjects wrote down the first word that came to mind, and assessed explicit memory with a cued-recall test in which the same cue was provided and subjects were instructed to try to remember the appropriate study-list target. Implicit memory was invariant across several elaborative and nonelaborative study tasks that significantly influenced explicit memory.

   A second type of dissociation between implicit and explicit memory involves the effect of study-test changes in modality of presentation and other types of surface information. As was noted earlier, priming effects on lexical decision and word identification tests are significantly reduced by study-test modality shifts (Clarke & Morton, 1983; Kirsner et al., 1983; Kirsner & Smith, 1974). Jacoby and Dallas (1981) compared the effects of modality shifts on implicit (word identification) and explicit (*yes/no* recognition) tasks. They found that changing modality of presentation from study (auditory) to test (visual) severely attenuated priming effects on word identification performance but had little or no effect on recognition performance. Graf, Shimamura, and Squire (1985) reported that priming effects on the stem-completion task were reduced by a study-test modality shift, whereas cued-recall performance was not significantly influenced by this manipulation, and Roediger and Blaxton (1987) found that priming of word-fragment completion performance was attenuated by modality shifts even though free-recall and recognition performance were largely unaffected. Along the same lines, several studies have shown that within the visual modality, priming effects on lexical decision, fragment completion, and reading tasks are highly sensitive to study-test changes of various types of surface information (Kolers, 1975, 1976; Roediger & Blaxton, 1987; Roediger & Weldon, 1987; Scarborough et al., 1979), whereas recall and recognition are either unaffected or slightly affected by such changes.

A third kind of evidence for implicit/explicit dissociations comes from studies that have manipulated retention interval. On both word-fragment completion (Komatsu & Ohta, 1984; Tulving et al., 1982) and word identification tests (Jacoby & Dallas, 1981), priming effects persist with little change across delays of days and weeks, whereas recognition memory declines across the same delays. In other situations, however, priming of word-stem completion (Graf & Mandler, 1984; Graf et al., 1984; Shimamura & Squire, 1984) and lexical decision (Forster & Davis, 1984) has proved to be a relatively transient phenomenon, decaying across delays of minutes and hours over which explicit remembering persists. Fourth, recent studies indicate that manipulations of retroactive and proactive interference that significantly impair explicit recall and recognition do not influence priming effects on either word-stem completion (Graf & Schacter, 1987) or word-fragment completion (Sloman, Hayman, Ohta, & Tulving, in press). A fifth and final type of evidence for dissociation between priming and remembering is the finding of statistical independence between performance on recognition tests and tests of word-fragment completion (Tulving et al., 1982), word-stem completion (Graf & Schacter, 1985), homophone spelling (Eich, 1984; Jacoby & Witherspoon, 1982), prototype identification (Metcalfe & Fisher, 1986), and reading of mirror inverted script (Kolers, 1976). In these experiments, successful performance on an implicit memory test was uncorrelated with success or failure on an explicit memory test.

Taken together, the foregoing studies provide impressive evidence that priming effects on implicit memory tests differ substantially from explicit recall and recognition. Other studies, however, have revealed several similarities between priming and remembering. First, under certain conditions manipulations of retention interval have parallel effects on priming effects and explicit memory (Jacoby, 1983a; Schacter & Graf, 1986a; Sloman et al., in press). Second, Jacoby (1983a) has shown that manipulating list context at the time of test, which is known to affect recognition memory, also affects performance on the word identification task: Identification performance was higher when 90% of tested words came from a previously studied list than when only 10% did. Third, both implicit and explicit memory are influenced by newly acquired associations between unrelated word pairs. On a variety of implicit memory tests, including word-stem completion (Graf & Schacter, 1985, 1987; Schacter & Graf, 1986a, 1986b), lexical decision (McKoon & Ratcliff, 1979, 1986), and reading of degraded word pairs (Moscovitch, Winocur, & McLachlan, 1986), more priming is observed when a target word is tested in the context of its study-list cue than when it is tested alone or in the presence of some other cue. Fourth, this phenomenon of *implicit memory for new associations* (cf. Graf & Schacter, 1985) resembles explicit remembering of new associations insofar as it depends on some degree of elaborative processing at the time of study. For example, Schacter and Graf observed associative effects on word completion performance after subjects had performed study tasks that required them to elaborate semantic links between two unrelated words, such as generating sentences or reading meaningful sentences (e.g., *The injured* OFFICER *smelled the* FLOWER). When subjects engaged in study tasks that prevented elaboration of semantic relations, such as comparing the number of vowels and consonants in the target words or reading anomalous sentences (e.g., *The dusky* COW *multiplied the* EMPLOYER), implicit memory for new associations was not observed. Schacter and

McGlynn (1987), using free-association and cued-recall tests, also found that both implicit and explicit memory for newly acquired associations depends on elaborative study processing. A fifth type of evidence showing a relation between implicit and explicit memory was reported by Johnston, Dark, & Jacoby (1985). They demonstrated that processes subserving implicit memory can affect performance on an explicit memory task: Recently studied words that were identified quickly on a word identification test were more likely to be given a recognition judgment of "old" than were more slowly identified words. These similarities between implicit and explicit memory have a number of implications that will be discussed later when alternative theoretical accounts of implicit memory are compared.

IMPLICIT MEMORY IN AMNESIA

The amnesic syndrome, which is produced by lesions to the medial temporal and diencephalic regions of the brain (e.g., Moscovitch, 1982; Rozin, 1976; Squire, 1986; Weiskrantz, 1985), is characterized by normal perceptual, linguistic, and intellectual functioning together with an inability to remember explicitly recent events and new information. Amnesic patients are seriously impaired on standard tests of explicit recall and recognition, and they perform disastrously in real-life situations that require explicit remembering, such as recollecting actions and events during a round of golf (Schacter, 1983). Beginning with the previously discussed clinical observations of Korsakoff (1889) and Claparède (1911/1951), instances of implicit memory by amnesic patients have been documented widely. Most modern studies of implicit memory in amnesia can be classified into two broad categories: skill learning or repetition priming.

Research on skill learning in amnesia was initiated by Milner and Corkin and their colleagues in the 1960s. They demonstrated that the profoundly amnesic patient H. M. could acquire motor skills such as pursuit rotor and mirror tracing, even though he did not remember explicitly that he had previously performed the task (Milner, 1962; Milner, Corkin, & Teuber, 1968). Robust learning of motor skills has been observed in various other amnesic patients (e.g., Butters, 1987; Eslinger & Damasio, 1986; Starr & Phillips, 1970). Amnesic patients have also exhibited normal or near-normal learning of perceptual and cognitive skills, including reading of mirror-inverted script (Cohen & Squire, 1980; Moscovitch, 1982), puzzle solving (Brooks & Baddeley, 1976), rule learning (Kinsbourne & Wood, 1975), and serial pattern learning (Nissen & Bullemer, 1987) , despite their failure to remember explicitly that they had previously performed the skills. Similar dissociations have been observed in drug-induced amnesia (Nissen, Knopman, & Schacter, in press) and multiple-personality amnesia (Nissen, Ross, Willingham, Mackenzie, & Schacter, in press).

The second major area of research on implicit memory in amnesia, concerned with repetition priming effects, was initiated by the important series of experiments conducted by Warrington and Weiskrantz (1968, 1970, 1974, 1978). They found that amnesic patients could show normal retention of a list of familiar words when tested with word-stem or fragment cues, whereas these same patients were profoundly impaired on free-recall and recognition tests. Indeed, Warrington and Weiskrantz (1968) noted that patients often did not remember that they had been shown any study-list items and treated the fragment test as a kind of "guessing game." In subsequent research using the fragment cuing procedure, amnesic patients' performance was sometimes impaired with respect to that of control subjects (e.g., Squire, Wetzel, & Slater, 1978).

It is now clear that whether or not amnesic patients show normal retention when tested with word fragments and various other cues depends critically on the implicit/explicit nature of the test. For example, Graf et al., (1984) demonstrated that when subjects were given explicit memory instructions—that is, they were told to use word stems as cues for *remembering* previously studied words—amnesics were impaired with respect to controls. By contrast, when subjects were given implicit memory instructions—that is, they were told to complete the stems with the first word that comes to mind—amnesics and controls showed comparable amounts of priming (see also Graf et al., 1985). In an early and often overlooked study, Gardner, Boller, Moreines, and Butters (1973) presented Korsakoff's syndrome amnesics and controls with a categorized word list. When subjects were subsequently given category cues and asked to respond with the first category member that came to mind, both amnesics and controls showed equivalent amounts of priming. When asked to remember list items in response to category cues, amnesics were impaired with respect to controls (see also Graf et al., 1985; see Kihlstrom, 1980, for priming of category production performance in hypnotic amnesia). Schacter (1985) found that amnesic patients showed normal priming effects after studying a list of common idioms (e.g., SOUR–GRAPES) and then writing down the first word that came to mind on a free-association test (e.g., SOUR–?). Amnesics were impaired, however, when instructed to try to use the same cues to remember study-list targets. Shimamura and Squire (1984) obtained a similar pattern of results with highly related paired associates (e.g., TABLE–CHAIR). On the basis of these studies, it seems reasonable to conclude that normal retention of a list of familiar items by amnesic patients occurs only when implicit tests are used. Consistent with this observation, amnesic patients have shown normal priming effects on various other implicit memory tests, including lexical decision (Moscovitch, 1982), perceptual identification (Cermak, Talbot, Chandler, & Wolbarst, 1985), and homophone spelling (Jacoby & Witherspoon, 1982; for more extensive review, see Schacter & Graf, 1986b; Shimamura, 1986).

In most of the priming experiments discussed thus far, study materials consisted of items with integrated or unitized preexisting memory representations, such as common words, linguistic idioms, or highly related paired associates. Recently, several investigators have examined whether amnesic patients show normal priming or implicit memory for novel information that does not have any preexisting representation as a unit in memory, such as nonwords or unrelated paired associates. The results thus far have been mixed. Cermak et al. (1985) found that amnesic patients do not show priming of nonwords on a perceptual identification task, and Diamond and Rozin (1984) obtained similar results when implicit memory was tested with three-letter stems. Using a word completion test, Graf and Schacter (1985) and Schacter and Graf (1986b) found that some amnesic patients—those with relatively mild memory disorders—showed normal implicit memory for a newly acquired association between unrelated words, whereas severely amnesic patients did not show implicit memory for new associations. Moscovitch et al. (1986) assessed implicit memory with a task that involved reading degraded pairs of unrelated words, and observed normal implicit memory for new associations in patients with severe memory disorders. McAndrews, Glisky, and Schacter (in press) investigated implicit memory for new information by presenting subjects with novel, difficult-to-comprehend sentences (e.g., *The haystack was important because the cloth ripped.*), and requiring them to generate cues that rendered the sentences comprehensible (e.g., *parachute*). They found that severely amnesic patients' ability to generate the correct cues was facilitated substantially by a single prior exposure to the cue-sentence pair, despite their complete lack of explicit memory for the sentences and cues.

The foregoing studies indicate that amnesic patients can show priming effects for newly acquired information, but they also suggest that such effects depend on the type of implicit memory test that is used and, in some instances, on the severity of amnesia. Another important issue concerning priming in amnesic patients concerns the duration of the phenomenon. Several investigators have reported that priming of word-completion performance in amnesic patients is a relatively transient phenomenon, lasting only a few hours (Diamond & Rozin, 1984; Graf et al., 1984; Rozin, 1976; Squire, Shimamura, & Graf, in press). By contrast, McAndrews et al. (in press) found that severely amnesic patients showed robust priming on their sentence puzzle task after a 1-week retention interval. These observations suggest that the duration of priming in amnesic patients may depend on the way that implicit memory is assessed and the nature of the target information.

In addition to skill learning and repetition priming phenomena, amnesic patients have also exhibited dissociations between implicit and explicit memory in various other situations. Schacter, Harbluk, and McLachlan (1984) demonstrated that amnesic patients could learn some fictitious information about people (e.g., *Bob Hope's father was a fireman*), but could not remember explicitly that they had just been told the information (see also Schacter & Tulving, 1982; Shimamura & Squire, 1987). Similarly, Luria (1976) observed that an amnesic patient produced bits and pieces of recently presented stories, even though he did not remember being told any stories. Glisky, Schacter, and Tulving (1986) showed that a densely amnesic patient could learn to program a microcomputer despite the patient's persistent failure to remember explicitly that he had ever worked on a microcomputer. Johnson, Kim, and Risse (1985) found that amnesics acquired preferences for previously exposed melodies, Crovitz, Harvey, and McClanahan (1979) demonstrated that amnesics could spot a hidden figure more quickly after a single exposure to it, and Weiskrantz and Warrington (1979) reported evidence of classical conditioning in amnesic patients—in all cases, with little or no explicit recollection of the experimental materials and of the learning episode itself.

SUMMARY OF CONTEMPORARY STUDIES

The research reviewed in the preceding five sections indicates that implicit memory has been documented across different tasks, materials, and subject populations. Although it is clear that a wide variety of phenomena can all be grouped together under the rather general heading of *implicit memory,* it is equally clear that there are differences among these diverse phenomena. One difference that may be significant theoretically concerns whether implicit memories are *accessible* or *inaccessible* explicitly—that is, whether or not information that is expressed implicitly can, under certain conditions, be remembered explicitly. Several studies have found substantial implicit memory when explicit recognition is at the chance level and explicit recall is at or close to the floor, thereby suggesting that the implicitly expressed information is inaccessible explicitly (e.g., Bargh & Pietromonaco, 1982; Eich, 1984; Graf et al., 1982, 1984; Kunst-Wilson & Zajonc, 1980; Lewicki, 1986; McAndrews et al., in press; Squire, Shimamura, & Graf, 1985). These findings come either from studies of amnesic patients or from experiments in which normal subjects are prevented from encoding target materials in a fully conscious or elaborative manner. By contrast, in studies of normal subjects that allow elaborative encoding of target materials, implicitly expressed information is generally accessible explicitly. For example, normal subjects who produce a previously studied word on a completion test following elaborative encoding are able to consciously remember having studied the word if an explicit recall test is given, whereas a densely amnesic patient who produces a recently studied word on a completion test cannot under any circumstances consciously or explicitly remember having studied the word.

The observation that many implicit memory phenomena in normal subjects fall into the category of "accessible explicitly" raises questions concerning the extent to which, and sense in which, such phenomena should be considered implicit. That is, if normal subjects *can* remember target information explicitly under appropriate test conditions, how can we be sure that they do not remember explicitly on a nominally implicit memory test? Some investigators have attempted to disguise the fact that previously presented items appear on a test by presenting an implicit memory task as one of several filler tasks during a retention interval, and by testing only a small proportion of previously studied items (e.g., Graf et al., 1984; Jacoby, 1983a; Schacter & Graf, 1986a). The point of these procedures is to prevent subjects from catching on concerning the nature of the test, or at least to discourage the use of explicit memory strategies. It seems quite likely, however, that subjects will "clue in" concerning the nature of the test once they have been exposed to, or have successfully produced, a number of list items. Nevertheless, the fact that several studies have shown differential effects of experimental variables on implicit and explicit memory tasks when identical test cues were provided, and only the implicit/explicit nature of test instructions were varied (e.g., Graf & Mandler, 1984; Schacter & Graf, 1986a), suggests that subjects do not deliberately use explicit memory strategies on implicit memory tasks. If subjects did use such strategies, we would expect to observe parallel effects of experimental variables when the same cues are provided on implicit and explicit tasks.

However, the foregoing considerations indicate only that it is possible to prevent intentional or *voluntary* explicit memory from influencing performance on implicit memory tests. It is possible that some instances of what appear to be implicit memory may be better described as *involuntary* explicit memory: cases in which a test cue leads to an unintentional but fully conscious and explicit "reminding" of the occurrence of a prior episode (cf. Ross, 1984). The possibility of confusing implicit memory with involuntary explicit memory would appear to be greatest in experiments with normal subjects that permit elaborative encoding of target materials. At present, we know little about the relation between implicit memory and involuntary explicit memory, but future research and theorizing should be directed toward this issue.

Another difference among the various implicit memory phenomena concerns whether or not target information acquired during a study episode is represented directly in consciousness at the time of test. For example, in repetition priming studies, the target material (i.e., *assassin*) is represented in consciousness at the time of test, such as when the subject completes a test fragment with a previously studied item. By contrast, in other situations target content is not represented in consciousness at the time of test, yet influences performance *indirectly*. For example, when subjects performing an impression-formation task rate a target person more negatively because of subliminal exposure to hostile words that cannot be recalled (e.g., Bargh & Pietromonaco, 1982), or when subjects make classification responses on the basis of rules that they cannot articulate (e.g., Lewicki, 1986; Reber, 1976), the influence of acquired information on implicit memory is indirect. Although we do not know whether direct and indirect expressions of implicit memory differ in theoretically significant ways, the issue has been previously overlooked and may be worth exploring in future studies.

The foregoing considerations also highlight the fact that we presently lack well-specified criteria for assessing whether subjects are explicitly aware of previous experiences at the time of test (Tulving, 1985c). Similar issues concerning criteria for determining awareness have been debated extensively in the literature on perception and learning without awareness (e.g., Cheesman & Merikle, 1986; Eriksen, 1960; Nisbett & Wilson, 1977), and memory researchers would do well to attempt to incorporate some of the lessons from these investigations into research on implicit memory.

THEORETICAL ACCOUNTS OF IMPLICIT MEMORY

In view of the diversity of phenomena that can be grouped under the rubric of implicit memory, it is perhaps not surprising that no single theory has addressed, much less accounted for, all or even most of the observations discussed in this article. Rather, different theoretical views have been advanced to accommodate different subsets of the data. However, one general idea that can be rejected on the basis of recent research is the threshold view discussed in the historical section. The finding that implicit memory is unaffected by experimental variables that have large effects on explicit memory, and that performance on implicit tests is often statistically independent of performance on explicit tests, is inconsistent with a threshold model in which implicit and explicit tests differ only in their sensitivity to the strength of memory traces. In this section, three more viable theoretical approaches to implicit memory phenomena are considered, which are referred to, respectively, as *activation, processing,* and *multiple memory system* accounts. Each of these views has been concerned primarily with repetition priming effects and with dissociations observed in amnesic patients.

Activation views hold that priming effects on implicit memory tests are attributable to the temporary activation of preexisting representations, knowledge structures, or logogens (e.g., Graf & Mandler, 1984; Mandler, 1980; Morton, 1979; Rozin, 1976). Activation is assumed to occur automatically, independently of the elaborative processing that is necessary to establish new episodic memory traces. An activated representation readily "pops into mind" on an implicit memory test, but it contains no contextual information about an item's occurrence as part of a recent episode and therefore does not contribute to explicit remembering of the episode.

Processing views seek to understand differences between implicit and explicit memory by explicating the nature of and relations between encoding and retrieval processes or procedures (e.g., Craik, 1983; Jacoby, 1983a, 1983b; Moscovitch et al., 1986; Roediger & Blaxton, 1987; Witherspoon & Moscovitch, 1986). Such views assume that both implicit and explicit memory rely on newly established episodic representations, and portray differences between them in terms of interactions between features of encoded representations and different demands posed by implicit and explicit tests. The best articulated version of this view relies on the distinction between *conceptually driven* processes and *data-driven* processes (Jacoby, 1983b; Roediger & Blaxton, 1987). Conceptually driven processes reflect subject-initiated activities such as elaborating, organizing, and reconstructing; data-driven processes are initiated and guided by the information or data that is presented in test materials. Although both explicit and implicit tests can have data-driven and conceptually driven components, it is argued that explicit memory tests typically draw primarily on conceptually driven processes, whereas implicit tests typically draw primarily on data-driven processes. Performance dissociations between implicit and explicit tests are thus attributed to differences between conceptually driven and data-driven processes.

Multiple memory system interpretations ascribe differences between implicit and explicit memory to the different properties of hypothesized underlying systems. For example, Squire and Cohen (1984) argued that conscious or explicit recollection is a property of, and supported by, a *declarative* memory system that is involved in the formation of new representations or data structures. By contrast, implicit memory phenomena such as learning of skills and repetition priming effects are attributed to a *procedural* system in which memory is expressed by online modification of procedures or processing operations. The distinction between episodic and semantic memory (Tulving, 1972, 1983) has also been invoked to account for dissociations on implicit and explicit tests (e.g., Cermak et al., 1985; Kinsbourne & Wood, 1975; Parkin, 1982; Schacter & Tulving, 1982; Tulving, 1983). The episodic memory system is viewed as the basis for explicit remembering of recent events, whereas semantic memory is seen as responsible for performance on tasks such as word completion, lexical decision, and word identification, which require subjects to make use of preexisting knowledge of words and concepts. A variety of other multiple memory system views have also been put forward (e.g., Johnson, 1983; O'Keefe & Nadel, 1978; Schacter & Moscovitch, 1984; Warrington & Weiskrantz, 1982).

Each of these three approaches is consistent with certain features of existing data and has difficulty accommodating others. Activation views account for the finding that priming of preexisting representations does not depend on elaborative processing (e.g., Graf et al., 1982; Jacoby & Dallas, 1981) and that under certain conditions, priming decays rapidly in both normals and amnesics (Cermak et al., 1985; Diamond &

Rozin, 1984; Graf et al., 1984; Graf & Mandler, 1984; Shimamura & Squire, 1984; Squire et al., in press). Activation accounts are also consistent with the finding that some severely amnesic patients who show normal priming of items with preexisting memory representations (e.g., familiar words, idioms) do not show normal priming of nonwords or unrelated paired associates (Cermak et al., 1985; Diamond & Rozin, 1984; Schacter, 1985; Schacter & Graf, 1986b). However, an activation view does not readily accommodate those cases in which amnesic patients do show implicit memory for new information (Graf & Schacter, 1985; McAndrews et al., in press; Moscovitch et al., 1986), and has difficulty accounting for the effect of newly acquired associations on implicit memory tests in normal subjects (Graf & Schacter, 1985, 1987; McKoon & Ratcliff, 1979, 1986; Schacter & Graf, 1986a, 1986b; see Mandler, in press, for discussion). The activation notion is also inconsistent with the persistence of facilitation on certain implicit memory tests over days, weeks, and months in normal subjects (Jacoby, 1983a; Jacoby & Dallas, 1981; Komatsu & Ohta, 1984; Schacter & Graf, 1986a; Sloman et al., in press; Tulving et al., 1982) and amnesic patients (Crovitz et al., 1979; McAndrews et al., in press).

The strengths and weaknesses of the conceptual versus data-driven processing view are a virtual mirror image of those of the activation view. With its heavy emphasis on an episodic basis of implicit memory, this notion accounts well for observations of persistence, associative effects, contextual sensitivity, and study–test interactions (see Jacoby, 1983b; Roediger & Blaxton, 1987, for elaboration). However, it is less able to handle the findings on short-lived activation, dependence of some priming effects on preexisting representations in amnesic patients, and differences between priming of new and old representations in normals (cf. Feustel et al., 1983; Schacter & Graf, 1986a). This view also has difficulty accounting for the finding that implicit memory for newly acquired associations, as indexed by performance on the stem completion task, depends on some degree of elaborative study processing (e.g., Schacter & Graf, 1986a). Because it has been argued that elaborative study processing should not affect performance on data-driven implicit memory tasks such as stem completion (e.g., Roediger & Weldon, 1987), the finding that some aspects of performance on an implicit test are elaboration dependent is puzzling. It is also important to note that this view does not speak directly to the key feature of implicit memory phenomena: the absence of conscious recollection of a prior experience at the time of test. That is, it is not clear why data-driven processing should be associated with lack of explicit recollection of a prior experience, whereas conceptually driven processing is generally associated with conscious recollection of a prior experience (see Jacoby, 1984, for relevant discussion).

The strengths and weaknesses of multiple memory system views differ somewhat from the foregoing. The procedural/declarative view has been primarily applied to phenomena observed in amnesic patients. The strength of this view is that it provides a straightforward account of *normal* perceptual-motor skill learning in amnesics who lack conscious recollection of prior episodes: Skill learning is assumed to depend on a procedural memory system that is spared in amnesic patients, but does not provide a basis for explicit remembering. It has also been suggested that procedural memory is responsible for priming effects (Cohen, 1984; Squire, 1986). However, recent evidence indicates that priming and skill learning can be dissociated experimentally (Butters, 1987). This hypothesis also cannot readily account for amnesic patients' failure to show priming for nonwords: If priming reflects the modification of procedures used to encode target stimuli, it should occur for both old and new information. Moreover, amnesic patients show implicit memory in situations in which it is unlikely that performance is mediated by the procedural system. For example, amnesics can retrieve newly acquired facts and vocabulary even though they have no explicit recollection of having learned the information (Glisky et al., 1986; Schacter et al., 1984). It does not seem reasonable to attribute the implicit memory observed here to the procedural system, because learning of new facts is allegedly the responsibility of declarative memory (Squire & Cohen, 1984).

Proponents of the episodic–semantic distinction can account for some priming phenomena by postulating that performance on completion and identification tests depends upon activation of the semantic memory system, whereas explicit recall and recognition depend on episodic memory. This account would then be characterized by similar strengths and weaknesses as the activation view discussed earlier. Several other difficulties in applying the episodic–semantic distinction to implicit memory phenomena have been discussed elsewhere (McKoon, Ratcliff, & Dell, 1986; Roediger & Blaxton, 1987; Schacter & Tulving, 1982; Squire & Cohen, 1984; Tulving, 1983, 1986).

The foregoing considerations indicate that although each of the three main theoretical views accommodates certain aspects of the data, no single theoretical position accounts satisfactorily for all of the existing findings concerning implicit memory.

IMPLICIT MEMORY: FUTURE DIRECTIONS

To conclude the article, I will first summarize key issues that need to be addressed in implicit memory research; I will then consider briefly a related domain of inquiry which may provide fruitful perspectives on implicit memory and suggest new directions for research.

EMPIRICAL AND THEORETICAL EXTENSIONS OF IMPLICIT MEMORY RESEARCH

One of the most striking features of the historical survey and review of current research is the sheer diversity of implicit memory phenomena that have been observed. The fact that implicit memory has been observed across a wide variety of tasks and subject populations has both empirical and theoretical implications. On the empirical side, it seems clear that a critical task for future research is to delineate systematically the similarities and differences among the various implicit memory tests that have been used. Within the domain of repetition priming, for example, it would be desirable to further explore the relations among word-stem and fragment completion, word identification, lexical decision, free association, and other implicit memory tasks; each of these tests may be tapping different aspects of implicit memory (cf. Witherspoon & Moscovitch, 1986). Such research could help to clarify a number of unresolved issues. Consider, for example, the time course of repetition priming effects on implicit memory tests. It was noted earlier that activation views are consistent with findings of rapid decay of priming. However, the meaning of *rapid decay* varies widely, from seconds or minutes in some lexical decision paradigms (e.g., Forster & Davis, 1984) to several hours in stem-completion paradigms (e.g., Diamond & Rozin, 1984; Graf & Mandler, 1984). Moreover, as discussed previously, priming in fragment completion, word identification, and other implicit memory paradigms can persist for days, weeks, and months (Jacoby, 1983a; McAndrews et al., in press; Schacter & Graf, 1986a; Sloman et al., in press; Tulving et al., 1982). To understand these differences in the time course of priming, researchers will need a better understanding of the nature of the information and processes tapped by different implicit memory tests.

It would also be desirable to attempt to relate the findings from priming studies to observations concerning implicit memory in other paradigms, such as implicit rule learning. One area that appears particularly promising concerns the role of implicit memory in affective and social phenomena such as mood states (Bowers, 1984), fears and phobias (Jacobs & Nadel, 1985), impression formation (Bargh & Pietromonaco, 1982), and self-conceptions (Markus & Kunda, 1986). As revealed in the historical section, many striking implicit memory phenomena were reported by investigators concerned with the role of unconscious influences in affective states (e.g., Freud, Janet), and experimental studies of this issue could provide key insights into the functions of implicit memory. A second, related area that has not yet been fully exploited concerns the role of implicit memory in functional amnesias. A few investigators have examined implicit memory in hypnosis (Kihlstrom, 1980, 1984; Williamsen et al., 1965), multiple personality (Nissen, Ross, Willingham, Mackenzie, & Schacter, in press), and alcohol and drug intoxication (Hashtroudi, Parker, DeLisi, Wyatt, & Mutter, 1984; Nissen, Knopman, & Schacter, in press), but much work remains to be done. Third, research concerning the development of implicit memory in young and old populations is needed. Schacter and Moscovitch (1984) argued that infants and very young children may be capable of implicit memory only. However, there has been virtually no research that has explored the issue directly. Several studies have reported that older adults show intact repetition priming (Graf & Schacter, 1985; Light, Singh, & Capps, 1986) but little else is known about the relation between aging and implicit memory.

On the theoretical side, the diversity of implicit memory phenomena suggests that attempts to account for all relevant obsevations with a single construct or dichotomy will probably not be entirely successful. As was evident in the discussion of theoretical alternatives, no single position convincingly handles all relevant data. Accordingly, it is worth entertaining the idea that there are multiple sources of implicit memory phenomena. For example, Schacter and Graf (1986b) argued that automatic, relatively short-lived priming effects depend on activation of preexisting representations, whereas longer lasting, elaboration-dependent effects may be based on specific components of newly created episodic representations (see also Schacter & Graf, 1986a; Forster & Davis, 1984). Similarly, it is possible that some implicit memory phenomena, such as perceptual-motor skill learning in amnesic patients, reflect the operation of a memory system that is distinct from the system subserving explicit recall and recognition whereas other implicit memory phenomena, such as associative effects on word-completion performance, depend on components of the same system that subserves recall and recognition. Unfortunately, firm criteria for distinguishing between multiple-system and single-system accounts do not exist, although some possibilities have been discussed (cf. Sherry & Schacter, in press; Tulving, 1985a). Nevertheless, in view of the diversity of implicit memory phenomena, the activation, processing, and multiple-memory system views need not be mutually exclusive. Each may account well for certain aspects of the data, and may be useful in generating different questions and problems for future research.

THE GENERALITY OF IMPLICIT/EXPLICIT DISSOCIATIONS: A THEORETICAL CHALLENGE

Recent research has revealed that implicit/explicit dissociations are not restricted to situations involving memory for recent events. These studies have produced dissociations that are remarkably similar to some of those discussed here in one crucial respect: Subjects demonstrate that they possess a particular kind of knowledge by their performance on a task, yet they are not consciously aware that they possess the knowledge and cannot gain access to it explicitly. In cognitive psychology, evidence of this kind, although somewhat controversial, has been provided by previously mentioned studies on perception without awareness (e.g., Cheesman & Merikle, 1986; Marcel, 1983).

Neuropsychological research has demonstrated that patients with various lesions and deficits show implicit knowledge of stimuli that they cannot explicitly perceive, identify, or process semantically. First, patients with lesions to primary visual projection areas, who do not have conscious perceptual experiences within their hemianopic field, nevertheless perform at above-chance levels when given forced-choice discrimination tests concerning locations, orientation, and other dimensions of a visual stimulus (e.g., Weiskrantz, 1986; see Campion, Latto, & Smith, 1983, for a critique). This phenomenon of "blind-sight" occurs in patients who claim that they are guessing the location and identity of the visual stimulus but do not "see" anything at all. A second, similar dissociation has been reported in patients with lesions of the right parieto-occipital cortex who have deficits orienting and attending to stimuli which are presented in their left visual fields. Such patients can make accurate same–different judgments regarding stimuli that are presented simultaneously in the left and right visual fields, despite the fact that they cannot state the identity of the stimulus in the left visual field and often deny the presence of any left-field stimulus (Volpe, LeDoux, & Gazzaniga, 1979). Third, patients with facial recognition deficits (prosopagnosia) show stronger galvanic skin responses to familiar than to unfamiliar faces, even though patients do not explicitly recognize any faces as familiar (Bauer, 1984; Tranel & Damasio, 1985). Fourth, alexic patients, who have serious problems reading common words, perform at above chance levels when required to make lexical decisions and semantic categorizations regarding words that they cannot explicitly or consciously identify (Coslett, 1986; Shallice & Saffran, 1986), or to point to objects corresponding to words that they deny seeing (Landis, Regard, & Serrant, 1980). Fifth, aphasic patients with severe comprehension deficits show semantic priming effects for related word pairs without conscious understanding of the semantic relation that links the words (Blumstein, Milberg, & Shrier, 1982; Milberg & Blumstein, 1981).

The foregoing phenomena differ from one another, and from the implicit memory phenomena discussed earlier, insofar as the performance of each type of patient reflects somewhat different residual or preserved capacities (for more detailed review, see Schacter, McAndrews, & Moscovitch, in press). The striking similarity, however, is that in all cases knowledge is expressed implicitly and does not give rise to a conscious experience of knowing, perceiving, or remembering. This observation suggests that conscious or explicit experiences of knowing, perceiving, or remembering are all in some way dependent upon the functioning of a common mechanism, a mechanism whose functioning is disrupted in various brain-damaged patients. Elsewhere, I have outlined a model that delineates some properties of this mechanism, describes how it is related to various memory structures, and suggests that it can be isolated or disconnected from specific memory and processing systems in different neuropsychological syndromes (Schacter, 1987). For the present purposes, the observation of implicit–explicit dissociations in multiple domains has several implications: It provides a possibly important clue for development of theories of implicit memory, it suggests that the study of implicit memory should be pursued in close conjunction with the study of related phenomena in normal and brain-damaged populations, and it highlights again the generality and pervasiveness of dissociations between implicit and explicit expressions of memory and knowledge.

REFERENCES

Adams, J. K. (1957). Laboratory studies of behavior without awareness. *Psychological Bulletin, 54,* 383–405.

Bargh, J. A., Bond, R. N., Lombardi, W. J., & Tota, M. E. (1986). The additive nature of chronic and temporary sources of construct accessibility. *Journal of Personality and Social Psychology, 50,* 869–878.

Bargh, J. A., & Pietromonaco, P. (1982). Automatic information processing and social perception: The influence of trait information presented outside of conscious awareness on impression formation. *Journal of Personality and Social Psychology, 43,* 437–449.

Barkworth, T. (1891). Some recent experiments in automatic writing. *Proceedings of the Society for Psychical Research, 7,* 23–29.

Bauer, R. M. (1984). Autonomic recognition of names and faces in prosopagnosia: A neuropsychological application of the guilty knowledge test. *Neuropsychologia, 22,* 457–469.

Bergson, H. (1911). *Matter and memory.* New York: Macmillan.

Binet, A. (1890). *On double consciousness.* Chicago: Open Court.

Blumstein, S. E., Milberg, W., & Shrier, R. (1982). Semantic processing in aphasia: Evidence from an auditory lexical decision task. *Brain and Language, 17,* 301–315.

Bowers, K. S. (1984). On being unconsciously influenced and informed. In K. S. Bowers & D. Meichenbaum (Eds.), *The unconscious reconsidered* (pp. 227–272). New York: Wiley.

Brewer, W. F. (1974). There is no convincing evidence for operant or classical conditioning in adult humans. In W. B. Weimer & D. S. Palermo (Eds.), *Cognition and the symbolic processes* (pp. 1–42). Hillsdale, NJ: Erlbaum.

Brooks, D. N., & Baddeley, A. D. (1976). What can amnesic patients learn? *Neuropsychologia, 14,* 111–122.

Brooks, L. (1978). Nonanalytic concept formation and memory for instances. In E. Rosch & B. B. Lloyd (Eds.), *Cognition and categorization* (pp. 169-211). Hillsdale, NJ: Erlbaum.

Bruce, V., & Valentine, T. (1985). Identity priming in the recognition of familiar faces. *British Journal of Psychology, 76,* 373-383.

Butters, N. (1987, February). *Procedural learning in dementia: A double dissociation between Alzheimer and Huntington's disease patients on verbal priming and motor skill learning.* Paper presented at the meeting of the International Neuropsychological Society, Washington, DC.

Campion, J., Latto, R., & Smith, Y. M. (1983). Is blindsight an effect of scattered light, spared cortex, and near-threshold vision? *The Behavioral and Brain Sciences, 6,* 423-486.

Carpenter, W. B. (1874). *Principles of mental physiology.* London: John Churchill.

Cermak, L. S., Talbot, N., Chandler, K., & Wolbarst, L. R. (1985). The perceptual priming phenomenon in amnesia. *Neuropsychologia, 23,* 615-622.

Cheesman, J., & Merikle, P. M. (1986). Word recognition and consciousness. In D. Besner, T. G. Waller, & G. E. Mackinnon (Eds.), *Reading research: Advances in theory and practice* (Vol. 5, pp. 311-352). New York: Academic Press.

Claparède, E. (1951). Recognition and 'me-ness.' In D. Rapaport (Ed.), *Organization and pathology of thought* (pp. 58-75). New York: Columbia University Press. (Reprinted from Archives de Psychologie, 1911, *11,* 79-90.)

Clarke, R. G. B., & Morton, J. (1983). Cross modality facilitation in tachistoscopic word recognition. *Quarterly Journal of Experimental Psychology, 35A,* 79-96.

Cofer, C. C. (1967). Conditions for the use of verbal associations. *Psychological Bulletin, 68,* 1-12.

Cohen, N. J. (1984). Preserved learning capacity in amnesia: Evidence for multiple memory systems. In L. R. Squire & N. Butters (Eds.), *Neuropsychology of memory* (pp. 83-103). New York: Guilford Press.

Cohen, N. J., & Squire, L. R. (1980). Preserved learning and retention of pattern-analyzing skill in amnesia: Dissociation of "knowing how" and "knowing that." *Science, 210,* 207-209.

Coslett, H. B. (1986, June). *Preservation of lexical access in alexia without agraphia.* Paper presented at the 9th European Conference of the International Neuropsychological Society, Veldhoven, The Netherlands.

Craik, F. I. M. (1983). On the transfer of information from temporary to permanent memory. *Philosophical Transactions of the Royal Society of London, 302,* 341-359.

Craik, F. I. M., & Tulving, E. (1975) Depth of processing and the retention of words in episodic memory. *Journal of Experimental Psychology: General, 104,* 268-294.

Crovitz, H. F., Harvey, M. T., & McClanahan, S. (1979). Hidden memory: A rapid method for the study of amnesia using perceptual learning, *Cortex, 17,* 273-278.

Darwin, E. (1794). *Zoonomia; or the laws of organic life.* (Vol. 1) London: J. Johnson.

Diamond, R., & Rozin, P. (1984). Activation of existing memories in the amnesic syndrome. *Journal of Abnormal Psychology, 93,* 98-105.

Dixon, N. F. (1971). *Subliminal perception: The nature of a controversy.* London: McGraw-Hill.

Dixon, N. F. (1981). *Preconscious processing.* New York: Wiley.

Dulany, D. E., Carlson, R. A., & Dewey, G. I. (1984). A case of syntactical learning and judgment: How conscious and how abstract? *Journal of Experimental Psychology: General, 113,* 541-555.

Dulany, D. E., Carlson, R. A., & Dewey, G. I. (1985). On consciousness in syntactic learning and judgment: A reply to Reber, Allen, and Regan. *Journal of Experimental Psychology: General, 114,* 25-32.

Dunn, R. (1845). Case of suspension of the mental faculties. *Lancet, 2,* 588-590.

Ebbinghaus, H. (1885). *Über das Gedächtnis* [Memory]. Leipzig: Duncker and Humbolt.

Eich, E. (1984). Memory for unattended events: Remembering with and without awareness. *Memory & Cognition, 12,* 105-111.

Ellenberger, H. F. (1970). *The discovery of the unconscious.* New York: Basic Books.

Erdelyi, M. H. (1970). Recovery of unavailable perceptual input. *Cognitive Psychology, 1,* 99-113.

Eriksen, C. W. (1960). Discrimination and learning without awareness: A methodological survey and evaluation. *Psychological Review, 67,* 279-300.

Eslinger, P. J., 7 Damasio, A. R. (1986). Preserved motor learning in Alzheimer's disease: Implications for anatomy and behavior. *The Journal of Neuroscience, 6,* 3006-3009.

Feustel, T. C., Shiffrin, R. M., & Salasoo, A. (1983). Episodic and lexical contributions to the repetition effect in word identification. *Journal of Experimental Psychology: General, 112,* 309-346.

Forbach, G. B., Stanners, R. F., & Hochhaus, L. (1974). Repetition and practice effects in a lexical decision task. *Memory & Cognition, 2,* 337-339.

Forster, K. I., & Davis, C. (1984). Repetition priming and frequency attenuation in lexical access. *Journal of Experimental Psychology: Learning, Memory, and Cognition, 10,* 680-698.

Fowler, C., Wolford, G., Slade, R., & Tassinary, L. (1981). Lexical access with and without awareness. *Journal of Experimental Psychology: General, 110,* 341-362.

Freud, S., & Breuer, J. (1966). *Studies on hysteria.* (J. Strachey, Trans.). New York: Avon Books.

Gardner, H., Boller, F., Moreines, J., & Butters, N. (1973). Retrieving information from Korsakoff patients: Effects of categorical cues and reference to the task. *Cortex, 9,* 165-175.

Giddan, N. S. (1967). Recovery through images of briefly flashed stimuli. *Journal of Personality, 35,* 1-19.

Giddan, N. S., & Eriksen, C. W. (1959). Generalization of response biases acquired with and without verbal awareness. *Journal of Personality, 27,* 104-115.

Glisky, E. L., Schacter, D. L., & Tulving, E. (1986). Computer learning by memory-impaired patients: Acquisition and retention of complex knowledge. *Neuropsychologia, 24,* 313-328.

Gordon, P. C., & Holyoak, K. J. (1983). Implicit learning and generalization of the "mere exposure" effect. *Journal of Personality and Social Psychology, 45,* 492-500.

Graf, P., & Mandler, G. (1984). Activation makes words more accessible, but not necessarily more retrievable. *Journal of Verbal Learning and Verbal Behavior, 23,* 553-568.

Graf, P., Mandler, G., & Haden, P. (1982). Simulating amnesic symptoms in normal subjects. *Science, 218,* 1243-1244.

Graf, P., & Schacter, D. L. (1985). Implicit and explicit memory for new associations in normal and amnesic subjects. *Journal of Experimental Psychology: Learning, Memory, and Cognition, 11,* 501-518.

Graf, P., & Schacter, D. L. (1987). Selective effects of interference on implicit and explicit memory for new associations. *Journal of Experimental Psychology: Learning, Memory, and Cognition, 13,* 45-53.

Graf, P., Shimamura, A. P., & Squire, L. R. (1985). Priming across modalities and priming across category levels: Extending the domain of preserved function in amnesia. *Journal of Experimental Psychology: Learning, Memory, and Cognition, 11,* 385-395.

Graf, P., Squire, L. R., & Mandler, G. (1984). The information that amnesic patients do not forget. *Journal of Experimental Psychology: Learning, Memory, and Cognition, 10,* 164-178.

Greenspoon, J. (1955). The reinforcing effect of two spoken sounds on the frequency of two responses. *American Journal of Psychology, 68,* 409-416.

Haber, R. N., & Erdelyi, M. H. (1967). Emergence and recovery of initially unavailable perceptual material. *Journal of Verbal Learning and Verbal Behavior, 6,* 618-628.

Haldane, E. S., & Ross, G. R. T. (Eds.). (1967). *The philosophical works of Descartes.* Cambridge: Cambridge University Press.

Hashtroudi, S., Parker, E. S., DeLisi, L. E., Wyatt, R. J., & Mutter, S. A. (1984). Intact retention in acute alcohol amnesia. *Journal of Experimental Psychology: Learning, Memory, and Cognition, 10,* 156-163.

Herbart, J. F. (1896). *A text-book in psychology.* New York: D. Appleton.

Hering, E. (1920). Memory as a universal function of organized matter. In S. Butler (Ed.), *Unconscious memory* (pp. 63-86). London: Jonathan Cape.

Holender, D. (1986). Semantic activation without conscious identification in dichotic listening, parafoveal vision, and visual masking: A survey and appraisal. *The Behavioral and Brain Sciences, 9,* 1-66.

Hull, C. L. (1933). *Hypnosis and suggestibility.* New York: Appleton Century.

Irwin, F. W., Kauffman, K., Prior, G., & Weaver, H. B. (1934). On 'learning without awareness of what is being learned.' *Journal of Experimental Psychology, 17,* 823-827.

Jacobs, W. J., & Nadel, L. (1985). Stress-induced recovery of fears and phobias. *Psychological Review 92,* 512-531.

Jacoby, L. L. (1983a). Perceptual enhancement: Persistent effects of an experience. *Journal of Experimental Psychology: Learning, Memory, and Cognition, 9,* 21-38.

Jacoby, L. L. (1983b). Remembering the data: Analyzing interactive processes in reading. *Journal of Verbal Learning and Verbal Behavior, 22,* 485-508.

Jacoby, L. L. (1984). Incidental versus intentional retrieval: Remembering and awareness as separate issues. In L. R. Squire & N. Butters (Eds.), *Neuropsychology of memory* (pp. 145-156). New York: Guilford Press.

Jacoby, L. L., & Dallas, M. (1981). On the relationship between autobiographical memory and perceptual learning. *Journal of Experimental Psychology: General, 110,* 306-340.

Jacoby, L. L., & Witherspoon, D. (1982). Remembering without awareness. *Canadian Journal of Psychology, 36,* 300-324.

Janet, P. (1893). L'amnésie continue [Continuous amnesia]. *Révue Générale Des Sciences, 4,* 167-179.

Janet, P. (1904). L'amnésie et la dissociation des souvenirs par l'émotion [Amnesia and the dissociation of memories by emotion]. *Journal de Psychologie Normale et Pathologique, 1,* 417-453.

Johnson, M. (1983). A multiple-entry, modular memory system. In G. H. Bower (Ed.), *The psychology of learning and motivation* (Vol. 17, pp. 81-123). New York: Academic Press.

Johnson, M. K., Kim, J. K., & Risse, G. (1985). Do alcoholic Korsakoff's syndrome patients acquire affective reactions? *Journal of Experimental Psychology: Learning, Memory, and Cognition, 11,* 27-36.

Johnston, W. A., Dark, V. J., & Jacoby, L. L. (1985). Perceptual fluency and recognition judgments. *Journal of Experimental Psychology: Learning, Memory, and Cognition, 11,* 3-11.

Kihlstrom, J. F. (1980). Posthypnotic amnesia for recently learned materials: Interactions with "episodic" and "semantic" memory. *Cognitive Psychology, 12,* 227-251.

Kihlstrom, J. F. (1984). Conscious, subconscious, unconscious: A cognitive perspective. In K. S. Bowers & D. Meichenbaum (Eds.), *The unconscious reconsidered* (pp. 149-211). New York: Wiley.

Kinsbourne, M., & Wood, F. (1975). Short term memory and the amnesic syndrome. In D. D. Deutsch & J. A. Deutsch (Eds.), *Short-term memory* (pp. 258-291). New York: Academic Press.

Kirsner, K., Milech, D., & Standen, P. (1983). Common and modality-specific processes in the mental lexicon. *Memory & Cognition, 11,* 621-630.

Kirsner, K., & Smith, M. C. (1974). Modality effects in word identification. *Memory & Cognition, 2,* 637-640.

Kolers, P. A. (1975). Memorial consequences of automatized encoding. *Journal of Experimental Psychology: Human Learning and Memory, 1,* 689-701.

Kolers, P. A. (1976). Reading a year later. *Journal of Experimental Psychology: Human Learning and Memory, 2,* 554-565.

Komatsu, S. I., & Ohta, N. (1984). Priming effects in word-fragment completion for short- and long-term retention intervals. *Japanese Psychological Research, 26,* 194-200.

Korsakoff, S. S. (1889). Etude médico-psychologique sur une forme des maladies de la mémoire [Medical-psychological study of a form of diseases of memory]. *Révue Philosophique, 28,* 501-530.

Krieckhaus, E. E., & Eriksen, C. W. (1960). A study of awareness and its effects on learning and generalization. *Journal of Personality, 28,* 503-517.

Kunst-Wilson, W. R., & Zajonc, R. B. (1980). Affective discrimination of stimuli that cannot be recognized. *Science, 207,* 557-558.

Lacey, J. L., & Smith, R. L. (1954). Conditioning and generalization of unconscious anxiety. *Science, 120,* 1045-1052.

Landis, T., Regard, M., & Serrant, A. (1980). Iconic reading in a case of alexia without agraphia caused by a brain tumor: A tachistoscopic study. *Brain and Language, 11,* 45-53.

Lazarus, R. S., & McCleary, R. (1951). Autonomic discrimination without awareness: A study of subception. *Psychological Review, 58,* 113-122.

Leibniz, G. W. (1916). *New essays concerning human understanding.* Chicago: Open Court.

Lewicki, P. (1985). Nonconscious biasing effects of single instances on subsequent judgments. *Journal of Personality and Social Psychology, 48,* 563-574.

Lewicki, P. (1986). Processing information about covariations that cannot be articulated. *Journal of Experimental Psychology: Learning, Memory, and Cognition, 12,* 135-146.

Light, L. L., Singh, A., & Capps, J. L. (1986). Dissociation of memory and awareness in young and older adults. *Journal of Clinical and Experimental Neuropsychology, 8,* 62-74.

Luria, A. R. (1976). *The neuropsychology of memory.* Washington, DC: V. H. Winston.

Maine de Biran. (1929). *The influence of habit on the faculty of thinking.* Baltimore: Williams & Wilkins.

Mandler, G. (1980). Recognizing: The judgment of previous occurrence. *Psychological Review, 87,* 252-271.

Mandler, G. (in press). Memory: Conscious and unconscious. In P. R. Solomon, G. R. Goethals, C. M. Kelley, & B. R. Stephens (Eds.), *Memory–An interdisciplinary approach.* New York: Springer-Verlag.

Mandler, G., Nakamura, Y., Van Zandt, B. J. S. (in press). Nonspecific effects of exposure on stimuli that cannot be recognized. *Journal of Experimental Psychology: Learning, Memory, and Cognition.*

Marcel, A. J. (1983). Conscious and unconscious perception: Experiments on visual masking and word recognition. *Cognitive Psychology, 15,* 197-237.

Markus, H., & Kunda, Z. (1986). Stability and malleability of the self-concept. *Journal of Personality and Social Psychology, 51,* 858-866.

Masson, M. E. J. (1984). Memory for the surface structure of sentences: Remembering with and without awareness. *Journal of Verbal Learning and Verbal Behavior, 23,* 579-592.

McAndrews, M. P., Glisky, E. L., & Schacter, D. L. (in press). When priming persists: Long-lasting implicit memory for a single episode in amnesic patients. *Neuropsychologia.*

McAndrews, M. P., & Moscovitch, M. (1985). Rule-based and exemplar-based classification in artificial grammar learning. *Memory & Cognition, 13,* 469-475.

McDougall, W. (1924). *Outline of psychology.* New York: Charles Scribner's Sons.

McKoon, G., & Ratcliff, R. (1979). Priming in episodic and semantic memory. *Journal of Verbal Learning and Verbal Behavior, 18,* 463-480.

McKoon, G., & Ratcliff, R. (1986). Automatic activation of episodic information in a semantic memory task. *Journal of Experimental Psychology: Learning, Memory, and Cognition, 12,* 108–115.

McKoon, G., Ratcliff, R., & Dell, G. (1986). A critical evaluation of the semantic–episodic distinction. *Journal of Experimental Psychology: Learning, Memory, and Cognition, 12,* 295–306.

Metcalfe, J., & Fisher, R. P. (1986). The relation between recognition memory and classification learning. *Memory & Cognition, 14,* 164–173.

Milberg, W., & Blumstein, S. E. (1981). Lexical decision and aphasia: Evidence for semantic processing. *Brain and Language, 14,* 371–385.

Milner, B. (1962). Les troubles de la mémoire accompagnant des lésions hippocampiques bilatérales (Disorders of memory accompanying bilateral hippocampal lesions]. In *Physiologie de l'hippocampe.* Paris: Centre National de la Recherche Scientifique.

Milner, B., Corkin, S., & Teuber, H. L. (1968). Further analysis of the hippocampal amnesic syndrome: 14 year follow-up study of H. M. *Neuropsychologia, 6,* 215–234.

Miss X. (1889). Recent experiments in crystal visions. *Proceedings of the Society for Psychical Research, 5,* 486–521.

Morton, J. (1979). Facilitation in word recognition: Experiments causing change in the logogen models. In P. A. Kolers, M. E. Wrolstad, & H. Bouma (Eds.), *Processing of visible language* (Vol. 1, pp. 259–268). New York: Plenum.

Moscovitch, M. (1982). Multiple dissociations of function in amnesia. In L. S. Cermak (Ed.), *Human memory and amnesia* (pp. 337–370). Hillsdale, NJ: Erlbaum.

Moscovitch, M., Winocur, G., & McLachlan, D. (1986). Memory as assessed by recognition and reading time in normal and memory-impaired people with Alzheimer's disease and other neurological disorders. *Journal of Experimental Psychology: General. 115,* 331–347.

Murrell, G. A., & Morton, J. (1974). Word recognition and morphemic structure. *Journal of Experimental Psychology, 102,* 963–968.

Neisser, U. (1954). An experimental distinction between perceptual processes and verbal response. *Journal of Experimental Psychology, 47,* 399–402.

Nelson, T. O. (1978). Detecting small amounts of information in memory: Savings for nonrecognized items. *Journal of Experimental Psychology: Human Learning and Memory, 4,* 453–468.

Nisbett, R. E., & Wilson, T. D. (1977). Telling more than we can know: Verbal reports on mental processes. *Psychological Review, 84,* 231–259.

Nissen, M. J., & Bullemer, P. (1987). Attentional requirements of learning: Evidence from performance measures. *Cognitive Psychology, 19,* 1–32.

Nissen, M. J., Knopman, D., & Schacter, D. L. (in press). Neurochemical dissociation of memory systems. *Neurology.*

Nissen, M. J., Ross, J. L., Willingham, D. B., Mackenzie, T. B., & Schacter, D. L. (in press). Memory and awareness in a patient with multiple personality disorder. *Brain and Cognition.*

O'Keefe, J., & Nadel, L. (1978). *The hippocampus as a cognitive map.* Oxford: Clarendon Press.

Osgood, C. E., & Hoosain, R. (1974). Salience of the word as a unit in the perception of language. *Perception & Psychophysics, 15,* 168–192.

Parkin, A. (1982). Residual learning capability in organic amnesia. *Cortex, 18,* 417–440.

Perry, C., & Laurence, J. R. (1984). Mental processing outside of awareness: The contributions of Freud and Janet. In K. S. Bowers & D. Meichenbaum (Eds.), *The unconscious reconsidered* (pp. 9–48). New York: Wiley.

Pine, F. (1960). Incidental stimulation: A study of preconscious transformations. *Journal of Abnormal and Social Psychology, 60,* 68–75.

Poetzl, O. (1960). The relationship between experimentally induced dream images and indirect vision. Monograph No. 7. *Psychological Issues, 2,* 41–120.

Prince, M. (1914). *The unconscious.* New York: Macmillan.

Reber, A. S. (1976). Implicit learning of synthetic languages: The role of instructional set. *Journal of Experimental Psychology: Human Learning and Memory, 2,* 88-94.

Reber, A. S., Allen, A., & Regan, S. (1985). Syntactical learning and judgment, still unconscious and still abstract: Comment on Dulany, Carlson, and Dewey. *Journal of Experimental Psychology: General, 114,* 17-24.

Roediger, H. L. III, & Blaxton, T. A. (1987). Retrieval modes produce dissociations in memory for surface information. In D. S. Gorfein & R. R. Hoffman (Eds.), *Memory and cognitive processes: The Ebbinghaus centennial conference* (pp. 349-379). Hillsdale, NJ: Erlbaum.

Roediger, H. L. III, & Weldon, M. S. (1987). Reversing the picture superiority effect. In M. A. McDaniel & M. Pressley (Eds.), *Imagery and related mnemonic processes: theories, individual differences, and applications* (pp. 151-174). New York: Springer-Verlag.

Rosenfeld, H. M., & Baer, D. M. (1969). Unnoticed verbal conditioning of an aware experimenter by a more aware subject: The double-agent effect. *Psychological Review, 76,* 425-432.

Ross, B. H. (1984). Remindings and their effects in learning a cognitive skill. *Cognitive Psychology, 16,* 371-416.

Rozin, P. (1976). The psychobiological approach to human memory. In M. R. Rosenzweig & E. L. Bennett (Eds.), *Neural mechanisms of learning and memory.* Cambridge, MA: MIT Press.

Salasoo, A., Shiffrin, R. M., & Feustel, T. (1985). Building permanent memory codes: Codification and repetition effects in word identification. *Journal of Experimental Psychology: General, 114,* 50-77.

Scarborough, D. L., Cortese, C., & Scarborough, H. S. (1977). Frequency and repetition effects in lexical memory. *Journal of Experimental Psychology: Human Perception and Performance, 3,* 1-17.

Scarborough, D. L., Gerard, L., & Cortese, C. (1979). Accessing lexical memory: The transfer of word repetition effects across task and modality. *Memory & Cognition, 7,* 3-12.

Schacter, D. L. (1982). *Stranger behind the engram: Theories of memory and the psychology of science.* Hillsdale, NJ: Erlbaum.

Schacter, D. L. (1983). Amnesia observed: Remembering and forgetting in a natural environment. *Journal of Abnormal Psychology, 92,* 236-242.

Schacter, D. L. (1985). Priming of old and new knowledge in amnesic patients and normal subjects. *Annals of the New York Academy of Sciences, 444,* 41-53.

Schacter, D. L. (1987, June). *On the relation between memory and consciousness: Dissociable interactions and conscious experience.* Paper presented at the Conference on Memory and Memory Dysfunction, Toronto, Ontario, Canada.

Schacter, D. L., & Graf, P. (1986a). Effects of elaborative processing on implicit and explicit memory for new associations. *Journal of Experimental Psychology: Learning, Memory, and Cognition, 12,* 432-444.

Schacter, D. L., & Graf, P. (1986b). Preserved learning in amnesic patients: Perspectives from research on direct priming. *Journal of Clinical and Experimental Neuropsychology, 8,* 727-743.

Schacter, D. L., Harbluk, J. L., & McLachlan, D. R. (1984). Retrieval without recollection: An experimental analysis of source amnesia. *Journal of Verbal Learning and Verbal Behavior, 23,* 593-611.

Schacter, D. L., McAndrews, M. P., & Moscovitch, M. (in press). Access to consciousness: Dissociations between implicit and explicit knowledge in neuropsychological syndromes. In L. Weiskrantz (Ed.), *Thought without language.* London: Oxford University Press.

Schacter, D. L., & McGlynn, S. M. (1987). *Implicit memory: Effects of elaboration depend on unitization.* Manuscript submitted for publication.

Schacter, D. L., & Moscovitch, M. (1984). Infants, amnesics, and dissociable memory systems. In M. Moscovitch (Ed.), *Infant memory* (pp. 173-216). New York: Plenum.

Schacter, D. L., & Tulving, E. (1982). Memory, amnesia, and the episodic/semantic distinction. In R. L. Isaacson & N. E. Spear (Eds.), *The expression of knowledge* (pp. 33-65). New York: Plenum Press.

Schneider, K. (1912). Über einige klinisch-pathologische Untersuchungsmethoden und ihre Ergebnisse. Zugleich ein Beitrag zur Psychopathologie der Korsakowschen Psychose [On certain clinical-pathological methods of research and their results. Together with a contribution to the psychopatholgy of Korsakoff's psychosis]. *Zeitschrift für Neurologie und Psychiatrie, 8,* 553-616.

Seamon, J. G., Brody, N., & Kauff, D. M. (1983). Affective discrimination of stimuli that are not recognized: Effects of shadowing, masking, and cerebral laterality. *Journal of Experimental Psychology: Learning, Memory, and Cognition, 9,* 544-555.

Shallice, T., & Saffran, E. (1986). Lexical processing in the absence of explicit word identification: Evidence from a letter-by-letter reader. *Cognitive Neuropsychology, 3,* 429-458.

Sherry, D. F., & Schacter, D. L. (in press). The evolution of multiple memory systems. *Psychological Review.*

Shevrin, H., & Fritzler, D. E. (1968). Visual evoked response correlates of unconscious mental processes. *Science, 161,* 295-298.

Shimamura, A. P. (1986). Priming effects in amnesia: Evidence for a dissociable memory function. *Quarterly Journal of Experimental Psychology, 38A,* 619-644.

Shimamura, A. P., & Squire, L. R. (1984). Paired-associate learning and priming effects in amnesia: A neuropsychological study. *Journal of Experimental Psychology: General, 113,* 556-570.

Shimamura, A. P., & Squire, L. R. (1987). A neuropsychological study of fact learning and source amnesia. *Journal of Experimental Psychology: Learning, Memory, and Cognition, 13,* 464-474.

Slamecka, N. J. (1985a). Ebbinghaus: Some associations. *Journal of Experimental Psychology: Learning, Memory, and Cognition, 11,* 414-435.

Slamecka, N. J. (1985b). Ebbinghaus: Some rejoinders. *Journal of Experimental Psychology: Learning, Memory, and Cognition, 11,* 496-500.

Sloman, S. A., Hayman, C. A. G., Ohta, N., & Tulving, E. (in press). Forgetting and interference in fragment completion. *Journal of Experimental Psychology: Learning, Memory, and Cognition.*

Squire, L. R. (1986). Mechanisms of memory. *Science, 232,* 1612-1619.

Squire, L. R., & Cohen, N. J. (1984). Human memory and amnesia. In J. McGaugh, G. Lynch, & N. Weinberger (Eds.), *Proceedings of the conference on the neurobiology of learning and memory* (pp. 3-64). New York: Guilford Press.

Squire, L. R., Shimamura, A. P., & Graf, P. (1985). Independence of recognition memory and priming effects: A neuropsychological analysis. *Journal of Experimental Psychology: Learning, Memory, and Cognition, 11,* 37-44.

Squire, L. R., Shimamura, A. P., & Graf, P. (in press). Strength and duration of priming effects in normal subjects and amnesic patients. *Neuropsychologia.*

Squire, L., Wetzel, C. D., & Slater, P. C. (1978). Anterograde amnesia following ECT: An analysis of beneficial effects of partial information. *Neuropsychologia, 16,* 339-348.

Start, A., & Phillips, L. (1970). Verbal and motor memory in the amnesic syndrome. *Neuropsychologia, 8,* 75-88.

Storms, L. H. (1958). Apparent backward associations: A situational effect. *Journal of Experimental Psychology, 55,* 390-395.

Thorndike, E. L., & Rock, R. T., Jr. (1934). Learning without awareness of what is being learned or intent to learn it. *Journal of Experimental Psychology, 17,* 1-19.

Tranel, D., & Damasio, A. R. (1985). Knowledge without awareness: An autonomic index of facial recognition by prosopagnosics. *Science, 228,* 1453-1454.

Tulving, E. (1972). Episodic and semantic memory. In E. Tulving & W. Donaldson (Eds.), *Organization of memory* (pp. 381-403). New York: Academic Press.

Tulving, E. (1983). *Elements of episodic memory.* Oxford: The Clarendon Press.

Tulving, E. (1985a). On the classification problem in learning and memory. In L.-G. Nilsson & T. Archer (Eds.), *Perspectives in learning and memory* (pp. 67-94). Hillsdale, NJ: Erlbaum.

Tulving, E. (1985b). Ebbinghaus's memory: What did he learn and remember? *Journal of Experimental Psychology: Learning, Memory, and Cognition, 11,* 485-490.

Tulving, E. (1985c). Memory and consciousness. *Canadian Psychology, 25,* 1-12.

Tulving, E. (1986). What kind of a hypothesis is the distinction between episodic and semantic memory? *Journal of Experimental Psychology: Learning, Memory, and Cognition, 12,* 307-311.

Tulving, E., Schacter, D. L., & Stark, H. A. (1982). Priming effects in word-fragment completion are independent of recognition memory. *Journal of Experimental Psychology: Learning, Memory, and Cognition, 8,* 336-342.

Volpe, B. T., LeDoux, J. E., & Gazzaniga, M. S. (1979). Information processing of visual stimuli in an 'extinguished' field. *Nature, 282,* 722-724.

Warrington, E. K., & Weiskrantz, L. (1968). New method of testing long-term retention with special reference to amnesic patients. *Nature, 217,* 972-974.

Warrington, E. K., & Weiskrantz, L. (1970). Amnesia: Consolidation or retrieval? *Nature, 228,* 628-630.

Warrington, E. K., & Weiskrantz, L. (1974). The effect of prior learning on subsequent retention in amnesic patients. *Neuropsychologia, 12, 419-428.*

Warrington, E. K., & Weiskrantz, L. (1978). Further analysis of the prior learning effect in amnesic patients. *Neuropsychologia, 16,* 169-176.

Warrington, E. K., & Weiskrantz, L. (1982). Amnesia: A disconnection syndrome? *Neuropsychologia, 20,* 233-248.

Weiskrantz, L. (1985). On issues and theories of the human amnesic syndrome. In N. M. Weinberger, J. L. McGaugh, & G. Lynch (Eds.), *Memory systems of the brain* (pp. 380-415). New York: Guilford Press.

Weiskrantz, L. (1986). *Blindsight.* New York: Oxford University Press.

Weiskrantz, L., & Warrington, E. K. (1979). Conditioning in amnesic patients. *Neuropsychologia, 17,* 187-194.

Williamsen, J. A., Johnson, H. J., & Eriksen, C. W. (1965). Some characteristics of posthypnotic amnesia. *Journal of Abnormal Psychology, 70,* 123-131.

Wilson, W. R. (1979). Feeling more than we can know: Exposure effects without learning. *Journal of Personality and Social Psychology, 37,* 811-821.

Winnick, W. A., & Daniel, S. A. (1970). Two kinds of response priming in tachistoscopic recognition. *Journal of Experimental Psychology, 84,* 74-81.

Witherspoon, D., & Moscovitch, M. (1986). *Independence between word fragment completion and perceptual identification.* Manuscript submitted for publication.

Young, A. W., McWeeny, K. H., Hay, D. C., & Ellis, A. W. (1986). Access to identity-specific semantic codes from familiar faces. *Quarterly Journal of Experimental Psychology, 38A,* 271-295.

QUESTIONS FOR FURTHER THOUGHT

1. What is implicit memory, and how does it differ from explicit memory?
2. What are some major techniques used to measure implicit memory?
3. How do the effects of amnesia typically differ for implicit versus explicit memory?
4. Does implicit memory differ from implicit learning?
5. Do differences between implicit and explicit memory performance indicate that human memory works through separate systems?

Revisiting a Century-Old Freudian Slip— From Suggestion Disavowed to the Truth Repressed

Kenneth Bowers and Peter Farvolden

INTRODUCTION

An individual is having difficulty in adjusting to the challenges life presents. Seeking help, the individual goes to a psychotherapist recommended by someone else. After a series of seemingly fruitless sessions, things suddenly take a dramatic turn. Perhaps under hypnosis, the individual starts recalling instances of sexual abuse by his or her parents during childhood. At first, these memories are vague and fleeting, but they become more vivid, more detailed, and more compelling over time. Soon, the individual starts to attribute present problems to the long-term effects of the sexual abuse. A series of confrontations between the individual and his or her parents may lead to a lawsuit. A once seemingly intact family is intact no longer.

This scenario has played out with increasing frequency in recent years. At issue is the validity or even reality of recalling what are usually called *repressed memories*, memories of events in the past that were allegedly repressed (pushed down into unconsciousness) for many years, only to surface again.

No consensus has emerged about whether repressed memories really exist, although cognitive psychologists agree about the extreme difficulty of showing their validity. Indeed, laboratory experiments can create false memories, memories of events people believe they have experienced but that were actually implanted for events that never occurred. In the following article, the authors provide a dispassionate and thorough review of the literature on repressed memories. Bowers and Farvolden do not come to any final conclusions, but they show the fragility of the evidentiary base that has been offered in support of the concept of repressed memories.

This article was written shortly before Bowers's death from cancer. Indeed, the editor of the journal in which the article was published moved up its publication to bring it out before Bowers died. It is a tribute to Bowers that, literally on his deathbed, he would produce an article that so completely, dispassionately, and sensibly reviewed work in a field that has been so marked by contention, distortion, and even, at times, selective reporting of data. The field will remember

Source: From Bowers, K. S., & Farvolden, P. (1996). Revisiting a century-old Freudian slip—From suggestion disavowed to the truth repressed. *Psychological Bulletin, 119,* 355–380. Copyright © 1996 by the American Psychological Association. Reprinted with permission.

Kenneth Bowers as someone who could rise above the fray and provide one of the few balanced accounts available of an extremely contentious literature.

———

The debate concerning recovered–false memories of childhood sexual abuse by adults in psychotherapy is rooted in different understandings of how memory and suggestion function. To help bridge that gap, the authors formulate a notion of repression that should be acceptable to most cognitive psychologists and to some clinicians. However, they also argue that repression of truly traumatic memories is rare. Many clinicians beginning with S. Freud have seriously underestimated the impact of suggestion on memory and belief. This underestimation has left adult patients vulnerable to suggested memories of childhood sexual abuse. Such suggested memories are then invoked as independent evidence for how adult psychopathology is rooted in such abuse. The authors propose some safeguards to mitigate against this confirmatory bias. ∎

Childhood sexual abuse has become a major social issue. This article is concerned with one especially controversial aspect of this issue—the status of repressed memories of childhood sexual abuse recovered by adults during the course of psychotherapy. On one hand, it is claimed that the prevalence of sexual abuse has been underestimated, in part because memory for it is typically repressed (Miller, 1986). According to this view, "retrieving memories of sexual abuse is an important part of the survivor's experience and one crucial to successful resolution of the trauma" (Olio, 1989, p. 99; see also Courtois, 1992). On the other hand, it has been argued that adult memories of sexual abuse are not so much recovered as iatrogenically created by therapists who are ideologically committed to the traumatic origins of adult psychopathology (Ofshe & Watters, 1994; Pendergrast, 1995). In turn, this argument is vigorously denounced as a backlash—as yet another attempt to minimize the incidence and prevalence of childhood sexual abuse. Here is but one example of such a reaction:

> I believe that many of the voices of the backlash are, if not perpetrators themselves, then apologists for perpetrators, whether knowingly or unknowingly, and it is this defense of the status quo and protection against the revelation of this secret that arouse such vituperative defense and counter-attack. (Bloom, 1994, p. 469; see also Conte, 1994; and Herman & Harvey, 1993)

Perhaps the most constructive reaction to such a comment is to acknowledge that the prevalence of childhood abuse considerably exceeds the prevalence of false memories of abuse.

However, critics of recovered memory (e.g., Crews, 1993, 1994a, 1994b; Ofshe & Singer, 1994; Pope, 1994) do not deny that child abuse is a problem; indeed, they often argue that false memories and accusations of sexual abuse are the worst enemy of genuine sexual abuse victims (e.g., E. F. Loftus, 1993). However, many critics do attack a central tenet of recovered-memory advocates, namely, the possibility that painful abuse memories can be repressed (E. M. Loftus & Ketcham, 1994; Ofshe & Watters, 1994). Skeptics argue that *repression* (or in some cases dissociation) of sexual abuse memories is a concept without any scientific merit (e.g., Holmes, 1974, 1990). Clearly, if repression does not exist, there can be no therapeutic recovery of repressed memories. Therefore, what appears to be a recovered memory of abuse can only be a false memory of abuse.

Amidst all the confusion this volatile issue has created, one thing has become increasingly clear: The nature of memory and the power of suggestion are unavoidably implicated in the debate over the validity of recovered memories of sexual abuse. Accordingly, a major goal of this article is to explore how different views of memory and suggestion contribute to the controversy. Whereas we agree that the risk of suggesting memories of abuse is considerable, we do not think it is necessary to abandon the notion of repression to make this point. Indeed, the claim for the therapeutic recovery of repressed memories of sexual abuse is logically independent of the claim that such memories are iatrogenically created. Accordingly, evidence for suggested–false memory is not automatically evidence against repressed–recovered memory, and vice versa.

In the first major section of this article, we attempt to formulate a notion of repression in a manner that should seem plausible to memory experts and at least some clinicians. The second major section of this article concerns the role of suggestion in psychotherapy. It begins with an historical review of Freud's (1905/1959c) 100-year-old theory of trauma and psychopathology—which serves as a model for today's trauma theorists. We examine how Freud was far more concerned than most current trauma therapists with the possibility that suggestive influences were at work in psychoanalytic therapy—although he ultimately and emphatically rejected this view. However, we argue that the grounds for this rejection have proved quite insufficient for the purpose of distinguishing between true and suggested *memories* of abuse. In the third and final section of this article, we note how repression and suggestion have implications for the conduct of contemporary psychotherapy.

First of all, however, we want to examine very briefly some issues regarding sexual abuse per se and how they relate to the debate under consideration.

SOME FINDINGS REGARDING SEXUAL ABUSE

There is a substantial literature on the incidence, prevalence, and effects of sexual abuse (e.g., Beitchman, Zucker, Hood, DaCosta, & Akman, 1991; Beitchman et al., 1992; Finkelhor, Hotaling, Lewis, & Smith, 1990; Haskell & Randall, 1993; Koss, Gidycz, & Wisniewski, 1987). Not surprisingly, the rates of reported abuse vary widely as a result of several factors, including what criteria were adopted for describing sexual abuse, whether the abuse was repeated, whether it was perpetrated by a father, whether coercion was involved, what the age of the victim was at the time of the abuse, and so forth (Beitchman et al., 1991, 1992). Various sample characteristics turn out to be crucial—for example, whether the participants are randomly selected from the population at large or from a clinic population, whether they are patients or student volunteers, whether they fill out questionnaires or are questioned in face-to-face interviews, and so on. Another important distinction concerns whether the data are based on children exposed to abuse who have come to the attention of social agencies (Ceci & Bruck, 1993a, 1993b) or on adult retrospective reports of sexual abuse experienced as children or as adolescents (e.g., Briere & Conte, 1993; Herman & Schatzow, 1987; Nash, Hulsey, Sexton, Harralson, & Lambert, 1993). In a somewhat different vein, recent evidence indicates that the reported incidence of child abuse is going up, whereas the corroboration of such reports is going down (Eckenrode, Powers, Doris, Munsch, & Bolger, 1993).

Sexual abuse that involves physical force or brutality is almost always traumatic, but when such brutality is absent, there is a wide spectrum of retrospective personal assessments of abuse incidents ranging from distinctly negative and traumatic to positive (Constantine, 1981; Levitt & Pinnell, 1995; Spence, 1994). Moreover, "many sexually abused children . . . are apparently asymptomatic" (Kendall-Tackett, Williams, & Finkelhor, 1993, p. 175). As well, the presumed negative effects of sexual abuse have been reported to be a more direct result of family pathology than of sexual abuse per se (Fromuth, 1986; Harter, Alexander, & Neimeyer, 1988; Nash et al., 1993).

These caveats do not render child sexual abuse any less egregious or the perpetrator of it any less accountable. Indeed, it is important to recognize that child sexual abuse should be condemned in its own right, not just in terms of its short- or long-term consequences for the abuse victim (Beitchman et al., 1991–1992). However, the fact that such abuse is not always traumatic does have an important implication for the topic at hand. If repression functions to keep traumatic memories from becoming conscious then the memory of sexual abuse that is not traumatic will presumably not be repressed. Such nontraumatic abuse may nevertheless be forgotten—for the same ordinary reasons that the name of one's second-grade teacher is forgotten. However, just as relevant reminders can accurately recover the name of a second-grade teacher, so too could they recall to mind an incident of sexual abuse. The point to emphasize is that such cued recall does not necessarily imply that the original forgetting was due to repression or that the things forgotten were originally traumatic. This is true even if the recalled incident generates in the remembering adult feelings of revulsion and distress that were absent when the childhood incident occurred (see Hacking, 1995).

Under the assumption that a particular person did in fact suffer nontraumatic child abuse that was subject to ordinary forgetting, it seems unlikely that the abuse would nevertheless engender serious psychopathology later on in life. Of course, an asymptomatic outcome of such abuse does not ordain a problem-free adulthood. However, there are adults who were sexually abused as children, and for some of them, the abuse incident(s) may well engender continuing adverse reactions, up to and including posttraumatic stress syndrome (PTSD; Eth, Randolph, & Brown, 1989; Horowitz, 1986; Meichenbaum, 1994; van der Kolk, 1994). Note that one of the main features of PTSD is recurrent, intrusive thoughts about the traumatic incident (van der Kolk & Saporta, 1991), which is virtually the opposite of repression. Nevertheless, there may be a few patients who handle memories of sexual abuse by blocking them out of their mind, either by repression or dissociation (Kaszniak, Nussbaum, Berren, & Santiago, 1988; Nash, 1994).

In summary, adults who seek therapy can be (a) people who have experienced traumatic childhood sexual abuse that they have never been able to forget, (b) people who have experienced traumatic childhood sexual abuse that they have successfully repressed, (c) people who experienced childhood sexual abuse that was not traumatic and that has been subject to ordinary forgetting, and (d) people who have never experienced childhood sexual abuse. There is no question that therapy must deal with the traumatic memories of people in the first category. Several problems arise with people in the last three categories, however. First, the relative frequency of patients in these three categories is typically difficult if not impossible to determine. Second, it is seldom if ever clear which of these three categories a particular patient belongs in. Third, the category a person belongs in presumably makes a great deal of difference in terms of how therapy should proceed. For example, consider a person who had been nontraumatically abused as a child and for whom the incident has been subject to ordinary forgetting. Successful therapeutic efforts to uncover the abuse incident is very apt to cause more problems than it solves. Under the injunction, "first do no harm," any effort to uncover memories of abuse in this case could be regarded as reflecting the therapist's needs and concerns rather than the patient's welfare. This would of course be even more true for patients in adult therapy who were in fact not abused as children.

Therapeutic efforts to uncover abuse perhaps makes some sense with patients who were in fact abused as children, for whom the abuse was experienced as traumatic, and who repressed the incident. As we have already stressed, however, it is unclear how many such people there are; it is also unclear how to distinguish them from people who were not abused or who simply forgot the abuse incident(s). However, it is our impression that trauma therapists regard patients in these latter two categories to be few in number compared with patients who have repressed memories of genuine sexual abuse experienced as children. This unverified and difficult-to-prove assumption evidently justifies their attempts to recover memories of abuse in a correspondingly high proportion of patients, even though

> there is not a single controlled study demonstrating any beneficial effect of therapeutic efforts to recover hidden memories of CSA [childhood sexual abuse] in clients who report no abuse history, and there is no convincing evidence to support the claim that practitioners can discriminate between clients with no awareness of abuse histories and clients with no abuse histories. (Lindsay, 1995, p. 288)

Critics of course regard the category of patients with repressed memories as virtually empty largely because they do not believe repression exists (e.g., E. M. Loftus & Ketcham, 1994; Ofshe & Watters, 1993, 1994).[1] What is the basis for such a reaction?

REPRESSED MEMORY

REPRESSION AND THE NATURE OF EVIDENCE

What is clear in surveying the literature on both sides of the repressed-memory controversy is how skeptics and advocates differ in what they count as evidence for repression. On the one hand, skeptics tend to regard laboratory investigations as the main, if not sole, venue to valid claims about human functioning. They look at the available evidence on repression and find it wanting (e.g., Bower, 1990; Crews, 1994a, 1994b; Grunbaum, 1984, 1986; Holmes, 1974, 1990). Many clinicians, on the other hand, are impressed with the various case reports indicating how people can defend against stressful thoughts or memories by rendering them unconscious, either by repression or some related means (e.g., Nemiah, 1984; Olio, 1989; Terr, 1990, 1994).

For instance, in the foreword of Diane Middlebrook's (1991) biography of the poet Anne Sexton, Martin Orne—who was the poet's therapist for many years—informs the reader that she "literally remembered almost nothing of relevance from one [therapy] session to the next" and that "Anne's severe memory problem . . . eventually [led] to an impasse in her therapy" (p. 15). As a consequence, Orne decided to tape-record their therapy sessions so that Sexton could review the previous hour's therapy before coming to the next session.[2] As clinicians, we see no reason to doubt Orne's observation that Sexton indeed had serious memory problems that went far beyond ordinary forgetting and that repression or dissociation were probably involved.

In another high-profile case, Gordon Bower (1981) reported that Sirhan Sirhan had absolutely no waking recall of actually shooting Robert F. Kennedy, even though he was able to "relive" the event under hypnosis. However, Bower continued, Sirhan

> denied that he had ever been hypnotized . . . , denied that it was his own voice on the tape recorder, and denied that it was his handwriting—he alleged that [the hypnotist] must have hired an actor or a handwriting specialist to mimic him. Sirhan eventually did accept the theory that he must have killed Bobby Kennedy. . . . But his belief was based on "hearsay," much as is my belief that I was born on a Wednesday evening—I must have been there but I sure cannot remember it. (p. 130)

The issue of just what constitutes evidence is central here. When preceded by the word *scientific,* the word *evidence* is valorized. Not all scientific evidence, however, is convincing or probing (e.g., Andreski, 1972; Lykken, 1968, 1991; Meehl, 1978, 1990), and many warranted beliefs do not need to be scientifically validated—for example, a belief that nettles sting, water slakes thirst, and losing at love hurts. More abstractly, the claim that mesmerism is the same phenomenon as hypnosis is widely accepted by scientists, even though this equivalence has never been established scientifically. Similarly, most people agree that witchcraft (in the supernatural sense) does not exist, even though this fact was never documented scientifically. Indeed, as Polanyi (1964) has pointed out,

> the destruction of belief in witchcraft during the sixteenth and seventeenth centuries was achieved in the face of an overwhelming, and still rapidly growing, body of evidence for its reality. Those who denied that witches existed did not attempt to explain this evidence at all, but successfully urged that it be disregarded. . . . [Ironically] one of the founders of the Royal Society, not unreasonably denounced this method as unscientific, on the ground of the professed empiricism of contemporary science. (p. 168)

Finally, claims based on careful clinical observation are not automatically rendered invalid simply because they are not confirmed in the laboratory. For instance, fugue states and psychogenic amnesia are genuine human conditions, their rarity notwithstanding (Schacter & Kihlstrom, 1989). It is simply not reasonable to maintain, in the presence of a person experiencing a psychogenic fugue, that there is no evidence for the existence of fugue states because the condition has not been confirmed in the laboratory.

Nevertheless, identifying a disorder is one thing; understanding it is quite another. In addition, scientifically controlled studies can make a major contribution to understanding various clinical disorders. For example, the florid manifestations of multiple personality disorder (MPD—renamed *dissociative identity disorder* [DID] in the *Diagnostic and Statistical Manual of Mental Disorders* [4th ed., *DSM-IV*], American Psychiatric Association, 1994) may be experienced by the patient as genuine, but we are not thereby obliged to invoke distinct personalities to account for different persona. Researchers have in fact clarified that explicit or conscious memory is more affected by alterations in personality than is implicit memory (Nissen, Ross, Willingham, Mackenzie, & Schacter, 1988). On the assumption that implicit memories are at least as pervasive and defining of a person as the memories he or she can explicitly recall, it seems likely that the different personalities of a patient with MPD (DID) share core features that help make the individual unique and singular, however multifarious he or she may appear to be at the level of explicit memory. This understanding of DID substantially qualifies the clinical understanding of it as an expression of distinct, independent personalities.

Other scientific studies of clinical syndromes (e.g., Kaszniak et al., 1988; Sackeim, Nordlie, & Gur, 1979; Schacter, Wang, Tulving, & Freedman, 1982) help to provide a more differentiated understanding of underlying mechanisms of overt behavior and subjective experience that are difficult or even impossible to appreciate without controlled observation. Yet, as seen in the next section, science at any given point in time is also limited in what it can unequivocally assert.

SITUATING REPRESSION

Scientific claims are always underdetermined by the available data so that science is at least in part a social and rhetorical process (Kuhn, 1962; Polkinghorne, 1983). Holton (1973) recognized this fact when he averred to the thematic dimension of science, which reflects "fundamental preconceptions of a stable and widely diffused kind that are not resolvable into or derivable from observation and analytic ratiocination" (p. 24). Among other things, such preconceptions establish in the scientist's mind the antecedent likelihood that certain things are likely true and worth pursuing, whereas other things are not.

In the minds of many laboratory scientists, repressed or dissociated trauma memories have a low antecedent likelihood of being valid, at least in part because they do not follow the usual rules of memory that are relatively easy to demonstrate in the laboratory, such as the fact that multiple exposure to information increases its memorability. By way of contrast, Terr (1994) has argued that single traumatic experiences are readily recalled—indeed are difficult to forget—whereas a repeated trauma (e.g., a young girl experiencing multiple molestations by her father) tends to be dissociated and virtually unavailable to recall. Terr's views have been quite influential in legal circles (Terr, 1994; Maclean, 1993; Spiegel & Scheflin, 1994), but it is not easy for memory researchers to accept the notion that memory for repeated trauma should differ so fundamentally from memory for nontraumatic events. In addition, Terr's claims about the nonmemorability of repeated trauma created an awkward inconsistency for her, as well. First, however, we have to consider the difference between repression and dissociation.

The terms *repression* and *dissociation* are sometimes used interchangeably, and even when this is not the case, the differences between them are often unclear (see Hilgard, 1977, for an important exception to this generalization). Some investigators (e.g., Erdelyi, 1990, p. 11) explicitly deny any formal distinction between repression and dissociation, emphasizing that they both function to keep things out of consciousness. However, in their coauthored book, *Studies in Hysteria,* Breuer and Freud (1893–1895/1955) had clearly different views of *why* material was not integrated into consciousness. Breuer's "hypnoid hysteria" represents an early, state-specific concept of memory. According to this view, when exogenous or endogenous information is processed in a state of reverie, hyperarousal, fatigue, and so forth, it often escapes integration into ordinary waking consciousness. Breuer acknowledged that his views on the subject were similar to Janet's (1901, 1907/1965) concept of dissociation, with one important exception: Breuer rejected Janet's claim that dissociation presupposed a biological weakness of mind. Janet's insistence on this point was probably a holdover from Jean Charcot's neurologizing of hysteria and hypnosis (see Shorter, 1992, chapter 7). Otherwise, the similarities between Janet and Breuer were striking compared with how they both differed from Freud's (1915/1959d) view of repression. For both Janet and Breuer, the disconnection of ideas from consciousness was a passive consequence of how they were processed in the first place. For Freud, repression involved an active eschewal of threatening information. Until fairly recently, Freud's notion of repression carried the day (Ellenberger, 1970; Perry & Laurence, 1984).

Terr (1994) was more explicit than many contemporary clinicians in distinguishing repression and dissociation. In effect, she proposed that *dissociation* involves inadequate processing of traumatic events at the time of their occurrence, whereas *repression* involves "block[ing] retrieval of something already fully registered and stored" (p. 70). One implication of Terr's views is that an "incident that engender[s] . . . repression may be recovered later, but any incidents that were part of the dissociated trance may be completely forgotten. Or, if remembered, they may be shrouded in a gauzelike haze" (p. 76).

Consider Terr's (1994) repression–dissociation distinction in the context of her insistence that a singular trauma is almost impossible to forget, whereas multiple traumas are dissociated and are therefore difficult or impossible to remember. From this juxtaposition, it seems to follow that memory for sexual abuse is either never forgotten (because it is a unique event) or unavailable to recall (because multiple incidents of abuse were dissociated at the time of their occurrence). What, then, are we to make of very clear and vivid memories of sexual abuse that are recovered many years later in the course of psychotherapy? Presumably, the only abuse memories that are inaccessible before therapy are those that have been dissociated; yet, according to Terr, dissociated memories are not just temporarily inaccessible to recall but also virtually unavailable (Tulving & Thomson, 1973). Accordingly, clear and vivid memories of sexual abuse retrieved during the course of psychotherapy are unlikely to be an accurate record of historical events.

Terr's (1994) theorizing thus led her to unintended conclusions that she could not possibly endorse, given her unequivocal committment to the position that clear, accurate memories of a singular trauma can be forgotten and then recovered, not only in therapy but sometimes spontaneously. For instance, Terr's expert testimony was largely responsible for the conviction of a man accused of murdering the childhood friend of his daughter. The main basis for Terr's testimony was the daughter's spontaneous, vivid, and detailed recollection of having witnessed her young friend's rape and murder 20 years earlier (Maclean, 1993; Spiegel & Scheflin, 1994). However, according to Terr's own theorizing, witnessing such a singular trauma should not be subject to repression, and if it were dissociated, it should not be available for such vivid, detailed recall 2 decades later. Accordingly, memory for the event was either never forgotten, unrecoverable, or invalid. The problem here is that Terr did not provide a viable concept of *repression*—one that can make a painful memory inaccessible without rendering it unavailable.

REPRESSION RECONSIDERED

As we indicate in more detail shortly, we view *repression* as motivated forgetting of information that is very threatening to one's self-esteem or self-concept (Erdelyi, 1985). Most of the time, however, the information repressed is not memory for a traumatic historical event but is instead an affectively loaded idea, memory, fantasy, or impulse (Davis, 1990; Weinberger, 1990). At a time when so much emphasis is placed on the recovery of repressed trauma memories, it is perhaps worthwhile to remind ourselves that Freud's segue from a trauma- to a conflict-based theory of adult psychopathology also shifted the burden of repression: No longer did it need to eradicate memory of historical trauma; it only had to filter, limit, or bias against consciousness of intrapsychic treats—provoked, as they often are by external stimulation. Given the essentially private and relatively evanescent nature of this latter material, the task of repression is perhaps less onerous than preventing truly traumatic memories from becoming conscious.

Indeed, as we have already mentioned, when it comes to a serious trauma, intrusive thoughts and memories of it are the most characteristic reaction, and there may be biological reasons why this is so (LeDoux, 1991, 1994; LeDoux, Romanski & Zagoraris, 1989; van der Kolk, 1994; van der Kolk & Saporta, 1991). Accordingly, repressing or dissociating memory of a traumatic event would seem to be a relatively rare event. There are some examples in the literature of amnesia for trauma among individuals who experienced combat (e.g., Grinker & Spiegel, 1945; Henderson & Moore, 1944; Kolb, 1988; see also an excellent review of functional amnesia by Schacter & Kihlstrom, 1989). As well, Williams (1994) presented some longitudinal data showing that 38% of 129 women did not report corroborated sexual abuse that they had experienced almost 2 decades earlier. Despite its superiority over strictly retrospective studies of child sexual abuse, it is not entirely clear whether and to what extent non-reported abuse in the Williams study was due to repression—as distinct from ordinary forgetting, infantile amnesia, embarrassment at mentioning the abuse incidents, and so on (Femina, Yeager, & Lewis, 1990; E. M. Loftus, Garry, & Feldman, 1994). As Kihlstrom (1995) has emphasized,

> better methodology is required to distinguish between those who do not recall actual abuse and those who do not report on it, and among the former, between memory failures that reflect repression, dissociation, and other pathological processes, and those that are benign. (p. 66)

For the most part, clinicians who advocate the importance and pervasivenss of repressed-trauma memories are hard put to provide convincing (i.e., corroborated) demonstrations of it. For instance, none of the people involved in the Chowchilla bus kidnapping have ever forgotten their near brush with death (Terr, 1981, 1983, 1990). Whereas Herman and Schatzow (1987) reported a high incidence of repressed memories of sexual abuse in 53 women in group therapy, these findings contrast sharply with results Herman and Hirschman (1981) reported earlier, wherein few if any of 40 incest victims were amnestic for their abuse. Indeed, neither *amnesia* nor *repression* is listed in the index of this earlier work.

Moreover, in a later book entitled *Trauma and Recovery,* Herman (1992) provided very little evidence for repressed trauma memories. Quite to the contrary, she asserted that "long after the danger is past, traumatized people relive the event as though it were continually recurring in the present" (p. 37). Even when talking about the constrictive effects of trauma, Herman's illustrative case material typically implied memory for the traumatic episode (e.g., a rape victim asserting that "I cut off all my hair. I did not want to be attractive to men" and "I would just stay home and I was just frightened," p. 46). One has to look very hard for examples of genuinely repressed trauma memories in this book, although there are many illustrations of how difficult it can be for individuals who have experienced trauma to give voice to unspeakable events they have experienced. However, one cannot infer repression from the fact that recurrent and intrusive memories of the unspeakable have for a long time remained unspoken. Even so, our point is not that repression of traumatic memories never occurs—only that it is rare.

Moreover, trauma sufficient to produce repressed memories of it is virtually impossible to demonstrate in the laboratory—even if there were no ethical proscriptions against doing so. After all, laboratory participants are very likely to assume that, whatever apparent dangers a laboratory investigation presents, built-in safety factors must be operative (e.g., Orne & Evans, 1965). Such an assumption should mitigate against laboratory-generated trauma sufficient to repress memory for it, even in the repression prone. However, it is arguably the case that repression of a lesser kind—for example, the tendency not to recall threatening thoughts and memories—has already been established in the laboratory (e.g., Davis, 1990; Weinberger, 1990).

All in all, it is perhaps not surprising that profound repression (or dissociation) of trauma memories, such as may occasionally be witnessed in a clinic, is virtually impossible to demonstrate in the lab. Ironically, because skeptics regard repressed trauma memories as very unlikely, they demand particularly high-quality evidence for the memories' existence. For many investigators, high-quality evidence means evidence from well-controlled experimental investigations. As we have just seen, however, well-controlled experimental findings that unequivocally demonstrate repressed trauma memories are most unlikely. Consequently, skeptics take the absence of such findings as evidence that repressed trauma memories do not exist. As clinicians, we are more sympathetic to clinical evidence for repressed trauma memories, and there is a plausible mental mechanism that renders repression totally nonproblematic, namely, thought avoidance (Bower, 1990; Erdelyi, 1993). A person who is struggling with difficult thoughts, memories, or both can attempt to put them out of his or her mind, with varying degrees of difficulty and success. If a person deliberately ejects anxiety-provoking thoughts, memories, or beliefs from consciousness frequently enough, the ejection can perhaps become habitual and automatic. In this way, the person eventually becomes unaware of both the disturbing thought and the fact that anything was (or is being) done to keep it from becoming conscious. As Erdelyi and Goldberg (1979) wittily put it, "this constitutes nothing other than an intrapsychic version of a 'cover-up' of the 'cover-up,' hardly a novel notion in this post-Watergate era" (p. 366).

The typical reaction of skeptics to this model of repression is to concede that something like this certainly occurs but that it is not repression; rather, it is motivated forgetting, suppression, or some other strategic mental maneuver (Ofshe & Watters, 1994). The repression that does not exist, according to skeptics, is an unconscious process over which a person has no control. However, when Freud (Breuer & Freud, 1893–1895/1955) first introduced the notion of repression, he described it as the intentional ejection of a painful thought or memory from consciousness. An editor's footnote to this original statement "clarified" that Freud's use of *intentional* in this context "merely indicates the existence of a motive and carries no implication of conscious intention" (p. 10). This comment is frankly revisionist, although clearly Freud himself later expanded the notion of repression in subsequent writing (e.g., Freud, 1915/1959d) and rather confused the issue in a manner that has been artfully exposed by Erdelyi (1985; see also Bowers, 1990, p. 152).

Still, one might reasonably ask how it is possible to avoid thinking of a thought or memory without first thinking about it. Does every attempt to avoid particular thoughts or memories paradoxically reinstate them (Wegner, 1994)? Research on the role of intuition in problem solving (Bowers, Farvolden, & Mermigis, 1994; Bowers, Regehr, Balthazard, & Parker, 1990) helps to clarify how this paradox can be finessed. One of several tasks used in these investigations involved presenting a series of word clues, each of them a low associate of the solution word. Participants were asked to respond to each successive clue with whatever word came to mind until they thought of the solution. In general, participants' responses associatively approached the solution closer and closer with each successive clue; nevertheless, participants sometimes reported that the solution just seemed to "pop" suddenly into their mind.

In the context of repression, the same process can work to engender avoidance of an idea or memory. Thus, if intuition is in part based on an approach to portend a solution as yet undiscovered, then repression may involve an avoidant reaction to portend a painful thought or memory (cf. Dollard & Miller, 1950). As Bowers (1984) has previously noted, what both repression and intuition have in common is a presentiment that currently emerging ideas are leading to something important that cannot be fully specified in advance, but which nontheless generates sufficient emotional valence to determine either avoidant or approach responses. (p. 244)

It is interesting in this regard that one of the defining criterion of PTSD is "persistent avoidance of stimuli *associated* [italics added] with the trauma" (*DSM-IV,* p. 428). The implication is surely that if one can avoid trauma-associated cues, there is a better chance of keeping trauma memories at bay. Indeed, it is claimed that the "avoidance of reminders may include amnesia for an important aspect of the traumatic event" (*DSM-IV,* p. 425). How is avoidance of reminders consistent with amnesia?

Although the initial act of repression may be volitional, intentional efforts to retrieve repressed memories may be unsuccessful simply because free recall in the absence of relevant cues is more difficult than cued recall. Moreover, in the absence of such cues, it would not necessarily be clear that there was an event to be recalled—and therefore little or no motivation to recover repressed memories. Indeed, the motivation is all in the direction of avoiding recall. Nevertheless, even for people with a "gift" for repression, sufficiently potent cues should simply overwhelm their motivated efforts to forget traumatic events. Thus, one way of getting combat survivors to recall trauma for which they are amnestic is to play recorded battle sounds when their critical reality testing is compromised by hypnosis or by drugs (Kolb, 1988). Recall that this was also the strategy that Orne (Middlebrook, 1991) used with his patient Anne Sexton—to play tapes of a previous session to remind her of what had happened and what progress had been made.

This relatively straightforward notion of repression is based on mental avoidance of threat and anxiety of a kind that Dollard and Miller (1950) emphasized years ago. This threat avoidance model of repression seems somehow insufficient to account for Sirhan Sirhan's massive repression of his assassination of Robert F. Kennedy—an event literally viewed by millions of people and the consequences for which were inescapable no matter what Sirhan believed. A qualitatively different kind of repression seems required; one has recently been proposed by R. V. Ramachandran (1995).

Some of Ramachandran's (1995) patients who have right parietal lesions denied their left-arm paralysis so totally and completely that they seemed to have no tacit, let alone explicit, awareness of their condition. In a series of tests, Ramachandran demonstrated how a small series of such patients maintained a clear conviction of their ability to use their left arm in the face of all evidence to the contrary—until one of the patients was administered a cold-water bath to her left ear. Under such vestibular stimulation, she acknowledged the problem that she had denied so tenaciously up until then. Unfortunately, the effects were short lasting. Not only did the patient eventually revert to denial of left-hand neglect but she also denied having an interim period of lucidity about her paralysis. Ramachandran

suggest[ed] that what one is really seeing is an amplified version of Freudian defense mechanisms . . . caught in *flagrant delicto;* mechanisms of the same sort that we all use in our daily lives. However, since the defenses are grotesquely exaggerated, studying them might give us for the first time an *experimental handle* on defense mechanisms, i.e., we might actually be able to study the rules governing their development by manipulating the stimulus contingencies in individual patients. (p. 26)

Ramachandran's (1995) article is much too rich and complex to review in detail, but it deserves a close reading by people who both agree and disagree with the entire notion of repression. For present purposes, the idea behind this second form of repression involves less threat avoidance per se than a total cognitive restructuring of evidence into a story that is most probable given conflicting evidence. The brain does this in the cognitive realm, just as it does in the visual domain. Thus, various visual illusions become an analogue for cognitive delusions, in that they both impose a most probable scenario onto a situation that is quite anomalous. The detection of a large-scale anomaly (such as a paralyzed left arm) recruits a virtual paradigm shift to protect the person from indecision and to promote and preserve a coherent account of the world and of the self. Ramachandran located this large-scale anomaly detector in the right hemisphere. Smaller scale anomaly detection he located in the left hemisphere, and he argued that these "innocent" repressions and rationalizations are part and parcel of everyday life for most individuals.

Among other things, the paradigm shift model of repression makes some sense out of Sirhan Sirhan's reaction to having assassinated R. F. Kennedy—that is, acknowledgment of the crime during hypnosis that was totally and unequivocally denied during a waking state (Dollard & Miller, 1950). In the context of such a momentous act, Sirhan just "chose" to stick with a story that best preserved his self-concept. Whether cold-water vestibular stimulation would have recovered the crime in a waking state remains a moot but intriguing question.

Whatever type of repression is suspected, the attempt to cue accurate memories risks suggesting false ones—an issue we consider later in some detail. However, even when suggested memories are not an issue—as is largely the case in individuals who experienced combat amnesia—there is "[no] guarantee that a recovered emotionally charged memory accurately reflects a psychologically traumatic incident" (Kolb, 1988, p. 273). Similar sentiments were expressed by a psychiatrist during an earlier war (McCurdy, 1918). More recently, Frankel (1994) has provided a critical analysis of "flashbacks," revealing them to be a problematic basis for establishing the historical accuracy of suddenly remembered events (Persinger, 1992). The important point is this: Endorsing the concept of repression does not commit theorists to the belief that recovered memories must be historically accurate in all particulars. A memory, by virtue of having been repressed, does not somehow escape the distortions and constructive features of memories in general (Bartlett, 1932; E. F. Loftus, 1993; Schacter, in press), and it is simply a mistake to assume that a sudden insight, flashback, or cathartic experience is self-validating. A couple of illustrations may make this point clearer.

Until the later part of the 19th century, all the known hydrocarbon molecules had a linear structure; however, the structure of benzene remained elusive. The story goes that one evening the Belgian chemist, Auguste Kekule, dreamt of snakes, at least one of which suddenly took its tail in its mouth, thereby forming a circle (Hein, 1966). Suddenly, Kekule appreciated the possibility that benzene might have a closed rather than a linear structure.[3] Subsequent work established the validity of this hypothesis.

We wish to emphasize about this incident that the snake dream was not evidence for the closed structure of benzene (see Hein, 1966); it functioned only to suggest a possible molecular structure for which independent evidence was required and obtained. Whereas this point is obvious enough vis-à-vis organic chemistry, it seems much harder to appreciate that the same point holds for psychology. For example, some reports (Ofshe & Watters, 1994; Terr, 1994; Wright, 1994) leave one with the distinct impression that fantasies, night dreams, or flashbacks—especially if they depict emotionally arousing or upsetting events—are often received as evidence for the historical reality of the events experienced (Courtois, 1991; Olio, 1989). A personal experience of Kenneth Bowers indicates just how problematic this view is.

About 15 years ago, he had an unusual dream, which delivered a thrilling and powerful insight—accompanied by absolute confidence in its truth. What he dreamed was this: Israel and Venezuela shared a common border. He was absolutely stunned by this revelation and asked himself over and over again: "How could I have lived more than 40 years and never realized this obvious fact before? Indeed, how could I be the very first person ever to see what was now so patently obvious." He was convinced that this insight was going to change the entire geopolitical situation in the Middle East. Venezuela had oil; Israel needed oil. Something could surely be worked out between the two countries who had no historical animosities. He was so excited by the dream that it woke him up. At first the transition from sleep to waking did nothing to diminish his confidence in this geographic insight. Only slowly did reality begin to seep in—in the form of the Atlantic Ocean, to say nothing of the Mediterranean Sea.

Now, consider a darker scenario. Suppose he had dreamt that he was sexually abused by his parents when he was 6 years old. Such a dream might well convince him that he had indeed been molested—*especially* if he had the "help" of a therapist who believed that most adult distress was rooted in childhood sexual abuse and that such dreams (among other things) revealed the nature and the perpetrator of the abuse. Where, may one ask, is the Atlantic Ocean when one really needs it; there would be nothing so formidable as 5,000 miles of water to challenge the conviction of having been molested. So, in effect, the content of the dream would become evidence for its validity. Surely the problems associated with this assumption are obvious.

Although recovered memories of abuse are never self-validating, this is quite different from insisting that they are always incorrect. However, their correctness needs to be independently established, rather than assumed. Corroborating memories of decades-old abuse can be an insurmountable obstacle for a therapist, who is in no position to play detective in any case. What complicates the situation is that many therapists accept such abuse memories at face value, in part because they feel they are rejecting the patient unless they confirm each and all of his or her ideas, memories, and beliefs (Olio, 1989). The therapist's acceptance of these conditions provides just the imprimatur that the patient requires to fully accept them as valid.

What this scenario leaves out is how the original emergence of the abuse memory may be suggested by the therapist in the first place, however unwittingly and unintentionally. In the next section, we examine this possibility at length.

SUGGESTION

We have previously mentioned that therapeutic efforts to recall repressed memories is a risk factor for suggesting them. It is time to examine this possibility more carefully. One way of doing so would be to review research showing how malleable memory is to postevent information (Garry, Loftus, & Brown, 1994; E. Loftus, 1979; Weingardt, Loftus, & Lindsay, 1995), to particular ways of processing information in an effort to recall it (e.g., Bartlett, 1932; Johnson, 1988a; Johnson, Hashtroudi, & Lindsay, 1993; Lindsay & Johnson, 1989; Ross, 1989), and to hypnotic or hypnosis-like suggestion (Labelle, Laurence, Nadon, & Perry, 1990; Laurence, Nadon, Nogrady, & Perry, 1986; Laurence & Perry, 1983; S. J. Lynn & Nash, 1993). In addition, there is a large literature on attitude, belief, and behavior change that is somewhat related to alterations of memory (Brown, 1995; Cialdini, 1993). As we discuss later, people can be convinced that something is true of their historical past even though they might not have a clear memory of the incident. There is no shortage of relevant research reviews of memory, however (see, e.g., Garry et al., 1994; Lindsay & Read, 1994); whereas we invoke such research, we do not attempt to duplicate such efforts.

Rather, we have chosen to proceed historically, focusing on some of Freud's 100-year-old contributions to the current debate regarding repressed versus suggested memories. Our reason for proceeding in this fashion is a considered judgment of what is most likely to register with practitioners. Just as laboratory scientists are apt to be unimpressed with the clinical evidence for repression, many practitioners are unimpressed with laboratory-based research on memory and suggestion. Indeed, if they are aware of such research at all, they often regard it as having little or no relevance to real-life memory—especially memory for previously repressed trauma. As Terr (1994) argued, "trauma sets up new rules for memory" (p. 52). So, whereas we certainly refer to relevant research, our main focus is to examine the clinical grounds for recovered memory of abuse.

PREAMBLE TO A 100-YEAR-OLD DEBATE

Leading advocates of repressed memory invoke Freud's (1896/1959a) chapter, "The Aetiology of Hysteria," as a kind of talisman for repressed trauma memories. Judith Herman (1992), who is a leader in the recovered-memory movement, argued that

> this paper still rivals contemporary clinical descriptions of the effects of childhood sexual abuse. It is a brilliant, compassionate, eloquently argued, closely reasoned document. Its triumphant title and exultant tone suggest that Freud viewed his contribution as the crowning achievement in the field. (p. 13)

Jeffrey Masson, whose book *The Assault on the Truth* in many ways inspired a return to Freud's (1896/1959a) traumatic theory of neurosis, simply referred to "The Aetiology of Hysteria" as "Freud's most brilliant" (Masson, 1985a, p. 26) chapter. In the context of the growing appreciation that sexual abuse of children is a serious problem, this early chapter seems to many people not only profound but prophetic.

However, there was a serious problem with Freud's (1896/1959a) trauma theory. As Alice Miller (1986) pointed out:

> In "The Aetiology of Hysteria" Freud is struggling with . . . resistance on the part of the public. He knows that he has hit upon a truth that concerns everyone, i.e., the consequences of childhood trauma for later life . . . , and at the same time he knows that the overwhelming majority of people will oppose him precisely because he is telling the truth. (p. 110)

According to theorists like Herman, Masson, and Miller, opposition to Freud's trauma theory led him to abandon it; for them, this recantation represents "a failure of courage" (Masson, 1985a, p. 190)—a particularly stinging criticism because courage has always been an important part of Freud's cachet (Gay, 1988; Jones, 1961). According to Masson, trauma theory was so badly received that only by abandoning it was Freud able to ensure the survival of psychoanalysis—the Mephistophelian implication was that Freud sacrificed Truth in the hopes of achieving lasting fame. Herman (1992) put a distinctly feminist spin on her assessment of Freud's change of heart: "Out of the ruins of the traumatic theory of hysteria, Freud created psychoanalysis. The dominant psychological theory of the next century was founded in the denial of women's reality" (p. 14). Courtois (1991) went even further: Feminists "view the [Oedipal] theory as nothing short of a cover-up that denies the reality of child sexual abuse while excusing its perpetrators" (p. 50).

It is not difficult to detect a sense of moral condemnation in these assessments of Freud's (1896/1959a) switch from a trauma-based to a conflict-based theory of adult neurosis. The grounds for this reaction are straightforward: Child sexual abuse occurs frequently and leaves lasting psychological scars—especially when abuse victims are unable to remember or speak of it (Summit, 1983). With considerable pain and anguish, Freud's patients (mostly women) revealed to him the abuse they had suffered as children, most often at the hands of their fathers. For a while, he listened to them. However, because such reports were so unpalatable and unpopular, Freud switched allegiances: Rather than speaking the truth on behalf of his patient, he courted the favor of his peers. He did so by rejecting the patients' abuse memories as accurate reflections of historical events and chose to regard them as fantasies instead. To have discovered the Truth and then abandoned it to curry favor with professional colleagues is morally reprehensible.

By implication, the moral high ground involves repossessing Freud's (1896/1959a) original insights into the traumatic origin of adult neurosis. Doing so restores the intellectual basis for trauma theory and therapy, thereby sanctioning therapeutic efforts to recover the historical basis of patients' "suffering." However, it is to be expected that the same forces are operating today as were operating in Freud's time to resist child sexual abuse as a pervasive and malignant reality in the lives of many patients seeking psychotherapy (Miller, 1986). These forces simply cannot be permitted to win a second time. Given the moral imperative that fuels trauma theory and practice, it is perhaps not surprising that research on memory and suggestion—which raises doubts about the historical accuracy of abuse memories—is typically dismissed as a dangerous irrelevancy.

It is the moral dimension of this debate that gives it such intensity. It is not simply a dispute over data and theory; it is a matter of Truth and how it affects people's lives. For recovered memory advocates, the Truth is the pervasiveness of child sexual abuse that has been denied by generations of practitioners, and more recently, by scientists—whose research on memory simply has not captured the malignant reality of how such abuse ruins people's lives. For some advocates of false memory, the Truth is that repression does not exist and that recovered memories of sexual abuse are the result of trauma ideology run amok. As the editors of a recent special issue of *Consciousness and Cognition* on the topic of recovered versus false memory put it: "We wanted vital social interest, but we got something closer to a religious war" (Banks & Pezdek, 1994, p. 265).

Our aim is to examine more closely the intellectual origins of repressed trauma and its alleged pathogenic significance. Insofar as current clinical practice is intellectually grounded in Freud's original trauma theory,[4] we focus on a good deal of our attention on its validity. If it is shown to be problematic, so too are the moral imperatives that are currently associated with it. However, we address not only Freud's early trauma views of psychopathology but his later conflict theory, as well. As we discuss later, there are legitimate grounds for questioning Freud's later conflict theory of psychopathology other than those forwarded by trauma theorists. What is more, the grounds for questioning the conflict theory are virtually identical to the grounds for questioning its precursor.

In none of what follows should it be inferred that we question the incidence, prevalence, and effects of actual childhood abuse. That is not the issue: Childhood sexual abuse is clearly a widespread societal problem. The issue we address is whether recovered memories of abuse that emerge in therapy 20–40 years after the alleged abuse incidents can be trusted as reflecting actual abuse, or whether the convictions of the therapist engender suggested abuse that is difficult or impossible for either therapist or patient to distinguish from the real thing.

REEXAMINING FREUD

In "The Aetiology of Hysteria," Freud (1896/1959a) presented his argument for a traumatic theory of hysteria, based on his findings from 18 patients with hysteria. This theory assumed that a child was a more or less passive "victim" of a premature sexual experience imposed by a trusted caretaker or by another child. Freud argued that for this trauma to result in hysterical symptoms later on in life, memory for such childhood incidents must be repressed.[5] In fact, "hysterical symptoms are derivatives of memories operating unconsciously" (Freud, 1896/1959a, p. 208); accordingly, the point of therapy is to convert "unconscious memories of infantile scenes into conscious recollection" (p. 207).

Freud made it clear that this is not easy work because hysterics "can be induced only under the very strongest compulsion of the treatment to engage in reproducing the scenes" (1896/1959a, p. 199). Although it is difficult to know exactly what Freud meant here, one plausible interpretation is that patients must visualize traumatic incidents as a way of remembering them. Indeed, on another occasion, Freud stated, "when memories return in the form of pictures our task is in general easier than when they return as thoughts" (Breuer & Freud, 1893–1895/1955, p. 280). If visualization of scenes as a way of recovering memory is what Freud had in mind, his comment must be seen in the light of the investigations of his near contemporary, Sir

Frederick Bartlett. On the basis of his memory research, Bartlett concluded that "the appearance of a visual image is followed by an increase of confidence entirely out of proportion to any objective accuracy that is thereby secured" (1932, p. 60; for a contemporary treatment of imagery–memory interface, see Dobson & Markham, 1993; Intraub & Hoffman, 1992; and Markham & Hynes, 1993). Thus, visualizing scenes of sexual abuse has a good chance of increasing a person's confidence that abuse occurred, even when it did not.

What is perhaps even more curious about Freud's (1896/1959a) "strongest compulsion" comment is this: It was offered as an argument against the possibility that the effects of treatment are due to suggestion. Here is what Freud has to say about this possibility:

> The behavior of the patients who reproduce these infantile experiences is in every respect incompatible with the assumption that the scenes are anything but a most distressing reality which is recalled with the utmost reluctance. Before they are analysed, the patients know nothing of these scenes; they are generally indignant if we tell them that something of the sort is now coming to light. . . . [W]hilst calling these infantile experiences into consciousness they experience the most violent sensations, of which they are ashamed and which they endeavor to hide, and they still try, even after going through them again and again in so convincing a fashion, to withhold belief by emphasizing the fact that *they have no feeling of recollecting these scenes as they had in the case of other forgotten material.* (Freud, 1896/1959a, p. 199, italics added)

Then, just to ensure there was no misunderstanding, Freud argued in a chapter 2 years later that therapists can

> boldly demand confirmation of our suspicions from the patient. We must not be led astray by initial denials. If we keep firmly to what we have inferred, we shall in the end conquer every resistance by emphasizing the unshakeable nature of our convictions. . . . Moreover, the idea that one might, by one's insistence, cause a patient who is psychically normal to accuse himself falsely of sexual misdemeanors—such an idea may safely be disregarded as an imaginary danger. (Freud, 1898/1955a, p. 269)

The irony of this last comment should not be lost. By the time the chapter containing this last quotation was published, Freud (1896/1959a) was privately beginning to think that the sexual incidents he pursued with such diligence and sense of discovery were instead the product of the patient's fantasy and imagination. As indicated by his letters to Wilhelm Fliess, this change in heart occurred in September of 1897 (Masson, 1985b, pp. 264–267). However, Freud did not publish his conversion to the conflict theory until 1905 in "Three Essays on the Theory of Sexuality" (Freud, 1905/1955). In a shorter essay also published in 1905, and entitled, "My Views on the Part Played by Sexuality in the Aetiology of the Neurosis," Freud (1905/1959c) entered a mea culpa, in which he recanted his traumatic theory in favor of a fantasy-based, conflict-theory of neurosis. In one critical passage, he stated,

> it happened by chance that my earlier, not very plentiful material contained a disproportionately large number of cases in whose infantile history seduction by adults or

other older children had played the chief part. I overestimated the frequency of these occurrences, which are otherwise quite authentic, and all the more so since I was not at this period able to discriminate between the deceptive memories of hysterics concerning their childhood and the memory-traces of actual happenings. (p. 276)

In this passage, Freud (1905/1959c) admitted to being fooled by the small number of hysterical cases on which he had based his earlier theory, acknowledged the authenticity of sexual seduction in those patients, and implicitly promised to deliver a clear basis for discriminating fantasies from actual seductions. As we discuss later, the unfulfilled nature of this promise continues to haunt contemporary psychotherapy.

According to several reviews (e.g., Crews, 1993; Powell & Boer, 1994; Schimek, 1987), there is a perverse irony involved in Freud's transition from the trauma to the conflict theory. The basic issue is this:

> Freud's conclusion that hysteria always requires the occurrence of sexual abuse in early childhood was not based directly on the patients' reports and conscious memories, but involved a great deal of selective interpretation and reconstruction. . . . By changing the original seduction theory, Freud did not suppress clear and unambiguous evidence; he only changed some aspects of his interpretation of the data—namely their ultimate origin in an internal fantasy rather than an external trauma. (Schimek, 1987, pp. 938-939)

Freud's reconstruction of his patients' trauma memories was based on their dreams, fantasies, and transference. Moreover, he "did not make . . . a distinction between what was consciously remembered, unconsciously reproduced, or mostly reconstructed" (Schimek, 1987, p. 947). In fact,

> it is clear that these "reproductions" were not presented and experienced as memories, thus were not acknowledged and recognized by the patient. It is *Freud* [italics added] who concluded that the material refers to a trauma that actually took place in the patient's early childhood. (Schimek, 1987, p. 943)

To summarize, although Freud often gave the impression that he reported uncovered memories of passively experienced sexual abuse experienced by his patients, he in fact *interpreted* various signs, symptoms, dreams, and fantasies as reflecting recovered memories of abuse. As Crews (1993) noted,

> Freud himself laid down the outlines of the seduction plots, which were then fleshed out from "clues" supplied by his bewildered and frightened patients, whose signs of distress he then took to be proof that his constructions were correct. (p. 62)

Crews then cited Esterson (1993) to devastating effect: "So having decided that his *own* constructions [about childhood abuse] are untrue, [Freud] concludes that they are not genuine occurrences, but are phantasies *of his patients!*" (p. 133). Powell and Boer (1994) concurred:

> Freud's apparent tendency to inform the patient explicity of his hypothesis and then aggressively demand that the patient produce memories to confirm that hypothesis

calls into question much of the clinical material he gathered at that time [i.e., when he was formulating his trauma theory]. (p. 1288)

It seems pretty clear that Freud's original trauma theory was problematic in a sense that he himself did not entirely appreciate. It was not just that his patients' memories of sexual abuse were confabulations; rather, there is considerable doubt about whether they had any such memories at all (see also Israels & Schatzman, 1993; Schatzman, 1992). By this understanding, Freud's abdication of his trauma theory was not nearly the cruel abandonment of abused patients as current recovered-memory advocates have argued.[6]

One small blessing of Freud's trauma theory was that such beliefs could, in principle, be independently corroborated—although the practical difficulties of doing so are formidable. However, the transition from a trauma-based seduction theory of neurosis to a conflict-based Oedipal theory renders corroboration all but impossible. Fantasied seductions can only be inferred rather than observed, so in the transition from his first to his second theory of hysterical neurosis, Freud asked the reader to abandon entirely historical truth for psychological or narrative truth. It is a vexing request (Spence, 1982, 1994).

Foremost among the difficulties presented by this transition is this: Whatever problems Freud may have had in defending his first theory against the charge of suggestion could only get worse with his second theory. If anything, he became more adamant in defending his second theory against such charges. Freud (1915–1917/1966) addressed this issue in chapter 28 of his book, *Introductory Lectures on Psychoanalysis,* written long after his shift from the traumatic to the conflict theory of neurosis:

> There is a risk that the influencing of our patient may make the objective certainty of our findings doubtful. . . . This is the objection that is most often raised against psycho-analysis [sic], and it must be admitted that, though it is groundless, it cannot be rejected as unreasonable. If it were justified, psycho-analysis would be nothing more than a particularly well-disguised and particularly effective form of suggestive treatment and we should have to attach little weight to all that it tells us about what influences our lives, the dynamics of the mind or the unconscious. That is what our opponents believe; and in especial they think that we have "talked" the patients into everything relating to the importance of sexual experiences. (p. 452)

According to Freud, "these accusations are contradicted more easily by an appeal to experience than by the help of theory" (Freud, 1915–1917/1966, p. 452). Experience taught him that the

> [patient's] conflicts will only be successfully resolved and his resistances overcome if the anticipatory ideas he is given tally with what is real in him. Whatever in the doctor's conjectures is inaccurate drops out in the course of the analysis; it has to be withdrawn and replaced by something more correct. (p. 452)

Then, just a little later in the same paragraph, Freud argued that

> at the end of an analytic treatment . . . if success is . . . obtained . . . , it rests, not on suggestion, but . . . [on] . . . overcoming . . . internal resistances, [and] on the internal change that has been brought about in the patient. (p. 453)

Finally, in one of his very late chapters, Freud made perhaps his last statements on the issue of suggestion:

> The danger of our leading a patient astray by suggestion, by persuading him to accept things which we ourselves believe but which he ought not to, has certainly been enormously exaggerated. An analyst would have had to behave very incorrectly before such a misfortune could overtake him; above all, he would have to blame himself with not allowing his patients to have their say. I can assert without boasting that such an abuse of "suggestion" has never occurred in my practice. (Freud, 1937/1959b, pp. 363–364)

Clearly in these passages, Freud (1937/1959b) felt that he had addressed and put to rest the issue of suggestion. Doing so was critical. For if patients merely internalize therapists' suggestions, then their memories or fantasies regarding childhood sexuality are not an independent confirmation of Freud's theories but are simply a perverse echo of them. Freud argued that his theory was saved from this dismal fate because incorrect interpretations would not "tally" with anything real in the patient and would, therefore, be rejected. In other words, only an accurate interpretation will "take"; if false, it would not be accepted or internalized as a suggestion.

It was philosopher of science Adolf Grunbaum (1984, 1986) who recently called attention to this tally argument. We agree that it is an important if not the sole basis for Freud's (1937/1959b) distinguishing what is true from what is false about the patient. We concur with Freud up to a point: It is also our experience that patients do not accept just any interpretation made about their inner life. However, it does not follow that whatever the patient ultimately does accept is True. But that is precisely what Freud's tally criterion seems to imply. If, for instance, a patient overcomes initial resistance to the idea that his or her difficulties have a sexual basis, the ultimate acceptance of this idea can *only* occur because some pre-existing sexual issue in the patient's makeup resonates with and confirms this interpretation.

As the quotations above make clear, Freud's (1937/1959b) understanding of this crucial matter depended on the fact that patients do not internalize suggestions that are untrue—a very dubious assumption indeed.[7] For instance, both Rossi and Erickson (Erickson & Rossi, 1980), and especially Janet (1925; Macmillan, 1991), reported therapy cases in which suggestion was successfully used to replace a particularly malignant history with a more benign one (see Perry, Laurence, D'Eon, & Tallant, 1988, for a review of these and other similar cases). However, as Freud fully appreciated, it would be mortally wounding to the psychoanalytic agenda if his interpretations were internalized as a suggestion, and he resisted this possibility with as much force and vigor as most of his patients resisted Freud's insistence on the sexual etiology of their difficulties.[8]

However, Freud *also* viewed patient resistance to his interpretations as further evidence that his theories were correct. Indeed, as some of the quotations above from Freud imply, it often seems that the more strongly his patients resisted, the more evidence it was that his theory and interpretation of the patients' difficulties were correct, and the more he pressed his patients to accept them. In other words, *both* resistance to his interpretations *and* acquiescence to them were accepted as validating his emerging theories. The upshot is that it was impossible for patients to say anything that could possibly disconfirm Freud's theory about why they were distressed. In addition, this, of course, puts psychoanalysis out of the reach of science (Popper, 1962).

In summary, our argument boils down to the fact that Freud has not successfully discriminated two quite different cases. In one case, a female patient reluctantly accepted an interpretation because it accurately identified and revealed the sexual origins of her difficulties. In the other case, the patient reluctantly accepted and internalized this view as a suggestion because it seemed to account for much of the patient's current distress and misery (Ganaway, 1989, 1994). In other words, Freud was unsuccessful in discriminating the patient's reluctant acceptance of the Truth from the patient's reluctant acceptance of suggestion. His inability in this regard should not be surprising; it is a profoundly difficult problem that continues to bedevil psychologists. Indeed, the tally argument's inability to clearly demarcate these two quite different possibilities remains a critically important issue in the current recovered-memory debate. That is, the mere fact that a patient in therapy recovers and accepts as true a memory that he or she was sexually molested as a child does not by itself clarify whether the remembered events actually happened, or whether they represent the suggestive impact of a therapist's conviction that childhood abuse is at the root of much adult "misery."

Although we are being critical of Freud here, we are not arguing that Freud's ideas were always wrongheaded—that, for instance, the sexual etiology of adult neurosis is totally and always fallacious, that incest or repression never occurs, or that memories of sexual abuse, even those recovered in therapy, are always mistaken. Rather, our point is that his tally criterion does not permit psychologists to distinguish clearly between when a particular patient accepts a Freudian interpretation of his or her difficulties because it is true and when it is accepted and internalized as a suggestion.

As some of the earlier quotations indicate, Freud at least struggled with the entire notion of suggestion (see Wachtel, 1993, chapter 9, for a sympathetic review of Freud's attempt to cope with suggestion in psychoanalysis). This struggle took place even though most research on social influence, on the vicissitudes of memory, and on suggestion was yet to be done. Curiously, contemporary trauma therapists, who do have the benefit of such research, seem to struggle much less than Freud did with the role of suggestion in psychotherapy. Instead, some combination of intellectual ignorance (of pertinent contemporary research), intellectual arrogance (simply dismissing all such research as irrelevant to psychotherapy), and intellectual laziness are involved in the presumption that psychological distress in adults is routinely rooted in childhood sexual abuse. Such a presumption implies that therapy can be reduced to the tenacious rooting out of such "victimization"—the strong assumption being that success in recovering memories of abuse is necessary for healing. Less dramatic perhaps, but certainly less freighted with presupposition, is the art of collaborating with patients in an attempt to help them deal better with current difficulties in living—whatever their source might be. Few people have been so articulate in espousing such a view as Paul Wachtel.

COUNTERVAILING CONSIDERATIONS

In chapter 9 of his *Therapeutic Communication,* Wachtel (1993) addressed forthrightly the smudged boundary between accurate attribution of a patient's present feelings and thoughts, on one hand, and suggesting the possibility that certain things might be true, on the other. Near the beginning of this chapter, he asserted that "an attributional comment will be useful . . . only if it addresses a tendency that is at least [a] potential [one] in the patient, if it has some ring of truth or familiarity to it" (p. 157). Later, he said that his preferred manner of communicating

> blurs boundaries. What is the therapist's viewpoint and what is the patient's is for the moment partially obscured. And of course, this is precisely its point: it is designed, in essence, to insert a new idea into the patient's inner dialogue, to encourage the patient to adopt a perspective from the therapist, to identify with a different point of view that, it is hoped, will be liberating. (p. 159)

Then, in the next paragraph, Wachtel (1993) continued,

> the therapist's comments . . . can easily be rejected if they are read as alien. And they are likely to be experienced as alien if they do not in fact resonate with some aspects of the patient's own aspirations, values, or vision of what is possible in his life. (p. 160)

The quotations above are clearly recognizable as a restatement of Freud's (1937/1959b) tally criterion. Later, Wachtel (1993) provided some indication of how his use of the tally criterion differs from Freud's:

> Thus, even if we attempt quite consciously to guide the patient in a particular direction—and it must always be in a direction that is our best guess as to what the patient would do if he were free of irrational anxiety or conflict, not what the therapist might prefer to do—we can be confident that the human tendency constantly and actively to organize and reinterpret material will assure that what follows will not be simple parroting of our message. The strongest likelihood, indeed, is that the suggestion the therapist makes will lead the patient in quite unanticipated directions. (p. 172)

Note the emphasis on how the patient will move in "unanticipated directions," rather than fulfilling the therapist's theoretical expectations. What is more, Wachtel's (1993) position clearly and honestly acknowledges—one might even say celebrates—suggestive influences in therapy. At the same time, Wachtel credited and respected the patient's inner experience as a corrective on interpretations that stray too far from what the patient can assimilate. However, when an interpretation is accepted by the patient, it can be because something true has been discerned, because a suggestion has been accommodated and internalized, or some combination thereof. So, unlike Freud (1937/1959b), Wachtel invoked the tally criterion, not to discriminate between interpretations that are True versus those that function merely as suggestions but rather, to protect the patient against untoward or pernicious suggestive influences. Insofar as therapy is conducted by humans, even this more realistic use of the tally criterion is by no means fail-safe. Nevertheless, on the assumption that suggestive influences in therapy are inevitable, contemporary trauma therapists have much to learn from Wachtel's approach to psychotherapy.

Wachtel (1993) challenged the traditional psychoanalytic assumption that therapy simply permits change without actively producing it. His sympathy with more behavioral views of therapy (Wachtel, 1977) allowed him to see this point clearly. However, he brought a psychodynamic sensibility to the behaviorist's agenda by focusing on the patient's *current* feelings and perceptions, which are doubtless related in some coherent way to the patient's historical past. However, unlike traditional psychoanalysis, he emphasized that therapeutic interventions have to tally only with the patient's current perception and experience, not with some historical event that is typically beyond independent corroboration, and the patient's memory for which is subject to all sorts of distortions. Moreover, when an interpretation is internalized, it does not imply that it is historically True; rather, the attributional–suggestive character of an interpretation is evaluated in terms of whether it encourages the patient to overcome fears and helps to alter maladaptive patterns of behavior.

By contrast, trauma therapy proceeds on the Freudian assumption that historical Truth is both knowable and necessary for healing and that in the context of psychotherapy, the tally criterion serves to demarcate what is true from what is false. Thus, Herman and Harvey (1993) argued that "therapists often make suggestions, but patients will respond only when those suggestions resonate with their own feelings and experiences. If a therapist is on the wrong track, most patients simply say so" (p. 6). So far, their position seems indistinguishable from Wachtel's (1977, 1993). However, they then go on to say: "If the therapist persists in pursuing a false hypothesis, therapy is ineffective, and the patient will usually look elsewhere for help" (p. 6). It seems such a small, inconsequential addendum, but notice how it implies—more in keeping with Freud than with Wachtel—that a false idea will not be assimilated and internalized as a suggestion. In the next section, we see where Herman (1992) went with this implication.

SEEKING AND UNCOVERING TRUTH

Secure in the notion that patients do not accept a "false hypothesis"—that the tally criterion serves to distinguish what is false from what is true—Herman (1992) asserted that the therapist must be committed "to truth-telling without evasion or disguise" (p. 135).

> From the outset, the therapist should place great emphasis on the importance of truth-telling and full disclosure, since the patient is likely to have many secrets, including secrets from herself. The therapist should make clear that the truth is a goal constantly to be striven for, and that while difficult to achieve at first, it will be attained more fully in the course of time. (p. 148)

Clearly, Herman (1992) sought historical truth—the existential facts of one's past (Spence, 1982). In doing so, she did not take seriously the possibility that the historical truth is likely to be some combination of unknowable and inaccurate.

Moreover, the way Herman (1992) framed the goals of therapy subtly implied that the historical facts uncovered in the course of therapy will likely be bad and that it will therefore take a good deal of time and emotional turmoil before the patient will be able to deal with them. Accordingly, any relatively benign account of distress that the patient forwards early on during the course of therapy is readily regarded as "denial"—that is, as a way of defending oneself against a far darker truth. Then, if and when something emotionally terrifying does eventually emerge, it is likely true. This conclusion is of course a non sequitur. Even under the pessimistic (Freudian) assumption that the truth is always bad, it does not follow that everything bad is true. However, in the absence of any independent corroboration of bad news (e.g., memories of sexual or physical abuse) that emerges during the course of therapy, the emotional upheaval that accompanies such "insight" is readily misappropriated as validating it.

Finally, "bad news" therapy obscures how a female patient, for example, was originally set up to expect something distressing, how within that context she has spent considerable time and emotional resources seeking a worst-case scenario for her difficulties, and that unless something bad eventually surfaces, she is apt to experience herself as having failed therapy. All in all, Herman's (1992) commitment to seeking and uncovering the Truth obscures the powerful suggestive impact that her therapeutic goals and procedures can implicitly have on her patients.

The problem of suggestion is especially evident in Herman's (1992) work with incest victims who are seen in group therapy. As Herman recounted in her book, "the goals most frequently chosen [by such groups] include recovering new memories or telling some part of the [trauma] story to another person" (p. 222). Furthermore, "the work of the group focuses on the shared experience of trauma in the past, not on interpersonal difficulties in the present" (p. 223). So, contra Wachtel (1993), the group focused on what was temporally remote and difficult (if not impossible) to verify, rather than on what was current and imminent in their lives. Among other things, this orientation generated increased solidarity with other group members and reduced the possibility of conflict among them. Participants who are on a common quest for external trauma that took place in the past are less likely to notice and respond insightfully to each others' present patterns of interpersonal interaction that maintain and exacerbate difficulties in living (Wachtel, 1993).

> The cohesion that develops in a trauma-focused group enables participants to embark upon the tasks of remembrance and mourning. The group provides a powerful stimulus for the recovery of traumatic memories. As each group member reconstructs [his or] her own narrative, the details of [the] story almost inevitably evoke new recollections in each of the listeners. In the incest survivor groups, virtually every member who has defined a goal of recovering memories has been able to do so. Women who feel stymied by amnesia are encouraged to tell as much of their story as they do remember. Invariably the group offers a fresh emotional perspective that provides a bridge to new memories. In fact, the new memories often come too fast. At times it is necessary to slow the process down in order to keep it within the limits of the individual's and the group's tolerance. (Herman, 1992, p. 224)

One can read this quotation as a straightforward account of truth seeking and truth telling by participants who have in fact experienced the trauma of incest. In that case, confiding the traumatic incident might be appropriate and healing (Pennebaker, 1989; Pennebaker & Susman, 1988; but see Greenberg & Stone, 1992, whose carefully designed study cast doubt on the benefits of disclosure). However, the quotation above can also be read as engendering suggested abuse in people who are "miserable" for other reasons. An emerging abuse narrative can be convincing in part because it is emotionally distressing (and must therefore be true) and in part because it is so readily accepted and endorsed by cohorts, who recognize the truth because "they've been there." Here is an example of this dynamic at work, taken from Herman's (1992) influential book:

Schatzow: *Is your question whether, in the process of recovering memories, people started out with images?*

Robin: *Yes.*

Leila: *I definitely did. I'd have little pieces, a dream and then a feeling.*

Robin: *Yeah. See, I had a whole story that happened, and this was like the missing piece of the story. My sister and I ended up in a foster home, and I never knew how that happened. My story at the time was that my father couldn't take care of us so he had to give us up against his will. But now as I recover more of these—images—whatever they are …*

Lindsay: *Happenings.*

Herman: *Experiences.*

Robin: *Thank you—now it seems that we were taken away from him. I have an image of running away from home and being out on the street and then I'm in the foster home. I had all those pieces together, even the part about running away, but I still didn't have the piece about the room. That just happened this week. It's still hard for me to believe that that happened to a little girl. I was only about ten years old.*

Leila: *That's how old I was too.*

Belle: *Jesus!*

Robin: *But can I believe it?*

Lindsay: *Yeah, do you believe it now?*

Robin: *It's still hard to believe it actually happened to me. I wish I could say I do and have a lot of conviction behind it, but I can't.*

Corinne: *It's enough that you know the image. I mean, you don't have to swear on a stack of bibles.*
[Laughter]

Robin: *Boy, am I glad you said that! (p. 226)*

The interactions above can be interpreted, à la Herman (1992), as a poignant example of how historically accurate incest memories are recovered; however, the succession of interchanges can also be read as a process of converting the possibility of incest into an image of incest, which in turn is transformed into a memory of abuse that did not in fact occur (see also Courtois, 1992; recall that casting thoughts into images increases the likelihood that they will be experienced as memories; Bartlett, 1932). These successive transformations were, of course, aided and abetted by group members who clearly had a psychological stake in uncovering such abuse—partly as a means for furthering group solidarity (Janis, 1972) and partly as reconfirmation of their own histories of abuse.

The problem created by such therapeutic interventions is exactly the same one that Freud (1896/1959a) was unable to resolve satisfactorily a century ago: We cannot discriminate between uncovered memories of genuine historical abuse, on one hand, and the internalization of suggested abuse, on the other. What is worse, the commitment of bad news therapy to Truth seeking and Truth telling obscures the possibility that suggestion might implicitly generate the abuse memories so keenly sought and told. The mere fact of repeatedly considering the possibility of abuse can increase its subsequent familiarity—a very hazardous state of affairs because research has shown that "a statement will seem true if it expresses facts that feel familiar" (Begg, Anas, & Farinacci, 1992, p. 446; see also Johnson, 1988b). Bad news therapy can thus both generate and reinforce the patient's emerging experience of remembered abuse—treating it as if its historical accuracy were beyond dispute.

The scenario above is especially problematic, given trauma therapists' prediliction for reading a variety of symptoms (e.g., eating disorders, dreams, and disruptions in intimate relations) as camouflaged mnemonic residues of past abuse (Bass & Davis, 1988; Blume, 1990; Courtois, 1992; Fredrickson, 1992) in much the same way that Freud's first theory did (Schimek, 1987). There can be no question that genuine trauma can leave people emotionally scarred, but it does not follow that all emotional problems are attributable to physical or sexual trauma (Tavris, 1993). Moreover, when an ideological commitment to the traumatic basis of adult neurosis insinuates itself into therapy, and the patient's difficulties are attributed to unremembered trauma, the possibility for false memories of abuse, beliefs in abuse, or both are enhanced considerably. Why is this so?

Recall that in Wachtel's (1977, 1993) use of the tally criterion, a patient's current feelings and perceptions may or may not tally with a therapist's attribution-suggestion. As we have seen, when an interpretation does not tally with the patient's present state of mind, it is rejected—and a therapist guided by the tally criterion would not insist on pursuing the matter. By contrast, therapists who are guided by a commitment to the traumatic origin of adult neurosis readily infer repression of abuse from a patient's resistance to such a proposal. In other words, the inability to recall abuse becomes evidence that it occurred (e.g., Bass & Davis, 1988). Such an interpretation perversely tallies with the patient's experience of not remembering the alleged abuse incident, thereby increasing the risk that the patient will falsely internalize the suggestion of abuse. Accordingly, invoking repressed memories of sexual abuse first subverts and then exploits the tally criterion.

To summarize, Wachtel (1977, 1993) fully recognized the role that suggestion inevitably plays in psychotherapy; but for him, the tally criterion served as a brake on the illicit or overweening impact of interpretation as a suggestion. His commitment was to help the patient, and in the context of this singular goal, the tally criterion represented the best way of respecting the boundary between the therapist's ideas and intuitions about the patient, on one hand, and the patient's identity, experience, and sense of self, on the other. By contrast, Herman's (1992) therapeutic commitment is divided between uncovering the Truth about a patient, on one hand, and helping the patient, on the other—as if the former were both knowable and necessary for the latter (see also Olio, 1989). In the context of this dual commitment, the tally criterion is easily subverted, becoming a blunt instrument of suggestion rather than a safeguard against its overweening influence.

In effect, trauma therapists' commitment to uncovering Truth makes them vulnerable to accepting their intuitions and hypotheses about the patient as true despite the absence of any independent corroboration (recall that Kekule's snake dream [Hein, 1966] was not evidence for the closed structure of benzene). Furthermore, such a commitment makes it difficult to recognize the possibility that intuitions about the traumatic source of psychological distress can unwittingly serve as the suggestive source of false abuse memories, beliefs, or both. Indeed, to the extent that suggestion is not recognized as intrinsic to psychotherapy, implicitly suggested effects are more readily accepted as independent confirmation of the therapist's intuitions—whatever those intuitions may be.

The argument above brings us to the following irony: Recognizing the inevitability of suggestive influences in psychotherapy helps minimize their untoward effects, whereas minimizing or denying the ubiquitous role of suggestion renders the therapist—and the patient—especially vulnerable to its unintended, unrecognized, and potentially damaging influence.[9] Thus, Wachtel (1993) fully recognized the inevitability of suggested effects in therapy—a recognition that was expressed in the special care with which he formulated and forwarded his therapeutic interpretations. Although such interpretations may suggest as much as they reveal, reliance on the tally criterion minimizes the likelihood that suggestion will become overbearing and pernicious in its impact. On one hand, in an important sense, Wachtel's appreciation of suggestive effects in therapy increases the likelihood that his interpretations will be true to the patient. On the other hand, Herman's (1992) commitment to uncovering the historical Truth about a patient risked subverting the tally criterion, which we think substantially increases the likelihood of engendering untoward suggested effects that are not recognized as such. By proceeding in this fashion, modern trauma therapists recapitulate a century-old Freudian slip—from dismissal of suggestion as a powerful determinant of memory and experience, to misappropriating implicitly suggested abuse memories as independent evidence for the trauma theory that anticipates, seeks, and generates them.

TYPES OF SUGGESTION

It is impossible to engage in suggestion-free psychotherapy—just as it is impossible for physicists to observe electrons without disturbing them in the process.[10] This Heisenberg-like indeterminancy can render it difficult or impossible to know in any given case whether psychotherapy has cued an accurate memory, on one hand, or suggested a false one, on the other (although see Person & Klar, 1994, who proposed grounds for such a distinction). Indeed, it may be possible to suggest amnesia for actual abuse (D. Spiegel, personal communication, May 5, 1995)—a possibility that coheres with Janet's (1925) and Erickson's (Erickson & Rossi, 1980) use of suggestion to replace a problematic history with a more benign one.

The indeterminacy regarding whether remembered abuse is real or suggested is disquieting. One reason why clinicians reject suggested abuse memories is that they do not appreciate how powerful suggestion can be in everyday life.

• • •

CONCLUDING REMARKS

People who are committed to the accuracy of recovered abuse memories are, for the most part, also committed to the authority of subjective experience as a means of knowing about oneself and the world—especially when such experience conforms to theoretical expectancies about the prevalence of abuse and the current reign of feminist victimology (Kaminer, 1993). There is an immediacy to experience that is lacking in relatively abstract considerations of how memory and suggestion can function to generate compelling but misleading beliefs and mnemonic experiences. Moreover, there is an understandable tendency for patients to externalize conflicts rather than to work them through (Ganaway, 1994)—a tendency that can be actualized in abuse memories that seem to explain one's current distress even while it creates other, potentially worse, problems. Moreover, calling a patient's subjective experience into question—however delicately and sensitively—can readily be viewed as a challenge not only to the patient's veracity but also to his or her integrity and even his or her very identity.

Consequently, in each case where memories of abuse are recovered in therapy, the immediacy and sanctity of personal experience are pitted against the relatively remote virtues of research-based findings concerned with memory and suggestion. The research tradition is not infallible, and conclusions based on it can be erroneous in any particular case. However, in the long run, it is the best safeguard against superstition and the perils of errant subjectivity. Based on controlled research, we know now that memory is not reproductive—that "memory is not so much like reading a book as it is like writing one from fragmentary notes" (Kihlstrom, 1994, p. 341); we know now that suggestions of various kinds can powerfully alter belief, behavior, and memory; we know now that such suggested effects can occur without intention. What is more, there is no good reason to assume that this knowledge suddenly becomes obsolete or irrelevant when recovered memory of sexual abuse is the issue, and it is simply irresponsible to suggest otherwise. Granted, a therapist's knowledge about memory and suggestion is no absolute guarantee in any particular case that a particular recovered memory of abuse is mistaken. However, surely there is an obligation for each such case to be evaluated in light of what therapists know about memory and suggestion—rather than simply deferring to a patient's compelling mnemonic experience that he or she was sexually abused.

It would of course be even more desirable if therapists generally were to become well-trained and informed about the nature of memory and suggestion and to take this knowledge into account whenever sexual abuse is suspected (see Dawes, 1994, about the parlous nature of present clinical training). Conducting therapy in light of this knowledge provides an important opportunity, challenge, and choice: Realizing how difficult or impossible it will be to distinguish between true and false memories of abuse, the therapist should balance in each case the potential for harm that would result from *not* recovering true memories of abuse against the potential problems that would result from recovering false memories of abuse. Then the therapist should proceed in a fashion that is least likely to produce harm.

REFERENCES

American Psychiatric Association. (1994). *Diagnostic and statistical manual of mental disorders* (4th ed.). Washington, DC: Author.

Andreski, S. (1972). *Social sciences as sorcery.* London: Andre Deutsch.

Banks, W. P., & Pezdek, K. (1994). The recovered memory/false memory debate. *Consciousness and Cognition, 3,* 265–268.

Barnes, M. (Director). (1982). *Hypnosis on trial* [Film].

Bartlett, F. C. (1932). *Remembering: A study in experimental and social psychology.* Cambridge, England: Cambridge University Press.

Bass, E., & Davis, L. (1988). *The courage to heal: A guide for women survivors of child sexual abuse.* New York: Harper & Row.

Begg, I. M., Anas, A., & Farinacci, S. (1992). Dissociation of processes in belief: Source of recollection, statement familiarity, and the illusion of truth. *Journal of Experimental Psychology: General, 121,* 446–458.

Beitchman, J. H., Zucker, K. J., Hood, J. E., DaCosta, G. A., & Akman, D. (1991). A review of the short-term effects of child sexual abuse. *Child Abuse and Neglect, 15,* 537–556.

Beitchman, J. H., Zucker, J. H., Hood, J. E., DaCosta, G. A., Akman, D., & Cassavia, E. (1992). A review of long-term effects of child sexual abuse. *Child Abuse and Neglect, 16,* 101–118.

Bloom, S. L. (1994). Hearing the survivor's voice: Sundering the wall of denial. *Journal of Psychohistory, 21,* 461–477.

Blume, S. E. (1990). *Secret survivors: Uncovering incest and its aftereffects in women.* New York: Ballantine Books.

Bower, G. H. (1981). Mood and memory. *American Psychologist, 36,* 129–148.

Bower, G. H. (1990). Awareness, the unconscious, and repression: An experimental psychologist's perspective. In J. L. Singer (Ed.), *Repression and dissociation: Implications for personality theory, psychopathology, and health* (pp. 209–231). Chicago: University of Chicago Press.

Bowers, K. S. (1984). On being unconsciously influenced and informed. In K. S. Bowers & D. Meichenbaum (Eds.), *The unconscious reconsidered* (pp. 227–272). New York: Wiley.

Bowers, K. S. (1990). Unconscious influences and hypnosis. In J. L. Singer (Ed.), *Repression and dissociation: Implications for personality theory, psychopathology, and health* (pp. 143–178). Chicago: University of Chicago Press.

Bowers, K. S., Farvolden, P., & Mermigis, L. (1994). Intuitive antecedents of insight. In S. M. Smith, T. M. Ward, & R. A. Finke (Eds.), *The creative cognition approach* (pp. 27–52). Cambridge, MA: MIT Press.

Bowers, K. S., Regehr, G., Balthazard, C., & Parker, K. (1990). Intuition in the context of discovery. *Cognitive Psychology, 22,* 72–110.

Brenneis, C. B. (1994). Belief and suggestion in the recovery of memories of childhood sexual abuse. *Journal of the American Psychoanalytic Association, 42,* 1027–1053.

Breuer, J., & Freud, S. (1955). Studies on hysteria. In J. Strachey (Ed.), *Standard edition of the complete psychological works of Sigmund Freud* (Vol. 2, pp. 1–310). London: Hogarth Press. (Original work published 1893–1895.)

Briere, J., & Conte, J. (1993). Self-reported amnesia for abuse in adults molested as children. *Journal of Traumatic Stress, 6,* 21–31.

Brown, D. (1995). Pseudomemories: The standard of science and the standard of care in trauma treatment. *American Journal of Clinical Hypnosis, 37,* 1–24.

Browne, M. W. (1988, April 16). The benzene ring: Dream analysis. *New York Times, C4,* p. 10.

Ceci, S. J., & Bruck, M. (1993a). Child witness: Translating research into policy. *Social Policy Report: Society for Research in Child Development, 7,* 1–30.

Ceci, S. J., & Bruck, M. (1993b). Suggestibility of the child witness: A historical review and synthesis. *Psychological Bulletin, 113,* 403–439.

Cialdini, R. (1993). *Influence: Science and practice* (3rd ed.). Glenview, IL: Harper-Collins.

Constantine, L. L. (1981). The effects of early sexual experiences: A review and synthesis of research. In L. L. Constantine & F. M. Martinson (Eds.), *Children and sex: New findings, new perspectives* (pp. 217–244). Boston: Little, Brown.

Conte, J. R. (1994). Child sexual abuse: Awareness and backlash. *Sexual Abuse of Children, 4,* 224–232.

Courtois, C. A. (1991). Theory, sequencing, and strategy in treating adult survivors. In J. Briere (Ed.), *Treating victims of child sexual abuse* (pp. 47–60). San Francisco: Jossey-Bass.

Courtois, C. A. (1992). The memory retrieval process in incest survivor therapy. *Journal of Child Sexual Abuse, 1,* 15–31.

Crews, F. (1993, November 18). The unknown Freud. *New York Review of Books,* pp. 55–66.

Crews, F. (1994a, November 17). The revenge of the repressed. *New York Review of Books,* pp. 55–60.

Crews, F. (1994b, December 1). The revenge of the repressed: Part 2. *New York Review of Books,* pp. 49–58.

Davis, P. J. (1990). Repression and the inaccessibility of emotional memories. In J. L. Singer (Ed.), *Repression and dissociation: Implications for personality theory, psychopathology, and health* (pp. 387–403). Chicago: University of Chicago Press.

Dawes, R. M. (1994). *House of cards: Psychology and psychotherapy built on myth.* New York: Free Press.

Dobson, M., & Markham, R. (1993). Imagery ability and source monitoring: Implications for eyewitness memory. *British Journal of Psychology, 32,* 111.

Dollard, J., & Miller, N. E. (1950). *Personality and psychotherapy: An analysis in terms of learning, thinking, and culture.* New York: McGraw-Hill.

Eckenrode, J., Powers, J., Doris, J., Munsch, J., & Bolger, N. (1993). Substantiation of child abuse and neglect reports. *Journal of Consulting and Clinical Psychology, 56,* 9–16.

Einhorn, H. J. (1986). Accepting error to make less error. *Journal of Personality Assessment, 50,* 387–395.

Ellenberger, H. (1970). *The discovery of the unconscious: The history and evolution of dynamic psychology.* New York: Basic Books.

Erdelyi, M. (1985). *Psychoanalysis: Freud's cognitive psychology.* New York: Freeman.

Erdelyi, M. H. (1990). Repression, reconstruction, and defense: History and integration of the psychoanalytic and experimental frameworks. In J. L. Singer (Ed.), *Repression and dissociation: Implications for personality theory, psychopathology, and health* (pp. 1–32). Chicago: University of Chicago Press.

Erdelyi, M. (1993). Repression: The mechanism and the defense. In D. M. Wegner & J. W. Pennebaker (Eds.), *Handbook of mental control* (pp. 126–148). Englewood Cliffs, NJ: Prentice-Hall.

Erdelyi, M. H., & Goldberg, B. (1979). Let's not sweep repression under the rug: Toward a cognitive psychology of repression. In J. F. Kihlstrom & F. J. Evans (Eds.), *Functional disorders of memory* (pp. 355–402). Hillsdale, NJ: Erlbaum.

Erickson, M. H., & Rossi, E. L. (1980). The February man: Facilitating new identity in hypnotherapy. In E. L. Rossie (Ed.), *The collected papers of Milton H. Erickson on hypnosis* (Vol. 4, pp. 525–542). New York: Irvington.

Esterson, A. (1993). *Seductive mirage: An exploration of the work of Sigmund Freud.* Chicago: Open Court.

Eth, S., Randolph, E. T., & Brown, J. A. (1989). Post-traumatic stress disorder. In J. G. Howells (Ed.), *Modern perspectives in the psychiatry of the neuroses* (pp. 210–234). New York: Brunner/Mazel.

Femina, D. D., Yeager, C. A., & Lewis, D. O. (1990). Child abuse: Adolescent records vs. adult recall. *Child Abuse and Neglect, 14,* 227-231.

Finkelhor, D., Hotaling, G., Lewis, I., & Smith, C. (1990). Sexual abuse in a national survey of adult men and women: Prevalence, characteristics, and risk factors. *Child Abuse and Neglect. 14,* 19-28.

Frankel, F. (1994). The concept of flashbacks in historical perspective. *International Journal of Clinical and Experimental Hypnosis, 42,* 321-336.

Fredrickson, R. (1992). *Repressed memories: A journey to recovery from sexual abuse.* New York: Simon & Schuster.

Freud, S. (1955). Three essays on the theory of sexuality. In J. Strachey (Ed. and Trans.), *The standard edition of the complete psychological works of Sigmund Freud* (Vol. 7, pp. 125-243). London: Hogarth Press. (Original work published 1905.)

Freud, S. (1959a). The aetiology of hysteria. In J. Riviere (Ed.), *Sigmund Freud: Collected papers* (Vol. 1, pp. 183-219). New York: Basic Books. (Original work published 1896.)

Freud, S. (1959b). Constructions in analysis. In J. Strachey (Ed.), *Sigmund Freud: Collected papers* (Vol. 5, pp. 358-371). New York: Basic Books. (Original work published 1937.)

Freud, S. (1959c). My views on the part played by sexuality in the aetiology of the neurosis. In J. Riviere (Trans.), *Sigmund Freud: Collected papers* (Vol. 1, pp. 272-283). New York: Basic Books. (Original work published 1905.)

Freud, S. (1959d). Repression. In E. Jones (Ed.), *Sigmund Freud: Collected papers* (Vol 4, pp. 84-97). New York: Basic Books. (Original works published 1915.)

Freud, S. (1966). The introductory lectures on psychoanalysis. In J. Strachev (Ed.), *The complete introductory lectures on psychoanalysis* (pp. 15-463). New York: Norton. (Original work published 1915-1917.)

Fromuth, M. E. (1986). The relationship of childhood sexual abuse with later psychological and sexual adjustment in a sample of college women. *Child Abuse and Neglect, 10,* 5-15.

Ganaway, G. K. (1989). Historical truth versus narrative truth: Clarifying the role of exogenous trauma in the etiology of multiple personality disorder and its variants. *Dissociation, 2,* 205-220.

Ganaway, G. K. (1994). Transference and countertransference shaping influences on dissociative syndromes. In S. J. Lynn & J. W. Rhue (Eds.), *Dissociation: Clinical and theoretical implications* (pp. 317-337). New York: Guilford Press.

Ganaway, G. K. (1995). Hypnosis, childhood trauma, and dissociative identity disorder. Toward an integrative theory. *International Journal of Clinical and Experimental Hypnosis, 43,* 127-144.

Garry, M., Loftus, E. M., & Brown, S. W. (1994). Memory: A river runs through it. *Consciousness and Cognition, 3,* 438-451.

Gay, P. (1988). *Freud: A life for our time.* New York: Norton.

Greenberg, M. A., & Stone, A. A. (1992). Emotional disclosure about traumas and its relation to health: Effects of previous disclosure and trauma severity. *Journal of Personality and Social Psychology, 63,* 75-84.

Grinker, R. R., & Spiegel, J. P. (1945). *Men under stress.* Philadelphia: Blakiston.

Grunbaum, A. (1984). *The foundations of psychoanalysis: A philosophical critique.* Berkeley: University of California Press.

Grunbaum, A. (1986). Precis of the foundations of psychoanalysis: A philosphical critique. *Behavioral and Brain Sciences, 9,* 217-284.

Hacking, I. (1995). *Rewriting the soul.* Princeton, NJ: Princeton University Press.

Harter, S., Alexander, P. C., & Neimeyer, R. A. (1988). Long-term effects of incestuous child abuse in college women: Social adjustment, social cognition, and family characteristics. *Journal of Consulting and Clinical Psychology, 56,* 5-8.

Haskell, L., & Randall, M. (1993). The Women's Safety Project: Summary of key statistical findings. In P. Marshall & M. A. Vaillancourt (Eds.), *Changing the landscape: Ending violence—Achieving equality: Final report of the Canadian Panel on Violence Against Women* (pp. A1–A18). Ottawa, Ontario, Canada: Minister of Supply and Services.

Hein, G. E. (1966). Kekule and the architecture of molecules. In R. F. Gould (Ed.), *Advances in chemistry series: Kekule centennial* (pp. 1–12). Washington, DC: American Chemical Society.

Henderson, J. L., & Moore, M. (1944). The psychoneurosis of war. *New England Journal of Medicine, 230,* 125–131.

Herman, J. L. (1992). *Trauma and recovery.* New York: Basic Books.

Herman, J. L., & Harvey, M. R. (1993). The false memory debate: Social science or social backlash. *Harvard Mental Health Letter, 9,* 4–6.

Herman, J. L., & Hirschman, L. (1981). *Father-daughter incest.* Cambridge, MA: Harvard University Press.

Herman, J. L., & Schatzow, E. (1987). Recovery and verification of memories of childhood sexual abuse. *Psychoanalytic Psychology: 4,* 1–14.

Hilgard, E. R. (1977). *Divided consciousness: Multiple controls in human thought and action.* New York: Wiley.

Holmes, D. S. (1974). Investigations of repression: Differential recall of material experimentally or naturally associated with ego threat. *Psychological Bulletin, 81,* 632–653.

Holmes, D. S. (1990). The evidence for repression: An examination of sixty years of research. In J. L. Singer (Ed.), *Repression and dissociation: Implications for personality theory, psychopathology, and health* (pp. 85–102). Chicago: University of Chicago Press.

Holton, G. (1973). *Thematic origins of scientific thought: Kepler to Einstein.* Cambridge, MA: Harvard University Press.

Horowitz, M. (1986). Stress-response syndromes. *Hospital and Community Psychiatry, 37,* 241–249.

Huston, W. (Producer and Director). (1948). *Let there be light* [Film]. (Available from the U.S. Army and International Historical Films.)

Intraub, H., & Hoffman, J. E. (1992). Reading and visual memory: Remembering scenes that were never seen. *American Journal of Psychology, 105,* 101–114.

Israels, H., & Schatzman, M. (1993). The seduction theory. *History of Psychiatry, 4,* 23–59.

Janet, P. (1901). *The mental state of hystericals.* New York: Putnam.

Janet, P. (1925). *Psychological healing* (Vol. 1). New York: Macmillan.

Janet, P. (1965). *The major symptoms of hysteria.* New York: Hafner. (Original work published 1907.)

Janis, I. L. (1972). *Victims of groupthink.* Boston: Houghton Mifflin.

Johnson, M. K. (1988a). Discriminating the origin of information in T. F. Oltmanns & B. A. Maher (Eds.), *Delusional beliefs* (pp. 34–65). New York: Wiley.

Johnson, M. K. (1988b). Reality monitoring: An experimental phenomenological approach. *Journal of Experimental Psychology: General, 117,* 390–394.

Johnson, M. K., Hashtroudi, S., & Lindsay, D. S. (1993). Source monitoring. *Psychological Bulletin, 114,* 3–28.

Jones, E. (1961). The life and times of Sigmund Freud. In L. Trilling & S. Marcus (Eds.), *The life and times of Sigmund Freud.* New York: Basic Books.

Kaminer, W. (1993). *I'm dysfunctional, you're dysfunctional: The recovery movement and other self-help fashions.* New York: Vintage Books.

Kaszniak, A. W., Nussbaum, P. D., Berren, M. R., & Santiago, J. (1988). Amnesia as a consequence of male rape: A case report. *Journal of Abnormal Psychology, 97,* 100–104.

Kendall-Tackett, K. A., Williams, L. M., & Finkelhor, D. (1993). Impact of sexual abuse on children: A review and synthesis of recent empirical studies. *Psychological Bulletin, 113.* 164–180.

Kihlstrom, J. F. (1994). Hypnosis, delayed recall, and the principles of memory. *International Journal of Clinical and Experimental Hypnosis, 42,* 337-345.

Kihlstrom, J. F. (1995). The trauma-memory argument. *Consciousness and Cognition, 4,* 65-67.

Kolb, L. C. (1988). Recovery of memory and repressed fantasy in combat-induced post-traumatic stress disorder of Vietnam veterans. In H. M. Pettinati (Ed.), *Hypnosis and memory* (pp. 265-274). New York: Guilford Press.

Koss, M. P., Gidycz, A., & Wisniewski, N. (1987). The scope of rape: Incidence and prevalence of sexual aggression and victimization in a national sample of higher education students. *Journal of Consulting and Clinical Psychology, 55,* 162-170.

Kuhn, T. S. (1962). *The structure of scientific revolutions.* Chicago: University of Chicago Press.

Labelle, L., Laurence, J., Nadon, R., & Perry, C. (1990). Hypnotizability, preference for an imagic cognitive style, and memory creation in hypnosis. *Journal of Abnormal Psychology, 99,* 222-228.

Laurence, J., Nadon, R., Nogrady, H., & Perry, C. (1986). Duality, dissociation, and memory creation in highly hypnotizable subjects. *International Journal of Clinical and Experimental Hypnosis, 34,* 295-310.

LeDoux, J. E. (1991). Systems and synapses of emotional memory. In L. R. Squire, N. M. Weinberger, G. Lynch, & J. L. McGaugh (Eds.), *Memory: Organization and locus of change* (pp. 205-216). New York: Oxford University Press.

LeDoux, J. E. (1994). Emotion, memory and the brain. *Scientific American, 270,* 50-57.

Levitt, E. E., & Pinnell, C. M. (1995). Some additional light on the childhood sexual abuse-psychopathology axis. *International Journal of Clinical and Experimental Hypnosis, 43,* 145-162.

Lindsay, D. S. (1995). Beyond backlash: Comments to Enns, McNeilly, Corkery, and Gilbert. *The Counseling Psychologist, 23,* 280-289.

Lindsay, D. S., & Johnson, M. K. (1989). The eyewitness suggestibility effect and memory for source. *Memory and Cognition, 17,* 349-358.

Lindsay, D. S., & Read, J. D. (1994). Psychotherapy and memories of childhood and sexual abuse: A cognitive perspective. *Applied Cognitive Psychology, 8,* 281-338.

Loftus, E. (1979). *Eyewitness testimony.* Cambridge, MA: Harvard University Press.

Loftus, E. F. (1993). The reality of repressed memories. *American Psychologist, 48,* 518-537.

Loftus, E. M., Garry, M., & Feldman, J. (1994). Forgetting sexual trauma: What does it mean when 38% forget? *Journal of Consulting and Clinical Psychology, 62,* 1177-1181.

Loftus, E. M., & Ketcham, K. (1994). *The myth of repressed memory: False memories and allegations of sexual abuse.* New York: St. Martin's Press.

Lykken, D. T. (1968). Statistical significance in psychological research. *Psychological Bulletin, 70,* 151-159.

Lykken, D. T. (1991). What's wrong with psychology anyway? In D. Cicchetti & W. M. Grove (Eds.), *Thinking clearly about psychology: Essays in honor of Paul E. Meehl* (Vol. 1, pp. 3-39). Minneapolis: University of Minnesota Press.

Lynn, S. J., & Nash, M. R. (1993). Truth in memory: Ramifications for psychotherapy and hypnotherapy. *American Journal of Clinical Hypnosis, 36,* 194-208.

Macmillan, M. (1991). *Freud evaluated: The completed arc.* Amsterdam: Elsevier.

Maclean, H. N. (1993). *Once upon a time: A true tale of memory, murder, and the law.* New York: HarperCollins.

Markham, R., & Hynes, L. (1993). The effect of vividness of imagery on reality monitoring. *Journal of Mental Imagery, 17,* 159-170.

Masson, J. M. (1985a). *The assault on truth; Freud's suppression of the seduction theory.* New York: Penguin Books.

Masson, J. M. (1985b). *The complete letters of Sigmund Freud to Wilhelm Fliess, 1887–1904.* Cambridge, MA: Belknap Press.

McCurdy, J. T. (1918). *War neurosis.* Cambridge, England: Cambridge University Press.

Meehl, P. E. (1978). Theoretical risks and tabular asterisks: Sir Karl, Sir Ronald, and the slow progress of soft psychology. *Journal of Consulting and Clinical Psychology, 46,* 806–834.

Meehl, P. E. (1990). Appraising and amending theories. The strategy of Lakatosian defense and two principles that warrant it. *Psychological Inquiry: 1,* 108–141.

Meichenbaum, D. (1994). *A clinical handbook/practical therapist manual for assessing and treating adults with post-traumatic stress disorder (PTSD).* Waterloo, Ontario, Canada: Institute Press.

Middlebrook, D. (1991). *Anne Sexton: A biography:* Boston: Houghton Mifflin.

Miller, A. (1986): *Thou shalt not be aware: Society's betrayal of the child.* New York: Meridian.

Nash, M. R. (1994). Memory distortion and sexual trauma: The problem of false negatives and false positives. *International Journal of Clinical and Experimental Hypnosis, 42,* 346–362.

Nash, M. R., Hulsey, T. L., Sexton, M. C., Harralson, T. I., & Lamert, W. (1993). Long-term sequelae of childhood sexual abuse: Perceived family environment, psychopathology, and dissociation. *Journal of Consulting and Clinical Psychology, 61,* 276–283.

Nemiah, J. C. (1984). The unconscious and psychopathology. In K. S. Bowers & D. Meichenbaum (Eds.). *The unconscious reconsidered* (pp. 49–87). New York: Wiley.

Nissen, M. J., Ross, J. L., Willingham, D. B., Mackenzie, T. B., & Schacter, D. L. (1988). Memory and awareness in a patient with multiple personality disorder. *Brain and Cognition, 8,* 117–134.

Ofshe, R. J., & Singer, M. T. (1994). Recovered-memory therapy and robust repression. *International Journal of Clinical and Experimental Hypnosis, 42,* 391–410.

Ofshe, R., & Watters, E. (1993). Making monsters. *Society, 30,* 4–16.

Ofshe, R., & Watters, E. (1994). *Making monsters: False memories, psychotherapy, and sexual hysteria.* New York: Scribner.

Olio, K. A. (1989). Memory retrieval in the treatment of adult survivors of sexual abuse. *Transactional Analysis Journal, 19,* 93–100.

Orne, M. T., & Evans, F. (1965). Social control in the psychological experiment. Antisocial behavior and hypnosis. *Journal of Personality and Social Psychology, 1,* 189–200.

Pendergrast, M. (1995). *Victims of memory: Incest accusations and shattered lives.* Hinesburg, VT: Upper Access.

Pennebaker, J. W. (1989). Confession, inhibition, and disease. In L. Berkowitz (Ed.), *Advances in experimental social psychology* (Vol. 22, pp. 211–244). New York: Academic Press.

Pennebaker, J. W., & Susman, J. R. (1988). Disclosure of trauma and psychosomatic processes. *Social Science and Medicine, 26,* 327–332.

Perry, C., & Laurence, J. (1984). Mental processing outside of awareness: The contributions of Freud and Janet. In K. Bowers & D. Meichenbaum (Eds.), *The unconscious reconsidered* (pp. 9–48). New York: Wiley.

Perry, C. W., Laurence, J., D'Eon, R., & Tallant, B. (1988). Hypnotic age regression techniques in the elicitation of memories: Applied uses and abuses. In H. M. Pettinati (Ed.), *Hypnosis and memory* (pp. 128–154). New York: Guilford Press.

Persinger, M. A. (1992). Neuropsychological profiles of adults who report "sudden remembering" of early childhood memories: Implications for claims of sex abuse and alien visitation/abduction experiences. *Perceptual Motor Skills, 75,* 259–266.

Person, E. S., & Klar. H. (1994). Establishing trauma: The difficulty distinguishing between memories and fantasies. *Journal of the American Psychoanalytic Association, 42,* 1055-1081.

Polanyi, M. (1964). *Personal knowledge: Towards a post-critical philosophy.* New York: Harper Torchbook.

Polkinghorne, D. (1983). *Methodology for the human sciences.* Albany: State University of New York Press.

Pope, H. G. (1994). "Recovered memories": Recent events and review of evidence. *Currents in Affective Illness, 13,* 5-12.

Popper, K. (1962). *Conjectures and refutations.* New York: Basic Books.

Powell, R. A., & Boer, D. P. (1994). Did Freud mislead patients to confabulate memories of abuse? *Psychological Reports, 74,* 1283-1298.

Raginsky, B. B. (1969). Hypnotic recall of aircrash cause. *International Journal of Clinical and Experimental Hypnosis, 17,* 1-19.

Ramachandran, V. S. (1995). Anosognosia in parietal lobe syndrome. *Consciousness and Cognition, 4,* 22-51.

Robinson, P. (1993). *Freud and his critics.* Berkeley: University of California Press.

Rocke, A. J. (1988, September 9). The man who dreamed benzene rings. *New York Times, A4,* p. 26.

Ross, M. (1989). Relation of implicit theories to the construction of personal histories. *Psychological Review, 96,* 341-357.

Sackeim, H. I., Nordlie, J. W., & Gur, R. C. (1979). A model of hysterical and hypnotic blindness: Cognition, motivation, and awareness. *Journal of Abnormal Psychology, 88,* 474-489.

Schacter, D. L. (in press). Memory distortion: History and current status. In D. L. Schacter, J. T. Coyle, G. D. Fischbach, M.-M. Mesulam, & L. E. Sullivan (Eds.), *Memory distortion: How minds, brains, and societies reconstruct the past.* Cambridge, MA: Harvard University Press.

Schacter, D. L., & Kihlstrom, J. F. (1989). Functional amnesia. In F. Boller & J. Grafman (Eds.), *Handbook of neuropsychology* (Vol. 3, pp. 209-231). Amsterdam: Elsevier.

Schacter, D. L., Wang, P. L., Tulving, E., & Freedman, M. (1982). Functional retrograde amnesia: A quantitative case study. *Neuropsychologia, 20,* 523-532.

Schatzman, M. (1992, March 21). Freud: Who seduced whom? *New Scientist,* 34-37.

Schimek, J. G. (1987). Fact and fantasy in the seduction theory: A historical review. *Journal of the American Psychoanalytic Association, 35,* 937-965.

Shorter, E. (1992). *From paralysis to fatigue: A history of psychosomatic illness in the modern era.* New York: Free Press.

Spence, D. P. (1982). *Narrative truth and historical truth: Meaning and interpretation in psychoanalysis.* New York: Norton.

Spence, D. P. (1994). Narrative truth and putative child abuse. *International Journal of Clinical and Experimental Hypnosis, 42,* 289-303.

Spiegel, D., & Scheflin, A. W. (1994). Dissociated or fabricated? Psychiatric aspects of repressed memory in criminal and civil cases. *International Journal of Clinical and Experimental Hypnosis, 42,* 411-432.

Tavris, C. (1993, January 3). Beware the incest survivor machine [Book review]. *New York Times,* p. 1.

Terr, L. (1981). Psychic trauma in children: Observations following the Chowchilla school-bus kidnapping. *American Journal of Psychiatry, 138,* 14-19.

Terr, L. (1983). Chowchilla revisited: The effects of psychic trauma four years after a school-bus kidnapping. *American Journal of Psychiatry, 140,* 1543-1550.

Terr, L. (1990). *Too scared to cry: Psychic trauma in childhood.* New York: Harper & Row.

Terr, L. (1994). *Unchained memories.* New York: Basic Books.

Tulving, E., & Thomson, D. M. (1973). Encoding specificity and retrieval processes in episodic memory. *Psychological Review, 80,* 352-373.

van der Kolk, B. A. (1994). The body keeps the score: Memory and the evolving psychobiology of posttraumatic stress. *Harvard Review of Psychiatry, I,* 253-265.

van der Kolk, B. A., & Saporta, J. (1991). The biological response to psychic trauma: Mechanisms and treatment of intrusion and numbing. *Anxiety Research, 4,* 199-212.

Wachtel, P. L. (1973). Psychodynamics, behavior therapy, and the implacable experimenter: An inquiry into the consistency of personality. *Journal of Abnormal Personality, 82,* 324-334.

Wachtel, P. L. (1977). *Psychoanalysis and behavior therapy.* New York: Basic Books.

Wachtel, P. L. (1993). *Therapeutic communication: Principles and effective practice.* New York: Guilford Press.

Wegner, D. M. (1994). Ironic processes of mental control. *Psychological Review, 101,* 34-52.

Weinberger, D. A. (1990). The construct validity of the repressive coping style. In J. L. Singer (Ed.), *Repression and dissociation: Implications for personality theory, psychopathology, and health* (pp. 337-386). Chicago: University of Chicago Press.

Weingardt, K. W., Loftus, E., & Lindsay, D. S. (1995). Misinformation revisited. *Memory and Cognition, 23,* 72-82.

Williams, L. M. (1994). Recall of childhood trauma: A prospective study of women's memories of child sexual abuse. *Journal of Consulting and Clinical Psychology, 62,* 1167-1176.

Wright, L. (1994). *Remembering satan.* New York: Knopf.

NOTES

1. We are aware of two films that include segments in which repressed memories are recovered by hypnosis. One is a U.S. Army film that concerns the recovery of traumatic events experienced by an American soldier in World War 2 (Huston, 1948). The other concerns a helicopter pilot who became amnesic for the events surrounding a helicopter accident, including the death of two friends (Barnes, 1982). The latter is particularly interesting, inasmuch as the events recalled under hypnosis were subsequently corroborated by reinvestigation of the accident debris. A somewhat similar incident was reported by Raginsky (1969).

2. These tape-recordings became an issue many years later, when Orne turned them over to Sexton's biographer. The American Psychiatric Association brought ethical charges against Orne for doing so, but he was eventually cleared of all of them.

3. According to a *New York Times* article by Malcom W. Browne (1988), some experts have questioned the authenticity of this anecdote on the grounds that Kekule used it to establish his priority in the discovery of the benzene ring, thereby eliminating the need to share credit for the discovery with foreign scientists. However, a letter written in response to this article (Rocke, 1988) argued that "in the five years or so that Dr. Wotiz has attempted to debunk the 'Kekule myth,' he has gained few converts among professional historians of science. I, and most of my peers who have researched this area, believe there is little evidence to deny the dream stories or Kekule's priority to benzene structure" (p. 26).

4. We appreciate that contemporary psychoanalysis is in many respects quite different from its Freudian forebear and that many of our comments regarding Freud's traumatic and conflict theory do not necessarily apply to people like Kernberg, Kohut, and other current progenitors of the Freudian legacy. Ganaway (1989, 1994, 1995) is a vocal exponent of this updated psychoanalytic view and is also one of the leading critics of the recovered-memory movement (see also Brenneis, 1994).

5. One implication of this position is that remembered abuse is not pathogenic. Accordingly, some contemporary trauma therapists evidently insist on seeking unremembered abuse, on the assumption that remembered abuse is an unlikely basis for current distress.

6. Robinson (1993) argued that Freud never completely gave up his trauma theory: "In view of Freud's revived hopes for the seduction theory after September 21, 1897, his long delay in confessing his departures from it, and his continuing belief, to the end of his life, that childhood seductions were real and consequential, we would be better advised to speak of a tension, rather than a categorical opposition, between the seduction theory and the Oedipus theory" (p. 170).

7. Robinson (1993) tried to defend Freud by arguing, contra Grunbaum (1984, 1986), that Freud did not make strong claims for the success of psychoanalysis implied by the tally argument, and that in fact the tally argument was more a casual expositional devise than a serious criterion for distinguishing what was true (and therapeutically effective) from what was false (and therapeutically ineffective). From our point of view, what Robinson's analysis missed is that the tally argument is Freud's chief defense against the possibility that participants could internalize a suggestion that was false—without regard to whether such an internalization was positive or negative in its impact.

8. Another historical figure felt even more strongly about suggestion. According to Janet (1925, pp. 63–64), Mary Baker Eddy, the founder of Christian Science, was adamant that her healing interventions were not due to "malicious magnetism." She put a contract out to have one of her students, Daniel Spofford, murdered because she suspected him of practicing such suggestive wizardry. The attempt failed, but it created a scandal; Mrs. Baker was ordered by the court to pay a fine.

9. This formulation of the issue owes a lot to an article by Einhorn (1986), "Accepting Error to Make Less Error."

10. We would like to thank our colleague William Corning for suggesting this analogy.

QUESTIONS FOR FURTHER THOUGHT

1. How do recovered memories differ from other memories?

2. How could one reliably identify genuine recovered memories?

3. How might therapists inadvertently create new memories that appear to be recovered memories?

4. What are the implications of this article for training therapists?

5. Are you convinced that repression of traumatic memories is a rare phenomenon? Why or why not?

5

CONCEPTS AND CATEGORIES

PRINCIPLES OF CATEGORIZATION
Eleanor Rosch

CONCEPTS AND CONCEPTUAL STRUCTURE
Douglas Medin

PRINCIPLES OF CATEGORIZATION

Eleanor Rosch

INTRODUCTION

When people place things into categories, what do they do and how do they do it? At one time, both this question and its answer seemed straightforward, even trivial, concerns. People simply assigned phenomena to categories according to the well-defined features that matched an object to a category. For example, grass might be placed into the category of "green things" because it is an example of a green thing, just as a cherry might be placed into the category of "red things" because it is red. What could be simpler than that?

In a set of classic studies, Eleanor Rosch showed that the process is not, in fact, such a simple one. Many categories are not so well-defined and clean-cut as they seem at first glance. For example, in some sense, lawn grass might be viewed as representing a better, more typical green than does a fresh olive, whose green color is, well, more olive-toned than that of the grass. Although a ripe tomato is generally red, the red it represents does not seem to most people to represent the category of "red" as well as does the red of the cherry.

Rosch showed that people make these mental gradations when they assign objects to categories. Their performance reflects their perception, for example, of a cherry as representing a better red than does a ripe tomato. The color of the cherry comes closer to representing a psychological *prototype* for redness.

Rosch and her colleagues also showed that in a hierarchy of categories, people hold in their heads what Rosch referred to as a *basic* level. For example, when you show someone a small, red, spherical fruit with a stem, that person is more likely to call it a "cherry" than to call it either a "fruit" or a "maraschino cherry." Basic-level categories tend to be those categories that, in people's lives, provide the most useful differentiations of classes of objects (i.e., they are the most inclusive levels of classification at which member objects share large numbers of attributes). Clearly, categorization is more complicated than it may first appear.

Rosch's work on concepts is probably among the most widely cited bodies of work in the entire field of cognitive psychology. The work turned on its head prior thinking about concepts. Before Rosch, most investigators of concepts were content to use abstract objects, such as squares and circles, in their studies of concept formation. After Rosch, few people used such stimuli; instead, they switched to the real-life stimuli Rosch decided to use. Rosch's work showed that most properties of objects cannot be seen as defining the objects. Thus, although most birds

Source: From "Principles of categorization." In E. Rosch & B. B. Lloyd (Eds.), (1978), *Cognition and categorization* (pp. 27–48). Hillsdale, NJ: Erlbaum. Reprinted with permission.

fly, not all do. Flying, therefore, is a characteristic but not a defining attribute of a bird. Investigators saw that Rosch was correct in her argument that most properties are characteristic rather than defining attributes.

Although some investigators no longer accept prototype models, even investigators who accept other models still cite Rosch's work as a basis of comparison for their own new models. When a work becomes a standard for the work that follows it, that work truly can be viewed as a classic.

———

The following is a taxonomy of the animal kingdom. It has been attributed to an ancient Chinese encyclopedia entitled the *Celestial Emporium of Benevolent Knowledge:*

> On those remote pages it is written that animals are divided into (a) those that belong to the Emperor, (b) embalmed ones, (c) those that are trained, (d) suckling pigs, (e) mermaids, (f) fabulous ones, (g) stray dogs, (h) those that are included in this classification, (i) those that tremble as if they were mad, (j) innumerable ones, (k) those drawn with a very fine camel's hair brush, (l) others, (m) those that have just broken a flower vase, (n) those that resemble flies from a distance (Borges, 1966, p. 108).

Conceptually, the most interesting aspect of this classification system is that it does not exist. Certain types of categorizations may appear in the imagination of poets, but they are never found in the practical or linguistic classes of organisms or of man-made objects used by any of the cultures of the world. For some years, I have argued that human categorization should not be considered the arbitrary product of historical accident or of whimsy but rather the result of psychological principles of categorization, which are subject to investigation. This chapter is a summary and discussion of those principles.

The chapter is divided into five parts. The first part presents the two general principles that are proposed to underlie categorization systems. The second part shows the way in which these principles appear to result in a basic and primary level of categorization in the levels of abstraction in a taxonomy. It is essentially a summary of the research already reported on basic level objects (Rosch, Mervis, Gray, Johnson, & Boyes-Braem, 1976). Thus the second section may be omitted by the reader already sufficiently familiar with that material. The third part relates the principles of categorization to the formation of prototypes in those categories that are at the same level of abstraction in a taxonomy. In particular, this section attempts to clarify the operational concept of prototypicality and to separate that concept from claims concerning the role of prototypes in cognitive processing, representation, and learning for which there is little evidence. The fourth part presents two issues that are problematical for the abstract principles of categorization stated in Part I: (1) the relation of context to basic level objects and prototypes; and (2) assumptions about the nature of the attributes of real-world objects that underlie the claim that there is structure in the world. The fifth part is a report of initial attempts to base an analysis of the attributes, functions, and contexts of objects on a consideration of objects as props in culturally defined events.

It should be noted that the issues in categorization with which we are primarily concerned have to do with explaining the categories found in a culture and coded by the language of that culture at a particular point in time. When we speak of the formation of categories, we mean their formation in the culture. This point is often misunderstood. The principles of categorization proposed are not as such intended to constitute a theory of the development of categories in children born into a culture nor to constitute a model of how categories are processed (how categorizations are made) in the minds of adult speakers of a language.

THE PRINCIPLES

Two general and basic principles are proposed for the formation of categories: The first has to do with the function of category systems and asserts that the task of category systems is to provide maximum information with the least cognitive effort; the second has to do with the structure of the information so provided and asserts that the perceived world comes as structured information rather than as arbitrary or unpredictable attributes. Thus maximum information with least cognitive effort is achieved if categories map the perceived world structure as closely as possible. This condition can be achieved either by the mapping of categories to given attribute structures or by the definition or redefinition of attributes to render a given set of categories appropriately structured. These principles are elaborated in the following.

Cognitive Economy. The first principle contains the almost common-sense notion that, as an organism, what one wishes to gain from one's categories is a great deal of information about the environment while conserving finite resources as much as possible. To categorize a stimulus means to consider it, for purposes of that categorization, not only equivalent to other stimuli in the same category but also different from stimuli not in that category. On the one hand, it would appear to the organism's advantage to have as many properties as possible predictable from knowing any one property, a principle that would lead to formation of large numbers of categories with as fine discriminations between categories as possible. On the other hand, one purpose of categorization is to reduce the infinite differences among stimuli to behaviorally and cognitively usable proportions. It is to the organism's advantage not to differentiate one stimulus from others when that differentiation is irrelevant to the purposes at hand.

Perceived World Structure. The second principle of categorization asserts that unlike the sets of stimuli used in traditional laboratory-concept attainment tasks, the perceived world is not an unstructured total set of equiprobable co-occurring attributes. Rather, the material objects of the world are perceived to possess (in Garner's, 1974, sense) high correlational structure. That is, given a knower who perceives the complex attributes of feathers, fur, and wings, it is an empirical fact provided by the perceived world that wings co-occur with feathers more than with fur. Given an actor with the motor programs for sitting, it is a fact of the perceived world that objects with the perceptual attributes of chairs are more likely to have functional sit-on-able-ness than objects with the appearance of cats. In short, combinations of what we perceive as the attributes of real objects do not occur uniformly. Some pairs, triples, etc., are quite probable, appearing in combination sometimes with one, sometimes another attribute; others are rare; others logically cannot or empirically do not occur.

It should be emphasized that we are talking about the perceived world and not a metaphysical world without a knower. What kinds of attributes *can* be perceived are, of course, species-specific. A dog's sense of smell is more highly differentiated than a human's, and the structure of the world for a dog must surely include attributes of smell that we, as a species, are incapable of perceiving. Furthermore, because a dog's body is constructed differently from a human's, its motor interactions with objects are necessarily differently structured. The "out there" of a bat, a frog, or a bee is surely more different still from that of a human. What attributes *will* be perceived given the ability to perceive them is undoubtedly determined by many factors having to do with the functional needs of the knower interacting with the physical and social environment. One influence on how attributes will be defined by humans is clearly the category system already existent in the culture at a given time. Thus, our segmentation of a bird's body such that there is an attribute called "wings" may be influenced not only by perceptual factors such as the Gestalt laws of form that would lead us to consider the wings as a separate part (Palmer, in press) but also by the fact that at present we already have a cultural and linguistic category called "birds." Viewing attributes as, at least in part, constructs of the perceiver does not negate the higher-order structural fact about attributes at issue, namely that the attributes of wings and feathers do co-occur in the perceived world.

These two basic principles of categorization, a drive toward cognitive economy combined with structure in the perceived world, have implications both for the level of abstraction of categories formed in a culture and for the internal structure of those categories once formed.

For purposes of explication, we may conceive of category systems as having both a vertical and horizontal dimension. The vertical dimension concerns the level of inclusiveness of the category—the dimension along which the terms *collie, dog, mammal, animal,* and *living thing* vary. The horizontal dimension concerns the segmentation of categories at the same level of inclusiveness—the dimension on which dog, cat, car, bus, chair, and sofa vary. The implication of the two principles of categorization for the vertical dimension is that not all possible levels of categorization are equally good or useful; rather, the most basic level of categorization will be the most inclusive (abstract) level at which the categories can mirror the structure of attributes perceived in the world. The implication of the principles of categorization for the horizontal dimension is that to increase the distinctiveness and flexibility of categories, categories tend to become defined in terms of prototypes or prototypical instances that contain the attributes most representative of items inside and least representative of items outside the category.

THE VERTICAL DIMENSION OF CATEGORIES: BASIC-LEVEL OBJECTS

In a programmatic series of experiments, we have attempted to argue that categories within taxonomies of concrete objects are structured such that there is generally one level of abstraction at which the most basic category cuts can be made (Rosch et al., 1976). By *category* is meant a number of objects that are considered equivalent. Categories are generally designated by names (e.g., *dog, animal*). A *taxonomy* is a system by which categories are related to one another by means of class inclusion. The greater the inclusiveness of a category within a taxonomy, the higher the level of abstraction. Each category within a taxonomy is entirely included within one other category (unless it is the highest-level category) but is not exhaustive of that more inclusive category (see Kay, 1971). Thus the term *level of abstraction* within a taxonomy refers to a particular level of inclusiveness. A familiar taxonomy is the Linnean system for the classification of animals.

Our claims concerning a basic level of abstraction can be formalized in terms of cue validity (Rosch et al., 1976) or in terms of the set theoretic representation of similarity provided by Tversky (1977). Cue validity is a probabilistic concept; the validity of a given cue x as a predictor of a given category y (the conditional probability of y/x) increases as the frequency with which cue x is associated with category y increases and decreases as the frequency with which cue x is associated with categories other than y increases (Beach, 1964a, 1964b; Reed, 1972). The cue validity of an entire category may be defined as the summation of the cue validities for that category of each of the attributes of the category. A category with high cue validity is, by definition, more differentiated from other categories than one of lower cue validity. The elegant formulization that Tversky provides is in terms of the variable "category resemblance," which is defined as the weighted sum of the measures of all of the common features within a category minus the sum of the measures of all of the distinctive features. Distinctive features include those that belong to only some members of a given category as well as those belonging to contrasting categories. Thus Tversky's formalization does not weight the effect of contrast categories as much as does the cue validity formulation. Tversky suggests that two disjoint classes tend to be combined whenever the weight of the added common features exceeds the weight of the distinctive features.

A working assumption of the research on basic objects is that (1) in the perceived world, information-rich bundles of perceptual and functional attributes occur that form natural discontinuities, and that (2) basic cuts in categorization are made at these discontinuities. Suppose that basic objects (e.g., chair, car) are at the most inclusive level at which there are attributes common to all or most members of the category. Then both total cue validities and category resemblance are maximized at that level of abstraction at which basic objects are categorized. This is, categories one level more abstract will be superordinate categories (e.g., furniture, vehicle) whose members share only a few attributes among each other. Categories below the basic level will be bundles of common and, thus, predictable attributes and functions but contain many attributes that overlap with other categories (for example, kitchen chair shares most of its attributes with other kinds of chairs).

Superordinate categories have lower total cue validity and lower category resemblance than do basic-level categories, because they have fewer common attributes; in fact, the category resemblance measure of items within the superordinate can even be negative due to the high ratio of distinctive to common features. Subordinate categories have lower total cue validity than do basic categories, because they also share most attributes with contrasting subordinate categories; in Tversky's terms, they tend to be combined because the weight of the added common features tend to exceed the weight of the distinctive features. That basic objects are categories at the level of abstraction that maximizes cue validity and maximizes category resemblance is another way of asserting that basic objects are the categories that best mirror the correlational structure of the environment.

We chose to look at concrete objects because they appeared to be a domain that was at once an indisputable aspect of complex natural language classifications yet at the same time were amenable to methods of empirical analysis. In our investigations of basic categories, the correlational structure of concrete objects was considered to consist of a number of inseparable aspects of form and function, any one of which could serve as the starting point for analysis. Four investigations provided converging operational definitions of the basic level of abstraction: attributes in common, motor movements in common, objective similarity in shape, and identifiability of averaged shapes.

Common Attributes. Ethnobiologists had suggested on the basis of linguistic criteria and field observation that the folk genus was the level of classification at which organisms had bundles of attributes in common and maximum discontinuity between classes. The purpose of our research was to provide a systematic empirical study of the co-occurrence of attributes in the most common taxonomies of biological and man-made objects in our own culture.

The hypothesis that basic level objects are the most inclusive level of classification at which objects have numbers of attributes in common was tested for categories at three levels of abstraction for nine taxonomies: tree, bird, fish, fruit, musical instrument, tool, clothing, furniture, and vehicle. Examples of the three levels for one biological and one nonbiological taxonomy are shown in Table 1. Criteria for choice of these

TABLE 1   Examples of Taxonomies Used in Basic Object Research

SUPERORDINATE	BASIC LEVEL	SUBORDINATE
Furniture	Chair	Kitchen chair
		Living-room chair
	Table	Kitchen table
		Dining-room table
	Lamp	Floor lamp
		Desk lamp
Tree	Oak	White oak
		Red oak
	Maple	Silver maple
		Sugar maple
	Birch	River birch
		White birch

specific items were that the taxonomies contain the most common (defined by word frequency) categories of concrete nouns in English, that the levels of abstraction bear simple class-inclusion relations to each other, and that those class-inclusion relations be generally known to our subjects (be agreed upon by a sample of native English speakers). The middle level of abstraction was the hypothesized basic level: For nonbiological taxonomies, this corresponded to the intuition of the experimenters (which also turned out to be consistent with Berlin's linguistic criteria); for biological categories, we assumed that the basic level would be the level of the folk generic.

Subjects received sets of words taken from these nine taxonomies; each subject's task was to list all of the attributes he could think of that were true of the items included in the class of things designated by each object name. Thus, for purposes of this study, attributes were defined operationally as whatever subjects agreed them to be with no implications for whether such analysis of an object could or could not be perceptually considered prior to knowledge of the object itself. Results of the study were as predicted: Very few attributes were listed for the superordinate categories, a significantly greater number listed for the supposed basic-level objects, and not significantly more attributes listed for subordinate-level objects than for basic-level. An additional study showed essentially the same attributes listed for visually present objects as for the object names. The single unpredicted result was that for the three biological taxonomies, the basic level, as defined by numbers of attributes in common, did not occur at the level of the folk generic but appeared at the level we had originally expected to be superordinate (e.g., *tree* rather than *oak*).

Motor Movements. Inseparable from the perceived attributes of objects are the ways in which humans habitually use or interact with those objects. For concrete objects, such interactions take the form of motor movements. For example, when performing the action of sitting down on a chair, a sequence of body and muscle movements are typically made that are inseparable from the nature of the attributes of chairs—legs, seat, back, etc. This aspect of objects is particularly important in light of the role that sensory–motor interaction with the world appears to play in the development of thought (Bruner, Olver, & Greenfield, 1966; Nelson, 1974; Piaget, 1952).

In our study of motor movements, each of the sets of words used in the previous experiment was administered to new subjects. A subject was asked to describe, in as much finely analyzed detail as possible, the sequences of motor movements he made when using or interacting with the object. Tallies of agreed upon listings of the same movements of the same body part in the same part of the movement sequence formed the unit of analysis. Results were identical to those of the attribute listings; basic objects were the most general classes to have motor sequences in common. For example, there are few motor programs we carry out to items of furniture in general and several specific motor programs carried out in regard to sitting down on chairs, but we sit on kitchen and living-room chairs using essentially the same motor programs.

Similarity in Shapes. Another aspect of the meaning of a class of objects is the appearance of the objects in the class. In order to be able to analyze correlational structures by different but converging methods, it was necessary to find a method of analyzing similarity in the visual aspects of the objects that was not dependent on subjects' descriptions, that was free from effects of the object's name (which would not have been the case for subjects' ratings of similarity), and that went beyond similarity of analyzable, listable attributes that had already been used in the first study described. For this purpose, outlines of the shape of two-dimensional representations of objects were used, an integral aspect of natural forms. Similarity in shape was measured by the amount of overlap of the two outlines when the outlines (normalized for size and orientation) were juxtaposed.

Results showed that the ratio of overlapped to nonoverlapped area when two objects from the same basic-level category (e.g., two cars) were superimposed was far greater than when two objects from the same superordinate category were superimposed (e.g., a car and a motorcycle). Although some gain in ratio of overlap to nonoverlap also occurred for subordinate category objects (e.g., two sports cars), the gain obtained by shifting from basic-level to subordinate objects was significantly less than the gain obtained by shifting from superordinate to basic-level objects.

Identifiability of Averaged Shapes. If the basic level is the most inclusive level at which shapes of objects of a class are similar, a possible result of such similarity may be that the basic level is also the most inclusive level at which an averaged shape of an object can be recognized. To test this hypothesis, the same normalized superimposed shapes used in the previous experiment were used to draw an average outline of the overlapped figures. Subjects were then asked to identify both the superordinate category and the specific object depicted. Results showed that basic objects were the most general and inclusive categories at which the objects depicted could be identified. Furthermore, overlaps of subordinate objects were no more identifiable than objects at the basic level.

In summary, our four converging operational definitions of basic objects all indicated the same level of abstraction to be basic in our taxonomies. Admittedly, the basic level for biological objects was not that predicted by the folk genus; however, this fact appeared to be simply accounted for by our subjects' lack of knowledge of the additional depth of real-world attribute structure available at the level of the folk generic (see Rosch et al., 1976).

IMPLICATIONS FOR OTHER FIELDS

The foregoing theory of categorization and basic objects has implications for several traditional areas of study in psychology; some of these have been tested.

Imagery. The fact that basic-level objects were the most inclusive categories at which an averaged member of the category could be identified suggested that basic objects might be the most inclusive categories for which it was possible to form a mental image isomorphic to the appearance of members of the class as a whole. Experiments using a signal-detection paradigm and a priming paradigm, both of which have been previously argued to be measures of imagery (Peterson & Graham, 1974; Rosch, 1975b), verified that, in so far as it was meaningful to use the term *imagery,* basic objects appeared to be the most abstract categories for which an image could be reasonably representative of the class as a whole.

Perception. From all that has been said of the nature of basic classifications, it would hardly be reasonable to suppose that in perception of the world, objects were first categorized either at the most abstract or at the most concrete level possible. Two separate studies of picture verification (Rosch et al., 1976; Smith, Balzano, & Walker, 1978) indicate that, in fact, objects may be first seen or recognized as members of their basic category, and that only with the aid of additional processing can they be identified as members of their superordinate or subordinate category.

Development. We have argued that classification into categories at the basic level is overdetermined because perception, motor movements, functions, and iconic images would all lead to the same level of categorization. Thus basic objects should be the first categorizations of concrete objects made by children. In fact, for our nine taxonomies, the basic level was the first named. Even when naming was controlled, pictures of several basic-level objects were sorted into groups "because they were the same type of thing" long before such a technique of sorting has become general in children.

Language. From all that has been said, we would expect the most useful and, thus, most used name for an item to be the basic-level name. In fact, we found that adults almost invariably named pictures of the subordinate items of the nine taxonomies at the basic level, although they knew the correct superordinate and subordinate names for the objects. On a more speculative level, in the evolution of languages, one would expect names to evolve first for basic-level objects, spreading both upward and downward as taxonomies increased in depth. Of great relevance for this hypothesis are Berlin's (1972) claims for such a pattern for the evolution of plant names, and our own (Rosch et al., 1976) and Newport and Bellugi's finding for American Sign Language of the Deaf, that it was the basic-level categories that were most often coded by single signs and super- and subordinate categories that were likely to be missing. Thus a wide range of converging operations verify as basic the same levels of abstraction.

THE HORIZONTAL DIMENSION: INTERNAL STRUCTURE OF CATEGORIES: PROTOTYPES

Most, if not all, categories do not have clear-cut boundaries. To argue that basic object categories follow clusters of perceived attributes is not to say that such attribute clusters are necessarily discontinuous.

In terms of the principles of categorization proposed earlier, cognitive economy dictates that categories tend to be viewed as being as separate from each other and as clear-cut as possible. One way to achieve this is by means of formal, necessary and sufficient criteria for category membership. The attempt to impose such criteria on categories marks virtually all definitions in the tradition of Western reason. The psychological treatment of categories in the standard concept-identification paradigm lies within this tradition. Another way to achieve separateness and clarity of actually continuous categories is by conceiving of each category in terms of its clear cases rather than its boundaries. As Wittgenstein (1953) has pointed out, categorical judgments become a problem only if one is concerned with boundaries—in the normal course of life, two neighbors know on whose property they are standing without exact demarcation of the boundary line. Categories can be viewed in terms of their clear cases if the perceiver places emphasis on the correlational structure of perceived attributes such that the categories are represented by their most structured portions.

By *prototypes of categories* we have generally meant the clearest cases of category membership defined operationally by people's judgments of goodness of membership in the category. A great deal of confusion in the discussion of prototypes has arisen from two sources. First, the notion of prototypes has tended to become reified as though it meant a specific category member or mental structure. Questions are than asked in an either-or fashion about whether something is or is not the prototype or part of the prototype in exactly the same way in which the question would previously have been asked about the category boundary. Such thinking precisely violates the Wittgensteinian insight that we can judge how clear a case something is and deal with categories on the basis of clear cases in the total absence of information about boundaries. Second, the empirical findings about prototypicality have been confused with theories of processing—that is, there has been a failure to distinguish the structure of categories from theories concerning the use of that structure in processing. Therefore, let us first attempt to look at prototypes in as purely structural a fashion as possible. We will focus on what may be said about prototypes based on operational definitions and empirical findings alone without the addition of processing assumptions.

Perception of typicality differences is, in the first place, an empirical fact of people's judgments about category membership. It is by now a well-documented finding that subjects overwhelmingly agree in their judgments of how good an example or clear a case members are of a category, even for categories about whose boundaries they disagree (Rosch, 1974, 1975a). Such judgments are reliable even under changes of instructions and items (Rips, Shoben, & Smith, 1973; Rosch, 1975a, 1975b; Rosch & Mervis, 1975). Were such agreement and reliability in judgment not to have been obtained, there would be no further point in discussion or investigation of the issue. However, given the empirical verification of degree of prototypicality, we can proceed to ask what principles determine which items will be judged the more prototypical and what other variables might be affected by prototypicality.

In terms of the basic principles of category formation, the formation of category prototypes should, like basic levels of abstraction, be determinate and be closely related to the initial formation of categories. For categories of concrete objects (which do not have a physiological basis, as categories such as colors and forms apparently do—Rosch, 1974), a reasonable hypothesis is that prototypes develop through the same principles such as maximization of cue validity and maximization of category resemblance[1] as those principles governing the formation of the categories themselves.

In support of such a hypothesis, Rosch and Mervis (1975) have shown that the more prototypical of a category a member is rated, the more attributes it has in common with other members of the category and the fewer attributes in common with members of the contrasting categories. This finding was demonstrated for natural language superordinate categories, for natural language basic-level categories, and for artificial categories in which the definition of attributes and the amount of experience with items was completely specified and controlled. The same basic principles can be represented in ways other than through attributes in common. Because the present theory is a structural theory, one aspect of it is that centrality shares the mathematical notions inherent in measures like the mean and mode. Prototypical category members have been found to represent the means of attributes that have a metric, such as size (Reed, 1972; Rosch, Simpson, & Miller, 1976).

In short, prototypes appear to be just those members of a category that most reflect the redundancy structure of the category as a whole. That is, if categories form to maximize the information-rich cluster of attributes in the environment and, thus, the cue validity or category resemblance of the attributes of categories, prototypes of categories appear to form in such a manner as to maximize such clusters and such cue validity still further within categories.

It is important to note that for natural language categories both at the superordinate and basic levels, the extent to which items have attributes common to the category was highly negatively correlated with the extent to which they have attributes belonging to members of contrast categories. This appears to be part of the structure of real-world categories. It may be that such structure is given by the correlated clusters of attributes of the real world, or such structure may be a result of the human tendency once a contrast exists to define attributes for contrasting categories so that the categories will be maximally distinctive. In either case, it is a fact that both representativeness within a category and distinctiveness from contrast categories are correlated with prototypicality in real categories. For artificial categories, either principle alone will produce prototype effects (Rosch, Simpson, & Miller, 1976; Smith & Balzano, personal communication, 1977) depending on the structure of the stimulus set. Thus to perform experiments to try to distinguish which principle is the *one* that determines prototype formation and category processing appears to be an artificial exercise.

· · ·

TWO PROBLEMATICAL ISSUES

The Nature of Perceived Attributes. The derivations of basic objects and of prototypes from the basic principles of categorization have depended on the notion of a structure in the perceived world—bundles of perceived world attributes that formed natural discontinuities. When the research on basic objects and their prototypes was initially conceived (Rosch et al., 1976a), I thought of such attributes as inherent in the real world. Thus, given an organism that had sensory equipment capable of perceiving attributes such as wings and feathers, it was a fact in the real world that wings and feathers co-occurred. The state of knowledge of a person might be ignorant of (or indifferent or inattentive to) the attributes or might know of the attributes but be ignorant concerning their correlation. Conversely, a person might know of the attributes and their correlational structure but exaggerate that structure, turning partial into complete correlations (as when attributes true only of many members of a category are thought of as true of all members). However, the environment was thought to constrain categorizations in that human knowledge could not provide correlational structure where there was none at all. For purposes of the basic object experiments, perceived attributes were operationally defined as those attributes listed by our subjects. Shape was defined as measured by our computer programs. We thus seemed to have our system grounded comfortably in the real world.

On contemplation of the nature of many of the attributes listed by our subjects, however, it appeared that three types of attributes presented a problem for such a realistic view: (1) some attributes, such as "seat" for the object "chair," appeared to have names that showed them not to be meaningful prior to knowledge of the object as chair; (2) some attributes such as "large" for the object "piano" seemed to have meaning only in relation to categorization of the object in terms of a superordinate category—piano is large for furniture but small for other kinds of objects such as buildings; (3) some attributes such as "you eat on it" for the object "table" were functional attributes that seemed to require knowledge about humans, their activities, and the real world in order to be understood. That is, it appeared that the analysis of objects into attributes was a rather sophisticated activity that our subjects (and indeed a system of cultural knowledge) might well be considered to be able to impose only *after* the development of the category system.

In fact, the same laws of cognitive economy leading to the push toward basic-level categories and prototypes might also lead to the definition of attributes of categories such that the categories once given would appear maximally distinctive from one another and such that the more prototypical items would appear even more representative of their own and less representative of contrastive categories. Actually, in the evolution of the meaning of terms in languages, probably both the constraint of real-world factors and the construction and reconstruction of attributes are continually present. Thus, given a particular category system, attributes are defined such as to make the system appear as logical and economical as possible. However, if such a system becomes markedly out of phase with real-world constraints, it will probably tend to evolve to be more in line with those constraints—with redefinition of attributes ensuing if necessary. Unfortunately, to state the matter in such a way is to provide no clear place at which we can enter the system as analytical scientists. What is the unit with which to start our analysis? Partly in order to find a more basic real-world unit for analysis than attributes, we have turned our attention to the contexts in which objects occur—that is, to the culturally defined events in which objects serve as props.

The Role of Context in Basic-Level Objects and Prototypes. It is obvious, even in the absence of controlled experimentation, that a man about to buy a chair who is standing in a furniture store surrounded by different chairs among which he must choose will think and speak about chairs at other than the basic level of "chair." Similarly, in regard to prototypes, it is obvious that if asked for the most typical African animal, people of any age will not name the same animal as when asked for the most typical American pet animal. Because interest in context is only beginning, it is not yet clear just what experimentally defined contexts will affect what dependent variables for what categories. But it is predetermined that there will be context effects for both the level of abstraction at which an object is considered and for which items are named, learned, listed, or expected in a category. Does this mean that our findings in regard to basic levels and prototypes are relevant only to the artificial situation of the laboratory in which a context is not specified?

Actually, both basic levels and prototypes are, in a sense, theories about context itself. The basic level of abstraction is that level of abstraction that is appropriate for using, thinking about, or naming an object in most situations in which the object occurs (Rosch et al., 1976). When a context is not specified in an experiment, people must contribute their own context. Presumably, they do not do so randomly. Indeed, it seems likely that, in the absence of a specified context, subjects assume what they consider the normal context or situation for occurrence of that object. To make such claims about categories appears to demand an analysis of the actual events in daily life in which objects occur.

THE ROLE OF OBJECTS IN EVENTS

The attempt we have made to answer the issues of the origin of attributes and the role of context has been in terms of the use of objects in the events of daily human life. The study of events grew out of an interest in categorizations of the flow of experience. That is, our initial interest was in the question of whether any of the principles of categorization we had found useful for understanding concrete objects appeared to apply to the cutting up of the continuity of experience into the discrete bounded temporal units that we call *events*.

Previously, events have been studied primarily from two perspectives in psychology. Within ecological and social psychology, an observer records and attempts to segment the stream of another person's behavior into event sequences (for example, Barker & Wright, 1955; Newtson, 1976). Within the artificial intelligence tradition, Story Understanders are being constructed that can "comprehend," by means of event scripts, statements about simple, culturally predictable sequences such as going to a restaurant (Schank, 1975).

The unit of the event would appear to be a particularly important unit for analysis. Events stand at the interface between an analysis of social structure and culture and an analysis of individual psychology. It may be useful to think of scripts for events as the level of theory at which we can specify how culture and social structure enter the individual mind. Could we use events as the basic unit from which to derive an understanding of objects? Could we view objects as props for the carrying out of events and have the functions, perceptual attributes, and levels of abstraction of objects fall out of their role in such events?

Our research to date has been a study rather than an experiment and more like a pilot study at that. Events were defined neither by observation of others nor by a priori units for scripts but introspectively in the following fashion. Students in a seminar on events were asked to choose a particular evening on which to list the events that they remembered of that day—e.g., to answer the question what did I do? (or what happened to me?) that day by means of a list of the names of the events. They were to begin in the morning. The students were aware of the nature of the inquiry and that the focus of interest was on the units that they would perceive as the appropriate units into which to chunk the days' happenings. After completing the list for that day, they were to do the same sort of lists for events remembered from the previous day, and thus to continue backwards to preceding days until they could remember no more days' events. They also listed events for units smaller and larger than a day: for example, the hour immediately preceding writing and the previous school quarter.

The results were somewhat encouraging concerning the tractability of such a means of study. There was considerable agreement on the kinds of units into which a day should be broken—units such as making coffee, taking a shower, and going to statistics class. No one used much smaller units: That is, units such as picking up the toothpaste tube, squeezing toothpaste onto the brush, etc., never occurred. Nor did people use larger units such as "got myself out of the house in the morning" or "went to all my afternoon classes." Furthermore, the units that were listed did not change in size or type with their recency or remoteness in time to the writing. Thus, for the time unit of the hour preceding writing, components of events were not listed. Nor were larger units of time given for a day a week past than for the day on which the list was composed. Indeed, it was dramatic how, as days further and further in the past appeared, fewer and fewer events were remembered although the type of unit for those that were remembered remained the same. That is, for a day a week past, a student would not say that he now only remembered getting himself out of the house in the morning (though such "summarizing" events could be inferred); rather he either did or did not remember feeding the cat that day (an occurrence that could also be inferred but for which inference and memory were introspectively clearly distinguishable). Indeed, it appeared that events such as "all the morning chores" as a whole do not have a memory representation separate from memory of doing the individual chores—perhaps in the way that superordinate categories, such as furniture, do not appear to be imageable per se apart from imaging individual items in the category. It should be noted that event boundaries appeared to be marked in a reasonable way by factors such as changes of the actors participating with ego, changes in the objects ego interacts with, changes in place, and changes in the type or rate of activity with an object, and by notable gaps in time between two reported events.

A good candidate for the basic level of abstraction for events is the type of unit into which the students broke their days. The events they listed were just those kinds of events for which Schank (1975) has provided scripts. A script of an event analyzes it into individual units of action; these typically occur in a predictable order. For example, the script for going to a restaurant contains script elements such as entering, going to a table, ordering, eating, and paying. Some recent research has provided evidence for the psychological reality of scripts and their elements (Bower, 1976).

Our present concern is with the role of concrete objects in events. What categories of objects are required to serve as props for events at the level of abstraction of those listed by the students? In general, we found that the event name itself combined most readily with superordinate noun categories; thus, one gets dressed with clothes and needs various kitchen utensils to make breakfast. When such activities were analyzed into their script elements, the basic level appeared as the level of abstraction of objects necessary to script the events; e.g., in getting dressed, one puts on pants, sweater, and shoes, and in making breakfast, one cooks eggs in a frying pan.

With respect to prototypes, it appears to be those category members judged the more prototypical that have attributes that enable them to fit into the typical and agreed upon script elements. We are presently collecting normative data on the intersection of common events, the objects associated with those events, and the other sets of events associated with those objects.[2] In addition, object names for eliciting events are varied in level of abstraction and in known prototypicality in given categories. Initial results show a similar pattern to that obtained in the earlier research in which it was found that the more typical members of superordinate categories could replace the superordinate in sentence frames generated by subjects told to "make up a sentence" that used the superordinate (Rosch, 1977). That is, the task of using a given concrete noun in a sentence appears to be an indirect method of eliciting a statement about the events in which objects play a part; that indirect method showed clearly that prototypical category members are those that can play the role in events expected of members of that category.

The use of deviant forms of object names in narratives accounts for several recently explored effects in the psychological literature. Substituting object names at other than the basic level within scripts results in obviously deviant descriptions. Substitution of superordinates produces just those types of narrative that Bransford and Johnson (1973) have claimed are not comprehended; for example, "The procedure is actually quite simple. First you arrange things into different groups. Of course, one pile may be sufficient [p. 400]." It should be noted in the present context that what Bransford and Johnson call *context cues* are actually names of basic-level events (e.g., washing clothes) and that one function of hearing the event name is to enable the reader to translate the superordinate terms into basic-level objects and actions. Such a translation appears to be a necessary aspect of our ability to match linguistic descriptions to world knowledge in a way that produces the "click of comprehension."

On the other hand, substitution of subordinate terms for basic-level object names in scripts gives the effect of satire or snobbery. For example, a review (Garis, 1975) of a pretentious novel accused of actually being about nothing more than brand-name snobbery concludes, "And so, after putting away my 10-year-old Royal 470 manual and lining up my Mongol number 3 pencils on my Goldsmith Brothers Formica imitation-wood desk, I slide into my oversize squirrel-skin L. L. Bean slippers and shuffle off to the kitchen. There, holding *Decades* in my trembling right hand, I drop it, *plunk,* into my new Sears 20-gallon, celadon-green Permanex trash can [p. 48]."

Analysis of events is still in its initial stages. It is hoped that further understanding of the functions and attributes of objects can be derived from such an analysis.

SUMMARY

The first part of this chapter showed how the same principles of categorization could account for the taxonomic structure of a category system organized around a basic level and also for the formation of the categories that occur within this basic level. Thus the principles described accounted for both the vertical and horizontal structure of category systems. Four converging operations were employed to establish the claim that the basic level provides the cornerstone of a taxonomy. The section on prototypes distinguished the empirical evidence for prototypes as structural facts about categories from the possible role of prototypes in cognitive processing, representation, and learning. Then we considered assumptions about the nature of the attributes of real-world objects and assumptions about context—insofar as attributes and contexts underlie the claim that there is structure in the world. Finally, a highly tentative pilot study of attributes and functions of objects as props in culturally defined events was presented.

REFERENCES

Barker, R., & Wright, H. (1955). *Midwest and its children.* Evanston, Ill.: Row-Peterson.

Beach, L. R. (1964a). Cue probabilism and inference behavior. *Psychological Monographs, 78* (Whole No. 582).

Beach, L. R. (1964b). Recognition, assimilation, and identification of objects. *Psychological Monographs, 78* (Whole No. 583).

Berlin, B. (1972). Speculations on the growth of ethnobotanical nomenclature. *Language in Society, 1,* 51-86.

Borges, J. L. (1966). *Other inquisitions 1937-1952.* New York: Washington Square Press.

Bower, G. (1976, September). *Comprehending and recalling stories.* Paper presented as Division 3 presidential address to the American Psychological Association, Washington, D.C.

Bransford, J. D., & Johnson, M. K. (1973). Considerations of some problems of comprehension. In W. Chase (Ed.), *Visual information processing.* New York: Academic Press.

Bruner, J. S., Olver, R. R., & Greenfield, P. M. (1966). *Studies in cognitive growth.* New York: Wiley.

Garis, L. (1975, March). The Margaret Mead of Madison Avenue. *Ms.,* 47-48.

Garner, W. R. (1974). *The processing of information and structure.* New York: Wiley.

Kay, P. (1971). Taxonomy and semantic contrast. *Language, 47,* 866-887.

Lakoff, G. Hedges: A study in meaning criteria and the logic of fuzzy concepts. *Papers from the eighth regional meeting, Chicago Linguistics Society.* Chicago: University of Chicago Linguistics Department, 1972.

Nelson, K. (1974). Concept, word, and sentence: Interrelation in acquisition and development. *Psychological Review, 81,* 267-285.

Neuman, P. G. (1974). An attribute frequency model for the abstraction of prototypes. *Memory and Cognition, 2,* 241-248.

Newtson, D. (1976). Foundations of attribution: The perception of ongoing behavior. In J. Harvey, W. Ickes, & R. Kidd (Eds.), *New directions in attribution research.* Hillsdale, N.J.: Erlbaum.

Palmer, S. (in press). Hierarchical structure in perceptual representation. *Cognitive Psychology.*

Peterson, M. J., & Graham, S. E. (1974). Visual detection and visual imagery. *Journal of Experimental Psychology, 103,* 509-514.

Piaget, J. (1952). *The origins of intelligence in children.* New York: International Universities Press.

Posner, M. I., Goldsmith, R., & Welton, K. E. (1967). Perceived distance and the classification of distorted patterns. *Journal of Experimental Psychology, 73,* 28-38.

Reed, S. K. (1972). Pattern recognition and categorization. *Cognitive Psychology, 3,* 382-407.

Rips, L. J., Shoben, E. J., & Smith, E. E. (1973). Semantic distance and the verification of semantic relations. *Journal of Verbal Learning and Verbal Behavior, 12,* 1-20.

Rosch, E. (1974). Linguistic relativity. In A. Silverstein (Ed.), *Human communication: Theoretical perspectives.* New York: Halsted Press.

Rosch, E. (1975a). Cognitive representations of semantic categories. *Journal of Experimental Psychology: General, 104,* 192-233.

Rosch, E. (1975b). The nature of mental codes for color categories. *Journal of Experimental Psychology: Human Perception and Performance, 1,* 303-322.

Rosch, E. (1977). Human categorization. In N. Warren (Ed.), *Advances in cross-cultural psychology* (Vol. 1). London: Academic Press.

Rosch, E., & Mervis, C. B. (1975). Family resemblances: Studies in the internal structure of categories. *Cognitive Psychology, 7,* 573-605.

Rosch, E., Mervis, C. B., Gray, W. D., Johnson, D. M., & Boyes-Braem, P. (1976). Basic objects in natural categories. *Cognitive Psychology, 8,* 382-439.

Rosch, E., Simpson, C., & Miller, R. S. (1976). Structural bases of typicality effects. *Journal of Experimental Psychology: Human Perception and Performance. 2,* 491-502.

Schank, R. C. (1975). The structure of episodes in memory. In D. G. Bobrow & A. Collins (Eds.), *Representation and understanding: Studies in cognitive science.* New York: Academic Press.

Smith, E. E., Balzano, G. J., & Walker, J. H. (1978). Nominal, perceptual, and semantic codes in picture categorization. In J. Cotton & R. Klatzky (Eds.), *Semantic factors in cognition.* Hillsdale, NJ: Erlbaum.

Tversky, S. (1977). Features of similarity. *Psychological Review, 84,* 327-352.

Wittgenstein L. (1953). *Philosophical investigations.* New York: Macmillan.

Notes

1. Tversky formalizes prototypicality as the member or members of the category with the highest summed similarity to all members of the category. This measure, although formally more tractable than that of cue validity, does not take account, as cue validity does, of an item's dissimilarity to contrast categories. This issue is discussed further later.

2. This work is being done by Elizabeth Kreusi.

QUESTIONS FOR FURTHER THOUGHT

1. What is a prototype?

2. What is a basic-level category, and how does it differ from categories at other levels?

3. What evidence does Rosch present to argue for the existence of prototypes in conceptual structure?

4. What is the principle of cognitive economy, and how does it influence category formation?

5. Why might traditional laboratory studies of concept learning fail to generalize to learning categories in the everyday world?

CONCEPTS AND CONCEPTUAL STRUCTURE

Douglas Medin

INTRODUCTION

The so-called *classical view* of concepts held that all instances or examples of a category share some common trait, and this trait holds the category together. According to this view, for example, all birds share a common set of features that jointly distinguish them from other categories. Eleanor Rosch and her colleagues, however, showed defects in the classical view of concepts and categories. For example, a robin and an ostrich are both birds, but to most people, a robin somehow seems to be a better example of a bird than does an ostrich.

Rosch therefore suggested an alternative conceptualization in which people decide on category membership based on resemblance to a prototype. In other words, a robin more resembles the prototype for a bird than does an ostrich, and hence it is a better or more typical instance of a bird.

In this article, Douglas Medin argues against both views of concepts and category membership. He points out, for example, that context effects can determine which of two concepts more typically represents a category. For example, consider the category of "beverage consumed during a break." For secretaries, tea is more typical than milk, but the reverse is true for young school children. Thus, no one prototype typifies beverage consumed during a break.

Medin suggested that recent theory and research support the notion that people refer to exemplar-based theories to decide whether and how well a concept fits a category. For example, such a theory specifies what constitutes a zebra. Generally, people expect a zebra to have stripes, but if someone paints the zebra a solid color, they still believe the animal to be a zebra, despite its loss of visible stripes. To determine category relationships, people generate exemplars that fit theories and assign category memberships based on the exemplars. For example, tea but not milk would be an exemplar in the category of beverages likely to be consumed by secretaries during their breaks, and the reverse would be true for school children.

Medin is considered a leader in work on concepts because of his instrumental role in moving the field beyond the prototype-based view to a theory-based view that emphasizes the importance of good exemplars of concepts rather than single prototypes of these concepts. Prototypes differ in important ways from exemplars. For one difference, theorists typically assume only one prototype for a concept, whereas multiple exemplars may typify varying criteria. For another

Source: From Medin, D. L. (1989). Concepts and conceptual structure. *American Psychologist, 44,* 1469–1481. Copyright © 1989 by the American Psychological Association. Reprinted with permission.

thing, the exemplars are actual examples, whereas a prototype may be an ideal-ized "average" of actual instances that itself does not exist. This article by Medin is important because it provides strong evidence for the utility of the theory-based view.

———

Research and theory on categorization and conceptual structure have recently undergone two major shifts. The first shift is from the assumption that concepts have defining properties (the classical view) to the idea that concept representations may be based on properties that are only characteristic or typ-ical of category examples (the probabilistic view). Both the probabilistic view and the classical view assume that categorization is driven by similarity rela-tions. A major problem with describing category structure in terms of similar-ity is that the notion of similarity is too unconstrained to give an account of conceptual coherence. The second major shift is from the idea that concepts are organized by similarity to the idea that concepts are organized around theories. In this article, the evidence and rationale associated with these shifts are described, and one means of integrating similarity-based and theory-driven categorization is outlined. ∎

What good are categories? Categorization involves treating two or more distinct entities as in some way equivalent in the service of accessing knowledge and making predictions. Take psychodiagnostic categories as an example. The need to access relevant knowledge explains why clinical psychologists do not (or could not) treat each individual as unique. Although one would expect treatment plans to be tai-lored to the needs of individuals, absolute uniqueness imposes the prohibitive cost of ignorance. Clinicians need some way to bring their knowledge and experience to bear on the problem under consideration, and that requires the appreciation of some similarity or relationship between the current situation and what has gone before. Although clinical psychologists may or may not use a specific categorization system, they must find points of contact between previous situations and the current con-text; that is, they must categorize. Diagnostic categories allow clinicians to predict the efficacy of alternative treatments and to share their experiences with other thera-pists. Yet another reason to categorize is to learn about etiology. People who show a common manifestation of some problem may share common precipitating condi-tions or causes. Ironically, the only case in which categorization would not be useful is where all individuals are treated alike; thus, categorization allows diversity.

More generally speaking, concepts and categories serve as building blocks for human thought and behavior. Roughly, a *concept* is an idea that includes all that is characteristically associated with it. A *category* is a partitioning or class to which some assertion or set of assertions might apply. It is tempting to think of categories as existing in the world and of concepts as corresponding to mental representations of them, but this analysis is misleading. It is misleading because concepts need not have real-world counterparts (e.g., unicorns) and because people may impose rather than discover structure in the world. I believe that questions about the nature of categories may be psychological questions as much as metaphysical questions. Indeed, for at least the last decade my colleagues and I have been trying to address the question of why we have the categories we have and not others. The world could be partitioned in a limitless variety of ways, yet people find only a miniscule subset of possible classifications to be meaningful. Part of the answer to the categorization question likely does depend on the nature of the world, but part also surely depends on the nature of the organism and its goals. Dolphins have no use for psychodiagnostic categories.

Given the fundamental character of concepts and categories, one might think that people who study concepts would have converged on a stable consensus with respect to conceptual structure. After all, Plato and Aristotle had quite a bit to say about concepts, medieval philosophers were obsessed with questions about universals and the essence of concepts, and concept representation remains as a cornerstone issue in all aspects of cognitive science. However, we have neither consensus nor stability. The relatively recent past has experienced at least one and probably two major shifts in thought about conceptual structure, and stability is the least salient attribute of the current situation. In the remainder of this article, I will briefly describe these shifts and then outline some ways of integrating the strong points of the various views.

THE FIRST SHIFT: CLASSICAL VERSUS PROBABILISTIC VIEWS

It is difficult to discuss concepts without bringing in the notion of similarity at some point. For example, a common idea is that our classification system tends to maximize within-category similarity relative to between-category similarity. That is, we group things into categories because they are similar. It will be suggested that alternative views of conceptual structure are associated with distinct (though sometimes implicit) theories of the nature of similarity.

THE CLASSICAL VIEW

The idea that all instances or examples of a category have some fundamental characteristics in common that determine their membership is very compelling. The classical view of concepts is organized around this notion. The classical view assumes that mental representations of categories consist of summary lists of features or properties that individually are necessary for category membership and collectively are sufficient to determine category membership. The category *triangle* meets these criteria. All triangles are closed geometric forms with three sides and interior angles that sum to 180 degrees. To see if something is a triangle one has only to check for these three properties, and if any one is missing one does not have a triangle.

What about other concepts? The classical view suggests that all categories have defining features. A particular person may not know what these defining features are but an expert certainly should. In our 1981 book, *Categories and Concepts,* Ed Smith and I reviewed the status of the classical view as a theory of conceptual structure. We concluded that the classical view was in grave trouble for a variety of reasons. Many of the arguments and counterarguments are quite detailed, but the most serious problems can be easily summarized.

1. Failure to Specify Defining Features. One glaring problem is that even experts cannot come up with defining features for most lexical concepts (i.e., those reflected in our language). People may believe that concepts have necessary or sufficient features (McNamara & Sternberg, 1983), but the features given as candidates do not hold up to closer scrutiny. For example, a person may list "made of wood" as a necessary property for violins, but not all violins are made of wood. Linguists, philosophers, biologists, and clinical psychologists alike have been unable to supply a core set of features that all examples of a concept (in their area of expertise) necessarily must share.

2. Goodness of Example Effects. According to the classical view, all examples of a concept are equally good because they all possess the requisite defining features. Experience and (by now) a considerable body of research undermines this claim. For example, people judge a robin to be a better example of bird than an ostrich is and can answer category membership questions more quickly for good examples than for poor examples (Smith, Shoben, & Rips, 1974). Typicality effects are nearly ubiquitous (for reviews, see Medin & Smith, 1984; Mervis & Rosch, 1981; Oden, 1987); they hold for the artistic style (Hartley & Homa, 1981), chess (Goldin, 1978), emotion terms (Fehr, 1988; Fehr & Russell, 1984), medical diagnosis (Arkes & Harkness, 1980), and person perception (e.g., Cantor & Mischel, 1977).

Typicality effects are not, in principle, fatal for the classical view. One might imagine that some signs or features help to determine the presence of other (defining) features. Some examples may have more signs or clearer signs pointing the way to the defining properties, and this might account for the difference in goodness of example judgments or response times. This distinction between identification procedures (how one identifies an instance of a concept) and a conceptual core (how the concept relates to other concepts) may prove useful if it can be shown that the core is used in some other aspect of thinking. It seems, however, that this distinction serves more to insulate the classical view from empirical findings, and Smith, Rips, and Medin (1984) argued that there are no sharp boundaries between core properties and those used for purposes of identification.

3. Unclear Cases. The classical view implies a procedure for unambiguously determining category membership; that is, check for defining features. Yet there are numerous cases in which it is not clear whether an example belongs to a category. Should a rug be considered furniture? What about a clock or radio? People not only disagree with each other concerning category membership but also contradict themselves when asked about membership on separate occasions (Barsalou, 1989; Bellezza, 1984; McCloskey & Glucksberg, 1978).

These and other problems have led to disenchantment with the classical view of concepts. The scholarly consensus has shifted its allegiance to an alternative, the probabilistic view.

THE PROBABILISTIC VIEW

The rejection of the classical view of categories has been associated with the ascendance of the probabilistic view of category structure (Wittgenstein, 1953). This view holds that categories are "fuzzy" or ill-defined and that categories are organized around a set of properties or clusters of correlated attributes (Rosch, 1975) that are only characteristic or typical of category membership. Thus, the probabilistic view rejects the notion of defining features.

The most recent edition of the *Diagnostic and Statistical Manual of Mental Disorders (DSM-IIIR,* American Psychiatric Association, 1987) uses criteria based on lists of characteristic symptoms or features to describe diagnostic categories and thereby endorses the probabilistic view. For example, a diagnosis of depression can be made if a dysphoric mood and any five of a set of nine symptoms are present nearly every day for a period of at least 2 weeks. Thus, two people may both be categorized as depressed and share only a single one of the nine characteristic symptoms!

The probabilistic view is perfectly at home with the typicality effects that were so awkward for the classical view. Membership in probabilistic categories is naturally graded, rather than all or none, and the better or more typical members have more characteristic properties than the poorer ones. It is also easy to see that the probabilistic view may lead to unclear cases. Any one example may have several typical properties of a category but not so many that it clearly qualifies for category membership.

In some pioneering work aimed at clarifying the structural basis of fuzzy categories, Rosch and Mervis (1975) had subjects list properties of exemplars for a variety of concepts such as *bird, fruit,* and *tool.* They found that the listed properties for some exemplars occurred frequently in other category members, whereas others had properties that occurred less frequently. Most important, the more frequently an exemplar's properties appeared within a category, the higher was its rated typicality for that category. The correlation between number of characteristic properties possessed and typicality rating was very high and positive. For example, robins have characteristic bird properties of flying, singing, eating worms, and building nests in trees, and they are rated to be very typical birds. Penguins have none of these properties, and they are rated as very atypical birds. In short, the Rosch and Mervis work relating typicality to number of characteristic properties put the probabilistic view on fairly firm footing.

1. Mental Representations of Probabilistic View Categories. If categories are not represented in terms of definitions, what form do our mental representations take? The term, *probabilistic view,* seems to imply that people organize categories via statistical reasoning. Actually, however, there is a more natural interpretation of fuzzy categories. Intuitively, probabilistic view categories are organized according to a *family resemblance* principle. A simple form of summary representation would be an example or ideal that possessed all of the characteristic features of a category. This summary representation is referred to as the *prototype,* and the prototype can be used to decide category membership. If some candidate example is similar enough to the prototype for a category, then it will be classified as a member of that category. The general notion is that, based on experience with examples of a category, people abstract out the central tendency or prototype that becomes the summary mental representation for the category.

A more radical principle of mental representation, which is also consistent with fuzzy categories, is the exemplar view (Smith & Medin, 1981). The exemplar view denies that there is a single summary representation and instead claims that categories are represented by means of examples. In this view, clients may be diagnosed as suicidal, not because they are similar to some prototype of a suicidal person, but because they remind the clinician of a previous client who was suicidal.

A considerable amount of research effort has been aimed at contrasting exemplar and prototype representations (see Allen, Brooks, Norman, & Rosenthal, 1988; Estes, 1986a, 1986b; Medin, 1986; Medin & Smith, 1984; Nosofsky, 1987, 1988a; and Oden, 1987). Genero and Cantor (1987) suggested that prototypes serve untrained diagnosticians well but that trained diagnosticians may find exemplars to be more helpful. For my present purposes, however, I will blur over this distinction to note that both prototype and exemplar theories rely on roughly the same similarity principle. That is, category membership is determined by whether some candidate is sufficiently similar either to the prototype or to a set of encoded examples, where similarity is based on matches and mismatches of independent, equally abstract, features.

2. Probabilistic View and Similarity. To give meaning to the claim that categorization is based on similarity, it is important to be specific about what one means by similarity. Although the consensus is not uniform, I believe that the modal model of similarity with respect to conceptual structure can be summarized in terms of the four assumptions as follows: (a) Similarity between two things increases as a function of the number of features or properties they share and decreases as a function of mismatching or distinctive features. (b) These features can be treated as independent and additive. (c) The features determining similarity are all roughly the same level of abstractness (as a special case they may be irreducible primitives). (d) These similarity principles are sufficient to describe conceptual structure, and therefore, a concept is more or less equivalent to a list of its features. This theory of similarity is very compatible with the notion that categories are organized around prototypes. Nonetheless, I will later argue that each of these assumptions is wrong or misleading and that to understand conceptual structure, theories of similarity are needed that reject each of these assumptions. Before outlining an alternative set of similarity assumptions, however, I will first describe a set of observations that motivate the second, still more recent, shift in thinking concerning conceptual structure.

PROBLEMS FOR PROBABILISTIC VIEW THEORIES

PROBLEMS FOR PROTOTYPES

Although the general idea that concepts are organized around prototypes remains popular, at a more specific, empirical level, prototype theories have not fared very well. First of all, prototype theories treat concepts as context-independent. Roth and

Shoben (1983), however, have shown that typicality judgments vary as a function of particular contexts. For example, tea is judged to be a more typical beverage than milk in the context of secretaries taking a break, but this ordering reverses for the context of truck drivers taking a break. Similarly, Shoben and I (Medin & Shoben, 1988) noted that the typicality of combined concepts cannot be predicted from the typicality of the constituents. As an illustrative example, consider the concept of *spoon.* People rate small spoons as more typical spoons than large spoons, and metal spoons as more typical spoons than wooden spoons. If the concept *spoon* is represented by a prototypic spoon, then a small metal spoon should be the most typical spoon, followed by small wooden and large metal spoons, and large wooden spoons should be the least typical. Instead, people find large wooden spoons to be more typical spoons than either small wooden spoons or large metal spoons (see also Malt & Smith, 1983). The only way for a prototype model to handle these results is to posit multiple prototypes. But this strategy creates new problems. Obviously one cannot have a separate prototype for every adjective–noun combination because there are simply too many possible combinations. One might suggest that there are distinct subtypes for concepts like *spoon,* but one would need a theory describing how and when subtypes are created. Current prototype models do not provide such a theory. A third problem for prototype theories grows out of Barsalou's work (1985, 1987) on goal-derived categories such as "things to take on a camping trip" and "foods to eat while on a diet." Barsalou has found that goal-derived categories show the same typicality effects as other categories. The basis for these effects, however, is not similarity to an average or prototype but rather similarity to an ideal. For example, for the category of things to eat while on a diet, typicality ratings are determined by how closely an example conforms to the ideal of zero calories.

Laboratory studies of categorization using artificially constructed categories also raise problems for prototypes. Normally many variables relevant to human classification are correlated and therefore confounded with one another. The general rationale for laboratory studies with artificially created categories is that one can isolate some variable or set of variables of interest and unconfound some natural correlations. Salient phenomena associated with fuzzy categories are observed with artificially constructed categories, and several of these are consistent with prototype theories. For example, one observes typicality effects in learning and on transfer tests using both correctness and reaction time as the dependent variable (e.g., Rosch & Mervis, 1975). A striking phenomenon, readily obtained, is that the prototype for a category may be classified more accurately during transfer tests than are the previously seen examples that were used during original category learning (e.g., Homa & Vosburgh, 1976; Medin & Schaffer, 1978; Peterson, Meagher, Chait, & Gillie, 1973).

Typicality effects and excellent classification of prototypes are consistent with the idea that people are learning these ill-defined categories by forming prototypes. More detailed analyses, however, are more problematic. Prototype theory implies that the only information abstracted from categories is the central tendency. A prototype representation discards information concerning category size, the variability of the examples, and information concerning correlations of attributes. The evidence suggests that people are sensitive to all three of these types of information (Estes, 1986b; Flannagan, Fried, & Holyoak, 1986; Fried & Holyoak, 1984; Medin, Altom, Edelson, &

Freko, 1982; Medin & Schaffer, 1978). An example involving correlated attributes pinpoints part of the problem. Most people have the intuition that small birds are much more likely to sing than large birds. This intuition cannot be obtained from a single summary prototype for birds. The fact that one can generate large numbers of such correlations is a problem for the idea that people reason using prototypes. More generally, prototype representations seem to discard too much information that can be shown to be relevant to human categorizations.

Yet another problem for prototypes is that they make the wrong predictions about which category structures should be easy or difficult to learn. One way to conceptualize the process of classifying examples on the basis of similarity to prototypes is that it involves a summing of evidence against a criterion. For example, if an instance shows a criterial sum of features (appropriately weighted), then it will be classified as a bird, and the more typical a member is of the category, the more quickly the criterion will be exceeded. The key aspect of this prediction is that there must exist some additive combination of properties and their weights that can be used to correctly assign instances as members or nonmembers. The technical term for this constraint is that categories must be *linearly separable* (Sebestyn, 1962). For a prototype process to work in the sense of accepting all members and rejecting all nonmembers, the categories must be linearly separable.

If linear separability acts as a constraint on human categorization, then with other factors equal, people should find it easier to learn categories that are linearly separable than categories that are not linearly separable. To make a long story short, however, studies employing a variety of stimulus materials, category sizes, subject populations, and instructions have failed to find any evidence that linear separability acts as a constraint on human classification learning (Kemler-Nelson, 1984; Medin & Schwanenflugel, 1981; see also Shepard, Hovland, & Jenkins, 1961).

The cumulative effect of these various chunks of evidence has been to raise serious questions concerning the viability of prototype theories. Prototype theories imply constraints that are not observed in human categorization, predict insensitivity to information that people readily use, and fail to reflect the context sensitivity that is evident in human categorization. Rather than getting at the character of human conceptual representation, prototypes appear to be more of a caricature of it. Exemplar models handle some of these phenomena, but they fail to address some of the most fundamental questions concerning conceptual structure.

EXEMPLAR-BASED THEORIES

The problems just described hold not only for prototype theories in particular but also for any similarity-based categorization model that assumes that the constituent features are independent and additive. To give but one example, one could have an exemplar model of categorization that assumes that, during learning, people store examples but that new examples are classified by "computing" prototypes and determining the similarity of the novel example to the newly constructed prototypes. In short, the central tendency would be abstracted (and other information discarded) at the time of retrieval rather than at the time of storage or initial encoding. Such a model would inherit all the shortcomings of standard prototype theories.

Some exemplar storage theories do not endorse the notion of feature independence (Hintzman, 1986; Medin & Schaffer, 1978), or they assume that classification is based on retrieving only a subset of the stored examples (presumably the most similar ones or, as a special case, the most similar one). The idea that retrieval is limited, similarity-based, and context-sensitive is in accord with much of the memory literature (e.g., Tulving, 1983). In addition, these exemplar models predict sensitivity to category size, instance variability, context, and correlated attributes. It is my impression that in head-to-head competition, exemplar models have been substantially more successful than prototype models (Barsalou & Medin, 1986; Estes, 1986b; Medin & Ross, 1989; Nosofsky, 1988a, 1988b; but see Homa, 1984, for a different opinion).

Why should exemplar models fare better than prototype models? One of the main functions of classification is that it allows one to make inferences and predictions on the basis of partial information (see Anderson, 1988). Here I am using *classification* loosely to refer to any means by which prior (relevant) knowledge is brought to bear, ranging from a formal classification scheme to an idiosyncratic reminding of a previous case (which, of course, is in the spirit of exemplar models; see also Kolodner, 1984). In psychotherapy, clinicians are constantly making predictions about the likelihood of future behaviors or the efficacy of a particular treatment based on classification. Relative to prototype models, exemplar models tend to be conservative about discarding information that facilitates predictions. For instance, sensitivity to correlations of properties within a category enables finer predictions: From noting that a bird is large, one can predict that it cannot sing. It may seem that exemplar models do not discard any information at all, but they are incomplete without assumptions concerning retrieval or access. In general, however, the pairs of storage and retrieval assumptions associated with exemplar models preserve much more information than prototype models. In a general review of research on categorization and problem-solving, Brian Ross and I concluded that abstraction is both conservative and tied to the details of specific examples in a manner more in the spirit of exemplar models than prototype models (Medin & Ross, 1989).

Unfortunately, context-sensitive, conservative categorization is not enough. The debate between prototype and exemplar models has taken place on a platform constructed in terms of similarity-based categorization. The second shift is that this platform has started to crumble, and the viability of probabilistic view theories of categorization is being seriously questioned. There are two central problems. One is that probabilistic view theories do not say anything about why we have the categories we have. This problem is most glaringly obvious for exemplar models that appear to allow any set of examples to form a category. The second central problem is with the notion of similarity. Do things belong in the same category because they are similar, or do they seem similar because they are in the same category?

DOES SIMILARITY EXPLAIN CATEGORIZATION?

1. Flexibility. Similarity is a very intuitive notion. Unfortunately, it is even more elusive than it is intuitive. One problem with using similarity to define categories is that similarity is too flexible. Consider, for example, Tversky's (1977) influential contrast model, which defines similarity as a function of common and distinctive features weighted for salience or importance. According to this model, similarity relationships will depend heavily on the particular weights given to individual properties or features. For example, a *zebra* and a *barber pole* would be more similar than a *zebra* and a *horse* if the feature "striped" had sufficient weight. This would not necessarily be a problem if the weights were stable. However, Tversky and others have convincingly shown that the relative weighting of a feature (as well as the relative importance of matching and mismatching features) varies with the stimulus context, experimental task (Gati & Tversky, 1984; Tversky, 1977), and probably even the concept under consideration (Ortony, Vondruska, Foss, & Jones, 1985). For example, common properties shared by a pair of entities may become salient only in the context of some third entity that does not share these properties.

Once one concedes that similarity is dynamic and depends on some (not well-understood) processing principles, earlier work on the structural underpinnings of fuzzy categories can be seen in a somewhat different light. Recall that the Rosch and Mervis (1975) studies asked subjects to list attributes or properties of examples and categories. It would be a mistake to assume that people had the ability to read and report their mental representations of concepts in a veridical manner. Indeed Keil (1979, 1981) pointed out that examples like *robin* and *squirrel* shared many important properties that almost never show up in attribute listings (e.g., has a heart, breathes, sleeps, is an organism, is an object with boundaries, is a physical object, is a thing, can be thought about, and so on). In fact, Keil argued that knowledge about just these sorts of predicates, referred to as *ontological knowledge* (Sommers, 1971), serves to organize children's conceptual and semantic development. For present purposes, the point is that attribute listings provide a biased sample of people's conceptual knowledge. To take things a step further, one could argue that without constraints on what is to count as a feature, any two things may be arbitrarily similar or dissimilar. Thus, as Murphy and I (Murphy & Medin, 1985) suggested, the number of properties that plums and lawn mowers have in common could be infinite: Both weigh less than 1,000 Kg, both are found on earth, both are found in our solar system, both cannot hear well, both have an odor, both are not worn by elephants, both are used by people, both can be dropped, and so on (see also Goodman, 1972; Watanabe, 1969). Now consider again the status of attribute listings. They represent a biased subset of stored or readily inferred knowledge. The correlation of attribute listings with typicality judgments is a product of such knowledge and a variety of processes that operate on it. Without a theory of that knowledge and those processes, it simply is not clear what these correlations indicate about mental representations.

The general point is that attempts to describe category structure in terms of similarity will prove useful only to the extent that one specifies which principles determine what is to count as a relevant property and which principles determine the importance of particular properties. It is important to realize that the explanatory work is being done by the principles which specify these constraints rather than the general notion of similarity. In that sense, similarity is more like a dependent variable than an independent variable.

| TABLE 1 | Comparison of Two Approaches to Concepts |

ASPECT OF CONCEPTUAL THEORY	SIMILARITY-BASED APPROACH	THEORY-BASED APPROACH
Concept representation	Similarity structure, attribute lists, correlated attributes	Correlated attributes plus underlying principles that determine which correlations are noticed
Category definition	Various similarity metrics, summation of attributes	An explanatory principle common to category members
Units of analysis	Attributes	Attributes plus explicitly represented relations of attributes and concepts
Categorization basis	Attribute matching	Matching plus inferential processes supplied by underlying principles
Weighting of attributes	Cue validity, salience	Determined in part by importance in the underlying principles
Interconceptual structure	Hierarchy based on shared attributes	Network formed by causal and explanatory links, as well as sharing of properties picked out as relevant
Conceptual development	Feature accretion	Changing organization and explanations of concepts as a result of world knowledge

2. Attribute Matching and Categorization. The modal model of similarity summarized in Table 1 invites one to view categorization as attribute matching. Although that may be part of the story, there are several ways in which the focus on attribute matching may be misleading. First of all, as Armstrong, Gleitman, and Gleitman (1983) emphasized, most concepts are not a simple sum of independent features. The features that are characteristically associated with the concept *bird* are just a pile of bird features unless they are held together in a "bird structure." Structure requires both attributes and *relations* binding the attributes together. Typical bird features (laying eggs, flying, having wings and feathers, building nests in trees, and singing) have both an internal structure and an external structure based on interproperty relationships. Building nests is linked to laying eggs, and building nests in trees poses logistical problems whose solution involves other properties such as having wings, flying, and singing. Thus, it makes sense to ask why birds have certain features (e.g., wings and feathers). Although people may not have thought about various interproperty relationships, they can readily reason with them. Thus, one can answer the question of why birds have wings and feathers (i.e., to fly).

In a number of contexts, categorization may be more like problem solving than attribute matching. Inferences and causal attributions may drive the categorization process. Borrowing again from work by Murphy and me (1985), "jumping into a swimming pool with one's clothes on" in all probability is not associated directly with the concept *intoxicated*. However, observing this behavior might lead one to classify the person as drunk. In general, real-world knowledge is used to reason about or explain properties, not simply to match them. For example, a teenage boy might show many of the behaviors associated with an eating disorder, but the further knowledge that the teenager is on the wrestling team and trying to make a lower weight class may undermine any diagnosis of a disorder.

3. Summary. It does not appear that similarity, at least in the form it takes in current theories, is going to be at all adequate to explain categorization. Similarity may be a by-product of conceptual coherence rather than a cause. To use a rough analogy, winning basketball teams have in common scoring more points than their opponents, but one must turn to more basic principles to explain why they score more points. One candidate for a set of deeper principles is the idea that concepts are organized around theories, and theories provide conceptual coherence. In the next section, I will briefly summarize some of the current work on the role of knowledge structures and theories in categorization and then turn to a form of rapprochement between similarity and a knowledge-based categorization principle.

THE SECOND SHIFT: CONCEPTS AS ORGANIZED BY THEORIES

KNOWLEDGE-BASED CATEGORIZATION

It is perhaps only a modest exaggeration to say that similarity gets at the shadow rather than the substance of concepts. Something is needed to give concepts life, coherence, and meaning. Although many philosophers of science have argued that observations are necessarily theory-labeled, only recently have researchers begun to stress that the organization of concepts is knowledge-based and driven by theories about the world (e.g., Carey, 1985; S. Gelman, 1988; S. Gelman & Markman, 1986a, 1986b; Keil, 1986, 1987; Keil & Kelly, 1987; Lakoff, 1987; Markman, 1987; Massey & R. Gelman, 1988; Murphy & Medin, 1985; Oden, 1987; Rips, 1989; Schank, Collins, & Hunter, 1986; and others).

The primary differences between the similarity-based and theory-based approaches to categorization are summarized in Table 1, taken from Murphy and Medin (1985). Murphy and Medin suggested that the relation between a concept and an example is analogous to the relation between theory and data. That is, classification is not simply based on a direct matching of properties of the concept with those in the example, but rather requires that the example have the right "explanatory relationship" to the theory organizing the concept. In the case of a person diving into a swimming pool with his or her clothes on, one might try to reason back to either causes or predisposing conditions. One might believe that having too much to drink impairs judgment and that going into the pool shows poor judgment. Of course, the presence of other information, such as the fact that another person who cannot swim has fallen into the pool, would radically change the inferences drawn and, as a consequence, the categorization judgment.

One of the more promising aspects of the theory-based approach is that it begins to address the question of why we have the categories we have or why categories are sensible. In fact, coherence may be achieved in the absence of any obvious source of similarity among examples. Consider the category composed of children, money, photo albums, and pets. Out of context the category seems odd. If one's knowledge base is enriched to include the fact that the category represents "things to take out of one's house in case of a fire," the category becomes sensible (Barsalou, 1983). In addition, one could readily make judgments about whether new examples (e.g., personal papers) belonged to the category, judgments that would not be similarity based.

Similarity effects can be overridden by theory-related strategies even in the judgments of young children. That fact was very nicely demonstrated by Gelman and Markman (1986a) in their studies of induction. Specifically, they pitted category membership against perceptual similarity in an inductive inference task. Young children were taught that different novel properties were true of two examples and then were asked which property was also true of a new example that was similar to one alternative but belonged to a different category, and one that was perceptually different from the other examples but belonged to the same category. For example, children might be taught that a (pictured) flamingo feeds its baby mashed-up food and that a (pictured) bat feeds its baby milk, and then they might be asked how a (pictured) owl feeds its baby. The owl was more perceptually similar to the bat than to the flamingo, but even 4-year-olds made inferences on the basis of category membership rather than similarity.

Related work by Susan Carey and Frank Keil shows that children's biological theories guide their conceptual development. For example, Keil has used the ingenious technique of describing transformations or changes such as painting a horse to look like a zebra to examine the extent to which category membership judgments are controlled by superficial perceptual properties. Biological theories determine membership judgments quite early on (Keil, 1987; Keil & Kelly, 1987). Rips (1989) has used the same technique to show that similarity is neither necessary nor sufficient to determine category membership. It even appears to be the case that theories can affect judgments of similarity. For example, Medin and Shoben (1988) found that the terms *white hair* and *grey hair* were judged to be more similar than *grey hair* and *black hair*, but that the terms *white clouds* and *grey clouds* were judged as less similar than *grey clouds* and *black clouds*. Our interpretation is that white and grey hair are linked by a theory (of aging) in a way that white and grey clouds are not.

The above observations are challenging for defenders of the idea that similarity drives conceptual organization. In fact, one might wonder if the notion of similarity is so loose and unconstrained that we might be better off without it. Goodman (1972) epitomized this attitude by calling similarity "a pretender, an imposter, a quack" (p. 437). After reviewing some reasons to continue to take similarity seriously, I outline one possible route for integrating similarity-based and theory-based categorization.

The Need for Similarity

So far I have suggested that similarity relations do not provide conceptual coherence but that theories do. Because a major problem with similarity is that it is so unconstrained, one might ask what constrains theories. If we cannot identify constraints on theories, that is, say something about why we have the theories we have and not others, then we have not solved the problem of coherence: It simply has been shifted to another level. Although I believe we can specify some general properties of theories and develop a psychology of explanation (e.g., Abelson & Lalljee, 1988; Einhorn & Hogarth, 1986; Hilton & Slugoski, 1986; Leddo, Abelson, & Gross, 1984), I equally believe that a constrained form of similarity will play an important role in our understanding of human concepts. This role is not to provide structure so much as it is to guide learners toward structure.

The impact of more direct perceptual similarity on the development of causal explanations is evident in the structure of people's naive theories. Frazer's (1959) cross-cultural analysis of belief systems pointed to the ubiquity of two principles, homeopathy and contagion. The principle of homeopathy is that causes and effects tend to be similar. One manifestation of this principle is homeopathic medicine, in which the cure (and the cause) are seen to resemble the symptoms. In the Azande culture, for example, the cure for ringworm is to apply fowl's excrement because the excrement looks like the ringworm. Schweder (1977) adduced strong support for the claim that resemblance is a fundamental conceptual tool of everyday thinking in all cultures, not just so-called *primitive* cultures.

Contagion is the principle that a cause must have some form of contact to transmit its effect. In general, the more contiguous (temporally and spatially similar) events are in time and space, the more likely they are to be perceived as causally related (e.g., Dickinson, Shanks, & Evenden, 1984; Michotte, 1963). People also tend to assume that causes and effects should be of similar magnitude. Einhorn and Hogarth (1986) pointed out that the germ theory of disease initially met with great resistance because people could not imagine how such tiny organisms could have such devastating effects.

It is important to recognize that homeopathy and contagion often point us in the right direction. Immunization can be seen as a form of homeopathic medicine that has an underlying theoretical principle to support it. My reading of these observations, however, is not that specific theoretical (causal) principles are constraining similarity but rather that similarity (homeopathy and contagion) acts as a constraint on the search for causal explanations. Even in classical conditioning studies, the similarity of the conditioned stimulus and the unconditioned stimulus can have a major influence on the rate of conditioning (Testa, 1974). Of course, similarity must itself be constrained for terms like *homeopathy* to have a meaning. Shortly, I will suggest some constraints on similarity as part of an effort to define a role for similarity in conceptual development.

Similarity is likely to have a significant effect on explanations in another way. Given the importance of similarity in retrieval, it is likely that explanations that are applied to a novel event are constrained by similar events and their associated explanations. For example, Read (1983) found that people may rely on single, similar instances in making causal attributions about behaviors. Furthermore, Ross (1984) and Gentner and Landers (1985) have found that superficial similarities and not just similarity with respect to deeper principles or relations play a major role in determining the remindings associated with problem solving and the use of analogy.

In brief, it seems that similarity cannot be banished from the world of theories and conceptual structures. But it seems to me that a theory of similarity is needed that is quite different in character from the one summarized in Table 1. I will suggest an alternative view of similarity and then attempt to show its value in integrating and explanation with respect to concepts.

SIMILARITY AND THEORY IN CONCEPTUAL STRUCTURE

A CONTRASTING SIMILARITY MODEL

The following are key tenets of the type of similarity theory needed to link similarity with knowledge-based categorization: (a) Similarity needs to include attributes, relations, and higher-order relations. (b) Properties in general are not independent but rather are linked by a variety of interproperty relations. (c) Properties exist at multiple levels of abstraction. (d) Concepts are more than lists. Properties and relations create depth or structure. Each of the four main ideas directly conflicts with the corresponding assumption of the theory of similarity outlined earlier. In one way or another all of these assumptions are tied to structure. The general idea I am proposing is far from new. In the psychology of visual perception, the need for structural approaches to similarity has been a continuing, if not major, theme (e.g., Biederman, 1985, 1987; Palmer, 1975, 1978; Pomerantz, Sager, & Stoever, 1977). Oden and Lopes (1982) have argued that this view can inform our understanding of concepts: "Although similarity must function at some level in the induction of concepts, the induced categories are not 'held together' subjectively by the undifferentiated 'force' of similarity, but rather by structural principles" (p. 78). Nonindependence of properties and simple and higher-order relations add a dimension of depth to categorization. Depth has clear implications for many of the observations that seem so problematic for probabilistic view theories. I turn now to the question of how these modified similarity notions may link up with theory-based categorization.

PSYCHOLOGICAL ESSENTIALISM

Despite the overwhelming evidence against the classical view, there is something about it that is intuitively compelling. Recently I and my colleagues have begun to take this observation seriously, not for its metaphysical implications but as a piece of psychological data (Medin & Ortony, 1989; Medin & Wattenmaker, 1987; Wattenmaker, Nakamura, & Medin, 1988). One might call this framework "psychological essentialism." The main ideas are as follows: People act as if things (e.g., objects) have essences or underlying natures that make them the thing that they are. Furthermore, the essence constrains or generates properties that may vary in their centrality. One of the things that theories do is to embody or provide causal linkages from deeper properties to more superficial or surface properties. For example, people in our culture believe that the categories *male* and *female* are genetically determined, but to pick someone out as male or female we rely on characteristics such as hair length, height, facial hair, and clothing that represent a mixture of secondary sexual characteristics and cultural conventions. Although these characteristics are more unreliable than genetic evidence, they are far from arbitrary. Not only do they have some validity in a statistical sense, but also they are tied to our biological and cultural conceptions of *male* and *female.*

It is important to note that psychological essentialism refers not to how the world is but rather to how people approach the world. Wastebaskets probably have no true essence, although we may act as if they do. Both social and psychodiagnostic categories are at least partially culture specific and may have weak if any metaphysical underpinnings (see also Morey & McNamara, 1987).

If psychological essentialism is bad metaphysics, why should people act as if things had essences? The reason is that it may prove to be good epistomology. One could say that people adopt an *essentialist heuristic,* namely, the hypothesis that things that look alike tend to share deeper properties (similarities). Our perceptual and conceptual systems appear to have evolved such that the essentialist heuristic is very often correct (Medin & Wattenmaker, 1987; Shepard, 1984). This is true even for human artifacts such as cars, computers, and camping stoves because structure and function tend to be correlated. Surface characteristics that are perceptually obvious or are readily produced on feature listing tasks may not so much constitute the core of a concept as point toward it. This observation suggests that classifying on the basis of similarity will be relatively effective much of the time, but that similarity will yield to knowledge of deeper principles. Thus, in the work of Gelman and Markman (1986a) discussed earlier, category membership was more important than perceptual similarity in determining inductive inferences.

RELATED EVIDENCE

The contrasting similarity principles presented earlier coupled with psychological essentialism provide a framework for integrating knowledge-based and similarity-based categorization. Although it is far short of a formal theory, the framework provides a useful perspective on many of the issues under discussion in this article.

1. Nonindependence of Features. Earlier I mentioned that classifying on the basis of similarity to a prototype was functionally equivalent to adding up the evidence favoring a classification and applying some criterion (at least X out of Y features). Recall also that the data ran strongly against this idea. From the perspective currently under consideration, however, there ought to be two ways to produce data consistent with prototype theory. One would be to provide a theory that suggests the prototype as an ideal or that makes summing of evidence more natural. For example, suppose that the characteristic properties for one category were as follows: It is made of metal, has a regular surface, is of medium size, and is easy to grasp. For a contrasting category, the characteristic properties were: It is made of rubber, has an irregular surface, is of small size, and is hard to grasp. The categories may not seem sensible or coherent, but suppose one adds the information that the objects in one category could serve as substitutes for a hammer. Given this new information, it becomes easy to add up the properties of examples in terms of their utility in supporting hammering. In a series of studies using the above descriptions and related examples, Wattenmaker, Dewey, Murphy, and I (1986) found data consistent with prototype theory when the additional information was supplied, and data inconsistent with prototype theory when only characteristic properties were supplied. Specifically, we found that linearly separable categories were easier to learn than nonlinearly separable catagories only when an organizing theme was provided (see also Nakamura, 1985).

One might think that prototypes become important whenever the categories are meaningful. That is not the case. When themes are provided that are not compatible with a summing of evidence, the data are inconsistent with prototype theories. For instance, suppose that the examples consisted of descriptions of animals and that the organizing theme was that one category consisted of prey and the other of predators. It is a good adaptation for prey to be armored and to live in trees, but an animal that is both armored and lives in trees may not be better adapted than an animal with either characteristic alone. Being armored and living in trees may be somewhat incompatible. Other studies by Wattenmaker et al. using directly analogous materials failed to find any evidence that linear separability (and, presumably, summing of evidence) was important or natural. Only some kinds of interproperty relations are compatible with a summing of evidence, and evidence favoring prototypes may be confined to these cases.

The above studies show that the ease or naturalness of classification tasks cannot be predicted in terms of abstract category structures based on distribution of features, but rather requires an understanding of the knowledge brought to bear on them, for this knowledge determines interproperty relationships. So far only a few types of interproperty relationships have been explored in categorization, and much is to be gained from the careful study of further types of relations (e.g., see Barr & Caplan, 1987; Chaffin & Herrmann, 1987; Rips & Conrad, 1989; Winston, Chaffin, & Herrmann, 1987).

2. Levels of Features. Although experimenters can often contrive to have the features or properties comprising stimulus materials at roughly the same level of abstractness, in more typical circumstances levels may vary substantially. This fact has critical implications for descriptions of category structure (see Barsalou & Billman, 1988). This point may be best represented by an example from some ongoing research I am conducting with Glenn Nakamura and Ed Wisniewski. Our stimulus materials consist of children's drawings of people, a sample of which is shown in Figure 1. There are two sets of five drawings, one on the left and one on the right. The task of the participants in this experiment is to come up with a rule that could be used to correctly classify both these drawings and new examples that might be presented later.

One of our primary aims in this study was to examine the effects of different types of knowledge structures on rule induction. Consequently, some participants were told that one set was done by farm children and the other by city children; some were told that one set was done by creative children and the other by noncreative children; and still others were told that one set was done by emotionally disturbed children and the other by mentally healthy children. The exact assignment of drawings

FIGURE 1   Children's drawings of people used in the rule induction studies by Nakamura, Wisniewski, and Medin.

was counterbalanced with respect to the categories such that half the time the draw-ings on the left of Figure 1 were labeled as done by farm children and half the time the drawings on the right were labeled as having been done by farm children.

Although we were obviously expecting differences in the various conditions, in some respects the most striking result is one that held across conditions. Almost without exception the rules that people gave had properties at two or three different levels of abstractness. For example, one person who was told the drawings on the left were done by city children gave the following rule:"The city drawings use more pro-files, and are more elaborate. The clothes are more detailed, showing both pockets and buttons, and the hair is drawn in. The drawings put less emphasis on proportion and the legs and torso are off." Another person who was told the same drawings were done by farm children wrote:"The children draw what they see in their normal life. The people have overalls on and some drawings show body muscles as a result of labor. The drawings are also more detailed. One can see more facial details and one drawing has colored the clothes and another one shows the body under the clothes." As one can see, the rules typically consist of a general assertion or assertions coupled with either an operational definition or examples to illustrate and clarify the asser-tion. In some cases, these definitions or examples extend across several levels of abstractness.

One might think that our participants used different levels of description because there was nothing else for them to do. That is, there may have been no low-level perceptual features that would separate the groups. In a followup study we pre-sented examples one at a time and asked people to give their rule after each example. If people are being forced to use multiple levels of description because simple rules will not work, then we should observe a systematic increase in the use of multiple levels across examples. In fact, however, we observed multiple levels of description as the predominant strategy from the first example on. We believe that multiple levels arise when people try to find a link between abstract explanatory principles or ideas (drawings reflect one's experience) and specific details of drawings.

There are several important consequences of multilevel descriptions. First of all, the relation across levels is not necessarily a subset, superset, or a part–whole rela-tion. Most of the time one would say that the lower level property "supports" the higher level property; for example, "jumping into a swimming pool with one's clothes on" supports poor judgment. This underlines the point that categorization often involves more than a simple matching of properties. A related point is that features are ambiguous in the sense that they may support more than one higher level prop-erty. When the drawings on the right were associated with the label *mentally healthy,* a common description was "all the faces are smiling." When the label for the same drawing was *noncreative,* a common description was "the faces show little vari-ability in expression." Finally, it should be obvious that whether a category description is disjunctive (e.g., pig's nose or cow's mouth or catlike ears) or conjunctive or defin-ing (e.g., all have animal parts) depends on the level with respect to which the rule is evaluated.

3. Centrality. If properties are at different levels of abstraction and linked by a variety of relations, then one might imagine that some properties are more central than others because of the role they play in conceptual structure. An indication that properties differ in their centrality comes from a provocative study by Asch and Zukier (1984). They presented people with trait terms that appeared to be contradictory (e.g., kind and vindictive) and asked participants if these descriptions could be resolved (e.g., how could a person be both kind and vindictive?). Participants had no difficulty integrating the pairs of terms, and Asch and Zukier identified seven major resolution strategies. For present purposes, what is notable is that many of the resolution strategies involve making one trait term more central than the other one. For example, one way of integrating *kind* and *vindictive* was to say that the person was fundamentally evil and was kind only in the service of vindictive ends.

In related work, Shoben and I (Medin & Shoben, 1988) showed that centrality of a property depends on the concept of which it is a part. We asked participants to judge the typicality of adjective noun pairs when the adjective was a property that other participants judged was not true of the noun representing the concept. For example, our participants judged that all bananas and all boomerangs are curved. Based on this observation, other participants were asked to judge the typicality of a straight banana as a banana or a straight boomerang as a boomerang. Other instances of the 20 pairs used include *soft knife* versus *soft diamond* and *polka dot fire hydrant* versus *polka dot yield sign*. For 19 of the 20 pairs, participants rated one item of a pair as more typical than the other. Straight banana, soft knife, and polka dot fire hydrant were rated as more typical than straight boomerang, soft diamond, and polka dot yield sign. In the case of boomerangs (and probably yield signs), centrality may be driven by structure–function correlations. Soft diamonds are probably rated as very atypical because hardness is linked to many other properties and finding out that diamonds were soft would call a great deal of other knowledge into question.

Most recently, Woo Kyoung Ahn, Joshua Rubenstein, and I have been interviewing clinical psychologists and psychiatrists concerning their understanding of psychodiagnostic categories. Although our project is not far enough along to report any detailed results, it is clear that the *DSM-IIIR* guidebook (American Psychiatric Association, 1987) provides only a skeletal outline that is brought to life by theories and causal scenarios underlying and intertwined with the symptoms that comprise the diagnostic criteria. Symptoms differ in the level of abstractness and the types and number of intersymptom relations in which they participate, and as a consequence, they differ in their centrality.

CONCLUSIONS

The shift to a focus on knowledge-based categorization does not mean that the notion of similarity must be left behind. But we do need an updated approach to, and interpretation of, similarity. The mounting evidence on the role of theories and explanations in organizing categories is much more compatible with features at varying levels linked by a variety of interproperty relations than it is with independent features at a single level. In addition, similarity may not so much constitute structure as point toward it. There is a dimension of depth to categorization. The conjectures about psychological essentialism may be one way of reconciling classification in terms of perceptual similarity or surface properties with the deeper substance of knowledge-rich, theory-based categorization.

REFERENCES

Abelson, R. P., & Lalljee, M. G. (1988). Knowledge-structures and causal explanation. In D. J. Hilton (Ed.), *Contemporary science and natural explanation: Commonsense conceptions of causality* (pp. 175–202). Brighton, England: Harvester Press.

Allen, S. W., Brooks, L. R., Norman, G. R., & Rosenthal, D. (1988, November). *Effect of prior examples on rule-based diagnostic performance.* Paper presented at the meeting of the Psychonomic Society, Chicago.

American Psychiatric Association. (1987). *Diagnostic and statistical manual of mental disorders* (rev. ed.). Washington, DC: Author.

Anderson, J. R. (1988). The place of cognitive architectures in a rational analysis. In *The Tenth Annual Conference of the Cognitive Science Society* (pp. 1–10). Montreal: University of Montreal.

Arkes, H. R., & Harkness, A. R. (1980). Effect of making a diagnosis on subsequent recognition of symptoms. *Journal of Experimental Psychology: Human Learning and Memory, 6,* 568–575.

Armstrong, S. L., Gleitman, L. R., & Gleitman, H. (1983). What some concepts might not be. *Cognition, 13,* 263–308.

Asch, S. E., & Zukier, H. (1984). Thinking about persons. *Journal of Personality and Social Psychology, 46,* 1230–1240.

Barr, R. A., & Caplan, L. J. (1987). Category representations and their implications for category structure. *Memory and Cognition, 15,* 397–418.

Barsalou, L. W. (1983). Ad hoc categories. *Memory and Cognition, 11,* 211–227.

Barsalou, L. W. (1985). Ideals, central tendency, and frequency of instantiation as determinants of graded structure in categories. *Journal of Experimental Psychology: Learning, Memory and Cognition, 11,* 629–654.

Barsalou, L. W. (1987). The instability of graded structure: Implications for the nature of concepts. In U. Neisser (Ed.), *Concepts and conceptual development: The ecological and intellectual factors in categorization* (pp. 101–140). Cambridge, England: Cambridge University Press.

Barsalou, L. W. (1989). Intra-concept similarity and its implications for inter-concept similarity. In S. Vosniadou & A. Ortony (Eds.), *Similarity and analogical reasoning* (pp. 76–121). Cambridge, England: Cambridge University Press.

Barsalou, L. W., & Billman, D. (1988, April). *Systematicity and semantic ambiguity.* Paper presented at a workshop on semantic ambiguity, Adelphi University.

Barsalou, L. W., & Medin, D. L. (1986). Concepts: Fixed definitions or dynamic context-dependent representations? *Cahiers de Psychologie Cognitive, 6,* 187–202.

Bellezza, F. S. (1984). Reliability of retrieval from semantic memory: Noun meanings. *Bulletin of the Psychonomic Society, 22,* 377–380.

Biederman, I. (1985). Human image understanding: Recent research and a theory. *Computer Vision, Graphics, and Image Processing, 32,* 29–83.

Biederman, I. (1987). Recognition-by-components: A theory of human image understanding. *Psychological Review, 94,* 115–147.

Cantor, N., & Mischel, W. (1977). Traits as prototypes: Effects on recognition memory. *Journal of Personality and Social Psychology, 35,* 38–48.

Carey, S. (1985). *Conceptual change in childhood.* Cambridge, MA: MIT Press.

Chaffin, R., & Herrmann, D. J. (1987). Relation element theory: A new account of the representation and processing of semantic relations. In D. Gorfein & R. Hoffman (Eds.), *Learning and memory: The Ebbinghaus centennial conference* (pp. 221–245). Hillsdale, NJ: Erlbaum.

Dickinson, A., Shanks, D., & Evenden, J. (1984). Judgment of act–outcomes contingency: The role of selective attribution. *Quarterly Journal of Experimental Psychology, 36A* (1), 29–50.

Einhorn, J. H., & Hogarth, R. M. (1986). Judging probable cause. *Psychological Bulletin, 99,* 3–19.

Estes, W. K. (1986a). Memory storage and retrieval processes in category learning. *Journal of Experimental Psychology: General, 115,* 155–175.

Estes, W. K. (1986b). Array models for category learning. *Cognitive Psychology, 18,* 500–549.

Fehr, B. (1988). Prototype analysis of the concepts of love and commitment. *Journal of Personality and Social Psychology, 55,* 557–579.

Fehr, B., & Russell, J. A. (1984). Concept of emotion viewed from a prototype perspective. *Journal of Experimental Psychology: General, 113,* 464–486.

Flannagan, M. J., Fried, L. S., & Holyoak, K. J. (1986). Distributional expectations and the induction of category structure. *Journal of Experimental Psychology: Learning, Memory and Cognition, 12,* 241–256.

Frazer, J. G. (1959). *The new golden bough.* New York: Criterion Books.

Fried, L. S., & Holyoak, K. J. (1984). Induction of category distribution: A framework for classification learning. *Journal of Experimental Psychology: Learning, Memory and Cognition, 10,* 234–257.

Gati, I., & Tversky, A. (1984). Weighting common and distinctive features in perceptual and conceptual judgments. *Cognitive Psychology, 16,* 341–370.

Gelman, S. A. (1988). The development of induction within natural kind and artifact categories. *Cognitive Psychology, 20,* 65–95.

Gelman, S. A., & Markman, E. M. (1986a). Categories and induction in young children. *Cognition, 23,* 183–209.

Gelman, S. A., & Markman, E. M. (1986b). Young children's inductions from natural kinds: The role of categories and appearances. *Child Development, 58,* 1532–1541.

Genero, N., & Cantor, N. (1987). Exemplar prototypes and clinical diagnosis: Toward a cognitive economy. *Journal of Social and Clinical Psychology, 5,* 59–78.

Gentner, D., & Landers, R. (1985). *Analogical reminding: A good match is hard to find.* Paper presented at the International Conference of Systems, Man and Cybernetics, Tucson, AZ.

Goldin, S. E. (1978). Memory for the ordinary: Typicality effects in chess memory. *Journal of Experimental Psychology: Human Learning and Memory, 4,* 605–616.

Goodman, N. (1972). Seven strictures on similarity. In N. Goodman (Ed.), *Problems and projects.* New York: Bobbs-Merrill.

Hartley, J., & Homa, D. (1981). Abstraction of stylistic concepts. *Journal of Experimental Psychology: Human Learning and Memory, 7,* 33–46.

Hilton, D. J., & Slugoski, B. R. (1986). Knowledge-based causal attribution: The abnormal conditions focus model. *Psychological Review, 93,* 75–88.

Hintzman, D. L. (1986). "Schema abstraction" in a multiple-trace memory model. *Psychological Review, 93,* 411–428.

Homa, D. (1984). On the nature of categories. In G. Bower (Ed.), *The psychology of learning and motivation* (Vol. 18, pp. 49–94). New York: Academic Press.

Homa, D., & Vosburgh, R. (1976). Category breadth and the abstraction of prototypical information. *Journal of Experimental Psychology: Human Learning and Memory 2,* 322–330.

Keil, F. C. (1979). *Semantic and conceptual development: An ontological perspective.* Cambridge, MA: Harvard University Press.

Keil, F. C. (1981). Constraints on knowledge and cognitive development. *Psychological Review, 88,* 197–227.

Keil, F. C. (1986). The acquisition of natural kind and artifact terms. In W. Demopoulos & A. Marras (Eds.), *Language learning and concept acquisition* (pp. 133–153). Norwood, NJ: Ablex.

Keil, F. C. (1987). Conceptual development and category structure. In U. Neisser (Ed.), *Concepts and conceptual development: Ecological and intellectual factors in categorization* (pp. 175–200). Cambridge, England: Cambridge University Press.

Keil, F. C., & Kelly, M. H. (1987). Developmental changes in category structure. In S. Harnad (Ed.), *Categorical perception: The groundwork of cognition* (pp. 491–510). Cambridge, England: Cambridge University Press.

Kemler-Nelson, D. G. (1984). The effect of intention on what concepts are acquired. *Journal of Verbal Learning and Verbal Behavior, 23,* 734–759.

Kolodner, J. L. (1984). *Retrieval and organizational structures in conceptual memory: A computer model.* Hillsdale, NJ: Erlbaum.

Lakoff, G. (1987). *Women, fire, and dangerous things: What categories tell us about the nature of thought.* Chicago: University of Chicago Press.

Leddo, J., Abelson, R. P., & Gross, P. H. (1984). Conjunctive explanation: When two explanations are better than one. *Journal of Personality and Social Psychology, 47,* 933–943.

Malt, B. C., & Smith, E. E. (1983). Correlated properties in natural categories. *Journal of Verbal Learning and Verbal Behavior, 23,* 250–269.

Markman, E. M. (1987). How children constrain the possible meanings of words. In U. Neisser (Ed.), *Concepts and conceptual development: The ecological and intellectual factors in categorization* (pp. 256–287). Cambridge, England: Cambridge University Press.

Massey, C. M., & Gelman, R. (1988). Preschoolers' ability to decide whether a photographed unfamiliar object can move itself. *Developmental Psychology, 24,* 307–317.

McCloskey, M., & Glucksberg, S. (1978). Natural categories: Well-defined or fuzzy sets? *Memory and Cognition, 6,* 462–472.

McNamara, T. P., & Sternberg, R. J. (1983). Mental models of word meaning. *Journal of Verbal Learning and Verbal Behavior, 22,* 449–474.

Medin, D. L. (1986). Commentary on "Memory storage and retrieval processes in category learning." *Journal of Experimental Psychology: General, 115* (4), 373–381.

Medin, D. L., Altom, M. W., Edelson, S. M., & Freko, D. (1982). Correlated symptoms and simulated medical classification. *Journal of Experimental Psychology: Learning, Memory and Cognition, 8,* 37–50.

Medin, D. L., & Ortony, A. (1989). *Psychological essentialism.* In S. Vosniadou & A. Ortony (Eds.), *Similarity and analogical reasoning* (pp. 179–195). New York: Cambridge University Press.

Medin, D. L., & Ross, B. H. (1989). The specific character of abstract thought: Categorization, problem-solving, and induction. In R. J. Sternberg (Ed.), *Advances in the psychology of human intelligence* (Vol. 5, pp. 189–223). Hillsdale, NJ: Erlbaum.

Medin, D. L., & Schaffer, M. M. (1978). A context theory of classification learning. *Psychological Review, 85,* 207–238.

Medin, D. L., & Schwanenflugel, P. J. (1981). Linear separability in classification learning. *Journal of Experimental Psychology: Human Learning and Memory, 7,* 355–368.

Medin, D. L., & Shoben, E. J. (1988). Context and structure in conceptual combination. *Cognitive Psychology, 20,* 158–190.

Medin, D. L., & Smith, E. E. (1984). Concepts and concept formation. In M. R. Rosenzweig & L. W. Porter (Eds.), *Annual Review of Psychology, 35,* 113–118.

Medin, D. L., & Wattenmaker, W. D. (1987). Category cohesiveness, theories, and cognitive archeology. In U. Neisser (Ed.), *Concepts and conceptual development: The ecological and intellectual factors in categories* (pp. 25–62). Cambridge, England: Cambridge University Press.

Mervis, C. B., & Rosch, E. (1981). Categorization of natural objects. In M. R. Rosenzweig & L. W. Porter (Eds.), *Annual Review of Psychology, 32,* 89–115.

Michotte, A. (1963). *Perception of causality.* London: Methuen.

Morey, L. C., & McNamara, T. P. (1987). On definitions, diagnosis, and DSM-III. *Journal of Abnormal Psychology, 96,* 283–285.

Murphy, G. L., & Medin, D. L. (1985). The role of theories in conceptual coherence. *Psychological Review, 92,* 289–316.

Nakamura, G. V. (1985). Knowledge-based classification of ill-defined categories. *Memory and Cognition, 13,* 377–384.

Nosofsky, R. M. (1987). Attention and learning processes in the identification and categorization of integral stimuli. *Journal of Experimental Psychology: Learning, Memory, and Cognition, 13,* 87–108.

Nosofsky, R. M. (1988a). Exemplar-based accounts of relations between classification, recognition, and typicality. *Journal of Experimental Psychology: Learning, Memory, and Cognition, 14,* 700–708.

Nosofsky, R. M. (1988b). Similarity, frequency, and category representations. *Journal of Experimental Psychology: Learning, Memory, and Cognition, 14,* 54–65.

Oden, G. C. (1987). Concept, knowledge, and thought. In M. R. Rosenzweig & L. W. Porter (Eds.), *Annual Review of Psychology, 38,* 203–227.

Oden, G. C., & Lopes, L. (1982). On the internal structure of fuzzy subjective categories. In R. R. Yager (Ed.), *Recent developments in fuzzy set and possibility theory* (pp. 75–89). Elmsford, NY: Pergamon Press.

Ortony, A., Vondruska, R. J., Foss, M. A., & Jones, L. E. (1985). Salience, similes, and the asymmetry of similarity. *Journal of Memory and Language, 24,* 569–594.

Palmer, S. E. (1975). Visual perception and world knowledge. In D. A. Norman & D. E. Rumelhart (Eds.), *Explorations in cognition* (pp. 279–307). San Francisco: W. H. Freeman.

Palmer, S. E. (1978). Structural aspects of visual similarity. *Memory and Cognition, 6,* 91–97.

Peterson, M. J., Meagher, R. B., Jr., Chait, H., & Gillie, S. (1973). The abstraction and generalization of dot patterns. *Cognitive Psychology, 4,* 378–398.

Pomerantz, J. R., Sager, L. C., & Stoever, R. G. (1977). Perception of wholes and their component parts: Some configural superiority effects. *Journal of Experimental Psychology: Human Perception and Performance, 3,* 422–435.

Read, S. J. (1983). Once is enough: Causal reasoning from a single instance. *Journal of Personality and Social Psychology, 45,* 323–334.

Rips, L. (1989). Similarity, typicality, and categorization. In S. Vosniadou & A. Ortony (Eds.), *Similarity and analogical reasoning* (pp. 21–59). New York: Cambridge University Press.

Rips, L. J., & Conrad, F. G. (1989). The folk psychology of mental activities. *Psychological Review, 96,* 187–207.

Rosch, E. (1975). Cognitive representations of semantic categories. *Journal of Experimental Psychology: General, 104,* 192–233.

Rosch, E., & Mervis, C. B. (1975). Family resemblances: Studies in the internal structure of categories. *Cognitive Psychology, 7,* 573–605.

Ross, B. H. (1984). Remindings and their effects in learning a cognitive skill. *Cognitive Psychology, 16,* 371–416.

Roth, E. M., & Shoben, E. J. (1983). The effect of context on the structure of categories. *Cognitive Psychology, 15,* 346–378.

Schank, R. C., Collins, G. C., & Hunter, L. E. (1986). Transcending induction category formation in learning. *The Behavioral and Brain Sciences, 9,* 639–686.

Schweder, R. A. (1977). Likeness and likelihood in everyday thought: Magical thinking in judgments about personality. *Current Anthropology, 18,* 4.

Sebestyn, G. S. (1962). *Decision-making processes in pattern recognition.* New York: Macmillan.

Shepard, R. H. (1984). Ecological constraints on internal representation: Resonant kinematics of perceiving, imagining, thinking, and dreaming. *Psychological Review, 19,* 417–447.

Shepard, R. N., Hovland, C. I., & Jenkins, H. M. (1961). Learning and memorization of classifications. *Psychological Monographs, 75,* (13, Whole No. 517).

Smith, E. E., & Medin, D. L. (1981). *Categories and concepts.* Cambridge, MA: Harvard University Press.

Smith, E. E., Rips, J. J., & Medin, D. W. (1984). A psychological approach to concepts: Comments on Rey's "Concepts and stereotypes." *Cognition, 17,* 265–274.

Smith, E. E., Shoben, E. J., & Rips, J. J. (1974). Structure and processes in semantic memory: A featural model for semantic decisions. *Psychological Review, 81,* 214–241.

Sommers, F. (1971). Structural ontology. *Philosophia, 1,* 21–42.

Testa, T. J. (1974). Causal relationships and the acquisition of avoidance responses. *Psychological Review, 81,* 491–505.

Tulving, E. (1983). *Elements of episodic memory.* New York: Oxford University Press.

Tversky, A. (1977). Features of similarity. *Psychological Review, 84,* 327–352.

Watanabe, S. (1969). *Knowing and guessing: A formal and quantitative study.* New York: Wiley.

Wattenmaker, W. D., Dewey, G. I., Murphy, T. D., & Medin, D. L. (1986). Linear separability and concept learning: Context, relational properties, and concept naturalness. *Cognitive Psychology, 18,* 158–194.

Wattenmaker, W. D., Nakamura, G. V., & Medin, D. L. (1988). Relationships between similarity-based and explanation-based categorization. In D. Hilton (Ed.), *Contemporary science and natural explanation: Commonsense conceptions of causality* (pp. 205–241). Brighton, England: Harvester Press.

Winston, M. E., Chaffin, R., & Herrmann, D. (1987). A taxonomy of part–whole relations. *Cognitive Science, 11,* 417–444.

Wittgenstein, L. (1953). *Philosophical investigations* (G. E. M. Anscombe, trans.). Oxford: Blackwell.

QUESTIONS FOR FURTHER THOUGHT

1. What main theories of concepts and conceptual structure does the article review, and how do they differ from one another?

2. What role does similarity play in the classical and probabilistic theories of conceptual structure?

3. What are key differences between concepts and categories?

4. What are some of the main problems for probabilistic theories of conceptual structure?

5. Might the classical view of conceptual structure be seen as a special case of the theory-based view? If so, how? If not, why not?

6

KNOWLEDGE REPRESENTATION AND EXPERTISE

MENTAL ROTATION OF THREE-DIMENSIONAL OBJECTS
Roger Shepard and Jacqueline Metzler

EXPERT PERFORMANCE: ITS STRUCTURE AND ACQUISITION
Anders Ericsson and Neil Charness

MENTAL ROTATION OF THREE-DIMENSIONAL OBJECTS

Roger Shepard and Jacqueline Metzler

INTRODUCTION

Is it possible that the representation of transformations of objects in the mind is an analogue process, much as such transformations would be in real world? Suppose, for example, you rotate an object such as a coffee cup. The cup will pass through an infinite number of intermediate states as it makes its way toward its destination, say, 90 degrees from its original position. When you visualize this rotation in your mind, does the visual image similarly pass through an infinite number of intermediate states, or does it pass through a set of discrete and potentially countable states that may, nevertheless, be experienced as analogue transformations?

In an ingenious study, Roger Shepard and Jacqueline Metzler provided suggestive evidence for analogue mental transformations of internal representations. Shepard and Metzler showed participants in their study pairs of pictures of three-dimensional objects. Half of the pairs showed the same objects, except that the second figure in each pair represented a rotated version of the first figure. Rotations of the second object in each "same" pair ranged from 0 to 180 degrees with respect to the first object. The other pairs combined nonidentical images. The object in the second position was a mirror image of the object in the first position, again with a range of orientations.

The crucial finding in the study was that the time required to recognize that two objects were the same was a linear function of the degree of discrepancy in angular orientation of the second figure with respect to the first. In other words, people seemed to be mentally rotating the objects to bring them into mental congruence, with a constant rate of rotation across the range from 0 to 180 degrees. These results, then, suggested the use of analogue representations in the mind.

This article is often considered to be one of the most important articles in cognitive psychology, first, because it provided truly compelling evidence for the existence of analogue representations of objects in the mind. Authors rarely can provide such a compelling demonstration of any phenomenon in so short a space! Second, the research employs a simple, elegant, and totally compelling design. One reads the article and wonders why no one thought of the idea before.

Source: Reprinted with permission from Shepard, R. N., & Metzler, J. (1971). Mental rotation of three-dimensional objects. *Science, 171*, 701–703. Copyright © 1971 American Association for the Advancement of Science.

Often, the best experiments are those that seem so obvious that many researchers wonder why they didn't think of them—but they didn't. Finally, the research showed that reaction-time measures could be used to investigate real-time mental processing of spatial images. Many later researchers would pick up on this idea and extend the use of reaction times to explore the characteristics of mental images.

———

The time required to recognize that two perspective drawings portray objects of the same three-dimensional shape is found to be (i) a linearly increasing function of the angular difference in the portrayed orientations of the two objects and (ii) no shorter for differences corresponding simply to a rigid rotation of one of the two-dimensional drawings in its own picture plane than for differences corresponding to a rotation of the three-dimensional object in depth. ■

Human subjects are often able to determine that 2 two-dimensional pictures portray objects of the same three-dimensional shape even though the objects are depicted in very different orientations. The experiment reported here was designed to measure the time that subjects require to determine such identity of shape as a function of the angular difference in the portrayed orientations of the 2 three-dimensional objects.

This angular difference was produced either by a rigid rotation of one or two identical pictures in its own picture plane or by a much more complex, nonrigid transformation of one of the pictures that correspond to a (rigid) rotation of the three-dimensional object in depth.

This reaction time is found (i) to increase linearly with the angular difference in portrayed orientation and (ii) to be no longer for a rotation in depth than for a rotation merely in the picture plane. These findings appear to place rather severe constraints on possible explanations of how subjects go about determining identity of shape of differently oriented objects. They are, however, consistent with an explanation suggested by the subjects themselves. Although introspective reports must be interpreted with caution, all subjects claimed (i) that to make the required comparison they first had to imagine one object as rotated into the same orientation as the other and that they could carry out this "mental rotation" at no greater than a certain limiting rate; and (ii) that, since they perceived the two-dimensional pictures as objects in three-dimensional space, they could imagine the rotation around whichever axis was required with equal ease.

In the experiment, each of eight adult subjects was presented with 1,600 pairs of perspective line drawings. For each pair, the subject was asked to pull a right-hand lever as soon as he determined that the two drawings portrayed objects that were congruent with respect to three-dimensional shape and to pull a left-hand lever as soon as he determined that the two drawings depicted objects of different three-dimensional shapes. According to a random sequence, in half of the pairs (the "same" pairs) the two objects could be rotated into congruence with each other (as in Figure 1, A and B), and

FIGURE 1   Examples of pairs of perspective line drawings presented to the subjects. (A) A "same" pair, which differs by an 80° rotation in the picture plane; (B) a "same" pair, which differs by an 80° rotation in depth; and (C) a "different" pair, which cannot be brought into congruence by any rotation.

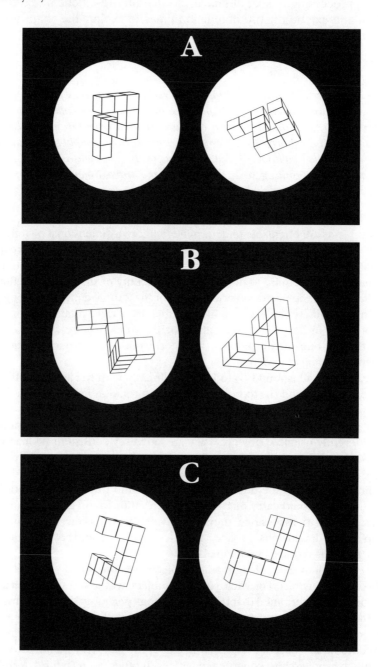

in the other half (the "different" pairs) the two objects differed by a reflection as well as a rotation and could not be rotated into congruence (as in Figure 1C).

The choice of objects that were mirror images or "isomers" of each other for the "different" pairs was intended to prevent subjects from discovering some distinctive feature possessed by only one of the two objects and thereby reaching a decision of noncongruence without actually having to carry out any mental rotation. As a further precaution, the ten different three-dimensional objects depicted in the various perspective drawings were chosen to be relatively unfamiliar and meaningless in overall three-dimensional shape.

Each object consisted of ten solid cubes attached face-to-face to form a rigid, armlike structure with exactly three right-angled "elbows" (see Figure 1). The set of all ten shapes included two subsets of five; within either subset, no shape could be transformed into itself or any other by any reflection or rotation (short of 360°). However, each shape in either subset was the mirror image of one shape in the other subset, as required for the construction of the "different" pairs.

For each of the ten objects, 18 different perspective projections—corresponding to one complete turn around the vertical axis by 20° steps—were generated by digital computer and associated graphical output.[1] Seven of the 18 perspective views of each object were then selected so as (i) to avoid any views in which some part of the object was wholly occluded by another part and yet (ii) to permit the construction of two pairs that differed in orientation by each possible angle, in 20° steps, from 0° to 180°. These 70 line drawings were then reproduced by photo-offset process and were attached to cards in pairs for presentation to the subjects.

Half of the "same" pairs (the "depth" pairs) represented two objects that differed by some multiple of a 20° rotation about a vertical axis (Figure 1B). For each of these pairs, copies of two appropriately different perspective views were simply attached to the cards in the orientation in which they were originally generated. The other half of the "same" pairs (the "picture-plane" pairs) represented two objects that differed by some multiple of a 20° rotation in the plane of the drawings themselves (Figure 1A). For each of these, one of the seven perspective views was selected for each object and two copies of this picture were attached to the card in appropriately different orientations. Altogether, the 1,600 pairs presented to each subject included 800 "same" pairs, which consisted of 400 unique pairs (20 "depth" and 20 "picture-plane" pairs at each of the 10 angular differences from 0° to 180°), each of which was presented twice. The remaining 800 pairs, randomly intermixed with these consisted of 400 unique "different" pairs, each of which (again) was presented twice. Each of these "different" pairs corresponded to one "same" pair (of either the "depth" or "picture-plane" variety) in which, however, one of the three-dimensional objects had been reflected about some plane in three-dimensional space. Thus the two objects in each "different" pair differed, in general, by both a reflection and a rotation.

The 1,600 pairs were grouped into blocks of not more than 200 and presented over 8 to 10 1-hour sessions (depending upon the subject). Also, although it is only of incidental interest here, each such block of presentations was either "pure," in that all pairs involved rotations of the same type ("depth" or "picture-plane"), or "mixed," in that the two types of rotation were randomly intermixed within the same block.

Each trial began with a warning tone, which was followed half a second later by the presentation of a stimulus pair and the simultaneous onset of a timer. The lever-pulling response stopped the timer, recorded the subject's reaction time, and terminated the visual display. The line drawings, which averaged between 4 and 5 cm in maximum linear extent, appeared at a viewing distance of about 60 cm. They were positioned, with a center-to-center spacing that subtended a visual angle of 9°, in two circular apertures in a vertical black surface (see Figure 1, A to C).

The subjects were instructed to respond as quickly as possible while keeping errors to a minimum. On the average, only 3.2 percent of the responses were incorrect (ranging from 0.6 to 5.7 percent for individual subjects). The reaction-time data presented below include only the 96.8 percent correct responses. However, the data for the incorrect responses exhibit a similar pattern.

In Figure 2, the overall means of the reaction times as a function of angular difference in orientation for all correct (right-hand) responses to "same" pairs are plotted separately for the pairs differing by a rotation in the picture plane (Figure 2A) and for the pairs differing by a rotation in depth (Figure 2B). In both cases, reaction time is a strikingly linear function of the angular difference between the 2 three-dimensional objects portrayed. The mean reaction times for individual subjects increased from a value of about 1 sec at 0° of rotation for all subjects to values ranging from 4 to 6 sec at 180° of rotation, depending upon the particular individual. Moreover, despite such variations in slope, the *linearity* of the function is clearly evident when the data are plotted separately for individual three-dimensional objects or for individual subjects. Polynomial regression lines were computed separately for each subject under each type of rotation. In all 16 cases, the functions were found to have a highly significant linear component ($p < .001$) when tested against deviations from linearity. No significant quadratic or higher-order effects were found ($p > .05$, in all cases).

The angle through which different three-dimensional shapes must be rotated to achieve congruence is not, of course, defined. Therefore, a function like those plotted in Figure 2 cannot be constructed in any straightforward manner for the "different" pairs. The *overall* mean reaction time for these pairs was found, however, to be 3.8 sec—nearly a second longer than the corresponding overall means for the "same" pairs. (In the postexperimental interview, the subjects typically reported that they attempted to rotate one end of one object into congruence with the corresponding end of the other object; they discovered that the two objects were *different* when, after this "rotation," the two free ends still remained noncongruent.)

Not only are the two functions shown in Figure 2 both linear, but they are very similar to each other with respect to intercept and slope. Indeed, for the larger angular differences, the reaction times were, if anything, somewhat shorter for rotation in depth than for rotation in the picture plane. However, since this small difference is either absent or reversed in four of the eight subjects, it is of doubtful significance. The determination of identity of shape may therefore be based, in both cases, upon a process of the same general kind. If we can describe this process as some sort of "mental rotation in three-dimensional space," then the slope of the obtained functions indicates that the average rate at which these particular objects can be thus "rotated" is roughly 60° per second.

FIGURE 2 Mean reaction times to two perspective line drawings portraying objects of the same three-dimensional shape. Times are plotted as a function of angular difference in portrayed orientation: (A) for pairs differing by a rotation in the picture plane only; and (B) for pairs differing by a rotation in depth. (The centers of the circles indicate the means and, when they extend far enough to show outside these circles, the vertical bars around each circle indicate a conservative estimate of the standard error of that mean based on the distribution of the eight component means contributed by the individual subjects.)

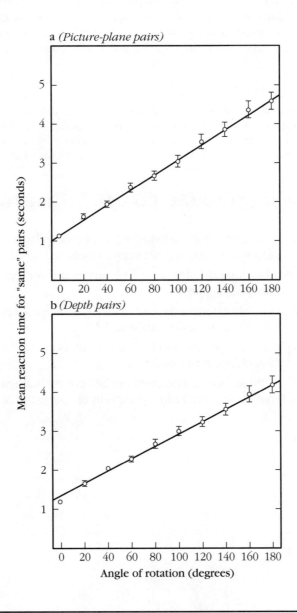

Of course the plotted reaction times necessarily include any times taken by the subjects to decide how to process the pictures in each presented pair as well as the time taken actually to carry out the process, once it was chosen. However, even for these highly practiced subjects, the reaction times were still linear and were no more than 20 percent lower in the "pure" blocks of presentations (in which the subjects knew both the axis and the direction of the required rotation in advance of each presentation) than in the "mixed" blocks (in which the axis of rotation was unpredictable). Tentatively, this suggests that 80 percent of a typical one of these reaction times may represent some such process as "mental rotation" itself, rather than a preliminary process of preparation or search. Nevertheless, in further research now underway, we are seeking clarification of this point and others.

NOTE

1. Mrs. Jih-Jie Chang of the Bell Telephone Laboratories generated the 180 perspective projections for us by means of the Bell Laboratories' Stromberg-Carlson 4020 microfilm recorder and the computer program for constructing such projections developed there by A. M. Noll. See, for example, A. M. Noll (1965). *Computers Automation 14,* 20.

QUESTIONS FOR FURTHER THOUGHT

1. In Shepard and Metzler's work, what is the relationship between the degree of discrepancy in angular orientation between two objects and reaction time?

2. How does speed of rotation outside the picture plane compare with speed of rotation within the picture plane?

3. How do subjects' introspective reports of their strategies compare with the data they produce in the mental-rotation task?

4. What activity besides time required to rotate an object contributes to response time on Shepard and Metzler's task?

5. How, if at all, might someone who does not believe in analogue mental representations of three-dimensional objects explain Shepard and Metzler's results?

EXPERT PERFORMANCE: ITS STRUCTURE AND ACQUISITION

Anders Ericsson and Neil Charness

INTRODUCTION

We know that people differ widely in their demonstrated levels of expertise in a broad variety of fields. For example, some chess players, musicians, athletes, and dancers display far superior performance compared to others. But what leads some people to become experts, while others remain as novices?

Psychologists have typically assumed that experts differ from novices largely in basic abilities. Experts become experts largely by virtue of being endowed with abilities that enable them to learn faster, to a higher level, or probably both, than other people. Although many and probably most psychologists still accept this view, Anders Ericsson and Neil Charness are among a group of psychologists who have presented a serious challenge to the abilities-based view. According to Ericsson and Charness, people become experts while others do not due to a single antecedent—deliberate practice.

Deliberate practice is practice in an activity in pursuit of a particular goal. In particular, effective practice is directed to produce a certain desired result. Thus, just playing a piece over and over again on the piano would not count as deliberate practice, but playing it with the intention of improving and correcting errors would count.

Ericsson and Charness review extensive evidence suggesting that experts in a wide variety of fields have spent substantially more time in deliberate practice than have novices. Many of these studies, but not all, are retrospective in focus. For example, in one study, Ericsson and his colleagues showed that a college student with an ordinary level of memory could be trained to become a mnemonist, remembering very long strings of numbers. Because the student, a runner, used running times as a basis for remembering the long strings of numbers, the skill did not transfer to other types of symbols, such as letters.

The Ericsson and Charness view may not be complete, but it presents a challenge to cognitive psychologists to show in what ways, if any, it needs to be supplemented. The importance of the work comes from its demonstration that, whether or not abilities matter, deliberate practice seems to be critically important in the acquisition of expertise. Indeed, the authors took the issue further, claiming that deliberate practice, rather than some kind of inborn talent, separates experts from novices in a wide variety of fields.

Source: From Ericsson, K. A., & Charness, N. (1994). Expert performance: Its structure and acquisition. *American Psychologist, 49,* 725–747. Copyright © 1994 by the American Psychological Association. Reprinted with permission.

Counter to the common belief that expert performance reflects innate abilities and capacities, recent research in different domains of expertise has shown that expert performance is predominantly mediated by acquired complex skills and physiological adaptations. For elite performers, supervised practice starts at very young ages and is maintained at high daily levels for more than a decade. The effects of extended deliberate practice are more far-reaching than is commonly believed. Performers can acquire skills that circumvent basic limits on working memory capacity and sequential processing. Deliberate practice can also lead to anatomical changes resulting from adaptations to intense physical activity. The study of expert performance has important implications for our understanding of the structure and limits of human adaptation and optimal learning. ■

In nearly every field of human endeavor, the performance of the best practitioners is so outstanding, so superior even to the performance of other highly experienced individuals in the field, that most people believe a unique, qualitative attribute, commonly called *innate talent,* must be invoked to account for this highest level of performance. Although these differences in performance are by far the largest psychologists have been able to reliably measure among healthy adults, exceptional performance has not, until recently, been extensively studied by scientists.

In the last decade, interest in outstanding and exceptional achievements and performance has increased dramatically. Many books have been recently published on the topic of genius (for example, Gardner, 1993a; Murray, 1989a; Simonton, 1984, 1988b; Weisberg, 1986, 1993), exceptionally creative individuals (D. B. Wallace & Gruber, 1989), prodigies (Feldman, 1986; A. Wallace, 1986), and exceptional performance and performers (Howe, 1990; Radford, 1990; Smith, 1983). Of particular interest to the general public has been the remarkable ability of idiot savants or savants, who in spite of a very low general intellectual functioning display superior performance in specific tasks and domains, such a mental multiplication and recall of music (Howe, 1990; Treffert, 1989). The pioneering research comparing the performance of experts and beginners (novices) by de Groot (1946/1978) and Chase and Simon (1973) has generated a great deal of research (Chi, Glaser, & Farr, 1988; Ericsson & Smith, 1991b). A parallel development in computer science has sought to extract the knowledge of experts by interviews (Hoffman, 1992) to build expert systems, which are computer models that are designed to duplicate the performance of these experts and make their expertise generally available. These efforts at artificial intelligence have been most successful in domains that have established symbolic representations, such as mathematical calculation, chess, and music (Barr & Feigenbaum, 1981–1982: Cohen & Feigenbaum, 1982), which incidentally are the main domains in which prodigies and savants have been able to display clearly superior performance (Feldman, 1980, 1986).[1]

The recent advances in our understanding of exceptional performance have had little impact on general theories in psychology. The new knowledge has not fulfilled the humanistic goals of gaining insights from the lives of outstanding people about how people might improve their lives. Maslow (1971) long ago eloquently expressed these goals:

> If we want to know how fast a human being can run, then it is no use to average out the speed of a "good sample" of the population; it is far better to collect Olympic gold medal winners and see how well they can do. If we want to know the possibilities for spiritual growth, value growth, or moral development in human beings, then I maintain that we can learn most by studying our moral, ethical, or saintly people.... Even when "good specimens," the saints and sages and great leaders of history, have been available for study, the temptation too often has been to consider them not human but supernaturally endowed. (p. 7)

The reasons for the lack of impact become clear when we consider the two most dominant approaches and their respective goals. The human information-processing approach, or the skills approach, has attempted to explain exceptional performance in terms of knowledge and skills acquired through experience. This approach, originally developed by Newell and Simon (1972), has tried to show that the basic information-processing system with its elementary information processes and basic capacities remains intact during skill acquisition and that outstanding performance results from incremental increases in knowledge and skill due to the extended effects of experience. By constraining the changes to acquired knowledge and skill, this approach has been able to account for exceptional performance within existing general theories of human cognition. According to this approach, the mechanisms identified in laboratory studies of learning can be extrapolated to account for expertise and expert performance by an incremental accumulation of knowledge and skill over a decade of intense experience in the domain. The long duration of the necessary period of experience and the presumed vast complexity of the accumulated knowledge has discouraged investigators from empirically studying the acquisition of expert performance. Similarly, individual differences in expert performance, when the amount of experience is controlled, have not been of major interest and have been typically assumed to reflect differences in the original structure of basic processes, capacities, and abilities.

The other major approach focuses on the individual differences of exceptional performers that would allow them to succeed in a specific domain. One of the most influential representatives of this approach is Howard Gardner, who in 1983 presented his theory of multiple intelligence in his book *Frames of Mind: The Theory of Multiple Intelligences* (hereinafter referred to as *Frames of Mind*). Gardner (1983, 1993a, 1993b) drew on the recent advances in biology and brain physiology about neural mechanisms and localization of brain activity to propose an account of the achievements of savants, prodigies, and geniuses in specific domains. He argued that exceptional performance results from a close match between the individual's intelligence profile and the demands of the particular domain. A major concern in this approach is the early identification and nurturing of children with high levels of the required intelligence for a specific domain. Findings within this approach have limited implications for the lives of the vast majority of children and adults of average abilities and talents.

In this article, we propose a different approach to the study of exceptional performance and achievement, which we refer to as the study of *expert performance*. Drawing on our earlier published research, we focus on reproducible, empirical phenomena of superior performance. We will thus not seriously consider anecdotes or unique events, including major artistic and scientific innovations, because they cannot be repeatedly reproduced on demand and hence fall outside the class of phenomena that can be studied by experimental methods. Our approach involves the identification of reproducible superior performance in the everyday life of exceptional performers and the capture of this performance under laboratory conditions. Later we show that the analysis of captured superior performance reveals that extended training alters the cognitive and physiological processes of experts to a greater degree than is commonly believed possible. In the final section of the article we review results from studying the lives of expert performers and identify the central role of large amounts of focused training (deliberate practice), which we distinguish from other forms of experience in a domain. The recent evidence for far-reaching effects of training leads us to start by reexamining the available evidence for innate talent and specific gifts as necessary conditions for attaining the highest levels of performance in a domain.

TRADITIONAL VIEW OF THE ROLE OF TALENT IN EXCEPTIONAL PERFORMANCE

Since the emergence of civilization, philosophers have speculated about the origin of highly desirable individual attributes, such as poetic ability, physical beauty, strength, wisdom, and skill in handiwork (Murray, 1989b). It was generally believed that these attributes were gifts from the gods, and it was commonly recognized that "On the whole the gods do not bestow more than one gift on a person" (Murray, 1989b, p. 11). This view persisted in early Greek thought, although direct divine intervention was replaced by natural causes. Ever since, there has been a bias toward attributing high abilities to gifts rather than experience, as expressed by John Stuart Mill, there is "a common tendency among mankind to consider all power which is not visibly the effect of practice, all skill which is not capable of being reduced to mechanical rules, as the result of a particular gift" (quoted in Murray, 1989b, p. 12).

One important reason for this bias in attribution, we believe, is linked to immediate legitimatization of various activities associated with the gifts. If the gods have bestowed a child with a special gift in a given art form, who would dare to oppose its development, and who would not facilitate its expression so everyone could enjoy its wonderful creations? This argument may appear strange today, but before the French Revolution the privileged status of kings and nobility and the birthright of their children were primarily based on such claims.

The first systematic development of this argument for gaining social recognition to artists can be found in classic work on *The Lives of the Artist* by Vasari (Bull, 1987), originally published in 1568. This book provided the first major biography of artists and is generally recognized as a major indirect influence on the layman's conceptions of artists even today (Barolsky, 1991). Although Vasari's expressed goal was simply to provide a factual history of art, modern scholars argue that "the *Lives* were partly designed to propagate ideas of the artist as someone providentially born with a vocation from heaven, entitled to high recognition, remuneration, and respect" (Bull, 1987, Vol. 2, p. xxvi). To support his claim, Vasari tried to identify early signs of talent and ability in the lives of the artists he described. When facts were missing, he is now known to have added or distorted material (Barolsky, 1991). For example,

Vasari dated his own first public demonstration of high ability to the age of 9, although historians now know that he was 13 years old at that event (Boase, 1979). His evaluations of specific pieces of art expressed his beliefs in divine gifts. Michelangelo's famous painting in the Sistine Chapel, the *Final Judgment,* was described by Vasari as "the great example sent by God to men so that they can perceive what can be done when intellects of the highest grade descend upon the earth" (quoted in Boase, 1979, pp. 251–252). Vasari also tried to establish a link between the noble families and the families of outstanding artists by tracing the heritage and family trees of the artists of his time to the great families of antiquity and to earlier great artists. However, much of the reported evidence is now considered to have been invented by Vasari (Barolsky, 1992). In the centuries following Vasari, our civilization underwent major social changes leading to a greater social mobility through the development of a skilled middle class and major progress in the accumulation of scientific knowledge. It became increasingly clear that individuals could dramatically increase their performance through education and training, if they had the necessary drive and motivation. Speculation on the nature of talent started to distinguish achievements due to innate gifts from other achievements resulting from learning and training. In 1759, Edward Young published a famous book on the origin of creative products, in which he argued that "An *Original* may be said to be of *vegetable* nature: it rises spontaneously from the vital root of Genius; it *grows,* it is not *made*" (quoted with original italics in Murray, 1989b, p. 28). Hence, an important characteristic of genius and talent was the apparent absence of learning and training, and thus talent and acquired skill became opposites (Bate, 1989). A century later Galton (1869/1979) presented a comprehensive scientific theory integrating talent and training that has continued to influence the conception of exceptional performance among the general population.

Sir Francis Galton was the first scientist to investigate empirically the possibility that excellence in diverse fields and domains has a common set of causes. On the basis of an analysis of eminent men in a wide range of domains and of their relatives, Galton (1869/1979) argued that three factors had to be present: innate ability, eagerness to work, and "an adequate power of doing a great deal of very laborious work" (p. 37). Because the importance of the last two factors—motivation and effort—had already been recognized (Ericsson, Krampe, & Heizmann, 1993), later investigators concentrated primarily on showing that innate abilities and capacities are necessary to attain the highest levels of performance.

Galton (1869/1979) acknowledged a necessary but not sufficient role for instruction and practice in achieving exceptional performance. According to this view, performance increases monotonically as a function of practice toward an asymptote representing a fixed upper bound on performance. Like Galton, contemporary researchers generally assume that training can affect some of the components mediating performance but cannot affect others. If performance achieved after extensive training is limited by components that cannot be modified, it is reasonable to assert that stable, genetically determined factors determine the ultimate level of performance. If all possible changes in performance related to training are attained after a fairly limited period of practice, this argument logically implies that individual differences in final performance must reflect innate talents and natural abilities.

The view that talent or giftedness for a given activity is necessary to attain the highest levels of performance in that activity is widely held among people in general. This view is particularly dominant in such domains of expertise as chess, sports, music, and visual arts, where millions of individuals are active but only a very small number reach the highest levels of performance.

One of the most prominent and influential scientists who draw on evidence from exceptional performance of artists, scientists, and athletes for a biological theory of talent is Howard Gardner. In *Frames of Mind,* Gardner (1983) proposed seven intelligences: linguistic, musical, spatial, logical–mathematical, bodily kinesthetic, and interpersonal and intrapersonal intelligence—each an independent system with its own biological bases (p. 68). This theory is a refinement and development of ideas expressed in an earlier book (Gardner, 1973), in which the talent position was more explicitly articulated, especially in the case of music. Gardner (1973) wrote,

> Further evidence of the strong hereditary basis of musical talent comes from a number of sources. Most outstanding musicians are discovered at an early age, usually before 6 and often as early as 2 or 3, even in households where relatively little music is heard. Individual differences are tremendous among children, and training seems to have comparatively little effect in reducing these differences. (p. 188)

He discussed possible mechanisms for talent in the context of music savants, who in spite of low intellectual functioning display impressive music ability as children: "it seems possible that the children are reflecting a rhythmic and melodic capacity that is primarily hereditary, and which needs as little external stimulation as does walking and talking in the normal child" (Gardner, 1973, p. 189). Although Gardner (1983) did not explicitly discuss his earlier positions, the evidence from prodigies and savants remains central. *Frames of Mind* contains a careful review of the then available research on the dramatic effects of training on performance. In particular, he reviewed the exceptional music performance of young children trained with the Suzuki method and noted that many of these children who began training without previous signs of musical talent attained levels comparable to music prodigies of earlier times and gained access to the best music teachers in the world. The salient aspect of talent, according to Gardner (1983), is no longer the innate structure (gift) but rather the potential for achievement and the capacity to rapidly learn material relevant to one of the intelligences. Gardner's (1983) view is consistent with Suzuki's rejection of inborn talent in music and Suzuki's (1963/1981) early belief in individual differences in innate general ability to learn, although Suzuki's innate abilities were not specific to a particular domain, such as music. However, in his later writings, Suzuki (1980/1981) argued that "every child can be highly educated if he is given the proper training" (p. 233), and he blamed earlier training failures on incorrect training methods and their inability to induce enthusiasm and motivation in the children. The clearest explication of Gardner's (1983) view is found when he discussed his proposal for empirical assessments of individuals' profiles in terms of the seven intelligences. He proposed a test in which "individuals were given the opportunity to learn to recognize certain patterns [relevant to the particular domain] and were tested on their capabilities to remember these from one day to the next" (p. 385). On the basis of tests for each of the intelligences, "intellectual profiles could be drawn up in the first year or two of life" (p. 386), although reliable assessments may have to wait until the preschool years because of "early neural and functional plasticity" (p. 386). Gardner's own hunch about strong intellectual abilities was that "an individual so blessed does not merely have an easy time learning new patterns; he learns them so readily that *it is virtually impossible for him to forget them*" (pp. 385–386).

Our reading of Gardner's (1993a, 1993b)[2] most recent books leads us to conclude that his ideas on talent have not fundamentally changed. According to Gardner's (1983) influential view, the evidence for the talent view is based on two major sources of data on performance: the performance of prodigies and savants and the ability to predict future success of individuals on the basis of early test results. Given that our knowledge about the exceptional performance of savants and prodigies and the predictive validity of tests of basic abilities and talents have increased considerably in the past decade, we briefly review the evidence or rather the lack of evidence for innate abilities and talent.

PERFORMANCE OF PRODIGIES AND SAVANTS

When the large collection of reports of amazing and inexplicable performance is surveyed, one finds that most of them cannot even be firmly substantiated and can only rarely be replicated under controlled laboratory conditions. Probably the best established phenomenon linked to talent in music is perfect pitch, or more accurately absolute pitch (AP). Only approximately 0.01% of the general population have AP and are able to correctly name each of the 64 different tones, whereas average musicians without AP can distinguish only approximately five or six categories of pitches when the pitches are presented in isolation (Takeuchi & Hulse, 1993). Many outstanding musicians display AP, and they first reveal their ability in early childhood. With a few exceptions, adults appear to be unable to attain AP in spite of extended efforts. Hence the characteristics of absolute pitch would seem to meet all of the criteria of innate talent, although there is some controversy about how useful this ability is to the expert musicians. In a recent review of AP, Takeuchi and Hulse (1993) concluded that the best account of the extensive and varied evidence points toward a theory that "states AP can be *acquired by anyone* [italics added], but only during a limited period of development" (p. 355). They found that all individuals with AP had started with music instruction early—nearly always before age five or six—and that several studies had been successful in teaching AP to 3- to 6-year-old children. At older ages, children perceive relations between pitches, which leads to accurate relative pitch, something all skilled musicians have. "Young children *prefer* to process absolute rather than the relative pitches of musical stimuli" (p. 356). Similar developmental trends from individual features to relational attributes are found in other forms of perception during the same age period (Takeuchi & Hulse, 1993). Rather than being a sign of innate talent, AP appears to be a natural consequence of appropriate instruction and of ample opportunities to interact with a musical instrument, such as a piano, at very young ages.

Other proposed evidence for innate talent comes from studies of prodigies in music and chess who are able to attain high levels of performance even as young children. In two influential books, Feldman (1980, 1986) showed that acquisition of skills in prodigies follows the same sequence of stages as in other individuals in the same domain. The primary difference is that prodigies attain higher levels faster and at younger ages. For example, an analysis of Picasso's early drawings as a child shows that he encountered and mastered problems in drawing in ways similar to less gifted individuals (Pariser, 1987). Feldman (1986) also refuted the myth that prodigies acquire their skills irrespective of the environment. In fact, he found evidence for the exact opposite, namely that "the more powerful and specific the gift, the more need for active, sustained and specialized intervention" (p. 123) from skilled teachers and parents. He described the classic view of gifts, in which parents are compelled to support their development, when he wrote, "When extreme talent shows itself it demands nothing less than the willingness of one or both of the parents to give up almost everything else to make sure that the talent is developed" (p. 122). A nice case in point is the child art prodigy Yani (Ho, 1989), whose father gave up his own painting career so as not to interfere with the novel style that his daughter was developing. Feldman (1980, 1986) argued that prodigious performance is rare because extreme talent for a specific activity in a particular child and the necessary environmental support and instruction rarely coincide.

Contrary to common belief, most child prodigies never attain exceptional levels of performance as adults (Barlow, 1952; Feldman, 1986). When Scheinfeld (1939) examined the reported basis of the initial talent assessment by parents of famous musicians, he found signs of interest in music rather than objective evidence of unusual capacity. For example, Fritz Kreisler was "playing violin" (p. 239) with two sticks at age 4, and Yehudi Menuhin had a "response to violins at concerts" (p. 239) at the age of 1½ years. Very early start of music instruction would then lead to the acquisition of absolute pitch. Furthermore, the vast majority of exceptional adult performers were never child prodigies, but instead they started instruction early and increased their performance due to a sustained high level of training (Bloom, 1985). The role of early instruction and maximal parental support appears to be much more important than innate talent, and there are many examples of parents of exceptional performers who successfully designed optimal environments for their children without any concern about innate talent (see Ericsson, Krampe, & Tesch-Römer, 1993, and Howe, 1990). For example, as part of an educational experiment, Laslo and Klara Polgar (Forbes, 1992) raised one of their daughters to become the youngest international chess grand master ever—she was even younger than Bobby Fischer, who was the youngest male achieving that exceptional level of chess-playing skill. In 1992 the three Polgar daughters were ranked first, second, and sixth in the world among women chess players, respectively.

Although scientists and the popular press have been interested in the performance of prodigies, they have been especially intrigued by so-called *savants*. Savants are individuals with low levels of general intellectual functioning who are able to perform at high levels in some special tasks. In a few cases the parents have reported that these abilities made their appearances suddenly, and they cited them as gifts from God (Ericsson & Faivre, 1988; Feldman, 1986). More careful study of the emergence of these and other cases shows that their detection may in some cases have been sudden, but the opportunities, support, and encouragement for learning had preceded the original performance by years or even decades (Ericsson & Faivre,

1988; Howe, 1990; Treffert, 1989). Subsequent laboratory studies of the performance of savants have shown them to reflect acquired skills. For example, savants who can name the day of the week of an arbitrary date (e.g., November 5, 1923) generate their answers using instructable methods that allow their performance to be reproduced by a college student after a month of training (for a review see Ericsson & Faivre, 1988). The only ability that cannot be reproduced after brief training concerns some savants' reputed ability to play a piece of music after a single hearing.

However, in a carefully controlled study of a music savant (J. L.), Charness, Clifton, and MacDonald (1988) showed that reproduction of short (2- to 12-note) tonal sequences and recall of from two to four chords (4 notes each) depended on whether the sequences or chords followed Western scale structure. Unfamiliar sequences that violated musical conventions were poorly recalled past 6 notes. Short, familiar sequences of notes and chords were accurately recalled, although recall dropped with length of sequence so that only 3 (of 24) 12-note familiar sequences were completely correct. Attempts to train J. L. to learn temporally static 16-note melodies were unsuccessful. Even in the case of the musical savant studied by Sloboda, Hermelin, and O'Conner (1985), who was able to memorize a new piece of music, there was a marked difference in success with a conventional versus a tonally unconventional piece. Thus, music savants, like their normally intelligent expert counterparts, need access to stored patterns and retrieval structures to enable them to retain long, unfamiliar musical patterns. Given that savants cannot read music—most of them are blind—they have to acquire new music by listening, which would provide motivation and opportunities for the development of domain-specific memory skills.

In summary, the evidence from systematic laboratory research on prodigies and savants provides no evidence for giftedness or innate talent but shows that exceptional abilities are acquired often under optimal environmental conditions.

PREDICTION OF FUTURE SUCCESS BASED ON INNATE ABILITIES AND TALENT

The importance of basic processes and capacities is central to many theorists in the human information-processing tradition. In conceptual analogies with computers, investigators often distinguish between hardware (the physical components of the computer) and software (computer programs and stored data). In models of human performance, "software" corresponds to knowledge and strategies that can be readily changed as a function of training and learning, and "hardware" refers to the basic elements that cannot be changed through training. Even theorists such as Chase and Simon (1973), who acknowledge that "practice is the major independent variable in the acquisition of skill" (p. 279), argue in favor of individual differences in talent that predispose people to be successful in different domains: "Although there clearly must be a set of specific aptitudes (e.g., aptitudes for handling spatial relations) that together comprise a talent for chess, individual differences in such aptitudes are largely overshadowed by immense differences in chess experience" (p. 297). Bloom (1985) went through many different domains to point out some necessary qualities that are likely to be mostly inborn, such as *"motor coordination, speed of reflexes,* and *hand–eye coordination"* (p. 546). These views were consistent with the available information at the time, such as high heritabilities for many of these characteristics. In their review of sport psychology, Browne and Mahoney (1984) argued for the importance of fixed physiological traits for elite performance of athletes and wrote that "there is good evidence that the limits of physiological capacity to become more efficient with training is determined by genetics" (p. 609). They cited research reporting that percentage of muscle fibers and aerobic capacity "are more than 90% determined by heredity for both male and female" (p. 609). However, more recent reviews have shown that heritabilities in random samples of twins are much lower and range between zero and 40% (Malina & Bouchard, 1991).

It is curious how little empirical evidence supports the talent view of expert and exceptional performance. Ever since Galton, investigators have tried to measure individual differences in unmodifiable abilities and basic cognitive and perceptual capacities. To minimize any influence from prior experience, they typically base their tests on simple tasks. They measure simple reaction time and detection of sensory stimuli and present meaningless materials, such as nonsense syllables and lists of digits, in tests of memory capacity. A recent review (Ericsson, Krampe, & Tesch-Römer, 1993) showed that efforts to measure talent with objective tests for basic cognitive and perceptual motor abilities have been remarkably unsuccessful in predicting final performance in specific domains. For example, elite athletes are able to react much faster and make better perceptual discriminations to representative situations in their respective domains, but their simple reaction times and perceptual acuity to simple stimuli during laboratory tests do not differ systematically from those of other athletes or control subjects (for reviews see Regnier, Salmela, & Russell, 1993, and Starkes & Deakin, 1985). Chess players' and other experts' superior memory for brief presentation of representative stimuli from their domains compared with that of novices is eliminated when the elements of the same stimuli are presented in a randomly arranged format (Chase & Simon, 1973; see Ericsson & Smith, 1991a, for a review). The performance of elite chess players on standard tests of spatial ability is not reliably different from control subjects (Doll & Mayr, 1987). The domain specificity of superior performance is striking and is observed in many different domains of expertise (Ericsson, Krampe, & Tesch-Römer, 1993).

This conclusion can be generalized with some qualifications to current tests of such general abilities as verbal and quantitative intelligence. These tests typically measure acquired knowledge of mathematics, vocabulary, and grammar by successful performance on items testing problem solving and comprehension. Performance during and immediately after training is correlated with IQ, but the correlations between this type of ability test and performance in the domain many months and years later is reduced (even after corrections for restriction of range) to such low values that Hulin, Henry, and Noon (1990) questioned their usefulness and predictive validity. At the same time, the average IQ of expert performers, especially in domains of expertise requiring thinking, such as chess, has been found to be higher than the average of the normal population and corresponds roughly to that of college students. However, IQ does not reliably discriminate the best adult performers from less accomplished adult performers in the same domain.

Even physiological and anatomical attributes can change dramatically in response to physical training. Almost everyone recognizes that regular endurance and strength training uniformly improves aerobic endurance and strength, respectively. As the amount and intensity or physical training is increased and maintained for long periods, far-reaching adaptations of the body result (see Ericsson, Krampe, & Tesch-Römer, 1993, for a review). For example, the sizes of hearts and lungs, the flexibility of joints, and the strength of bones increase as the result of training, and the nature and extent of these changes appear to be magnified when training overlaps with physical development during childhood and adolescence. Furthermore, the number of capillaries supplying blood to trained muscles increases, and muscle fibers can change their metabolic properties from fast twitch to slow twitch. With the clear exception of height, a surprisingly large number of anatomical characteristics show specific changes and adaptations to the specific nature of extended intense training, which we describe in more detail later in this article.

If one accepts the necessity of extended intense training for attaining expert performance—a claim that is empirically supported later in this article—then it follows that currently available estimates of heritability of human characteristics do not generalize to expert performance. An estimate of heritability is valid only for the range of environmental effects for which the studied subjects have been exposed. With a few exceptions, studies of heritabilities have looked only at random samples of subjects in the general population and have not restricted their analyses to individuals exposed to extended training in a domain. The remaining data on exceptional and expert performers have not been able to demonstrate systematic genetic influences. Explanations based on selective access to instruction and early training in a domain provide as good or in some cases better accounts of familial relations of expert performers, such as the lineage of musicians in the Bach family (see Ericsson, Krampe, & Tesch-Römer, 1993, for a review).

In summary, we argue that the traditional assumptions of basic abilities and capacities (talent) that may remain stable in studies of limited and short-term practice do not generalize to superior performance acquired over years and decades in a specific domain. In addition, we will later review evidence showing that acquired skill can allow experts to circumvent basic capacity limits of short-term memory and of the speed of basic reactions, making potential basic limits irrelevant. Once the potential for change through practice is recognized, we believe that a search for individual differences that might be predictive of exceptional and expert performance should focus on the factors advocated by Charles Darwin (quoted in Galton, 1908) in a letter to Galton after reading the first part of Galton's (1869/1979) book: "You have made a convert of an opponent in one sense, for I have always maintained that excepting fools, men did not differ much in intellect, only in zeal and hard work; I still think this is an *eminently* important difference" (p. 290). In commenting on Darwin's remark, Galton (1908) agreed but argued that "character, including the aptitude for work, is heritable" (p. 291). On the basis of their review, Ericsson, Krampe, and Tesch-Römer (1993) found that motivational factors are more likely to be the locus of heritable influences than is innate talent. We explicate the connection between these "motivational" factors and the rate of improving performance in a specific domain in the last section of this article.

There are two parts to the remaining portion of this article. First, we show that it is possible to study and analyze the mechanisms that mediate expert performance. We also show that the critical mechanisms reflect complex, domain-specific cognitive structures and skills that performers have acquired over extended periods of time. Hence, individuals do not achieve expert performance by gradually refining and extrapolating the performance they exhibited before starting to practice but instead by restructuring the performance and acquiring new methods and skills. In the final section, we show that individuals improve their performance and attain an expert level, not as an automatic consequence of more experience with an activity but rather through structured learning and effortful adaptation.

THE STUDY OF EXPERT PERFORMANCE

The conceptions of expert performance as primarily an acquired skill versus a reflection of innate talents influence how expert performance and expert performers are studied. When the goal is to identify critical talents and capacities, investigators have located experts and then compared measurements of their abilities with those of control subjects on standard laboratory tests. Tests involve simple stimuli and tasks in order to minimize any effects of previously acquired knowledge and skill. Given the lack of success of this line of research, we advocate a different approach that identifies the crucial aspects of experts' performance that these experts exhibit regularly at a superior level in their domain. If experts have acquired their superior performance by extended adaptation to the specific constraints in their domains, we need to identify representative tasks that incorporate these constraints to be able to reproduce the natural performance of experts under controlled conditions in the laboratory. We illustrate this method of designing representative test situations with several examples later in this section. Once the superior performance of experts can be reliably reproduced in a test situation, this performance can then be analyzed to assess its mediating acquired mechanisms. Following Ericsson and Smith (1991a), we define *expert performance* as consistently superior performance on a specified set of representative tasks for the domain that can be administered to any subject. The virtue of defining expert performance in this restricted sense is that the definition both meets all the criteria of laboratory studies of performance and comes close to meeting those for evaluating performance in many domains of expertise.

PERCEIVED EXPERTS VERSUS CONSISTENT EXPERT PERFORMANCE

In many domains, rules have evolved and standardized conditions and fair methods have been designed for measuring performance. The conditions of testing in many sports and other activities, such as typing competitions, are the same for all participating individuals. In other domains, the criteria for expert performance cannot be easily translated into a set of standardized tasks that captures and measures that performance. In some domains, expert performance is determined by judges or by the results of competitive tournaments. Psychometric methods based on tournament results, most notably in chess (Elo, 1986), have successfully derived latent measures of performance on an interval scale. In the arts and sciences, selected individuals are awarded prizes and honors by their peers, typically on the basis of significant achievements such as published books and research articles and specific artistic performances.

Some type of metric is of course required to identify *superior performance.* The statistical term *outlier* may be a useful heuristic for judging superior performance. Usually, if someone is performing at least two standard deviations above the mean level in the population, that individual can be said to be performing at an expert level. In the domain of chess (Elo, 1986), the term *expert* is defined as a range of chess ratings (2000–2199) approximately two to three standard deviations (200 rating points) above the mean (1600 rating points) and five to six standard deviations above the mean of chess players starting to play in chess tournaments.

In most domains, it is easier to identify individuals who are socially recognized as experts than it is to specify observable performance at which these individuals excel. The distinction between the perception of expertise and actual expert performance becomes increasingly important as research has shown that the performance of some individuals who are nominated as experts is not measurably superior. For example, studies have found that financial experts' stock investments yield returns that are not consistently better than the average of the stock market, that is, financial experts' performance does not differ from the result of essentially random selection of stocks. When successful investors are identified and their subsequent investments are tracked, there is no evidence for sustained superiority. A large body of evidence has been accumulated showing that experts frequently do not outperform other people in many relevant tasks in their domains of expertise (Camerer & Johnson, 1991). Experts may have much more knowledge and experience than others, yet their performance on critical tasks may not be reliably better than that of nonexperts. In summary, researchers cannot seek out experts and simply assume that their performance on relevant tasks is superior; they must instead demonstrate this superior performance.

IDENTIFYING AND CAPTURING EXPERT PERFORMANCE

For most domains of expertise, people have at least an intuitive conception of the kind of activities at which an expert should excel. In everyday life, however, these activities rarely have clearly defined starting and end points, nor do the exact external conditions of a specific activity reoccur. The main challenge is thus to identify particular well-defined tasks that frequently occur and that capture the essence of expert performance in a specific domain. It is then possible to determine the contexts in which each task naturally occurs and to present these tasks in a controlled context to a larger group of experts.

De Groot's (1946/1978) research on expertise in chess is generally considered the pioneering effort to capture expert performance. Ability in chess playing is determined by the outcomes of chess games between opponents competing in tournaments. Each game is different and is rarely repeated exactly except for the case of moves in the opening phase of the game. De Groot, who was himself a chess master, determined that the ability to play chess is best captured in the task of selecting the next move for a given chess position taken from the middle of the game between two chess masters. Consistently superior performance on this task for arbitrary chess positions logically implies a very high level of skill. Researchers can therefore elicit experts' superiority in performing a critical task by presenting the same unfamiliar chess position to any number of chess players and asking them to find the best next move. De Groot demonstrated that performance on this task discriminates well between chess players at different levels of skill and thus captures the essential phenomenon of ability to play this game.

In numerous subsequent studies, researchers have used a similar approach to study the highest levels of thinking in accepted experts in various domains of expertise (Chi et al., 1988; Ericsson & Smith, 1991b). If expert performance reflects extended adaptation to the demands of naturally occurring situations, it is important that researchers capture the structure of these situations in order to elicit maximal performance from the experts. Furthermore, if the tasks designed for research are sufficiently similar to normal situations, experts can rely on their existing skills, and no experiment-specific changes are necessary. How similar these situations have to be to real-life situations is an empirical question. In general researchers should strive to define the simplest situation in which experts' superior performance can still be reliably reproduced.

DESCRIPTION AND ANALYSIS OF EXPERT PERFORMANCE

The mere fact that it is possible to identify a set of representative tasks that can elicit superior performance from experts under standardized conditions is important. It dramatically reduces the number of contextual factors that can logically be essential for reproducing that superior performance. More important, it allows researchers to reproduce the phenomenon of expert performance under controlled conditions and in a reliable fashion. Researchers can thus precisely describe the tasks and stimuli and can theoretically determine which mechanisms are capable of reliably producing accurate performance across the set of tasks. Part of the standard methodology in cognitive psychology is to analyze the possible methods subjects could use to generate the correct response to a specific task, given their knowledge about procedures and facts in the domain. The same methodology can be applied to tasks that capture expert performance. Because, however, the knowledge experts may apply to a specific task is quite extensive and complex, it is virtually impossible for nonexperts to understand an analysis of such a task. Instead of describing such a case, we illustrate the methodology and related issues with a relatively simple skill, mental multiplication.

MENTAL MULTIPLICATION: AN ILLUSTRATION OF TEXT ANALYSIS

In a study of mental multiplication, the experimenter typically reads a problem to a subject: What is the result of multiplying 24 by 36? The subject then reports the correct answer—864. It may be possible that highly experienced subjects recognize that particular problem and retrieve the answer immediately from memory. That possibility is remote for normal subjects, and one can surmise that they must calculate the answer by relying on their knowledge of the multiplication table and familiar methods for complex multiplication. The most likely method is the paper-and-pencil method taught in the schools, where 24×36 is broken down into 24×6 and 24×30 and the products are added together (illustrated as Case B in Table 1). Often students are told to put the highest number first. By this rule, the first step in solving 24×36 is to rearrange it as 36×24 and then break it down as 36×4 and 36×20 (Case A). More sophisticated subjects may recognize that 24×36 is equivalent to $(30 - 6) \times (30 + 6)$ and use the formula $(a - b) \times (a + b) = a^2 - b^2$, thus calculating 24×36 as $30^2 - 6^2 = 900 - 36 = 864$ (Case C). Other subjects may recognize other shortcuts, such as $24 \times 36 = (2 \times 12) \times (3 \times 12) = 6 \times 12^2 = 6 \times 144$ (Case D). Skilled mental calculators often prefer to calculate the answer in the reverse order, as is illustrated in Case E. Especially for more complex problems this procedure allows them to report the first

---

TABLE 1 Five Possible Methods of Mentally Multiplying 24 by 36 and a Think-Aloud Protocol From a Subject Generating the Correct Answer

MENTAL MULTIPLICATION	THINK-ALOUD PROTOCOL
Method A 24 $\times\ 36$ 144 72 864	36 times 24 4 carry the—no wait 4 carry the 2 14
Method B 36 $\times\ 24$ 144 72 864	144 0 36 times 2 is 12 6 72 720 plus 144
Method C $24 \times 36 =$ $= (30 - 6) \times (30 + 6) =$ $= 30^2 - 6^2 =$ $= 900 - 36 = 864$	4 uh, uh 6 8 uh, 864
Method D $24 \times 36 = 2 \times 12 \times 3 \times 12 =$ $= 6 \times 12^2 = 6 \times 144 = 864$	
Method E $\begin{array}{r} AB \\ \times\ CD \\ \hline 100 \times A \times C \\ 10 \times A \times D \\ 10 \times C \times B \\ B \times D \end{array}$ $\begin{array}{r} 24 \\ \times\ 36 \\ \hline 600 \\ 120 \\ 120 \\ 24 \\ \hline 864 \end{array}$	

digit of the final result long before they have completed the calculation of the remaining digits. Because most people expect that the entire answer has to be available before the first digit can be announced, the last method gives the appearance of faster calculation speeds.

An investigator cannot determine on which of the methods in Table 1 a subject relied. However, if the subject was instructed to think aloud (see Ericsson & Simon, 1993, for the detailed procedure) while completing the mental multiplication, the investigator could record in detail the mediating sequences of the subject's thoughts, as is illustrated in the right panel of Table 1. Although methodologically rigorous methods for encoding and evaluating think-aloud protocols are available (Ericsson & Simon, 1993), the visual match between Case B and the protocol in Table 1 is sufficiently clear for the purposes of our illustration. Even with a less detailed record of the verbalized intermediate products in the calculation, it is possible to reject most of the alternative methods as being inconsistent with a recorded protocol.

THINK-ALOUD PROTOCOLS AND TASK ANALYSIS IN RESEARCH ON EXPERT PERFORMANCE

Since the demise of introspective analysis of consciousness around the turn of the century, investigators have been reluctant to consider any type of verbal report as valid data on subjects' cognitive processes. More recently, investigators have been particularly concerned that having subjects generate verbal reports changes the underlying processes. In a recent review of more than 40 experimental studies comparing performance with and without verbalization, Ericsson and Simon (1993) showed that the structure of cognitive processes can change if subjects are required to explain their cognitive processes. In contrast, if subjects were asked simply to verbalize the thoughts that come to their attention (think aloud), Ericsson and Simon found no reliable evidence that structural changes to cognitive processing occurred. Thinking aloud appears only to require additional time for subjects to complete verbalization and therefore leads to somewhat longer solution times in some cases.

A critical concern in applying this methodology to expert performance is how much information the think-aloud protocols of experts contain about the mediating cognitive processes. Obviously, many forms of skilled perceptual–motor performance are so rapid that concurrent verbalization of thought would seem impossible. We later consider alternative methodologies for such cases; but for a wide range of expert performance, think-aloud protocols have provided a rich source of information on expert performance. In his work on chess masters, de Groot (1946/1978) instructed his subjects to think aloud as they identified the best move for chess positions. From an analysis of the verbal reports, de Groot was able to describe how his subjects selected their moves. First, they familiarized themselves with the position and extracted the strengths and weaknesses of its structure. Then they systematically explored the consequences of promising moves and the opponent's likely countermoves by planning several moves ahead. From subjects' verbalizations, de Groot and subsequent investigators (Charness, 1981a) have been able to represent the sequences of moves subjects explored as search trees and to measure the amount and depth of planning for chess players at different levels of expertise (see Figure 1). The results of these analyses show that the amount and depth of search increase as a function of chess expertise to a given point (the level of chess experts); thereafter, no further systematic differences were found (Charness, 1989). That the very best chess players still differ in their ability to find and selectively explore the most promising moves suggests that the structure of their internal representations of chess positions differs.

FIGURE 1 Chess position presented to players with instruction to select best next move by white (top panel).

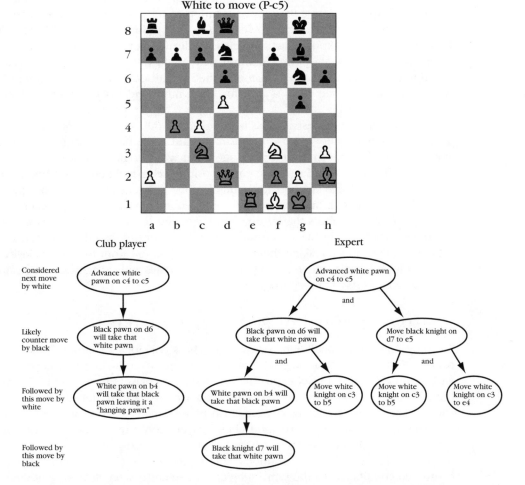

Note: Think-aloud protocols of a good club player (chess rating = 1657) and a chess expert (chess rating = 2004) collected by Charness (1981a) are shown in the bottom panel to illustrate differences in evaluation and planning for one specific move, P-c5 (white pawn from c4 to c5), the best move for this position. Reported considerations for other potential moves have been omitted. The chess expert considers more alternative move sequences, some of them to a greater depth than the club player does. From "Search in Chess: Age and Skill Differences" by N. Charness, 1981, *Journal of Experimental Psychology: Human Perception and Performance, 7,* p. 469. Copyright © 1981 by the American Psychological Association.

The central importance of experts' representations of solutions is revealed by verbal reports in other domains such as physics and medical diagnosis. When novices in physics solve a problem, they typically start with the question that asks for, say, a velocity; then they try to recall formulas for calculating velocities and then construct step by step a sequence of formulas by reasoning backward from the goal to the information given in the problem. In contrast, more experienced subjects proceed by forward reasoning. As they read the description of the problem situation, an integrated representation is generated and updated, so when they finally encounter the question in the problem text, they simply retrieve a solution plan from memory (Larkin, McDermott, Simon, & Simon, 1980). This finding suggests that experts form an immediate representation of the problem that systematically cues their knowledge, whereas novices do not have this kind of orderly and efficient access to their knowledge. Similarly, medical experts comprehend and integrate the information they receive about patients to find the correct diagnosis by reasoning forward, whereas less accomplished practitioners tend to generate plausible diagnoses that aid their search for confirming and disconfirming evidence (Patel & Groen, 1991).

Experts' internal representations of the relevant information about the situation are critical to their ability to reason, to plan out, and to evaluate consequences of possible actions. Approximately 100 years ago Binet was intrigued by some chess players' claims that they could visualize chess positions clearly when they played chess games without a visible chessboard (blindfold chess). Binet (1894) and subsequently Luria (1968) studied individuals with exceptional memory abilities who claimed to visualize as mental images the information presented to them. These claims, if substantiated, would imply that some individuals have sensory-based memory akin to photographic memory, making them qualitatively different from the vast majority of human adults. To gain understanding of these processes and capacities, investigators have turned to tests of perception and memory.

IMMEDIATE MEMORY OF PERCEIVED SITUATIONS

To study subjects' immediate perceptions of chess positions, de Groot (1946/1978) restricted the presentation to 2-15 sec and then removed the chess positions from view. Even after such a brief exposure, the best chess players were able to describe the structures of the chess positions and could reproduce the locations of all the chess pieces almost perfectly. Weaker chess players' memory was much worse, and generally the amount of information chess players could recall was found to be a function of skill. In a classic study, Chase and Simon (1973) studied subjects' memory for briefly presented chess positions and replicated de Groot's findings under controlled conditions. To the same subjects, Chase and Simon also presented chess positions with randomly rearranged chess pieces. Memory for these scrambled positions was uniformly poor and did not differ as a function of skill. This finding has been frequently replicated and shows that the superior memory for briefly presented chess positions is not due to any general memory ability, such as photographic memory, but depends critically on subjects' ability to perceive meaningful patterns and relations between chess pieces. Originally, Chase and Simon proposed that experts' superior short-term memory for chess positions was due to their ability to recognize configurations of chess pieces on the basis of their knowledge of vast numbers of specific patterns of pieces. With greater knowledge of more complex and larger configurations of chess pieces (chunks), an expert could recall more individual chess pieces with the same number of chunks. Hence Chase and Simon could account for very large individual differences in memory for chess positions within the limits of the capacity of normal short-term memory (STM), which is approximately seven chunks (Miller, 1956).

The Chase–Simon theory has been very influential. It gives an elegant account of experts' superior memory only for representative stimuli from their domains, and not even for randomly rearranged versions of the same stimuli (see Ericsson & Smith, 1991a, for a summary of the various domains of expertise in which this finding has been demonstrated). At that time Chase and Simon (1973) believed that storage of new information in long-term memory (LTM) was quite time consuming and that memory for briefly presented information could be maintained only in STM for experts and nonexperts alike. However, subsequent research by Chase and Ericsson (1982) on the effects of practice on a specific task measuring the capacity of STM has shown that through extended practice (more than 200 hours), it is possible for subjects to improve performance by more than 1,000%. These improvements are not mediated by increasingly larger chunks in STM but reflect the acquisition of memory skills that enable subjects to store information in LTM and thereby circumvent the capacity constraint of STM. Hence, with extensive practice, it is possible to attain skills that lead to qualitative, not simply quantitative, differences in memory performance for a specific type of presented information.

From experimental analysis of their trained subjects and from a review of data on other individuals with exceptional memory, Chase and Ericsson (1982; Ericsson, 1985) extracted several general findings of skilled memory that apply to all subjects. Exceptional memory is nearly always restricted to one type of material, frequently random sequences of digits. The convergence of acquired memory skills and alleged exceptional memory was demonstrated when the trained subjects performed tasks given previously to "exceptional" subjects. Figure 2 (middle panel) shows a matrix that Binet presented visually to his subjects. Below the matrix are several orders in which the same subjects were asked to recall the numbers from the matrix that they memorized. Ericsson and Chase (1982) found that their subjects matched or surpassed the exceptional subjects both in the speed of initial memorization and in the speed of subsequent recall. A detailed analysis contrasting the speed for different orders to recall showed the same pattern in trained and exceptional subjects, both of whom recalled by rows faster than by columns. Consistent with their acquired memory skill, the trained subjects encoded each row of the matrix as a group by relying on their extensive knowledge of facts relevant to numbers. They then associated a cue corresponding to the spatial location of each row with a retrieval structure illustrated in the top panel of Figure 2. To recall numbers in flexible order, subjects retrieved the relevant row using the corresponding retrieval cue and then extracted the desired next digit or digits. The high correlation between the recall times predicted from this method and the recall times observed for both exceptional and trained subjects imply that these groups have similar memory representation. When

| FIGURE 2 | Twenty-five-digit matrix used by Binet to test memory experts. |

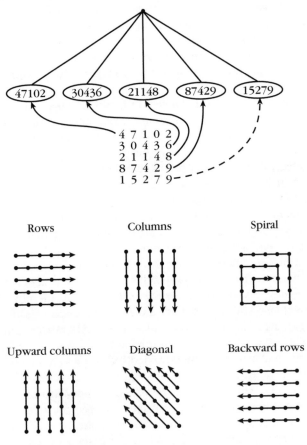

Note: Binet asked subjects to repeat the entire matrix in various orders shown at the bottom or to repeat individual rows as five-digit numbers. The top panel shows trained subjects' representation of the matrix as a sequence of rows, with all digits in a row stored together in an integrated memory encoding.

the biographical background of individuals exhibiting exceptional memory performance was examined, Ericsson (1985, 1988) found evidence for extended experience and practice with related memory tasks. Hence, these exceptional individuals and the trained college students should be viewed as expert performers on these laboratory tasks, where the same type of memory skills has been acquired during extended prior experience.

Acquired memory skill (skilled memory theory, Ericsson & Staszewski, 1989; and long-term working memory, Ericsson & Kintsch, 1994) accounts well even for the superior memory of experts. In many types of expert performance, research has shown that working memory is essentially unaffected by interruptions, during which the experts are forced to engage in an unrelated activity designed to eliminate any continued storage of information in STM. After the interruption and after a brief delay involving recall and reactivation of relevant information stored in LTM, experts can resume activity without decrements in performance. Storage in LTM is further evidenced by experts' ability to recall relevant information about the task even when they are unexpectedly asked for recall after the task has been completed. The amount recalled is found to increase as a function of the level of expert performance in chess (Charness, 1991).

The critical aspect of experts' working memory is not the amount of information stored per se but rather how the information is stored and indexed in LTM. In support of this claim, several cases have been reported in which nonexperts have been able to match the amount of domain-specific information recalled by experts, but without attaining the expert's sophisticated representation of the information. After 50 hours of training on memory for presented chess positions, a college student with minimal knowledge of chess was able to match the performance of chess masters (Ericsson & Harris, 1990). However, an analysis of how the chess position was encoded revealed that the trained subject focused on perceptually salient patterns in the periphery of the chess board, whereas the chess master attended to the central aspects critical to the selection of the next moves (Ericsson & Harris, 1990). When told explicitly to memorize presented medical information, medical students match or even surpass medical experts (Patel & Groen, 1991; Schmidt & Boshuizen, 1993). However, the medical experts are more able than medical students to identify and recall the important pieces of presented information. Medical experts also encode more general clinical findings, which are sufficient for reasoning about the case but not specific enough to recall or reconstruct the detailed facts presented about the medical patient (Boshuizen & Schmidt, 1992; Groen & Patel, 1988).

Experts acquire skill in memory to meet specific demands of encoding and accessibility in specific activities in a given domain. For this reason, their skill does not transfer from one domain to another. The demands for storage of intermediate products in mental calculation differ from the demands of blindfold chess, wherein the chess master must be able not simply to access the current position but also to plan and accurately select the best chess moves. The acquisition of memory skill in a domain is integrated with the acquisition of skill in organizing acquired knowledge and refining of procedures and strategies, and it allows experts to circumvent limits on working memory imposed by the limited capacity of STM.

PERCEPTUAL–MOTOR SKILL IN EXPERT PERFORMANCE

In many domains, it is critical that experts respond not just accurately but also rapidly in dynamically changing situations. A skilled performer needs to be able to perceive and encode the current situation as well as to select and execute an action or a series of actions rapidly. In laboratory studies of skill acquisition, investigators have been able to demonstrate an increase in the speed of perceptual–motor reactions as a direct function of practice. With extensive amounts of practice, subjects are able to evoke automatically the correction reaction to familiar stimulus situations. This analysis of perceived situations and automatically evoked responses is central to our understanding of skilled performance, yet it seems to be insufficient to account for the speeds observed in many types of expert performance. The time it takes to respond to a stimulus even after extensive training is often between 0.5 and 1.0 sec, which is too slow to account for a return of a hard tennis serve, a goalie's catching a hockey puck, and fluent motor activities in typing and music.

The standard paradigm in laboratory psychology relies on independent trials in which the occurrence of the presented stimulus, which the subject does not control, defines the beginning of a trial. In contrast, in the perceptual environment in everyday life, expert performance is continuous and changing, and experts must be able to recognize if and when a particular action is required. Most important, it is possible for the expert to analyze the current situation and thereby anticipate future events. Research on the return of a tennis serve shows that experts do not wait until they can see the ball approaching them. Instead they carefully study the action of the server's racquet and are able to predict approximately where in the service area the tennis ball will land even before the server has hit the ball. Abernethy (1991) has recently reviewed the critical role of anticipation in expert performance in many racquet sports. Similarly, expert typists are looking well ahead at the text they are typing in any particular instant. The difference between the text visually fixated and the letters typed in a given instant (eye–hand span) increases with the typists' typing speed. High-speed filming of the movements of expert typists' fingers shows that their fingers are simultaneously moved toward the relevant keys well ahead of when they are actually struck. The largest differences in speed between expert and novice typists are found for successive keystrokes made with fingers of different hands because the corresponding movements can overlap completely after extended typing practice. When the typing situation is artificially changed to eliminate looking ahead at the text to be typed, the speed advantage of expert typists is virtually eliminated (Salthouse, 1991a). Similar findings relating the amount of looking ahead and speed of performance apply to reading aloud (Levin & Addis, 1979) and sight-reading in music (Sloboda, 1985).

In summary, by successfully anticipating future events and skillfully coordinating overlapping movements, the expert performer is able to circumvent potential limits on basic elements of serial reactions.

GENERAL COMMENTS ON THE STRUCTURE OF EXPERT PERFORMANCE

Recent studies of expert performance have questioned the talent-based view that expert performance becomes increasingly dependent on unmodified innate components. Although these studies have revealed how beginners acquire complex cognitive structures and skills that circumvent the basic limits confronting them, researchers have not uncovered some simple strategies that would allow nonexperts to rapidly acquire expert performance, except in a few isolated cases, such as the sexing of chickens (Biederman & Shiffrar, 1987). Analyses of exceptional performance, such as exceptional memory and absolute pitch, have shown how it differs from the performance of beginners and how beginners can acquire skill through instruction in the correct general strategy and corresponding training procedures (Howe, 1990). However, to attain exceptional levels of performance, subjects must in addition undergo a very long period of active learning, during which they refine and improve their skill, ideally under the supervision of a teacher or coach. In the following section, we describe the particular activities (deliberate practice) that appear to be necessary to attain these improvements (Ericsson, Krampe, & Tesch-Römer, 1993).

By acquiring new methods and skills, expert performers are able to circumvent basic, most likely physiological, limits imposed on serial reactions and working memory. The traditional distinction between physiological (unmodifiable physical) and cognitive (modifiable mental) factors that influence performance does not seem valid in studies of expert performance. For the purposes of the typical 1-hour experiment in psychology, changes in physiological factors might be negligible; but once we consider extended activities, physiological adaptations and changes are not just likely but virtually inevitable. Hence, we also consider the possibility that most of the physiological attributes that distinguish experts are not innately determined characteristics but rather the results of extended, intense practice.

ACQUISITION OF EXPERT PERFORMANCE

A relatively uncontroversial assertion is that attaining an expert level of performance in a domain requires mastery of all of the relevant knowledge and prerequisite skills. Our analysis has shown that the central mechanisms mediating the superior performance of experts are acquired; therefore acquisition of relevant knowledge and skills may be the major limiting factor in attaining expert performance. Some of the strongest evidence for this claim comes from a historical description of how domains of expertise evolved with increased specialization within each domain. To measure the duration of the acquisition process, we analyze the length of time it takes for the best individuals to attain the highest levels of performance within a domain. Finally we specify the type of practice that seems to be necessary to acquire expert performance in a domain.

EVOLUTION OF DOMAINS OF EXPERTISE AND THE EMERGENCE OF SPECIALIZATION

Most domains of expertise today have fairly long histories of continued development. The knowledge in natural science and calculus that represented the cutting edge of mathematics a few centuries ago and that only the experts of that time were able to master is today taught in high school and college (Feldman, 1980). Many experts today are struggling to master the developments in a small subarea of one of the many natural sciences. Before the 20th century, it was common for musicians to compose and play their own music; since then, distinct career patterns have emerged for composers, solo performers, accompanists, teachers, and conductors. When Tchaikovsky asked two of the greatest violinists of his day to play his violin concerto, they refused, deeming the score unplayable (Platt, 1966). Today, elite violinists consider the concerto part of their standard repertory. The improvement in music training has been so considerable that according to Roth (1982), the virtuoso Paganini "would indeed cut a sorry figure if placed upon the modern concert stage" (p. 23). Paganini's techniques and Tchaikovsky's concerto were deemed impossible until other musicians figured out how to master and describe them so that students could learn them, as well. Almost 100 years ago the first Olympic Games were held, and results on standardized events were recorded. Since then records for events have been continuously broken and improved. For example, the winning time for the first Olympic Marathon is comparable to the current qualifying time for the Boston Marathon, attained by many thousands of amateur runners every year. Today, amateur athletes cannot successfully compete with individuals training full time, and training methods for specific events are continuously refined by professional coaches and trainers.

In all major domains there has been a steady accumulation of knowledge about the domain and about the skills and techniques that mediate superior performance. This accumulated experience is documented and regularly updated in books, encyclopedias, and instructional material written by masters and professional teachers in the domain. During the last centuries the levels of performance have increased, in some domains dramatically so. To attain the highest level of performance possible in this decade, it is necessary both to specialize and to engage in the activity full time.

MINIMUM PERIOD OF ATTAINMENT OF EXPERT PERFORMANCE

Another measure of the complexity of a domain is the length of time it takes an individual to master it and attain a very high level of performance or make outstanding achievements. Of particular interest is how fast the most "talented" or best performers can attain an international level of performance. In their classic study on chess, Simon and Chase (1973) argued that a 10-year period of intense preparation is necessary to reach the level of an international chess master and suggested similar requirements in other domains. In a review of subsequent research. Ericsson, Krampe, and Tesch-Römer (1993) showed that the 10-year rule is remarkably accurate, although there are at least some exceptions. However, even those exceptions, such as Bobby Fischer, who started playing chess very early and attained an international level at age 15, are only about a year shy of the 10-year requirement. Winning international competitions in sports, arts, and science appears to require at least 10 years of preparation and typically substantially longer. In the sciences and some of the arts, such as literature, the necessary preparation overlaps so much with regular education that it is often difficult to determine a precise starting point. However, when the time interval between scientists' and authors' first accepted publication and their most valued publication is measured, it averages more than 10 years and implies an even longer preparation period (Raskin, 1936). Even for the most successful ("talented") individuals, the major domains of expertise are sufficiently complex that mastery of them requires approximately 10 years of essentially full-time preparation, which corresponds to several thousands of hours of practice.

PRACTICE ACTIVITIES TO ATTAIN EXPERT PERFORMANCE

In almost every domain, methods for instruction and efficient training have developed in parallel with the accumulation of relevant knowledge and techniques. For many sports and performance arts in particular, professional teachers and coaches monitor training programs tailored to the needs of individuals ranging from beginners to experts. The training activities are designed to improve specific aspects of performance through repetition and successive refinement. To receive maximal benefit from feedback, individuals have to monitor their training with full concentration, which is effortful and limits the duration of daily training. Ericsson, Krampe, and Tesch-Römer (1993) referred to individualized training on tasks selected by a qualified teacher as *deliberate practice*. They argued that the amount of this type of practice should be closely related to the level of acquired performance.

From surveys of the kinds of activities individuals engage in for the popular domains, such as tennis and golf, it is clear that the vast majority of active individuals spend very little if any time on deliberate practice. Once amateurs have attained an acceptable level of performance, their primary goal becomes inherent enjoyment of the activity, and most of their time is spent on playful interaction. The most enjoyable states of play are characterized as flow (Csikszetmihalyi, 1990), when the individual is absorbed in effortless engagement in a continuously changing situation. During play even individuals who desire to improve their performance do not encounter the same or similar situations on a frequent and predictable basis. For example, a tennis player wanting to improve a weakness, such as a backhand volley, might encounter a relevant situation only once per game. In contrast, a tennis coach would give that individual many hundreds of opportunities to improve and refine that type of shot during a training session.

Work, another type of activity, refers to public performances, competitions, and other performances motivated by external social and monetary rewards. Although work activities offer some opportunities for learning, they are far from optimal. In work activities, the goal is to generate a quality product reliably. In several domains, such as performance arts and sports, there is a clear distinction between training before a performance and the performance itself. During the performance itself, opportunities for learning and improvements are minimal, although the problems encountered can be addressed during training following the performance. Most occupations and professional domains pay individuals to generate efficiently services and products of consistently high quality. To give their best performance in work activities, individuals rely on previously well-entrenched methods rather than exploring new methods with unknown reliability. In summary, deliberate practice is an effortful activity motivated by the goal of improving performance. Unlike play, deliberate practice is not inherently motivating; and unlike work, it does not lead to immediate social and monetary rewards (Ericsson, Krampe, & Tesch-Römer, 1993).

Individualized training of students, who begin as very young children under the supervision of professional teachers and coaches, is a relatively recent trend in most major domains. It was only in 1756, for example, that Wolfgang Amadeus Mozart's father published the first book in German on teaching students to play the violin. Before organized education became the norm, people acquired skill through apprenticeship, working as adolescents with skilled performers, frequently one of their parents. Recently there has been a lot of interest in this type of learning environment within the framework of situated cognition (Lave, 1988; Lave & Wenger, 1991). A significant element of apprenticeship is the imitation of skilled performers and careful study and copying of their work. In the arts, the study and imitation of masterpieces has a long history. For example, Benjamin Franklin (1788/1986) described in his autobiography how he tried to learn to write in a clear and logical fashion. He would read through a passage in a good book to understand it rather than memorize it and then try to reproduce its structure and content. Then he would compare his reproduction with the original to identify differences. By repeated application of this cycle of study, reproduction, and comparison with a well-structured original, Franklin argued that he acquired his skill in organizing thoughts for speaking and writing.

With the advent of audio and video recording, which have opened new possibilities for repeated study of master artists' performance, reproduction and comparison have been extended to allow individualized study and improvement of performance. This general method is central to achieving expert performance in chess. Advanced chess players spend as many as 4 hours a day studying published games between international chess masters (Forbes, 1992). The effective component of this type of study is predicting the chess master's next move without looking ahead. If the prediction is wrong, the advanced player examines the chess position more deeply to identify the reasons for the chess master's move. The activity of planning and extended evaluation of chess games is likely to improve a player's ability to internally represent chess positions, a memory skill that we discussed earlier in this article. This form of self-directed study has most of the characteristics of deliberate practice, but it is probably not as effective as individualized study guided by a skilled teacher. It is interesting to note that most of the recent world champions in chess were at one time tutored by chess masters (Ericsson, Krampe, & Tesch-Römer, 1993).

Deliberate practice differs from other domain-related activities, because it provides optimal opportunities for learning and skill acquisition. If the regular activities in a domain did not offer accurate and preferably immediate feedback or opportunities for corrected repetitions, improvements in performance with further experience would not be expected from learning theory. Most amateurs and employees spend very small amounts of time on deliberate efforts to improve their performance, once it has reached an acceptable level. Under these conditions only weak relations between amount of experience and performance would be predicted, which is consistent with the empirical data. Recent research has explored the question whether deliberate practice can account for the attainment of elite performance levels and for individual differences among expert-level performers. According to the framework proposed by Ericsson, Krampe, and Tesch-Römer (1993), the primary mechanism creating expert-level performance in a domain is deliberate practice.

ACQUIRING ELITE PERFORMANCE

Why do individuals even begin to engage in deliberate practice, when this activity is not inherently enjoyable? From many interviews, Bloom (1985) found that international-level performers in several domains start out as children by engaging in playful activities in the domain (see Phase 1 in Figure 3). After a period of playful and enjoyable experience, they reveal "talent" or promise. At this point, parents typically suggest that their children take lessons from a teacher and engage in limited amounts of deliberate practice. The parents help their children acquire regular habits of practice and teach them that this activity has instrumental value by noticing improvements in performance. The next phase (Bloom, 1985) is an extended period of preparation and ends with the individual's commitment to pursue activities in the domain on a full-time basis. During this period, the daily amounts of deliberate practice are increased, and more advanced teachers and training facilities are sought out. Occasionally, parents even move to a different region of the country to provide their child with the best training environment. In the next phase, the individual makes a full-time commitment to improving performance. This phase ends when the individual either can make a living as a professional performer in the domain or terminates full-time engagement in the activity. Bloom (1985) found that during this phase, nearly all of the individuals who ultimately reach an international-level performance work with master teachers who either themselves had reached that level or had previously trained other individuals to that level. All through their development, international-level performers are provided with the best teachers for their current levels of performance and engage in great amounts of deliberate practice.

| **FIGURE 3** | Three phases of development of expert performance followed by a qualitatively different phase of efforts to attain eminent achievements. |

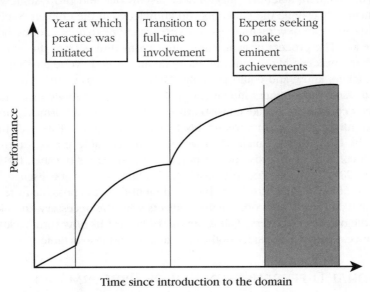

Note: From "Can We Create Gifted People?" by K. A. Ericsson, R. Th. Krampe, and S. Heizmann in *The Origins and Development of High Ability* (pp. 222–249), 1993, Chichester, England: Wiley. Copyright © 1993 by Ciba Foundation. Adapted by permission.

The dilemma in most domains of expertise is that millions of young individuals enter these domains with aspirations to reach the highest levels of performance, but by definition only a very small number can succeed. Given the low probability of ultimate success, parents and coaches have been very much interested in identifying these select individuals as early as possible and giving them encouragement, support, and the best learning opportunities. The consistent failures to identify specific "talents" in children is not surprising when one considers the qualitative changes occurring during the long period of development. In many domains, international performers start practice at age 4 to 6, when it is unclear what kind of objective evidence of talent and promise they could possibly display. Available descriptions suggest that children this young display interest and motivation to practice rather than exceptional performance. Once deliberate practice has begun, the primary measure of acquired skill and talent is the current level of performance compared with that of other children of comparable ages in the neighborhood. Only later at age 10 to 12 do the children typically start participating in competitions, where their performance is compared with that of other successful children from a larger geographical area. As performance level and age increase, the criteria for evaluating performance also change. In the arts and sciences, technical proficiency is no longer enough, and adult criteria of abstract understanding and artistic expression are applied.

During the first three phases of development, individuals master the knowledge and skills that master teachers and coaches know how to convey. To achieve the highest level (eminent performance), individuals must enter a fourth phase, going beyond the available knowledge in the domain to produce a unique contribution to the domain. Eminent scientists make major discoveries and propose new theories that permanently change the concepts and knowledge in the domain. Similarly, eminent artists generate new techniques and interpretations that extend the boundaries for future art. The process of generating innovations differs from the acquisition of expertise and mastery. Major innovations by definition go beyond anything even the master teachers know and could possibly teach. Furthermore, innovations are rare, and it is unusual that eminent individuals make more than a single major innovation during their entire lives. Unlike consistently superior expert performance, innovation occurs so infrequently and unpredictably that the likelihood of its ever being captured in the laboratory is small. However, it is still possible through retrospective analysis of concurrent records, such as notebooks and diaries (Gruber, 1981; Wallace & Gruber, 1989), to reconstruct the processes leading up to major discoveries. Once the context of a particular discovery has been identified, it is possible to reconstruct the situation and study how other naive subjects with the necessary knowledge can uncover the original discovery (Qin & Simon, 1990). Let us now turn back to expert performance, which we consider both reproducible and instructable.

INDIVIDUAL DIFFERENCES IN EXPERT PERFORMANCE

Biographies of international-level performers indicate that a long period of intense, supervised practice preceded their achievements. The simple assumption that these levels of deliberate practice are necessary accounts for the fact that the vast majority of active individuals who prematurely stop practicing never reach the highest levels of performance. However, in most major domains, a relatively large number of individuals continue deliberate practice and thus meet the criterion of necessity. Within this group striking individual differences in adult performance nonetheless remain.

Ericsson, Krampe, and Tesch-Römer (1993) hypothesized that differences in the amount of deliberate practice could account for even the individual differences among the select group of people who continue a regimen of deliberate practice. The main assumption, which they called the *monotonic benefits assumption,* is that individuals' performances are a monotonic function of the amount of deliberate practice accumulated since these individuals began deliberate practice in a domain. The accumulated amount of deliberate practice and the level of performance an individual achieves at a given age is thus a function of the starting age for practice and the weekly amount of practice during the intervening years. This function is illustrated in Figure 4. The second curve has been simply moved horizontally to reflect a later starting age, and the third curve reflects in addition a lower weekly rate of practice.

To evaluate these predictions empirically, it is necessary to measure the amount of time individuals spend on various activities, in particular deliberate practice. One way

FIGURE 4   Relations between age and performance.

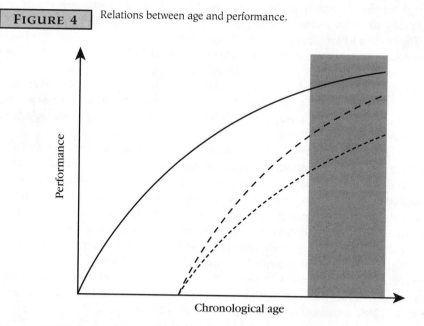

Note: The late period involving selection to the best music academies has been shaded. Solid line: Performance associated with an early starting age and a high level of practice. Dashed line: Performance for an equally high level of practice but a later starting age. Dotted line: Performance associated with the same late starting age but a lower level of practice. The slope of the dashed line appears steeper than that of the solid line. However, the horizontal distance between these two curves is constant. From "Can We Create Gifted People?" by K. A. Ericsson, R. Th. Krampe, and S. Heizmann in *The Origins and Development of High Ability* (pp. 222–249), 1993, Chichester, England: Wiley. Copyright © 1993 by Ciba Foundation. Adapted by permission.

of doing so, which is to have them keep detailed diaries, has a fairly long tradition in studies of time budgeting in sociology (Juster & Stafford, 1985). In most domains with teachers and coaches, deliberate practice is regularly scheduled on a daily basis, and advanced performers can accurately estimate their current and past amounts of practice as well as their starting ages and other characteristics of their practice history.

In a comprehensive review of studies comparing starting ages and amount of weekly practice for international, national, and regional-level performers in many different domains, Ericsson, Krampe, and Tesch-Römer (1993) found that performers who reached higher levels tended to start practicing as many as from 2 to 5 years earlier than did less accomplished performers. Individuals who attained higher levels of performance often spent more time on deliberate practice than did less accomplished individuals, even when there was no difference in the total time both groups spent on domain-related activities. Differences in the amount of deliberate practice accumulated during their development differentiated groups of expert performers at various current levels of performance. The three graphs in Figure 4 illustrate how simple differences in starting ages and weekly amounts of practice can yield very stable differences in amounts of training and performance levels.

Everyone recognizes that maturational factors affect performance. For this reason, competitions are nearly always structured by groups of contestants with the same ages. By the time individuals approach their middle to late teens (the shaded area in Figure 4) and are applying for scholarships and admission to the studios of master teachers and the best training environments, large differences in past practice and acquired skill are already present. Ericsson, Krampe, and Tesch-Römer (1993) found that by age 20, the top-level violinists in their study had practiced an average of more than 10,000 hours, approximately 2,500 hours more than the next most accomplished group of expert violinists and 5,000 hours more than the group who performed at the lowest expert level.

In summary, evidence from a wide range of domains shows that the top-level experts have spent a very large amount of time improving their performance and that the total amount accumulated during development is several years of additional full-time practice more than that of other less accomplished performers. This difference is roughly equivalent to the difference between freshmen and seniors in a highly competitive college. In these environments, where the best opportunities for further development are offered only to the individuals with the best current performance, it may be difficult for individuals with less prior practice and lower levels of performance even to secure situations in which they can practice full time. It is virtually impossible for them to catch up with the best performers because those performers maintain their lead through continuous practice at optimal levels.

STRUCTURE OF PRACTICE IN THE DAILY LIVES OF ELITE PERFORMERS

From analyses of diaries and other sources of biographical material, Ericsson, Krampe, and Tesch-Römer (1993) concluded that expert performers design their lives to optimize their engagement in deliberate practice. Expert musicians in their study spent approximately 4 hours a day—every day including weekends—on deliberate practice.

Practice sessions were approximately 1 hour long, followed by a period of rest. Performers practiced most frequently during the morning, when independent research indicates that individuals have the highest capacity for complex, demanding activity during the day (Folkard & Monk, 1985). All the expert musicians reported on the importance of sleep and rest in maintaining their high levels of daily practice. The expert musicians in the two best groups, who practiced longer each day, slept more than those in the least accomplished group and also slept more than other reference groups of subjects of comparable age. The additional sleep was primarily from an afternoon nap. Expert subjects maximize the amount of time they can spend on deliberate practice when they can fully focus on their training goals without fatigue. Many master teachers and coaches consider practice while fatigued and unfocused not only wasteful but even harmful to sustained improvements.

Focused, effortful practice of limited duration has been found to be important in a wide range of domains of expertise. Interestingly the estimated amount of deliberate practice that individuals can sustain for extended periods of time does not seem to vary across domains and is close to 4 hours a day (Ericsson, Krampe, & Tesch-Römer, 1993).

The effort and intensity of deliberate practice is most readily observable for perceptual–motor behavior in sports and performance arts. One goal of most of the practice activities is to push the limits of performance to higher levels by, for example, stretching in ballet, or repeated maximal efforts until exhaustion during interval training in running and weight lifting. It is well-known that intense exercise increases endurance and the size of muscles. However, recent research in sports physiology has shown that anatomical changes in response to extended intense exercise are more far-reaching than commonly believed. Within a few weeks of vigorous training, the number of capillaries supplying blood to the trained muscles increases. Longitudinal studies show that after years of "elite-level" endurance training, the heart adapts and increases in size to values outside the normal range for healthy adults. The metabolism and general characteristics of muscle fibers also change—from slow-twitch to fast-twitch or vice versa. Most interestingly, these changes are limited only to those muscles that are trained and critical to the particular sports event for which the athlete is preparing. Many of these changes appear to increase when practice overlaps with the body's development during childhood and adolescence. For example, the flexibility required for elite performance in ballet requires that dancers begin practicing before age 10 or 11. With the exception of height, the characteristics that differentiate elite athletes and performance artists from less accomplished performers in the same domains appear to reflect the successful adaptations of the body to intense practice activities extended over many years (Ericsson, Krampe, & Tesch-Römer, 1993).

These physiological adaptations are not unique to expert performers. Similar but smaller changes are found for individuals who train at less intense levels. Similar extreme adaptations are seen in individuals living under extreme environmental conditions, such as at very high altitudes, or coping with diseases, such as partial blockages of the blood supply to the heart. Many occupation-specific problems that expert performers experience in middle age also seem to result from related types of (mal)adaptive processes.

It is becoming increasingly clear that maximizing the intensity and duration of training is not necessarily good. Expert performers have a constant problem with avoiding strains and injuries and allowing the body enough time to adapt and recuperate. Even in the absence of physical injuries, an increasing number of athletes and musicians overtrain and do not allow themselves enough rest to maintain a stable equilibrium from day to day. Sustained overtraining leads to burnout, for which the only known remedy is to terminate practice completely for long periods. It appears that top-level adult experts practice at the highest possible level that can be sustained for extended periods without burnout or injury. Hence, it may be extremely difficult to consistently practice harder and improve faster than these individuals already do.

EXPERT PERFORMANCE FROM A LIFE SPAN PERSPECTIVE

Elite performers in most domains are engaged essentially full time from childhood and adolescence to late adulthood. The study of expert performers therefore offers a unique perspective on life span development and especially on the effects of aging. Many studies have examined the performance of experts as a function of age or of the ages when experts attained their best performance or their highest achievement. It is extremely rare for performers to attain their best performance before reaching adulthood, but it is not necessarily the case that performance continues to improve in those who keep exercising their skills across the life span. Rather, a peak age for performance seems to fall in the 20s, 30s, and 40s, as Lehman (1953) first noted. The age distributions for peak performance in vigorous sports are remarkably narrow and centered in the 20s with systematic differences between different types of sports (Schultz & Curnow, 1988). In vigorous sports, it is rare for elite athletes above age 30 to reach their personal best or even in many cases remain competitive with younger colleagues. Although less pronounced, similar age distributions centered somewhere in the 30s are found for fine motor skills and even predominantly cognitive activities, such as chess, science, and the arts. Simonton (1988a) has argued that the relative decline with age may be slight and may be attributable to the fact that total creative output for artists and scientists declines, although the probability of achieving an outstanding performance remains constant. Thus the frequency of producing an outstanding work declines with age. Perhaps the best evidence for decline with age is Elo's (1965) analysis of the careers of grand master chess players. As seen in Figure 5 (from Charness & Bosman, 1990), there is a peak for chess players in their 30s, although performance at 63 years of age is no worse than that at 21 years. The peak age for creative achievement differs considerably between domains. In pure mathematics, theoretical physics, and lyric poetry, the peak ages for contributions occur in the late 20s and early 30s. In novel writing, history, and philosophy, the peaks are less pronounced and occur in the 40s and early 50s (Simonton, 1988a). Even within domains, the peak age for performance seems to vary systematically with the types of demands placed on the performer. In international-level tournament chess, individuals typically play chess games for 4 to 5 hours daily for more than a week. Furthermore, tournament chess makes strong demands on working memory and, to some extent, on speed of processing, when players attempt to choose the best moves by

| **FIGURE 5** | Grand master performance by age. |

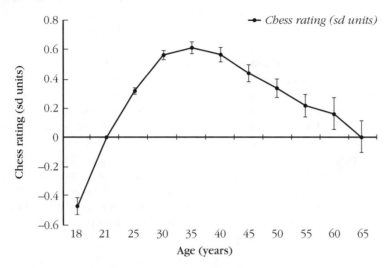

Note: Chess ratings scaled in standard deviation units, with performance at age 21 for each individual set to zero (data from Elo, 1965). Averaged scores across grand masters are shown with standard error bars. From "Expertise and Aging, Life in the Lab" (p. 358) by N. Charness and E. A. Bosman in *Aging and Cognition: Knowledge Organization and Utilization,* T. H. Hess (Ed.), 1990, Amsterdam: Elsevier. Copyright © 1990 by Elsevier. Adapted by permission.

searching through the problem spaces of possible moves. On average, a tournament chess player has approximately 3 min to consider each move (when normal time controls are used). In "postal chess," players have several days to make each move. Because deliberation times are longer and the players can use external memory to maintain the results of analysis, ascension to the world postal chess championship occurs much later, near 46 years of age as compared with 30 years of age for tournament chess (Charness & Bosman, 1990).

To researchers on aging, the decline in expert performance in old age, which in many domains is often relatively slight, is less interesting than expert performers' ability to maintain a very high level of performance during ages when beginners and less accomplished performers display clear effects of aging. A common hypothesis related to the notion of innate talent is that experts generally age more slowly than other performers, and thus no observable impairments would be expected. However, this hypothesis is not consistent with recent research on expert performance in chess (Charness, 1981b), typing (Bosman, 1993; Salthouse, 1984), and music (Krampe, 1994). The superior performance of older experts is found to be restricted to relevant tasks in their domains of expertise. For unrelated psychometric tasks and some tasks related to occupational activities, normal age-related decline is observed (Salthouse, 1991b).

The mediating mechanisms in younger and older experts' performance have been examined in laboratory studies developed under the expert performance approach. In typing, older experts who type at the same speed as younger experts are found to have larger eye–hand spans that permit older experts to compensate through advance preparation (Bosman, 1993; Salthouse, 1984). Older chess experts' ability to select the best chess move is associated with less planning than that of younger experts at an equivalent skill level. This suggests that older chess experts compensate through more extensive knowledge of chess (Charness, 1981a). Comparisons of older and younger expert pianists' ability to perform simple and complex sequences of keystrokes requiring bimanual coordination reveal no or small differences, whereas the same comparisons between older and younger amateur pianists reveal clear decrements with age that increase with the complexity of the tasks (Krampe, 1994). Such age effects require greater diversity in the models proposed to explain expertise. It is now evident that at least in typing and chess, two individuals at the same level of skill can achieve their performance through mechanisms with different structure. Although it is convenient to collapse a measure of expertise onto a unidimensional scale (such as chess rating or net words per minute for typing), this is an oversimplification that may obscure individual differences in the underlying processes that mediate same-level performance.

THE ROLE OF DELIBERATE PRACTICE

In the previous sections, we described the evidence for the necessity of deliberate practice for initially acquiring expert performance. The maintenance of expert performance could be due to the unique structure of the mechanisms acquired in expert performance or to a level of deliberate practice maintained during adulthood or both.

That most marked age-related decline is generally observed in perceptual–motor performance displayed in many types of sports. High levels of practice are necessary to attain the physiological adaptations that are found in expert performers, and the effects of practice appear to be particularly large when intense practice overlaps with physical development during childhood and adolescence. Most of these adaptations require that practice is maintained; if not, the changes revert to normal values, although for some anatomical changes many years of no practice appear necessary before the revision is completed. Hence, much of the age-related decline in performance may reflect the reduction or termination of practice. Studies of master athletes show that older athletes do not practice at the same intensity as the best young athletes. When older master athletes are compared with young athletes training at a similar level, many physiological measurements do not differ between them. However, at least some physiological functions, such as maximum heart rate, show an age-related decline independent of past or current practice. In summary, the ability to retain superior performance in sports appears to depend critically on maintaining practice during adulthood (Ericsson, 1990).

Evidence on the role of early and maintained practice in retaining cognitive aspects of expertise is much less extensive. Takeuchi and Hulse's (1993) recent review of absolute (perfect) pitch shows that children can easily acquire this ability at around the ages of 3 to 5. Acquisition of the same ability during adulthood is very difficult and time consuming. Some other abilities, such as the acquisition of second languages (especially accents and pronunciation), appear easier to acquire at young rather than adult ages. Whether early acquisition of abilities, per se, translates into better retention into old age is currently not known.

Virtually by definition, expert performers remain highly active in their domains of expertise. With increasing age, they typically reduce their intensive work schedules, a change in life style that is consistent with the decrease observed in their productivity (Simonton, 1988a). Roe (1953) found that eminent scientists reduce their levels of work during evenings and weekends. Information about distribution of time among different types of activities and especially the amount of time spent on maintaining and improving performance is essentially lacking. However, Krampe (1994) collected both diaries and retrospective estimates of past practice for older expert pianists. Consistent with the lack of performance differences between younger and older pianists in tasks relevant to piano playing, Krampe found that the older experts still practiced approximately 10 hours a week and spent more than 40 additional hours a week on other music-related activities. In addition, he found that individual differences in performance among older pianists could be predicted well by the amount of practice during the past 10 years. Whether a reduction in practice by older chess players and typists accounts for the differences between younger and older experts in these fields cannot currently be answered, given the lack of longitudinal data on performance and practice.

The study of expert performance over the life span of the performers is needed. This perspective is quite likely to provide new insights into the plasticity of the structure of human performance as a function of different developmental phases. Through investigation of focused sustained practice, it may be possible to determine which aspects can and, at least with the current training methods, cannot be modified to enhance current and future performance. Of particular practical and theoretical interest are those factors that enable experts to retain and maintain superior performance into old age.

SUMMARY AND CONCLUSION

The differences in performance between experts and beginners are the largest that have been reliably reproduced with healthy, normal adults under controlled test conditions. From the life-long efforts of expert performers who continuously strive to improve and reach their best performance, one can infer that expert performance represents the highest performance possible, given current knowledge and training methods in the domain. Individuals' acquisition of expert performance is thus a naturally occurring experiment for identifying the limits of human performance. It is hard to imagine better empirical evidence on maximal performance except for one critical flaw. As children, future international-level performers are not randomly assigned to their training conditions. Hence, one cannot rule out the possibility that there is something different about those individuals who ultimately reach expert-level performance.

Nevertheless, the traditional view of talent, which concludes that successful individuals have special innate abilities and basic capacities, is not consistent with the reviewed evidence. Efforts to specify and measure characteristics of talent that allow early identification and successful prediction of adult performance have failed. Differences between expert and less accomplished performers reflect acquired knowledge and skills or physiological adaptations effected by training, with the only confirmed exception being height.

Most plausible loci of individual differences are factors that predispose individuals toward engaging in deliberate practice and enable them to sustain high levels of practice for many years. Differences in these factors clearly have, in part, an environmental origin and can be modified as the level of practice is slowly increased with further experience. However, some of these factors, such as preferred activity level and temperament, may have a large genetic component. Furthermore, there may need to be a good fit between such predisposing factors and the task environment (along the lines of Thomas & Chess's, 1984, temperament–environment fit model) for expert-level performance to develop.

For a long time, the study of exceptional and expert performance has been considered outside the scope of general psychology because such performance has been attributed to innate characteristics possessed by outstanding individuals. A better explanation is that expert performance reflects extreme adaptations, accomplished through life-long effort, to demands in restricted, well-defined domains. By capturing and examining the performance of experts in a given domain, researchers have identified adaptive changes with physiological components as well as the acquisition of domain-specific skills that circumvent basic limits on speed and memory. Experts with different teachers and training histories attain their superior performance after many years of continued effort by acquiring skills and making adaptations with the same general structure. These findings imply that in each domain, there is only a limited number of ways in which individuals can make large improvements in performance. When mediating mechanisms of the same type are found in experts in very different domains that have evolved independently from each other, an account of this structure based on shared training methods is highly unlikely.

There is no reason to believe that changes in the structure of human performance and skill are restricted to the traditional domains of expertise. Similar changes should be expected in many everyday activities, such as thinking, comprehension, and problem solving, studied in general psychology. However, people acquire everyday skills under less structured conditions that lack strict and generalizable criteria for evaluation. These conditions also vary among individuals because of their specific living situations. In contrast, stable expert performance is typically restricted to standardized situations in a domain. Hence, the criteria for expert performance offer a shared goal for individuals in a domain that directs and constrains their life-long efforts to attain their maximal performance. Even when scientific investigators' ultimate goal is to describe and understand everyday skills, they are more likely to succeed by studying because the former is acquired under much more controlled and better understood conditions and achieved at higher levels of proficiency in a specific domain.

We believe that studies of the acquisition and structure of expert performance offer unique evidence on many general theoretical and applied issues in psychology. Extended deliberate practice gives near maximal values on the possible effects of environmental variables (in interaction with developmental variables) relevant to theoretical claims for invariant cognitive capacities and general laws of performance. We will significantly advance our knowledge of the interaction between environment and development by observing the effects of training during the early development of expert performers and the effects of maintaining training for older experts in late adulthood. The study of expert performance complements cross-cultural studies of environmental influences on thinking and cognition. The relation between language and thinking, traditionally restricted to comparisons between different languages (Hunt & Agnoli, 1991), should be particularly suitable for study in the context of expertise, where domain-specific names, concepts, and knowledge are explicated in training manuals and books and subjects with differing levels of mastery of the vocabulary and where "language" of the domain can be easily found.

For applied psychologists the study of expert performers and their master teachers and coaches offers a nearly untapped reservoir of knowledge about optimal training and specific training methods that has been accumulated in many domains for a long time. Across very different domains of expert performance, Ericsson, Krampe, and Tesch-Römer (1993) uncovered evidence for intriguing invariances in the duration and daily scheduling of practice activities. Further efforts to investigate training and development of training methods and to derive principles that generalize across domains should be particularly fruitful. Most important, a better understanding of social and other factors that motivate and sustain future expert performers at an optimal level of deliberate practice should have direct relevance to motivational problems in education, especially in our school system.

In conclusion, an analysis of the acquired characteristics and skills of expert performers as well as their developmental history and training methods will provide us with general insights into the structure and limits of human adaptations.

REFERENCES

Abernethy, B. (1991). Visual search strategies and decision-making in sport. *International Journal of Sport Psychology, 22,* 189-210.

Barlow, F. (1952). *Mental prodigies.* New York: Greenwood Press.

Barolsky, P. (1991). *Why Mona Lisa smiles and other tales by Vasari.* University Park: Pennsylvania State University Press.

Barolsky, P. (1992). *Giotto's father and the family of Vasari's Lives.* University Park: Pennsylvania State University Press.

Bar, A., & Feigenbaum, E. A. (Eds.). (1981-1982). *The handbook of artificial intelligence* (Vols. 1-2). Stanford, CA: HeurisTech Press.

Bate, J. (1989). Shakespeare and original genius. In P. Murray (Ed.), *Genius: The history of an idea* (pp. 76-97). Oxford: Basil Blackwell.

Biederman, I., & Shiffrar, M. M. (1987). Sexing day-old chicks: A case study and expert systems analysis of a difficult perceptual-learning task. *Journal of Experimental Psychology: Learning, Memory, and Cognition, 13,* 640-645.

Binet, A. (1894). *Psychologie des grands calculateurs et joueurs d'echecs* [Psychology of great mental calculators and chess players]. Paris: Libraire Hachette.

Bloom, B. S. (1985). Generalizations about talent development. In B. S. Bloom (Ed.), *Developing talent in young people* (pp. 507-549). New York: Ballantine Books.

Boase, T. S. R. (1979). *Giorgio Vasari: The man and the book.* Princeton, NJ: Princeton University Press.

Boshuizen, H. P. A., & Schmidt, H. G. (1992). On the role of biomedical knowledge in clinical reasoning by experts, intermediates, and novices. *Cognitive Science, 16,* 153-184.

Bosman, E. A. (1993). Age-related differences in motoric aspects of transcription typing skill. *Psychology and Aging, 8,* 87-102.

Browne, M. A., & Mahoney, M. J. (1984). Sport psychology. *Annual Review of Psychology, 35,* 605-625.

Bull, G. (1987). *A translation of Giorgio Vasari's* Lives of the artist (2 vols.). New York: Viking Penguin.

Camerer, C. F., & Johnson, E. J. (1991). The process–performance paradox in expert judgment: How can the experts know so much and predict so badly? In K. A. Ericsson & J. Smith (Eds.), *Toward a general theory of expertise: Prospects and limits* (pp. 195-217). Cambridge, England: Cambridge University Press.

Charness, N. (1981a). Search in chess: Age and skill differences. *Journal of Experimental Psychology: Human Perception and Performance, 7,* 467-476.

Charness, N. (1981b). Visual short-term memory and aging in chess players. *Journal of Gerontology, 36,* 615-619.

Charness, N. (1989). Expertise in chess and bridge. In D. Klahr & K. Kotovsky (Eds.), *Complex information processing: The impact of Herbert A. Simon* (pp. 183-208). Hillsdale, NJ: Erlbaum.

Charness, N. (1991). Expertise in chess: The balance between knowledge and search. In K. A. Ericsson & J. Smith (Eds.), *Toward a general theory of expertise: Prospects and limits* (pp. 39-63). Cambridge, England: Cambridge University Press.

Charness, N., & Bosman, E. A. (1990). Expertise and aging: Life in the lab. In T. H. Hess (Ed.), *Aging and cognition: Knowledge organization and utilization* (pp. 343-385). Amsterdam: Elsevier.

Charness, N., Clifton, J., & MacDonald, L. (1988). Case study of a musical mono-savant. In L. K. Obler & D. A. Fein (Eds.), *The exceptional brain: Neuropsychology of talent and special abilities* (pp. 277-293). New York: Guilford Press.

Chase, W. G., & Ericsson, K. A. (1982). Skill and working memory. In G. H. Bower (Ed.), *The psychology of learning and motivation* (Vol. 16, pp. 1-58). New York: Academic Press.

Chase, W. G., & Simon, H. A. (1973). The mind's eye in chess. In W. G. Chase (Ed.), *Visual information processing* (pp. 215-281). New York: Academic Press.

Chi, M. T. H., Glaser, R., & Farr, M. J. (Eds.), (1988). *The nature of expertise,* Hillsdale, NJ: Erlbaum.

Cohen, P. R., & Feigenbaum, E. A. (Eds.), (1982). *The handbook of artificial intelligence* (Vol. 3). Stanford, CA: HeurisTech Press.

Csikszentmihalyi, M. (1990). *Flow: The psychology of optimal experience.* New York: Harper & Row.

de Groot, A. (1978). *Thought and choice and chess.* The Hague: Mouton. (Original work published 1946.)

Doll, J., & Mayr, U. (1987). Intelligenz und Schachleistung—Eine untersuchung an Schachexperten [intelligence and achievement in chess: A study of chess masters]. *Psychologische Beiträge, 29,* 270-289.

Elo, A. E. (1965). Age changes in master chess performances. *Journal of Gerontology, 20,* 289-299.

Elo, A. E. (1986). *The rating of chessplayers, past and present* (2nd ed.). New York: Arco.

Ericsson, K. A. (1985). Memory skill. *Canadian Journal of Psychology, 39* (2), 188-231.

Ericsson, K. A. (1988). Analysis of memory of performance in terms of memory skill. In R. J. Sternberg (Ed.), *Advances in the psychology of human intelligence* (Vol. 4, pp. 137-179). Hillsdale, NJ: Erlbaum.

Ericsson, K. A. (1990). Peak performance and age: An examination of peak performance in sports. P. B. Baltes & M. M. Baltes (Eds.), *Successful aging: Perspectives from the behavioral sciences* (pp. 164-195). New York: Cambridge University Press.

Ericsson, K. A., & Chase, W. G. (1982). Exceptional memory. *American Scientist, 70,* 607-615.

Ericsson, K. A., & Faivre, I. A. (1988). What's exceptional about exceptional abilities? In I. K, Obler & D. Fein (Eds.), *The exceptional brain: Neuropsychology of talent and special abilities* (pp. 436-473). New York: Guilford Press.

Ericsson, K. A., & Harris, M. S. (1990, November). *Expert chess memory without chess knowledge: A training study.* Poster presented at the 31st Annual Meeting of the Psychonomic Society, New Orleans, LA.

Ericsson, K. A., & Kintsch, W. (1994). *Long-term working memory* (ICS Tech. Report No. 94-01). Boulder: University of Colorado, Institute of Cognitive Science.

Ericsson, K. A., Krampe, R. Th., & Heizmann, S. (1993). Can we create gifted people? In CIBA Foundation Symposium 178, *The origins and development of high ability* (pp. 222-249). Chichester, England: Wiley.

Ericsson, K. A., Krampe, R. Th., & Tesch-Römer, C. (1993). The role of deliberate practice in the acquisition of expert performance. *Psychological Review, 100.* 363-406.

Ericsson, K. A., & Simon, H. A. (1993). *Protocol analysis: Verbal reports as data* (rev. ed.). Cambridge, MA: MIT Press.

Ericsson, K. A., & Smith, J. (1991a). Prospects and limits of the empirical study of expertise: An introduction. In K. A. Ericsson & J. Smith (Eds.), *Toward a general theory of expertise: Prospects and limits* (pp. 1-39). Cambridge, England: Cambridge University Press.

Ericsson, K. A., & Smith, J. (Eds.). (1991b). *Toward a general theory of expertise: Prospects and limits.* Cambridge, England: Cambridge University Press.

Ericsson, K. A., & Staszewski, J. (1989). Skilled memory and expertise: Mechanisms of exceptional performance. In D. Klahr & K. Kotovsky (Eds.), *Complex information processing: The impact of Herbert A. Simon* (pp. 235-267). Hillsdale, NJ: Erlbaum.

Feldman, D. H. (1980). *Beyond universals in cognitive development.* Norwood, NJ: Ablex.

Feldman, D. H. (1986). *Nature's gambit: Child prodigies and the development of human potential.* New York: Basic Books.

Feng, J. (1984). Foreword. In L. Shufen & J. Cheng'an (Eds.), *Yani's monkeys* (pp. 1-2). Beijing, China: Foreign Languages Press.

Folkard, S., & Monk, T. H. (1985). Circadian performance rhythms. In S. Folkard & T. H. Monk (Eds.), *Hours of work* (pp. 37-52). Chichester, England: Wiley.

Forbes, C. (1992). *The Polgar sisters: Training or genius?* New York: Henry Holt.

Franklin, B. (1986). *The autobiography and other writings.* New York: Penguin Books. (Autobiography originally published 1788.)

Galton, F. (1979). *Hereditary genius: An inquiry into its laws and consequences.* London: Julian Friedman. (Original work published 1869.)

Galton, F. (1908). *Memories of my life.* London: Methuen.

Gardner, H. (1973). *The arts and human development.* New York: Wiley.

Gardner, H. (1983). *Frames of mind: The theory of multiple intelligences.* New York: Basic Books.

Gardner, H. (1993a). *Creating minds.* New York: Basic Books.

Gardner, H. (1993b). *Multiple intelligences: The theory in practice.* New York: Basic Books.

Groen, G. J., & Patel, V. L. (1988). The relationship between comprehension and reasoning in medical expertise. In M. T. H. Chi, R. Glaser, & M. J. Farr (Eds.), *The nature of expertise* (pp. 287-310). Hillsdale, NJ: Erlbaum.

Gruber, H. E. (1981). *Darwin on man: A psychological study of scientific creativity* (2nd ed.). Chicago: University of Chicago Press.

Ho,W.-C. (Ed.). (1989). *Yani:The brush of innocence.* New York: Hudson Hills.

Hoffman, R. R. (Ed.). (1992). *The psychology of expertise: Cognitive research and empirical AI.* New York: Springer-Verlag.

Howe, M. J. A. (1990). *The origins of exceptional abilities.* Oxford: Basil Blackwell.

Hulin, C. L., Henry, R. A., & Noon, S. L. (1990). Adding a dimension: Time as a factor in the generalizability of predictive relationships. *Psychological Bulletin, 107,* 328-340.

Hunt, E., & Agnoli, F. (1991). The Whorfian hypothesis: A cognitive psychology perspective. *Psychological Review, 98,* 377-389.

Juster, F. T., & Stafford, F. P. (Eds.). (1985). *Time, goods and well-being.* Ann Arbor: University of Michigan, Institute for Social Research.

Krampe, R. Th. (1994). *Maintaining excellence: Cognitive-motor performance in pianists differing in age and skill level.* Berlin: Edition Sigma.

Larkin, J. H., McDermott, J., Simon, D. P., & Simon, H. A. (1980). Models of competence in solving physics problems. *Cognitive Science, 4,* 317-345.

Lave, J. (1988). *Cognition in practice.* Cambridge, England: Cambridge University Press.

Lave, J., & Wenger, E. (1991). *Situated learning: Legitimate peripheral participation.* Cambridge, England: Cambridge University Press.

Lehman, H. C. (1953). *Age and achievement.* Princeton, NJ: Princeton University Press.

Levin, H., & Addis, A. B. (1979). *The eye-voice span.* Cambridge, MA: MIT Press.

Luria, A. R. (1968). *the mind of a mnemonist.* New York: Avon.

Malina, R. M., & Bouchard, C. (1991). *Growth, maturity, and physical activity.* Champaign, IL: Human Kinetics.

Maslow, A. H. (1971). *The farther reaches of human nature.* New York: Viking.

Miller, G. A. (1956). The magical number seven, plus or minus two: Some limits on our capacity for processing information. *Psychological Review, 63,* 81-97.

Murray, P. (Ed.). (1989a). *Genius:The history of an idea.* Oxford: Basil Blackwell.

Murray, P. (1989b). Poetic genius and its classic origins. In P. Murray (Ed.), *Genius:The history of an idea* (pp. 9-31). Oxford: Basil Blackwell.

Newell, A., & Simon, H. A. (1972). *Human problem solving.* Englewood Cliffs, NJ: Prentice-Hall.

Pariser, D. (1987). The juvenile drawings of Klee, Toulouse-Lautrec, and Picasso. *Visual Arts Research, 13,* 53-67.

Patel, V. L., & Groen, G. J. (1991). The general and specific nature of medical expertise: A critical look. In K. A. Ericsson & J. Smith (Eds.), *Toward a general theory of expertise* (pp. 93-125). Cambridge, England: Cambridge University Press.

Platt, R. (1966). General introduction. In J. E. Meade & A. S. Parkes (Eds.), *Genetic and environmental factors in human ability* (pp. ix-xi). Edinburgh: Oliver & Boyd.

Qin,Y., & Simon, H. A. (1990). Laboratory replication of scientific discovery process. *Cognitive Science, 14,* 281-312.

Radford, J. (1990). *Child prodigies and exceptional early achievers.* New York: Free Press.

Raskin, E. (1936). Comparison of scientific and literary ability: A biographical study of eminent scientists and letters of the 19th century. *Journal of Abnormal and Social Psychology, 31,* 20-35.

Regnier, G., Salmela, J., & Russell, S. J. (1993). Talent detection and development in sport. In R. N. Singer, M. Murphy, & L. K. Tennant (Eds.), *Handbook of research in sport psychology* (pp. 290-313). New York: Macmillan.

Roe, A. (1953). A psychological study of eminent psychologists and anthropologists, and a comparison with biological and physical scientists. *Psychological Monographs: General and Applied, 67* (whole No. 352), 1-55.

Roth, H. (1982). *Master violinist in performance.* Neptune City, NJ: Paganinia.

Salthouse, T. A. (1984). Effects of age and skill in typing. *Journal of Experimental Psychology: General, 13,* 345–371.

Salthouse, T. A. (1991a). Expertise as the circumvention of human processing limitations. In K. A. Ericsson & J. Smith (Eds.), *Toward a general theory of expertise: Prospects and limits* (pp. 286–300). Cambridge, England: Cambridge University Press.

Salthouse, T. A. (1991b). *Theoretical perspectives on cognitive aging.* Hillsdale, NJ: Erlbaum.

Sheinfeld, A. (1939). *You and heredity.* New York: Frederick A. Stokes.

Schmidt, H. G., & Boshuizen, H. P. A. (1993). On the origin of intermediate effects in clinical case recall. *Memory & Cognition, 21,* 338–351.

Schulz, R., & Curnow, C. (1988). Peak performance and age among superathletes: Track and field, swimming, baseball, tennis, and golf. *Journal of Gerontology: Psychological Sciences, 43,* 113–120.

Simon, H. A., & Chase, W. G. (1973). Skill in chess. *American Scientist, 61,* 394–403.

Simonton, D. K. (1984). *Genius, creativity, and leadership: Historiometric inquiries.* Cambridge, MA: Harvard University Press.

Simonton, D. K. (1988a). Age and outstanding achievement: What do we know after a century of research? *Psychological Bulletin, 104,* 251–267.

Simonton, D. K. (1988b). *Scientific genius: A psychology of science.* Cambridge, England: Cambridge University Press.

Sloboda, J. A. (1985). *The musical mind: the cognitive psychology of music.* Oxford: Oxford University Press.

Sloboda, J. A., Hermelin, B., & O'Connor, N. (1985). An exceptional musical memory. *Music Perception, 3,* 155–170.

Smith, S. B. (1983). *The great mental calculators.* New York: Columbia University Press.

Starkes, J. L., & Deakin, J. M. (1985). Perception in sport: A cognitive approach to skilled performance. In W. F. Straub & J. M. Williams (Eds.), *Cognitive sport psychology* (pp. 115–128). Lansing, NY: Sports Science Associates.

Suzuki, S. (1981). Every child can become rich in musical sense. In E. Hermann (Ed.), *Shinichi Suzuki: The man and his philosophy* (pp. 136–141). Athens, OH: Ability Development Associates. (Originally presented in 1963.)

Suzuki, S. (1981). Discovery of the law of ability and the principle of ability development: Proof that talent is not inborn. In E. Hermann (Ed.), *Shinichi Suzuki: The man and his philosophy* (pp. 233–246). Athens, OH: Ability Development Associates. (Originally presented in 1980.)

Takeuchi, A. H., & Hulse, S. H. (1993). Absolute pitch. *Psychological Bulletin, 113,* 345–361.

Thomas, A., & Chess, S. (1984). Genesis and evolution of behavioral disorders: From infancy to early adult life. *American Journal of Psychiatry, 141,* 1–9.

Treffert, D. A. (1989). *Extraordinary people: Understanding "idiot savants."* New York: Harper & Row.

Wallace, A. (1986). *The prodigy.* New York: Dutton.

Wallace, D. B., & Gruber, H. E. (Eds.). (1989). *Creative people at work.* New York: Oxford University Press.

Weisberg, R. W. (1986). *Creativity: Genius and other myths.* New York: Freeman.

Weisberg, R. W. (1993). *Creativity: Beyond the myth of genius.* New York: Freeman.

NOTES

1. The field of visual art my offer at least one recent exception (Feldman, 1986). The Chinese girl Yani produced some acclaimed paintings between the ages of three and six (Ho, 1989), but matters are complicated by the fact that these paintings were selected by her father (a

professional painter) from more than 4,000 paintings completed by Yani during this 3-year-old period (Feng. 1984).

2. In his recent book *Creating Minds,* Gardner (1993a) examined the lives of seven great innovators, such as Einstein, Picasso, Stravinsky, and Gandhi. Each was selected to exemplify outstanding achievements in one of seven different intelligences. Gardner's careful analysis reveals that the achievements of each individual required a long period of intense preparation and required the coincidence of many environmental factors. Striking evidence for traditional talent, such as prodigious achievements as a child, is notably absent, with the exception of Picasso. The best evidence for talent, according to Gardner, is their rapid progress once they made a commitment to a particular domain of expertise. These findings are not inconsistent with Gardner's views on talent because innovation and creation of new ideas are fundamentally different from high achievements in a domain due to talent. Gardner wrote, "in the case of a universally acclaimed prodigy, the prodigy's talents mesh perfectly with current structure of the domain and the current tastes of the field. Creativity, however, does not result from such perfect meshes" (pp. 40–41).

QUESTIONS FOR FURTHER THOUGHT

1. What do Ericsson and Charness believe is the role of innate talents in the acquisition of expertise?

2. How does deliberate practice differ from just plain old "practice"?

3. How are think-aloud protocols different from the introspective analyses of consciousness that were popular a century ago?

4. What are implications of Ericsson and Charness's views for developing skill at a profession?

5. How might someone who believes strongly in the importance of innate talents account for Ericsson and Charness's results?

7

LANGUAGE

CONSTRUCTING INFERENCES DURING NARRATIVE TEXT COMPREHENSION
Arthur Graesser, Murray Singer, and Tom Trabasso

LEXICAL ACCESS DURING SENTENCE COMPREHENSION: (RE)CONSIDERATION OF CONTEXT EFFECTS
David Swinney

Constructing Inferences During Narrative Text Comprehension

Arthur Graesser, Murray Singer, and Tom Trabasso

Introduction

The following sentence is from a newspaper account of a rescue at sea:

> A 300-pound man found floating in 54-degree waters off Long Island was saved by his fat, according to doctors.

The sentence appears to mean that the man's excessive fat saved him from hypothermia, the often lethal reduction in body temperature that accompanies immersion in cold water. The sentence does not state this fact explicitly, however; rather, the hypothermia-related account is based on an inference generated in part by the reference to the 54 degree temperature of the water. It is at least possible that the man was saved by his fat providing additional buoyancy to save him from drowning or by providing a large store of energy.

A subsequent sentence reveals the accuracy of the hypothermia-related explanation:

> Just as a whale or polar bear is shielded from the cold, this man's fat actually saved him from freezing to death.

Much of the meaning that people derive when reading or listening is based on inferences they themselves generate rather than on explicit statements. Graesser, Singer, and Trabasso provide a theory that accounts for inferences readers make when they read for meaning. Their theory assumes that readers actively construct a representation of the meaning of a text that (a) addresses the readers' goals, (b) coherently combines general and specific information, and (c) explains why events are mentioned in the text.

Text comprehension is a very complex process. The Graesser, Singer, and Trabasso article is an important one in cognitive psychology, because it proposes a plausible model of this process, marshals diverse kinds of past evidence to support the model, and provides additional new evidence that is consistent with the model but not with plausible alternative models.

———

Source: From Graesser, A. C., Singer, M., & Trabasso, T. (1994). Constructing inferences during narrative text comprehension. *Psychological Review, 101,* 371–395. Copyright © 1994 by the American Psychological Association. Reprinted with permission.

The authors describe a constructionist theory that accounts for the knowledge-based inferences that are constructed when readers comprehend narrative text. Readers potentially generate a rich variety of inferences when they construct a referential situation model of what the text is about. The proposed constructionist theory specifies that some, but not all, of this information is constructed under most conditions of comprehension. The distinctive assumptions of the constructionist theory embrace a principle of search (or effort) after meaning. *According to this principle, a reader attempts to construct a meaning representation that addresses the reader's goals, that is coherent at both local and global levels, and that explains why actions, events, and states are mentioned in the text. This study reviews empirical evidence that addresses this theory and contrasts it with alternative theoretical frameworks.* ∎

An adequate psychological theory of text comprehension should be able to account for the generation of inferences when readers construct a *situation model* of what a text is about. A situation model is a mental representation of the people, setting, actions, and events that are mentioned in explicit clauses or that are filled in inferentially by world knowledge (Bower, 1989; Garnham & Oakhill, in press; Glenberg, Meyer, & Lindem, 1987; Johnson-Laird, 1983; Kintsch, 1988; Morrow, Greenspan, & Bower, 1987; Singer, 1990; van Dijk & Kintsch, 1983). For example, suppose that an adult reads a novel. Several classes of knowledge-based inferences are potentially constructed during comprehension: The goals and plans that motivate characters' actions, characters' knowledge and beliefs, traits, emotions, the causes of events, properties of objects, spatial relationships among entities, expectations about future episodes in the plot, referents of nouns and pronouns, attitudes of the writer, emotional reactions of the reader, and so on. Some of these inferences are normally generated "on-line" (i.e., during the course of comprehension), whereas others are normally "off-line" (i.e., generated during a later retrieval task but not during comprehension). Researchers in cognitive psychology and discourse processing have attempted to identify and explain which classes of inferences are normally generated on-line (Balota, Flores d'Arcais, & Rayner, 1990; Graesser & Bower, 1990; Graesser & Kreuz, 1993; Kintsch, 1993; Magliano & Graesser, 1991; McKoon & Ratcliff, 1992; Singer, 1988, in press; Whitney, 1987).

In this article, we present a constructionist theory that makes decisive predictions about the classes of inferences that are constructed on-line during the comprehension of narrative text. One of the shortcomings of early constructionist theories (Anderson & Ortony, 1975; Bartlett, 1932; Bransford, Barclay, & Franks, 1972; Schmidt, 1982; Weimer & Palermo, 1974) is that they failed to make specific predictions about the inferences and meaning representations that are constructed during encoding. Because of this shortcoming, some researchers (e.g., McKoon & Ratcliff, 1992) have concluded that constructionist theories assume that a complete, lifelike cognitive representation is constructed and that virtually all classes of inferences are generated on-line. During the past decade, however, the research conducted by constructionist theorists has revealed that only a subset of inferences are on-line. The constructionist theory presented in the present article accommodates these empirical findings and thereby positions constructionism on more solid footing.

   The proposed constructionist theory embraces a principle that has a long history in experimental psychology and that distinguishes it from other contemporary psychological theories in discourse processing: *Search (or effort) after meaning* (Bartlett, 1932; Berlyne, 1949, 1960; Spiro, 1980; Stein & Trabasso, 1985). A more precise specification of this search-after-meaning principle has three critical assumptions:

1. *The reader goal assumption.* The reader constructs a meaning representation that addresses the reader's goals. These goals and meaning representations are normally pitched at deep levels of processing (e.g., semantics and the referential situation model) rather than at shallow levels (e.g., wording and syntax).

2. *The coherence assumption.* The reader attempts to construct a meaning representation that is coherent at both local and global levels. *Local coherence* refers to structures and processes that organize elements, constituents, and referents of adjacent clauses or short sequences of clauses. Global coherence is established when local chunks of information are organized and interrelated into higher order chunks.

3. *The explanation assumption.* The reader attempts to explain why actions, events, and states are mentioned in the text. These explanations involve naive theories of psychological and physical causality in an effort to achieve coherence in understanding.

Thus, readers attempt to construct a meaningful referential situation model that addresses the readers' goals, that is coherent, and that explains why actions, events, and states are mentioned in the text.

   Previous constructionist theories have either explicitly or implicitly adopted one or more of these assumptions. The proposed constructionist theory is distinctive because it explicitly adopts all three assumptions and it directly focuses on the problem of inference generation. Previous constructionist theories have been vague or indecisive in delimiting the classes of inferences that are generated on-line. This was not a salient objective for these theories in the past because there was very little research on inference generation two decades ago. Now that inference generation has received more attention in the fields of experimental psychology, cognitive science, and discourse processing, it is time to sort out what a constructionist theory would provide. The three assumptions of the search-after-meaning principle empower a constructionist framework to make decisive predictions about inference generation.

   A constructionist theory that embraces the search-after-meaning principle offers predictions that are not uniquely shared by alternative theoretical frameworks in the discourse-processing literature. By way of illustration, the proposed constructionist theory predicts that the following three classes of inferences are generated on-line under most processing conditions:

1. *Superordinate goals* of characters that motivate explicit actions in the text. For example, the superordinate goal of "getting revenge" motivates the action of a victim killing a villain; getting revenge explains why the victim kills the villain.

2. *Causal antecedents* that explain why an action, event, or state is explicitly mentioned in the text. For example, the event of a character becoming ill is explained by the causal antecedent "the character went bankrupt."

3. *Global thematic inferences* that integrate major chunks of the text or that convey the point of a message. For example, a story might be an instantiation of the virtue "practice what you preach."

In contrast, the theory predicts that readers do not normally construct inferences that forecast future episodes in the plot and inferences that track the spatial locations of objects within a spatial region.

According to the proposed constructionist theory, those inferences that are predicted to be generated on-line are not generated under all conditions of reading. Readers abandon such attempts at search after meaning under one or more of the following conditions: (a) if the reader is convinced that the text is "inconsiderate" (i.e., lacks global coherence and a message), (b) if the reader lacks the background knowledge that permits the establishment of explanations and global coherence, or (c) if the reader has goals that do not require the construction of a meaningful situation model (e.g., proofreading the text for spelling errors).

Our primary focus is on narrative text rather than on other discourse genres (such as expository, persuasive, and descriptive texts). This emphasis is nonarbitrary. Narrative text has a close correspondence to everyday experiences in contextually specific situations (Britton & Pelligrini, 1990; Bruner, 1986; Kintsch, 1980; Nelson, 1986; Schank, 1986). Both narrative texts and everyday experiences involve people performing actions in pursuit of goals, the occurrence of obstacles to goals, and emotional reactions to events. Knowledge about these actions, goals, events, and emotions are deeply embedded in our perceptual and social experience because it is adaptive to understand the actions and events in our social and physical environment. The inferencing mechanisms and world knowledge structures that are tapped during the comprehension of everyday experiences are also likely to be tapped during the comprehension of narratives; there is no justifiable reason to believe that readers would turn off these pervasive interpretive mechanisms during reading. Of course, this claim does not imply that there is a perfect overlap between the inferences generated during everyday experiences and the inferences generated during narrative comprehension. In particular, global thematic inferences may not be generated when we comprehend activities in the world because people coordinate multiple agendas in a complex, dynamic world.

In contrast to narrative text, expository text is decontextualized and is normally written to inform the reader about new concepts, generic truths, and technical material (Brewer, 1980; Bruner, 1986; Nystrand, 1986). The typical reader does not have extensive background knowledge about the topics in expository texts, so readers generate fewer inferences than they generate during the comprehension of narrative text (Britton & Gülgöz, 1991; Graesser, 1981). Narrative text is an important genre to study, given that we are interested in inference generation and the construction of referential situation models.

One major goal of this article is to present a constructionist theory that makes decisive predictions about the knowledge-based inferences that are generated on-line during narrative comprehension. These knowledge-based inferences are critical building blocks in the referential situation model that readers construct. It is beyond the scope of this article to dissect the vast number of shallow-level inferences that are needed to "flesh out" linguistic code and explicit propositional code. It is widely acknowledged that most of these shallow-level inferences are reliably generated on-line (Frazier & Flores d'Arcais, 1989; Perfetti, 1993; Swinney & Osterhout, 1990), perhaps automatically (McKoon & Ratcliff, 1992). Most of the uncertainty and controversy addresses the status of deeper knowledge-based inferences that presumably are generated during the construction of situation models. It is also beyond the scope of this article to discriminate between those inferences that are automatically versus strategically generated on-line. The distinction between automatic and strategic inferences was central to McKoon and Ratcliff's (1992) *minimalist hypothesis*, but it is not central to the proposed constructionist theory. Instead, the relevant contrast is between on-line and off-line inferences while readers *comprehend* text.

A greater appreciation of the constructionist theory is achieved when it is contrasted with alternative hypotheses, models, and theories. Therefore, in this article, we compare the predictions of the constructionist theory with the predictions of alternative theoretical frameworks: an explicit textbase position, a minimalist hypothesis, a current-state selection (CSS) strategy, a prediction–substantiation model, and a promiscuous inference generation position. The fact that these frameworks furnish different predictions about the on-line status of inferences supports the claim that the constructionist theory offers nontrivial predictions.

A second major goal of this article is to review the empirical evidence that tests the proposed constructionist theory and alternative theoretical frameworks. As it turns out, the fact that we are investigating knowledge-based inferences has some critical methodological consequences. In particular, a satisfactory empirical test of these models must ensure that the readers have adequate world knowledge to generate the inferences. We therefore advocate a *three-pronged method* (Magliano & Graesser, 1991; Suh & Trabasso, 1993; Trabasso & Suh, 1993) that coordinates (a) the collection of verbal protocols that expose candidate inferences, (b) the articulation of alternative theoretical frameworks concerning inference generation, and (c) the collection of time-based behavioral measures that test which inferences in (a) are actually generated on-line. The verbal protocols involve a think-aloud task or a question-answering task, while a normative group of subjects reads text, sentence by sentence. If an inference is exposed by these verbal protocols, then there is some assurance that the readers have adequate background knowledge to make the inference.

In this article, we do not articulate the constructionist theory to the point of covering all levels of language processing and of furnishing a detailed processing trace of the construction of inferences. In principle, the constructionist theory could be integrated with more comprehensive psychological models of text processing, such as Kintsch's construction–integration model (Kintsch, 1988), Just and Carpenter's READER model (1992), or Gernsbacher's structure-building framework (Gernsbacher, 1990). In principle, we also could present a detailed processing model that traces the construction of particular inferences on the basis of the text, relevant world knowledge structures, and the reader's goals (see Graesser & Clark, 1985, for one attempt). Although it is beyond the scope of this article to furnish this level of detail, the key components of a processing mechanism are described in sufficient detail to show how it narrows down the set of potential knowledge-based inferences.

COMPREHENSION AND KNOWLEDGE-BASED INFERENCES

It is important to clarify what we mean by "comprehension" and "knowledge-based inferences" because they are central ideas in the constructionist theory. As mentioned earlier, the constructionist theory is applicable only in cases when the reader attempts to comprehend the meaning of a text. All bets are off when, for example, the reader is merely proofreading the text for spelling errors or the reader is scanning the text for a particular word. As mentioned earlier, the constructionist theory makes predictions about those knowledge-based inferences that participate in the construction of a situation model. The distinctive properties of the theory are not pitched at the shallow-level inferences that are needed to construct syntactic code, propositional code, and the explicit textbase.

WHAT DOES IT MEAN TO COMPREHEND?

Comprehension has traditionally been one of the elusive, controversial constructs in cognitive science (Kintsch, 1980; Schank, 1986; Weizenbaum, 1976; Winograd & Flores, 1986). It is perhaps impossible to propose a definition that is complete and that would be accepted by all researchers in all disciplines. Everyone agrees that comprehension consists of the construction of multilevel representations of texts. Everyone agrees that comprehension improves when the reader has adequate background knowledge to assimilate the text, but what else exists or occurs when comprehension succeeds? How does a researcher determine whether a computer really understands a text or whether one person really understands another person?

Comprehension improves to the extent that the reader constructs more levels of representations and more inferences at each level. To illustrate some multiple levels of representation, consider the following short text.

> The truck driver saw the policeman hold up his hand. The truck driver's vehicle stopped, but a car rear-ended the truck driver.

The *textbase* level of representation would include a propositional description of the explicit text (Kintsch, 1992; Kintsch & van Dijk, 1978). For example, the first sentence would have the following propositional representation:

PROPOSITION 1: saw (truck driver, PROPOSITION 2)

PROPOSITION 2: hold-up (policeman, hand)

Each proposition has a predicate (i.e., verb, adjective, or connective) and one or more arguments (i.e., noun or embedded proposition). The textbase level would also connect the explicit sentences by argument overlap. The first sentence would be connected to the second sentence by the overlapping argument "truck driver."

The textbase provides a shallow representation of the explicit text but does not go the distance in capturing the deeper meaning of the text. Deeper meaning is achieved by computing a *referential* specification for each noun. For example, the car would rear-end the vehicle of the truck driver rather than the body of the truck driver. Deeper comprehension is achieved when the reader constructs *causes and motives* that explain why events and actions occurred. Readers would infer that an abrupt stop of the truck caused the car to rear-end the truck, even though the text never states that there was an abrupt stop. The reader would infer that the truck driver had the goal of stopping the truck and performed some intentional action to stop it, even though this was never explicitly stated. Deeper comprehension is achieved when the reader infers the *global message,* or *point,* of the text, such as "accidents occur even when people follow society's rules." However, this level of representation may be difficult to construct without the pragmatic context of the text, such as who wrote the text, why it was written, who read the text, and why it was read. Nevertheless, according to our definition of comprehension, readers attempt to construct representations at all of these levels.

A definition of comprehension is incomplete without a principled way of determining what content to elaborate at the various levels. The proposed constructionist theory was indeed developed to provide a more discriminating specification of content elaboration. Most readers would not normally construct a detailed description of the subplan that the truck driver executed to stop the truck (e.g., he moved his foot to the brake pedal, he pumped the brake, he calculated the distance between the truck and the policeman). These details would normally be omitted from the constructed representation. Yet it might be important to construct these details when the reader is an insurance agent trying to settle an insurance claim for the accident. Thus, the goals of the reader and the pragmatic context of the message must also be considered. It is widely acknowledged that it is not sufficient to build a theory of comprehension on the basis of the text alone.

Some researchers have enriched the definition of comprehension by adopting a "systemic" perspective that appeals to the notion of *harmony* (i.e., congruity, compatibility, and synchrony). One sense of harmony addresses the global coherence of the text; comprehension succeeds when there is harmony among explicit ideas within the text (Britton & Eisenhart, 1993). A second sense of harmony addresses the compatibility among the three major components of a communication system: the author, the text, and the reader (Britton & Gülgöz, 1991; Rosenblatt, 1978; Tierney & Shanahan, 1991). That is, comprehension succeeds to the extent that there is harmony among three representations: (a) the author's intended meaning of the text, (b) the explicit text, and (c) the reader's constructed meaning of the text. Writers compose the content and wording of text in service of their communication goals, whereas readers attempt to recover the writers' goals during comprehension. Comprehension breaks down to the extent that there is discord among the author's intended meaning, the explicit text, and the reader's constructed meaning. Inconsiderate text is incoherent and underspecified, so it fails to deliver a successful transmission of information from author to reader.

There are several important benefits when comprehension succeeds. The reader draws inferences that are relevant and correct. The reader asks good questions that tap potential knowledge gaps, anomalies, and contradictions. The reader's answers to questions are relevant, correct, and informative. The reader can paraphrase the message and generate good summaries. In fact, inference generation, question asking, question answering, paraphrasing, and summary generation have traditionally been the litmus tests of whether computers can understand text in the field of artificial intelligence (Kass, 1992; Lehnert, Dyer, Johnson, Young, & Harley, 1983; Schank & Abelson, 1977). When comprehension succeeds, the reader is able to detect whether an incoming statement in the text involves a contradiction, anomaly, or irrelevancy with respect to the earlier information (Glenberg, Wilkinson, & Epstein, 1982; Graesser & McMahen, 1993; Markman, 1979; Otero & Kintsch, 1992). However, sometimes comprehension does not succeed, and the reader settles for a simplistic, shallow representation of the text. A reader may have the illusion of successful comprehension even though the reader's simplistic representation fails to capture all of the explicit text and the depth of the material (Glenberg & Epstein, 1987; Weaver, 1990).

WHAT IS A KNOWLEDGE-BASED INFERENCE?

The purpose of this section is to delimit the classes of inferences that our constructionist theory addresses rather than to offer a complete and perfectly accurate taxonomy of inferences. Researchers in psycholinguistics and discourse processing have proposed several taxonomies of inferences (Clark, 1977; Graesser & Kreuz, 1993; Harris & Monaco, 1978; Kintsch, 1993; Magliano & Graesser, 1991; Nicholas & Trabasso, 1981; Reiger, 1975; Singer, 1988), but a consensus has hardly emerged.

Knowledge-based inferences are constructed when background knowledge structures in long-term memory (LTM) are activated, and a subset of this information is encoded in the meaning representation of the text. The meaning representation includes both the textbase and the referential situation model (Kintsch, 1988, 1992, 1993; Kintsch, Welsch, Schmalhofer, & Zimny, 1990; Schmalhofer & Glavanov, 1986; van Dijk & Kintsch, 1983). The background knowledge consists of specific and generic knowledge structures that are relevant to the text. The specific knowledge structures include memory representations of particular experiences, of other texts, and of previous excerpts within the same text. The generic knowledge structures include schemata (J. M. Mandler, 1984; Rumelhart & Ortony, 1977), scripts (Bower, Black, & Turner, 1979; Schank & Abelson, 1977), frames (Minsky, 1975), stereotypes (Wyer & Gordon, 1984), and other structured packets of generic knowledge. Most background knowledge structures are meaningful and contextually rich. That is, they are grounded in experience, with content organized by meaningful relations, for example, a script of eating at a restaurant. These rich structures furnish much of the content needed to interpret, explain, predict, and understand narrative events. However, other background knowledge structures are abstract and decontextualized, such as the schema for the rhetorical format of a fairy tale (J. M. Mandler, 1984; Stein & Glenn, 1979). Background knowledge structures (either specific or generic) are activated through pattern recognition processes by explicit content words, combinations of content words, and interpreted text constituents. When a background knowledge structure is very familiar and therefore overlearned, much of its content is automatically activated in working memory (WM) at very little cost to the processing resources in WM (Graesser & Clark, 1985; Kintsch, 1988, 1993).

When a knowledge-based inference is directly inherited or copied from a background knowledge structure, the process of incorporating it into the meaning representation of the text imposes small or intermediate costs to WM. However, sometimes a novel knowledge-based inference is constructed. A novel inference is a product of several incremental, cognitive cycles of searching memory and accumulating information from multiple information sources (Just & Carpenter, 1992). The precise mechanisms of constructing these novel knowledge-based inferences are not well understood, although several researchers have offered speculations (Graesser & Clark, 1985; Graesser & Zwaan, in press; Johnson-Laird, 1983; Schank & Abelson, 1977; Wilensky, 1983). These novel knowledge-based inferences are believed to place more burdens on WM. A potential inference has a lower likelihood of being generated online to the extent that its generation imposes greater demands on WM.

Examples of knowledge-based inferences are presented in the context of the following parable by Ambrose Bierce, entitled "How Leisure Came."

> A Man to Whom Time Was Money, and who was bolting his breakfast in order to catch a train, had leaned his newspaper against the sugar bowl and was reading as he ate. In his haste and abstraction, he stuck a pickle-fork into his right eye, and on removing the fork the eye came with it. In buying spectacles, the needless outlay for the right lens soon reduced him to poverty, and the Man to Whom Time Was Money had to sustain life by fishing from the end of the wharf.

Table 1 presents 13 classes of inferences and examples of these inferences in the context of this passage. These 13 classes are defined according to the content of the inference and its relation to the explicit text. These classes do not exhaust all of the potential inferences during comprehension, but they do provide an initial foundation for discussing the constructionist theory.

The order in which the inference classes are listed in Table 1 is not altogether arbitrary. Inference classes 1, 2, and 3 are needed to establish local coherence, whereas inference classes 3 and 4 are critical for establishing explanations. Classes 4, 5, and 6 are important for establishing global coherence. Classes 7 through 11 are elaborative inferences that are not needed for establishing coherent explanatory meaning representations. Classes 12 and 13 address the pragmatic communicative exchange between reader and author. The order of listing the inference classes is weakly correlated with the amount of attention that the inference classes have received in the psychological literature. Referential inferences (class 1) have received the most attention, whereas inferences about author intent and attitude (class 13) have received the least attention. The local inferences that are elicited by one or two sentences have received more attention than the global inferences. Inferences that are elicited from rich textual cues have received more attention than inferences that are remotely derived from the text by virtue of background knowledge structures.

The researchers' preferences in the selection of inferences to investigate can be attributed both to methodology and to theory. The most familiar and defensible research methods in experimental psychology carefully manipulate stimulus texts, so there is a preference for investigating local text-bound inferences. Early theories in psycholinguistics, text linguistics, and reading focused on inferences that were derived symbolically from explicit linguistic elements (Brady & Berwick, 1983; Brown & Yule, 1983; Katz & Fodor, 1963; Kempson, 1977). These inferences were derived by rules, meaning postulates, and compositional analyses that stripped away most of world knowledge. It is very tedious and difficult to specify the numerous knowledge structures associated with text, so theorists and empirical researchers have normally avoided a systematic analysis of world knowledge. Nevertheless, a mature theory of inference generation would need to analyze world knowledge in detail. Consequently, some researchers have pursued rather ambitious projects that map out the world knowledge structures that participate in text comprehension (Alterman, 1985; Dahlgren, 1988; Graesser & Clark, 1985; Mannes & Kintsch, 1991; Schank & Abelson, 1977). Clearly, it is important not to confuse the likelihood that a class of inferences is generated on-line and the amount of attention that the class of inferences has received in the scientific literature.

There is an important distinction between *text-connecting* inferences and *extra-textual* inferences (Graesser & Bower, 1990; Singer, & Ferreira, 1983; Trabasso & Suh, 1993). In the case of a text-connecting inference, the current clause being comprehended is related to a previous explicit statement in the text; the previous statement is reinstated (i.e., activated or reactivated) and is inferentially linked to the current clause. The referential inferences (class 1 in Table 1) are always text-connecting inferences. In the case of extratextual inferences, the inference is copied or derived from generic and specific knowledge structures that are relevant to the explicit text.

The taxonomy in Table 1 does not include some classes of inferences that normally are difficult to generate and are therefore off-line. First, there are logic-based inferences, which are derived from systems of domain-independent formal reasoning, such as propositional calculus, predicate calculus, and theorem proving (Newell & Simon, 1972; Rips, 1990). Second, there are quantitative inferences and statistical inferences that are products of complex formulae and mathematical procedures (Kahneman, Slovic, & Tversky, 1982). These inferences are usually a struggle to generate (Bruner, 1986; Graesser & Clark, 1985; Kintsch, 1993; Schank, 1986), as everyone who has attempted to solve analytical brain teasers and algebra word problems knows. Of course, this does not mean that these inferences are never generated during the comprehension of narrative text (Lea, O'Brien, Fisch, Noveck, & Braine, 1990).

For the convenience of communication, we consider whether each class of inferences is in one of two discrete states: on-line versus off-line. However, there undoubtedly is a probabilistic continuum between on-line and off-line. The continuum can be attributed to fluctuations in reader abilities, reader goals, text materials, samples of inferences, experimental tasks, and so on. The continuum can also be explained by the theoretical possibility that inferences are encoded to some degree rather than all-or-none (Gernsbacher, 1990; Kintsch, 1988; McKoon & Ratcliff, 1992; Sharkey & Sharkey, 1992). The degree to which an inference is encoded might be strengthened or attenuated as more information is received. Technically speaking, when we claim that a class of inferences is generated on-line, our intention is to convey that it has a substantially higher strength of encoding or higher likelihood of being generated than the contrast classes of inferences that are off-line. A full-blown theory would account for likelihood of generation, the strength of encoding, the time-course of generation, and the exact locus of generation (within the text) for each class of inference.

| TABLE 1 | | Inferences Relevant to "How Leisure Came" | |

TYPE OF INFERENCE	BRIEF DESCRIPTION	TEXT THAT ELICITS THE INFERENCE	INFERENCE
Class 1: Referential	A word or phrase is referentially tied to a previous element or constituent in the text (explicit or inferred).	". . . on removing the *fork* the eye came with *it*"	*Fork* is the referent for *it*.
Class 2: Case structure role assignment	An explicit noun phrase is assigned to a particular case structure role, e.g., agent, recipient, object, location, time.	"the man leaned his newspaper against the sugarbowl"	*Against the sugarbowl* is assigned to a location role.
Class 3: Causal antecedent	The inference is on a causal chain (bridge) between the current explicit action, event, or state and the previous passage context.	"In his haste and abstraction, he stuck a pickle fork into his right eye . . ."	The man was careless and mis-aimed his fork.
Class 4: Superordinate goal	The inference is a goal that motivates an agent's intentional action.	"A Man to Whom Time Was Money, and who was bolting his breakfast in order to catch a train . . ."	The man wanted to get to work and earn money.
Class 5: Thematic	This is a main point or moral of the text.	The entire passage	Haste makes waste.
Class 6: Character emotional reaction	The inference is an emotion experienced by a character, caused by or in response to an event or action.	". . . the needless outlay . . . reduced him to poverty"	The man became sad.
Class 7: Causal consequence	The inference is on a forecasted causal chain, including physical events and new plans of agents. These inferences do not include the character emotions in class 6.	". . . on removing the fork the eye came with it"	The man became blind in his right eye.
Class 8: Instantiation of noun category	The inference is a subcategory or a particular exemplar that instantiates an explicit noun or an implicit case role that is required by the verb.	". . . breakfast . . ."	Bacon and eggs

(Continued)

TABLE 1	Inferences Relevant to "How Leisure Came" *(Continued)*		
TYPE OF INFERENCE	**BRIEF DESCRIPTION**	**TEXT THAT ELICITS THE INFERENCE**	**INFERENCE**
Class 9: Instrument	The inference is an object, part of the body, or resource used when an agent executes an intentional action.	". . . the Man to Whom Time Was Money had to sustain life by fishing from the end of a wharf"	The man used a rod and reel (to fish).
Class 10: Subordinate goal–action	The inference is a goal, plan, or action that specifies how an agent's action is achieved.	". . . who was bolting his breakfast"	The man grasped his fork and moved it toward his mouth.
Class 11: State	The inference is an ongoing state, from the time frame of the text, that is not causally related to the story plot. The states include an agent's traits, knowledge, and beliefs; the properties of objects and concepts; and the spatial locations of entities.	". . . the Man to Whom Time Was Money had to sustain life by fishing from the end of a wharf"	Fishermen are poor; the city has a wharf.
Class 12: Emotion of reader	The inference is the emotion that the reader experiences when reading a text.	". . . on removing the fork the eye came with it"	The reader is disgusted.
Class 13: Author's intent	The inference is the author's attitude or motive in writing.	The entire passage	Bierce wants to lambaste workaholics.

A CONSTRUCTIONIST THEORY OF INFERENCE GENERATION

As discussed earlier, the proposed constructionist theory emphasizes Bartlett's (1932) principle of search (or effort) after meaning. This principle embraces the reader goal assumption, the coherence assumption, and the explanation assumption. We elaborate on these distinctive characteristics of the constructionist theory in this section. In addition to these distinctive characteristics, the theory adopts some components, assumptions, and predictions that are widely accepted by psychological researchers in discourse processing (Gernsbacher, 1990; Just & Carpenter, 1992; Kintsch, 1988; Sanford & Garrod, 1981; Singer, 1990; van Dijk & Kintsch, 1983). These uncontroversial assumptions are succinctly enumerated in this section before turning to the theory's distinctive characteristics.

Uncontroversial Components and Assumptions

1. *Information sources.* The three main information sources include the *text* (i.e., graphemes, phonemes, syntax, lexical items, propositions, and clauses), the relevant *background knowledge structures* (both specific and generic), and the *pragmatic context* of the message (i.e., the author, reader, setting, and purpose of the exchange).

2. *Levels of cognitive representation.* Following Kintsch and his colleagues (Kintsch, 1988, 1992; van Dijk & Kintsch, 1983), three levels of code are constructed as a result of comprehension: the *surface code* (i.e., the exact wording and syntax), the *textbase* (explicit text propositions plus inferences needed for text cohesion), and the *situation model.*

3. *Memory stores.* There are three memory stores: *short-term memory* (STM; which holds the most recent clause), *working memory* (WM; which holds approximately the last two sentences, plus information that is actively recycled in WM), and *long-term memory* (LTM). It should be noted that some models do not distinguish between STM and WM.

4. *Discourse focus.* Attention may be focused on any of the three levels of cognitive representation (see assumption 2). From the standpoint of the situation model, the discourse focus is analogous to a mental camera that scans across the scenario and zooms in on particular characters, actions, events, spatial regions, and hot spots (Bower, 1989).

5. *Convergence and constraint satisfaction.* Both the explicit information and inferences receive more strength of encoding to the extent that they are activated by several information sources (i.e., there is convergence), and they satisfy the conceptual constraints imposed by the various information sources (Golden & Rumelhart, 1991; Graesser & Clark, 1985; Kintsch, 1988; Mannes & Kintsch, 1991; Sharkey & Sharkey, 1992; St. John, 1991).

6. *Repetition and automaticity.* Repetition increases the speed of accessing knowledge structures and the elements within a knowledge structure. In the case of an automatized package of knowledge (e.g., a familiar generic knowledge structure), the content is wholistically accessed and activated at little cost to the processing resources in WM.

Distinctive Components and Assumptions of the Theory

The proposed constructionist theory embraces the search-after-meaning principle (Bartlett, 1932; Berlyne, 1949; Spiro, 1980; Stein & Trabasso, 1985). At a general level, this search-after-meaning principle asserts that comprehenders attempt to construct meaning out of text, social interactions, and perceptual input. The principle has three assumptions that empower the constructionist theory with distinctive predictions: (7) satisfaction of reader goals, (8) achievement of both local and global coherence, and (9) explanation of explicit information.

It is important to emphasize that the search-after-meaning principle is an effort, not necessarily an achievement. In most reading contexts, the fruits of these efforts are realized because writers–authors construct messages to be understood. However, there are conditions that prevent the reader from constructing a meaning representation that provides coherence, that explains the explicit text, and that satisfies the reader's goals. If the reader fails to devote any effort, then these inferences are not drawn. The inferences are not generated if the reader is given insufficient time for comprehension. A globally coherent message is not constructed if the text is choppy, incoherent, and pointless. An explanation may not be generated when there is a random sequence of events or a puzzling sequence of propositions that satisfy a researcher's counterbalancing constraints. Inferences are not constructed without the prerequisite background knowledge structures.

7. *Satisfaction of reader goals.* When readers comprehend a text, they are motivated by one or more goals. In some contexts, the goals are ill-defined and general. This is the case when an adult reads the morning newspaper to become informed about current events and when a person reads a novel to be entertained. The reader must understand the meaning of the text under these conditions. In other contexts, the reader's goals are specific. This is the case when a reader tries to determine whether it is a good time to invest some money in the stock market (while reading a newspaper) and when a reader tries to form a mental picture of what a character looks like (while reading a novel). According to the reader goal assumption, readers are persistent in their attempts to satisfy their goals and therefore will construct inferences that address these goals.

We distinguish among three levels of goal specificity: default, genre-based, and idiosyncratic. At the first, most undifferentiated, level, the reader's goal is to construct a meaningful situation model that is compatible with the text. This level is the least constrained and is regarded as the default level.

At the next level, there are goals associated with the genre of the text. Readers of fictive narrative have the goal of being entertained in some fashion (e.g., excited, enthralled, amused, or frightened), whereas readers of expository text have the goal of being informed about events and facts in the real world (Brewer, 1980; Kintsch, 1980; Pearson & Fielding, 1991; Zwaan, 1993). Brewer (1990) has contrasted four "discourse forms" that reflect different goals of reading text: to entertain, to persuade, to inform, and to have an aesthetic–literary impact. Zwaan's (1993) experiments on reading and memory have demonstrated that substantially different information is extracted from a text when it is called a *newspaper article* versus a *literary story.*

The final level of goal specificity involves idiosyncratic reader goals. These goals may lead the reader to construct virtually any type of code (i.e., surface or textbase versus situation model) and virtually any dimension of the situation model (e.g., spatiality, causality, plans, or traits of characters). An adequate account of idiosyncratic goals would need to incorporate a general theory of human motivation, which is quite outside the boundaries of our constructionist theory. The constructionist theory offers a priori predictions about inference generation in the context of default goals and genre-specific goals, whereas its predictions are ad hoc in the context of idiosyncratic goals. The ad hoc prediction is that inferences are generated if they are directly relevant to the idiosyncratic goals.

Reader goals must be carefully analyzed in the experiments conducted by researchers in discourse processing. The task demands constrain the goals that readers adopt and therefore the inferences that they construct. Readers may not generate deep inferences, for example, if the tests, materials, and tasks only require shallow processing. Unfortunately, this has been the case in a significant proportion of experiments on inference processing (see Magliano & Graesser, 1991). For example, suppose that an experiment is conducted in which the reader's task is to recognize whether character A or B is activated by a pronoun *she*. Suppose further that the words are presented very quickly (250 msec per word), and the reader is asked to recognize which of two words had been presented, as quickly as possible (namely, character A versus B after presenting *she*). Shallow processing is sufficient to complete this task because (a) the task merely involves the recognition of explicit text, (b) the material is quickly presented, (c) shallow processing is satisfactory for performance, and (d) the recognition test requires the discrimination of only two characters. The reader might adopt an artificial reading strategy that is similar to monitoring a list of unrelated items. The reader might be frustrated from having the normal comprehension goal of constructing a meaningful situation model. In contrast, a meaningful situation model would be constructed in a task that allows readers to read at their normal pace and that tests them on deep inferences relevant to the situation model.

8. *Local and global coherence.* The comprehender attempts to build a meaning representation that establishes local and global coherence among the events, actions, and states in the text. Once again, this does not mean that a coherent representation is necessarily achieved at all levels, however. If the reader believes that the text is not considerate and lacks global coherence, then the comprehender settles for local coherence. If the reader believes that the text lacks local coherence, then the reader regards the text as incoherent. Stated differently, the reader attempts to construct the most global meaning representation that can be managed on the basis of the text and the reader's background knowledge structures. A globally coherent cognitive representation is successfully achieved when the following conditions are met: (a) the textual features support global coherence, (b) the reader has the prerequisite background knowledge, and (c) the reader does not have a specific goal that prevents understanding of the material. When there is a breakdown in one or more of these conditions, the reader settles for local coherence or gives up trying to achieve any coherence at all.

Coherence is achieved to the extent that elements and constituents in a text are conceptually connected by virtue of background knowledge structures, the constructed situation model, linguistic features of the text, or all three. There is an imprecise but important distinction between local and global coherence. Local coherence is achieved when conceptual connections relate the content of adjacent text constituents (i.e., a phrase, proposition, or clause) or short sequences of constituents. For example, in the story "How Leisure Came," there is a causal connection between the "man's haste and abstraction" and the event "he stuck a pickle fork into his right eye."

Global coherence is achieved to the extent that most or all of the constituents can be linked together by one or more overarching themes. For example, the theme "haste makes waste" ties together most of the content of "How Leisure Came."

Features of the explicit text have a prominent role in the construction of local coherence (de Beaugrande, 1980; Halliday & Hasan, 1976; Kintsch & van Dijk, 1978; Mann & Thompson, 1986). In fact, the term *cohesion* is sometimes reserved for local connections that are based entirely or primarily on linguistic and textual features, as opposed to the situation model and background knowledge. Referential cohesion is established, for example, when an explicit noun in a sentence is connected referentially to a previous noun phrase or proposition in the text. Another example of cohesion is when a connective (e.g., *because, so, and, therefore*) explicitly links adjacent clauses with a particular type of conceptual relation.

Nevertheless, features of language and the explicit text do not go the distance in establishing local coherence. Sometimes readers need to infer the relations between constituents. The classes of inferences that are important for establishing a local coherence are referential inferences (class 1 in Table 1), case structure role assignments (class 2), and those causal antecedent inferences (class 3) that connect adjacent constituents. There is substantial evidence that the process of inferring these relations increases comprehension time (Bloom, Fletcher, van den Broek, Reitz, & Shapiro, 1990; Haberlandt & Bingham, 1978; Keenan, Baillet, & Brown, 1984; Myers, 1990; Myers, Shinjo, & Duffy, 1987; Singer, 1990).

The establishment of global coherence involves the organization of local chunks of information into higher order chunks. For example, a moral, main point, or theme of a text (class 5 in Table 1) organizes many of the events and episodes in narrative. A higher order chunk has its tentacles attached to constituents that span large stretches of text. As a consequence, readers sometimes need to link an incoming constituent to an excerpt much earlier in the text; the earlier excerpt is in LTM but no longer in WM. In these situations, reinstatement searches are executed to fetch the earlier text and to place it in WM. These reinstatement searches take additional processing time (Bloom et al., 1990; Dopkins, Klin, & Myers, 1993; Fletcher & Bloom, 1988; Kintsch & van Dijk, 1978; Singer, 1990, 1993; Suh & Trabasso, 1993; van den Broek & Lorch, 1993).

Detailed analyses of global coherence are available in several fields: text linguistics (Grimes, 1975; Halliday & Hasan, 1976), artificial intelligence (Dyer, 1983; Hobbs, 1979; Lehnert, 1981), education (Meyer, 1985), and cognitive psychology (J. M. Mandler, 1984; van Dijk & Kintsch, 1983). Some global structures are contextually specific and detailed, such as a script for eating at a restaurant (Schank & Abelson, 1977). Others are abstract frames. In one type of REVENGE structure, for example, characters A and B have a positive bond, character C harms B for unjustifiable reasons, and subsequently character A harms character C. Readers infer these global structures and thereby construct thematic inferences (class 5 in Table 1). Unfortunately, there have been very few empirical tests of whether these inferences are generated on-line (Seifert, McKoon, Abelson, & Ratcliff, 1986).

Although it is beyond the scope of this article to provide a detailed account of the representation and processing assumptions of the constructionist theory, it is worthwhile to point out briefly how coherence could be achieved computationally. Coherent representations have traditionally been expressed in a symbolic form and have been constructed by procedures that manipulate symbols (Dyer, 1983; Fletcher, 1986; Golden & Rumelhart, 1991; Graesser & Clark, 1985; Kintsch & van Dijk, 1978; Lehnert, 1981; Trabasso, van den Broek, & Suh, 1989; van Dijk & Kintsch, 1983). That is, the textbase, situation model, and background knowledge structures have consisted of structured packages of nodes (i.e., nouns, states, events, or goals) that are connected by relational arcs of different categories. The global structures have either been tree hierarchies or nonhierarchical networks. The process of constructing the coherent representations during comprehension has normally consisted of recursive transition networks or production systems (Allen, 1987; Anderson, 1983; Just & Carpenter, 1992).

More recently, researchers have adopted connectionist architectures for computing coherence (Britton & Eisenhart, 1993; Holyoak & Thagard, 1989; Kintsch, 1988; Read & Marcus-Newhall, 1993; Rumelhart & McClelland, 1986). In Kintsch's (1988) construction–integration model, for example, all N nodes in the total node space (involving the textbase, situation model, and background knowledge) are connected with one another in an $N \times N$ connectivity matrix. Each connection between two nodes is assigned a positive excitatory weight, a negative inhibitory weight, or a zero weight. As each constituent in the text is interpreted, the activation values of the nodes in the node space are modified by a spreading activation process through the node space, as stipulated by the connectivity matrix; a parallel constraint satisfaction process settles on activation values for the nodes by converging on the best compromise of the constraints imposed by positive, negative, and zero-weight connections. After the last clause in the text is comprehended, each of the N nodes has a final activation value. Those nodes that meet some criterion of activation are included in the final coherent meaning representation, whereas the other nodes are not included.

According to the constructionist theory, a computational model would need to be designed in a manner that ensures that readers make every effort to establish both local and global coherence. In Kintsch's construction–integration model, for example, there would need to be a special set of nodes in the node space and connections in the connectivity matrix that explicitly capture the coherence assumption. Similarly, the model would need to be augmented with a special set of nodes and connections that incorporate the reader goal assumption and the explanation assumption. In other words, the three distinctive assumptions of the constructionist theory do not naturally emerge from the version of the construction–integration model reported in Kintsch (1988).

9. *Explanation.* Comprehenders attempt to explain *why* episodes in the text occur and *why* the author explicitly mentions particular information in the message. Thus, comprehension is typically guided by why-questions rather than other types of questions (e.g., what-happens-next, how, where, or when). There is extensive evidence that causal explanations of actions, events, and states play a central role in our understanding of narrative (Black & Bower, 1980; Bloom et al., 1990; Bower et al., 1979; Fletcher, 1986; Graesser, 1981; Rumelhart, 1975; Schank, 1986; Singer, 1990; Trabasso & Sperry, 1985; Trabasso et al., 1989; van den Broek, 1990). The importance of causal explanations is also bolstered by theories outside of the discourse-processing arena. For example, it is compatible with theories of causal

attribution in social psychology (Hastie, 1983; Hilton, 1990; McLaughlin, 1990; Pennington & Hastie, 1986; Read, 1987; Read & Marcus-Newhall, 1993) and with theories of planning and mundane reasoning in artificial intelligence (Kuipers, 1985; Mooney, 1990; Schank, 1986).

Researchers have analyzed the information that is accessed when individuals answer why-questions (Graesser, 1981; Graesser & Clark, 1985; Graesser & Franklin, 1990; Graesser & Hemphill, 1991; Graesser, Lang, & Roberts, 1991; Graesser, Robertson, & Anderson, 1981; Lehnert, 1978; Schanks & Abelson, 1977). Explanations of why involuntary events occur include their causal antecedents and enabling states (class 3 in Table 1). The reasons why characters perform intentional actions include their superordinate goals (class 4) and the causal antecedents that trigger these goals (class 3). Regarding goals, superordinate goals are appropriate answers to why-questions but not subordinate goals and subplans. For example, consider the following question in the context of the "How Leisure Came" story: "Why did the man buy spectacles?" Appropriate answers to this why-question would include the superordinate goal "in order to improve his eyesight" but not the subordinate goal "in order to pay the doctor." Regarding causal chains, causal antecedents are appropriate answers to why-questions but not causal consequences. An appropriate answer to the example question would be the causal antecedent "because his right eye was damaged" but not the causal consequence "because he was reduced to poverty." Therefore, the claim that comprehension is guided by why-questions rather than other types of questions substantially narrows down the set of inferences that readers normally construct.

Comprehenders are particularly sensitive to actions and events in the world, rather than to constancies and ongoing states. This is because changes frequently convey new and interesting information: discrepancies from normal states in the world, violations of normative standards, danger, obstacles to an agent's goals, goal conflicts between agents, methods of repairing planning failures, emotions that are triggered by goal failures, and abnormal occurrences that have adaptive significance to the organism. The comprehender's attention is captured and explanations are sought when there is an abnormal deviation from the homeostatic balance in a physical, social, or psychological system (Berlyne, 1960; Cheng & Holyoak, 1985; Hart & Honore, 1985; Hilton, 1990; Lazarus, 1991; Mackie, 1980; G. Mandler, 1976). States become important only to the extent that they enable actions and events that dynamically unfold. It should be noted that the state inferences in Table 1 (class 11) do not include those states that enable actions and events.

Explicit actions and events are easy to explain when they are motivated or caused by a previous event, action, or state mentioned in the text. Explicit events and states are also easy to explain when they are very typical of the activated scripts and other background knowledge structures. For example, drinking a glass of wine is a very typical action in a BAR script. Such an action is stored in the generic script for BARS and in thousands of specific experiences involving bars. In contrast, the same voluntary action of drinking wine would be more difficult to explain if it could not be causally linked to the previous text and if it was not typical knowledge in the background knowledge structures (such as a person drinking wine in the context of a classroom). There is a coherence break when an incoming clause cannot be readily explained by prior text or by background knowledge structures. When these coherence breaks occur, the comprehender attempts to piece together an explanation from fragments of information in the activated information sources. It takes more time to explain these atypical actions and events (Bower et al., 1979; Hastie, 1983), but this atypical information is more distinctive and discriminable in memory than is the typical information (Bower et al., 1979; Graesser, Gordon, & Sawyer, 1979; Hastie, 1983). If the reader's attempt to explain an incoming clause fails, the reader may wait for the subsequent text to explain it (Stein & Trabasso, 1985).

A pragmatic level of explanation must also be considered when readers comprehend explicit actions, events, and states in the text. The reader considers why the author would bother mentioning the information conveyed in each explicit clause. Readers normally follow the Gricean postulate that whatever the author expresses is relevant and important (Grice, 1975; Roberts & Kreuz, 1993; Sperber & Wilson, 1986). When static information is presented at the beginning of the novel (e.g., a description of the protagonist's house), the author is presumably supplying a rich setting to anchor the story world. An explicit state might also be intended as a clue that ends up solving a mystery (e.g., there was a red stain on the shirt of a character).

A PROCESSING MODEL FOR THE CONSTRUCTIONIST THEORY

We present a processing model at this point to clarify what cognitive mechanisms would be involved in the production of inferences. The processing model would apply to situations where readers are attempting to comprehend considerate narrative text, without any idiosyncratic comprehension goals. We do not present a complete processing model. Instead, we briefly sketch a simple model that captures those inferences that are products of the explanation assumption and global coherence. These inferences are the most distinctive in the sense that they are not predicted to be generated by a number of alternative models of inference generation. Our processing model could be expanded to accommodate idiosyncratic reader goals and the establishment of local coherence; however, the resulting inferences would be generated by most theoretical frameworks and therefore are not particularly controversial.

Our processing model is built on the computational platform of Just and Carpenter's READER model (1992). There is a set of production rules that scan and operate on the contents of WM at each comprehension cycle, as text is comprehended online. The grain size of the comprehension cycle is defined as an explicit action, event, goal, or state in the discourse focus. A production rule has an "IF (condition, cognitive processes)" composition. If the specified conditions are met, then the cognitive processes are executed; if the conditions are not met, then the processes are not executed. All of the production rules are evaluated and executed in parallel, as is assumed in the READER model. The production rules are "soft" rules rather than "hard," brittle rules. That is, a condition is satisfied when there is a configuration of WM content that meets or exceeds some activation threshold; when cognitive processes are executed, the activation values of WM content are modified.

The READER model assumes that there is a limited supply of processing resources in WM. For the present purposes, it is not necessary to declare the precise upper bound in the capacity limitations. However, a few points need to be made about the amount of resources that are consumed by particular cognitive processes. According to the model, the process of accessing and utilizing generic information sources places very little demand on WM because this information is overlearned and automatized (see assumption 6). Access to generic information in LTM is very quick and executed in a parallel, rather than a serial, fashion. Access to specific information sources in LTM is accomplished more slowly (in parallel); the utilization of content within a specific information source is comparatively time consuming, at times in a serial fashion, and places more demands on WM. Therefore, it takes a noticeable amount of time to reinstate information that appeared much earlier in the text being read, after the information exits WM. Comprehension processes, including inference generation, slow down to the extent that the demands on WM approach the upper bound of capacity limitations. When the demands on WM exceed the upper bound, there is a catastrophic deterioration of comprehension, and few inferences are constructed. It should be noted, once again, that these assumptions are compatible with the basic processing mechanism of Just and Carpenter's (1992) READER model.

In Table 2, we present six production rules that implement the explanation assumption and the global coherence assumption. For each rule, there is a specification of the condition element, a succinct description of the cognitive processes, and an elaborated description of these processes. The condition element for rules A, B, C, and D declares the type of statement in the discourse focus (i.e., action, goal or state versus event) that "fires" the production rule. For rules E and F, the rule is fired when particular content in WM has an activation level that reaches some threshold. When a production rule is fired, various cognitive processes are executed: (a) searching for information sources in LTM and WM, (b) searching for information within information sources, (c) increasing the activation value of content in WM, and (d) verifying whether potential inferences are compatible with constraints of the WM content that is highly active. All six production rules are evaluated and possibly fired at each comprehension cycle, as text is comprehended on-line, statement by statement.

Production rules A, B, C, and F handle the explanation-based inferences. These inferences are needed to explain *why* characters perform actions, *why* events occur, and *why* information is explicitly stated in the text. Production rule A generates superordinate goals (i.e., motives) of character actions and goals. Production rule B generates causal antecedents of actions, goals, and events. Production rule C generates inferences that explain why statements are explicitly mentioned in the text. According to production rule F, these inferences are encoded in the situation model if their activation values meet some threshold.

All six production rules are needed to establish global coherence. According to production rule E, global plot structures are activated when WM contains a particular configuration of actions, goals, events, states, and emotions. Some of this WM content was established by explicit text and some by inferences: goal inferences through rule A, action/event/state inferences through rule B, and emotional reactions of characters through rule D. A global structure is constructed in the situation model if its activation value meets some threshold. Production rule C generates genre schemata, such as a schema for a mystery story, or a schema for a joke. Once again, a genre schema ends up being encoded if its activation value in WM manages to meet some threshold.

TABLE 2   Production Rules of the Constructionist Theory That Model the Process of Explanation and Establishing Global Coherence

PRODUCTION RULE	CONDITION	SUCCINCT DESCRIPTION OF COGNITIVE PROCESSES	ELABORATED DESCRIPTION OF COGNITIVE PROCESSES
A	Explicit statement in the discourse focus is an intentional action (A) or goal (G) of a character.	Explain why the character performed action A or has goal G.	1. Search information sources in WM and LTM for plausible superordinate goals of A or G. 2. Increase the activation of superordinate goals in WM to the extent that (a) they are in multiple information sources and (b) they are compatible with the constraints of WM content that meet some threshold of activation.
B	Explicit statement in the discourse focus is an intentional action (A), a goal (G), or an event (E).	Explain why the character performed action A, why the character has goal G, or why event E occurred.	1. Search information sources in WM and LTM for plausible causal antecedents of A, G, or E. 2. Increase the activation of the causal antecedents in WM to the extent that (a) they are in multiple information sources and (b) they are compatible with the constraints of WM content that meet some threshold of activation.
C	Any explicit statement (S) in the discourse focus.	Explain why the writer mentions S.	1. Search text genre schemas in LTM that would accommodate S. 2. Increase the activation of the genre schema to the extent that it is compatible with the constraints of S and with WM content that meets some threshold of activation.
D	Explicit statement in the discourse focus is an intentional action (A) or an event (E).	Track the emotional reactions of characters.	1. Search information sources in WM and LTM for salient emotional reactions of characters to A or E. 2. Increase the activation of the emotional reactions in WM to the extent that (a) they are in multiple information sources and (b) they are compatible with the constraints of WM content that meet some threshold of activation.

(Continued)

TABLE 2	Production Rules of the Constructionist Theory That Model the Process of Explanation and Establishing Global Coherence *(Continued)*

PRODUCTION RULE	CONDITION	SUCCINCT DESCRIPTION OF COGNITIVE PROCESSES	ELABORATED DESCRIPTION OF COGNITIVE PROCESSES
E	WM contains a particular configuration (C) of goals, actions, events, emotions, and/or states that meet some threshold of activation.	Create global structures.	1. Search for information sources in LTM that match configuration C. 2. Increase the activation of the information source in WM to the extent that it is compatible with the constraints of WM content that meet some activation threshold.
F	An implicit statement or structure in WM meets some activation threshold.	Construct inferences that receive high activation in WM.	The implicit statement or structure is constructed as an inference in the situation model.

Note. WM = working memory; LTM = long-term memory.

The six production rules implement the reader's active comprehension strategies when reading narrative text. As we discuss later, other models of inference generation do not postulate this ensemble of production rules. For example, McKoon and Ratcliff's (1992) minimalist hypothesis does not highlight these classes of inferences as being important for text comprehension. Except for the causal antecedent inferences, all elaborative inferences have an equivalent status in the minimalist hypothesis, namely that they are not consistently made during comprehension. If we were to implement the minimalist hypothesis in the form of a production system model, then the only production rules would be B and F. However, even rule B would need to be modified because the minimalist hypothesis states that a causal antecedent inference is made only under two conditions: (a) when the inference establishes local text coherence or (b) when there is a break in local text coherence that prompts a strategic search for causal antecedents (in the prior text or other information sources). The condition element of the production rules would need to be tuned to these discriminations. Unlike the minimalist hypothesis, the constructionist model always searches generic and specific information sources for causal antecedents of explicit events, actions, and goals; the search occurs regardless of whether or not there is a break in local text coherence. In summary, alternative models of inference generation would not have exactly the same set of production rules and the condition elements would not be tuned in exactly the same way. In a subsequent section, we examine assumptions and predictions of some alternative models.

PREDICTIONS OF THE CONSTRUCTIONIST THEORY

The constructionist theory makes distinctive predictions about which classes of inferences are likely to be generated on-line during the comprehension of narrative text. As discussed earlier, there undoubtedly is a continuum between on-line and off-line, but we assume a discrete demarcation for ease of communication.

In many contexts, readers have a general goal of reading a coherent text for understanding or for entertainment (rather than an idiosyncratic goal). The default or genre-based level of goal specificity would apply, as discussed earlier, and the predictions of the constructionist theory are clear-cut. The theory predicts that the following classes of inferences are generated on-line: referential (class 1), case structure role assignment (class 2), causal antecedent (class 3), superordinate goal (class 4), thematic (class 5), and character's emotion reaction (class 6). The referential, case structure, and causal antecedent inferences (classes 1, 2, and 3) are needed to establish local coherence in the text. The inferences that assign case structure roles to explicit noun phrases and prepositional phrases establish local coherence within a clause. The referential inferences and causal antecedent inferences are prevalent when establishing local coherence between clauses. The causal antecedent and superordinate goal inferences (classes 3 and 4, respectively) are needed to explain why involuntary events occur and why characters perform intentional actions. Thematic inferences (class 5) are generated during the establishment of global coherence. The emotional reactions of characters (class 6) and the superordinate goals (class 4) also play a prominent role in global plot configurations of stories (Dyer, 1983; Lehnert, 1981; Stein & Levine, 1991) and are therefore needed for the establishment of global coherence. Interesting story plots involve goal conflicts and salient emotional reactions of characters to episodes in the story world.

The constructionist theory predicts that several classes of "elaborative" inferences in Table 1 are not normally generated on-line: causal consequences (class 7), instantiations of noun categories (class 8), instruments (class 9), subordinate goals/actions (class 10), and states (class 11). These inferences are not needed to construct a coherent explanation of the explicit content in the narrative, so they have a lower likelihood of being generated on-line.

An elaborative inference in one of the above five classes might be constructed on-line by virtue of convergence and constraint satisfaction (see assumption 5). This occurs when an inference receives a high strength of activation from multiple information sources, and it satisfies the constraints from multiple information sources. It is important to point out that there are theoretical and empirical criteria for identifying these elaborative inferences that are products of convergence and constraint satisfaction (Graesser & Clark, 1985; Kintsch, 1988; Mannes & Kintsch, 1991). Therefore, the predictions of the constructionist theory remain tractable.

As a case in point, causal consequence inferences are normally not constructed on-line according to the constructionist theory. That is, readers do not forecast a hypothetical plot that involves new plans of agents and long event chains into the future. According to the constructionist theory, the only causal consequences that are generated on-line are (a) superordinate goals of existing plans that may end up being achieved in the future plot (class 4 inferences), (b) emotional reactions of characters to events and actions (class 6 inferences), and (c) causal consequences that have a high strength of encoding by virtue of assumption 5. Researchers have frequently proposed that causal consequences are not made on-line because there are too many alternative hypothetical plots that could potentially be forecasted, because most of these alternatives would end up being erroneous when the full story is known, or because it takes a large amount of cognitive resources to forecast a single hypothetical plot (Graesser & Clark, 1985; Johnson-Laird, 1983; Kintsch, 1988; Potts, Keenan, & Golding, 1988; Reiger, 1975). However, a causal consequence inference is likely to be generated on-line if it is highly constrained by context and there are few if any alternative consequences that would be likely to occur (Keefe & McDaniel, 1993; McKoon & Ratcliff, 1986; Murray, Klin, & Myers, 1991; van den Broek, 1990).

In some contexts, readers are motivated by idiosyncratic goals. They are predicted to generate those classes of inferences that are directly relevant to the idiosyncratic goals. For example, if their goal is to gain a vivid mental picture of the spatial setting and to track the location of objects, then spatial state inferences (class 11 in Table 1) would be constructed on-line even though it is time consuming to generate such inferences (Morrow et al., 1987; Morrow, Bower, & Greenspan, 1989; Perrig & Kintsch, 1985). However, spatial inferences are not normally generated on-line when readers read naturalistic stories for understanding and entertainment (Zwaan & Van Oostendorp, 1993). In some contexts, the reader's idiosyncratic goals are pitched at a shallow level of comprehension, such as proofreading a manuscript for spelling errors or performing in an experimental task that involves word recognition. In such cases, the reader would not construct a meaningful situation model, and virtually none of the inferences in Table 1 would be generated on-line. Therefore, there is not an invariant set of on-line inferences when considering all of the reader goals that potentially motivate reading. However, there are clear-cut predictions when the reader goals are pitched at a default level or a genre-based level of goal specificity.

The status of author intent or attitude (class 13) is uncharted at this point of inference research. There has been very little theoretical discussion of the psychological impact of author intent and attitude (Hunt & Vipond, 1986; Rosenblatt, 1978) and no empirical research investigating on-line processing. From one perspective, the reader is expected to generate inferences about author intent and attitude because it explains why the author expresses particular clauses in the text and why the author wrote the text. From another perspective, however, there are several reasons for being pessimistic about the likelihood of generating these inferences on-line. There rarely is a rich pragmatic context that anchors communication between the author and reader of a story, so there is very little information to support such inferences. In fact, the author of a text is normally invisible to the reader. There are cases in which there is a rich pragmatic context, for example, a letter to a friend or a politician writing a story to be read by a constituency; in these cases, readers are predicted to generate inferences and explanations about author intent and attitude on-line. A second reason to be pessimistic is that the reader may fail to achieve a globally coherent interpretation of the text per se; establishing a globally coherent message is presumably a prerequisite or corequisite of computing author intent and attitude. There is yet a third reason to be pessimistic. People do not normally construct author intent and attitude when they observe events and actions in the everyday world, so this cognitive skill is not overlearned through everyday experience.

The status of reader emotions (class 12) is also uncharted. In one sense, reader emotions are reactions of the reader to the text rather than inferences per se. The reader experiences suspense, surprise, fear, curiosity, amusement, and other emotions while reading episodes in the narrative (Brewer & Ohtsuka, 1988; Graesser, Long, & Mio, 1990; Jose & Brewer, 1984). The reader may identify with a character and empathetically experience some semblance of the character's emotions. These reader reactions do not refer directly to the situation model depicted in the story plot, so they are not really knowledge-based inferences. In another sense, however, they are inferences that refer to the pragmatic context of the author–message–reader system. Authors write texts to elicit particular reader emotions, readers have these emotions, and readers cognitively acknowledge (consciously or unconsciously) that they are experiencing these manipulated emotions. Readers may experience the appropriate emotion during an episode, with elevated physiological arousal, in a manner carefully crafted by the author (Beach & Brown, 1987). Alternatively, readers may cognitively infer that they should be having a particular emotion during a particular episode, even though they are not physiologically aroused or in the mind-set of experiencing the appropriate emotion. When a reader reads a story for a second or third time, the reader may cognitively infer that an episode is surprising or suspenseful even though the entire story is known and there is no uncertainty about the plot (Gerrig, 1989). Clearly, the phenomenon of reader emotion is complex. For this reason, the constructionist theory does not offer a decisive prediction about its processing status (i.e., on-line versus off-line).

In summary, the constructionist theory predicts that six classes of inferences are normally generated on-line (1, 2, 3, 4, 5, and 6) and five classes are off-line (7, 8, 9, 10, and 11). These predictions prevail when reading narrative under the default and genre-based reading goals. All things being equal, there should be a higher strength of encoding for the first six classes than for the second five classes. A decisive prediction is not offered for inferences referring to reader emotion (class 12) and to author intent and attitude (class 13).

• • •

EMPIRICAL EVIDENCE FOR THE CONSTRUCTIONIST THEORY

There have been some lively debates over the proper measures and experimental designs that test whether or not a class of inferences is generated on-line (Graesser & Bower, 1990; Keenan, Golding, Potts, Jennings, & Aman, 1990; Magliano & Graesser, 1991; McKoon & Ratcliff, 1989, 1990; Potts et al., 1988; Singer, 1988). However, in this article, we do not dissect the methodological problems with each of the existing measures and tasks. There does not appear to be a perfect measure and task; there are merely trade-offs, each with some benefits and some shortcomings. The evidence presented in this section is based on empirical studies that have minimal methodological problems. An ideal dependent measure would tap processes that occur during the course of comprehension rather than reconstructive processes well after comprehension is completed; this eliminates recall and summarization tasks in which data are collected after a reader finishes comprehending a text. An ideal dependent measure would track the time-course of various cognitive processes by charting response times. Such measures include self-paced reading times for text segments (e.g., words, clauses, and sentences), gaze durations on words in eye-tracking studies, lexical-decision latencies on test words (i.e., whether a test string is a word or a nonword), naming latencies on test words, latencies to verify whether a test statement is true or false, latencies to decide whether a test segment had been presented earlier (i.e., recognition memory), or speeded recognition judgments under a deadline procedure. Moreover, an ideal experimental design would eliminate or control extraneous variables.

To test whether knowledge-based inferences are generated on-line, it is critical to demonstrate that subjects have a sufficient knowledge base and sufficient information sources to produce the inferences. It would be pointless to test whether readers generate an inference if they do not have the prerequisite world knowledge or if an inference test item (i.e., a word or statement) fails to match any cognitive representation that a reader could manage to construct. There is one, very critical, methodological implication of this note of caution: Experimenters should not generate their own inference test items and assume that the subjects are actually making these inferences, particularly if the experimenter ends up concluding that the inference class is not generated on-line. The experimenter must validate that the inferences could be generated by the designated reader population if the readers had sufficient time to do so.

In light of the above cautionary note, researchers have sometimes collected verbal protocols from readers during comprehension to validate that the readers could potentially generate the inferences under investigation. These verbal protocols are collected while the reader comprehends the text sentence by sentence or clause by clause. In think-aloud tasks, the readers express whatever comes to mind as each explicit clause is comprehended (Beach & Brown, 1987; Daly, Weber, Vargelisti, Maxwell, & Neel, 1989; Ericsson, 1988; Ericsson & Simon, 1980; Fletcher, 1986; Olson, Duffy, & Mack, 1984; Suh & Trabasso, 1993; Trabasso & Suh, 1993). In question-answering tasks, the readers answer particular questions about each clause, such as why, how, and what-happens-next (Graesser, 1981; Graesser & Clark, 1985). In question-asking tasks, the reader asks questions that come to mind about each sentence (Collins, Brown, & Larkin, 1980; Olson, Duffy, & Mack, 1985). These verbal protocols expose potential knowledge-based inferences. The researcher has some assurance that the inference could be made, that the reader population has the prerequisite world knowledge, and that the inference is expressible in language. The researcher can measure the proportion of subjects who produce the inference at particular points in the text that elicit the inference.

Of course, the fact that an inference is expressed in verbal protocols does not imply that the inferences are normally generated on-line. It is possible that readers adopt unnatural reading strategies when producing the verbal protocols (Nisbett & Wilson, 1977). Therefore, it is necessary to test the on-line status of candidate inferences by collecting appropriate measures from a separate group of readers who do not supply verbal protocols. Such measures include sentence reading times, gaze durations on words, lexical-decision latencies or naming latencies on test items in a secondary task, latencies in making recognition memory judgments on words or sentences, and so on. Researchers have satisfactorily demonstrated that particular classes of inferences exposed by verbal protocols do in fact predict these on-line temporal measures collected from a different group of readers (Graesser, Haberlandt, & Koizumi, 1987; Long, Golding, & Graesser, 1992; Long & Golding, 1993; Magliano, Baggett, Johnson, & Graesser, 1993; Millis, Morgan, & Graesser, 1990; Olson et al., 1984; Sharkey & Sharkey, 1992; Suh & Trabasso, 1993). These studies have shown that some, but not all, classes of inferences from the verbal protocols are generated on-line. Therefore, theories of inference generation can be tested by coordinating verbal protocol analyses and on-line temporal measures, as we illustrate later. Magliano and Graesser (1991) have advocated the implementation of a three-pronged method that coordinates (a) the collection of verbal protocols to expose potential inferences, (b) theories of discourse processing that make distinctive predictions about which classes of inferences are generated on-line, and (c) the collection of on-line temporal measures to assess whether a class of inferences is actually made on-line.

At this stage of development, most investigations of inference generation have not used the three-pronged method. It takes considerable effort to collect and analyze the verbal protocols, so most researchers have resisted the temptation to pursue the methodology. However, we believe that the most compelling evidence involves the collection of these protocols to ensure that readers have sufficient knowledge to make these inferences. Once we are satisfied that the readers can make these inferences under unlimited time constraints, we can then collect time-based behavioral measures to investigate the time-course of generating these inferences.

This section has three parts. In the first subsection, we review empirical tests of inference processing in studies that used time-based behavioral measures to tap on-line processing but did not adopt the three-pronged method. The focus is on inference classes 1 through 4 and 6 through 11 because there are essentially no adequate empirical tests of classes 5, 12, and 13. In the second subsection, we report a study that adopted the three-pronged method to investigate text-connecting inferences during narrative comprehension. As mentioned earlier, these inferences specify how explicit clauses in the text are connected conceptually. In the third subsection, we report studies that used the three-pronged method to investigate extratextual inferences during narrative comprehension. As reported below, the available evidence supports the constructionist theory to a greater extent than the alternative theoretical positions presented in the previous section.

EVIDENCE FROM STUDIES THAT DO NOT USE THE THREE-PRONGED METHOD

The constructionist theory predicts that the following five inference classes are generated on-line (under normal comprehension conditions in which the reader is not tuned to generate a particular class of inferences): referential inferences, case structure role assignments, causal antecedents, characters' emotional reactions, and superordinate goals. In fact, there is empirical support for these predictions in studies that have used the time-based behavioral measures described above. Support has accrued in the case of referential inferences (Bever & McElree, 1988; Dell, McKoon, & Ratcliff, 1983; Duffy & Rayner, 1990; Gernsbacher, 1990; McKoon & Ratcliff, 1992; O'Brien, Duffy, & Myers, 1986; Sanford & Garrod, 1981), case role assignments (Frazier & Flores d'Arcais, 1989; Just & Carpenter, 1980; Swinney & Osterhout, 1990), causal antecedents (Bloom et al., 1990; Fletcher & Bloom, 1988; McKoon & Ratcliff, 1986, 1989; Myers et al., 1987; Potts et al., 1988; Singer, Halldorson, Lear, & Andrusiak, 1992; van den Broek & Lorch, 1993), superordinate goals (Dopkins et al., 1993), and characters' emotional reactions (Gernsbacher, Goldsmith, & Robertson, 1992).

· · ·

A STUDY OF TEXT-CONNECTING INFERENCES USING THE THREE-PRONGED APPROACH

Suh and Trabasso (1993) have used the three-pronged method to investigate text-connecting inferences during the comprehension of more lengthy narrative texts. A discourse model predicted the points in the text where particular text-connecting inferences would be constructed on-line. Specifically, they were interested in the process of reinstating superordinate goals that were explicitly mentioned earlier in the text. Think-aloud protocols were collected from a group of subjects while they comprehended the stories, sentence by sentence. The content extracted from these verbal protocols confirmed the predicted text-connecting inferences of the discourse model; that is, superordinate goals were reinstated by explicit clauses at predictable text locations. A separate group of readers provided recognition test decisions and latencies for test statements at different points in the text (instead of providing verbal protocols). The patterns of recognition decisions and latencies confirmed the model's predictions regarding the locations in the text where the superordinate goals are reinstated.

In Table 3, we present two versions of an example story that was investigated by these researchers (Suh & Trabasso, 1993; Trabasso & Suh, 1993). In the hierarchical version, Jimmy has a main (superordinate) goal of wanting to buy a bike. Jimmy tries to get his mother to buy the bike, but this strategy fails because she refuses. Later on in the story, after the main goal is presumably no longer in WM, Jimmy tries a second approach to getting the bike by asking for a job, earning money, and purchasing the bike by himself. Many of the actions in the second half of the hierarchical story should reinstate Jimmy's goal of buying a bike (G11; see Table 3). In contrast, this goal should not be reinstated by these actions in the second half of the sequential story version. Jimmy's goal of buying the bike is satisfied early in the sequential version of the story because Jimmy's mother agrees to get the bike for Jimmy.

The discourse model of Suh and Trabasso (1993) predicts that the superordinate goal will be reinstated by particular story actions in the hierarchical version. Reinstatement of this goal supports global coherence. It should be noted that the

| **TABLE 3** | Hierarchical and Sequential Versions of the Jimmy Story (Suh & Trabasso, 1993) |

CATEGORY	SENTENCE
	Hierarchical Version
S11	Once there was a boy named Jimmy.
E11	One day, Jimmy saw his friend Tom riding a new bike.
G11	Jimmy wanted to buy a bike.
A11	Jimmy spoke to his mother.
O11	Jimmy's mother refused to get a bike for him.
R11	Jimmy was very sad.
E21	The next day, Jimmy's mother told him that he should have his own savings.
G21	Jimmy wanted to earn some money.
A21	Jimmy asked for a job at a nearby grocery store.
A22	Jimmy made deliveries for the grocery store.
O21	Jimmy earned a lot of money.
A31	Jimmy went to the department store.
A32	Jimmy walked to the second floor.
O31	Jimmy bought a new bike.
	Sequential Version
S11	Once there was a boy named Jimmy.
E11	One day, Jimmy saw his friend Tom riding a new bike.
G11	Jimmy wanted to buy a bike.
A11	Jimmy spoke to his mother.
O11	Jimmy's mother got a bike for him.
R11	Jimmy was very happy.
E21	The next day, Jimmy's mother told him that he should have his own savings.
G21	Jimmy wanted to earn some money.
A21	Jimmy asked for a job at a nearby grocery store.
A22	Jimmy made deliveries for the grocery store.
O21	Jimmy earned a lot of money.
A31	Jimmy went to the department store.
A32	Jimmy walked to the second floor.
O31	Jimmy bought a new basketball.

Note. S = setting; E = event; G = goal; A = attempt; O = outcome; R = reaction. The first number after the letter indicates the episode to which the statement belongs. The second number indicates the cumulative number of times that the statement's category has occurred in that episode. For example, A32 refers to the second attempt in the third episode.

superordinate goal should be reinstated even though there is no break in local coherence. All of the sentences in both stories are locally coherent by virtue of argument repetition (Halliday & Hasan, 1976; Kintsch & van Dijk, 1978): The subject of each sentence after sentence 1 is Jimmy. According to the minimalist hypothesis and the CSS strategy, the global goal inference should not be reinstated because there is no break in local coherence or causal coherence.

One prong of the three-pronged method addresses theory. The theoretical predictions of Suh and Trabasso (1993) were based on a discourse theory that specifies in detail how the content of the stories are organized into causal network structures and how the structures are constructed during comprehension (Trabasso & Suh, 1993; Trabasso & van den Broek, 1985; Trabasso et al., 1989). Each sentence is classified by its role in an episodic structure. That is, it is assigned to one of six main categories: settings (S), events (E), goals (G), attempts (A), outcomes (O), and reactions (R). Settings introduce characters and indicate the spatial-temporal context of the story. Events have an impact on characters and influence goals. Goals are desired and valued states, activities, objects, and resources. Attempts are actions carried out to achieve goals. Outcomes index the success or failure of a goal being achieved. Reactions are emotions and cognitions that evaluate events and outcomes. The numbers in the lettered subscripts in Table 3 refer to the episode in which the sentence occurs (the first digit) and the ordinal number of a particular category within an episode (the second digit). For example, G_{21} is the second episode's first goal statement and A_{32} is the third episode's second attempt statement. Trabasso's discourse theory specifies how the sentences are connected with different categories of causal arcs and how these connections are built on-line during comprehension. The discourse theory predicts that G_{11} should be causally linked (on-line) to sentences A_{11}, G_{21}, A_{31}, and A_{32} in the hierarchical version but only to sentence A_{11} in the sequential version.

Another prong of the three-pronged method states that verbal protocols should be collected to confirm that the theoretically predicted inferences are generated on-line. Suh and Trabasso (1993) collected think-aloud protocols as subjects read the stories sentence by sentence. After a subject read each sentence, the subject told the experimenter what his or her understanding of the story was in the context of the story, no matter how obvious it was to the subject. The protocols were tape recorded and analyzed. The theoretical prediction is that the superordinate goal (G_{11}, Jimmy wanting to buy a bike) should frequently be mentioned when A_{11}, G_{21}, A_{31}, and A_{32} are comprehended in the hierarchical version and when A_{11} is comprehended in the sequential version. This prediction was confirmed. The likelihoods of mentioning G_{11} were 1.00, 0.92, 0.58, and 0.92 for the respective actions in the hierarchical version, and 0.92, 0.29, 0.04, and 0.17 in the sequential version. The verbal protocols clearly confirmed the predictions of the discourse theory.

The other prong of the three-pronged method states that time-based behavioral measures should be collected to more rigorously assess whether an inference is actually made on-line. Suh and Trabasso (1993) collected recognition decisions and latencies for test items that were interspersed with the sentences during comprehension. Test statements were presented after story sentences, and subjects decided as quickly as possible whether the test statement was presented earlier in the text (by pressing a "yes" or a "no" key). A critical test item was the G_{11} goal sentence. The recognition latency was expected to be shorter if the reader had reinstated G_{11} during the comprehension of a story sentence. The results confirmed the predictions of the discourse model. Recognition latencies (in msec) were 973, 986, and 1,084 for the critical test item after A_{11}, G_{21}, and A_{32}, respectively, in the hierarchical version; the corresponding latencies were 980, 1,123, and 1,209 in the sequential version.

• • •

STUDIES OF EXTRATEXTUAL INFERENCES USING THE THREE-PRONGED METHOD

Graesser and his colleagues have used the three-pronged method to investigate extra-textual inferences during the comprehension of short narrative texts (Graesser et al., 1987; Long & Golding, 1993; Long et al., 1992; Long, Golding, Graesser, & Clark, 1990; Magliano et al., 1993) and short expository texts (Millis, 1989; Millis et al., 1990). They focused on five classes of inferences because the status of these classes discriminated among alternative theoretical positions: superordinate goals (class 4), subordinate goals (class 10), causal antecedents (class 3), causal consequences (class 7), and states (class 11). Below, we present an example story and an example inference in each of these five classes:

THE CZAR AND HIS DAUGHTER

Once there was a Czar who had three lovely daughters. One day the three daughters went walking in the woods. They were enjoying themselves so much that they forgot the time and stayed too long. A dragon kidnapped the three daughters. As they were being dragged off they cried for help. Three heroes heard their cries and set off to rescue the daughters. The heroes came and fought the dragon and rescued the maidens. Then the heroes returned the daughters to their palace. When the Czar heard of the rescue, he rewarded the heroes.

Inferences when comprehending "The dragon kidnapped the daughters":

1. Superordinate goal: The dragon wanted to eat the daughters.
2. Subordinate goal: The dragon grabbed the daughters.
3. Causal antecedent: The dragon saw the daughters.
4. Causal consequence: Someone rescued the daughters.
5. State: The dragon had scales.

The first prong of the method addresses theory. The theoretical predictions were discussed earlier in this article.

The second prong of the three-pronged method involved the collection of question-answering protocols while readers comprehended the stories clause by clause. After reading each clause (that referred to an action, event, or state), the subjects answered questions about the clause. One group answered a why-question, a second group answered a how-question, and a third group answered a what-happened-next question. The question categories were selected to extract particular types of extratextual inferences. As discussed earlier, research on human question answering has strongly established that why, how, and what-happened-next questions are selective in extracting particular inferences (Graesser & Franklin, 1990; Graesser et al., 1981, 1991; Graesser & Murachver, 1985). Why-questions expose superordinate goals and causal antecedents; how-questions expose subordinate goals/actions and causal antecedent events; what-happened-next questions expose causal consequences. States are exposed by more than one of these question categories and can be distinguished by content.

A *constructive history chart* was prepared for each of the inferences that was elicited by the question-answering protocols. The chart identified which explicit clauses in the text elicited a particular inference, the type of question that elicited it, and the proportion of subjects who articulated the inference in the question-answering protocols. The point in the story where an inference first emerged was particularly informative. In fact, all experiments that collected time-based measures tested an inference when it first emerged in the situation model, as manifested in the question-answering protocols.

Whenever Graesser and his colleagues evaluated the on-line status of classes of inferences, they always equilibrated the classes of inference test items on the proportion of subjects who produced the item in the question-answering task (Graesser & Franklin, 1990; Graesser et al., 1981, 1991; Graesser & Murachver, 1985). Inference test items were also equilibrated on a number of extraneous measures, such as word length, word frequency, and word class (i.e., nouns, verbs versus adjectives).

The third prong of the three-pronged method involved the collection of lexical-decision latencies or naming latencies for test words during the comprehension of the stories. Long et al. (1992) reported a study that adopted the three-pronged methodology to test whether superordinate goal inferences and subordinate action inferences are generated on-line when stories are comprehended. According to the constructionist theory, superordinate goals should be generated on-line because they explain why characters perform intentional actions. In contrast, subordinate actions should not be generated because they do not explain why actions occur; subordinate actions merely elaborate the details about how actions are executed. Long et al. used question-answering protocols to extract a sample of superordinate goals and subordinate actions associated with explicit actions in the test. Why-questions uncovered the superordinate goals, whereas how-questions uncovered the subordinate actions. The two samples of inferences were equilibrated on a number of extraneous variables, such as production likelihood in the question-answering protocols, word frequency, word length, and word class.

Long et al. (1992) collected word-naming latencies to test whether inference words are generated on-line during comprehension. A test word was presented 500 msec after each sentence in a story was read. The subjects were instructed to say the test word aloud as quickly as possible. The test word was sometimes a word that came from a superordinate goal and sometimes a word from a subordinate goal/action. These items were new inferences constructed for the first time in the story by explicit target actions. There also was a control condition in which the superordinate and subordinate inferences were named in an unrelated passage context. Therefore, an *inference activation score* could be computed for each test word by subtracting the naming latency of the word in the inference context from the naming latency of the word in an unrelated context. This computation of inference activation scores has been used by other researchers who have collected lexical-decison latencies to study inference processing (Kintsch, 1988; Sharkey & Sharkey, 1992; Till, Mross, & Kintsch, 1988). Long et al. (1992) reported significantly higher inference activation scores for superordinate goal words than for subordinate goal/action words (which in turn were essentially zero). Using the same design, Long et al. reported a similar pattern of data when lexical decisions were collected instead of naming latencies. The activation scores showed the following pattern: superordinate goal > subordinate goal/action > 0.

In another study, Long and Golding (1993) reported that superordinate goals are constructed very quickly (within 750 msec) in the case of fast readers with good comprehension. In contrast, inference activation scores were essentially zero in the case of subordinate goal/actions for all readers and in the case of superordinate goals for readers who are not fast, good comprehenders. Precise control over reading time was accomplished by implementing a rapid serial visual presentation (RSVP) rate of 250 msec per word. There was precise control over the time-course of inference activation by imposing a short 200-msec stimulus onset asynchrony (SOA) between the final word of the sentence and the test word. The results of these investigations of superordinate and subordinate goals are compatible with the constructionist theory and incompatible with most of the alternative theoretical positions (i.e., explicit textbase position, minimalist hypothesis, and promiscuous inference generation position).

Magliano et al. (1993) tested whether causal antecedent and causal consequence inferences are generated on-line and also determined the time-course of their activation. They manipulated inference category (causal antecedent versus causal consequence), RSVP rate (250 versus 400 msec), and SOA interval (250, 400, 600, and 1,200 msec). Lexical-decision latencies were collected on test items after each sentence, following the same procedure as the studies presented above. The results indicated that there was a threshold of 400 msec after stimulus presentation (either RSVP or SOA) before causal antecedents were generated, whereas causal consequence inferences were never generated on-line.

Studies using the three-pronged method have revealed that state inferences are not generated on-line. Long et al. (1990) compared causal antecedent event inferences with state inferences in a study that collected lexical-decision latencies. Latencies were shorter for test words that referred to causal antecedent event inferences than for those referring to state inferences. Graesser et al. (1987) collected word reading times using a moving window method and focused on times for end-of-clause words. It was assumed that inferences are generated primarily at end-of-clause words, following the results of previous research (Haberlandt & Graesser, 1985; Just & Carpenter, 1980; Kintsch & van Dijk, 1978). Graesser et al. (1987) found that end-of-clause reading times were predicted by the number of new goal inferences and causal antecedent event inferences that were constructed during the comprehension of the clause but not by the number of state inferences.

In summary, Graesser's research on extratextual inferences using the three-pronged method was compatible with the predictions of the constructionist theory and one version of the CSS strategy (i.e., the CSS + Goal strategy). Superordinate goals and causal antecedents are generated on-line, whereas subordinate goals/actions, causal consequences, and states do not tend to be generated on-line. Stated differently, the first two inference classes have substantially higher encoding strengths than do the latter three classes.

• • •

Summary of Empirical Findings

This section has presented evidence for the constructionist theory of inference generation. Although most of the available research has been on short texts that do not use the three-pronged method, a few studies have adopted the methodology that coordinates theory, the collection of verbal protocols, and the collection of time-based behavioral measures.

• • •

In closing, it would appear that the proposed constructionist theory provides the best foundation for predicting and explaining inference generation during the comprehension of narrative text. Readers construct rather rich situation models during the comprehension of narrative. However, it is not the case that the reader constructs a complete lifelike rendition of the story, as if a camera captured all pictorial details in fine detail and a narrator tracked the minds of all of the characters. Instead, a predictable subset of the situation is preserved and another subset never makes it into the meaning representation. The search-after-meaning principle goes a long way in distinguishing what knowledge is in the representation versus what is out.

REFERENCES

Allen, J. (1987). *Natural language understanding.* Menlo Park, CA: Benjamin/Cummings.

Alterman, R. (1985). A dictionary based on concept coherence. *Artificial Intelligence, 25,* 153-186.

Anderson, J. R. (1983). *The architecture of cognition.* Cambridge, MA: Harvard University Press.

Anderson, R. C., & Ortony, A. (1975). On putting apples into bottles—A problem of polysemy. *Cognitive Psychology, 7,* 167-180.

Balota, D. A., Flores d'Arcais, G. B., & Rayner, K. (Eds.). (1990). *Comprehension processes in reading.* Hillsdale, NJ: Erlbaum.

Bartlett, F. C. (1932). *Remembering: A study in experimental and social psychology.* Cambridge, England: Cambridge University Press.

Beach, R., & Brown, R. (1987). Discourse conventions and literary inference. Toward a theoretical model. In R. J. Tierney, P. L. Anders, & J. N. Mitchell (Eds.), *Understanding readers' understanding: Theory and practice* (pp. 147-174). Hillsdale, NJ: Erlbaum.

Berlyne, D. E. (1949). 'Interest' as a psychological concept. *British Journal of Psychology, 39,* 184-195.

Berlyne, D. E. (1960). *Conflict, arousal, and curiosity.* New York: McGraw-Hill.

Bever, T. G., & McElree, B. (1988). Empty categories access their antecedents during comprehension. *Linguistic Inquiry, 19,* 35-44.

Black, J. B., & Bower, G. H. (1980). Story understanding and problem solving. *Poetics, 9,* 223-250.

Bloom, C. P., Fletcher, C. R., van den Broek, P., Reitz, L., & Shapiro, B. P. (1990). An on-line assessment of causal reasoning during comprehension. *Memory & Cognition, 18,* 65-71.

Bower, G. H. (1989). Mental models in text understanding. In A. F. Bennett & K. M. McConkey (Eds.), *Cognition in individual and social contexts* (pp. 129-144). Amsterdam: Elsevier.

Bower, G. H., Black, J. B., & Turner, T. J. (1979). Scripts in memory for text. *Cognitive Psychology, 11,* 177-220.

Brady, M., & Berwick, R. (1983). *Computational models of discourse.* Cambridge, MA: MIT Press.

Bransford, J. D., Barclay, J. R., & Franks, J. J. (1972). Sentence memory: A constructive versus interpretive approach. *Cognitive Psychology, 3,* 193-209.

Brewer, W. F. (1980). Literary theory, rhetoric, and stylistics: Implications of psychology. In R. J. Spiro, B. C. Bruce, & W. F. Brewer (Eds.), *Theoretical issues in reading comprehension* (pp. 221–239). Hillsdale, NJ: Erlbaum.

Brewer, W. F., & Ohtsuka, K. (1988). Story structure, characterization, just world organization, and reader affect in American and Hungarian short stories. *Poetics, 17,* 395–415.

Britton, B. K., & Eisenhart, F. J. (1993). Expertise, text coherence, and constraint satisfaction: Effects on harmony and settling rate. In *Proceedings of the Fifteenth Annual Conference of the Cognitive Science Society* (pp. 266–271). Hillsdale, NJ: Erlbaum.

Britton, B. K., & Gülgöz, S. (1991). Using Kintsch's computational model to improve instructional text: Effects of repairing inference calls on recall and cognitive structure. *Journal of Educational Psychology, 83,* 329–404.

Britton, B. K., & Pelligrini, A. D. (1990). *Narrative thought and narrative language.* Hillsdale, NJ: Erlbaum.

Brown, G., & Yule, G. (1983). *Discourse analysis.* Cambridge, England: Cambridge University Press.

Bruner, J. (1986). *Actual minds, possible worlds.* Cambridge, MA: Harvard University Press.

Cheng, P. W., & Holyoak, K. J. (1985). Pragmatic reasoning schemas. *Cognitive Psychology, 17,* 391–416.

Clark, H. H. (1977). Bridging. In P. N. Johnson-Laird & P. C. Wason (Eds.), *Thinking: Readings in cognitive science* (pp. 243–263). Cambridge, England: Cambridge University Press.

Collins, A. M., Brown, J. S., & Larkin, K. M. (1980). Inferences in text understanding. In R. J. Spiro, B. C. Bruce, & W. F. Brewer (Eds.), *Theoretical issues in reading comprehension* (pp. 385–407). Hillsdale, NJ: Erlbaum.

Dahlgren, K. (1988). *Naive semantics for natural language understanding.* Norwell, MA: Kluwer Academic

Daly, J. A., Weber, D. J., Vangelisti, A. L., Maxwell, M., & Neel, H. (1989). Concurrent cognitions during conversations: Protocol analysis as a means of exploring conversations. *Discourse Processes, 12,* 227–244.

de Beaugrande, R. (1980). *Text, discourse, and process.* Norwood, NJ: Ablex.

Dell, G., McKoon, G., & Ratcliff, R. (1983). The activation of antecedent information during the processing of anaphoric reference in reading. *Journal of Verbal Learning and Verbal Behavior, 22,* 121–132.

Dopkins, S., Klin, C., & Myers, J. L. (1993). Accessibility of information about goals during the processing of narrative texts. *Journal of Memory and Language, 19,* 70–80.

Duffy, S. A., & Rayner, K. (1990). Eye movements and anaphor resolution: Effects of antecedent typicality and distance. *Language and Speech, 33,* 103–119.

Dyer, M. G. (1983). *In-depth understanding: A computer model of integrated processing for narrative comprehension.* Cambridge, MA: MIT Press.

Ericsson, K. A. (1988). Current verbal reports of text comprehension: A review. *Text, 8,* 295–325.

Ericsson, K. A., & Simon, H. A. (1980). Verbal reports as data. *Psychological Review, 87,* 215–251.

Fletcher, C. R. (1986). Strategies for the allocation of short-term memory during comprehension. *Journal of Memory and Language, 25,* 43–58.

Fletcher, C. R., & Bloom, C. P. (1988). Causal reasoning in the comprehension of simple narrative texts. *Journal of Memory and Language, 27,* 235–244.

Frazier, L., & Flores d'Arcais, G. B. (1989). Filler driven parsing: A study of gap filling in Dutch. *Journal of Memory and Language, 28,* 331–344.

Garnham, A., & Oakhill, J. (in press). The mental models theory of language comprehension. In B. K. Britton & A. C. Graesser (Eds.), *Models of understanding text.* Hillsdale, NJ: Erlbaum.

Gernsbacher, M. A. (1990). *Language comprehension as structure building.* Hillsdale, NJ: Erlbaum.

Gernsbacher, M. A., Goldsmith, H. H., & Robertson, R. R. (1992). Do readers mentally represent character's emotional states? *Cognition and Emotion, 6,* 89-112.

Gerrig, R. J. (1989). Suspense in the absence of uncertainty. *Journal of Memory and Language, 28,* 633-648.

Glenberg, A. M., & Epstein, W. (1987). Inexpert calibration of comprehension. *Memory & Cognition, 15,* 84-93.

Glenberg, A. M., Meyer, M., & Lindem, K. (1987). Mental models contribute to foregrounding during text comprehension. *Journal of Memory and Language, 26,* 69-83.

Glenberg, A. M., Wilkinson, A. C., & Epstein, W. (1982). The illusion of knowing: Failure in the self-assessment of comprehension. *Memory & Cognition, 10,* 597-602.

Golden, R. M., & Rumelhart, D. E. (1991). A distributed representation and model for story comprehension and recall. In *Proceedings of the Thirteenth Annual Conference of the Cognitive Science Society* (pp. 7-12). Hillsdale, NJ: Erlbaum.

Graesser, A. C. (1981). *Prose comprehension beyond the word.* New York: Springer-Verlag.

Graesser, A. C., & Bower, G. H. (Eds.). (1990). *Inferences and text comprehension.* San Diego, CA: Academic Press.

Graesser, A. C., & Clark, L. F. (1985). *Structures and procedures of implicit knowledge.* Norwood, NJ: Ablex.

Graesser, A. C., & Franklin, S. P. (1990). QUEST: A cognitive model of question answering. *Discourse Processes, 13,* 279-304.

Graesser, A. C., Gordon, S. E., & Sawyer, J. D. (1979). Memory for typical and atypical actions in scripted activities: Test of a script pointer + tag hypothesis. *Journal of Verbal Learning and Verbal Behavior, 18,* 319-332.

Graesser, A. C., Haberlandt, K., & Koizumi, D. (1987). How is reading time influenced by knowledge-based inferences and world knowledge? In B. K. Britton & S. M. Glynn (Eds.), *Executive control processes in reading* (pp. 217-251). Hillsdale, NJ: Erlbaum.

Graesser, A. C., & Hemphill, D. (1991). Question answering in the context of scientific mechanisms. *Journal of Memory and Language, 30,* 186-209.

Graesser, A. C., & Kreuz, R. J. (1993). A theory of inference generation during text comprehension. *Discourse Processes, 16,* 145-160.

Graesser, A. C., Lang, K. L., & Roberts, R. M. (1991). Question answering in the context of stories. *Journal of Experimental Psychology: General, 120,* 254-277.

Graesser, A. C., Long, D. L., & Mio, J. (1990). Humor and wit in comprehension. *Poetics, 18,* 143-164.

Graesser, A. C., & McMahen, C. L. (1993). Anomalous information triggers questions when adults solve problems and comprehend stories. *Journal of Educational Psychology, 85,* 136-151.

Graesser, A. C., & Murachver, T. (1985). Symbolic procedures of question answering. In A. C. Graesser & J. B. Black (Eds.), *The psychology of questions* (pp. 15-88). Hillsdale, NJ: Erlbaum.

Graesser, A. C., Robertson, S. P., & Anderson, P. A. (1981). Incorporating inferences in narrative representations: A study of how and why. *Cognitive Psychology, 13,* 1-26.

Graesser, A. C., & Zwaan, R. A. (in press). Inference generation and the construction of situation models. In C. A. Weaver, S. Mannes, & C. R. Fletcher (Eds.), *Discourse comprehension: Strategies and processing revisited.* Hillsdale, NJ: Erlbaum.

Grice, H. P. (1975). Logic and conversation. In P. Cole & J. L. Morgan (Eds.), *Syntax and semantics: Speech acts* (Vol. 3, pp. 41-58). San Diego, CA: Academic Press.

Grimes, J. (1975). *The thread of discourse.* The Hague: Mouton.

Haberlandt, K., & Bingham, G. (1978). Verbs contribute to the coherence of brief narratives: Reading related and unrelated sentence triplets. *Journal of Verbal Learning and Verbal Behavior, 17,* 419–425.

Haberlandt, K., & Graesser, A. C. (1985). Component processes in text comprehension and some of their interactions. *Journal of Experimental Psychology: General, 114,* 357–374.

Halliday, M. A. K., & Hasan, R. (1976). *Cohesion in English.* London: Longmans.

Harris, R. J., & Monaco, G. E. (1978). The psychology of pragmatic implications: Information processing between the lines. *Journal of Experimental Psychology: General, 107,* 1–22.

Hart, M. L. A., & Honore, A. M. (1985). *Causation in the law.* Oxford: Clarendon.

Hastie, R. (1983). Social inference. *Annual Review of Psychology, 34,* 511–542.

Hilton, D. J. (1990). Conversational processes and causal explanation. *Psychological Bulletin, 107,* 110–119.

Hobbs, J. R. (1979). Coherence and coreference. *Cognitive Science, 3,* 67–90.

Holyoak, K. J., & Thagard, P. (1989). Analogical mapping by constraint satisfaction. *Cognitive Science, 13,* 295–355.

Hunt, R. A., & Vipond, D. (1986). Evaluations in literary reading. *Text, 6,* 53–71.

Johnson-Laird, P. N. (1983). *Mental models.* Cambridge, MA: Harvard University Press.

Jose, P. E., & Brewer, W. F. (1984). Development of story liking: Character identification, suspense, and outcome resolution. *Developmental Psychology, 20,* 911–924.

Just, M. A., & Carpenter, P. A. (1980). A theory of reading: From eye fixations to comprehension. *Psychological Review, 87,* 329–354.

Just, M. A., & Carpenter, P. A. (1992). A capacity theory of comprehension: Individual differences in working memory. *Psychological Review, 99,* 122–149.

Kahneman, D., Slovic, P., & Tversky, A. (1982). *Judgments under uncertainty: Heuristics and biases.* Cambridge, England: Cambridge University Press.

Kass, A. (1992). Question asking, artificial intelligence, and human creativity. In T. W. Lauer, E. Peacock, & A. C. Graesser (Eds.), *Questions and information systems* (pp. 303–360). Hillsdale, NJ: Erlbaum.

Katz, J. J., & Fodor, J. A. (1963). The structure of semantic theory. *Language, 39,* 170–210.

Keefe, D. E., & McDaniel, M. (1993). The time course and durability of predictive inferences. *Journal of Memory and Language, 32,* 446–463.

Keenan, J. M., Baillet, S. D., & Brown, P. (1984). The effects of causal cohesion on comprehension and memory. *Journal of Verbal Learning and Verbal Behavior, 23,* 115–126.

Keenan, J. M., Golding, J. M., Potts, G. R., Jennings, T. M., & Aman, C. T. (1990). Methodological issues in evaluating the occurrence of inferences. In A. C. Graesser & G. H. Bower (Eds.), *Inferences and text comprehension* (pp. 295–312). San Diego, CA: Academic Press.

Kempson, R. M. (1977). *Semantic theory.* Cambridge, England: Cambridge University Press.

Kintsch, W. (1980). Learning from text, levels of comprehension, or: Why anyone would read a story anyway. *Poetics, 9,* 87–98.

Kintsch, W. (1988). The role of knowledge in discourse comprehension: A constructive-integration model. *Psychological Review, 95,* 163–182.

Kintsch, W. (1992). How readers construct situation models for stories: The role of syntactic cues and causal inferences. In A. F. Healy, S. M. Kosslyn, & R. M. Shiffrin (Eds.), *From learning processes to cognitive processes: Essays in honor of William K. Estes* (Vol. 2, pp. 261–278). Hillsdale, NJ: Erlbaum.

Kintsch, W. (1993). Information accretion and reduction in text processing: Inferences. *Discourse Processes, 16,* 193–202.

Kintsch, W., & van Dijk, T. A. (1978). Toward a model of text comprehension and production. *Psychological Review, 85,* 363–394.

Kintsch, W., Welsch, D., Schmalhofer, F., & Zinny, S. (1990). Sentence memory: A theoretical analysis. *Journal of Memory and Language, 29,* 133–159.

Kuipers, B. (1985). Commonsense reasoning about causality: Deriving behavior from structure. In D. G. Bobrow (Ed.), *Qualitative reasoning about physical systems* (pp. 169-204). Cambridge, MA: MIT Press.

Lazarus, R. S. (1991). *Emotion and adaptation.* London: Oxford University Press.

Lea, R. B., O'Brien, D. P., Fisch, S. M., Noveck, I. A., & Braine, M. D. S. (1990). Predicting propositional logic inferences in text comprehension. *Journal of Memory and Language, 29,* 361-387.

Lehnert, W. G. (1978). *The process of question answering.* Hillsdale, NJ: Erlbaum.

Lehnert, W. G. (1981). Plot units and narrative summarization. *Cognitive Science, 5,* 283-331.

Lehnert, W. G., Dyer, M. G., Johnson, P. N., Young, C. J., & Harley, S. (1983). BORIS: An experiment in in-depth understanding of narratives. *Artificial Intelligence, 20,* 15-62.

Long, D. L., & Golding, J. M. (1993). Superordinate goal inferences: Are they automatically generated during comprehension? *Discourse Processes, 16,* 55-73.

Long, D. L., Golding, J. M., & Graesser, A. C. (1992). The generation of goal related inferences during narrative comprehension. *Journal of Memory and Language, 5,* 634-647.

Long, D. L., Golding, J. M., Graesser, A. C., & Clark, L. F. (1990). Goal, event, and state inferences: An investigation of inference generation during story comprehension. In A. C. Graesser & G. H. Bower (Eds.), *Inferences and text comprehension* (pp. 89-107). San Diego, CA: Academic Press.

Mackie, J. L. (1980). *The cement of the universe: A study of causality.* Oxford: Clarendon.

Magliano, J. P., Baggett, W. B., Johnson, B. K., & Graesser, A. C. (1993). The time course of generating causal antecedent and causal consequence inferences. *Discourse Processes, 16,* 35-53.

Magliano, J. P., & Graesser, A. C. (1991). A three-pronged method for studying inference generation in literary text. *Poetics, 20,* 193-232.

Mandler, G. (1976). *Mind and emotion.* New York: Wiley.

Mandler, J. M. (1984). *Stories, scripts, and scenes: Aspects of schema theory.* Hillsdale, NJ: Erlbaum.

Mann, W. C., & Thompson, S. A. (1986). Relational propositions in discourse. *Discourse Processes, 9,* 57-90.

Mannes, S. M., & Kintsch, W. (1991). Routine computing tasks: Planning as understanding. *Cognitive Science, 15,* 305-342.

Markman, E. M. (1979). Realizing that you don't understand: Elementary school children's awareness of inconsistencies. *Child Development, 50,* 643-655.

McKoon, G., & Ratcliff, R. (1986). Inferences about predictable events. *Journal of Experimental Psychology: Learning, Memory, and Cognition, 12,* 82-91.

McKoon, G., & Ratcliff, R. (1989). Assessing the occurrence of elaborative inference with recognition: Compatibility checking versus compound cue theory. *Journal of Memory and Language, 28,* 547-563.

McKoon, G., & Ratcliff, R. (1992). Inference during reading. *Psychological Review, 99,* 440-466.

McLaughlin, M. L. (1990). Explanatory discourse and causal attribution. *Text, 10,* 63-68.

Meyer, B. J. F. (1985). Prose analysis: Purpose, procedures, and problems. In B. K. Britton & J. B. Black (Eds.), *Understanding expository text* (pp. 11-64). Hillsdale, NJ: Erlbaum.

Millis, K. K. (1989). *The time course of constructing bridging and expectation knowledge-based inferences during the comprehension of expository text.* Unpublished doctoral dissertation, Memphis State University, Memphis, TN.

Millis, K. K., Morgan, D., & Graesser, A. C. (1990). The influence of knowledge-based inferences on the reading time of expository text. In A. C. Graesser & G. H. Bower (Eds.), *Inferences and text comprehension* (pp. 197-212). San Digeo, CA: Academic Press.

Minsky, M. (1975). A framework for representing knowledge. In P. H. Winston (Ed.), *The psychology of computer vision* (pp. 211-277). New York: McGraw-Hill.

Mooney, R. J. (1990). *A general explanation-based mechanism and its application to narrative understanding.* San Mateo, CA: Morgan Kaufman.

Morrow, D. G., Bower, G., & Greenspan, S. (1989). Updating situation models during narrative comprehension. *Journal of Memory and Language, 28,* 292-312.

Morrow, D. G., Greenspan, S. L., & Bower, G. H. (1987). Accessibility and situation models in narrative comprehension. *Journal of Memory and Language, 26,* 165-187.

Murray, J. D., Klin, C. M, & Myers, J. L. (1991, November). *Forward inferences about specific events during reading.* 32nd Annual Meeting of the Psychonomic Society, San Francisco, CA.

Myers, J. L. (1990). Causal relatedness and text comprehension. In D. A. Balota, G. B. Flores d'Arcais, & K. Rayner (Eds.), *Comprehension processes in reading* (pp. 361-375). Hillsdale, NJ: Erlbaum.

Myers, J. L., Shinjo, M., & Duffy, S. A. (1987). The role of causal relatedness and memory. *Journal of Memory and Language, 4,* 453-465.

Nelson, K. (1986). *Event knowledge: Structure and function in development.* Hillsdale, NJ: Erlbaum.

Newell, A., & Simon, H. A. (1972). *Human problem-solving.* Englewood Cliffs, NJ: Prentice-Hall.

Nicholas, D. W., & Trabasso, T. (1981). Towards a taxonomy of inferences. In F. Wilkening, J. Becker, & T. Trabasso (Eds.), *Information integration by children* (pp. 243-266). Hillsdale, NJ: Erlbaum.

Nisbett, R. E., & Wilson, T. D. (1977). Telling more than we know: Verbal reports on mental processes. *Psychological Review, 84,* 231-279.

Nystrand, M. (1986). *The structure of written communication: Studies in reciprocity between writers and readers.* Norwood, NJ: Ablex.

O'Brien, E. J., Duffy, S. A., & Myers, J. L. (1986). Anaphoric inference during reading. *Journal of Experimental Psychology: Learning, Memory, and Cognition, 12,* 346-352.

Olson, G. M., Duffy, S. A., & Mack, R. L. (1984). Thinking out loud as a method for studying real-time comprehension processes. In D. E. Kieras & M. Just (Eds.), *New methods in the study of immediate processes in comprehension* (pp. 253-286). Hillsdale, NJ: Erlbaum.

Olson, G. M., Duffy, S. A., & Mack, R. L. (1985). Question asking as a component of text comprehension. In A. C. Graesser & J. B. Black (Eds.), *The psychology of questions* (pp. 219-226). Hillsdale, NJ: Erlbaum.

Otero, J., & Kintsch, W. (1992). Failures to detect contradictions in a text: What readers believe versus what they read. *Psychological Science, 3,* 229-235.

Pearson, P. D., & Fielding, L. (1991). Comprehension instruction. In R. Barr, M. L. Kamil, P. Mosenthal, & P. D. Pearson (Eds.), *Handbook of reading research* (Vol. 2, pp. 815-860). New York: Longman.

Pennington, N., & Hastie, R. (1986). Evidence evaluation in complex decision making. *Journal of Personality and Social Psychology, 51,* 242-258.

Perfetti, C. A. (1993). Why inferences might be restricted. *Discourse Processes, 16,* 181-192.

Perrig, W., & Kintsch, W. (1985). Propositional and situational representations in text. *Journal of Memory and Language, 26,* 165-187.

Potts, G. R., Keenan, J. M., & Golding, J. M. (1988). Assessing the occurrence of elaborative inferences: Lexical decision versus naming. *Journal of Memory and Language, 27,* 399-415.

Read, S. J. (1987). Constructing causal scenarios: A knowledge structure approach to causal reasoning. *Journal of Personality and Social Psychology, 52,* 288-302.

Read, S. J., & Marcus-Newhall, A. (1993). Explanatory coherence in social explanations: A parallel distributed processing account. *Journal of Personality and Social Psychology, 65,* 429-447.

Reiger, C. (1975). *Conceptual memory and inference. Conceptual information processing.* Amsterdam: North-Holland.

Rips, L. J. (1990). Reasoning. *Annual Review of Psychology, 41,* 321-354.

Roberts, R. M., & Kreuz, R. J. (1993). Nonstandard discourse and its coherence. *Discourse Processes, 16,* 451-464.

Rosenblatt, L. (1978). *The reader, the text, the poem.* Carbondale: Southern Illinois University Press.

Rumelhart, D. E. (1975). Notes on a schema for stories. In D. G. Bobrow & A. M. Collins (Eds.), *Representation and understanding: Studies in cognitive science* (pp. 211–236). San Diego, CA: Academic Press.

Rumelhart, D. E., & McClelland, J. L. (1986). *Parallel distributed processing: Explorations in the microstructure of cognition* (Vol. 1). Cambridge, MA: MIT Press.

Rumelhart, D. E., & Ortony, A. (1977). The representation of knowledge in memory. In R. C. Anderson, R. J. Spiro, & W. E. Montague (Eds.), *Schooling and the acquisition of knowledge* (pp. 99–135). Hillsdale, NJ: Erlbaum.

Sanford, A. J., & Garrod, S. C. (1981). *Understanding written language: Explorations in comprehension beyond the sentence.* New York: Wiley.

Schank, R. C. (1986). *Explanation patterns: Understanding mechanically and creatively.* Hillsdale, NJ: Erlbaum.

Schank, R. C., & Abelson, R. (1977). *Scripts, plans, goals and understanding: An inquiry into human knowledge structures.* Hillsdale, NJ: Erlbaum.

Schmalhofer, F., & Glavanov, D. (1986). Three components of understanding a programmer's manual: Verbatim, propositional, and situational representations. *Journal of Memory and Language, 25,* 279–294.

Schmidt, S. J. (1982). *Foundations for the empirical study of literature: The components of a basic theory.* Hamburg, Germany: Helmut Buske Verlag.

Seifert, C. M., McKoon, G., Abelson, R. P., & Ratcliff, R. (1986). Memory connections between thematically similar episodes. *Journal of Experimental Psychology: Learning, Memory, and Cognition, 12,* 220–231.

Sharkey, A. J. C., & Sharkey, N. E. (1992). Weak contextual constraints in text and word priming. *Journal of Memory and Language, 31,* 543–572.

Singer, M. (1988). Inferences in reading. *Reading Research: Advances in Theory and Practice, 6,* 177–219.

Singer, M. (1990). *Psychology of language.* Hillsdale, NJ: Erlbaum.

Singer, M. (1993). *Validation of motion bridging inferences in brief texts.* Manuscript submitted for publication.

Singer, M. (in press). Discourse inference processes. In M. Gernsbacher (Ed.), *Handbook of psycholinguistics.* San Diego, CA: Academic Press.

Singer, M., & Ferreira, F. (1983). Inferring consequences in story comprehension. *Journal of Verbal Learning and Verbal Behavior, 22,* 437–448.

Singer, M., Halldorson, M., Lear, J. C., & Andrusiak, P. (1992). Validation of causal bridging inferences in discourse understanding. *Journal of Memory and Language, 31,* 507–524.

Sperber, D., & Wilson, D. (1986). *Relevance: Communication and cognition.* Cambridge, MA: Harvard University Press.

Spiro, R. J. (1980). Constructive processes in prose comprehension and recall. In R. J. Spiro, B. C. Bruce, & W. F. Brewer (Eds.), *Theoretical issues in reading comprehension: Perspectives from cognitive psychology, linguistics, artificial intelligence, and education* (pp. 245–278). Hillsdale, NJ: Erlbaum.

Stein, N. L., & Glenn, C. G. (1979). An analysis of story comprehension in elementary school children. In R. O. Freedle (Ed.), *New directions in discourse processing* (Vol. 2, pp. 53–120). Norwood, NJ: Ablex.

Stein, N. L., & Levine, L. J. (1991). Making sense out of emotion: The representation and use of goal-structured knowledge. In W. Kessen, A. Ortony, & F. I. M. Craik (Eds.), *Memories, thoughts, and emotions: Essays in honor of George Mandler* (pp. 295–322). Hillsdale, NJ: Erlbaum.

Stein, N. L., & Trabasso, T. (1985). The search after meaning: Comprehension and comprehension monitoring. In F. J. Morrison, C. Lord, & D. Keating (Eds.), *Applied developmental psychology* (Vol. 2, pp. 33–58). San Diego, CA: Academic Press.

St. John, M. F. (1991). The story Gestalt: A model of knowledge inference processes in text comprehension. In *Proceedings of the Thirteenth Annual Conference of the Cognitive Science Society* (pp. 25–30). Hillsdale, NJ: Erlbaum.

Suh, S. Y., & Trabasso, T. (1993). Inferences during reading: Converging evidence from discourse analysis, talk-aloud protocols, and recognition priming. *Journal of Memory and Language, 32,* 279–300.

Swinney, D., & Osterhout, L. (1990). Inference generation during auditory language comprehension. In A. Graesser & G. Bower (Eds.), *Inferences and text comprehension* (pp. 17–33). San Diego, CA: Academic Press.

Tierney, R. J., & Shanahan, T. (1991). Research on the reading/writing relationship: Interactions, transactions, and outcomes. In R. Barr, M. L. Kamil, P. Mosenthal, & P. D. Pearson (Eds.), *Handbook of reading research* (Vol. 2, pp. 246–280). New York: Longman.

Till, R. E., Mross, E. F., & Kintsch, W. (1988). Time course of priming for associate and inference words in a discourse context. *Memory & Cognition, 16,* 283–298.

Trabasso, T., & Sperry, L. (1985). Causal relatedness and importance of story events. *Journal of Memory and Language, 24,* 595–611.

Trabasso, T., & Suh, S. Y. (1993). Using talk-aloud protocols to reveal inferences during comprehension of text. *Discourse Processes, 16,* 3–34.

Trabasso, T., & van den Broek, P. (1985). Causal thinking and the representation of narrative events. *Journal of Memory and Language, 24,* 612–630.

Trabasso, T., van den Broek, P., & Suh, S. Y. (1989). Logical necessity and transitivity of causal relations in stories. *Discourse Processes, 12,* 1–26.

van den Broek, P. (1990). Causal inferences and the comprehension of narrative text. In A. C. Graesser & G. H. Bower (Eds.), *Inferences and text comprehension* (pp. 175–196). San Diego, CA: Academic Press.

van den Broek, S., & Lorch, R. F. (1993). Network representations of causal relations in memory for narrative texts: Evidence from primed recognition. *Discourse Processes, 16,* 75–98.

van Dijk, T. A., & Kintsch, W. (1983). *Strategies of discourse comprehension.* San Diego, CA: Academic Press.

Weaver, C. A., III (1990). Constraining factors in calibration of comprehension. *Journal of Experimental Psychology: Learning, Memory, and Cognition, 16,* 214–222.

Weimer, W. B., & Palermo, D. S. (1974). *Cognition and symbolic processes.* Hillsdale, NJ: Erlbaum.

Weizenbaum, J. (1976). *Computer power and human reason: From judgment to calculation.* New York: Freeman.

Whitney, P. (1987). Psychological theories of elaborative inferences: Implications for schema-theoretic views of comprehension. *Reading Research Quarterly, 22,* 299–310.

Wilensky, R. (1983). *Planning and understanding.* Reading, MA: Addison-Wesley.

Winograd, T., & Flores, F. (1986). *Understanding computers and cognition: A new foundation for design.* Norwood, NJ: Ablex.

Wyer, R., & Gordon, S. E. (1984). The cognitive representation of social information. In R. Wyer & T. Srull (Eds.), *Handbook of social cognition* (pp. 73–150). Hillsdale, NJ: Erlbaum.

Zwaan, R. A. (1993). *Aspects of literary comprehension: A cognitive approach.* Philadelphia: John Benjamins.

Zwaan, R. A., & Van Oostendorp, H. (1993). Do readers construct spatial representations in naturalistic story comprehension? *Discourse Processes, 16,* 125–143.

QUESTIONS FOR FURTHER THOUGHT

1. What makes a theory "constructionist"?

2. Describe how Graesser and his colleagues theorize that individuals construct inferences during narrative text comprehension.

3. How might reading purpose affect inferences constructed during text comprehension?

4. Does the researchers' account of reader's goals accurately represent your goals when reading?

5. How might you apply the theory of Graesser and his colleagues to improve your own reading comprehension?

Lexical Access During Sentence Comprehension: (Re)Consideration of Context Effects

David Swinney

INTRODUCTION

Suppose a friend tells you that her parents bugged her when she was in high school. How do you determine whether she means that her parents used electronic devices to intercept her phone conversations or that her parents annoyed her?

The simple answer is that you rely on the context of the sentence to decide on the intended meaning, but how specifically do you do the information processing involved? When you hear your friend say the word *bugged,* do you access all possible meanings of the word and then decide which is the most likely, or do you access only the most likely meaning? Swinney used a clever experiment to determine which of these alternatives is the correct one.

Undergraduates were asked to listen to passages that contained words with multiple meanings, such as the following:

Rumor had it that, for years, the government building had been plagued with problems.

The man was not surprised when he found several spiders, roaches, and other *bugs* in the corner of his room.

Here the word *bugs* is intended to mean the insect rather than listening devices or errors in computer code.

At the same time undergraduates listened to passages, they also looked for letter strings to be presented on a computer screen in front of them. Their task, called the *lexical decision task,* was to indicate as quickly as possible by pushing one of two buttons whether the letter strings were words or nonwords. Swinney manipulated the relation between words presented in the lexical decision task and meanings of the ambiguous words of the passages the undergraduates heard. For example, the word *spy* presented in the lexical decision task is related to the listening device meaning of *bugs,* whereas the word *ant* is related to the insect meaning.

Source: From Swinney, D. A. (1979). Lexical access during sentence comprehension: (Re)consideration of context effects. *Journal of Verbal Learning and Verbal Behavior, 18,* 645–659. Reprinted with permission of Academic Press, Inc.

Swinney determined which meanings of words such as *bugs* were being accessed by looking for the speeds of lexical decisions about words related to different meanings, such as *spy* and *ant*. Also, Swinney varied whether the letter string for the lexical decision task appeared simultaneously with hearing the target word or after a delay of four syllables, allowing him to look for changes in the answer to the question of which meanings were accessed over time.

The question of how people disambiguate meaning of words had been puzzling psychologists for a long time but psychologists had not come up with a satisfactory way of addressing the problem. Swinney's work had great impact when it was published because it provided, at long last, a paradigm for addressing a long-standing, important question. The results indicated that multiple meanings of words are accessed initially—outside of conscious awareness—but within a quarter of a second, only the meaning that fits the context remains active. The paradigm introduced by Swinney was then adopted by many other researchers, as well.

———

The effects of prior semantic context upon lexical access during sentence comprehension were examined in two experiments. In both studies, subjects comprehended auditorily presented sentences containing lexical ambiguities and simultaneously performed a lexical decision task upon visually presented letter strings. Lexical decisions for visual words related to each of the meanings of the ambiguity were facilitated when these words were presented simultaneous with the end of the ambiguity (experiment 1). This effect held even when a strong biasing context was present.... Arguments are made for autonomy of the lexical access process of a model of semantic context effects. ■

Sentence comprehension requires the integration of information derived from a number of ongoing cognitive processes. It is clear, for example, that semantic and syntactic contexts interact with moment-to-moment comprehension processes to affect our interpretation of individual words and sentences; observations that contexts act to determine essential interpretations abound in the literature. However, while this effect is well documented, the process by which it occurs is not. Until the manner in which contexts exert their effects (i.e., the nature of information interaction) can be detailed, claims relying on the concept of "contextual determination" are empty and merely beg the question. Certainly, any attempt at a performative description of sentence comprehension must incorporate the details of this process. One of the important debates arising from concern over how (and when) contexts have their effects involves the question of whether comprehension processes are, in general, of a highly interactive, directable, nature (so that any stage of a process can come under the direction of some other, contextual, process: e.g., Marslen-Wilson, 1975; Marslen-Wilson & Welsh, 1978; Swinney & Hakes, 1976; Jenkins, 1977) or whether these processes are basically isolable and autonomous (so that context effects exert themselves only on the output of these processes; see, for example, Forster, 1976; Garrett, 1978).

One domain in which some effort has been made to examine this question is that of lexical access. The studies of interest have typically examined the processing of lexical ambiguities during sentence comprehension. Experiments involving a number of different tasks have shown that the occurrence of an ambiguous word, in comparison with that of an unambiguous control word, increases the processing complexity of an unbiased sentence (e.g., Foss, 1970; Foss & Jenkins, 1973; Holmes, Arwas, & Garrett, 1977; Chodorow, 1973). Such an increase presumably reflects comprehension processes which, at least momentarily, are involved in the retrieval and consideration of the several meanings of an ambiguous word. This effect occurs even though most people eventually become aware of only a single meaning for ambiguities in these conditions. The question of interest, then, is one of exactly how and when a biasing context aids in the final selection of a single relevant reading for an ambiguous word. It is particularly important to examine the nature of these effects for the most critical of contextual conditions for the issues raised here, that in which the biasing context occurs prior to the ambiguity.

Two general classes of hypotheses have been offered in explanation of such effects. The first of these, which have variously been termed "prior decision" (Foss & Jenkins, 1973) or "unitary perception" hypotheses are all versions of the highly interactive sentence processing view (see also Hogaboam & Perfetti, 1975; MacKay, 1970; Schvaneveldt, Meyer, & Becker, 1976). These hold that prior contextual information can act to direct lexical access so that only a single, relevant reading is ever accessed for an ambiguity. It is important to note that the nature of the claim made by such hypotheses is not limited to ambiguity alone; rather, it is a claim that lexical access, in general, is a contextually restricted, nonindependent process. The alternative class of hypotheses—postdecision or multiple-meaning hypotheses—holds that prior context has its effect only after all information is accessed for an ambiguity. Under these hypotheses, lexical access is viewed as an independent and relatively autonomous process in which context has its effects only following complete access of all the information about a word.

Data exist which appear to support both classes of hypotheses. Several studies (e.g., Conrad, 1974; Foss & Jenkins, 1973; Holmes et al., 1977; Lackner & Garrett, 1972; Cutler & Foss, 1974) have reported support for the Postdecision Hypothesis. However, a number of these utilized tasks which appear likely to have led subjects to employ some very specialized processing strategies (see Swinney & Hakes, 1976, for further discussion). Further, even the most compelling of the remainder have supported the Postdecision Hypothesis largely by virtue of failing to find support for the Prior Decision Hypothesis; they have not actually demonstrated the access of more than a single meaning for an ambiguity in the presence of a prior, biasing context.[1] Studies by Foss and Jenkins (1973) and Cutler and Foss (1974) provide good examples of this point. Both papers reported that phoneme monitoring latencies increased in the presence of an ambiguity (in comparison with an unambiguous control word) in an unbiased sentential context. Further, both studies failed to find any decrement in the ambiguity effect when a biasing context was introduced. Because such a decrement was expected if the Prior Decision Hypothesis was true, they interpreted this failure as support for the Postdecision Hypothesis. Unfortunately, support by default can often prove, for a number of reasons, to be a treacherous position to take. The work of Swinney and Hakes (1976), in fact, demonstrated that the ambiguity effect does decrease significantly in the presence of a *strongly* biased context, a result which forced reinterpretation of these previous results. The Swinney and Hakes (1976) result thus appeared to provide strong evidence that context can, at least under some conditions, direct the lexical access process; context would appear to be capable of interaction with lexical information during the access phase.

In spite of the intuitive appeal of this result, and its accordance with the highly interactive view of sentence perception, two problems deserve some consideration. First, it is obvious that the tasks used to study any process, and particularly those used to obtain on-line measures of comprehension (i.e., tasks examining the process during its operation, in contrast to examinations made after it is finished), must be appropriately applied in order to detect that process. This fact would appear to hold particular importance for examinations of ambiguity processing which use the phoneme monitoring task. The phoneme target in such monitoring studies, of necessity, occurs "downstream" from the ambiguity which is being examined (it usually begins the word following the ambiguity). The temporal gap between occurrence of the ambiguity and detection of the phoneme target in a following word is, thus, fairly extensive relative to the magnitude of the effects reported with this task. It is hoped that the problem here is self-evident: Claims related to lexical access which rely on monitoring data all contain the key assumption that the task actually measures lexical *access* and not some process that occurs *following* access. However, it is at least possible that the phoneme monitoring task actually reflects some type of postaccess decision process. If so, in situations where a prior biasing context is not very strong, as was the case in the Foss and Jenkins (1973) study, this postaccess decision process might take a relatively long time to complete, long enough so that the phoneme monitor decision for the following word is engaged while this process is still at work. Such a situation would thus produce the typical ambiguity effect. However, in the presence of a very strong biasing context (the Swinney & Hakes, 1976 study) this postaccess decision process could occur sufficiently quickly so as to reduce the processing load caused by the ambiguity prior to the time when the phoneme monitor task comes into play. In short, it may be that the phoneme monitoring task does not actually reflect the access of information for ambiguous (or other) words preceding the phoneme target but, rather, that it reflects postaccess processing. See Cairns and Hsu (1979) and Swinney (1976) for related arguments. If true, the task is not appropriate for examination of the hypotheses under question.

The second of the problems surrounding some of the previous work has arisen from recent examinations of the phoneme monitoring task (which has provided the bulk of the on-line evidence in this field). Both Mehler, Segui, and Carey (1978) and Newman and Dell (1978) have convincingly demonstrated that the ambiguity effects reported by Foss (1970), Foss and Jenkins (1973), and Cairns and Kamerman (1975) are all confounded with length and phonological properties of the initial phoneme of the ambiguity, its control, and the word preceding the ambiguity. When these factors were carefully examined, it appeared as though the ambiguity processing effects could be accounted for largely on the basis of these confounding variables. While the existence of some effect of ambiguity upon sentential processing has not been disproved, the role of the phoneme monitoring task in reflecting such an effect is certainly open to question. It should be noted that the claims of confounding asserted for the above-mentioned studies do not apply as strongly to the Swinney and Hakes (1976) results.[2]

The key to examining the experimental hypotheses in question, and to resolving the problems raised above, lies in increasing the sensitivity of the experimental task. In order to be able to provide positive evidence for the Postdecision Hypothesis, the experimental task should be capable of reflecting access of each of the several meanings of an ambiguous word. In addition, the task must be flexible enough to minimize the temporal gap between occurrence of the ambiguous word and the measure of access. Finally, the task must be applicable during sentence comprehension, and not just after the sentence has already been processed. To these ends, a task was devised which coupled the auditory presentation of an ambiguous sentence with a visual, lexical decision task. Recent work with cross-modality semantic priming has demonstrated that visual lexical decisions are facilitated following auditory processing of a related word (Swinney, Onifer, Prather, & Hirshkowitz, 1979). This finding fits well with the visual mode priming effect reported by Meyer and his associates (e.g., Meyer, Schvaneveldt, & Ruddy, 1972, 1975) and others (Fishler, 1977; Tweedy, Lapinski, & Schvaneveldt, 1977). In fact, the data suggest that cross-modal facilitation effects are at least as robust as those found solely within the visual modality. Several characteristics of the cross-modal priming task are worthy of note. One is that semantic priming holds when the primed (facilitated) word is presented visually during auditory sentence comprehension. The second is that subjects in this task are typically not aware of any particular relationship between the visually presented material and the auditory sentential material. (See the Results and Discussion sections for further explanation.) The semantic priming effect to be used here, much like that demonstrated in other studies, can thus occur as an automatic process, one not under control of conscious direction (see, for example, Fishler, 1977; Neely, 1977). In short, the task reflects the access of auditory (priming) words through the relative facilitation of lexical decisions made to visual words, without drawing particular attention to the relationships involved.

The major advantages of this task are, first, that the visual word can be presented simultaneously with the offset of the ambiguous word in the sentence (thus overcoming distance problems faced by the phoneme monitoring task), second, that it can be used during (rather than after) comprehension, and third, that it minimizes the possibility of attention being drawn to the experimental variables, a situation that has often compromised the results of previous experiments. Finally, this task can be used to measure activation of *each* of the meanings of an auditorily presented ambiguity. If a strong sentential context causes only a single reading to ever be accessed for an ambiguity in a sentence then only lexical decisions for visually presented words related to *that* reading of the ambiguity will be facilitated. On the other hand, if both (or several) readings of an ambiguity are accessed, even in the presence of a strong biasing context, then visual words related to each reading will display some facilitation in the concurrent lexical decision task.

In order to give the hypotheses under investigation a strong test, materials used in this first experiment were taken from the Swinney and Hakes (1976) study which had produced results supporting the Prior Effect Hypothesis.

EXPERIMENT 1

METHOD

Design and Materials. Sentential materials for this study were taken, with a few changes and additions, from those used in the Swinney and Hakes (1976) study. These consisted of 36 sets of sentence pairs (two sentences presented sequentially) each set having four variations. The four variations derive from a factorial combination of two variables: ambiguity and context.

The ambiguity variable was composed of two conditions: inclusion of either an ambiguous word or an unambiguous control word which was roughly synonymous with one reading of the ambiguity. These words were all nouns and all appeared in the predicate of the second sentence of each sentence pair. Ambiguous and control words were matched for frequency, using the Kučera and Francis (1967) norms, and for length in syllables. All ambiguous words were approximately equibiased, as determined by a pretest in which 44 subjects recorded their first interpretations of auditorily presented experimental sentences from the "no content" condition (see below). The maximum proportion attained for any single reading of any of the ambiguities ranged between .50 and .70.

The context variable comprised two conditions: either no disambiguating context, or a prior, strongly predictive disambiguating context. The latter was determined using a criterion (discussed at length in Swinney & Hakes, 1976) in which the context was not only more related to one meaning of the ambiguity than the others, but, as judged by two judges, was strongly predictive of one meaning of the ambiguity by virtue of being highly associated with that meaning and being incompatible with other possible meanings.

For each sentence pair, a set of three words (to be presented visually) was prepared. One of these words was related to the contextually biased reading of the ambiguity in the sentence, one was related to the "other," contextually inappropriate reading of the ambiguity, and the third was not related to any meaning of the ambiguity. The specific degree of relatedness of each visual word to its paired reading of the ambiguity was not specifically controlled. (All such materials, however, appeared to hold a moderate degree of relatedness.) The three words of each set were yoked for length and frequency. (Only moderate-frequency words were utilized.) All words used in these conditions were then compared in an independent, isolated lexical decision task. The experimental words, along with 36 other words and 44 nonword letter strings, were presented visually in random order to 24 subjects. Reaction times to make a word/nonword (lexical) decision were compared for words comprising the three conditions of experimental words. The mean times for these conditions were 0.661, 0.664, and 0.657 sec, respectively. Both multiple t test comparisons and analysis of variance, $F(2, 46) = 0.918$, revealed no significant differences between reaction times to words in these three conditions.

The four sentence variations and the set of three words paired with them are presented schematically in Table 1. The symbol "Δ" represents the point at which one of the three words would be presented visually during the auditory comprehension of the sentence.

TABLE 1	Schematized Sample of Experimental Materials	

	Ambiguity Condition	
CONTEXT CONDITION	**AMBIGUOUS**	**UNAMBIGUOUS**
No context	Rumor had it that, for years, the government building had been plagued with problems. The man was not surprised when he found several bugs$_\Delta$ in the corner of his room.	Rumor had it that, for years, the government building had been plagued with problems. The man was not surprised when he found several insects$_\Delta$ in the corner of his room.
Biasing context	Rumor had it that, for years, the government building had been plagued with problems. The man was not surprised when he found several spiders, roaches, and other bugs$_\Delta$ in the corner of his room.	Rumor had it that, for years, the government building had been plagued with problems. The man was not surprised when he found several spiders, roaches, and other insects$_\Delta$ in the corner of his room.

Visual words displayed at Δ ANT   (contextually related)
SPY   (contextually inappropriate)
SEW   (unrelated)

Four tape recordings were made from the sentential materials. Each tape contained one variation of each of the 36 sentence pairs chosen so that the four types of variation were equally represented on each tape. All tapes also included 46 filler sentence pairs, randomly interspersed among the test sentence pairs. Filler sentence pairs were identical for each tape.

For presentation purposes, three separate lists were created from the words and nonwords which were to be presented visually. Each list contained only one of the three visual words which were created in conjunction with each sentence pair. The three visual word conditions were equally represented on each list. Half of the materials on each list were words (36 experimental materials, and 2 words which were paired with filler sentences) and the other half (32) were nonwords (paired with filler sentences). For six of the filler sentences, no visual word appeared on the screen.

Thus, there were 12 presentation conditions: each of 3 lists paired with each of the 4 tape conditions. A 1,000-Hz signal was placed on a separate channel of the tape exactly coincident with the *offset* of each ambiguous or control word in the experimental sentential materials, and with the offset of a pseudorandomly chosen word in the filler sentences. These signals, inaudible to the subjects, signaled a PDP8/e computer to present the appropriate visual word and to start the timing mechanism which measured the latencies for the subject's lexical decisions. (See Onifer, Hirshkowitz, & Swinney, 1978, for discussion of hardware and software involved in this procedure.)

Subjects. Eighty-four undergraduates from Tufts University participated in partial fulfillment of a course requirement. Seven subjects were randomly assigned to each of the 12 experimental conditions. Data for six additional subjects were omitted from analysis for failure to achieve a score of at least 85% correct on the comprehension test.

Procedure. The subjects were seated in front of a CRT screen and listened through headphones to the 82 binaurally presented sentence pairs. Subjects were tested in groups of up to 3 at a time: each subject was in a booth isolating him/her from other subjects in a group. Subjects were instructed to listen carefully to each sentence and to understand it. They were told that they would be tested on their comprehension during the experiment, and that the result of this test was crucial to their successful participation in this experiment.

In addition, subjects were told that they had a second task. It was explained that a string of letters would appear on the screen during some of the sentences they listened to and that they were to decide as quickly as possible whether each letter string formed a word or not. No hint was given that words and sentences might be related and, in the five practice trials, no such relationship existed.

At both the midpoint and the end of the experimental session, subjects were given a sheet of paper containing 21 sentence pairs. They were required to decide whether each of these was either identical or similar to sentences they had heard, or whether the sentence had not occurred at all in the experiment. These materials were scored on a percentage correct basis. At the end of the experimental session, subjects were questioned about whether they had noticed ambiguities in the sentence materials and about whether they thought the words on the screen related in any specific fashion to the sentences they had heard.

RESULTS

The mean reaction times for the 12 experimental conditions, calculated across all materials and subjects, are presented in Table 2. It is apparent that lexical decisions for words related to *both* readings of the ambiguity are facilitated (relative to decisions for an unrelated control word) in conditions containing a lexical ambiguity and no biasing context. Similarly, and of greatest interest, this same effect holds for the condition in which there's strongly biasing semantic context present; lexical decisions for words related to both the contextually relevant and the contextually

TABLE 2   Mean Reaction Times (in milliseconds) for Conditions of the Ambiguity × Context × Visual Word Interaction: Experiment 1

		Visually Presented Words		
AMBIGUITY CONDITION	CONTEXT CONDITION	CONTEXTUALLY RELATED	CONTEXTUALLY INAPPROPRIATE	UNRELATED
Ambiguous	Biasing context	890	910	960
	No context	916	925	974
Unambiguous	Biasing context	887	958	963
	No context	914	967	972

inappropriate meanings of the ambiguity appear to be facilitated compared to decisions for unrelated control words. The effects for both of the unambiguous conditions also appear quite straightforward: Lexical decisions for the "related" word appear to be facilitated, but those for the other two words are not. Thus, by inspection, the results appear to support the Postdecision Hypothesis; even a very strong semantic context apparently does not direct lexical access. Statistical analysis supports this contention.

An analysis of variance revealed that main effects for Context, Ambiguity, and Visual Word Type were each significant for analyses employing both subjects and materials as random factors, Min $F'(1, 79) = 7.01$, $p < .01$; Min $F'(1, 86) = 6.32$, $p < .025$; Min $F'(2, 188) = 52.6$, $p < .001$, respectively. Both the Context × Visual Word Type and the Context × Ambiguity interactions failed to reach significance, Min F' $(1, 119) = 0.42$; Min $F'(1, 74) = 0.1$, respectively. Most revealing for the present purposes, however, was the fact that Ambiguity interacted significantly with Visual Word Type, Min $F'(2, 157) = 4.71$, $p < .01$, but that the Context × Ambiguity × Visual Word Type interaction was not significant, Min $F'(2, 161) = 0.04$.

In order to examine the predicted effects, planned multiple comparisons were made on the relevant Visual Word Type categories for each of the Ambiguity × Context conditions. For the condition containing a biasing context and an ambiguity, reaction times to visual words in both the contextually related and contextually inappropriate categories were significantly faster than latencies for unrelated words, $t(83) = -6.1$, $p < .0009$; $t(83) = -5.04$, $p < .0009$, respectively. The contextually related and contextually inappropriate categories, however, did not differ from each other in this condition, $t(83) = -1.05$. This same overall configuration of results held for the no context condition containing an ambiguity, $t(83) = -5.2$, $p < .0009$; $t(83) = -4.94$, $p < .0009$, $t(83) = -0.98$, respectively. In the unambiguous conditions, reaction times to the contextually related words were significantly faster than those for the unrelated words in both the biasing context, $t(83) = -7.4$, $p < .0009$, and no context, $t(83) = -5.16$, $p < .0009$, conditions. However, reaction times to contextually related words differed significantly from contextually inappropriate words in each context condition, $t(83) = -7.2$, $p < .0009$; $t(83) = -5.2$, $p < .0009$, respectively. In neither case did reaction times to the contextually inappropriate words differ from those to the unrelated words, $t(83) = -0.55$; $t(83) = -0.6$, respectively.[3,4]

The post-test questionnaires were evaluated in order to determine whether subjects noticed any specific relationship between words in the sentence and the visually presented words. Of the 84 subjects, only 11 thought they noticed any time-locked relationship between materials in the sentence and the visual words. However, the relationships these subjects reported were almost entirely unrelated to the experimental manipulations; it appears that perceptual displacement typically occurs in this task, and that subjects report seeing the visual words one to two syllables downstream from where they actually occur. Thus, reported relationships are most typically unrelated to the experimental manipulations. (Because the ratio of related materials to unrelated materials is kept low, a strategy of attempting to relate visual words to immediately preceding auditory material would actually be detrimental rather than facilatory to task performance.) Because these 11 "aware" subjects came from eight different materials conditions, analysis of their data could only be made by comparison with data obtained from the same subject-group conditions. In these comparisons there was only a single case in which the basic direction of effects for Ambiguity, Context, and Visual Word Type did not hold. However, it is notable that the facilitation for the contextually inappropriate visual word condition did not appear to be nearly so robust for "aware" subjects as it was for the "unaware" subjects, although these differences were not statistically significant.

Similarly, only 3 of the 84 subjects reported that they had noticed ambiguities in the materials during the experiment; due to the small number of cases, no further analysis of this factor was undertaken.

DISCUSSION

The results of experiment 1 provide fairly strong support for a model of sentential processing in which lexical *access* is an autonomous process; because semantic facilitation was observed for lexical decisions to words related to both the contextually relevant and the contextually inappropriate meanings of the ambiguities, even in the presence of the very strong prior semantic contexts, it appears reasonable to conclude that semantic context does not *direct* lexical access. Rather, immediately following occurrence of an ambiguous word, all meanings for that word seem to be momentarily accessed during sentence comprehension. Thus, the results which were previously obtained with the phoneme monitoring task would appear to be the consequence of some process which occurred following lexical access rather than a reflection of the access process itself (see also Cairns & Hsu, 1979, for arguments supporting this position). It seems likely that semantic context has its effects upon a postaccess decision process, one which eventuates in the choosing of a single reading for an ambiguity. Certainly, a number of intriguing questions now present themselves. Foremost among these is one concerning the nature of the information interaction which occurs during this posited postaccess decision process.

In order to further investigate this, a second experiment was performed which focused on the time course of this process. The experiment also had the goal of providing further information concerning the cross-modal priming task. Cairns and Kamerman (1976) reported that the increased sentential processing complexity caused by an ambiguity disappears approximately two syllables following the ambiguity, when measured by the phoneme monitoring task. If these results are valid (again, see Newman & Dell, 1978) then any lexical ambiguity is apparently resolved by that time, even when no overtly biasing context is present. Even if these phoneme monitoring data are questionable, it is clear that lexical ambiguity must be resolved relatively quickly, certainly by the end of the clause containing that ambiguity (see, e.g., Foss, Bever, & Silver, 1968; Bever, Garrett, & Hurtig, 1973). It is thus important to determine the rate and manner in which the nonrelevant reading(s) of an ambiguity is (are) discarded during this postaccess decision process. Available data do not permit us to even determine whether contextually irrelevant readings remain available at some level for processing or whether they are irretrievably lost to the comprehension device. Experiment 2 examines these questions utilizing the same basic experimental design as was used in experiment 1. In this experiment, however, the visual (primed) materials appear three syllables following occurrence of the ambiguous word in the sentence as well as immediately following it. If the contextually inappropriate meanings of an ambiguous word are immediately discarded or suppressed, then we should find that only the contextually relevant visual materials will be facilitated in this experiment. On the other hand, if all meanings of the ambiguous word remain under consideration until the end of the clause containing the ambiguity, then words related to both the contextually appropriate and the contextually inappropriate meanings of the ambiguous word should be facilitated.

• • •

GENERAL DISCUSSION

In all, the results from both of these experiments provide strong support for the conclusion that the *access* process for lexical items is isolable and autonomous at least with respect to effects of semantic context. That is, semantic contexts do not appear to direct lexical access, as was predicted by the Prior Decision Hypothesis. Thus, the access operation appears to be a stimulus (form)-driven process for which the entire inventory of information stored for a lexical form is made available to the sentence comprehension device. The results also support the existence of a postaccess decision process which acts to select a single meaning from those originally and momentarily accessed for involvement in further processing. This decision process apparently is completed at least by the time that three syllables of additional information have been processed (approximately 750–1,000 msec), even when no biasing context is present.

A few general comments concerning the posited postaccess decision process are in order. First, the normal time course of access, activation, and deactivation (for inappropriate meanings) in this process is clearly underestimated in this study. It is likely to be far less than the approximately 750–1,000 msec found in experiment 2. Further as this decision process takes place within a 1,000-msec period even for conditions containing no biasing context, one would expect it to be far faster in normal situations, where a context is typically present. Second, the nature of the decision process which chooses the relevant meaning of the ambiguity deserves some consideration. It may be that the process acts to suppress the level of activation of unchosen meanings. On the other hand, it may be that the single meaning which is chosen for an ambiguity is somehow made available to further (higher order) sentential processes in a manner which simply ignores the unchosen meanings. (For example, it could be that both meanings of the ambiguity are still somewhat activated following access, but that the relevant meaning is shifted to what might be considered the "current" level of processing; presumably, it would be just this "current" level which can provide automatic semantic priming.) At present, there are no data which will allow us to directly choose between these quite different alternatives, and it is clear that further work on the nature of this decision process is in order.

Finally, because most words can, in fact, have different meanings (be these merely the different senses of a word or the totally different meanings comprising an unsystematic lexical ambiguity), it seems reasonable to suggest that the postaccess decision process posited here may be a general process. For any word, some subset of all the information which is originally accessed for that word may be selected for further processing and integration into ongoing sentential analysis. If so, only a single meaning for an ambiguous word, and only a single "sense" of an unambiguous word, would thus come to conscious awareness following this postaccess decision process. Semantic contexts apparently aid this selection process; the more the context restricts or determines the relevant sense of a word, the quicker the decision process will presumably take place. This model would fit with approaches taken by a number of authors (e.g., Collins & Loftus, 1975; Morton, 1969) on the access of semantic memory. It should be noted that while semantic contexts apparently do not affect access, there may be other types of information that will act upon the access phase of word recognition. Syntactic information, for example, may well serve to direct access in a way that semantic context cannot (see, e.g., Fay, 1976; Garrett, 1978; Prather & Swinney, 1977; Ryder, 1978).

The model just sketched is, admittedly, underdetermined by the data. The nature of the claim being made is that sentence comprehension is not a totally interactive process; that is, that all kinds of information do not interact at all levels of processing. Certainly, it suggests that lexical access is basically a "bottom-up" or stimulus-driven process. This, however, is not at all to claim that this accessed information does not interact with other information. In fact, the data presented here could fit well with certain types of interactive models, such as that presented by Marslen-Wilson and his associates (e.g., Marslen-Wilson, 1975; Marslen-Wilson & Welsh, 1978), provided that certain constraints are placed on the interactions occurring around the access phase. In sum, however, these data appear to provide some evidence for autonomy of the lexical access process during sentence comprehension.

REFERENCES

Bever, T. G., Garrett, M. F., & Hurtig, R. The interaction of perceptual processes and ambiguous sentences. *Memory and Cognition,* 1973, *1,* 227–286.

Cairns, H. S., & Hsu, J. R. Effects of prior context upon lexical access during sentence comprehension: A replication and reinterpretation. *Journal of Psycholinguistic Research,* 1979, in press.

Cairns, H. S., & Kamerman, J. Lexical information processing during sentence comprehension. *Journal of Verbal Learning and Verbal Behavior,* 1975, *14,* 170–179.

Chodorow, M. *Using time-compressed speech to measure the effects of ambiguity.* Quarterly Progress Report No. 116, Massachusetts Institute of Technology, 1973. Pp. 235–240.

Collins, A. M., & Loftus, E. F. A spreading activation theory of semantic processing. *Psychological Review,* 1975, *82,* 407–428.

Conrad, C. Context effects in sentence comprehension: A study of the subjective lexicon. *Memory and Cognition,* 1974, *2,* No. 1A, 130–138.

Cutler, A., & Foss, D. J. *Comprehension of ambiguous sentences. The locus of context effects.* Paper presented at the Midwestern Psychological Association, Chicago, Ill., May 1974.

Fay, D. *The role of grammatical category in the mental lexicon.* Paper presented at the Midwestern Psychological Association, Chicago, Ill., May 1976.

Fishler, I. Semantic facilitation without association in a lexical decision task. *Memory and Cognition,* 1977, *5,* 333–339.

Forster, K. I. Accessing the mental lexicon. In R. J. Wales & E. Walker (Eds.), *New approaches to language mechanisms.* Amsterdam: North-Holland, 1976.

Foss, D. J. Some effects of ambiguity upon sentence comprehension. *Journal of Verbal Learning and Verbal Behavior,* 1970, *9,* 699–706.

Foss, D. J., Bever, T. G., & Silver, M. The comprehension and verification of ambiguous sentences. *Perception and Psychophysics,* 1968, *4,* 304–306.

Foss, D. J., & Jenkins, C. Some effects of context on the comprehension of ambiguous sentences. *Journal of Verbal Learning and Verbal Behavior,* 1973, *12,* 577–589.

Garrett, M. F. Word and sentence perception. In R. Held, H. W. Liebowitz, & H. L. Teuber (Eds.), *Handbook of sensory physiology,* Vol. VIII: *Perception.* Berlin: Springer-Verlag, 1978.

Hogaboam, T., & Perfetti, C. Lexical ambiguity and sentence comprehension. *Journal of Verbal Learning and Verbal Behavior,* 1975, *14,* 265–274.

Holmes, V. M., Arwas, R., & Garrett, M. F. Prior context and the perception of lexically ambiguous sentences. *Memory and Cognition,* 1977, *5,* 103–110.

Jenkins, J. *Context conditions meaning.* Invited address delivered at Midwestern Psychological Association. Chicago, Ill., May 1977.

Kirk, R. *Experimental design: Procedures for the behavioral sciences.* Belmont, CA: Brooks/Cole, 1968.

Kučera, H., & Francis, W. *Computational analysis of present-day American English.* Providence, RI: Brown Univ. Press, 1967.

Lackner, J. R., & Garrett, M. F. Resolving ambiguity: Effects of biasing context in the unattended ear. *Cognition,* 1972, *1,* 359–372.

MacKay, D. G. Mental diplopia: Towards a model of speech perception at the semantic level. In G. B. Flores d'Arcais & W. J. Levelt (Eds.), *Advances in psycholinguistics.* Amsterdam: North-Holland, 1970.

Marslen-Wilson, W. D. Sentence perception as an interactive parallel process. *Science,* 1975, *189,* 226–228.

Marslen-Wilson, W. D., & Welsh, A. Processing interactions and lexical access during word recognition in continuous speech. *Cognitive Psychology,* 1978, *10.*

Mehler, J., Segui, J., & Carey, P. Tails of words: Monitoring ambiguity. *Journal of Verbal Learning and Verbal Behavior,* 1978, *17,* 29–35.

Meyer, D., Schvaneveldt, R., & Ruddy, M. *Activation of lexical memory.* Paper presented at the Meeting of the Psychonomic Society, St. Louis, Mo., 1972.

Meyer, D. E., Schvaneveldt, R. W., & Ruddy, M. G. Loci of contextual effects on visual word recognition. In P. M. A. Rabbit & S. Dornic (Eds.), *Attention and performance V.* London/New York: Academic Press, 1975.

Morton, J. The interaction of information in word recognition. *Psychological Review,* 1969, *60,* 329–346.

Neely, J. Semantic priming and retrieval from lexical memory: Roles of inhibitionless spreading activation and limited capacity attention. *Journal of Experimental Psychology: General,* 1977, *106,* 226–254.

Newman, J. E., & Dell, G. S. The phonological nature of phoneme monitoring: A critique of some ambiguity studies. *Journal of Verbal Learning and Verbal Behavior,* 1978, *17,* 359–374.

Onifer, W., Hirshkowitz, M., & Swinney, D. A miniprocessor PDP8/e-based system for investigations of on-line language processing: Automated program for psycholinguistic experiments (APPLE). *Behavior Research Methods and Instrumentation,* 1978, *10* (2), 307–308.

Prather, P., & Swinney, D. *Some effects of syntactic context upon lexical access.* Paper presented at the American Psychological Association, San Francisco. August 1977.

Ryder, J. The effects of semantic and syntactic ambiguity on lexical processing. Unpublished paper. Psychology Department, Brandeis University, 1978.

Schvaneveldt, R., Meyer, D., & Becker, C. Lexical ambiguity, semantic context, and visual word recognition. *Journal of Experimental Psychology: Human Perception and Performance,* 1976, *2,* 243–256.

Swinney, D. *Does context direct lexical access?* Paper presented at Midwestern Psychological Association, Chicago, Ill., May 1976.

Swinney, D., & Hakes, D. Effects of prior context upon lexical access during sentence comprehension. *Journal of Verbal Learning and Verbal Behavior,* 1976, *15,* 681–689.

Swinney, D., Onifer, W., Prather, P., & Hirshkowitz, M. Semantic facilitation across sensory modalities in the processing of individual words and sentences. *Memory and Cognition,* 1979, 7 (3), 159–165.

Tweedy, L., Lapinski, R., & Schvaneveldt, R. Semantic context effects upon word recognition. *Memory and Cognition,* 1977, *5,* 84–89.

NOTES

1. The experiment by Lackner and Garrett (1972) may be an exception to the particular problems stated here. However, their data do not actually allow a decision concerning whether context acted in a prior access or post access fashion. See comments in Holmes, Arwas, and Garrett (1977) and Lackner and Garrett (1972).

2. Newman and Dell (1978) point to the apparent direct relationship between the magnitude of the obtained ambiguity effect and the magnitude of the difference in the number of phonological features shared between the target phoneme and the initial phoneme of the ambiguous and unambiguous control words. A similar direct relationship was shown to hold between the magnitude of the obtained ambiguity effect and the amount by which the length of the unambiguous control word exceeded that of the ambiguous word. The Swinney and Hakes (1976) materials have smaller differences between ambiguous and nonambiguous control words (on both the phonological and the length criteria) than any of the studies examined by Newman and Dell, and yet their data show the *largest* ambiguity effect of any of these studies. Further, and perhaps most importantly, the Swinney and Hakes (1976) results showed a decrement in this ambiguity effect in the face of a strong biasing context. Note that this change in the ambiguity effect occurs over sets of materials in which the critical phonemic and length features are identical. If the phoneme monitoring data is not reflecting an ambiguity processing effect, it is difficult to see what the basis for the observed decrement could be. Newman and Dell suggest that the semantic contexts may be attentuating a phonological search effect associated with the phoneme monitoring task rather than an ambiguity processing effect. However, that claim appears rather unlikely, particularly given that the decrement in processing latency occurs in the presence of semantic contexts which are in sentences which precede those containing the ambiguity and target phoneme. It would appear that a more parsimonious account of the results is that while length and phonological properties of the word preceding the target phoneme undoubtedly effect the phoneme monitoring task, the task also, given appropriate circumstances, reflects lexical processing complexity.

3. It should be noted that the only appropriate comparisons to make for these data are those given. Because the level of associativity of the contextually related and contextually inappropriate words to each of the meanings of the ambiguity are not equated (a nearly impossible task given the other, more critical, constraints required in matching these words; see Design and Materials section), the appropriate comparisons are just those which examine for evidence of facilitation priming between each of these visual words and its control. Levels of such facilitation cannot be meaningfully examined by direct comparison of reaction

times to the "related" and "inappropriate" words or by comparison of the relative degree of facilitation for each of these words compared to its control (although these have been given in a few cases above, just for general interest purposes.) This is, again, because the absolute degree of associativity of each visual word to its related sense of the ambiguity differ by an unknown amount. In addition, although the reaction times for the contextually related words are beguilingly similar for the ambiguous and nonambiguous conditions, no interpretable comparisons between these conditions are possible; the facilitation of the "contextually related" words occurs in response to different auditory contexts in the ambiguous and unambiguous conditions (e.g., to the word *bug* in the one and *insect* in the other, in the materials sample in Table 1.) It is interesting to note that reaction times to the control words, which are legitimate sources for comparison, are remarkably similar for the ambiguous and unambiguous conditions. However, overall, the only relevant and interpretable comparisons are those involving the search for presence or absence of significant facilitation priming for the "related" and "inappropriate" visual words in each of the individual experimental conditions; such evidence is sufficient and appropriate for examining the issues addressed in this paper.

4. Although all paired comparisons made by multiple *t* tests were both planned and necessary in order to examine the hypotheses under question, a more conservative test, the Bonferroni *t* (Kirk, 1968), was also applied to the data. For this test, the critical value of *d* for $\alpha = .05$, was 46.1. As can be seen by inspection, all comparisons which were significant under the standard *t* tests were also significant under the Bonferroni *t* analysis.

QUESTIONS FOR FURTHER THOUGHT

1. How does Swinney believe that people handle lexical ambiguities?

2. What evidence does Swinney present in favor of his theory of how people handle lexical ambiguity?

3. What is the likely reason that multiple meanings do not remain active indefinitely, or at least until they definitely are ruled out by new information?

4. How do subjects' activities in Swinney's experiments differ from ordinary listening or reading comprehension situations? Do any differences have implications for the applicability of the results to ordinary listening or reading comprehension?

5. How does the evidence Swinney presents rule out models that are alternatives to his own?

8

PROBLEM SOLVING

UNDERSTANDING AND SOLVING WORD ARITHMETIC PROBLEMS
Walter Kintsch and James Greeno

INTUITION IN INSIGHT AND NONINSIGHT PROBLEM SOLVING
Janet Metcalfe and David Weibe

Understanding and Solving Word Arithmetic Problems

Walter Kintsch and James Greeno

INTRODUCTION

The vast majority of studies in the field of cognitive psychology focus specifically on a single area of inquiry, such as attention, perception, memory, problem solving, or language. In contrast, much of the cognitive work people do in daily life requires an integration of processes, knowledge, and strategies from two or more areas. For example, as you read this paragraph, you are using at least a modicum of attention, some fancy perceptual apparatus, language processes, memory for the meanings of printed words, and if the meaning is unclear, perhaps some problem solving, as well. What kinds of issues are encountered when someone attempts to integrate concepts from two or more areas of inquiry for the purpose of accounting for performance on realistic cognitive tasks?

Kintsch and Greeno present a model of understanding and solving word arithmetic problems. Problems of the sort, "Jill has seven puppies and sells four of them. How many puppies does she have left?" require reading comprehension as well as arithmetic operations. The model Kintsch and Greeno propose is a hybrid that incorporates a model of comprehension, procedures for representing mathematical relations, and procedures for actually solving the represented problem. To test their model, Kintsch and Greeno developed a computer simulation of the model that makes predictions about the difficulty of different kinds of word arithmetic problems. The model's predictions are generally consistent with observed data.

It is difficult to formulate a compelling model in a single domain of cognitive psychology, and the Kintsch and Greeno model is especially impressive because it integrates two domains—text comprehension and mathematical reasoning. Indeed, the model results from collaboration between investigators in each of these fields, Kintsch specializing in text comprehension and Greeno in mathematical reasoning. Many real-world tasks actually do require individuals to cross domains, so the model proposed here serves as a bellwether for a direction in which models in cognitive psychology need to go—toward integration across traditionally separate domains of inquiry.

Source: From Kintsch, W., & Greeno, J. G. (1985). Understanding and solving word arithmetic problems. *Psychological Review, 92,* 109–129. Copyright © 1993 by the American Psychological Association. Reprinted with permission.

A processing model is presented that deals explicitly with both the text-comprehension and problem-solving aspects of word arithmetic problems. General principles from a theory of text processing (van Dijk & Kintsch, 1983) are combined with hypotheses about semantic knowledge for understanding problem texts (Riley, Greeno, & Heller, 1983) in an integrated model of problem comprehension. The model simulates construction of cognitive representations that include information that is appropriate for problem-solving procedures that children use. Several information-processing steps are distinguished, and various levels of representation are described. The model provides an analysis of processing requirements, including requirements for short-term memory that differ among types of problems. Predictions about difficulty of problems based on these processing differences are generally consistent with data that have been reported. ■

The question that we address in this article is the interaction between comprehension and problem solving. Theories of problem-solving processes have been developed in detail (e.g., Brown & Burton, 1978; Greeno, 1978; Newell & Simon, 1972), as have theories of processes of language comprehension (e.g., Anderson, 1976; Kintsch & van Dijk, 1978; Norman & Rumelhart, 1975; Schank, 1972; Winograd, 1972). These two lines of theory come together in analyses of the representation of problems, especially when text is used to present problem information or instructions (e.g., Hayes & Simon, 1974). Particular progress has been made in analyzing problem understanding in domains with formal methods for problem solving. Several studies have considered word problems in algebra or physics, which require representations of problem texts that can be coordinated with formulas (Bobrow, 1968; deKleer, 1975; Hinsley, Hayes, & Simon, 1977; Larkin, McDermott, Simon, & Simon, 1980; Novak, 1976; Paige & Simon, 1966).

In this article, we consider word problems in arithmetic, which require representations that can be used to choose operations such as addition, subtraction, or counting of objects. There is a considerable body of research on solutions of simple arithmetic word problems, including recent contributions by Carpenter and Moser (1982), DeCorte and Vershaffel (1981), Nesher (1982), Nesher, Greeno, and Riley (1982), Vergnaud (1982), and Wolters (1983). Problems have been classified according to the semantic relations among quantities in the problems, and data have been obtained that show (a) how difficult different kinds of problems are for children of variant ages, (b) what kinds of solution processes are used for different problems, and (c) what kinds of errors occur. Information-processing models that simulate solutions of word problems have been developed by Riley, Greeno, and Heller (1983) and by Briars and Larkin (in press). These models provide hypotheses about information structures formed in representing problems, inferences that are made, and counting operations that are performed on sets of objects that are represented. These models also give plausible explanations of the relative difficulty of different kinds of problems, based on assumptions that more complex processes and structures are needed to solve the more difficult problems.

The model that we present in this article includes a more thorough analysis of processes of text comprehension than has been provided in earlier investigations of arithmetic word problems.[1] We use the general theory of text comprehension developed by Kintsch and van Dijk (1978) and van Dijk and Kintsch (1983), along with Riley et al.'s (1983) assumptions about the semantic knowledge required for representing the problems and the processes of operating on the numbers in problems to find the answers. Both of the previous models are extended by this synthesis. We show that Riley et al.'s assumptions of semantic structure and problem-solving processes in arithmetic are compatible with general assumptions about text comprehension. We also show that van Dijk and Kintsch's assumptions about text comprehension can be applied in analyzing the task of understanding arithmetic-problem texts, a domain with rather different characteristics from the narrative and expository materials considered previously.

According to van Dijk and Kintsch (1983), memory representations of texts have two components: a propositional structure of information that is in the text in a specified sense, and a situation model that is derived from the text, wholly or in part. The propositional structure, or textbase, is obtained by constructing a coherent conceptual representation of the text, called a *microstructure,* and then deriving from the microstructure a hierarchical macrostructure that corresponds to the essential ideas expressed in the text. The situation model includes inferences that are made using knowledge about the domain of the text information. It is a representation of the content of a text, independent of how the text was formulated and integrated with other relevant experiences. Its structure is adapted to the demands of whatever tasks the reader expects to perform.

The task of comprehending a problem text is to construct from the verbal form of the problem a conceptual representation upon which problem-solving processes can operate. In the case of arithmetic, the reader's understanding includes conceptual relations among quantities that guide the choice of calculations to be performed. Nesher and Teubal (1975) presented a particularly clear discussion of the need for such a representation, intervening between the problem text and problem-solving operations. Following van Dijk and Kintsch (1983), we propose a dual representation, including a propositional textbase and a situation model, or problem model, that includes information that is inferred from the reader's knowledge in the domain of arithmetic problems.

Comprehension strategies are involved in the construction of this multilayered problem representation, and the strategies used in comprehending arithmetic word problems constitute a particular focus of our analysis. In reading a story, the comprehension strategies include looking for the motives of characters, outcomes of actions, and episode boundaries (Kintsch, 1977). The resulting macrostructure contains information about who did what and why. A professional reading a stock market report uses different strategies to find out about sales or capitalization of a company, providing a macrostructure that contains salient information about the company's standing (Kozminsky, Kintsch, & Bourne, 1981). In reading word arithmetic problems, yet different strategies are used, with the purpose of creating the kind of problem representation required for successful solution. We hypothesize that the general features of the comprehension process are alike in these three cases, but the content of the comprehension strategies, the nature of the knowledge structures involved, and the form of the resulting macrostructures are task and goal specific.

We suppose that children's experience in solving word problems results in their acquiring a special set of strategies for constructing mental representations of texts that are suitable for applying mathematical operations such as addition and subtraction. That is, readers learn not to use normal comprehension strategies that are appropriate, say, for reading stories or essays, but rather to analyze the text in a specialized way (cf. Kane, 1968; Nesher & Teubal, 1975). Arithmetic word problems also have special presuppositions that children presumably learn to apply (Nesher & Katriel, 1977). These features of word arithmetic problems make them particularly attractive for use in modeling the comprehension process; the very fact that comprehension strategies and presuppositions are unusual and distinct makes them easier to identify and characterize than more widely used, all-purpose strategies that tend to be taken for granted. Understanding and solving word problems can be considered a form of "expert" performance, in the sense used in the literature on problem solving in physics (e.g., Larkin et al., 1980; Chi, Feltovich, & Glaser, 1981), and our model provides an analysis of specialized expert knowledge in relation to the general process of text comprehension.

THE MODEL

The main components of the model that we present are a set of knowledge structures and a set of strategies for using these knowledge structures in building a representation and in solving the problem.[2] The representation is a dual one: On one side, we have the textbase representing the textual input, and on the other side an abstract problem representation, the problem model, which contains the problem-relevant information from the textbase in a form suitable for calculational strategies that yield the problem solution.

Problem representations are built in several information-processing steps, which do not necessarily occur in a strict sequence. The verbal input is transformed into a conceptual representation of its meaning, a list of propositions. The propositions are organized into a task-specific macrostructure that highlights the general concepts and relations that are mentioned in the text. The salient general concepts in the arithmetic problems we analyze are sets and relations among sets. We refer to this organized set of propositions as the *textbase*.

Coordinated with the representation of propositions is a second structure, the problem model, which reflects knowledge of the information needed to solve the problem. In constructing the problem model, the reader infers information that is needed for solving the problem but is not included in the textbase, and excludes information in the textbase that is not required for solution of the problem.

The model includes three sets of knowledge structures used in representing and solving problems. First, there is a set of propositional frames, used in translating sentences into propositions. Second, there is a set of schemata that represent properties and relations of sets in general form. These schemata are used in constructing macrostructures and problem models. Finally, there is a set of schemata that represent counting and arithmetic operations in general form. Specific versions of these action schemata are used in calculating the solutions of problems.

Table 1 shows a list of problems that we use in illustrating the model's operation. These problems can be thought of as prototypes for word problems that can be solved with a single addition or subtraction operation. In Riley et al.'s (1983) study, problems of these 14 types were given to school children in grades K–3. Problems varied in the states used to identify sets (possession, as in Table 1, or location), in the kinds of objects, and in the names of individuals or locations used to specify sets.

TABLE 1   Types of Word Problems

CATEGORY AND PROBLEM	CATEGORY AND PROBLEM
Change	**Subset unknown**
Result unknown	2. Joe and Tom have eight marbles altogether.
1. Joe had three marbles.	Joe has three marbles.
Then Tom gave him five more marbles.	How many marbles does Tom have?
How many marbles does Joe have now?	
	Compare
2. Joe had eight marbles.	Difference unknown
Then he gave five marbles to Tom.	1. Joe has eight marbles.
How many marbles does Joe have now?	Tom has five marbles.
	How many marbles does Joe have more than Tom?
Change unknown	
3. Joe had three marbles.	2. Joe has eight marbles.
Then Tom gave him some more marbles.	Tom has five marbles.
Now Joe has eight marbles.	How many marbles does Tom have less than Joe?
How many marbles did Tom give him?	
	Compared quality unknown
4. Joe had eight marbles.	3. Joe has three marbles.
Then he gave some marbles to Tom.	Tom has three more marbles than Joe.
Now he has three marbles.	How many marbles does Tom have?
How many marbles did he give to Tom?	
	4. Joe has eight marbles.
State Unknown	Tom has five marbles less than Joe.
5. Joe had some marbles.	How many marbles does Tom have?
Then Tom gave him five more marbles.	
Now Joe has eight marbles.	
How many marbles did Joe have in the beginning?	Referent unknown
	5. Joe has eight marbles.
6. Joe had some marbles.	He has five more marbles than Tom.
Then he gave five marbles to Tom.	How many marbles does Tom have?
Now Joe has three marbles.	
How many marbles did Joe have in the beginning?	6. Joe has three marbles.
	He has five marbles less than Tom.
Combine	How many marbles does Tom have?
Superset unknown	
1. Joe has three marbles.	
Tom has five marbles.	
How many marbles do they have altogether?	

The representations that the model constructs for these problems refer to sets of objects, properties that distinguish the sets, quantities associated with the sets, and relations among the sets. We suppose that children understand words such as *have, give, all, more,* and *less* in a general way when they begin school. We suppose further that through instruction in arithmetic and word problems, students can learn to treat these words in a special, task-specific way. This includes learning to represent propositions involving having, giving, and so on with arguments that refer to sets of objects. It also includes extensions of the ordinary use of terms such as *all* and *more* to more complicated constructions involving sets, denoted by *altogether* and *more than.* Another component of learning involves comprehension strategies, where children learn to pay attention to numbers and relations among sets, rather than, for example, to Joe's motives in giving Tom some marbles, or the possibility that Tom would rather have apples than marbles.

The model that we present has a single set of knowledge structures and processes, which we suggest may typify the comprehension ability of children at about the second-grade level. We propose this model as a prototype that shows how text-processing knowledge can interact with strategies involving higher order concepts and knowledge of problem-solving operations. Models analogous to the one that we present could be constructed to correspond to different levels of knowledge and skill, with less sophisticated knowledge assumed for younger children and more abstract and general representations for older children and adults. For example, it might be appropriate to assume that kindergarten and first-grade children lack a definite schema for representing sets, and instead solve problems by assembling and counting individual items, as Briars and Larkin (in press) postulated. Indeed, Riley et al. (1983) proposed a sequence of models that simulate different levels of problem-solving performance, with increasing success corresponding to more elaborate problem representations. The model that we present corresponds to the most advanced of Riley et al.'s models, which can solve all of the problems in Table 1.

INTRODUCTORY EXAMPLE

We begin with an example to show the kinds of representations that we assume to be constructed. The knowledge structures and processes needed to construct these representations are then described.

The problem we use for the example is the first problem in the Combine category in Table 1. Table 2 shows (a) the propositions in the text sentence, (b) the strategies that organize these propositions into a coherent, task-specific textbase, and (c) the contents of the problem model. (The fourth column, short-term buffer, is discussed in the Processing Requirements section of this article.)

The first three propositions are obtained from the sentence "Joe has three marbles." The proposition THREE (MARBLES) cues representation of a set. In the propositional textbase, the three propositions are sorted into the *object, quantity,* and *specification* slots. The arguments, *marbles, 3,* and *Joe,* are taken from propositions in the textbase and assigned to appropriate slots of a set schema in the problem model. At this time, the *role* slots of the set schema are empty in both the textbase and the problem model.

TABLE 2   Representation of Combine Problem 1

PROPOSITIONAL TEXTBASE	STRATEGIES	PROBLEM MODEL	SHORT-TERM BUFFER
	Joe has three marbles.		
P1 x_1 = Joe			
P2 HAVE(x_1, P3)			
P3 THREE (MARBLES)	MAKE-SET:		
S1-Obj: P3 ———————————→		marbles	
Quan:		→ 3	
Spec: P1 @ P2 ——————————→		→ Joe	
Role:		?	
	Tom has five marbles.		
P4 x_2 = Tom			S1: role = ?
P5 HAVE(x_2, P6)			
P6 FIVE (MARBLES)	MAKE-SET:		
S2-Obj: P6 ———————————→		marbles	
Quan:		→ 5	
Spec: P4 @ P5 ——————————→		→ Tom	
Role:		?	
	How many marbles do they have altogether?		
P7 HOWMANY (MARBLES)			S2: role = ?
P8 HAVE-ALTOGETHER			
(x_1 & x_2, P7)	MAKE-SET:		
S3-Obj: P7 ———————————→		marbles	
Quan:		→ goal	
Spec: P8 ——————————————→		→ Joe & Tom	
Role:		→ superset	
	SUPERSET		
		Request SUBSET (Joe)	
		SUBSET (Tom)	
	SUBSET (Tom)	S2: role = subset	
REINSTATE S1			
	SUBSET (Joe)	S1: role = subset	
			SUPERSET:
			S3: goal, super
	SOLVE: COUNT-ALL (S1, S2)		S2: 5, sub
			S1: 3, sub

Note. Obj = object; Quan = quantity; Spec = specification.

Propositions P4–P6 are obtained from the sentence "Tom has five marbles," and a second set is represented in both the textbase and the problem model, with propositions as arguments in the slots of the textbase and more concise arguments in the problem model.

Propositions P7 and P8 are taken from the question "How many marbles do they have altogether?" A third set representation is added to the textbase and the problem model, with the specification of P8 in the textbase and the argument *Joe & Tom* in the problem model. The quantitative proposition HOW MANY (MARBLES) cues identifying the quantity of set S3 as the problem goal. The HAVE-ALTOGETHER proposition cues assignment of the role of S3 as a superset.

When a superset is created, the model posts a request to assign subset roles to other sets in its representation. Specifications of these subsets are *Joe* and *Tom*, obtained from the specification of S3. Appropriate sets are already represented, so the subset role is assigned to S1 and S2. These roles are in the problem model and not in the textbase because they are added as inferences based on schemata, rather than being derived from the text directly.

Once the complete superset schema has been filled in, with the goal of computing the quantity of the superset, a calculational strategy is triggered that provides the answer to the problem. In this case, the strategy is COUNT-ALL, as is described below.

PROPOSITIONAL FRAMES AND SCHEMATA

Set Schema. The keystone of knowledge for representing problems, in our analysis is a schema for representing sets, shown in Table 3. A set is represented with four attributes, the slots that are shown in Table 3. The object slot holds the intension of the set, a common noun that refers to the kind of objects that the set contains. Quantity holds the cardinality of the set, if it is given numerically, or the term SOME or HOWMANY, a placeholder for a number in an indefinite statement or a question. Specification holds information that distinguishes the set from others, such as the owner of the set and indexical information such as the set's location or the time that is specified. Role holds a relational term that identifies the set's role in a higher level structure that includes other sets.

Propositional Frames. Table 4 lists the propositional frames needed to understand the problems in Table 1. The first column gives labels for the frames. The second column gives propositions that could be obtained from the problem texts in Table 1 by a simple parser, and that serve as the input for our model. The meaning postulates given in the third column indicate translation rules that relate the terms in propositions to the schemata.

TABLE 3	Set Schema
SLOT	**VALUE**
Object	<cnoun>
Quantity	<number>, SOME, HOWMANY
Specification	<owner>, <location>, <time>
Role	start, transfer, result; superset, subset; largeset, smallset, difference

	TABLE 4	Propositional Frames and Their Meaning Postulates[a]
FRAME TYPE	**PROPOSITION**	**MEANING POSTULATE**
Existential	x = Joe	—
	x = Tom	—
Quantity	<number> (<cnoun>)	Obj; <cnoun>; quan; <number>
	SOME (<cnoun>)	Obj; <cnoun>
	HOWMANY (<cnoun>)	Obj; <cnoun>; quan; goal
Possession	HAVE [x, P(Quan)]	Spec: x
	GIVE [x, x, P(Quan)]	Spec: x
	HAVE-ALTOGETHER [x, x, P(Quan)]	Spec: x & x
Compare	HAVE-MORE-THAN [x, x, P(Quan)]	Spec: x/x
	HAVE-LESS-THAN [x, x, P(Quan)]	Spec: x/x
Time	PAST(P)	Spec: past
	BEGINNING(P)	Spec: past
	THEN(P_i, P_j,)	Spec: after Si
	NOW(P)	Spec: present

Note. Obj = object; Quan = quantity; Spec = specification.
[a]The meaning postulates specify attributes of sets in the problem model.

A proper name states that an individual exists; we denote this as assignment of a value to a variable, which enables reference to the individual in other propositions.

Numbers occur in the problem texts along with kinds of objects, for example, *five marbles.* These phrases are cues to assign the common noun to the object slot of a set schema, and the number as the quantity in that schema. A phrase such as *some marbles* cues assignment of a kind of object to a set with the quantity slot left empty. A phrase such as *how many marbles* cues assignment of a kind of object to a set, with a goal of finding the quantity of that set.

Possession and time propositions are used to assign specifications of sets. For example, propositions from "Joe had five marbles" would include PAST{HAVE[JOE, FIVE(MARBLES)]}, which would cue *Joe* and *past* as specifications of the set of marbles.

For the possession frames in Table 4, the notation P(Quan) denotes a proposition in the quantity group. A set that is given to someone is specified as belonging to the recipient. We use a conjunction of owners to specify a union of sets owned by two individuals, as in "Joe and Tom have eight marbles altogether."

The comparison frames are cued by sentences such as "Tom has three more marbles than Joe" or "How many marbles does Joe have more than Tom?" In our analysis, the HAVE-MORE-THAN proposition has three arguments. The variables x_i and x_j refer to specifications of the two sets that are being compared, for example, *Tom* and *Joe*. The third argument is the quantitative proposition associated with the comparison. The set difference of the two comparison sets is represented as a set in its own right, mainly for notational economy.[3] The specification of a difference set is given as x_i/x_j or x_j/x_i, with the larger set's specification given first. For example, if Tom has more marbles than Joe, then the difference set's specification is Tom/Joe.

For the time frames in Table 4, P indicates that a proposition is an argument for the time proposition. For example, in PAST{HAVE[JOE,FIVE(MARBLES)]}, the argument is the proposition HAVE[JOE,FIVE(MARBLES)].

Higher Order Schemata. Each of the problem texts in Table 1 presents information and a question about three sets. Relations among these sets are critical for deciding how to solve the problem. The model includes five higher order schemata that are used to include these relations in representations of problems.

The TRANSFER schema is needed for the representation of the Change problems in Table 1. First, there is a *start* set of certain objects; then some other objects of the same kind, the *transfer* set, are given to the owner of the start set; this creates the *result* set. This scenario is represented by the TRANSFER-IN schema. Alternatively, the owner of the start set may give some objects away to someone else, so that the start set is reduced by that amount; in this case the TRANSFER-OUT schema applies. The objects, specifications, and quantities of the sets involved are always derived from appropriate propositions in the textbase; GIVE propositions cue transfer sets, and the roles of start and result are assigned on the basis of temporal propositions in the text.

The PART–WHOLE schema also involves three sets; two have the role *subset* and one has the role *superset.* The subsets are associated with HAVE propositions with individual owners. The superset role is assigned to a set specified as belonging to the two individuals.

The MORE-THAN and LESS-THAN schemata include a *largeset*, a *smallset*, and a *difference.* The HAVE-MORE-THAN proposition provides the specification and quantity for the difference, and it specifies the sets that should be assigned the roles of largeset and smallset.

COMPREHENSION STRATEGIES

Textbases are constructed by arranging the propositions of a text into a coherent network on the basis of appropriate knowledge schemata. Various strategies are used to decide which schemata to employ for that purpose, as described by van Dijk and Kintsch (1983). In word problems such as those in Table 1, the SET schema is always used as the basic structure of information. Thus, the textbase for these problems consists of several interrelated set schemata, the slots of which are filled with text propositions.

The strategies that are used to achieve this are given in Table 5. The first column lists the names of the production strategies and substrategies that are needed for the problems in Table 1. The second column shows the propositions that must be present in a textbase or derivable from the textbase to apply these productions. In general,

TABLE 5   Arithmetic Strategies

STRATEGY AND CONDITION	ACTION
MAKE-SET	
$Q(<cnoun>)$	Represent set: S
TRANSFERSET	
Si: Spec = GIVE $[x_j, x_k, Q(y)]$	Si: Role = transfer/out
Sj: Spec = x_j before Si	Sj: Role = start
	Request RESULTSET (x_j)
Si: $Spec$ + GIVE $[x_j, x_k, Q(y)]$	Si: Role = transfer/in
Sk: $Spec = x_k$, before Si	Sk: Role = start
	Request RESULTSET (x_k)
RESULTSET	
S: Spec = x, present	S: Role = result
DIFFERENCESET	
S: Spec = HAVE-MORE-THAN $[x_i, x_j, Q(y)]$	S: Role = difference
	Request LARGESET (x_i)
	SMALLSET (x_j)
S: Spec = HAVE-LESS-THAN $[x_i, x_j, Q(y)]$	S: Role = difference
	Request LARGESET (x_j)
	SMALLSET (x_i)
LARGESET	
S: Spec = x	S: Role = largeset
SMALLSET	
S: Spec = x	S: Role = smallset
SUPERSET	
Si: Spec = HAVE-ALTOGETHER $[x_i \& x_j, Q(y)]$	Si: Role = superset
	Request SUBSET (x_i)
	SUBSET (x_j)
Si: Role = start	Si: Role = subset
Sj: Role = transfer/in	Sj: Role = subset
Sk: Role = result	Sk: Role = superset
Si: Role = start	Si: Role = superset
Sj: Role = transfer/out	Sj: Role = subset
Sk: Role = result	Sk: Role = subset
Si: Obj = y	Si: Role = superset
Spec = x	Infer
Role = largeset	HAVE $[x, Q_j(y)]$—Sp
Sj: Quan = $Q_j(y)$	HAVE $[x, Q_k(y)]$—Sq
Role = smallset	Sp: Role = subset
Sk: Quan = $Q_k(y)$	Sq: Role = subset
Role = difference	
SUBSET	
S: Spec = x	S: Role = subset

Note. Spec = specification; Obj = object; Quan = quantity.

main strategies are triggered by propositions that are found in the textbase. A main strategy can request a substrategy, and the model attempts to derive information to match the condition of the substrategy. The final column shows the actions that are carried out. These actions are in addition to assignments that are made according to the meaning postulates shown in Table 4.

The MAKE-SET strategy is cued by a quantitative proposition about some kind of object, for example, FIVE(MARBLES) or HOWMANY(MARBLES). The action of MAKE-SET is to form a data structure for representing a specific set, both in the propositional textbase and in the problem model, with the slots object, quantity, specification, and role. Any propositions already in memory that fit into the slots are assigned to them in the textbase, and appropriate translations into the problem model are made. For example, if propositions FIVE(MARBLES) and HAVE(JOE,FIVE(MARBLES)) are in memory when a set is formed, these propositions will be assigned as the object and specification slots in the textbase, and the arguments, 5 and *Joe,* will be transferred to the quantity and specification slots in the problem model.

The TRANSFERSET strategy assigns roles to sets according to the TRANSFER-IN and TRANSFER-OUT schemata. The strategy is cued by a GIVE proposition along with an existing set that is associated with one of the individuals involved in the GIVE proposition. GIVE, along with a set owned by the agent of GIVE (earlier in time), results in assigning *transfer/out* as the role of the set specified by the GIVE proposition, and assigning *start* to the other set. GIVE, along with a set owned by the patient of GIVE (earlier in time), results in assigning transfer/in as the role of the set specified by the GIVE proposition, and assigning start to the other set. A substrategy is requested for assigning the role of *result* to another set. RESULTSET requires a set that matches the *transfer* set in objects and owner, with a time specification that is later than the transfer set; this set is given the role of result.

The DIFFERENCE strategy assigns roles according to the MORE-THAN and LESS-THAN schemata. It is cued by a HAVE-MORE-THAN or HAVE-LESS-THAN proposition, and assigns *difference* as the *role* of the set specified by the proposition. Two substrategies are requested: LARGESET and SMALLSET. These assign the appropriate roles to the two sets that are compared.

The SUPERSET strategy assigns roles according to the PART–WHOLE schema. SUPERSET is cued by a proposition of HAVE-ALTOGETHER with an owner specification that is a conjunction of two individuals. The set for which the proposition is the specification is given the role of superset, and the SUBSET substrategy is requested. The substrategy requires sets that match the superset's kind of objects and the individual owners; these are given the role subset.

SUPERSET is also used to form representations with the PART–WHOLE schema when representations with other schemata are not sufficient for problems to be solved. This condition arises when the problem solver lacks operations for the specific combinations of information in the representation. One such conversion takes information in a TRANSFER schema. If a transfer/in occurred, the result set becomes the superset, and the start and transfer sets become the subsets. If a transfer/out occurred, the start set becomes the superset and the transfer and result sets are the subsets.

Another conversion takes information in a DIFFERENCE schema. In this case, the largeset is considered as a pair of subsets, one equal to the smallset and the other equal to the difference. The subsets are added by inference to the problem representation. In the PART–WHOLE representation, the largeset becomes the superset. Two propositions are inferred, both involving the specification of the largeset. One says that the largeset's owner also owns a set equal in quantity to the smallset, and the other says that the largeset's owner also owns a set equal in quantity to the difference. These propositions trigger the MAKE-SET strategy, which forms representations of the two subsets, and SUPERSET assigns the role of subset to both of them.

It is not always the case that children use the correct knowledge structures, even when they solve a problem correctly. Thus, there is some evidence (Riley et al., 1983) that children treat Combine problems as transfer problems, and hence solve such problems correctly before they ever have acquired a true SUPERSET schema. Similarly, Compare 3 and 4 problems may be treated as transfer problems sometimes, so that these problems are solved correctly in the absence of any real understanding of the MORE-THAN and LESS-THAN relations, which are difficult for young children.

Note that some role assignments are directly supported by linguistic cues in the text (e.g., "in the beginning" identifies a start set, "altogether" a superset), whereas others must be inferred without direct linguistic support (e.g., the subsets in Combine problems, and the largeset and smallset in Compare problems).

PROBLEM-SOLVING PROCEDURES

The model as described thus far constructs representations of problems with the information needed to determine how to solve them. We now consider the procedures necessary to solve the problems in Table 1, based on the information in the representations.

The procedures that we discuss correspond to addition and subtraction of numbers, but we formulate them as operations of counting sets of discrete objects. Procedures of addition and subtraction of numbers would do as well, formally, but counting operations have been considered by other theorists (Briars & Larkin, in press; Riley et al., 1983), partly because they can be used by children who have not yet learned formal arithmetic. The procedures that we include are a subset of those identified by Carpenter and Moser (1983) in a study of the problem-solving performance of primary-grade children.

We include one procedure corresponding to addition, called *count-all*. To apply count-all to the x and y arguments, form a set by counting out x objects, then form another set by counting out y objects, and finally count the union of the two sets.

We postulate four procedures that correspond to subtraction. One of these is called *separate-from*. To apply separate-from to x and y, with x the larger argument, form a set with x objects, then remove y objects, and finally count the objects that remain. A second procedure that corresponds to subtraction is called *separate-to*. To apply this to x and y, form a set with x objects, then remove objects until y objects remain, and finally, count the objects that were removed.

A third procedure for subtraction is called *add-on*. To apply add-on to x and y, with x larger, count out a set with y, then add objects to the set until the total of x has been reached, and then count the objects that were added. The final procedure is called *match-separate*. To apply match-separate to x and y, form a set with x objects

TABLE 6	Problem-Solving Procedures: Change Problems, TRANSFER Schema

PROBLEM TYPE	START	TRSF/IN	TRSF/OUT	RESULT	REPRESENTATIVE PROCEDURE
1	K	K		U	COUNT-ALL (st, trsf/in)
2	K		K	U	SEPARATE-FROM (st, trsf/out)
3	K	U		K	ADD-ON (res, st)
4	K		U	K	SEPARATE-TO (st, res)
5	U	K		K	(convert)
6	U		K	K	(convert)

Note. K indicates roles with known values; U indicates roles for which values are to be computed; st = start; trsf/in = transfer in; trsf/out = transfer out; res = result.

and another set with y objects. Next, form a subset of the larger set, equal in size to the smaller set. Finally, count the members of the larger set that are not in the matched subset.

In our model, procedures are associated with schemata by procedural attachments. The information in a procedural attachment includes the consequence of performing the procedure and prerequisite conditions for its performance, stated in terms of the schema's components. The attachment also includes a subprocedure for identifying the arguments of the procedure, and a connection with the action sequence that constitutes performance of the procedure (cf. Greeno, 1983). This structure of procedural knowledge was developed by Sacerdoti (1977). The relation of procedures to schemata is similar to that discussed by Bobrow and Winograd (1979).

Tables 6, 7, and 8 show the five problem-solving procedures, along with the problem situations that they are associated with in our model. For those problem types for which procedures are specified, the procedures are the modal choices made by the first- and second-grade students studied by Carpenter and Moser (1983). Thus, Tables 6–8 are really incomplete: Instead of associating a single procedure with each problem situation, a complete model would specify a probability distribution over several procedures for each problem, which would of course be grade dependent.[4]

TABLE 7	Problem-Solving Procedures: Combine Problems, PART–WHOLE Schema

PROBLEM TYPE	SUBSET 1	SUBSET 2	SUPERSET	
1	K	K	U	COUNT-ALL (sub1, sub 2)
2	K	U	K	SEPARATE-FROM (sup, sub1)

Note. K indicates roles with known values; U indicates roles for which values are to be computed; sub1 = subset 1; sub2 = subset 2; sup = superset.

| TABLE 8 | Problem-Solving Procedures: Compare Problems, MORE–LESS Schema | | | |

PROBLEM TYPE	LARGESET	SMALLSET	DIFFERENCE	
1	K	K	U	MATCH-SEPARATE (lg, sm)
2	K	K	U	MATCH-SEPARATE (lg, sm)
3	U	K	K	(convert)
4	K	U	K	(convert)
5	K	U	K ·	(convert)
6	U	K	K	(convert)

Note. K indicates roles with known values; U indicates roles for which values are to be computed; lg = largeset; sm = smallset.

The entries in Tables 6, 7, and 8 indicate which roles of schemata correspond to prerequisites and consequences of the procedures in the procedural attachments. K is used to indicate roles in which known values are prerequisites; U is used to indicate roles for which values are consequences. For example, in the model the count-all, add-on, and separate-from procedures are all attached to the TRANSFER/IN schema. The prerequisites of count-all are known values of the start and transfer/in roles, and the consequence of count-all is a value for the result role. When the problem solver has a problem represented with the TRANSFER schema, with the goal of finding the result and with known values in the start and the transfer/in roles, the count-all procedure is chosen, and the known values are used as arguments.

For the problem types with (convert) entered as the procedure, we postulate that there is no problem-solving procedure available for those specific combinations of information given in the problem. When this occurs, the problem solver forms a problem model using the PART–WHOLE schema, using the SUPERSET strategy discussed earlier. Our decision to assume that these problem types require conversion is based on the fact that these problem types are relatively difficult for children (e.g., Riley et al., 1983). Unfortunately, observations of children's procedures in solving these problem types are not available.

PROCESSING REQUIREMENTS

Our discussion thus far has dealt with the nature of problem representations and the knowledge and strategies used in forming representations of problems and solving them. We now consider differences among the problem types in the demands on resources that occur during the process of comprehension. Specifically, we focus on differences in the loads on short-term memory that occur, according to the model that we have developed.

The processing model that we use is that of van Dijk and Kintsch (1983), which is an elaboration of an earlier model by Kintsch and van Dijk (1978). Propositions are constructed on-line when reading or listening to a sentence. The set-building strategies are triggered by certain constellations of propositions. Whenever a proposition is completed that triggers one of the set-building strategies, the appropriate set is formed and the propositions currently being processed are assigned their places in the various slots of the set schema. Propositions that are formed after a schema has been established are inserted into the existing schema if appropriate, or else they are held in the short-term buffer until a new schema is formed that will accept them.

When a new set is formed, the former schema that was active in the buffer is displaced, unless the old set can be incorporated as a component of a higher order schema that is formed, such as a TRANSFER or SUPERSET schema. In that case, the new higher order chunk is formed in the short-term buffer, where it remains until a unit is generated that does not belong to it. Whenever a new chunk displaces an unrelated old one from the short-term buffer, the displaced chunk is stored in episodic text memory. (This term is used for convenience of reference, without implying that episodic text memory is a store separate from a person's other memories.) Retrieval from episodic text memory is possible via pattern matching of some content cue, or via temporal cues that are effective for short delays.

The contents of the short-term buffer change continuously, but its capacity is limited, though not necessarily fixed. (As Kintsch & Polson, 1979, have shown in another context, there may be trade-offs between the capacity of the short-term buffer and the other resource demands on the system, so that if the task to be performed is a difficult one, fewer resources are available for actively maintaining information in the buffer.) Following van Dijk and Kintsch (1983), we assume that the buffer may contain a single chunk plus one or more active requests for missing information. When one of the set-building strategies is triggered, the new chunk that is formed absorbs the previously unassigned propositions and perhaps the previous chunk, too, if the new chunk is based on a higher order schema that subsumes the schema of the previous chunk.

Building a chunk can impose considerable demands, in part because of requests that may have to be retained in the buffer in an active state. Requests that occur for arithmetic problems involve sets with unspecified roles in higher order schemata. For example, when a transfer set is formed, based on a proposition about giving some objects, a start set and a result set are then needed. In the Change problems of Table 1, the start set is specified first, so that slot in the TRANSFER schema can be filled with a set already in the buffer. The request for the result set is placed in the buffer and requires resources to be maintained.

To illustrate these processing assumptions, refer to Table 2, which traces construction of the representation of Combine Problem 1. The first sentence is "Joe has three marbles." When this is processed, the MAKE-SET strategy is triggered, and a chunk for set S1 is placed in the short-term buffer. The second sentence, "Tom has five marbles," triggers MAKE-SET again, to represent the set of Tom's marbles, S2. Because no higher order strategy is triggered, the chunk for S2 replaces the chunk for S1 in the short-term buffer. The third sentence is the question, "How many marbles do they have altogether?" This triggers MAKE-SET to form a chunk for S3, the set belonging to Joe and Tom. It also triggers the SUPERSET strategy, which assigns the role superset to S3 and requests two subsets with Joe and Tom, respectively, as their specifications.

The set associated with Tom is in the short-term buffer and is assigned the role of sub-set. The set associated with Joe has to be retrieved from episodic memory to be integrated into the PART–WHOLE structure by assigning it a subset role.

Table 9 shows the contents of the short-term buffer after each sentence of the various problem types. We discuss some of these in detail in the Examples section.

Table 10 summarizes some processing aspects that might be related to problem difficulty. The last two rows of the table are data from Riley et al. (1983), showing proportions of children who solved the various problems with objects available for use as counters.[5] Riley et al. attributed differences in problem difficulty to the differences in knowledge structures that the various problems require, and we agree that availability of the required schemata plays a major role. At the same time, differences in processing load appear to play a role, as well. As the size of the chunks that must be maintained in the short-term buffer increases and the number of active requests increases, solution probabilities generally decrease. The need to reinstate an already inactive unit from episodic memory does not appear to be related to problem difficulty (as it was in Miller & Kintsch, 1980); however, the texts of these problems are extremely brief, so that temporal retrieval cues could still be highly effective when reinstatements are needed.

Interesting interactions between knowledge structures and processing are suggested by the difference between the Change 3–4 and Change 5–6 problems and the difference between Compare 3–4 and Compare 5–6. In our model, the 3–4 and 5–6 types in each category have similar processing requirements, although Change 5–6 require a conversion that Change 3–4 do not. In addition, note in Table 1 that for Change 3–4, the first set is formed from the sentence "Joe had three marbles," whereas for Change 5–6, the first set is formed from "Joe had some marbles." It is quite possible that young children have not yet learned to interpret *some* as a quantifying determiner and fail to form a chunk using the SET schema when they read about *some*

TABLE 9   Contents of the Short-Term Buffer

PROBLEM TYPES	AFTER FIRST SENTENCE	AFTER SECOND SENTENCE	AFTER QUESTION
Change 1–4[a]	SET	TRANSFER (two sets) Request one set	TRANSFER (three sets)
Change 5–6[a]	SET	TRANSFER (two sets) Request one set	PART–WHOLE (three sets)
Combine 1	SET	SET	PART–WHOLE (three sets)
Combine 2	PART–WHOLE (one set) Request two sets	PART–WHOLE (two sets) Request one set	PART–WHOLE (three sets)
Compare 1–2	SET	SET	DIFFERENCE (three sets)
Compare 3–6	SET	DIFFERENCE (two sets) Request one set	PART–WHOLE (three sets)

[a]Change 3–6 include a third sentence. Short-term memory holds a TRANSFER schema with three sets after that sentence is processed.

| TABLE 10 | Processing Characteristics of Word Arithmetic Problems |

	Change			Combine		Compare		
VARIABLE	1–2	3–4	5–6	1	2	1–2	3–4	5–6
Knowledge-base schema used								
Transfer	x	x	x					
Part–whole			x	x	x		x	x
More/less-than						x	x	x
Processing statistics								
No. of inferences	0.00	0.00	0.00	2.00	2.00	2.00	4.00	4.00
No. of reinstatements	0.00	0.00	0.00	1.00	0.00	1.00	0.00	0.00
Conversion	0.00	0.00	1.00	0.00	0.00	0.00	1.00	1.00
Short-term buffer load								
Average chunk size	2.00	2.25	2.25	1.67	2.00	1.67	2.00	2.00
No. of requests	1.00	1.00	1.00	0.00	3.00	0.00	1.00	1.00
Proportion correct								
First grade	1.00	0.56	0.28	1.00	0.39	0.28	0.17	0.11
Second grade	1.00	1.00	0.80	1.00	0.70	0.85	0.80	0.65

marbles. This would result in an increased memory load for problems containing *some* because unattached propositions would have to be carried along over two cycles in Change 3-4 and over three cycles in Change 5-6, whereas no such problems would arise for Change 1-2. Similar considerations apply to Compare 5-6 type problems, where the second sentence gives the difference between two sets when the referent set has not been mentioned previously.

Support for the model provided by the analyses of Table 8 must be regarded as preliminary and, at most, suggestive. We include these results to illustrate implications of the model regarding information-processing requirements, and to indicate that detailed experimental tests of these implications could provide useful information about interactions between processing requirements and knowledge structures.

• • •

DISCUSSION

Our goal was to develop a model that constructs representations of word problems with the information needed for successful solution, using a general model of text processing. One benefit of the product is an integration of theoretical ideas developed in different contexts. The theoretical effort also provides a test of both the general ideas about text comprehension in van Dijk and Kintsch's (1983) model, and the hypotheses about semantic structures needed for understanding word problems postulated by Riley et al. (1983). The outcome indicates that van Dijk and Kintsch's model of text processing has sufficient generality to apply comfortably to the semi-technical subject matter of arithmetic problems. It also indicates that the structures hypothesized by Riley et al. can be formed with processes of language comprehension that can be assumed plausibly to be available for the task.

In this final section, we discuss two sets of issues. First, we discuss special characteristics of the information in problem texts and the processes of comprehending this information. Then we discuss ways in which our analysis could be extended naturally to cover a broader range of problems and levels of knowledge and skill in comprehension.

SPECIAL CHARACTERISTICS OF WORD PROBLEMS

We discuss three features of the word-problem domain: reference to sets, special presuppositions, and special comprehension strategies.

Reference to sets plays a key role in the representation of word problems in arithmetic. In our model, we have chosen a representation that makes reference to sets part of the textbase, with a SET schema that is activated by propositions with quantitative terms. This is consistent with a formal analysis by Johnson and Greeno (1983) in which numerals and the terms *some* and *how many* are treated as determiners, and plural terms such as *marbles* are treated as common nouns. Then, phrases such as *some marbles* and *five marbles* are syntactically analogous to phrases such as *a marble,* forming noun terms. Semantically, although a single noun term with a determiner implies the existence of an individual object, a plural noun term such as *five marbles* implies the existence of a set.

An alternative assumption can be made that plural nouns such as *marbles* function as noun terms. This interpretation is preferred by linguists in formal semantics (e.g., Carlson, 1977), in part because it permits a straightforward analysis of sentences such as "Joe collects marbles" and "Marbles are round." (Singular common nouns cannot function independently of determiners as subject or object terms.) If plurals are noun terms, then numerals and the terms *some* and *how many* do not function as determiners. One possibility that works is for them to function as adjectival modifiers, so that *five marbles* is syntactically analogous to *glass marbles,* although a different semantic analysis is required. If this interpretation is used in comprehension of word problems, reference to sets does not occur in the propositional textbases, and considerably more work has to be done by the interpretive processes that form the problem models.

We suppose that the noun-term interpretation of plurals is standard, as linguists have concluded. That implies that if our characterization of word-problem comprehension is correct, then it must result from a specialized comprehension process. The process is specialized at a deep level, involving the syntax and semantics of word classes, as well as at the level of higher order interpretive schemata. We conjecture that acquisition of this specialized comprehension knowledge is an important, although not universal, achievement for school children in their experience with word problems.

A second issue in the comprehension of word problems involves a set of presuppositions. Nesher and Katriel (1977) noted that word problems can be solved only under a set of presuppositions that involves completeness of the propositions in the problems. In effect, these presuppositions say that all of the information relevant to solving the problem has been given. For example, for "Joe had three marbles; then Tom gave him five more marbles; how many marbles does Joe have now?" it is assumed that Joe did not lose any of his original three marbles, and that he did not win or lose any in a game.

Another presupposition involves representation of numbers. Strictly, a sentence such as "Joe has three marbles" only says that Joe has *at least* three marbles; he might have four, five, or any larger number, and the sentence "Joe has three marbles" would be true. Texts of problems presuppose that "*n* things" means "exactly *n* things," unless this is specifically denied by a modifier such as *at least* or *at most.*

A third issue involves specialized strategies for extracting information from text that is relevant to the problem-solving task. If the sentence "Then Tom gave Joe some marbles" were encountered in a story, it would be propositionalized in the same way as it is in our model. However, in the context of a story, different aspects of our knowledge of *giving* might be used in the comprehension process. For example, Tom might expect to obtain something in exchange, or at least would count on Joe's gratitude. In word problems, instead, the reader is only concerned with a few, special aspects of meaning of these rich natural-language concepts, namely, those related to mathematical sets, their cardinalities, and relations among them. Note that the meaning postulates in Table 4 do not represent the whole meanings of propositions as they are used in natural language, but only those aspects that are relevant to understanding word arithmetic problems. Thus, an expert problem solver presumably has to learn to interpret problems using a specialized knowledge base, ignoring many features that would ordinarily be relevant to the interpretation of text. Objects, persons, actions, and their relations are relevant only insofar as they specify features of sets in the problems.

EXTENSIONS

We have worked out the details of our model for the problems in Table 1. We conclude now by discussing extensions that would be required to expand the domain of problems that the model could understand and solve.

First, a large domain of problems can be generated with minor variations of the problems in Table 1 by changing names of persons and kinds of objects, and by adding one or more ways of specifying sets such as location. This domain, which was sampled in Riley et al.'s (1983) empirical study, among others, could be covered by our model simply by adding the propositional frames needed to interpret the terms of the propositions so that representations of sets and set relations could be obtained.

There are problems that are close relatives of types in Table 1, but that are not similar enough to be handled by the comprehension structures that we have postulated. One example is the equalizing problem, studied by Carpenter and Moser (1982); for example, "Joe has three marbles; Tom has eight; How many marbles should Joe get to have as many as Tom?" The problem has the structure of a Compare problem, with the difference unknown. It could also be interpreted as a Change problem, with *have as many as Tom* used to identify the result as a set of eight marbles, and with the question interpreted as setting the goal of finding the transfer quantity. For our model to achieve either interpretation, it would need additional conditions for applying the comprehension strategies that it uses to assign roles to sets in higher order schematic strategies.

Our analysis would have to be extended substantially to account for higher levels of skill. In our present model, the cues for representation of problem texts are quite specific, and the process of comprehension is strongly bottom-up in character. This is inconsistent with an ability to interpret a wide variety of problem texts in terms of an additive relation among quantities; for example, it seems unlikely that specific super-set cues exist for a problem such as the following: "27 cars went into the parking structure, and 18 came out; how many times did a car pass through the gate?" (cf. Nesher & Katriel, 1977). We speculate that in a mature comprehension system, processing occurs in a more top-down fashion, including hypotheses about quantitative relations based on schemata of additive part–whole relations and other general structures, and active processing involving attempts to find arguments for general quantitative relations and operations. Thus, in the problem about the parking structure, superset and subset roles would be assigned on the basis of a semantic analysis of the situation, noting that *passed through the gate* is implied by both *went into* and *came out,* rather than on the basis of specific textural cues. Even so, extensions of the model in this direction appear quite feasible.

Another extension involving additional top-down processing would involve a nontrivial role for macrostrategies. The problems that we have analyzed are short ones that were prepared so that they do not contain any extraneous material. Everything that is said is problem relevant. Thus, in these problems the microstructures and the macrostructures are identical. No operations of deletion or construction are needed to reduce the texts to their essential components.

Obviously, one could paraphrase these problems in such a way that the problem-relevant information would be embedded in a more elaborate textual matrix, say an interesting little story. We would expect that such an elaboration should make the problems harder to solve. There would be several reasons for this presumptive outcome in our model. First, the macro-operators of deletion, construction, and generalization would have to be used to reduce the text to its problem-relevant aspects, constituting a further demand on resources and a potential source of errors. For example, deletion would be needed to remove from the macrostructure propositions that cannot be assigned to slots in the various set schemata, leaving the relevant schematic skeleton of the microstructure.

In addition, however, a quite different problem might arise because of competition from task-inappropriate macro-operators. The formal cues in a story that trigger many macro-operators must be suppressed in comprehending arithmetic word problems. Concerns about the motives of characters, narrative categories, and the like, interfere with the proper understanding of these problems. However, because such normal comprehension strategies are highly automatized, their deliberate suppression may be required, at least until the task-appropriate strategies begin to dominate the learner's repertoire of strategies in this particular context.

Finally, we have not addressed questions about different developmental levels of knowledge and skill in solving arithmetic word problems. Our model of understanding and problem solving represents a level of skill that is sufficiently advanced to solve all of the problems that were used by Riley et al. (1983). We have given a simplified account of the process, especially regarding problem-solving processes. We have included only counting processes involving objects, omitting counting without objects and recall of arithmetic facts, used frequently by children, especially those old enough to solve the hardest problems in the set (Carpenter & Moser, 1983). A thorough analysis of problem-solving procedures requires a significant theoretical effort, but we expect that it would result in extensions that would be compatible with the general features of our analysis of comprehension processes.

Riley et al. (1983) formulated models of semantic structures and processes adequate for solving subsets of the problems that Riley's subjects were given. The models differ in the degree of dependence on external representations of problem information and in the power of inferential processes involving assignment of roles in schemata. We have not worked out alternative versions of our model to correspond to different levels of success in understanding and solving problems, but that would seem to be a feasible project. For example, dependence on external representations could be modeled by formulating versions of strategies such as TRANSFERSET and SUPERSET that would modify existing set representations destructively, increasing or decreasing existing sets, rather than forming new sets with specified relations to existing sets.

Although the techniques introduced here have been applied in an admittedly very simple situation, their potential may be far greater. The principles involved in the comprehension and utilization of technical prose, in general, are largely the same as the ones we have encountered here. When dealing with technical texts, it makes no sense to separate questions of comprehension from questions of use; the latter presuppose the former, but the nature of comprehension itself is determined by the purposes for which the text is read. It is not enough to just look at knowledge structures and problem-solving procedures; one must also identify the aspects of the textual input that govern the use of these knowledge structures and operations. It is not enough to have a SUPERSET schema; strategies are also required to build such a structure from a given problem text, and their use must be sufficiently automatized so that enough mental resources remain available to satisfy memory demands when the problem is presented in a nonoptimal way. Errors may reflect lack of knowledge, but at other times, merely the limited information-processing capacity of the human organism. These issues have been illustrated here with relatively simple word arithmetic problems, but the principle involved pertains to a large and very important domain of texts that make demands both on problem solving and comprehension.

REFERENCES

Anderson, J. R. (1976). *Language, memory, and thought.* Hillsdale, NJ: Erlbaum.

Bobrow, D. G. (1968). Natural-language input for a computer problem-solving system. In M. Minsky (Ed.), *Semantic information processing* (pp. 135–215). Cambridge, MA: MIT Press.

Bobrow, D. G., & Winograd, T. (1979). KRL: Another perspective. *Cognitive Science, 3,* 29–42.

Briars, D. J., & Larkin, J. H. (in press). An integrated model of skill involving elementary word problems. *Cognition and Instruction.*

Brown, J. S., & Burton, R. R. (1978). Diagnostic models for procedural bugs in basic mathematical skills. *Cognitive Science, 2,* 155-192.

Carlson, G. N. (1977). A unified analysis of the English bare plural. *Linguistics and Philosophy, 1,* 413-457.

Carpenter, T. P., & Moser, J. M. (1982). The development of addition and subtraction problem-solving skills. In T. P. Carpenter, J. M. Moser, & T. Romberg (Eds.), *Addition and subtraction: A cognitive perspective* (pp. 9-24). Hillsdale, NJ: Erlbaum.

Carpenter, T. P., & Moser, J. M. (1983). The acquisition of addition and subtraction concepts. In R. Lesh & M. Landau (Eds.), *Acquisition of mathematics concepts and processes* (pp. 7-44). New York: Academic Press.

Chi, M. T. H., Feltovich, P. J., & Glaser, R. (1981). Categorization and representation of physics problems by experts and novices. *Cognitive Science, 5,* 121-152.

DeCorte, E., & Vershaffel, L. (1981). Children's solution processes in elementary arithmetic problems: Analysis and improvement. *Journal of Educational Psychology, 6,* 765-779.

deKleer, J. (1975). *Qualitative and quantitative knowledge in classical mechanics* (Tech. Rep. AI-TR-352). Cambridge, MA: Artificial Intelligence Laboratory.

Greeno, J. G. (1983). Forms of understanding on mathematical problem solving. In S. G. Paris, G. M. Olson, & H. W. Stevenson (Eds.), *Learning and motivation in the classroom* (pp. 83-111). Hillsdale, NJ: Erlbaum.

Greeno, J. G. (1978). Understanding and procedural knowledge in mathematics education. *Educational Psychologist, 12,* 262-283.

Hayes, J. R., & Simon, H. A. (1974). Understanding written problem instructions. In L. W. Gregg (Ed.), *Knowledge and cognition* (pp. 167-200). Hillsdale, NJ: Erlbaum.

Hinsley, D., Hayes, J. R., & Simon, H. A. (1977). From words to equations: Meaning and representation in algebra word problems. In P. A. Carpenter, & M. A. Just (Eds.), *Cognitive processes in comprehension* (pp. 89-106). Hillsdale, NJ: Erlbaum.

Johnson, W. L., & Greeno, J. G. (1983, August). *Competence for understanding arithmetic word problems.* Presented at the meeting of Mathematical Psychology Society, Boulder, CO.

Kane, R. (1968). The readability of mathematical English. *Journal of Research in Science Teaching, 5,* 296-298.

Kintsch, W. (1977). On comprehending stories. In M. A. Just, & P. A. Carpenter (Eds.), *Cognitive processes in comprehension* (pp. 33-62). Hillsdale, NJ: Erlbaum.

Kintsch, W., & Polson, P. G. (1979). On nominal and functional serial position curves: Implications for short-term memory models? *Psychological Review, 86,* 407-413.

Kintsch, W. & van Dijk, T. A. (1978). Toward a model of text comprehension and production. *Psychological Review, 85,* 363-394.

Kozminsky, E., Kintsch, W., & Bourne, L. E., Jr. (1981). Decision making with texts: Information analysis and schema acquisition. *Journal of Experimental Psychology: General, 3,* 363-380.

Larkin, J. G., McDermott, J., Simon, D. P., & Simon, H. A. (1980). Models of competence involving physics problems. *Cognitive Science, 4,* 317-345.

Miller, J. R., & Kintsch, W. (1980). Readability and recall of short prose passages: A theoretical analysis. *Journal of Experimental Psychology: Human Learning and Memory, 6,* 335-354.

Nesher, P. (1982). Levels of description in the analysis of addition and subtraction. In T. P. Carpenter, J. M. Moser, & T. Romberg (Eds.), *Addition and subtraction: A cognitive perspective* (pp. 25-38). Hillsdale, NJ: Erlbaum.

Nesher, P., Greeno, J. G., & Riley, M. S. (1982). The development of semantic categories for addition and subtraction. *Experimental Studies in Mathematics, 13,* 373-394.

Nesher, P., & Katriel, T. A. (1977). A semantic analysis of addition and subtraction word problems in arithmetic. *Educational Studies in Mathematics, 8,* 251–269.

Nesher, P., & Teubal, E. (1975). Verbal cues as an interfering factor in verbal problem solving. *Educational Studies in Mathematics, 6,* 41–51.

Newell, A., & Simon, H. A. (1972). *Human problem solving.* Englewood Cliffs, NJ: Prentice-Hall.

Norman, D. A., & Rumelhart, D. E. (1975). *Explorations in cognition.* San Francisco: Freeman.

Novak, G. S. (1976). Computer understanding of physics problems stated in natural language. *American Journal of Computational Linguistics,* Microfiche 53.

Paige, J. M., & Simon, H. A. (1966). Cognitive processes involving algebra word problems. In B. Kleinmuntz (Ed.), *Problem solving* (pp. 51–118). New York: Wiley.

Riley, M. S., Greeno, J. G., & Heller, J. I. (1983). Development of children's problem-solving ability in arithmetic. In H. P. Ginsburg (Ed.), *The development of mathematical thinking* (pp. 153–196). New York: Academic Press.

Sacerdoti, E. D. (1977). *A structure for plans and behavior.* New York: Elsevier-North Holland.

Schank, R. C. (1972). Conceptual dependency: A theory of natural language understanding. *Cognitive Psychology, 3,* 552–631.

van Dijk, T. A., & Kintsch, W. (1983). *Strategies of discourse comprehension.* New York: Academic Press.

Vergnaud, G. (1982). A classification of cognitive tasks and operations of thought involved in addition and subtraction problems. In T. P. Carpenter, J. M. Moser, & T. Romberg (Eds.), *Addition and subtraction: A cognitive perspective* (pp. 39–59). Hillsdale, NJ: Erlbaum.

Winograd, T. (1972). *Understanding natural language.* New York: Academic Press.

Wolters, M. A. D. (1983). The part–whole schema and arithmetic problems. *Educational Studies in Mathematics, 2,* 127–138.

NOTES

1. Riley et al.'s (1983) model is given conceptual representations of problems that are transformed in various ways to arrive at problem solutions, but no explicit account is given of how the conceptual representations are derived from problem texts. Briars and Larkin's model takes English-language input and creates problem representations, but their text-processing assumptions were designed for the arithmetic-problem task, rather than being related to general principles of text comprehension.

2. A simulation of this model has been written by C. R. Fletcher in INTERLISP. It runs on any XEROX LISP machine. A technical report describing this simulation, as well as copies of the program, can be obtained by writing to W. Kintsch.

3. An alternative would be to represent MORE-THAN and LESS-THAN as relations between sets. This would be more economical in some ways, but would require a more complicated use of the role slots in schemata for sets, allowing relations among sets other than those that are required for the higher order schemata.

4. Even then Tables 6–8 would still present only a highly simplified picture of the relation between problem types and procedures that Carpenter and Moser (1983) observed. We have included only a few of the procedures that children used; in addition to using objects to represent problems, children also used procedures involving counting without objects and simple retrieval of addition or subtraction facts. The choice of a procedure depended on factors such as the sizes of numbers in the problems, in addition to the problem types. A complete analysis of the process of choosing procedures is an important theoretical problem, but is beyond the scope of this article.

5. The pattern of these results, though not the actual percentage-correct values, appears to be highly stable: Nesher et al. (1982, Tables 3 and 4) summarize nine studies with children from K to 6, which corroborate the results shown here.

QUESTIONS FOR FURTHER THOUGHT

1. Summarize the main aspects of the Kintsch–Greeno model of how people understand and solve word arithmetic problems.

2. What is the role of knowledge in the solution of word arithmetic problems?

3. How is knowledge represented by the model?

4. Is the scientific importance of the model enhanced by its implementation in a computer simulation?

5. How might one design an experiment to falsify at least one aspect of the Kintsch–Greeno model?

INTUITION IN INSIGHT AND NONINSIGHT PROBLEM SOLVING

Janet Metcalfe and David Weibe

INTRODUCTION

Some problems seem to require fairly routine processes for their solutions. These problems are sometimes referred to as *well-structured problems,* because the representation of the problem situations are straightforward and because they include clear paths that, if discovered, eventually lead to their solutions.

Well-structured problems are sometimes compared with *ill-structured problems,* which lack any straightforward problem representations and any clearly specifiable paths toward solutions. Such problems are also called *insight problems.*

Psychologists disagree about whether the processes required to solve insight problems differ fundamentally from the processes required to solve the more conventional, well-structured problems. A series of studies by Janet Metcalfe and her colleagues has provided some of the strongest evidence to date that people employ fundamentally different processes for solving the two kinds of problems.

Metcalfe and Weibe had individuals solve both insight and noninsight problems. As they solved these problems, the subjects provided what are called "feeling-of-warmth" ratings. The individuals indicated at frequent intervals how "warm" (close) they felt to solutions.

The resultant feeling-of-warmth ratings showed dramatically different patterns for the two kinds of problems. For noninsight problems, feeling-of-warmth ratings increased gradually over time as individuals approached solutions. For the insight problems, in contrast, feeling-of-warmth ratings generally remained low and constant until right before individuals reached solutions, at which point they rapidly increased. These results suggested to Metcalfe and Weibe a difference in the way people processed information in the two kinds of problems.

For years, psychologists have argued whether insightful problem solving differs qualitatively from noninsightful problem solving, but much of the argumentation never went beyond words. No one had supplied compelling scientific demonstrations to support one side or the other. Indeed, a disappointingly high ratio of theory to data characterized the study of insight. The work of Metcalfe and Weibe brought the study of insightful problem solving into a new era. These researchers not only showed a difference between insightful and noninsightful problem solving, but they showed that insightful problem solving could be studied in a scientifically rigorous way. Although some investigators have interpreted

Source: From Metcalfe, J. & Weibe, D. (1987). Intuition in insight and noninsight problems. *Memory & Cognition, 15,* 238–246, reprinted by permission of Psychonomic Society, Inc.

Metcalfe and Weibe's findings in ways other than the interpretation of the authors, all these investigators have had to contend with these striking and impressive findings. Work is often viewed as classic when all scientists studying a phenomenon—whether they agree with the work or not—must contend with it or be viewed as unscholarly by failing to account for it, one way or another.

———

People's metacognitions, both before and during problem solving, may be of importance in motivating and guiding problem-solving behavior. These metacognitions could also be diagnostic for distinguishing among different classes of problems, each perhaps controlled by different cognitive processes. In the present experiments, intuitions on classic insight problems were compared with those on noninsight and algebra problems. The findings were as follows: (1) subjective feeling of knowing predicted performance on algebra problems but not on insight problems; (2) subjects' expectations of performance greatly exceeded their actual performance, especially on insight problems; (3) normative predictions provided a better estimate of individual performance than did subjects' own predictions, especially on the insight problems; and, most importantly, (4) the patterns-of-warmth ratings, which reflect subjects' feelings of approaching solution, differed for insight and noninsight problems. Algebra problems and noninsight problems showed a more incremental pattern over the course of solving than did insight problems. In general, then, the data indicated that noninsight problems were open to accurate predictions of performance, whereas insight problems were opaque to such predictions. Also, the phenomenology of insight-problem solution was characterized by a sudden, unforeseen flash of illumination. We propose that the difference in phenomenology accompanying insight and noninsight problem solving, as empirically demonstrated here, be used to define insight. ∎

The rewarding quality of the experience of insight may be one reason why scientists and artists alike are willing to spend long periods of time thinking about unsolved problems. Indeed, creative individuals often actively seek out weaknesses in theoretical structures, areas of unresolved conflict, and flaws in conceptual systems. This tolerance and even questing for problems carries the risk that a particular problem may have no solution or that the investigator may be unable to uncover it. For instance, it was thought for many years that Euclid's fifth postulate might be derivable even though no one was able to derive it (see Hofstadter, 1980). The payoff for success, however, is the often noted "discovery" experience for the individual and (perhaps) new knowledge structures for the culture. This special mode of discovery may be qualitatively different from more routine analytical thinking.

Bergson (1902) differentiated between an intuitive mode of inquiry and an analytical mode. Many other theorists have similarly emphasized the importance of a method of direct apperception, variously called *restructuring, intuition, illumination,* or *insight* (Adams, 1979; Bruner, 1966; Davidson & Sternberg, 1984; Dominowski, 1981; Duncker, 1945; Ellen, 1982; Gardner, 1978; Koestler, 1977; Levine, 1986; Maier, 1931; Mayer, 1983; Polya, 1957; Sternberg, 1986; Sternberg & Davidson, 1982; Wallas, 1926). Polanyi (1958) noted:

> We may describe the obstacle to be overcome in solving a problem as a "logical gap," and speak of the width of the logical gap as the measure of the ingenuity required for solving the problem. "Illumination" is then the leap by which the logical gap is crossed. It is the plunge by which we gain a foothold at another shore of reality. (p. 123)

Sternberg (1985) said that "significant and exceptional intellectual accomplishment—for example, major scientific discoveries, new and important inventions, and new and significant understandings of major literary, philosophical, and similar work—almost always involve [sic] major intellectual insights" (p. 282). Arieti (1976) stated that "the experience of aesthetic insight—that is, of creating an aesthetic unity—is a strong emotional experience. . . . The artist feels almost as if he had touched the universal" (p. 186). Although these major insights are of crucial importance both to the person and to the culture, their unpredictable and subjective nature presents difficulties for rigorous investigation. Sternberg and Davidson (1982) suggested that solving small insight puzzles may serve as a model for scientific insight. We shall adopt this approach in the present paper.

Despite the importance attributed to the process of insight, there is little empirical evidence for it. In fact, Weisberg and Alba (1981a) claimed correctly that there was no evidence whatsoever (see also Weisberg & Alba, 1981b, 1982). Since that time, two studies investigating the metacognitions that precede and accompany insight problem solving have provided some data favoring the construct. In the first study (Metcalfe, 1986a), feeling-of-knowing performance was compared on classical insight problems and on general information memory questions (Nelson & Narens, 1980). In the problem-solving phase of the study, subjects were given insight problems to rank order in terms of the likelihood of solution. On the memory half of the study, trivia questions that subjects could not answer immediately (e.g., "What is the name of the villainous people who lived underground in H. G. Wells's book *The Time Machine?*") were ordered in terms of the likelihood of remembering the answers on the second test. The memory part of the study was much like previous feeling-of-knowing experiments on memory (e.g., Gruneberg & Monks, 1974; Hart, 1967; Lovelace, 1984; Nelson, Leonesio, Landwehr, & Narens, 1986; Nelson, Leonesio, Shimamura, Landwehr, & Narens, 1982; Schacter, 1983). Metcalfe found that the correlation between predicted solution and actual solution was not different from zero for the insight problems, although this correlation, as in other research, was substantial for the memory questions. Metcalfe interpreted these data as indicating that insightful solutions could not be predicted in advance, which would be expected if insight problems were solved by a sudden "flash of illumination." However, the data may have resulted from a difference between problem solving in general and memory retrieval, rather than a difference between insight and noninsight problem-solving processes.

In a second study (Metcalfe, 1986b), subjects were instructed to provide estimates of how close they were to the solutions to problems every 10 sec during the problem-solving intervals. These estimates are called *feeling-of-warmth* (Simon, Newell, & Shaw, 1979) ratings. If the problems were solved by what subjectively is a sudden flash of insight, one would expect that the warmth ratings would be fairly low and constant until solution, at which point they would jump to a high value. This is what was found in the experiment. On 78% of the problems and anagrams for which subjects provided the correct solutions, the progress estimates increased by no more than 1 point, on a 10-point scale, over the entire solution interval. On those problems for which the wrong answer was given, however, the warmth protocols showed a more incremental pattern. Thus, it did not appear to be the case that there were no circumstances at all under which an incremental pattern would appear. It appeared with incorrect solutions. However, in that study, the incremental pattern may have been attributable to a special decision-making strategy, rather than to an incremental problem-solving process. Thus, whether noninsight problems show a warmth pattern different from that of insight problems is still unclear.

A straightforward comparison of the warmth ratings produced during solution of insight and noninsight problems is, therefore, important and has not been attempted previously. Simon (1977, 1979) provided several models that apply to incremental problems such as algebra, chess, and logic problems. Basically, Simon et al. (1979) proposed that people are able to use a directed-search strategy in problem solving (as opposed to an exhaustive search through all possibilities, which in many cases would be impossible) because they are able to compare their present state with the goal state. If a move makes the present state more like a goal state (i.e., if the person gets "warmer"), that move is taken. Simon et al. (1979) provided several think aloud protocols that suggest that this "functional" or "means–end" analysis of reducing differences can be applied to a wide range of analytical problems. They noted that the Logic Theorist (a computer program that uses this heuristic) "can almost certainly transfer without modification to problem solving in trigonometry, algebra, and probably other subjects such as geometry and chess" (p. 157). If this monitoring process is guiding human problem solving, then the warmth ratings should increase to reflect subjects' increasing nearness to the solutions. Of course, if insight problems are solved by some nonanalytical, sudden process, as previous research suggests, we would expect to find a difference, depending on problem type, in the warmth protocols.

The experiments described below explored the metacognitions exhibited by subjects on insight and on noninsight problems. Experiment 1 compared warmth ratings during the solution of insight problems with those produced during the solution of noninsight problems. The noninsight problems were the type that have been analyzed and modeled by programs that use a functional analysis. Thus, we expected to find that subjects' warmth ratings would increment gradually over the course of the problem-solving intervals. We expected that warmth ratings on the insight problems would, in contrast, increase rapidly only when the solution was given. Experiment 2 used algebra problems rather than the multistep problems that have been modeled with search-style programs. Algebra problems may be more characteristic of the sorts of problems people solve daily than are (at least some of) the multistep problems used in experiment 1. As noted above, however, because the means–end search strategy should be applicable to algebra problems, incremental warmth protocols were expected. For these reasons, as well as their availability, algebra problems were worth investigating. In addition to examining warmth ratings during the course of problem solving, experiment 2 also investigated other predictors of performance: subjects' feeling-of-knowing rankings, normative predictors of performance, and subjective estimations of the likelihood of success. We expected that noninsight problems would show more incremental warmth protocols than would insight problems. We also expected that people would have more accurate metacognitions (about how well they would be able to solve problems and which problems they would be able to solve) for the noninsight than for the insight problems.

EXPERIMENT 1

METHOD

Subjects. Twenty-six volunteers were paid $4 for a 1-h session of problem solving. Seven of these subjects either produced no correct answers on one of the insight or the noninsight problems or produced correct answers immediately, so that no warmth protocols could be obtained for the solution interval. Thus, 19 subjects produced usable data.

Materials. Ten problems, provided on 3 × 5 in. cards, were given in random order to the subjects for solution one at a time. Half of these problems were noninsight problems, and half were insight problems. The noninsight problems were designated as such because past literature had labeled them as multistep problems or because they had been analyzed by incremental or search models such as those of Karat (1982) or Simon (1977, 1979). The noninsight problems are reproduced in Appendix A. The insight problems were chosen because they had been considered to be insight problems by other authors or by the sources from which they were taken. However, we felt free to eliminate problems that in our previous experiments (Metcalfe, 1986a, 1986b) had been designated by subjects as "grind-out-the-solution" problems rather than insight problems. Our criterion for calling a problem an insight problem was not well-defined. This lack of definition may well be one reason that research on insight has progressed so slowly. We shall return to this point in our conclusion. The insight problems we used are reproduced in Appendix B.

Procedure. The subjects were told that they would be asked to solve a number of problems, one at a time. Once they had the answer, they were to write it down so that the experimenter could ascertain whether it was right or wrong. If the experimenter had any doubt about the correctness of the answer, she asked the subject for clarification before proceeding to the next problem. During the course of solving, the subjects were asked to provide warmth ratings to indicate their perceived nearness to the solution. These ratings were marked by the subject with a slash on a 3-cm visual analogue scale on which the far left end was "cold," the far right end was "hot," and intermediate degrees of warmth were to be indicated by slashes in the middle range. Altogether, there were 40 lines that could be slashed for each problem (to allow for the maximum amount of time that a subject was permitted to work on a given problem); these lines were arranged vertically on an answer sheet. The subjects were told to put their first rating at the far left end of the visual analogue scale. They then worked their way down the sheet marking warmth ratings at 15-sec intervals, which were indicated by a click given by the experimenter. Because it requires less attention on the part of the subject, is nonsymbolic, and apparently is less distracting and intrusive, this visual-analogue-scale technique for assessing warmth is superior to the Metcalfe (1986b) technique of writing down numerals.

RESULTS

The probability level of $p \leq .05$ was chosen for significance. The increments in the warmth ratings were assessed in two ways. First, the angle subtended from the first rating to the last rating before the rating given with the answer in a particular protocol for a particular problem was measured. (We refer to this henceforth as the "angular warmth"). Second, the difference between the first slash or rating and the last rating before the rating given with the answer was measured. (We refer to this as the "differential warmth"). These two methods can yield different results because angular warmth, unlike differential warmth, varies according to the total time spent solving the problem. For example, consider two protocols, both of which start at the far left end of the scale and both of which have the warmth immediately before the answer given as a slash in the exact center of the scale. Let the first protocol have a total time of 1 min and the second a total of 2 min. When these two are ranked according to differential warmth, they will be tied, or be considered to be equally incremental. When they are ranked according to angular warmth, however, the first protocol will be said to be more incremental than the second. Thus, the differential warmth measure considers the total solving time (whatever it is) to be the unit of analysis, whereas the angular warmth measure gives an indication of the increment in warmth per unit of real time. We could not decide which method was more appropriate, so we used both.

The correctly solved problems were separately rank ordered from greatest to least on each of the angular warmth and the differential warmth measures, for each subject. Then a Goodman and Kruskal gamma correlation (see Nelson, 1984, 1986), comparing the rank orderings of the increment in warmth (going from most incremental to least) and problem type was computed. These gammas were treated as summary data scores for each subject. A positive correlation (which is what was expected) indicates that the noninsight problems tended to have more incremental warmth protocols than did the insight problems. The overall correlation on the angular warmth measure was .26, which is significantly different from zero [$t(18) = 2.02$, $MSe = .32$]. The overall correlation on the differential warmth measure was .23, which was also significantly different from zero [$t(18) = 1.63$, $MSe = .37$, by a one-tailed test].

Thus, the warmth protocols of the insight problems in experiment 1 showed a more sudden achievement of solution than did those of the noninsight problems. This is precisely what was expected given that the insight problems involved sudden illumination and the noninsight problems did not.

EXPERIMENT 2

METHOD

Subjects. Seventy-three University of British Columbia students in introductory psychology participated in exchange for a small bonus course credit. To allow assessment of performance on the feeling-of-knowing tasks detailed below, it was necessary that the subjects correctly solve at least one insight and one algebra problem, and that they miss at least one insight and one algebra problem. Twenty-one subjects failed to get at least one algebra or one insight problem correct, and so were dropped from the analyses. Four subjects got all the algebra problems correct and were dropped. This left 48 subjects who provided usable feeling-of-knowing data.

For warmth-rating data to be usable, it was necessary that the subjects get at least one insight and one algebra problem correct with at least three warmth ratings. Thirty-nine subjects provided usable data for this analysis.

Materials. The materials were classical insight problems (reproduced in Appendix B) and algebra problems selected from a high school algebra textbook (reproduced in Appendix C). The insight problems were selected, insofar as possible, to require little cognitive work other than the critical insight. Weisberg and Alba (1981b) argued against the idea of insight because they found that providing the clue or "insight" considered necessary to solve a problem did not ensure problem solution. Sternberg and Davidson (1982) pointed out that this failure of the clue to result in immediate problem solution may have occurred not because there was no process of insight, but rather because there were a number of additional processes involved in solving the problem as well as insight. In an attempt to circumvent such additional processes, we tried to use problems that were minimal.

Procedure and Design. The subjects were shown a series of insight or algebra problems, one at a time, randomly ordered within insight or algebra problem-set blocks. If they knew the answer to the problem, either from previous experience or by figuring it out immediately, the problem was eliminated from the test set. Once five unsolved problems (either insight or algebra, depending on order of presentation condition) had been accumulated, the experimenter arranged in a circle the 3×5 in. index cards on which the problems were typed and asked the subjects to rearrange them into a line going from the problem they thought they were most likely to be able to solve in a 4-min interval to that which they were least likely to be able to solve. This ranking represents the subjects' feelings that they will know (or feeling-of-knowing) ordering. The five cards were reshuffled, and the subjects were asked to assess the probability that they could solve each problem. The cards were shuffled again and then presented one at a time for solution. Every 15 sec during the course of solving, the subjects were told to indicate their feeling of warmth (i.e., their perceived closeness to solution) by putting a slash through a line that was 3 cm long, as in experiment 1. The subjects were not told explicitly to anchor the first slash at the far left of the scale, but they tended to do so. Altogether, there were 17 lines that could be slashed for each problem. The subjects continued through the set of five test problems until they had either written a solution or exhausted the time on each. Then the procedure was repeated with the other set of problems (either insight or algebra). The order of problem set (insight or algebra) was counterbalanced across subjects. The subjects were tested individually in 1-h sessions.

RESULTS

Warmth Ratings. The gammas computed on the angular warmth measures indicated that the insight problems showed a less incremental slope than did the algebra problems: Mean $G = .35$, which is significantly greater than zero [$t(37) = 3.10$, $MSe = .49$]. Gammas computed on the differential warmth measure showed the same pattern: Mean $G = .32$, which is also significantly greater than zero [$t(37) = 2.56$, $MSe = .58$].

Figure 1 provides a graphical representation of the subjects' warmth values for insight and algebra problems during the minute before the correct solution was given. The histograms in Figure 1 contain data from all subjects who had ratings in the specified intervals. To convert the visual analogue scale to a numerical scale, the 3-cm rating lines were divided into seven equal regions, and a slash occurring anywhere within one of these regions was given the appropriate numerical warmth value. Thus, ratings of 7 could occur before a solution was given because the subjects could, and did, provide ratings that were almost, but not quite, at the far right end of the scale. The trends of the distributions, over the last minute of solving time, going from the bottom to the top panel in Figure 1, tell the same story as the angular and differential warmth measures: There was a gradual increment in warmth with algebra problems but little increasing warmth with the insight problems.

Feeling of Knowing on Ranks. A Goodman and Kruskal gamma correlation was computed between the rank ordering given by the subject and the response (correct or incorrect) on each problem, for each of the two sets of problems. Then an analysis of variance was performed on these scores; the factors were order of presentation of problem block (either algebra first or insight first—between subjects) and problem type (algebra or insight—within subjects). There was a significant difference in gamma between the algebra problems (Mean $G = .40$) and the insight problems (Mean $G = .08$) [$F(1,46) = 6.46, MSe = .77$]. The correlation on the algebra problems was greater than zero [$t(46) = 4.6, MSe = .36$], whereas the correlation for the insight problems was not [$t(46) = .08, MSe = .47$]. This latter result replicates Metcalfe (1986a). Thus, it appears that the subjects fairly accurately predicted which algebra problems they would be able to solve later, but were unable to predict which insight problems they would solve.

Feeling of Knowing on Probabilities. The problems in each set were ranked according to the stated probability that they would be solved, and another gamma was computed on the data so arranged. Because the correlation cannot be computed if the identical probabilities are given for all problems (in either set), 4 subjects had to be eliminated from this analysis, leaving 44 subjects. Because there could be ties in

FIGURE 1	Frequency histograms of warmth ratings for correctly solved insight and algebra problems in experiment 2. The panels, from bottom to top, give the ratings 60, 45, 30, and 15 sec before solution. As shown in the top panel, a 7 rating was always given at the time of solution.

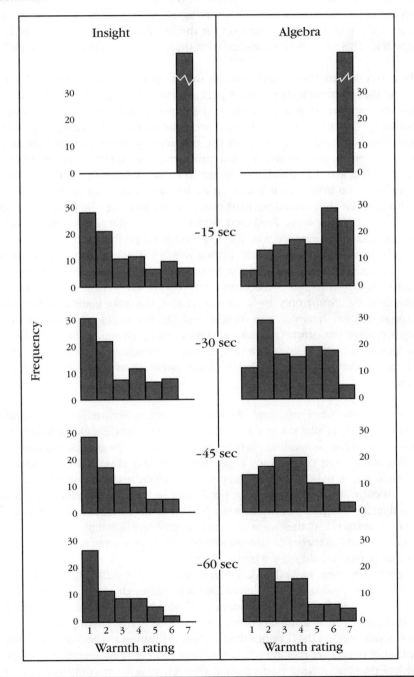

the probability estimates, and because there could be some inconsistency between the rankings and the estimates, the results are not identical to those presented above. As before, the difference between the algebra problems (Mean $G = .40$) and the insight problems (Mean $G = .15$) was significant [$F(1,42) = 2.8, MSe = .99$ one-tailed]. The correlation for the algebra problems was significantly greater than zero [$t(42) = 3.82, MSe = .48$], whereas the correlation for the insight problems was not [$t(42) = 1.2, MSe = .65$]. This analysis is consistent with the analysis conducted on the ranks.

Calibration. To compare the subjects' overall ability (Lichtenstein, Fischoff, & Phillips, 1982) to predict how well they would perform on the insight versus the algebra problems, the mean value was computed for the five probability estimates (one for each problem). This mean was compared with the actual proportion of problems that each subject solved correctly. Both the predicted performance and the actual performance were better on the algebra problems than on the insight problems [$F(1,46) = 54.67, MSe = .11$]. Previous research had shown that subjects overestimated their ability more on insight problems than on memory questions (Metcalfe, 1986a), and we thought that they would perhaps overestimate more on the insight problems than on the algebra problems. Predicted performance on the insight problems was .59, whereas actual performance was only .34. Predicted performance was .73 on the algebra problems, whereas actual performance was .55. The interaction showing that there was greater overestimation on the insight than on the algebra problems was significant [$F(1,46) = 3.18, MSe = .08$, one-tailed]. This result is fairly weak. Not only is the interaction significant only by a one-tailed test, but also, insofar as the actual performance differed between the insight and algebra problems, the interaction involving predicted performance could be eliminated by changing the scale. Despite these hedges, the result suggests that people may overestimate their ability more on insight than on algebra problems. None of the interactions with order of set was significant.

Personal Versus Normative Predictions. We looked at normative predictions because it was possible that there was no, or a very diffuse, underlying difficulty structure (or a restricted range in the probability correct) with the insight problems, and hence the zero feeling-of-knowing correlations could simply reflect that lack of structure, or range. In addition, there is the interesting possibility that the normative predictions of problem difficulty are more accurate at predicting individual behavior in particular situations than are subjects' self-evaluations. Nelson et al. (1986) found such an effect with memory retrieval. If this were the case in problem solving, as well, then the experimenter would in theory be able to predict better than a person him- or herself whether that person would solve a particular problem.

The problems were ranked ordered in terms of their difficulty by computing across subjects the probability of solution for each. Although ideally difficulty should have been computed from an independent pool of subjects, this was not cost effective. Thus, there is a small artificial correlation induced in this ranking because a subject's own results made a 2.1%, rather than a 0% contribution to the difficulty ranking. To see whether normative ranking was better than subjective judgment as a predictor of individual problem-solving performance, two gammas were compared. The first

TABLE 1	Mean Gamma Correlations Between Personal and Normative Predictions and Actual Performance for Insight and Algebra Problems in Experiment 2	

	Type of Prediction	
	PERSONAL	**NORMATIVE**
Insight	.08	.77
Algebra	.40	.60

was based on the normative ranking against the individual's performance, and the second was based on the subject's own feeling-of-knowing rank ordering against his or her performance. The normative probabilities were a much better predictor of subjects' individual performance than their own feelings of knowing. The normative correlation for the insight problems was .77; for the algebra problems, it was .60. These correlations indicate that there was sufficient range in the difficulty of the problems (both insight and algebra) that overall frequency correct was a good predictor of individual performance. The zero feeling-of-knowing correlation, discussed earlier, is therefore probably not attributable to a restricted range of insight-problem difficulty. The interaction between personal versus normative gammas as a function of problem type was significant [$F(1,46) = 10.13$, $MSe = 1.13$]. Table 1 gives the means. The idea that subjects may have privileged access to idiosyncratic information that makes them especially able to predict their own performance was overwhelmingly wrong in this experiment.

DISCUSSION

This study shows that there is an empirically demonstrable distinction between problems that people have thought were insight problems and those that are generally considered not to require insight, such as algebra or multistep problems. The above experiments showed that people's subjective metacognitions were predictive of performance on the noninsight problems, but not on the insight problems. In addition, the warmth ratings that people produced during noninsight problem solving showed a more incremental pattern, in both experiments, than did those problems that were preexperimentally designated as involving insight. These findings indicate in a straightforward manner that insight problems are, at least subjectively, solved by a sudden flash of illumination; noninsight problems are solved more incrementally.

A persistent problem has blocked the study of the process of insight: How can we ascertain when we are dealing with an insight problem? Let us now propose a solution. Given that the warmth protocols differentiate between problems that seem to be insight problems and those that do not, we may use the warmth protocols themselves in a diagnostic manner. If we find problems (or indeed problems for particular individuals) that are accompanied by step-function warmth protocols during the solution interval, we may define those problems as being insight problems for those people. Thus, we propose that insight be defined in terms of the antecedent phenomenology that may be monitored by metacognitive assessments by the subject. Adopting this solution may have interesting (although as yet unexplored) consequences. Perhaps the underlying processes involved in solving an insight problem are qualitatively different from those involved in solving a noninsight problem. It may (or may not) be that contextual or structural novelty is essential for insight. Perhaps there is a class of problems that provoke insights for all people. But perhaps insight varies with the level of skill within a particular problem-solving domain. If so, we might be able to use the class of problems that provoke insight for an individual to denote the individual's conceptual development in the domain in question. Perhaps this person–problem interaction will provide some optimal difficulty level for motivating a person and therefore have pedagogical consequences. Insight problems may be especially challenging to people, and their solution distinctly pleasurable. Of course, many other possibilities present themselves for future consideration. The process of insight has heretofore been virtually opaque to scientific scrutiny. Differentiating insight problems from other problems by the phenomenology that precedes solution may facilitate illumination of the process of insight.

REFERENCES

Adams, J. L. (1979). *Conceptual blockbusting.* New York: Norton.

Arietti, S. (1976). *Creativity: The magic synthesis.* New York: Basic Books.

Bergson, H. (1902). *An introduction to metaphysics.* New York: Putnam.

Bruner, J. (1966). *On knowing: Essays for the left hand.* Cambridge, MA: Harvard University Press.

Davidson, J. E., & Sternberg, R. J. (1984). The role of insight in intellectual giftedness. *Gifted Child Quarterly, 28,* 58–64.

deBono, E. (1967). *The use of lateral thinking.* New York: Penguin.

deBono, E. (1969). *The mechanism of mind.* New York: Penguin.

Dominowski, R. L. (1981). Comment on an examination of the alleged role of "fixation" in the solution of "insight" problems. *Journal of Experimental Psychology: General, 110,* 199–203.

Duncker, K. (1945). On problem solving. *Psychological Monographs, 58* (5, Whole No. 270).

Ellen, P. (1982). Direction, past experience, and hints in creative problem solving: Reply to Weisberg and Alba. *Journal of Experimental Psychology: General, III,* 316–325.

Fixx, J. F. (1972). *More games for the superintelligent.* New York: Popular Library.

Gardner, M. (1978). *Aha! Insight.* New York: Freeman.

Gruneberg, M. M., & Monks, J. (1974). Feeling of knowing in cued recall. *Acta Psychologica, 38,* 257–265.

Hart, J. T. (1967). Memory and the memory-monitoring process. *Journal of Verbal Learning & Verbal Behavior, 6,* 685–691.

Hofstadter, D. R. (1980). *Gödel, Escher, Bach: An eternal golden braid.* New York: Vintage Books.

Karat, J. (1982). A model of problem solving with incomplete constraint knowledge. *Cognitive Psychology, 14,* 538–559.

Koestler, A. (1977). *The act of creation.* London: Picadoo.

Levine, M. (1986). *Principles of effective problem solving.* Unpublished manuscript, State University of New York at Stonybrook.

Lichtenstein, S., Fischoff, B., & Phillips, L. D. (1982). Calibration of probabilities: The state to the art to 1980. In D. Kahneman, P. Slovic, & A. Tversky (Eds.), *Judgment under uncertainty: Heuristics and biases.* Cambridge: Cambridge University Press.

Lovelace, E. A. (1984). Metamemory: Monitoring future recallability during study. *Journal of Experimental Psychology: Learning, Memory, & Cognition, 10,* 756-766.

Luchins, A. S. (1942). Mechanization in problem solving. *Psychological Monographs, 54* (6, Whole No. 248).

Maier, N. R. F. (1931). Reasoning in humans: II. The solution of a problem and its appearance in consciousness. *Journal of Comparative Psychology, 12,* 181-194.

Mayer, R. E. (1983). *Thinking, problem solving, cognition.* New York: Freeman.

Metcalfe, J. (1986a). Feeling of knowing in memory and problem solving. *Journal of Experimental Psychology: Learning, Memory, & Cognition, 12,* 288-294.

Metcalfe, J. (1986b). Premonitions of insight predict impending error. *Journal of Experimental Psychology: Learning, Memory, & Cognition, 12,* 623-634.

Nelson, T. O. (1984). A comparison of current measures of the accuracy of feeling of knowing prediction. *Psychological Bulletin, 95,* 109-133.

Nelson, T. O. (1986). ROC curves and measures of discrimination accuracy: A reply to Swets. *Psychological Bulletin, 100,* 128-132.

Nelson, T. O., Leonesio, R. J., Landwehr, R. S., & Narens, L. (1986). A comparison of three predictors of an individual's memory performance. The individual's feeling of knowing versus the normative feeling of knowing versus base-rate item difficulty. *Journal of Experimental Psychology: Learning, Memory, & Cognition, 12,* 279-287.

Nelson, T. O., Leonesio, R. J., Shimamura, A. P., Landwehr, R. F., & Narens, L. (1982). Overlearning and the feeling of knowing. *Journal of Experimental Psychology: Learning, Memory, & Cognition, 8,* 279-288.

Nelson, T. O., & Narens, L. (1980). Norms of 300 general-information questions: Accuracy of recall, latency of recall, and feeling-of-knowing ratings. *Journal of Verbal Learning & Verbal Behavior, 19,* 338-368.

Polanyi, M. (1958). *Personal knowledge: Towards a post-critical philosophy.* Chicago: University of Chicago Press.

Polya, G. (1957). *How to solve it.* Princeton, NJ: Princeton University Press.

Restle, F., & Davis, J. H. (1962). Success and speed of problem solving by individuals and groups. *Psychological Review, 69,* 520-536.

Schacter, D. L. (1983). Feeling of knowing in episodic memory. *Journal of Experimental Psychology: Learning, Memory, & Cognition, 9,* 39-54.

Simon, H. (1977). *Models of discovery.* Dordrecht, The Netherlands: Reidel.

Simon, H. (1979). *Models of thought.* New Haven, CT: Yale University Press.

Simon, H., Newell, A., & Shaw, J. C. (1979). The process of creative thinking. In H. Simon (Ed.), *Models of thought* (pp. 144-174). New Haven, CT: Yale University Press.

Sternberg, R. J. (1985). *Beyond IQ.* Cambridge, MA: Cambridge University Press.

Sternberg, R. J. (1986). *Intelligence applied.* San Diego: Harcourt Brace Jovanovich.

Sternberg, R. J., & Davidson, J. E. (1982, June). The mind of the puzzler. *Psychology Today, 16,* 37-44.

Travers, K. J., Dalton, L. C., Bruner, V. F., & Taylor, A. R. (1976). *Using advanced algebra.* Toronto: Doubleday.

Wallas, G. (1926). *The art of thought.* New York: Harcourt.

Weisberg, R. W., & Alba, J. W. (1981a). An examination of the alleged role of "fixation" in the solution of several "insight" problems. *Journal of Experimental Psychology: General, 110,* 169-192.

Weisberg, R. W., & Alba, J. W. (1981b). Gestalt theory, insight, and past experience: Reply to Dominowski. *Journal of Experimental Psychology: General, 110,* 193-198.

Weisberg, R. W., & Alba, J. W. (1982). Problem solving is not like perception: More on Gestalt theory. *Journal of Experimental Psychology: General, 111,* 326-330.

APPENDIX A
INCREMENTAL PROBLEMS

1. If the puzzle you solved before you solved this one was harder than the puzzle you solved after you solved the puzzle you solved before you solved this one, was the puzzle you solved before you solved this one harder than this one (Restle & Davis, 1962)?

2. Given containers of 163, 14, 25, and 11 ounces, and a source of unlimited water, obtain exactly 77 ounces of water (Luchins, 1942).

3. Given state:

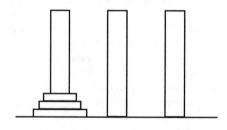

Goal state:

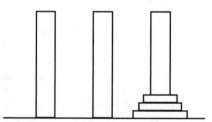

Allowable moves: Move only one disc at a time; take only the top disc on a peg; never place a larger disc on top of a smaller one (e.g., Karat, 1982; Levine, 1986).

4. Three people play a game in which one person loses and two people win each round. The one who loses must double the amount of money that each of the other two players has at that time. The three players agree to play three games. At the end of the three games, each player has lost one game and each person has $8. What was the original stake of each player (R. Thaler, personal communication, September 1986)?

5. Next week I am going to have lunch with my friend, visit the new art gallery, go to the social security office, and have my teeth checked at the dentist. My friend cannot meet me on Wednesday; the social security office is closed weekends; the

dentist has office hours only on Tuesday, Friday, and Saturday; the art gallery is closed Tuesday, Thursday, and weekends. What day can I do everything I have planned? (Sternberg & Davidson, 1982)?

APPENDIX B
INSIGHT PROBLEMS

1. A prisoner was attempting to escape from a tower. He found in his cell a rope which was half long enough to permit him to reach the ground safely. He divided the rope in half and tied the two parts together and escaped. How could he have done this (experiments 1 and 2; Restle & Davis, 1962)?

2. Water lilies double in area every 24 hours. At the beginning of summer there is one water lily on the lake. It takes 60 days for the lake to become completely covered with water lilies. On which day is the lake half covered (experiments 1 and 2; Sternberg & Davidson, 1982)?

3. If you have black socks and brown socks in your drawer, mixed in a ratio of 4 to 5, how many socks will you have to take out to make sure that you have a pair the same color (experiments 1 and 2; Sternberg & Davidson, 1982)?

4. The triangle shown below points to the top of the page. Show how you can move three circles to get the triangle to point to the bottom of the page (experiments 1 and 2; deBono, 1969).

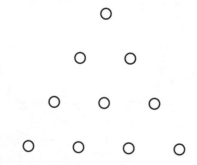

5. A landscape gardener is given instructions to plant four special trees so that each one is exactly the same distance from each of the others. How is he able to do it (experiments 1 and 2; deBono, 1967)?

6. A man bought a horse for $60 and sold it for $70. Then he bought it back for $80 and sold it for $90. How much did he make or lose in the horse trading business (experiment 2; deBono, 1967)?

7. A woman has four pieces of chain. Each piece is made up of three links. She wants to join the pieces into a single closed loop of chain. To open a link costs 2 cents and to close a link costs 3 cents. She only as 15 cents. How does she do it (experiment 2; deBono, 1967)?

APPENDIX B (CONTINUED)

8. Without lifting your pencil from the paper show how you could join all 4 dots with 2 straight lines (experiment 2; M. Levine, personal communication, October 1985).

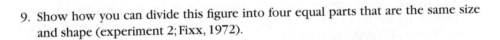

9. Show how you can divide this figure into four equal parts that are the same size and shape (experiment 2; Fixx, 1972).

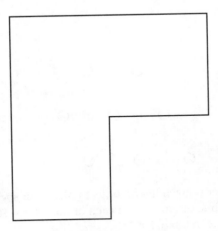

10. Describe how to cut a hole in a 3 × 5 in. card that is big enough for you to put your head through (experiment 2; deBono, 1969).

11. Show how you can arrange 10 pennies so that you have 5 rows (lines) of 4 pennies in each row (experiment 2; Fixx, 1972).

12. Describe how to put 27 animals in 4 pens in such a way that there is an odd number of animals in each pen (experiment 2; L. Ross, personal communication, December 1985).

APPENDIX C
MATH PROBLEMS (TAKEN FROM TRAVERS, DALTON, BRUNER, & TAYLOR, 1976)

1. $(3x^2 + 2x + 10)(3x) =$
2. $(2x + y)(3x - y) =$
3. Factor: $16y^2 - 40yz + 25z^2$
4. Solve for x:

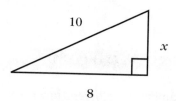

5. $18x^2 + \dfrac{24x}{3x} =$
6. Factor: $x^2 + 6x + 9$
7. Solve for x:
   $\frac{1}{5}x + 10 = 25$
8. $\dfrac{-6x^2y^4}{3x^5y^3} =$
9. $\sqrt[3]{-27} =$
10. $\sqrt[6]{25} =$
11. Solve for $x, y,$ and z:
    $x + 2y - z = 13$
    $2x + y + z = 8$
    $3x - y = 2z = 1$
12. $\sqrt[9]{1{,}000} =$
13. Solve for m:
    $\dfrac{m - 3}{2m} - \dfrac{m - 2}{2m + 1} = 0$
14. $\sqrt{-121} =$
15. Solve for a and b:
    $3a + 6b = 5$
    $2a - b = 1$
16. $\sqrt[4]{16} =$
17. $(\sqrt[6]{2^2})\ (\sqrt[6]{2^3}) =$
18. $(a^2)(a^7) =$

APPENDIX C (CONTINUED)

19. $\dfrac{(a^2)}{(a^6)} =$

20. Find cos θ

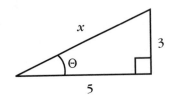

QUESTIONS FOR FURTHER THOUGHT

1. Why do Metcalfe and Weibe believe that fundamentally different processes are involved in the solution of insight versus nonsight problems?

2. How are feeling-of-warmth ratings critical to the conclusions that Metcalfe and Weibe reach?

3. What role does metacognition play in distinguishing insight and noninsight problems?

4. What is an important practical problem faced by researchers who wish to study insight?

5. How might someone who believes that people apply fundamentally the same solution processes in insight and noninsight problems question Metcalfe and Weibe's interpretation of their results?

9

REASONING, JUDGMENT, AND DECISION MAKING

REASONING ABOUT A RULE
Peter Wason

CHOICES, VALUES, AND FRAMES
Daniel Kahneman and Amos Tversky

REASONING ABOUT A RULE

Peter Wason

INTRODUCTION

Are people natural logical reasoners, or is logical reasoning a skill that they learn, perhaps only as a result of explicit instruction? Many experts have believed that logical reasoning is a natural skill. For example, George Boole (1854/1951) entitled a famous book on logic *The Laws of Thought*, implying that formal logic merely mirrors the natural laws of human thinking. Jean Piaget (1972), the famous Swiss developmental psychologist, believed for most of his life that everyone develops the ability to reason logically around the age of 11 or 12 years, when people enter what Piaget called the *stage of formal operations*. Even today, most economists operate under the assumption that people are naturally rational thinkers, and some psychologists, such as Jonathan Baron (1985), have suggested that rational thought underlies human intelligence.

This study was one of a series performed by Peter Wason that suggested that, whatever else they may be, people are not natural logical reasoners. Consider the statement, "If P, then Q." Wason showed, as most people would expect, that people know that to show the truth of this statement, they need to show that Q always follows from P. For example, if the abstract statement above is concretized as "If it rains, then the ground will be wet," we need to show that every time it rains, the ground will be wet. This inference is called *modus ponendo ponens* in logic. What very few people realize, however, is that a second statement must also be shown to be true: "If not Q, then not P," or, "If the ground is not wet, then it is not raining." This statement is called *modus tollendo tollens* in logic. Although the two statements are logically equivalent, people do not spontaneously see the equivalence, nor often see it even when given information (what Wason calls *therapy*) to help them see the equivalence.

Wason used what has come to be called the *Wason card-selection task* to show a curious failing in people's ability to reason logically, even with the help of guidance. This task quickly became, and probably still is, the single most widely used task in studies of deductive reasoning. For this reason alone, the work is a classic. But at least one other reason reinforces the work's importance. The main result showed that models that view people as "logical" or "rational" thinkers just cannot accurately portray the truth. In fact, people may know the implications of affirming the antecedent ("If X is true, then Y is true. . . . X is true") in conditional reasoning, but they generally do not know the implications of denying the consequent ("If X is true, then Y is true. . . . Y is not true"). Thus, models that view people as logicians in action give inadequate accounts of how they actually reason.

―

Source: From Wason, P. (1968). Reasoning about a rule. *Quarterly Journal of Experimental Psychology, 20*, 273–281. Reprinted by permission of The Experimental Psychology Society.

Two experiments were carried out to investigate the difficulty of making the contrapositive inference from conditional sentences of the form, "if P then Q." This inference, that not-P follows from not-Q, requires the transformation of the information presented in the conditional sentence. It is suggested that the difficulty is due to a mental set for expecting a relation of truth, correspondence, or match to hold between sentences and states of affairs. The elicitation of the inference was not facilitated by attempting to induce two kinds of therapy designed to break this set. It is argued that the subjects did not give evidence of having acquired the characteristics of Piaget's "formal operational thought." ∎

INTRODUCTION

This investigation is concerned with the difficulty of making a particular type of inference from conditional sentences, statements of material implication of the form, "if P then Q" (P⊃ Q).

Within the propositional calculus, the truth table for the conditional counts the following combinations of the components of the sentences as true: PQ, $\bar{P}$Q, $\bar{P}\bar{Q}$ (where $\bar{P}$ stands for not-P and $\bar{Q}$ for not-Q), and only the one combination, P$\bar{Q}$, as false. It follows that only values of P and values of $\bar{Q}$ allow a valid inference. In other words, a valid inference depends crucially upon the *possibility* of meeting the falsifying contingency, P$\bar{Q}$. It rests simply upon the denial of this contingency. $\bar{P}$ comes out true whether it is associated with Q or $\bar{Q}$, and Q comes out true whether it is associated with P or $\bar{P}$. For example, suppose someone says, "if John is a stockbroker, then he is bound to read the *Financial Times*." If John isn't a stockbroker, or if he does read the *Financial Times,* the conditional statement (to the logician) is inevitably true. But if he is a stockbroker, or if he never reads the *Financial Times,* then there are grounds for verifying or falsifying the conditional statement. Hence, logically, only two forms of inference are valid: "P⊃ Q and P . . . Q" (*modus ponens*) and "P⊃ Q and $\bar{Q}$ . . . $\bar{P}$" (*modus tollens* or contrapositive). The other two forms of inference, "P⊃ Q, and $\bar{P}$ . . . $\bar{Q}$" (denial of the antecedent) and "P⊃ Q and Q . . . P" (affirmation of the consequent) are fallacious.

In a task consisting of sentences expressed in everyday terms the author (Wason, 1964) has shown that the affirmation of the consequent occurs significantly more frequently than the denial of the antecedent. In an abstract task the occurrence of all four types of inference has been investigated in a pilot study (Wason, 1966). The subjects were presented with the following sentence, "if there is a vowel on one side of the card, then there is an even number on the other side," together with four cards each of which had a letter on one side and a number on the other side. On the front of the first card appeared a vowel (P), on the front of the second a consonant ($\bar{P}$), on the front of the third an even number (Q), and on the front of the fourth an odd number ($\bar{Q}$). The task was to select all those cards, but only those cards, which would have to be turned over in order to discover whether the experimenter was lying in making the conditional sentence. The results of this study, and that of a replication by Hughes (1966), showed the same relative frequencies of cards selected. Nearly all subjects select P, from 60 to 75 percent, select Q; only a minority select $\bar{Q}$, and hardly any select $\bar{P}$. Thus two errors are committed: The consequent is fallaciously affirmed, and the contrapositive is withheld. This type of task will be called henceforth the *selection task.* These errors seem to be enduring and deep. Hughes has shown that they often persist for 15 trials, even when the subjects turn over all the cards after each trial and evaluate the conditional sentence with respect to them.

A theory to explain these results has been postulated (Wason, 1966). It rests on two assumptions. The first assumption is that individuals are not constrained by the rules of the propositional calculus. They implicitly assume that a conditional sentence can have three outcomes or truth values. PQ is true, $P\bar{Q}$ is false, and $\bar{P}$ with either Q or $\bar{Q}$ is irrelevant. This interpretation is not original: It has been debated in the history of logic since the Stoic and Megarian schools. The assumption explains why the consequent is affirmed—Q is selected in order to see whether it is associated with P making the conditional true. It also explains why the antecedent is so infrequently denied—$\bar{P}$ is irrelevant to the truth or falsity of the sentence.

The second assumption explains the infrequency of the contrapositive inference—why $\bar{P}$ is so seldom deduced from $\bar{Q}$. This assumption is that individuals are biased, through a long learning process, to expect a relation of truth, correspondence, or match to hold between sentences and states of affairs. In adult experience, truth is encountered more frequently than falsity, and we seldom use a proposition or judgment that something is false in order to make a deduction. The semantic concept of falsity is logically equivalent to the syntactic concept of negation, and it has been shown that both cause difficulty when sentences have to be evaluated or constructed (Wason, 1959, 1961; Wason & Jones, 1963). Both concepts are relevant to the selection task. A value of $\bar{Q}$ represents a mismatch between a state of affairs visible on the card and a clause in the conditional sentence. This mismatch has to be recognized as such by transforming the information in the relevant clause from Q to $\bar{Q}$. In other words, a state of affairs (x) has to be seen not simply as x but as $\bar{Q}$. In doing this, the individual presumably makes a judgment of falsity by uttering a covert negative sentence to himself. The difficulties involved in doing all this are assumed to be sufficient to account for the relative failure to select $\bar{Q}$.

According to this theory, the affirmation of the consequent—the deduction of P from Q—is a plausible inference. But the withholding of the contrapositive remains irrational and is consequently a factor of much greater interest. The present investigation is concerned with the effects of therapies designed to correct the bias toward truth or correspondence and thus facilitate the elicitation of the contrapositive inference.

EXPERIMENT 1

THE PROJECTION OF FALSITY

It was predicted that if individuals were to "project falsity," i.e. to say what values, if any, associated with the given values, P, $\bar{P}$, Q, $\bar{Q}$, would make a conditional sentence *false,* then they would more readily select $\bar{Q}$ to determine whether the sentence was in fact true or false. P is the only value associated with $\bar{Q}$ which could make a conditional sentence false. Hence if individuals were to project P on to a value of $\bar{Q}$, they might be more likely to select $\bar{Q}$ as informative.

METHOD

Design. In the experimental group, the subjects first carried out a selection task. They decided which of four cards (P, $\bar{\text{P}}$, Q, $\bar{\text{Q}}$) would enable them to determine whether a given conditional sentence was true or false, if they were to know the values on the backs of the cards. They were then invited to say what values, if any, on the backs of the cards would render the sentences false. They then revised their initial selections of the cards, if they wished to do so, and finally evaluated the sentence with respect to the values on both sides of all four cards, i.e. they turned over each card and evaluated the sentence as true or false with respect to it. In the control group, the procedure was similar, but instead of projecting falsity, the subjects were simply asked to think again about their initial selections, i.e. to revise them, "because people often do this task too quickly and get it wrong."

Subjects. Thirty-six first year psychology and statistics students of University College London.

Material. Two conditional sentences were typed on separate cards (5 × 3 in): (1) "If there is a D on one side of any card, then there is a 3 on its other side," (2) "If there is a 3 on one side of any card, then there is a D on its other side." These two sentences were used as a control for the order in which the two items were mentioned. Associated with each sentence were four cards (2 × 2 in). The cards associated with sentence (1) had the following letters and numbers on their fronts, and (in brackets) the following on their backs: D(3), 3(K), B(5), 7(D). The following cards were associated with sentence (2): 3(D), K(3), 5(B), D(7). It will be appreciated that both sets of cards conform to only one of the two possible combinations of values of the antecedent and consequent: P(Q), Q($\bar{\text{P}}$), $\bar{\text{P}}$($\bar{\text{Q}}$), $\bar{\text{Q}}$(P). The other combination was not used: P($\bar{\text{Q}}$), Q(P), $\bar{\text{P}}$(Q), $\bar{\text{Q}}$($\bar{\text{P}}$).

Procedure. The subjects were allocated alternately to the groups and tested individually. Half the subjects in each group were tested with sentence (1) and half with sentence (2). The sentence was placed on the desk and the four test cards were placed in a line in a random order face upward in front of the sentence. The subjects were told that cards with letters on their fronts had numbers on their backs and *vice versa.* In the selection task, the experimenter pointed to each card in turn and asked the subject whether knowing what was on the other side would enable him to find out whether the sentence was true or false. During the projection of falsity, in the experimental group, the experimenter pointed to each card and asked the subject to name a letter (or number) on the other side which would make the sentence false, or to say "none," if none would do so.

RESULTS

Two subjects, both in the control group, seemed unable to comply with the instructions and were hence rejected.

Tables 1 and 2 show the frequency of the responses in the different phases of the task for the experimental and control groups, respectively. It will be noted immediately that, by comparing the frequencies in the diagonal cells, there is a greater tendency for the initial and revised selections of the cards to conform in the control group than in the experimental group. Inspection shows that the frequency of selecting $\bar{Q}$ increases over the task from five to eight in the experimental group and from two to three in the control group. The prediction that the selection of $\bar{Q}$ would be facilitated significantly in the experimental group is not confirmed.

Table 1 shows that in the experimental group, 13 subjects did not select $\bar{Q}$ initially, and that of these, five did not project P on to $\bar{Q}$ and eight did project it. But of these eight, only three included a value of $\bar{Q}$ in their revised selection. Thus, the therapy of falsifying the values cannot always be induced, and even when it is induced it is by no means effective.

Table 1 shows that the most frequent projection of falsity was on to all four values (P, $\bar{P}$, Q, $\bar{Q}$). But only one of the six subjects responsible for doing this subsequently selected all four values in their revised selection. It is evident that in these cases, falsification did not render all the values acceptable for testing the truth or falsity of the sentence. The invitation to project falsity in these cases seemed to result in an arbitrary or indiscriminate response which had no bearing on subsequent behaviour.

It will be noted that the P and Q pair is selected with the greatest frequency in both the experimental group (eight cases) and in the control group (10 cases).

Table 3 is the frequency distribution of the evaluation of the contingencies as true, false, or irrelevant for the combined groups.

TABLE 1 Frequency of Initial Selections, Projections of Falsity and Revised Selections in the Experimental Group

INITIAL SELECTION	PROJECTION OF FALSITY	*Revised Selection*							
		PQ	P	PQ$\bar{Q}$	P$\bar{P}$Q	P$\bar{P}$Q$\bar{Q}$	P$\bar{Q}$	N	N
P Q	P Q	2				1		3	
	P$\bar{P}$Q$\bar{Q}$	4				1		5	8
P	P Q	1						1	
	P	1						1	
	P $\bar{Q}$						1	1	4
	P$\bar{P}$Q$\bar{Q}$	1						1	
P Q$\bar{Q}$	P		1					1	
	P $\bar{Q}$			1				1	3
	P Q$\bar{Q}$			1				1	
P$\bar{P}$Q	P $\bar{Q}$						1	1	1
P$\bar{P}$Q$\bar{Q}$	$\bar{P}$ $\bar{Q}$						1	1	
	P Q$\bar{Q}$						1	1	2
	N	9	1	2	0	2	4	18	18

TABLE 2	Frequency of Initial and Revised Selections in the Control Group

				Revised Selection			
INITIAL SELECTION	PQ	P	PQ̄	PP̄	PQQ̄	P̄PQQ̄	N
P Q	9					1	10
P	1	2					3
P Q̄			1				1
P P̄				1			1
P Q Q̄					1		1
P P̄ Q Q̄							0
N	10	2	1	1	1	1	16

It will be noted that the author's theory is corroborated with respect to the evaluation of the PQ, PQ̄, and P̄Q̄ contingencies, but is refuted with respect to the evaluation of the P̄Q contingency. This was evaluated as making the sentence false by 22 subjects and by only 10 subjects. This result is particularly interesting because, on the revised selection, P̄ was selected only four times out of 34, and yet, when it is associated with Q there is a much greater tendency for it to be judged as relevant to the falsity of the sentence.

This experiment has shown the inadequacy of projecting falsity as a therapy for the elicitation of the contrapositive inference, and that some subjects cannot even perform the therapeutic exercise. Two further pilot studies were carried out which revealed one interesting phenomenon. In the first study, the four values were presented on separate trials and a few subjects, when presented with P̄ and Q̄, said they did not need to turn these over because they already falsified the conditional sentence. In the second study, the subjects were asked to pick out only those values

TABLE 3	Frequency of the Evaluations in the Combined Groups

PQ	P̄Q	PQ̄	P̄Q̄	N
t	f	f	i	15
t	i	f	i	9
t	f	f	t	3
t	t	f	t	2
t	f	f	f	2
i	f	f	i	1
t	f	i	i	1
t	i	t	i	1
				34

Note. t = true, f = false, i = irrelevant.

which "could break the rule" (i.e., falsify the conditional sentence). Four subjects selected *only* values of $\bar{P}$ and $\bar{Q}$ and refused to turn them over because they claimed this was useless. "It doesn't make any difference—the two I have chosen do break the rule." "There is no rule regarding that card ($\bar{P}$)." Thus, in a small minority of subjects, the concept of something following a rule appears to be inadequately conceived, for to know what could follow a rule is to know what could break that rule.

EXPERIMENT 2

THE RESTRICTED CONTINGENCY PROGRAM

It was predicted that if subjects were initially allowed to evaluate examples of the four contingencies with respect to a given conditional sentence, and were, in addition, told that only one contingency falsified the sentence, then they would subsequently select values of $\bar{Q}$ within the same task to a greater extent than those who had not had this experience. The term, *restricted* is used because the intention of this program was not to teach the truth table for the conditional, but to make the subject aware that only the $P\bar{Q}$ contingency falsified the sentence. It was reasoned that if the subject knows in advance that $\bar{Q}$ is crucial for falsification, then he might select it as potentially informative.

METHOD

Design. The experimental group first received the program and then carried out a selection task with the same material. The control group carried out a selection task without receiving the program.

Subjects. Twenty-six first-year psychology students at the University of Edinburgh.

Material. Two conditional sentences were typed on separate cards similar to those used in experiment 1. (1) "If there is a square on one side of the card, then there is a red scribble on the other side," (2) "If there is a red scribble on one side of a card, then there is a square on the other side." Four program cards were prepared for the experimental group which had the following stimuli on either side: (*a*) square, yellow scribble, (*b*) square, red scribble, (*c*) rectangle, red scribble, (*d*) hexagon, brown scribble. Eight similar cards were prepared for the selection task, the items mentioned first being on the front of the cards, and the items mentioned second (in brackets) being on the back: (*a*) square (red scribble), (*b*) square (brown scribble), (*c*) red scribble (square), (*d*) red scribble (hexagon), (*e*) green scribble (rectangle), (*f*) parellelogram (yellow scribble), (*g*) triangle (red scribble), (*h*) blue scribble (square). It will be appreciated that these cards represent both combinations of values of the antecedent and consequent: $P(Q), P(\bar{Q}), \bar{P}(Q), \bar{P}(\bar{Q}), Q(P), Q(\bar{P}), \bar{Q}(P), \bar{Q}(\bar{P})$.

Procedure. The subjects were allocated alternately to the groups and tested individually. Six subjects in the experimental group were tested with sentence (1) and seven with sentence (2), these proportions being reversed in the control group.

Before presenting the conditional sentence, the subjects in both groups examined the cards briefly to familiarize them with the fact that there was always a geometric shape on one side and a colored scribble on the other side.

In the experimental group, the conditional sentence was presented, and the four program cards were handed to the subjects who were asked to pick out "the one card which makes the rule false" (i.e. falsifies the conditional sentence). They were then asked to pick out any which "prove the rule true." It was explained to them that their decisions meant that the converse of the sentence could not be assumed—"that the rule only held one way." The subjects in the control group were given a similar amount of time to understand the conditional sentence without any explanation of its meaning.

The selection task had three phases which were the same for both groups.

Phase 1. The eight selection task cards were placed on the desk front side up in a random array, and the subject was asked to pick out "all those cards, but only those cards, which would show you, if you knew what was on the other side, that the rule was true or false."

Phase 2. The subject was asked to turn over all those cards which he had selected and evaluate the conditional sentence with respect to each: "tell me whether each proves the rule true or proves it false."

Phase 3. The subject was invited to project falsity onto the residual cards (i.e., those cards which had not been selected). Each pair of cards (representing the same value) was pointed to in turn, starting with the $\overline{Q}$ cards, if these had not been selected: "could anything on the back of those cards make the rule false?"

RESULTS

In the programming in the experimental group, all the subjects picked out the $P\overline{Q}$ card without hesitation as the only falsifying instance, and they all picked out PQ as the only verifying instance.

Table 4 is the frequency distribution of the choices made in the selection task for both groups. (All subjects were consistent in picking out both instances of any value which they selected.)

	EXPERIMENTAL GROUP	CONTROL GROUP	N
TABLE 4 Frequencies of Values Selected in Both Groups			
P Q	6	6	12
P	5	4	9
P $\overline{Q}$	1	1	2
P $\overline{P}$	1	1	2
P $\overline{P}$ Q $\overline{Q}$	0	1	1
			26

It is at once apparent that there is little difference in the results of the two groups and that the treatment given to the experimental group failed in its effects.

Table 5 is the frequency distribution of the evaluation of the contingencies and the projections of falsity onto the residual values in the combined groups. An empty cell in the evaluation task means that at least one of the values associated with that cell was absent from both sides of a selected card. An empty cell in the falsification task, however, means that a value on the front of a card, associated with that cell, had been selected (and evaluated), and hence was no longer available for the projection of falsity. A dash in a cell means that a subject denied that any value associated with the value in that cell would falsify the rule, and an entry of a value in a cell means that it, associated with the value in that cell, would falsify the rule. It will be noted that the selected values, other than P which was always selected, correspond to the *empty* cells in the falsification task.

It is of particular interest to note that six out of a possible 17 subjects failed to say that P, projected on to $\bar{Q}$, would falsify the rule and that 8 of the 10 subjects, who had claimed that Q($\bar{P}$) falsified the rule subsequently said that no value associated with $\bar{P}$ would falsify the rule.

Only nine of the 24 subjects, who had not selected $\bar{Q}$, said that they were aware of having made a mistake in the selection task.

TABLE 5   Frequency of the Evaluations of the Contingencies and of the Projection of Falsity on Residual Values in the Combined Groups

Evaluation Task				Falsification Task			
PQ	$\bar{P}Q$	$P\bar{Q}$	$\bar{P}\bar{Q}$	$\bar{P}$	Q	$\bar{Q}$	N
t		f		—	—	P	6
t	f	f		—		—	5
t	f	f		—		P	3
t	i	f		—		P	2
t		f	i	—	—		2
t	f	f		Q		P	2
t	f	f	t		$\bar{P}$	P	1
t		f		—	—	—	1
t		f		—	$\bar{P}$	P	1
t	i	f	i	—		P	1
t		f		Q	$\bar{P}$	P	1
t	f	f	i				1
							26

Note. t = true, f = false, i = irrelevant. No P column is included under falsification because all subjects selected P.

GENERAL DISCUSSION

The results show that two kinds of therapy do not facilitate the act of making the contrapositive inference, the selection of $\overline{Q}$, but they do show phenomena of considerable interest. The selection task was not meaningless to the subjects. Their results are far from random. In the combined experiments, 50 percent initially select just P and Q out of the possible 15 combinations of values which could have been selected. This marked tendency to pick out only those values which are mentioned in the conditional sentence suggests that the selection task seemed deceptively easy. Its real meaning, the challenge which it implies, escaped the subjects to a large extent. But the selection of P and Q, which is so resistant to therapy, is consistent with the theory that individuals are biased through a long learning process to seek and expect a simple correspondence to hold between sentences and states of affairs. The introspections corroborate the theory. "You first of all accept all the cards as true—you don't make any allowances for any of them being wrong until you turn them over." "A rule is a rule, so looking at it frankly the ones with squares will have red scribbles on the back." "I feel very unhappy about my original choice, but yes, I would still choose the same ones if I had to do the task again." One subject twice projected truth instead of falsity before he could be prevailed upon to comply with the instructions.

It is a reasonable inference that this set for truth inhibits the perception of a card as being an exemplar of $\overline{Q}$. Even when it is recognized as such it is not always used to make a deduction. In the results of the combined experiments, 16.7 percent of the subjects select $\overline{Q}$. But of those who do not initially select it, 30.6 percent fail to project P onto it as a means of falsifying the conditional sentence. This seems extraordinarily capricious. It is as if someone had said that any number other than 3 on the other side of D would falsify the conditional and in the next breath denied that any letter on the other side of 7 would do so. However, once the drift of the subjects' reasoning is apparent, the logical discrepancies begin to look more plausible. P(Q) and Q(P) come to the same thing when the cards are turned over: They both verify the rule. When $Q(\overline{P})$ is turned over it certainly doesn't verify the rule—hence it must falsify it. But of course, there is nothing on the other side of $\overline{P}$ which would falsify the rule because there is nothing on the other side which could verify it. One might risk a general statement about this. Suppose that a rule is confirmed whenever one state of affairs (*y*) depends upon another (*x*); and suppose initially one has access to either *x* or *y* but not both. If *y* is obtained, then there is an expectancy that *x* will be found to have been associated with it, thus confirming the rule; but if *x* is found not to have been associated with *y*, we are tempted to say that the rule has been refuted. However, if initially *x* is not obtained, no such expectancy is generated, and we are less inclined to say that, if *y* were to follow, the rule would be refuted. If *y* is not obtained initially, nothing seems to follow about the rule at all.

The results, however, are still disquieting. If Piaget is right (Inhelder and Piaget, 1958), then the subjects in the present investigation should have reached the stage of formal operations. A person who is thinking in these terms will take account of the possible and the hypothetical by formulating propositions about them. He will be able to isolate the variables in a problem and subject them to a combinatorial analysis.

But this is exactly what the subjects in the present experiment singularly fail to do. The variables in the present tasks are abstract but they are distinct and susceptible to symbolic manipulation. Could it then be that the stage of formal operations is not completely achieved at adolescence, even among intelligent individuals?

It may not, however, be the concept of implication which causes difficulty so much as its customary verbal guise: "if P then Q." That form of words suggests that the consequent follows the antecedent in time, or even that there is a causal relation between them. Other expressions have been tested. Hughes (1966) has shown that the logically equivalent expression, "Q if P," causes, if anything, even more difficulty. But implication can be formulated with simpler logical connectives, e.g., "$\bar{P}$ or Q" (either not-P or Q), "$-(P\bar{Q})$" (it is not the case that P and not-Q). P. N. Johnson-Laird (personal communication) has reported that the mode of formulation makes a considerable difference when the contingencies have to be evaluated. We intend to test these and other formulations to see whether similar differences can be detected in selection tasks. This problem may be generalized. Is it the formal structure of rules which is responsible for their difficulty, or is it the words with which we express these rules? If the latter, what words illuminate the structure?

REFERENCES

Hughes, M. A. M. (1966). *The use of negative information in concept attainment.* Unpublished Ph.D. thesis, University of London.

Inhelder, B., and Piaget, J. (1958). *The growth of logical thinking.* New York: Basic Books.

Wason, P. C. (1959). The processing of positive and negative information. *Quart. J. Exp. Psychol., 11,* 92–107.

Wason, P. C. (1961). Response to affirmative and negative binary statements. *Brit. J. Psychol., 52,* 133–142.

Wason, P. C., and Jones, S. (1963). Negatives: Denotation and connotation. *Brit. J. Psychol., 54,* 299–307.

Wason, P. C. (1964). The effect of self-contradiction on fallacious reasoning. *Quart. J. Exp. Psychol., 16,* 30–34.

Wason, P. C. (1966). Reasoning. In Foss, B. (Ed.), *New horizons in psychology,* Harmondsworth: Penguin.

QUESTIONS FOR FURTHER THOUGHT

1. What is the main finding of the Wason studies?
2. Why do the Wason studies call into question whether people are truly logical reasoners?
3. How did subjects respond on Wason's task if not with logical reasoning?
4. How informative were subjects' intuitions about their performance?
5. How might problem content affect the results of reasoning in the Wason task?

CHOICES, VALUES, AND FRAMES

Daniel Kahneman and Amos Tversky

INTRODUCTION

When people choose between two or more plans of action, they consider the plans, decide which represents the best of the alternatives available, and select it; what's important, of course, is the plan, not the way the plan is presented, right? Wrong!

In a series of ground-breaking studies, Daniel Kahneman and Amos Tversky showed that the way a plan is presented powerfully affects how favorably the plan is viewed. In other words, the actual words used to present the option have a major effect on how attractive it appears to be. As a result, studies of judgment should not consider what a plan is without evaluating how the plan is worded to avoid seriously distorting psychologists' understanding of how people process information in tasks requiring judgment and decision making. The difference made by the wording of a problem can be understood in terms of what Kahneman and Tversky called *framing effects*.

Suppose you are given a choice between two public-health programs for saving the lives of people threatened by a killer disease. Under one program, 200 lives will be saved; another offers a ⅓ probability that 600 lives will be saved and a ⅔ probability that no people will be saved. Most people prefer the first program.

Now suppose, instead, you are given a choice between a first program, in which 400 people will die, and a second program that offers a ⅓ probability that nobody will die and a ⅔ probability that 600 people will die. Most people prefer the second program.

Oddly, people prefer the first program in the first problem and the second program in the second problem, even though the first programs in the two problems are formally identical to each other, as are the second programs in the two problems. When people are presented with the problem in terms of gains (saving lives), they are risk-adverse, but when they are presented with essentially the same problem in terms of losses (losing lives), they take risks. Their decision depends on how the problem is framed.

Kahneman and Tversky's work on framing has become widely cited throughout the entire field of psychology, as well as in the field of economics. It shows that the choice people have to make is no more important than the way the choice is presented to them. We cannot simply look at the conceptual deep structure of a decision problem. The same person may arrive at opposing decisions, depending upon the way the problem is framed. We need to know how the problem is framed by the decision maker, because this information may determine its outcome, regardless of its underlying structure.

Source: Reprinted with permission from Kahneman, D., & Tversky, A. (1984). Choices, values, and frames. *American Psychologist, 39,* 341–350.

We discuss the cognitive and the psychophysical determinants of choice in risky and riskless contexts. The psychophysics of value induce risk aversion in the domain of gains and risk seeking in the domain of losses. The psychophysics of chance induce overweighting of sure things and of improbable events, relative to events of moderate probability. Decision problems can be described or framed in multiple ways that give rise to different preferences, contrary to the invariance criterion of rational choice. The process of mental accounting, in which people organize the outcomes of transactions, explains some anomalies of consumer behavior. In particular, the acceptability of an option can depend on whether a negative outcome is evaluated as a cost or as an uncompensated loss. The relation between decision values and experience values is discussed. ∎

Making decisions is like speaking prose—people do it all the time, knowingly or unknowingly. It is hardly surprising, then, that the topic of decision making is shared by many disciplines, from mathematics and statistics, through economics and political science, to sociology and psychology. The study of decisions addresses both normative and descriptive questions. The normative analysis is concerned with the nature of rationality and the logic of decision making. The descriptive analysis, in contrast, is concerned with people's beliefs and preferences as they are, not as they should be. The tension between normative and descriptive considerations characterizes much of the study of judgment and choice.

Analyses of decision making commonly distinguish risky and riskless choices. The paradigmatic example of decision under risk is the acceptability of a gamble that yields monetary outcomes with specified probabilities. A typical riskless decision concerns the acceptability of a transaction in which a good or a service is exchanged for money or labor. In the first part of this article, we present an analysis of the cognitive and psychophysical factors that determine the value of risky prospects. In the second part, we extend this analysis to transactions and trades.

RISKY CHOICE

Risky choices, such as whether or not to take an umbrella and whether or not to go to war, are made without advance knowledge of their consequences. Because the consequences of such actions depend on uncertain events such as the weather or the opponent's resolve, the choice of an act may be construed as the acceptance of a gamble that can yield various outcomes with different probabilities. It is therefore natural that the study of decision making under risk has focused on choices between simple gambles with monetary outcomes and specified probabilities, in the hope that these simple problems will reveal basic attitudes toward risk and value.

We shall sketch an approach to risky choice that derives many of its hypotheses from a psychophysical analysis of responses to money and to probability. The psychophysical approach to decision making can be traced to a remarkable essay that Daniel Bernoulli published in 1738 (Bernoulli 1738/1954) in which he attempted to explain why people are generally averse to risk and why risk aversion decreases with increasing wealth. To illustrate risk aversion and Bernoulli's analysis, consider the choice between a prospect that offers an 85% chance to win $1,000 (with a 15% chance to win nothing) and the alternative of receiving $800 for sure. A large majority of people prefer the sure thing over the gamble, although the gamble has higher (mathematical) expectation. The expectation of a monetary gamble is a weighted average, where each possible outcome is weighted by its probability of occurrence. The expectation of the gamble in this example is .85 × $1,000 + .15 × $0 = $850, which exceeds the expectation of $800 associated with the sure thing. The preference for the sure gain is an instance of risk aversion. In general, a preference for a sure outcome over a gamble that has higher or equal expectation is called *risk aversion,* and the rejection of a sure thing in favor of a gamble of lower or equal expectation is called *risk seeking.*

Bernoulli suggested that people do not evaluate prospects by the expectation of their monetary outcomes, but rather by the expectation of the subjective value of these outcomes. The subjective value of a gamble is again a weighted average, but now it is the subjective value of each outcome that is weighted by its probability. To explain risk aversion within this framework, Bernoulli proposed that subjective value, or utility, is a concave function of money. In such a function, the difference between the utilities of $200 and $100, for example, is greater than the utility difference between $1,200 and $1,100. It follows from concavity that the subjective value attached to a gain of $800 is more than 80% of the value of a gain of $1,000. Consequently, the concavity of the utility function entails a risk averse preference for a sure gain of $800 over an 80% chance to win $1,000, although the two prospects have the same monetary expectation.

It is customary in decision analysis to describe the outcomes of decisions in terms of total wealth. For example, an offer to bet $20 on the toss of a fair coin is represented as a choice between an individual's current wealth *W* and an even chance to move to *W* + $20 or to *W* − $20. This representation appears psychologically unrealistic: People do not normally think of relatively small outcomes in terms of states of wealth but rather in terms of gains, losses, and neutral outcomes (such as the maintenance of the status quo). If the effective carriers of subjective value are changes of wealth rather than ultimate states of wealth, as we propose, the psychophysical analysis of outcomes should be applied to gains and losses rather than to total assets. This assumption plays a central role in a treatment of risky choice that we called *prospect theory* (Kahneman & Tversky, 1979). Introspection as well as psychophysical measurements suggest that subjective value is a concave function of the size of a gain. The same generalization applies to losses, as well. The difference in subjective value between a loss of $200 and a loss of $100 appears greater than the difference in subjective value between a loss of $1,200 and a loss of $1,100. When the value functions for gains and for losses are pieced together, we obtain an *S*-shaped function of the type displayed in Figure 1.

The value function shown in Figure 1 is (a) defined on gains and losses rather than on total wealth, (b) concave in the domain of gains and convex in the domain of losses, and (c) considerably steeper for losses than for gains. The last property, which we label *loss aversion,* expresses the intuition that a loss of $X is more aversive than

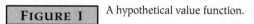

FIGURE 1   A hypothetical value function.

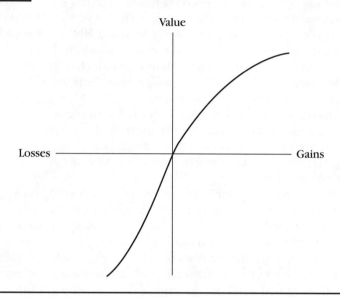

a gain of $X is attractive. Loss aversion explains people's reluctance to bet on a fair coin for equal stakes: The attractiveness of the possible gain is not nearly sufficient to compensate for the aversiveness of the possible loss. For example, most respondents in a sample of undergraduates refused to stake $10 on the toss of a coin if they stood to win less than $30.

The assumption of risk aversion has played a central role in economic theory. However, just as the concavity of the value of gains entails risk aversion, the convexity of the value of losses entails risk seeking. Indeed, risk seeking in losses is a robust effect, particularly when the probabilities of loss are substantial. Consider, for example, a situation in which an individual is forced to choose between an 85% chance to lose $1,000 (with a 15% chance to lose nothing) and a sure loss of $800. A large majority of people express a preference for the gamble over the sure loss. This is a risk-seeking choice because the expectation of the gamble (−$850) is inferior to the expectation of the sure loss (−$800). Risk seeking in the domain of losses has been confirmed by several investigators (Fishburn & Kochenberger, 1979; Hershey & Schoemaker, 1980; Payne, Laughhunn, & Crum, 1980; Slovic, Fischhoff, & Lichtenstein, 1982). It has also been observed with nonmonetary outcomes, such as hours of pain (Erakar & Sox, 1981) and loss of human lives (Fischhoff, 1983; Tversky, 1977; Tversky & Kahneman, 1981). Is it wrong to be risk averse in the domain of gains and risk seeking in the domain of losses? These preferences conform to compelling intuitions about the subjective value of gains and losses, and the presumption is that people should be entitled to their own values. However, we shall see that an *S*-shaped value function has implications that are normatively unacceptable.

To address the normative issue, we turn from psychology to decision theory. Modern decision theory can be said to begin with the pioneering work of von Neumann and Morgenstern (1947), who laid down several qualitative principles, or axioms, that should govern the preferences of a rational decision maker. Their axioms included transitivity (if A is preferred to B, and B is preferred to C, then A is preferred to C), and substitution (if A is preferred to B, then an even chance to get A or C is preferred to an even chance to get B or C), along with other conditions of a more technical nature. The normative and the descriptive status of the axioms of rational choice have been the subject of extensive discussions. In particular, there is convincing evidence that people do not always obey the substitution axiom, and considerable disagreement exists about the normative merit of this axiom (e.g., Allais & Hagen, 1979). However, all analyses of rational choice incorporate two principles: *dominance* and *invariance*. Dominance demands that if prospect A is at least as good as prospect B in every respect and better than B in at least one respect, then A should be preferred to B. Invariance requires that the preference order between prospects should not depend on the manner in which they are described. In particular, two versions of a choice problem that are recognized to be equivalent when shown together should elicit the same preference even when shown separately. We now show that the requirement of invariance, however elementary and innocuous it may seem, cannot generally be satisfied.

FRAMING OF OUTCOMES

Risky prospects are characterized by their possible outcomes and by the probabilities of these outcomes. The same option, however, can be framed or described in different ways (Tversky & Kahneman, 1981). For example, the possible outcomes of a gamble can be framed either as gains and losses relative to the status quo or as asset positions that incorporate initial wealth. Invariance requires that such changes in the description of outcomes should not alter the preference order. The following pair of problems illustrates a violation of this requirement. The total number of respondents in each problem is denoted by N, and the percentage who chose each option is indicated in parentheses.

> Problem 1 ($N = 152$): Imagine that the United States is preparing for the outbreak of an unusual Asian disease, which is expected to kill 600 people. Two alternative programs to combat the disease have been proposed. Assume that the exact scientific estimates of the consequences of the programs are as follows:
>
> If Program A is adopted, 200 people will be saved. (72%)
>
> If Program B is adopted, there is a one third probability that 600 people will be saved and a two thirds probability that no people will be saved. (28%)
>
> Which of the two programs would you favor?

The formulation of Problem 1 implicitly adopts as a reference point a state of affairs in which the disease is allowed to take its toll of 600 lives. The outcomes of the programs include the reference state and two possible gains, measured by the number of lives saved. As expected, preferences are risk averse: A clear majority of respondents prefer saving 200 lives for sure over a gamble that offers a one-third chance of saving 600 lives. Now consider another problem in which the same cover story is followed by a different description of the prospects associated with the two programs:

Problem 2 (*N* = 155): If Program C is adopted, 400 people will die. (22%)

If Program D is adopted, there is a one third probability that nobody will die and a two thirds probability that 600 people will die. (78%)

It is easy to verify that options C and D in Problem 2 are undistinguishable in real terms from options A and B in Problem 1, respectively. The second version, however, assumes a reference state in which no one dies of the disease. The best outcome is the maintenance of this state and the alternatives are losses measured by the number of people that will die of the disease. People who evaluate options in these terms are expected to show a risk-seeking preference for the gamble (option D) over the sure loss of 400 lives. Indeed, there is more risk seeking in the second version of the problem than there is risk aversion in the first.

The failure of invariance is both pervasive and robust. It is as common among sophisticated respondents as among naive ones, and it is not eliminated even when the same respondents answer both questions within a few minutes. Respondents confronted with their conflicting answers are typically puzzled. Even after rereading the problems, they still wish to be risk averse in the "lives saved" version; they wish to be risk seeking in the "lives lost" version; and they also wish to obey invariance and give consistent answers in the two versions. In their stubborn appeal, framing effects resemble perceptual illusions more than computational errors.

The following pair of problems elicits preferences that violate the dominance requirement of rational choice.

Problem 3 (*N* = 86): Choose between:

E. 25% chance to win $240 and
    75% chance to lose $760   (0%)

F. 25% chance to win $250 and
    75% chance to lose $750   (100%)

It is easy to see that F dominates E. Indeed, all respondents chose accordingly.

Problem 4 (*N* = 150): Imagine that you face the following pair of concurrent decisions. First examine both decisions, then indicate the options you prefer.

Decision (i) Choose between:
A. a sure gain of $240   (84%)
B. 25% chance to gain $1,000 and
    75% chance to gain nothing   (16%)

Decision (ii) Choose between:

    C. a sure loss of $750   (13%)

    D. 75% chance to lose $1,000 and

         25% chance to lose nothing   (87%)

As expected from the previous analysis, a large majority of subjects made a risk-averse choice for the sure gain over the positive gamble in the first decision, and an even larger majority of subjects made a risk-seeking choice for the gamble over the sure loss in the second decision. In fact, 73% of the respondents chose A and D and only 3% chose B and C. The same pattern of results was observed in a modified version of the problem, with reduced stakes, in which undergraduates selected gambles that they would actually play.

Because the subjects considered the two decisions in Problem 4 simultaneously, they expressed in effect a preference for A and D over B and C. The preferred conjunction, however, is actually dominated by the rejected one. Adding the sure gain of $240 (option A) to option D yields a 25% chance to win $240 and 75% to lose $760. This is precisely option E in Problem 3. Similarly, adding the sure loss of $750 (option C) to option B yields a 25% chance to win $250 and 75% chance to lose $750. This is precisely option F in Problem 3. Thus, the susceptibility to framing and the *S*-shaped value function produce a violation of dominance in a set of concurrent decisions.

The moral of these results is disturbing: Invariance is normatively essential, intuitively compelling, and psychologically unfeasible. Indeed, we conceive only two ways of guaranteeing invariance. The first is to adopt a procedure that will transform equivalent versions of any problem into the same canonical representation. This is the rationale for the standard admonition to students of business, that they should consider each decision problem in terms of total assets rather than in terms of gains or losses (Schlaifer, 1959). Such a representation would avoid the violations of invariance illustrated in the previous problems, but the advice is easier to give than to follow. Except in the context of possible ruin, it is more natural to consider financial outcomes as gains and losses rather than as states of wealth. Furthermore, a canonical representation of risky prospects requires a compounding of all outcomes of concurrent decisions (e.g., Problem 4) that exceeds the capabilities of intuitive computation even in simple problems. Achieving a canonical representation is even more difficult in other contexts such as safety, health, or quality of life. Should we advise people to evaluate the consequence of a public health policy (e.g., Problems 1 and 2) in terms of overall mortality, mortality due to diseases, or the number of deaths associated with the particular disease under study?

Another approach that could guarantee invariance is the evaluation of options in terms of their actuarial rather than their psychological consequences. The actuarial criterion has some appeal in the context of human lives, but it is clearly inadequate for financial choices, as has been generally recognized at least since Bernoulli, and it is entirely inapplicable to outcomes that lack an objective metric. We conclude that frame invariance cannot be expected to hold and that a sense of confidence in a particular choice does not ensure that the same choice would be made in another frame. It is therefore good practice to test the robustness of preferences by deliberate attempts to frame a decision problem in more than one way (Fischhoff, Slovic, & Lichtenstein, 1980).

The Psychophysics of Chances

Our discussion so far has assumed a Bernoullian expectation rule according to which the value, or utility, of an uncertain prospect is obtained by adding the utilities of the possible outcomes, each weighted by its probability. To examine this assumption, let us again consult psychophysical intuitions. Setting the value of the status quo at zero, imagine a cash gift, say of $300, and assign it a value of 1. Now imagine that you are given a ticket to a lottery that has a single prize of $300. How does the value of the ticket vary as a function of the probability of winning the prize? Barring utility for gambling, the value of such a prospect must vary between zero (when the chance of winning is nil) and 1 (when winning $300 is a certainty).

Intuition suggests that the value of the ticket is not a linear function of the probability of winning, as entailed by the expectation rule. In particular, an increase from 0% to 5% appears to have a larger effect than an increase from 30% to 35%, which also appears smaller than an increase from 95% to 100%. These considerations suggest a category-boundary effect: A change from impossibility to possibility or from possibility to certainty has a bigger impact than a comparable change in the middle of the scale. This hypothesis is incorporated into the curve displayed in Figure 2, which plots the weight attached to an event as a function of its stated numerical probability. The most salient feature of Figure 2 is that decision weights are regressive with respect to stated probabilities. Except near the endpoints, an increase of .05 in the probability of winning increases the value of the prospect by less than 5% of the value of the prize. We next investigate the implications of these psychophysical hypotheses for preferences among risky options.

| FIGURE 2 | A hypothetical weighting function. |

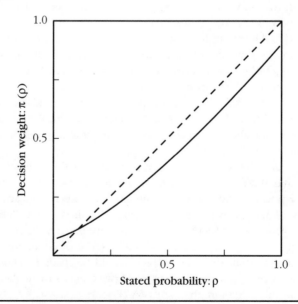

In Figure 2, decision weights are lower than the corresponding probabilities over most of the range. Underweighting of moderate and high probabilities relative to sure things contributes to risk aversion in gains by reducing the attractiveness of positive gambles. The same effect also contributes to risk seeking in losses by attenuating the aversiveness of negative gambles. Low probabilities, however, are overweighted, and very low probabilities are either overweighted quite grossly or neglected altogether, making the decision weights highly unstable in that region. The overweighting of low probabilities reverses the pattern described above: It enhances the value of long shots and amplifies the aversiveness of a small chance of a severe loss. Consequently, people are often risk seeking in dealing with improbable gains and risk averse in dealing with unlikely losses. Thus, the characteristics of decision weights contribute to the attractiveness of both lottery tickets and insurance policies.

The nonlinearity of decision weights inevitably leads to violations of invariance, as illustrated in the following pair of problems:

Problem 5 ($N = 85$): Consider the following two-stage game. In the first stage, there is a 75% chance to end the game without winning anything and a 25% chance to move into the second stage. If you reach the second stage you have a choice between:

A.	a sure win of $30	(74%)
B.	80% chance to win $45	(26%)

Your choice must be made before the game starts, i.e., before the outcome of the first stage is known. Please indicate the option you prefer.

Problem 6 ($N = 81$): Which of the following options do you prefer?

C.	25% chance to win $30	(42%)
D.	20% chance to win $45	(58%)

Because there is one chance in four to move into the second stage in Problem 5, prospect A offers a .25 probability of winning $30, and prospect B offers .25 × .80 = .20 probability of winning $45. Problems 5 and 6 are therefore identical in terms of probabilities and outcomes. However, the preferences are not the same in the two versions: A clear majority favors the higher chance to win the smaller amount in Problem 5, whereas the majority goes the other way in Problem 6. This violation of invariance has been confirmed with both real and hypothetical monetary payoffs (the present results are with real money), with human lives as outcomes, and with a nonsequential representation of the chance process.

We attribute the failure of invariance to the interaction of two factors: the framing of probabilities and the nonlinearity of decision weights. More specifically, we propose that in Problem 5, people ignore the first phase, which yields the same outcome regardless of the decision that is made, and focus their attention on what happens if they do reach the second stage of the game. In that case, of course, they face a sure gain if they choose option A and an 80% chance of winning if they prefer to gamble. Indeed, people's choices in the sequential version are practically identical to the choices they make between a sure gain of $30 and an 85% chance to win $45.

Because a sure thing is overweighted in comparison with events of moderate or high probability (see Figure 2) the option that may lead to a gain of $30 is more attractive in the sequential version. We call this phenomenon the *pseudo-certainty* effect because an event that is actually uncertain is weighted as if it were certain.

A closely related phenomenon can be demonstrated at the low end of the probability range. Suppose you are undecided whether or not to purchase earthquake insurance because the premium is quite high. As you hesitate, your friendly insurance agent comes forth with an alternative offer: "For half the regular premium you can be fully covered if the quake occurs on an odd day of the month. This is a good deal because for half the price you are covered for more than half the days." Why do most people find such probabilistic insurance distinctly unattractive? Figure 2 suggests an answer. Starting anywhere in the region of low probabilities, the impact on the decision weight of a reduction of probability from p to $p/2$ is considerably smaller than the effect of a reduction from $p/2$ to 0. Reducing the risk by half, then, is not worth half the premium.

The aversion to probabilistic insurance is significant for three reasons. First, it undermines the classical explanation of insurance in terms of a concave utility function. According to expected utility theory, probabilistic insurance should be definitely preferred to normal insurance when the latter is just acceptable (see Kahneman & Tversky, 1979). Second, probabilistic insurance represents many forms of protective action, such as having a medical checkup, buying new tires, or installing a burglar alarm system. Such actions typically reduce the probability of some hazard without eliminating it altogether. Third, the acceptability of insurance can be manipulated by the framing of the contingencies. An insurance policy that covers fire but not flood, for example, could be evaluated either as full protection against a specific risk, (e.g., fire) or as a reduction in the overall probability of property loss. Figure 2 suggests that people greatly undervalue a reduction in the probability of a hazard in comparison to the complete elimination of that hazard. Hence, insurance should appear more attractive when it is framed as the elimination of risk than when it is described as a reduction of risk. Indeed, Slovic, Fischhoff, and Lichtenstein (1982) showed that a hypothetical vaccine that reduces the probability of contracting a disease from 20% to 10% is less attractive if it is described as effective in half of the cases than if it is presented as fully effective against one of two exclusive and equally probable virus strains that produce identical symptoms.

FORMULATION EFFECTS

So far we have discussed framing as a tool to demonstrate failures of invariance. We now turn attention to the processes that control the framing of outcomes and events. The public health problem illustrates a formulation effect in which a change of wording from "lives saved" to "lives lost" induced a marked shift of preference from risk aversion to risk seeking. Evidently, the subjects adopted the descriptions of the outcomes as given in the question and evaluated the outcomes accordingly as gains or losses. Another formulation effect was reported by McNeil, Pauker, Sox, and Tversky (1982). They found that preferences of physicians and patients between hypothetical therapies for lung cancer varied markedly when their probable outcomes were described in terms of mortality or survival. Surgery, unlike radiation therapy, entails a risk of death during treatment. As a consequence, the surgery option was relatively less attractive when the statistics of treatment outcomes were described in terms of mortality rather than in terms of survival.

A physician, and perhaps a presidential advisor as well, could influence the decision made by the patient or by the president, without distorting or suppressing information, merely by the framing of outcomes and contingencies. Formulation effects can occur fortuitously, without anyone being aware of the impact of the frame on the ultimate decision. They can also be exploited deliberately to manipulate the relative attractiveness of options. For example, Thaler (1980) noted that lobbyists for the credit card industry insisted that any price difference between cash and credit purchases be labeled a cash discount rather than a credit card surcharge. The two labels frame the price difference as a gain or as a loss by implicitly designating either the lower or the higher price as normal. Because losses loom larger than gains, consumers are less likely to accept a surcharge than to forego a discount. As is to be expected, attempts to influence framing are common in the marketplace and in the political arena.

The evaluation of outcomes is susceptible to formulation effects because of the nonlinearity of the value function and the tendency of people to evaluate options in relation to the reference point that is suggested or implied by the statement of the problem. It is worthy of note that in other contexts, people automatically transform equivalent messages into the same representation. Studies of language comprehension indicate that people quickly recode much of what they hear into an abstract representation that no longer distinguishes whether the idea was expressed in an active or in a passive form and no longer discriminates what was actually said from what was implied, presupposed, or implicated (Clark & Clark, 1977). Unfortunately, the mental machinery that performs these operations silently and effortlessly is not adequate to perform the task of recoding the two versions of the public-health problem or the mortality-survival statistics into a common abstract form.

TRANSACTIONS AND TRADES

Our analysis of framing and of value can be extended to choices between multiattribute options, such as the acceptability of a transaction or a trade. We propose that, in order to evaluate a multiattribute option, a person sets up a mental account that specifies the advantages and the disadvantages associated with the option, relative to a multiattribute reference state. The overall value of an option is given by the balance of its advantages and its disadvantages in relation to the reference state. Thus, an option is acceptable if the value of its advantages exceeds the value of its disadvantages. This analysis assumes psychological—but not physical—separability of advantages and disadvantages. The model does not constrain the manner in which separate attributes are combined to form overall measures of advantage and of disadvantage, but it imposes on these measures assumptions of concavity and of loss aversion.

Our analysis of mental accounting owes a large debt to the stimulating work of Richard Thaler (1980, in press), who showed the relevance of this process to consumer behavior. The following problem, based on examples of Savage (1954) and Thaler (1980), introduces some of the rules that govern the construction of mental accounts and illustrates the extension of the concavity of value to the acceptability of transactions.

> Problem 7: Imagine that you are about to purchase a jacket for $125 and a calculator for $15. The calculator salesman informs you that the calculator you wish to buy is on sale for $10 at the other branch of the store, located 20 minutes drive away. Would you make a trip to the other store?

This problem is concerned with the acceptability of an option that combines a disadvantage of inconvenience with a financial advantage that can be framed as a *minimal, topical,* or *comprehensive* account. The minimal account includes only the differences between the two options and disregards the features that they share. In the minimal account, the advantage associated with driving to the other store is framed as a gain of $5. A topical account relates the consequences of possible choices to a reference level that is determined by the context within which the decision arises. In the preceding problem, the relevant topic is the purchase of the calculator, and the benefit of the trip is therefore framed as a reduction of the price, from $15 to $10. Because the potential saving is associated only with the calculator, the price of the jacket is not included in the topical account. The price of the jacket, as well as other expenses, could well be included in a more comprehensive account in which the saving would be evaluated in relation to, say, monthly expenses.

The formulation of the preceding problem appears neutral with respect to the adoption of a minimal, topical, or comprehensive account. We suggest, however, that people will spontaneously frame decisions in terms of topical accounts that, in the context of decision making, play a role analogous to that of "good forms" in perception and of basic-level categories in cognition. Topical organization, in conjunction with the concavity of value, entails that the willingness to travel to the other store for a saving of $5 on a calculator should be inversely related to the price of the calculator and should be independent of the price of the jacket. To test this prediction, we constructed another version of the problem in which the prices of the two items were interchanged. The price of the calculator was given as $125 in the first store and $120 in the other branch, and the price of the jacket was set at $15. As predicted, the proportions of respondents who said they would make the trip differed sharply in the two problems. The results showed that 68% of the respondents ($N = 88$) were willing to drive to the other branch to save $5 on a $15 calculator, but only 29% of 93 respondents were willing to make the same trip to save $5 on a $125 calculator. This finding supports the notion of topical organization of accounts, since the two versions are identical both in terms of a minimal and a comprehensive account.

The significance of topical accounts for consumer behavior is confirmed by the observation that the standard deviation of the prices that different stores in a city quote for the same product is roughly proportional to the average price of that product (Pratt, Wise, & Zeckhauser, 1979). Since the dispersion of prices is surely controlled by shoppers' efforts to find the best buy, these results suggest that consumers hardly exert more effort to save $15 on a $150 purchase than to save $5 on a $50 purchase.

The topical organization of mental accounts leads people to evaluate gains and losses in relative rather than in absolute terms, resulting in large variations in the rate at which money is exchanged for other things, such as the number of phone calls made to find a good buy or the willingness to drive a long distance to get one. Most consumers will find it easier to buy a car stereo system or a Persian rug, respectively, in the context of buying a car or a house than separately. These observations, of course, run counter to the standard rational theory of consumer behavior, which assumes invariance and does not recognize the effects of mental accounting.

The following problems illustrate another example of mental accounting in which the posting of a cost to an account is controlled by topical organization:

Problem 8 ($N = 200$): Imagine that you have decided to see a play and paid the admission price of $10 per ticket. As you enter the theater, you discover that you have lost the ticket. The seat was not marked, and the ticket cannot be recovered.

Would you pay $10 for another ticket?
  Yes (46%)   No (54%)

Problem 9 ($N = 183$): Imagine that you have decided to see a play where admission is $10 per ticket. As you enter the theater, you discover that you have lost a $10 bill.

Would you still pay $10 for a ticket for the play?
  Yes (88%)   No (12%)

The difference between the responses to the two problems is intriguing. Why are so many people unwilling to spend $10 after having lost a ticket, if they would readily spend that sum after losing an equivalent amount of cash? We attribute the difference to the topical organization of mental accounts. Going to the theater is normally viewed as a transaction in which the cost of the ticket is exchanged for the experience of seeing the play. Buying a second ticket increases the cost of seeing the play to a level that many respondents apparently find unacceptable. In contrast, the loss of the cash is not posted to the account of the play, and it affects the purchase of a ticket only by making the individual feel slightly less affluent.

An interesting effect was observed when the two versions of the problem were presented to the same subjects. The willingness to replace a lost ticket increased significantly when that problem followed the lost-cash version. In contrast, the willingness to buy a ticket after losing cash was not affected by prior presentation of the other problem. The juxtaposition of the two problems apparently enabled the subjects to realize that it makes sense to think of the lost ticket as lost cash, but not vice versa.

The normative status of the effects of mental accounting is questionable. Unlike earlier examples, such as the public-health problem, in which the two versions differed only in form, it can be argued that the alternative versions of the calculator and ticket problems differ also in substance. In particular, it may be more pleasurable to save $5 on a $15 purchase than on a larger purchase, and it may be more annoying to pay twice for the same ticket than to lose $10 in cash. Regret, frustration, and self-satisfaction can also be affected by framing (Kahneman & Tversky, 1982). If such secondary consequences are considered legitimate, then the observed preferences do not violate the criterion of invariance and cannot readily be ruled out as inconsistent or erroneous. On the other hand, secondary consequences may change upon reflection. The satisfaction of saving $5 on a $15 item can be marred if the consumer discovers that she would not have exerted the same effort to save $10 on a $200 purchase. We do not wish to recommend that any two decision problems that have the same primary consequences should be resolved in the same way. We propose, however, that systematic examination of alternative framings offers a useful reflective device that can help decision makers assess the values that should be attached to the primary and secondary consequences of their choices.

LOSSES AND COSTS

Many decision problems take the form of a choice between retaining the status quo and accepting an alternative to it, which is advantageous in some respects and disadvantageous in others. The analysis of value that was applied earlier to unidimensional risky prospects can be extended to this case by assuming that the status quo defines the reference level for all attributes. The advantages of alternative options will then be evaluated as gains and their disadvantages as losses. Because losses loom larger than gains, the decision maker will be biased in favor of retaining the status quo.

Thaler (1980) coined the term *endowment effect* to describe the reluctance of people to part from assets that belong to their endowment. When it is more painful to give up an asset than it is pleasurable to obtain it, buying prices will be significantly lower than selling prices. That is, the highest price that an individual will pay to acquire an asset will be smaller than the minimal compensation that would induce the same individual to give up that asset, once acquired. Thaler discussed some examples of the endowment effect in the behavior of consumers and entrepreneurs. Several studies have reported substantial discrepancies between buying and selling prices in both hypothetical and real transactions (Gregory, 1983; Hammack & Brown, 1974; Knetsch & Sinden, in press). These results have been presented as challenges to standard economic theory, in which buying and selling prices coincide except for transaction costs and effects of wealth. We also observed reluctance to trade in a study of choices between hypothetical jobs that differed in weekly salary (S) and in the temperature (T) of the workplace. Our respondents were asked to imagine that they held a particular position (S_1, T_1) and were offered the option of moving to a different position (S_2, T_2), which was better in one respect and worse in another. We found that most subjects who were assigned to (S_1, T_1) did not wish to move to (S_2, T_2), and that most subjects who were assigned to the latter position did not wish to move to the former. Evidently, the same difference in pay or in working conditions looms larger as a disadvantage than as an advantage.

In general, loss aversion favors stability over change. Imagine two hedonically identical twins who find two alternative environments equally attractive. Imagine further that by force of circumstance the twins are separated and placed in the two environments. As soon as they adopt their new states as reference points and evaluate the advantages and disadvantages of each other's environments accordingly, the twins will no longer be indifferent between the two states, and both will prefer to stay where they happen to be. Thus, the instability of preferences produces a preference for stability. In addition to favoring stability over change, the combination of adaptation and loss aversion provides limited protection against regret and envy by reducing the attractiveness of foregone alternatives and of others' endowments.

Loss aversion and the consequent endowment effect are unlikely to play a significant role in routine economic exchanges. The owner of a store, for example, does not experience money paid to suppliers as losses and money received from customers as gains. Instead, the merchant adds costs and revenues over some period of time and only evaluates the balance. Matching debits and credits are effectively cancelled prior to evaluation. Payments made by consumers are also not evaluated as losses but as alternative purchases. In accord with standard economic analysis, money is naturally viewed as a proxy for the goods and services that it could buy. This mode of evaluation is made explicit when an individual has in mind a particular alternative, such as "I can either buy a new camera or a new tent." In this analysis, a person will buy a camera if its subjective value exceeds the value of retaining the money it would cost.

There are cases in which a disadvantage can be framed either as a cost or as a loss. In particular, the purchase of insurance can also be framed as a choice between a sure loss and the risk of a greater loss. In such cases the cost–loss discrepancy can lead to failures of invariance. Consider, for example, the choice between a sure loss of $50 and a 25% chance to lose $200. Slovic, Fischhoff, and Lichtenstein (1982) reported that 80% of their subjects expressed a risk-seeking preference for the gamble over the sure loss. However, only 35% of subjects refused to pay $50 for insurance against a 25% risk of losing $200. Similar results were also reported by Schoemaker and Kunreuther (1979) and by Hershey and Schoemaker (1980). We suggest that the same amount of money that was framed as an uncompensated loss in the first problem was framed as the cost of protection in the second. The modal preference was reversed in the two problems because losses are more aversive than costs.

We have observed a similar effect in the positive domain, as illustrated by the following pair of problems:

Problem 10: Would you accept a gamble that offers a 10% chance to win $95 and a 90% chance to lose $5?

Problem 11: Would you pay $5 to participate in a lottery that offers a 10% chance to win $100 and a 90% chance to win nothing?

A total of 132 undergraduates answered the two questions, which were separated by a short filler problem. The order of the questions was reversed for half the respondents. Although it is easily confirmed that the two problems offer objectively identical options, 55 of the respondents expressed different preferences in the two versions. Among them, 42 rejected the gamble in Problem 10 but accepted the equivalent lottery in Problem 11. The effectiveness of this seemingly inconsequential manipulation illustrates both the cost–loss discrepancy and the power of framing. Thinking of the $5 as a payment makes the venture more acceptable than thinking of the same amount as a loss.

The preceding analysis implies that an individual's subjective state can be improved by framing negative outcomes as costs rather than as losses. The possibility of such psychological manipulations may explain a paradoxical form of behavior that could be labeled the *dead-loss effect*. Thaler (1980) discussed the example of a man who develops tennis elbow soon after paying the membership fee in a tennis club and continues to play in agony to avoid wasting his investment. Assuming that the individual would not play if he had not paid the membership fee, the question arises: How can playing in agony improve the individual's lot? Playing in pain, we suggest, maintains the evaluation of the membership fee as a cost. If the individual were to stop playing, he would be forced to recognize the fee as a dead loss, which may be more aversive than playing in pain.

CONCLUDING REMARKS

The concepts of utility and value are commonly used in two distinct senses: (a) *experience value*, the degree of pleasure or pain, satisfaction or anguish in the actual experience of an outcome; and (b) *decision value*, the contribution of an anticipated outcome to the overall attractiveness or aversiveness of an option in a choice. The distinction is rarely explicit in decision theory because it is tacitly assumed that decision values and experience values coincide. This assumption is part of the conception of an idealized decision maker who is able to predict future experiences with perfect accuracy and evaluate options accordingly. For ordinary decision makers, however, the correspondence of decision values between experience values is far from perfect (March, 1978). Some factors that affect experience are not easily anticipated, and some factors that affect decisions do not have a comparable impact on the experience of outcomes.

In contrast to the large amount of research on decision making, there has been relatively little systematic exploration of the psychophysics that relate hedonic experience to objective states. The most basic problem of hedonic psychophysics is the determination of the level of adaptation or aspiration that separates positive from negative outcomes. The hedonic reference point is largely determined by the objective status quo, but it is also affected by expectations and social comparisons. An objective improvement can be experienced as a loss, for example, when an employee receives a smaller raise than everyone else in the office. The experience of pleasure or pain associated with a change of state is also critically dependent on the dynamics of hedonic adaptation. Brickman & Campbell's (1971) concept of the hedonic treadmill suggests the radical hypothesis that rapid adaptation will cause the effects of any objective improvement to be short-lived. The complexity and subtlety of hedonic experience make it difficult for the decision maker to anticipate the actual experience that outcomes will produce. Many a person who ordered a meal when ravenously hungry has admitted to a big mistake when the fifth course arrived on the table. The common mismatch of decision values and experience values introduces an additional element of uncertainty in many decision problems.

The prevalence of framing effects and violations of invariance further complicates the relation between decision values and experience values. The framing of outcomes often induces decision values that have no counterpart in actual experience.

For example, the framing of outcomes of therapies for lung cancer in terms of mortality or survival is unlikely to affect experience, although it can have a pronounced influence on choice. In other cases, however, the framing of decisions affects not only decision but experience, as well. For example, the framing of an expenditure as an uncompensated loss or as the price of insurance can probably influence the experience of that outcome. In such cases, the evaluation of outcomes in the context of decisions not only anticipates experience but also molds it.

REFERENCES

Allais, M., & Hagen, O. (Eds.). (1979). *Expected utility hypotheses and the Allais paradox.* Hingham, MA: D. Reidel Publishing.

Bernoulli, D. (1954). Exposition of a new theory on the measurement of risk. *Econometrica 22,* 23–36. (Original work published 1738.)

Brickman, P., & Campbell, D. T. (1971). Hedonic relativism and planning the good society. In M. H. Appley (Ed.), *Adaptation-level theory: A symposium* (pp. 287–302). New York: Academic Press.

Clark, H. H., & Clark, E. V. (1977). *Psychology and language.* New York: Harcourt Brace Jovanovich.

Erakar, S. E., & Sox, H. C. (1981). Assessment of patients' preferences for therapeutic outcomes. *Medical Decision Making, 1,* 29–39.

Fischhoff, B. (1983). Predicting frames. *Journal of Experimental Psychology: Learning, Memory, and Cognition, 9,* 103–116.

Fischhoff, B., Slovic, P., & Lichtenstein, S. (1980). Knowing what you want: Measuring labile values. In T. Wallsten (Ed.), *Cognitive processes in choice and decision behavior* (pp. 117–141). Hillsdale, NJ: Erlbaum.

Fishburn, P. C., & Kochenberger, G. A. (1979). Two-piece von Neumann-Morgenstern utility functions. *Decision Sciences, 10,* 503–518.

Gregory, R. (1983). *Measures of consumer's surplus: Reasons for the disparity in observed values.* Unpublished manuscript, Keene State College, Keene, NH.

Hammack, J., & Brown, G. M., Jr. (1974). *Waterfowl and wetlands: Toward bioeconomic analysis.* Baltimore: Johns Hopkins University Press.

Hershey, J. C., & Schoemaker, P. J. H. (1980). Risk taking and problem context in the domain of losses: An expected-utility analysis. *Journal of Risk and Insurance, 47,* 111–132.

Kahneman, D., & Tversky, A. (1979). Prospect theory: An analysis of decision under risk. *Econometrica, 47,* 263–291.

Kahneman, D., & Tversky, A. (1982). The simulation heuristic. In D. Kahneman, P. Slovic, & A. Tversky (Eds.), *Judgment under uncertainty: Heuristics and biases* (pp. 201–208). New York: Cambridge University Press.

Knetsch, J., & Sinden, J. (in press). Willingness to pay and compensation demanded: Experimental evidence of an unexpected disparity in measures of value. *Quarterly Journal of Economics.*

March, J. G. (1978). Bounded rationality, ambiguity, and the engineering of choice. *Bell Journal of Economics, 9,* 587–608.

McNeil, B., Pauker, S., Sox, H., Jr., & Tversky, A. (1982). On the elicitation of preferences for alternative therapies. *New England Journal of Medicine, 306,* 1259–1262.

Payne, J. W., Laughhunn, D. J., & Crum, R. (1980). Translation of gambles and aspiration level effects in risky choice behavior. *Management Science, 26,* 1039–1060.

Pratt, J. W., Wise, D., & Zeckhauser, R. (1979). Price differences in almost competitive markets. *Quarterly Journal of Economics, 93,* 189–211.

Savage, L. J. (1954). *The foundation of statistics.* New York: Wiley.

Schlaifer, R. (1959). *Probability and statistics for business decisions.* New York: McGraw-Hill.

Schoemaker, P. J. H., & Kunreuther, H. C. (1979). An experimental study of insurance decisions. *Journal of Risk and Insurance, 46,* 603–618.

Slovic, P., Fischhoff, B., & Lichtenstein, S. (1982). Response mode, framing, and information-processing effects in risk assessment. In R. Hogarth (Ed.), *New directions for methodology of social and behavioral science: Question framing and response consistency* (pp. 21–36). San Francisco: Jossey-Bass.

Thaler, R. (1980). Toward a positive theory of consumer choice. *Journal of Economic Behavior and Organization, 1,* 39–60.

Thaler, R. (in press). Using mental accounting in a theory of consumer behavior. *Journal of Marketing.*

Tversky, A. (1977). On the elicitation of preferences: Descriptive and prescriptive considerations. In D. Bell, R. L. Kenney, & H. Raiffa (Eds.), *Conflicting objectives in decisions. International Series on Applied Systems Analysis* (pp. 209–222). New York: Wiley.

Tversky, A., & Kahneman, D. (1981). The framing of decisions and the psychology of choice. *Science, 211,* 453–458.

von Neumann, J., & Morgenstern, O. (1947). *Theory of games and economic behavior* (2nd ed.). Princeton, NJ: Princeton University Press.

QUESTIONS FOR FURTHER THOUGHT

1. What is framing, and how does it affect decision making?

2. Why do you think that framing so strongly influences people's choices and decisions?

3. When is framing most likely to have a large effect on decision making?

4. When is framing least likely to have a large effect on decision making?

5. If you wanted to convince someone not to take a risky course of action, how would you frame the problem facing the person to discourage the risky choice?

10

COGNITIVE DEVELOPMENT

NETWORK REPRESENTATIONS OF A CHILD'S DINOSAUR KNOWLEDGE
Michelene Chi and Randi Koeske

A CHARACTERISTIC-TO-DEFINING SHIFT IN THE DEVELOPMENT OF WORD MEANING
Frank Keil and Nancy Batterman

NETWORK REPRESENTATIONS OF A CHILD'S DINOSAUR KNOWLEDGE

Michelene Chi and Randi Koeske

INTRODUCTION

We know that children as well as adults tend to recall more familiar words better than they recall less familiar words. But why do we obtain such a difference? What is it about the more familiar words that makes them easier to recall? And for how long a period of time does this differential memorability extend?

In a now-famous study, Michelene Chi and Randi Koeske set out to address these questions. In the course of the study, they also showed that an intensive study of a single participant (a 4½-year-old boy interested in dinosaurs) can tell us more than we might expect possible.

The investigators presented the child with a free-recall task in which two lists of dinosaurs—one list comprising more well-known dinosaurs, and the other, less well-known dinosaurs—were to be learned. A year later the child was asked to name dinosaurs (the ones that the child had seen the year before in the recall task).

Chi and Koeske found that the list of more familiar dinosaurs was better recalled at the time of learning and then better remembered a year later. More importantly, they found that the more familiar dinosaurs could be characterized by an internal semantic network representation with more and stronger links, and more internal cohesion in terms of higher-order groupings and specific patterns of interlinkages. These results suggest that the superior recall of more familiar words is due to specific and identifiable aspects of the internal representations of these words and their interconnections.

———

A young child's knowledge of 40 dinosaurs was elicited from two tasks. The data gathered from these knowledge-production protocols were used to map two interrelated semantic networks of dinosaurs, viewed as concept nodes connected by links. The two mappings corresponded to two sets of dinosaurs (20 each), partitioned on the basis of external criteria: mother's subjective

Source: From Chi, M. T. H., & Koeske, R. D. (1983). Network representations of a child's dinosaur knowledge. *Developmental Psychology, 19,* 29–39. Copyright © 1983 by the American Psychological Association. Reprinted with permission.

judgment of the child's knowledge of each dinosaur and the frequency of mention in the child's dinosaur books. Comparisons of the structure of the two mappings were based on three attributes: (a) number of links, (b) strength of links, and (c) the internal cohesion of the network in terms of higher order groupings and specific patterns of interlinkages. The validity of the differential structures of the two mappings was verified by the corresponding differential memory performance. The better structured set of dinosaurs was more easily remembered and retained by the child over a year than the less structured set of dinosaurs. ■

More and better structured knowledge has been a pervasive concept generally used for interpreting better memory performance. In the traditional list-learning literature, it has long been known that within an age group, the more knowable a list is, the better the recall. However, the literature on verbal learning is generally not explicit about what *knowable* means other than that it can be indexed by a number of measures, such as familiarity, meaningfulness, imagery values, frequency, and so on.

The term *more knowledge* has also been used as an explanation of better memory performance of individuals with greater skills. For example, chess experts can recall a greater number of pieces from a chess position than novices, and this ability has been related to the size of their knowledge base for chess patterns as well as the size of each pattern (Chase & Simon, 1973). That is, the expert has many more patterns or chunks that he or she recognizes, and the chunks also contain more pieces. Hence, skill differences in the domain have been attributed to a difference in the quantity of knowledge and not differences in the way that chess patterns are represented. Both the expert and novice players' knowledge of chess can be represented in the same way, namely, chunks or units of knowledge unified by relations such as color, proximity, locations, and so on (for more details, see Chase & Chi, 1981). Also, the structure of the representations may differ between experts and novices in that the configurations of their patterns may be different. However, because the exact nature of the experts' and novices' patterns is not specified, it is not clear whether the novices' knowledge base is deficient in (a) having fewer total number of patterns, (b) having smaller patterns, (c) having patterns with different configurations from those of the experts, or (d) all of the above.

Recently, the same interpretation has been used by developmentalists to explain memory performance differences between age groups (Chi, 1976, 1981; Dempster, 1978; Lindberg, 1980). It has been shown that a child's poorer memory performance, when compared with adults', may reflect in general his or her lack of knowledge. However, the deficiency in children's knowledge is usually not specified in an exact way, or else it is specified in the same way as the chunk structures discussed by Chase and Simon (1973; see Chi, 1978). Again, age differences, like skill differences, are attributable to a difference in the quantity of knowledge, and references to structural differences in the knowledge representation are made only in a global way.

By structural differences, we do not mean that there is a change in the representation of knowledge, as other developmentalists have done. In the developmental literature, the term *structural change* is often equated with the term *representational change*. That is, a representational change is often conceived of as the availability of new structures (Fischer, 1980; Halford & Wilson, 1980; Piaget, 1970). Keil (1981), for example, refers to "radical restructuring" or "fundamental reorganization of conceptual framework" as representational change (p. 200). It is perhaps unfortunate that we use the term *structure* as referring to something distinct from representation. But by structure, we refer to the properties of a representation.

Perhaps two examples will clarify the intended meaning here. A dramatic illustration of representational change would be the change in children's reliance on a predominantly imaginal mode of representation to a symbolic or linguistic mode (Bruner, Olver, & Greenfield, 1966; Piaget, 1971). It has been assumed that children are incapable of encoding or representing certain concepts until the nature of their representation changes to conform with the concepts (see further discussions by Carey, in press; Keil, 1981; Mandler, in press).

An example of structural (but not representational) change is the commonly discussed change concerning the modification of conceptual representation from a predominantly linear mode to a hierarchical, treelike structure. The treelike nature of conceptual representation is usually revealed by measuring agreement among subjects concerning the degree of relatedness among concepts. Relatedness or clustering is indexed by the proximity of the concepts during sorting and recall. Adults typically recall and sort concepts in clusters corresponding to taxonomic groupings, and this can be captured in a hierarchical tree structure (Friendly, 1977; Johnson, 1967). Furthermore, skilled adults' structure will be more treelike than less-skilled adults' (McKeithen, Reitman, Rueter, & Hirtle, 1981). In the developmental work, one could also say that the structure changes with increasing age, becoming more hierarchical, suggesting greater agreement among subjects, greater taxonomic clustering, and better fit of the data to a tree structure (Corsale & Ornstein, 1980). But the nature of the representation remains the same, consisting of concept nodes and links.

Perhaps a better term to use would be *organizational* rather than *structural change*. But the implications of organizational change seem more limited, referring predominantly to reorganizing existing knowledge, without an explicit reference to the possibility of adding or deleting knowledge, as well. *Organization* sometimes also refers predominantly to the quantity or amount rather than the more qualitative aspects of reorganization. Hence, it is preferable to preserve the term *structural change* to refer to the kind of organizational changes to be discussed in this article. (For further discussion of the relation between structural and representational change, see Chi & Rees, in press.)

The present research is concerned with elucidating what constitutes better structure rather than more knowledge or representational change. This will be done by assessing and comparing the knowledge structures of two subsets of a domain of knowledge that a child possesses: a subset he or she knows more about and a subset he or she knows less about. The assumption is that the same kind of representation underlies the two subsets of a knowledge domain. The goal, then, is to identify the attributes of a knowledge structure that make one subset of knowledge more structured than another subset. Subsequent memory performance differences on the two subsets will be used as an index of the validity of the assessed structures.

Although this is not a developmental study, developmental extrapolations are intended. Age groups are not compared, because age differences (as well as skill differences) tend to produce results that are dominated by the older age group's greater knowledge, and any structural change that may exist is often overshadowed by this greater knowledge. Age groups are also not compared for another reason, namely, that age trends are often contaminated by changes in other factors, such as strategic usage and memory capacity. By studying differences in the attributes of a knowledge structure within a single child, we will be able to assume that strategic usage and capacity limitation remain relatively invariant under different stimulus conditions. The implications of the present results for development will be discussed later.

Because strategic usage and capacity limitation are ignored, this study focuses only on the role of knowledge, narrowly defined as knowledge of concepts. Concepts are represented as a semantic mapping of nodes and their related properties in a network of nodes and links (Anderson, 1976; Collins & Loftus, 1975; Collins & Quillian, 1969; Norman & Rumelhart, 1975). Attributes of the network structure will be assessed by the number of links between nodes, the strength of linkages, and the cohesiveness of the entire collection of concept nodes in semantic memory.

METHOD

SUBJECTS

To evaluate the effect of knowledge on memory performance in a child, it is necessary to select a domain in which a young child could be expert. A 4½-year-old boy who had been exposed to dinosaur information for about 1½ years was chosen. Like many children of his age, he was very interested in dinosaurs and was highly motivated to learn about them. His parents read dinosaur books to him often during this period (an average of 3 hours per week), and he had a collection of nine dinosaur books and various plastic models for use in play.

TASKS TO ELICIT KNOWLEDGE

Two tasks were used to elicit which dinosaurs the child knew and what he knew about each. The production task, conducted first, simply asked the child to generate the names of all the dinosaurs he knew. To maintain his interest, whenever he generated a particular name, a plastic model of the named dinosaur was handed to him. In this manner, the production task became a collectionlike game. When the child paused for a long time (about 10 sec), the experimenter would probe with a particular dinosaur, such as "How about Stegosaur?" This production task was conducted for six sessions, spanning about 2 weeks. A total of 46 distinct names were generated (including a few names of extinct mammals), with about 25 dinosaurs generated at each session.

To gain information about what the child knew about each dinosaur, a clue game was devised in which the chooser generated a list of properties (usually two or three) and the guesser identified the dinosaur to which these properties belonged. For example, the experimenter (or the child) might say, "I am thinking about a plant-eating dinosaur, and his nickname means double beam." By alternating roles between the experimenter and the child, information was obtained about the child's recognition and spontaneous generation of a subset of the dinosaurs and their properties.

STIMULI

The stimuli used for both the semantic mapping and the memory tasks (to be described) were 40 dinosaurs selected from the 46 generated during the production task. Six names were discarded for a variety of reasons. Some, for example, referred to extinct mammals (such as Wooly Rhinoceros) that are often mentioned along with dinosaurs in the dinosaur books.

The 40 dinosaurs were grossly partitioned into a better known and a lesser known list of 20 each, based on two external criteria: mother's judgment and frequency. The mother subjectively judged whether a given dinosaur could be considered better known (List A) or lesser known (List B) to the child. After the mother's judgments were made, frequency of the two lists was determined by measuring the proportion of the child's nine books that mentioned each dinosaur. List A dinosaurs were mentioned on the average in 50% of the nine books, and List B dinosaurs were mentioned in 20% of the books. Thus, the frequency of mention of the two lists was consistent with the mother's judgment of the child's knowledge of each dinosaur. The two lists of dinosaurs are shown in Table 1.

TASKS TO MEASURE MEMORY PERFORMANCE

Two tasks were used to measure memory performance. The recall task consisted of presenting each list of 20 dinosaur names (Lists A and B in Table 1) orally at a rate of 3 sec per item, after which the child was asked to free recall the names just presented. Three free-recall trials were presented for each type of list, separately, on consecutive days. The order of items (within each list) was randomized for each presentation.

The naming task, conducted a year after the recall task, was aimed at measuring the amount of retention. It consisted of presenting a picture of a dinosaur to the child and requiring him to name the dinosaur. Since the child could name pictures of all the dinosaurs used in this study, any loss after a year would be attributable to forgetting.

MAPPING THE SEMANTIC NETWORK

Dinosaur–Dinosaur Links. The sequencing of dinosaurs generated in the production task was taken as evidence of dinosaur–dinosaur linkages. For example, if Triceratops and Stegosaur were generated in succession, a link between the two was assumed to be present in the semantic network. No link was mapped between two dinosaurs mentioned in sequence if the sequence was interrupted by the experimenter's prompt, which usually occurred after the child paused for 10 or more sec. Multiple links between a given pair of dinosaurs were represented in the network when the pairing was mentioned several times throughout the six sessions of protocols. Thus, the frequency of mention in the protocol was taken as a measure of the strength of linkages.

TABLE 1	**Dinosaur Categories and Their Members**	

DINOSAUR CATEGORY	LIST A	LIST B
Armored	Ankylosaur Glyptodont Monoclonius[a] Protoceratops Stegosaur[a] Styracosaur[a] Triceratops[a]	Polacanthus[a]
Duckbills	Iguanodon Lambeosaur Pachycephalosaur Trachodon	Camptosaur Corythosaur Parasaurolophus Plateosaur[a]
Giant meat eaters	Allosaur Tyrannosaur	Ceratosaur[a] Gorgosaur
Water-dwelling reptiles	Plesiosaur	Archelon[a] Elasmosaur Icthyosaur[a] Mosasaur Tylosaur
Early meat eaters	Dimetrodon	Sphenacodon
Lightweight bird or egg eaters		Compsognathus Ornitholestes[a] Oviraptor Saltoposuchus[a] Struthiomimus
Giant plant eaters	Brachiosaur[a] Brontosaur[a] Diplodocus[a]	
Flying reptiles	Archeopteryx Rhamphorhyncus	
Ancient precursors		Diplocaulus Seymouria

[a]Indicates the targets.

Dinosaur–Property Links. The dinosaur-property linkages were derived from the clue game. For simplicity, no discriminations were made between those properties that the child could recognize (i.e., generated by the experimenter) versus those that he could generate. Properties that were mentioned across several different dinosaurs were depicted as linked together in the semantic network. For example, "eats plants" was a property that was associated in the protocols with several dinosaurs, such as Brachiosaur, Triceratops, and Stegosaur. "Eats plants" was thus viewed as a common property shared by all of those dinosaurs, and in Figure 1 it is mapped as a shared diet node.

Six key types of property nodes were generated or recognized by the child in the clue game: appearance, such as "a small head"; defense mechanism, such as "it has horns"; diet, such as "eats plants"; habitat, such as "lives in the water"; locomotion, such as "walking on hind feet"; and nickname, such as "three-horned face" for Triceratops. These property nodes are labeled by the appropriate letters in the figure and attached to the dinosaurs with which they were associated. When it is ambiguous whether a property (such as spines) should be classified as an appearance or defense mechanism node, both labels are provided in the figure. A few additional properties peculiar to only one or two dinosaurs were also mentioned, and these are labeled as other nodes.

The rationale underlying the methodology of mapping is loosely based on assumptions of a spreading activation model of memory (Anderson, 1976; Collins &

FIGURE 1   Network representation for the target dinosaurs from the better-known list. (A = armored; P = giant plant eaters; a = appearance; d = defense mechanism; di = diet; h = habitat; l = locomotion; n = nickname; o = other)

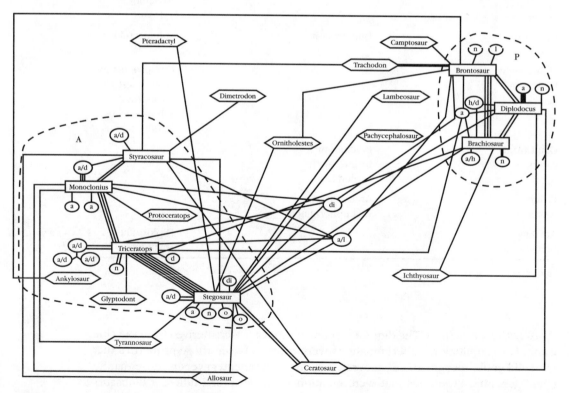

Loftus, 1975). Thus, dinosaurs were viewed as linked together if they were mentioned in succession, because presumably the mentioning of one dinosaur triggered the activation of a closely related dinosaur. Also, identical properties mentioned in association with several dinosaurs were linked as sharing the same property, because it is assumed that nodes in memory are nonredundant.

Groupings. Another way to discuss the structure of a semantic network is in terms of higher order units. It is assumed that concepts fall into internal units or groups. From our own knowledge of dinosaurs and the way they were categorized informally in the child's books, we imposed an organization on these mappings by classifying the total set of 40 dinosaurs into nine groups. Table 1 shows the category names and their members. Using this procedure, each list of 20 dinosaurs could be classified into seven of these nine groups, thus indicating that the two lists were partially overlapping in terms of the dinosaur groups sampled.

Selection of Subsets: Targets. Two problems arise if mapping of all List A dinosaurs is compared with that of List B dinosaurs. First, the child undoubtedly knew more about the List A dinosaurs, as a whole, than the List B dinosaurs, because List A dinosaurs, on the average, were mentioned more frequently in the nine books than the List B dinosaurs. Further, more information was provided in the books about the List A dinosaurs. Assuming that a child can only learn and remember a subset of what is presented, the amount of property information known about the List B dinosaurs must necessarily be less than the amount of property information known about the List A dinosaurs. Thus, differences in the two mappings would undoubtedly be contaminated by this factor.

The second concern about analyzing and comparing the mappings of the entire sets of 20 dinosaurs is a methodological one. That is, because there was no control over which dinosaurs the child would choose to include in the clue game, many dinosaurs were not sampled. Hence, we do not have a complete assessment of the child's knowledge of properties for all 40 dinosaurs. Thus, to eliminate biases solely to the number of times particular dinosaurs were mentioned (thus producing a sampling bias and inflating the amount of information known about the List A dinosaurs), two subsets of seven dinosaurs were selected from each of the 20-item lists. These subsets of dinosaurs (henceforth referred to as the *targets;* see Table 1) were matched on the frequency with which they were sampled by both the experimenter and the child during the clue game. Hence, the actual mappings in Figures 1 (the better-known List A) and 2 (the lesser-known List B) are only for the target dinosaurs and all of their associated links (both dinosaur–dinosaur and dinosaur–property).

In the figures, target dinosaurs are enclosed in rectangles, nontarget dinosaurs (those that are mentioned in association with the targets) are enclosed in hexagons, properties are enclosed in ovals, and groupings are circumscribed by large circles. Figures 1 and 2, although mapped separately, are not intended to indicate that the two representations are distinct in memory. We conceive of one interrelated network for all 40 dinosaurs. The two parts have simply been separated for ease of analysis. In fact, we have attempted to map the network so that identical nodes on Figures 1 and 2 appear in approximately the same location. To see the interrelated network, Figures 1

FIGURE 2

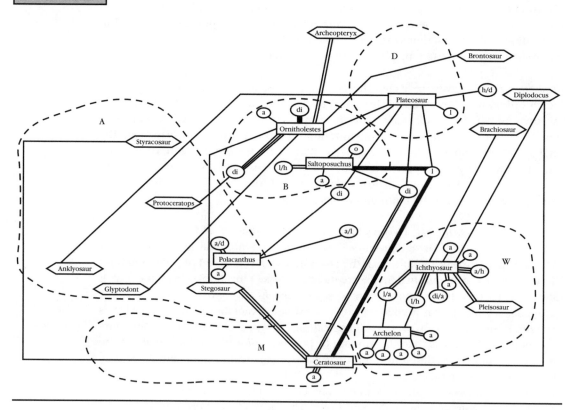

and 2 can be overlaid, one on top of the other, and redundant nodes should overlap. This is merely our attempt to indicate that the two mappings represent an interrelated semantic network in memory.

To summarize, dinosaur concepts were linked when they were mentioned by the child in succession in the production protocols, and properties were linked to dinosaurs when they were identified or generated by the child in the clue game protocols. Then, the entire set of 40 dinosaurs was partitioned into nine groups. For simplicity, the network was mapped separately for the two lists. Furthermore, to reduce differences between the two mappings that might arise only from having more property information in the better-known List A dinosaurs, 7 targets from each list of 20 were selected and mapped in detail in Figures 1 and 2. These subsets of 7 were matched on the frequency with which they were sampled in the clue game protocols. Because the selection criteria for the targets were controlled on the basis of the amount of information known, the resulting distribution of the targets among the groupings was not uniform (see Table 1). This variability has to be tolerated when working only with what the child knows.

RESULTS

COMPARISON OF THE TWO MAPPINGS: TARGETS

Links. Since the two target sets were chosen to minimize differences in the amount of property information, it is not surprising that they do not differ in the average number of property nodes associated with each target dinosaur ($M = 5.1, SD = 1.70$, for Figure 1; $M = 4.7, SD = 1.57$, for Figure 2). What does differ between the two mappings is the average number of links associated with each target dinosaur (15.86 for Figure 1, 10.00 for Figure 2), $t(12) = 4.81, p < .01$. Because there were no differences in the number of property nodes associated with each target dinosaur, this difference in linkages arose from a higher proportion of links between dinosaurs (59% in Figure 1 versus 21% in Figure 2), $t(12) = 5.39, p < .01$. A difference between the two subsets also occurred for the strength of the linkages, as indexed by the frequency of mention in the protocols. All of the List A target dinosaurs in Figure 1 have multiple links to at least one other target dinosaur, whereas none of the List B target dinosaurs in Figure 2 does. In sum, the target dinosaurs of the better-known List A mapping are more strongly interlinked than the targets in List B.

Groupings. To provide some psychological reality to the assumed groupings, the semantic mapping needs to show some measure of greater cohesion among target dinosaurs within a group and less cohesion among targets between groups. The validity of the groupings is quite strong in the list A target dinosaurs. List A targets fall into two categories: armored dinosaurs and large plant eaters. Two measures of cohesion within groups can be discerned. First, target dinosaurs showed multiple direct (dinosaur–dinosaur) links to target dinosaurs within the same group and either no direct or only single links to targets of the other group. The targets in Group A, for example, shared on the average three links with each other. Second, targets within a group shared more properties with each other than targets in different groups. That is, there were more indirect (dinosaur–property–dinosaur) links within than between groups (see Figure 1).

This pattern of differential interlinkages among targets (i.e., more links within a group than between groups) is not apparent for the lesser-known List B dinosaurs. The seven List B targets fall into five groups. Since five groups are present with only seven targets, one would not expect a strong pattern of interconnections. However, even for those groups that do contain two members, no apparent pattern of strong interlinkages within groups was present. For example, there were no direct dinosaur–dinosaur links in Figure 2 between the targets within either Group B (light-weight bird or egg eaters) or Group W (water-dwelling reptiles), nor was there evidence of greater property sharing among the targets within as opposed to between groups. There seemed to be just as much sharing of properties (indirect links) among targets of different groups (such as between Group B and Group M, giant meat eaters) as there was within a group (such as Group W). This suggests that the internal cohesiveness of the List B groups was less well-defined, with more uniform interconnections among dinosaurs of different groups.

COMPARISON OF THE TWO MAPPINGS: ENTIRE SETS

Further evidence that groupings are stronger for the better-known dinosaurs can be discerned by examining the overall pattern of linkages for all 40 dinosaurs. There are eight direct (dinosaur-to-dinosaur) linkages between members of the three main groups in List A (armored, duckbills, and giant plant eaters), to which 70% of these dinosaurs belong, whereas there are only two such direct linkages between members of the three groups in List B (lightweight bird or egg eaters, duckbills, and water-dwelling reptiles), to which 70% of those dinosaurs belong. Moreover, seven indirect linkages between the same three dinosaur groups in List A exist, because they explicitly share common properties. Only two such indirect linkages exist between dinosaurs in the three main groups of List B. Again, the greater amount of direct and indirect linkages among List A dinosaurs suggests that they tend to form more cohesive and interconnected units, whereas dinosaurs in List B tend to form a more weakly and uniformly connected whole.

In sum, the two semantic mappings of the better- and lesser-known target dinosaurs did not differ in the total number of target dinosaur nodes (seven in each subset) or the average number of property nodes (about five) per dinosaur node. Nor did the two sets of 20 dinosaurs differ in the total number of groupings into which each set could be classified (nine in each set). These differences were controlled to a certain degree, because the focus of this research was not on identifying trivial differences in knowing more (i.e., having more nodes or more groups in memory). In general, such differences were considered self-evident and less interesting psychologically. Instead, the interest was in how the organization of knowledge might differ for items judged more or less knowable.

The results suggest that in the semantic mappings of the target subsets, the better-known mapping (compared with the lesser-known) has (a) a greater total number of interdinosaur links, (b) greater strength of linkages, and (c) greater cohesion of target dinosaurs, defined in terms of stronger within-group and weaker between-groups direct and indirect links. This latter difference is also apparent when the entire sets of dinosaurs are compared. It is postulated here that these three attributes can be used to characterize the properties of a better-structured knowledge base.

RECALL AND RETENTION

The child's memory performance on the two lists showed marked differences. The dinosaurs recalled from List A numbered 10, 8, and 9 (out of 20) across the three trials, compared with 6, 4, and 3 from List B, $t(4) = 5.83, p < .01$. In both cases, targets from each list were recalled proportionally to the frequency of targets in each list (35% of each list were targets). That is, of the dinosaurs recalled on each trial, 39% were targets from List A and 31% were targets from List B. The intrusion rates were also low on an absolute basis; for List A, there were on the average 1.3 intrusions across the three trials, and for List B, there were 2.0 intrusions.

If the experimenter-imposed groupings mentioned in previous sections match well with the child's own groupings, then presumably the recall order should reflect clustering according to groupings. Clustering was measured by the number of successive dinosaurs recalled from the same group, using Bousfield's (1953) ratio of repetition (RR) scoring. All intrusions were ignored, but repeated items were included in the calculation. List A recall trials had on the average an RR score of .67, whereas list B recall trials had on the average an RR score of .17. Although the greater clustering of the better-known list is consistent with the notion that List A dinosaurs represent a more cohesive and better-structured set of items, this particular analysis may be questionable, because the underlying assumption of equal distribution is not met. Further, as Murphy (1979) has noted, an RR score is confounded with the amount of recall.

The child's memory after a year of infrequent exposure to dinosaurs was measured by his ability to name a dinosaur when a picture of it was presented. Eleven of the 20 List A dinosaurs were identified correctly by name, whereas only 2 of the 20 List B dinosaurs were correctly named, $x^2(1) = 9.23, p < 0.005$. One interpretation of name identification is that it requires the association of the visual appearance or properties of a dinosaur with the name of the dinosaur. The greater retention of the better known dinosaurs is consistent with the interpretation that properties of the better known dinosaurs were attached with greater strength than the dinosaurs of the lesser known list.

In sum, the better recall, clustering, and retention performance of the child on List A dinosaurs may be interpreted to derive from two sources. First, better memory for the better known dinosaurs could arise from knowing more in the simple sense, that is, knowing more properties about each dinosaur. Although we did not quantify precisely how much more the child knew about List A dinosaurs, this assumption is fairly conservative. However, we believe that the more potent source affecting recall is not knowing more in the simple sense.

Rather, we offer the second interpretation that better recall and retention of list of items may be influenced by how well the composition of the list of items matches the structure of the knowledge base, defined here in terms of the number of direct and indirect links among dinosaur concepts, the strength of linkages, and the particular pattern of intra- and interlinkages, which delineates the cohesion of groupings. Because the mappings of the List A dinosaurs (at least the targets) are more structured than those of List B, this is correlational evidence that such structures might have induced the memory performance patterns. However, there is more concrete evidence favoring the second interpretation, namely, that targets were not recalled to a greater degree than nontargets. This suggests that knowing more property information per se about the targets did not facilitate their recall.

DISCUSSION

It has long been known in the adult literature that knowledge facilitates recall. Chi (1976) has suggested that knowledge may also underlie developmental trends in memory. That is, adults may generally perform better than children on memory tasks because they know more than the children. In fact, recent evidence has shown that the commonly observed developmental improvements in memory performance are no longer obtained when children know more than the adults (Chi, 1978) or when children and adults are not tested on the same set of stimuli (Lindberg, 1980). That is, if adults and children are tested on stimulus material that they each know, then their memory performances are comparable, because what is considered familiar to the adults may not be familiar to children (Chi, 1981; Dempster, 1978).

In this study, we were not interested in capturing more knowledge in the sense of a larger quantity of knowledge or larger sized structures, nor were we interested in depicting knowledge differences as a change in the representation. Further, we did not specify the quality of structure in terms of quantities, such as larger group sizes or larger numbers of groups. Rather, we postulated that the entire network has the same representation for more and less knowable sets of dinosaurs. The difference between them lies in the particular configuration of nodes and links. Comparisons of the two knowledge sets were then based on a set of attributes identified from the protocol data as relevant for distinguishing the cohesiveness of the structure. Therefore, this research has developed procedures for eliciting the semantic representation of a knowledge domain as well as suggested measures for quantifying important features of knowledge organization, such as density, strength, and cohesiveness.

This study is unique in another way: It mapped the semantic network of conceptual knowledge from protocol data generated by a subject. In the majority of the existing research in which semantic networks are depicted, they are generally constructed from the researcher's assumptions or theory of structure. Then the validity of the structures is tested with specific tasks (the top-down approach). For example, Collins and Quillian (1969) constructed a hierarchical network and tested its structure with sentence verification tasks. Likewise, Gentner (1975) constructed networks for possessive verbs such as *give* and *take* and tested their order of acquisition in terms of children's comprehension. This study, in contrast, did not construct a semantic network from our analyses or intuition. Instead, a network was constructed from the child's protocols, and attributes of interest that might define differences between structures were sought (the bottom-up approach). The only aspect of the network that was top-down was the groupings.

This study was also able to focus only on the representation of concepts, ignoring the role of strategic usage and memory capacity by considering the performance of a very young child and examining only within-subject variations. By choosing a 4-year-old and examining only within-subject performance, it can be assumed with some degree of confidence that the standard adult retrieval strategies are not effectively used (Myers & Perlmutter, 1978).

Therefore, differential recall, retention, and clustering measures on two subsets of a knowledge domain can hardly be attributed to differential application of retrieval strategies. Even if retrieval strategies were available to the child, there is no logical reason why a child would apply them differentially, that is, in one subset of the knowledge domain and not another. In addition, capacity issues can be ignored when only within-subject comparisons are made. We offer the implication that developmentally, if strategic usage and capacity limitations do play a role in memory performance, their effects may appear enhanced because of the concurrent changes in the knowledge structures with increasing age.

In sum, we think such detailed analyses of the knowledge base have provided insights into the exact nature of a child's performance on memory and other cognitive tasks as well as highlighted the important attributes that may define and discriminate the structure of knowledge representation.

REFERENCES

Anderson, J. R. *Language, memory and thought.* Hillsdale, NJ: Erlbaum, 1976.

Bousfield, W. A. The occurrences of clustering in the recall of randomly arranged associates. *Journal of General Psychology,* 1953, *49,* 229–240.

Bruner, J. S., Olver, R. R., & Greenfield, P. M. *Studies in cognitive growth.* New York: Wiley, 1966.

Carey, S. Are children fundamentally different kinds of thinkers and learners than adults? In S. Chipman, J. Segal, & R. Glaser (Eds.), *Thinking and learning skills: Current research and open questions* (Vol. 2). Hillsdale, NJ: Erlbaum, in press.

Chase, W. G., & Chi, M. T. H. Cognitive skill: Implications for spatial skill in large-scale environments. In J. Harvey (Ed.), *Cognition, social behavior, and the environment.* Hillsdale, NJ: Erlbaum, 1981.

Chase, W. G., & Simon, H. A. Perception in chess. *Cognitive Psychology,* 1973, *4,* 55–81.

Chi, M. T. H. Short-term memory limitations in children: Capacity or processing deficits? *Memory and Cognition,* 1976, *4,* 559–572.

Chi, M. T. H. Knowledge structures and memory development. In R. Siegler (Ed.), *Children's thinking: What develops?* Hillsdale, NJ: Erlbaum, 1978.

Chi, M. T. H. Knowledge development and memory performance. In M. P. Friedman, J. P. Das, & N. O'Connor (Eds.), *Intelligence and learning.* New York: Plenum Press, 1981.

Chi, M. T. H., & Rees, E. A learning framework for development. In M. T. H. Chi (Ed.), *Trends in memory development.* Basel: Karger, in press.

Collins, A. M., & Loftus, E. F. A spreading-activation theory of semantic processing. *Psychological Review,* 1975, *82,* 407–428.

Collins, A. M., & Quillian, M. R. Retrieval time from semantic memory. *Journal of Verbal Learning and Verbal Behavior,* 1969, *8,* 240–247.

Corsale, K., & Ornstein, P. Developmental changes in children's use of semantic information in recall. *Journal of Experimental Child Psychology,* 1980, *30,* 231–245.

Dempster, F. M. Memory span and short-term memory capacity: A developmental study. *Journal of Experimental Child Psychology,* 1978, *26,* 419–431.

Fischer, K. W. A theory of cognitive development: The control and construction of hierarchies of skills. *Psychological Review,* 1980, *87,* 477–531.

Friendly, M. L. In search of the M-Gram: The structure of organization in free recall. *Cognitive Psychology,* 1977, *9,* 188–249.

Gentner, D. Evidence for the psychological reality of semantic components: The verbs of possession. In D. A. Norman & D. E. Rumelhart (Eds.), *Explorations in cognition.* San Francisco: Freeman, 1975.

Halford, G. S., & Wilson, W. H. A category theory approach to cognitive development. *Cognitive Psychology,* 1980, *12,* 356–411.

Johnson, S. C. Hierarchical clustering schemes. *Psychometrika,* 1967, *32,* 241–254.

Keil, F. C. Constraints on knowledge and cognitive development. *Psychological Review,* 1981, *88,* 197–227.

Lindberg, M. A. Is knowledge base development a necessary and sufficient condition for memory development? *Journal of Experimental Child Psychology,* 1980, *30,* 401–410.

Mandler, J. M. Representation. In J. H. Flavell & E. M. Markman (Eds.), *Cognitive development.* New York: Wiley, in press.

McKeithen, K. B., Reitman, J. S., Rueter, H. H., & Hirtle, S. C. Knowledge organization and skill differences in computer programmers. *Cognitive Psychology,* 1981, *13,* 307–325.

Murphy, M. D. Measurement of category clustering in free recall. In C. R. Puff (Ed.), *Memory organization and structure.* New York: Academic Press, 1979.

Myers, N. A., & Perlmutter, M. Memory in the years from two to five. In P. A. Ornstein (Ed.), *Memory development in children.* Hillsdale, NJ: Erlbaum, 1978.

Norman, D. A., & Rumelhart, D. E. *Explorations in cognition.* San Francisco: Freeman, 1975.

Piaget, J. Piaget's theory. In P. Mussen (Ed.), *Carmichael's manual of child psychology.* New York: Wiley, 1970.

Piaget, J. The theory of stages in cognitive development. In D. R. Green, M. P. Ford, & G. B. Flamer (Eds.), *Measurement and Piaget.* New York: McGraw-Hill, 1971.

QUESTIONS FOR FURTHER THOUGHT

1. Why did the child dinosaur expert in the Chi and Koeske study show better memory for dinosaurs from the better-structured set?

2. What are the general implications of the Chi and Koeske findings for a theory of memory development?

3. How might the Chi and Koeske findings be applied to help children improve learning effectiveness in school?

4. Does Chi and Koeske's account of memory performance have implications for other areas, such as differences in performance between adults and children on IQ tests?

5. Why might advancing age lead to a decline in recall performance (assuming that Chi and Koeske's findings apply across the life span)?

A Characteristic-to-Defining Shift in the Development of Word Meaning

Frank Keil and Nancy Batterman

INTRODUCTION

Psychologists generally distinguish between defining features of a concept, on the one hand, and characteristic features, on the other. Defining features are ones that unequivocally identify something: They are individually necessary and jointly sufficient for identifying an object or other thing. For example, all mammals give birth to live young, so giving birth to live young is a defining feature of a mammal. A particular animal may share many attributes in common with a mammal, but if it does not give birth to live young, it is not a mammal. Characteristic features, on the other hand, are typical of a given concept, but not essential to defining it. For example, many mammals walk on four legs, but an animal does not have to walk on four legs in order to be classified as a mammal.

Frank Keil and Nancy Batterman suggested that young children do not distinguish between defining and characteristic features. Indeed, they are as likely or more likely to believe that characteristic features are defining ones than to correctly identify defining features. In order to illustrate their point, they presented children of varying ages with problems that required the children to distinguish between the two kinds of features. For example, a nice-looking old lady might be seen robbing a TV or a suspicious-looking person might be seen fixing it. The young children were more likely than the older ones to identify the suspicious-looking person as a thief than to identify the nice-looking old lady as the thief, even though only the latter was shown engaged in thievery.

The work of Rosch (described earlier) showed the importance of characteristic features to adults' representations of the meanings of concepts. The work of Keil and Batterman shows that, for children, characteristic features strongly dominate in their mental representations. Indeed, children may misunderstand what is presented to them and opt for characteristic rather than defining features if the characteristic and defining features contradict each other. This stunning demonstration has made the Keil–Batterman paper a classic in the field of cognitive development.

Source: From Keil, F. C., & Batterman, N. (1984). A characteristic-to-defining shift in the development of word meaning. *Journal of Verbal Learning and Verbal Behavior, 23,* 221–236. Reprinted with permission of Academic Press, Inc.

*Many word meanings seem to mix two representational types, sometimes
known as* characteristic *and* defining *features. It is proposed that meanings
typically develop from representations in which characteristic features predominate to those in which defining features become more central. (The same
shift can also be described without the assumption of featural decomposition
of meaning.) A study with preschool and elementary school children confirmed this proposal by showing that children's judgments of whether brief
stories described valid instances of a concept shifted in a manner predicted by
these hypotheses.* ■

Researchers who study the acquisition of word meaning generally adopt one of
two positions: either (1) the acquisition of word meaning can be explained by
the gradual addition or subtraction of discrete criterial semantic features (e.g., Clark,
1973) or (2) word meanings develop through experience with exemplars that generate a prototype structure from which meaning emanates (e.g., Anglin, 1977). These
views seem contradictory to one another and have led to sharp disagreements about
how word meanings are acquired. It may be, however, that both views are correct
and that both types of representation predominate at different times in the acquisition of most word meanings.

Many word meanings appear to be initially represented in a noncriterial manner
where familiar instances are the primary influences on lexical structure. Later, more
criterial, definitional aspects of meaning may be the primary determinants of word
usage. This view has several related precursors. An early version was proposed by
Vygotsky (1934/1962), who argued that the young child's word meanings undergo a
fundamental change in their nature from poorly organized representations that originate from familiar instances to more rule-governed meanings. Vygotsky explicitly
cites the example of a child who judged that a kinship term such as "aunt" was seen
as meaning people of the female sex with a particular age range and disposition. Only
later do the children master the abstract rules that strictly decide kinship relations.

Vygotsky's view differs from the one advanced here in two important ways:
(1) He tended to view this process as a general monolithic ability related to the emergence of egocentric speech. By contrast, the shift proposed here occurs at different
ages with different conceptual domains depending on factors related to the nature of
the domains themselves and to the words mapped onto them. (2) Vygotsky did not
recognize that even while some aspects of children's word meanings might be completely instance bound, in other respects, the meanings might be governed by necessary relations and rules.

Since Vygotsky, there have been several views of perceptual and conceptual
development that suggest patterns analogous to the characteristic-to-defining shift for
word meaning. One of the most frequent proposals has been that of a progression
from wholistic to analytical representations. Werner (1948) originally proposed such
a shift, and Bruner, Olver, Greenfield, et al. (1966) and Gibson (1969) have offered
modified accounts for conceptual and perceptual development. Gibson (1969), however, focused more on the structure of the information that is learned and thus was
less convinced than Werner and Bruner of an across-the-board, stage-like shift.

The relation of wholistic-to-analytic shifts to characteristic-to-defining shifts in word meaning can be better understood by considering a recent series of studies on perceptual development conducted by Kemler and Smith (Kemler & Smith, 1978; Kemler, 1983b; Smith, 1981). Kemler (1983a), for example, cites Vygotsky's earlier work as well as Garner's (1974) integral/separable distinction in an attempt to explain developmental changes in classification in which younger children tend to sort objects on the basis of overall similarity over several dimensions (where no one dimension is criterial) while older children group objects more along a few strict dimensions. Thus, Kemler shows that young children may sort together objects A and B, which are close to each other in a multidimensional stimulus space but which share no common dimensional values, while older children might sort together objects A and C, which, while farther apart overall in the space, share the same value on some dimension. Kemler and Smith have shown such a shift using perceptual features such as facial features, shape, color, etc.

The relation to the characteristic-to-defining contrast can be seen in both Kemler's and Smith's discussions of Rosch's work. They point out how many of the analytic classes for adults seemed to be treated in a more prototype-like fashion by children, where no one perceptual dimension is crucial for membership in a class but rather a weighted sum of several dimensions seems to be the primary determinant of sorting. In the perceptual domain, then, this account describes a shift from attending to several features that are characteristic of an object to a few more criterial (e.g., defining) features.

This sort of shift may be closely related to a phenomenon in the acquisition of word meaning. Carey (1978), for example, argues that even meanings as apparently analytic as "tall" may be initially represented mostly in terms of examples, and often quite haphazard examples at that. Thus, the meaning of "tall" might be inextricably bound up with the objects it denotes and a tall man might be understood as being tall in a different way from a tall chair (e.g., "tall" might refer to head-to-toe extent for man, but imply overall size for a chair). Carey provided some initial support for this haphazard-example hypothesis and also demonstrated that, later on, missing semantic features also seemed to be involved.

Keil and Carroll (1980) followed up on Carey's proposal by examining the child's understanding of "tall" in two studies that presented a large number of different, potentially tall objects. The most significant finding was that, if ambiguous visual figures were presented, children correctly understood "tall" with one biasing context and misunderstood "tall" with another context, even though the exact same perceptual display was used in both cases. A second result was that, at later ages, the children seemed to switch to more rule-governed, criterial forms of representation, even though specific rules were sometimes incorrect (e.g., "tall" = "narrow"). Finally, throughout this example-to-rule-based representational change, the children maintained an invariant set of features describing "tall" as a spatial property of physical objects. Thus, some aspects of meaning remain invariant and criterial throughout development; a point to which we will return later.

Unfortunately, the paradigms used in the Carey study and in the Keil and Carroll study are limited to a small range of dimensional terms whose meanings can be assessed by having subjects make judgments about simple visual displays. Most concepts do not lend themselves to such analyses, and the question arises as to how one can test for an analogous representational shift for them. A slight reconceptualization of the phenomenon, however, suggests several research strategies.

Research in semantic memory has for some time recognized what seem to be two different specific features in semantic memory networks: defining and characteristic features (e.g., Smith, 1978). The distinction has also been referred to as the dictionary–encyclopedia distinction, although that description is a misnomer, because dictionaries frequently employ characteristic features in their definitions (e.g., entries with "typically" will usually refer to characteristic features). The distinction asserts that some aspects of meaning consist of necessary attributes that must be present 100% of the time for a concept to be instantiated. These are the defining features. The characteristic features are typically associated with a concept, or are "characteristic" of it, but no one feature is absolutely necessary. They are responsible, at least in one view, for generating the Roschean prototypes that seem to be associated with so many concepts (cf. Rosch & Mervis, 1975).

Many controversies involving this distinction remain. Some (e.g., MacNamara, 1971) argue that the distinction is bogus and that all features can be viewed as characteristic with different probabilistic weights ranging from quite low to an almost perfect co-occurrence with instances of the concept. Others (e.g., Katz, 1972; Glass & Holyoak, 1975) argue that this is an in-principle distinction and that the two types of features have very different linguistic and psychological properties.

On a related note, concepts vary considerably in the extent to which they employ each of the two types of features. Armstrong, Gleitman, and Gleitman (1983), for example, have demonstrated that well-defined concepts such as "triangle" and "odd number," even while having characteristic features associated with them that generate prototype-like data, are not treated as fuzzy concepts by subjects, who rely exclusively on the defining features when making judgments about meaning. On the other hand, a number of philosophers (e.g., Kripke, 1972; Putnam, 1975) and some psychologists (e.g., Rosch, 1978) argue that many of the so-called "natural kind" terms seem to have no defining or necessary features whatsoever.

These controversies, however, are mostly orthogonal to the developmental proposal made here. Regardless of whether there is a strict dichotomy between defining and characteristic features or a smooth continuum, and regardless of the extent to which individual concepts rely on one or the other type of feature, there are good reasons for suspecting that there is a developmental shift from representations based mostly on characteristic features to those relying more on defining features. These shifts may be restricted to concepts that have a mixture of both types of features (or, alternatively, to those that have a reasonable range along the defining-to-characteristic continuum). We will argue, however, that an analogous shift may occur for most concepts.

It is proposed that children's early conceptual representations often tend to be overwhelmed by characteristic features so that the presence or absence of defining features may be completely ignored or that they are treated as merely characteristic. After the child progresses through some sort of transitional state, the reverse situation holds. This proposal is further supported by a recent study in which Landau (1982) had children select which of several pictures was a better instance of a "grandmother" where some pictures had "symptoms" (i.e., characteristic features) of the kinship term and others suggested "criteria" (i.e., defining features). There was a strong shift toward criterion-based choices with increasing age. There was also indications that changes in how the task was perceived might have influenced the shift, a point which is discussed further below.

There is one last theoretical point that must be dealt with before turning to an examination of how such a claim might be evaluated. It concerns the entire notion of features and the decomposition of word meaning into discrete elements or atoms, whether they are necessary or only probabilistic. In an eloquent essay, Bolinger (1965) criticized what he calls the *atomization of meaning* by arguing that the decomposition of meaning into discrete, criterial components rarely seems to capture the full meaning of words. More recently Fodor, Garrett, Walker, & Parkes (1980) have attacked the notion of definitional decomposition and have empirically challenged the assumption that there are either real-time processing or representational sorts of evidence for the decomposition of concepts such as "kill" into "cause-to-die" (see also Armstrong et al., 1983, and Carey, 1982).

Fodor et al. argue that meaning is better characterized as an inferential network composed of inferential links known as *meaning postulates*. Meaning postulates allow one to make inferences about what is entailed by a word either in isolation or in a sentential context but do not represent the decompositional elements that comprise word meaning. While Fodor et al. do not discuss it explicitly, one can imagine an analogous network of inferences that are not necessary entailments but are probabilistic associations. Such notions are quite common in cognitive psychology research (e.g., Anderson & Bower, 1973).

These alternatives to a feature decomposition approach illustrate that it is not necessary to state the developmental phenomenon in terms of defining and characteristic features. The same defining/characteristic distinction can be represented in an inferential network. Nonetheless, for simplicity of exposition, the studies reported herein will be described in terms of defining and characteristic features.

Preliminary evidence for the characteristic-to-defining shift has been gathered in some informal studies with 36 preschoolers. The children were simply asked to give definitions of concepts to see if the definitions change with age in a manner that reflects this shift. A wide range of concepts having a mix of defining and characteristic features, such as "island," "advertisement," and "uncle," was used. For the most part, the preschoolers mentioned only characteristic features in their definitions. Thus, several preschoolers defined an "island" as a warm place, a place where people dance with no clothes, or a place with palm trees and beaches. Virtually none of them stated that water had to be on all sides. Similarly, "uncles" were friends, usually male, and usually in a certain age range. "Advertisements," when understood at all, were described in terms of familiar advertising techniques. One child said that it was kind of show with singing and dancing and "when they usually announced a number at the end."

These definitions, while suggestive of a characteristic-to-defining shift, cannot be conclusive evidence in their own right for several reasons: (1) The quantitative reporting of such definitions is difficult given the wide individual differences among young children in the types of definitions they offer (e.g., some children give very peculiar demands on the children that may distort their true knowledge of word meanings. The characteristic-to-defining shift might reflect a changing response bias rather than a change in representation. There is, therefore, a need for tasks that more closely approximate natural language usage. (3) If one wants to assess the extent to which children are relying on one type of feature versus another, one needs stimulus material that will differentially emphasize these features.

In the present study, these problems were overcome by using a different technique, one which described situations or events to children and asked them to make judgments. For each concept, two stories were devised. One story (the −characteristic/ +defining case) had correct defining features but lacked important characteristic features. The other story had salient characteristic features but had incorrect defining ones (the +characteristic/ −defining case). It was predicted that young children would accept the +characteristic/ −defining stories as valid instances of the concepts and reject the −characteristic/ +defining ones, while older children would do the opposite. No clear predictions were made as to how the transition might be achieved. However, since the transition seems to be dependent on the particular features used, it was felt that the shift might occur at different ages for different concepts.

METHODS

SUBJECTS

Sixteen children at each of three grades, K, 2, and 4, participated as subjects. The average ages were 5 years, 7 months; 7 years, 11 months; and 9 years, 9 months, respectively. In addition 39 preschool children participated in a modified version of the elementary school task (the average age was 4 years, 5 months).

STIMULI

The 17 terms selected for use in the study are shown in Table 1. The selection of the terms proceeded according to several criteria: (1) The terms should be ones that were likely to be familiar even to preschoolers. (2) The terms must have clear defining and characteristic features both of which are salient to adult users of the words. (3) The features should enable two stories to be constructed that allow one of the two types of features to be emphasized while the other is suppressed.

These selection criteria clearly did not result in a fully representative sample of natural language terms. Many terms seem to have only one sort of feature and not the other. In fact, the conceptual domains that lend themselves to these special kinds of terms are interesting in their own right (they include kinship terms, terms for social conventions, and financially and morally related concepts). It is beyond the scope of this paper to consider the reasons why such domains generate these special terms. Other classes of terms, natural kind terms, will be considered briefly later as a potential exception class with no defining features.

The stories constructed for the terms were approximately 20 sec in length. The +characteristic/ −defining and −characteristic/ +defining stories are shown in Table 2.

TABLE 1	List of Terms Used

Lie
Robber
Menu
Jail
Twins
Sign
Taxi
Hat
Mailman
Factory
Island
Lunch
Vacation
Church
Uncle
Museum
News

Research on moral reasoning (Kun, Parsons, & Ruble, 1974) and narrative recall (Brown, 1976) suggests that the order of presentation of elements in a story can markedly influence comprehension and recall. In particular, younger children tend to notice and remember primarily the terminal elements of the story. Because of this effect, defining features were generally presented at the end of each story. This ensured that any trend among the younger children of ignoring defining features could not be attributed to the order of placement of those features in the story. If anything, this stimulus configuration is conservative in that it works against the developmental hypothesis. The story was also repeated several times to further reduce order of presentation effects.

As can be seen from the stories, the +characteristic/ −defining story not only failed to have the appropriate defining features, it had ones that were contradictory to the meaning of the word. By contrast, the −characteristic/ +defining story had features that were atypical of most instances of the concept and correct defining features.

PROCEDURE

Each child was seen individually for either a ½ hour session or for two such sessions conducted over successive school days. The stories were presented in semirandom order with the main constraint on order being that the +characteristic/ −defining and the −characteristic/ +defining stories be at least eight items apart in the stimulus set. Children were read a story and then asked if the thing described could be an "x," where "x" was the term for which the story was constructed. When necessary, children's answers were followed with probe questions to clarify ambiguous responses and to ensure that the children were attending to the task.

TABLE 2   Pairs of Stories Used for Each of the Terms

+Characteristic/ −Defining	−Characteristic/ +Defining
This girl hated a boy in her class because he was so mean and did really nasty things to her. She wanted to get him into trouble, so she told the teacher all the nasty things the boy had really done. Could that be a lie?	This little boy always got good grades in school and prizes for being so smart. The other children were jealous of him because of it, and he didn't want to make them feel bad and wanted them to be his friends. So, one time, when he really got a good mark on a test, he told them that he got a bad mark so they'd be his friend. Could that be a lie?
This smelly, mean old man with a gun in his pocket came to your house one day and took your colored television set because your parents didn't want it anymore and told him that he could have it. Could he be a robber?	This very friendly and cheerful woman came up to you and gave you a hug, but then she disconnected your toilet bowl and took it away without permission and never returned it. Could she be a robber?
Suppose a waitress handed you something shaped like this (experimenter handed subject a piece of paper folded in half) that had written inside the restaurant's history—when it was built, the names of the waitresses and cooks, etc., but it didn't say anything about food inside. Could that be a menu?	If there was this seashell sitting on a table in a restaurant, and on it was listed all the meals and foods that the restaurant served, could that be a menu?
There is this ugly building in the slums with bars on every window and rats who live in the corners. The men who live there are so poor they can only eat bread and water. They are allowed to leave the building whenever they want to. Could that be a jail?	There is this beautiful castle with horses and a swimming pool, and really delicious food. The people who live there can use all of these great things, but they are never allowed to leave unless they get special permission. They can only stay in the castle if they've done something wrong. Could that be a jail?
These two girls look alike, dress alike, do well in the same subjects in school, like the same vegetables, and live in the same house. One of them, however, is two years older than the other one. Could these be twin sisters?	There are these two girls who were born at the same time on the same day in the same room from the same mommy, but one of them lives in California and the other one lives in New York. Could these be twin sisters?
There is this big thing on the highway shaped like this (experimenter held up rectangular piece of paper) that was built to keep the sun out of the driver's eyes, but it has no writing on it. Could that be a sign?	There is this giant cupcake sitting in the middle of your street. Everyday, they put out a fresh one because people come and nibble on it. In bright orange frosting, the cupcake says, "Sally's Bakeshop—one block that-a-way." Could that be a sign?
Your next door neighbor painted his car yellow with black and white checks around the edges. The car even has a white bump on top. He likes to put on his cap and uniform and drive all over town everyday. He never gives strangers rides, though, because he thinks it's too dangerous. Could that be a taxi?	This purple car with three wheels and rainbows painted on the tires is driven around by a woman in a nightgown and a football helmet. Whenever you want to go somewhere, you wave to her and she takes you wherever you want to go as long as you pay her. Could that be a taxi?
There is this black thing made of felt and shaped like this with a brim around the edges (experimenter held up sketch of hat) that people put ashes from their cigarette in. Could that be a hat?	This man strapped a ribbon around a garbage can lid and tied it around his head to keep out the sun and the rain and the snow. Could that be a hat?
This man drives by in a red, white, and blue truck everyday. His job is to clean out mailboxes with a special vacuum cleaner. He pulls his truck right up to your mailbox and sticks his vacuum cleaner in to get out all the dirt and dust from your mailbox. Could that be a mailman?	This person dressed in bright orange shorts who goes around on rollerskates comes to your door every day at around 1 o'clock in the morning bringing you letters and packages. Could that be mailman?

(Continued)

TABLE 2	Pairs of Stories Used for Each of the Terms (*Continued*)

+Characteristic/ −Defining	−Characteristic/ +Defining
There is this big, concrete ugly building with lots of smoke stacks and chimneys on the roof. It is a warehouse where things are stored to keep warm. Nothing is ever made there, and no one ever goes in or out of the building. Could that be a factory?	There is this beautiful house in the woods. Inside, people dress in beautiful clothes, tuxedoes and evening gowns, and from 9 to 5 everyday sit on comfortable couches making buttons. Some pour the wax, some put the buttons in boxes so they can be sold to the stores. Could that be a factory?
There is this place that sticks out of the land like a finger. Coconut trees and palm trees grow there, and the girls sometimes wear flowers in their hair because it's so warm all the time. There is water on all sides except one. Could that be an island?	On this piece of land, there are apartment buildings, snow, and no green things growing. This piece of land is surrounded by water on all sides. Could that be an island?
It's 6 o'clock in the morning. You got up early because you're going on a trip, and you're really hungry. You make yourself a tunafish sandwich, french fries, and an ice cream soda. Could that be lunch?	It's 12 o'clock in the afternoon and the sun is shining really bright. You already ate something today, but you're still very hungry so you decide to eat pancakes with syrup, orange juice, scrambled eggs, cereal, and milk. Could that be lunch?
This family leads a very interesting life. They try out different hotels all over the United States. They stay in them, eat their fine foods, and rate them so that other people know whether they are good places to stay or not. They write a book about this, and get paid for doing it. Could that be a vacation?	This man decided not to go to work 1 week. He stayed at home, watched television, slept, and ate, but then his television broke down and he was sad and bored. Could that be a vacation?
This beautiful building with a point on the top and stained glass windows and a bell was built to take care of delicate plants. Nobody ever goes inside the building, and a man takes care of the plants by sticking a hose in through the beautiful stained glass windows with scenes from the Bible on them. Could that be a church?	There is this huge tent with red and white stripes that floats in the middle of the ocean. People come there by boat every Sunday to sing and pray and talk about God. Could that be a church?
This man your daddy's age loves you and your parents and loves to visit and bring presents, but he's not related to your parents at all. He's not your mommy or daddy's brother or sister or anything like that. Could that be an uncle?	Suppose your mommy has all sorts of brothers, some very old and some very, very young. One of your mommy's brothers is so young he's only 2 years old. Could that be an uncle?
There is this beautiful building with columns. Mr. Johnson lives there, but he has a big problem. There are all these cracks in his floors and his walls. So, he covers them with paintings and statues, and he never lets anyone inside to see them. Could that be a museum?	There is this small, wooden shack in the countryside. People come from all over and pay 50¢ to get inside and see the interesting display of dirty shirts with rings around the collar and spots and stains. Could that be a museum?
You turn on the radio and there is this man talking very seriously about foreign countries, wars, fires, and robberies. He is reading from a book that was written last year. Could that be news?	You turn on the TV and these children are singing and dancing to loud rock and roll music—and they're singing everything that happened in the world that day—the weather, the fires, the robberies. They even sometimes hold up crayon drawings to show what they were talking about. Could that be news?

The procedure had to be modified with the preschoolers, many of whom were unable to complete the task or who found the story presentation format awkward. In such cases spontaneous definitions as well as more informal bits of information about the concept were also requested. These differences in procedure, as well as the large number of missing cases, resulted in the data for the preschoolers being evaluated independently of those for the elementary school children.

SCORING

All transcripts were scored independently by two judges according to a 3-point scoring system:

A score of 1 was given to children who seemed to rely solely on characteristic features in making their judgments of whether the story described an instance of the queried term. Thus, if a +characteristic/ −defining story was deemed a valid instance of the term, or if a −characteristic/ +defining story was deemed an invalid instance, a score of 1 was given.

A score of 2 was given for a class of related responses. Most common were those cases where a child referred to both characteristic and defining features and indicated that both were necessary for the story to be an instance of the concept. These scores were more common in the −characteristic/+defining cases, where a child would explicitly state that, in addition to the defining features, certain characteristic features were also required. A score of 2 was also given for cases where the child seemed to rely primarily on defining features, but incorrect ones (e.g., an uncle is your father's father). Finally, a score of 2 was assigned in those cases where a child oscillated between a correct and incorrect response.

A score of 3 was given for those cases where defining features seemed to predominate. Thus, the −characteristic/ +defining stories were judged to be valid instances of the term while the +characteristic/ −defining stories were not.

Missing or unscorable responses were coded as blanks to be handled by repeated measures ANOVA with incomplete cells.

Using this scheme, the two scorers agreed on 91% of all scores. The remaining disagreements were resolved through discussion. In virtually all cases, the resolution was deemed appropriate by both scorers.

RESULTS

The overall results are summarized in Figure 1.

There are three points to notice in this overview of the data: (1) There was a significant increase in performance with age, $F(2,30) = 16.86, p < .001$, with older children judging more of the −characteristic/+defining stories and fewer of the +characteristic/ −defining stories to be acceptable. (2) There was a significant main effect of story type, with +characteristic/−defining stories receiving higher scores than −characteristic/ +defining ones, $F(1,30) = 39.01, p < .001$. That is, the children were more likely to reject a +characteristic/ −defining story than to accept a −characteristic/ +defining story. (3) There was no significant interaction between

FIGURE 1 Summary graph showing mean scores for all tests as functions of school grade and story type.

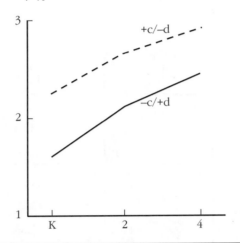

story type and age, $F(2,30) = .24, p > .05$. (The analyses were done with repeated measures ANOVA in which subjects with missing data were excluded.)

These results, however, are only a crude summary, and a more detailed concept by concept analysis is also necessary. Figure 2 shows the developmental patterns for each of the 17 concepts.

Thirteen of the seventeen cases showed significant overall increases with age; two of the exceptions were significant at the .06 level. The two other exceptions were "robber" and "hat." Fourteen of the seventeen cases showed significant main effects, with +characteristic/−defining stories having higher scores than −characteristic/+defining stories. The three exceptions were "lie," "vacation," and "twins," which showed no significant differences. In only three cases was there a significant age by story type interaction. These results, then, indicate that the general developmental patterns were also reflected in almost every instance.

The order of emergence of the shift across terms can be calculated by rank ordering the mean levels of performance at an intermediate age, such as grade 2. When this is done, the order shown in Table 3 is found.

The overall results are easier to interpret if a few excerpts from the transcripts are used to illustrate the developmental patterns. Consider, first, some responses by kindergartners indicating a heavy reliance on characteristic features:

Uncle (−characteristic/ +defining)
    E. *Could he be an uncle?*
    C. *No ... because he's little and 2 years old.*
    E. *How old does an uncle have to be?*
    C. *About 24 or 25.*
    E. *If he's 2 years old can he be an uncle?*
    C. *No ... he can be a cousin.*

FIGURE 2   Each graph shows the mean scores on each of the two story types as a function of school grade.

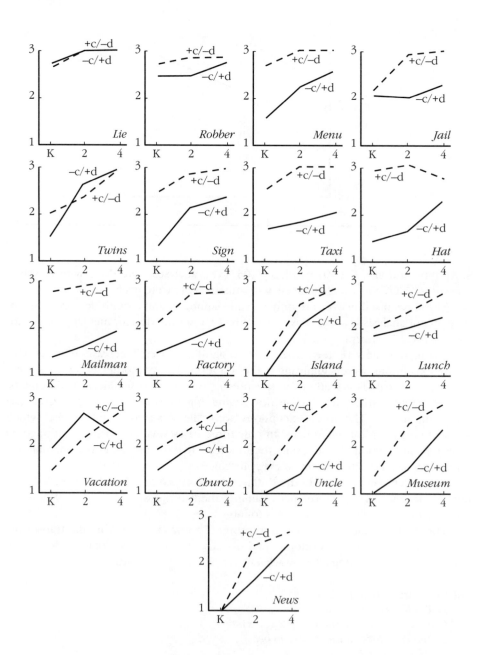

TABLE 3	
TERM	**OVERALL MEAN SCORE**
Lie	2.90
Robber	2.71
Menu	2.53
Jail	2.40
Twins	2.39
Sign	2.39
Taxi	2.33
Hat	2.30
Mailman	2.27
Factory	2.23
Island	2.17
Lunch	2.17
Vacation	2.12
Church	2.10
Uncle	1.98
Museum	1.91
News	1.86

Robber (–characteristic/ +defining)

    E. *Could she be a robber?*

    C. *No ... 'cause robbers, they have guns and they do stickups, and this woman didn't do that, and she didn't have a gun, she didn't do a stickup.*

    E. *Does a robber have to have a gun?*

    C. *Yes ... 'cause robbers kill sometimes.*

    E. *(Repeats story.) Could she be a robber?*

    C. *No.*

Museum (–characteristic/ +defining)

    E. *Could that be a museum?*

    C. *No ... a museum is something with dinosaur bones.*

    E. *Well suppose (repeats story). Could that be a museum ... can they have dirty shirts?*

    C. *No, that's a laundromat!*

Consider, second, what seem to be transitional stages where either both sets of features or idiosyncratic defining features are used. The following excerpts are taken from the second grade transcripts:

Factory (–characteristic/ +defining)

    E. *Is that a factory?*

    C. *No ... because you have to make things.*

    E. *They're making buttons. Is that a factory?*

    C. *No ... it's a house. Factories have to make all sorts of things.*

    E. *More things than buttons?*

    C. *Yes.*

Lunch (−characteristic/ +defining)

    E. *Could that be a lunch?*

    C. *No ... because lunch you have to have sandwiches and stuff like that.*

    E. *Can you have cereal for lunch?*

    C. *No.*

    E. *Can you have pancakes for lunch?*

    C. *No.*

    E. *Well how do you know if something is lunch or not?*

    C. *If the time says 12:00.*

    E. *This was 12:00.*

    C. *Well I don't think so.*

    E. *(Repeats story.) Is that lunch?*

    C. *I know ... that one is not lunch ... you have to eat sandwiches in lunch.*

    E. *Can you have anything else?*

    C. *You can have drinks, but not breakfast.*

Twin Sisters (+characteristic/ −defining)

    E. *Could they be twin sisters?*

    C. *No, because one is older.*

    E. *What are twin sisters?*

    C. *The same amount.*

    E. *Do twin sisters have to wear the same clothes?*

    C. *Yes.*

    E. *Do they have to live in the same house?*

    C. *Yes.*

Finally, some excerpts from the fourth graders' transcripts where defining features seem to predominate:

Uncle (−characteristic/ +defining)

    E. *Is he an uncle?*

    C. *Yes ... because he's still my mother's brother.*

    E. *Can an uncle be any age?*

    C. *Yes.*

Island (−characteristic/ +defining)

    E. *Could that be an island?*

    C. *Yes ... because it's surrounded by water ... An island's just a piece of land surrounded by water.*

Church (−characteristic/ +defining)

    E. *Could that be a church?*

    C. *Yeah ... I guess so 'cause they're talking about God and stuff like that and they pray.*

    E. *Could a church be a red and white tent in the middle of the ocean?*

    C. *I don't know.*

    E. *But this place is (repeats story). Is it a church?*

    C. *Sort of ... but it's not on ground.*

    E. *Does a church have to be on ground?*

C. *I guess it doesn't have to be . . . it could be out in the ocean.*
E. *(Repeats story once more.) So is this place a church or not?*
C. *Yeah, it's a church.*

The preschool data were generally in accord with the elementary school data. The children for the most part relied on characteristic rather than defining features. Thus only 4 of the 39 preschoolers gave more responses relying primarily on defining features than on characteristic ones. The differences between +characteristic/ −defining and −characteristic/ +defining stories were less than for older children, and were not significant. This lack of difference, however, may be a floor effect since the preschoolers tended to rely so heavily on characteristic features that they were almost always wrong.

GENERAL DISCUSSION

The results confirm the presence of a characteristic-to-defining shift in the acquisition of word meaning. In 14 of the 17 cases, there was a clear increase of scores with age, indicating a switch from responses based only on characteristic features to ones relying more on defining features. In several cases, the shift was sufficiently dramatic that almost none of the kindergartners attended to the defining features while virtually all the fourth graders did.

While the precise nature of the representations for these words and how they change cannot be unambiguously determined at this point (are they feature based, dimensional, or exemplar based? [cf. Smith & Medin, 1981]), the protocols and the developmental patterns suggest an important role for familiar exemplars rather than simple collections of feature sets. Children who are in the most immature stage of development frequently access highly specific exemplars to justify their responses rather than some sort of typicality statement (e.g., "it usually has y"). Thus, a child denies that a person is an uncle because he is not like the child's own uncle. Similarly, a child might deny that a −characteristic/ +defining island is an island by pointing out how different it is from islands that the child has experienced before. The "tall" study of Keil and Carroll (1980) provides more support for an exemplar-based view, as the early uses of "tall" were tightly bound to specific instances of "tall" things.

Children's early biases toward exemplar-based representations may be related to the wholistic-to-analytic distinction discussed by Kemler and Smith (1978). If a child who is unfamiliar with a domain is unable to classify by specific dimensions and can only use overall similarity, it is as if the child cannot decompose objects but can only evaluate them as integrated wholes. If so, then nondecomposable, exemplar-based representations would be an excellent way of storing their knowledge.

Why is there an early bias toward exemplar-based representations and why is there a shift? One account might argue that young children in general are more wholistic and that the shift reflects a stage-like change in the nature of their representations (cf. Werner, 1948; Bruner et al., 1966). However, the findings that the shift occurs at different ages for different words sheds doubt on such an explanation.

Instead, an account is suggested whereby individuals who are unfamiliar with a concept start with exemplar-based representations but shift to representations with more analytic/defining components as more knowledge is acquired. If such an account is correct, then two predictions follow: (1) In a domain with which adults are unfamiliar, exemplar-based representations should predominate early on with a shift occurring as more knowledge is acquired. (2) Even young children might show more analytic representations if they are very familiar with a domain.

A study by Chi, Feltovich, and Glaser (1981) provides support for the first prediction, as it showed that novices and experts classify physics problems in a manner analogous to a characteristic-to-defining shift. Novices tended to group together problems based on how they were typically instantiated (e.g., "ramp" or "pendulum" problems), while experts tended to classify according to more defining principles such as whether Newton's Second Law or the Law of Conservation of Energy was involved. Evidence for the second prediction is suggested by Chi (in press), as well, who notes that the representations of a young dinosaur expert seem to differ from those of more naive subjects by being more principled in nature: a hierarchical, taxonomic system was apparently imposed on the dinosaurs and the features in the hierarchy were defining in nature.

It would be an oversimplification, however, to suggest that the characteristic-to-defining shift is merely an expert/novice difference and that adults could be shown to make judgments just like children with highly unfamiliar concepts. This is because most concepts are not isolated entities but are parts of semantic fields or other relational systems. An individual with rich and detailed knowledge about many members of a semantic field who is learning a new word for some entity in that field is in a very different position from someone who has little or no knowledge of the field and is learning the same new word. Thus, adults might differ radically from children, even though they are both learning a new word, and possibly a new concept, if that word is easily mapped by the adult onto a highly familiar semantic field while it is not by the child.

There are at least three other classes of alternative explanations as to why the shift occurs. One class refers to possible correlates of defining and characteristic features. For example, most of the characteristic features were primarily perceptual in nature, while most of the defining features were conceptual and not directly observable. Thus, the shift might represent an increasing ability to understand and attend to aspects of concepts that are not directly perceivable. This account would tend to place most of the source of the shift in the concepts of the objects themselves and less in the nature of the mapping of words onto concepts.

We suspect that the perceptual/conceptual contrast is not the sole basis for the shift, however. To the extent that the Kemler and Smith work is analogous, it illustrates a shift where both sorts of features are equally perceptual. Moreover, for the few terms in this study where both features were perceptual (e.g., island), the shift was still observed. Finally, the Keil and Carroll (1980) study with the concept of "tall" documents a shift where representations before and after the shift are perceptually based, albeit much less instance bound in later cases. Given, however, the high correlation in this study between the characteristic/defining and the perceptual/conceptual distinctions, further empirical work is needed to assess the relation between the two. Fortunately, there are several words where the characteristic and defining features are both perceptual (e.g., cooking terms) or both conceptual (moral acts) and these can be used to decide the issue.

A second class of alternative explanations argues that the shift reflects less the ways in which word meanings are represented and more how the children perceive the demands of the task used in this study. Perhaps either their concept of how to give a definition or their understanding of what the experimenter has in mind changes, but not their representations. Other researchers (Kossan, 1978; Landau, 1982) have found some evidence for such changes in studies on word meaning acquisition. Such an account is not fully compatible with the details of this study, however. In particular, the shift is not seen at the same time for all concepts. Its occurrence is apparently dictated by intrinsic properties of the concepts themselves. If the shifts reflected a change in perceived task demands, they should occur at roughly the same time for all concepts. In addition, a wide variety of different measures and tasks have documented what appear to be closely analogous shifts. Thus, in tasks ranging from giving definitions, to judging stories as describing valid instances (pilot and study reported here), to comparative judgments of perceptual displays (Keil & Carroll, 1980; Carey, 1978), to similarity judgments (Kemler, 1983b), to classification tasks (Smith, 1981), analogous results have been found. If the shift is so task-dependent, one would expect to see it to be more susceptible to changes in the task. Nonetheless, given that the influence of task constraint has repeatedly been shown to be so powerful in cognitive development research, it should not be completely ruled out here.

A final class of explanations argues that the shift reflects the changing nature of the input children receive. Perhaps adults do not provide defining features to children until fairly late in development after giving them many characteristic features. There is, after all, some evidence that adults do give different semantic information to older and younger children (e.g., Anglin, 1977). Even if the parents were to change in this manner, however (which is not at all clear), the reason why they change might well be a consequence of something they have discovered about changes in the children's representations. Two research projects are now examining parents' explanations to children and should address this alternative explanation.

In addition to the shift itself, a second finding of this study was better performance on the +characteristic/ −defining stories than on the −characteristic/ +defining stories. This difference may be caused by children who are in a transitional stage where both the defining features and the characteristic features are believed to be essential for a word's meaning. Such children reject the +characteristic/ −defining story, usually by referring exclusively to the defining features. Their responses were given a score of 3, or a 2 if they explicitly say that both the defining and characteristic features are needed. By contrast, when presented with the −characteristic/ +defining story, they incorrectly reject the story as not describing an instance of the concept, because it lacks certain characteristic features. They then receive a score of 1 if no reference to defining features is made or a score of 2 if both types are explicitly mentioned as being essential. Thus, if several children were in such a transitional state, scores on the +characteristic/ −defining stories would be inflated and those on the −characteristic/ +defining deflated.

It is logically possible that the transitional stage might instead involve children for whom either just defining or just characteristic features are sufficient for describing a valid instance of the concept. Such cases would result in higher scores on the −characteristic/ +defining stories than on the +characteristic/ −defining ones. Since this never occurred, it appears that children make the transition by requiring both types of features rather than one or the other. The reason for this preference will have to be uncovered by future studies.

The account described so far suggests that early representations involve solely characteristic attributes, and that only with time and accretion of knowledge and the relevant principles do more defining properties play a role in word meaning. This is an oversimplification, however. In addition to the defining and characteristic aspects of word meaning, which are usually easily accessible and used to judge the truth value of sentences in which these meanings occur, other aspects of word meaning seem to form a deeper background and are presupposed rather than used directly in the verification of a sentence. Many investigators in philosophy and linguistics (Russell, 1924; Ryle, 1938; Sommers, 1963; Allwood, Andersson, & Dahl, 1977; Katz, 1972) and some in psychology (Bever & Rosenbaum, 1971; Keil, 1979) have referred to such a distinction between presupposed aspects of word meaning and more directly accessed information. This kind of presupposed knowledge has sometimes been called *ontological knowledge* (Sommers, 1963) in that it consists of information about the most basic categories of discourse such as events, physical objects, and abstract entities.

In the present study, children often exhibited a set of presuppositions about the general category of things to which a word referred while nonetheless filling out the details completely in terms of characteristic features. For example, while children might show a wide range of views of what islands were like, all of them knew that they were some kind of geographical entity. An informal study was conducted with eight children from each of the grades in the study reported in this article. After taking part in the main study, these 24 children were asked to make a judgment about each of the terms in combination with a predicate from a different ontological category, (e.g., "the jail is hungry," or "the lunch was sorry"). Children at all ages were highly successful at such anomaly judgments even though many of them concerned highly abstract, nonperceptible properties of objects such as the ability to grow, the ability to have emotions, and the distinction between mechanical versus biological innards.

In short, at the level of presupposed basic categorical information, children at the youngest ages may attribute criterial properties to words (e.g., all objects denoted by a word must have mass, color, or emotions, and objects in other categories must not), and they use this knowledge to make anomaly judgments. More extensive work is needed to see if children are using these "ontological" properties as a basic framework within which the characteristic-to-defining shift can occur, but the results of this informal study are compatible with such a view.

A final issue concerns the generality of the results in light of the special set of concepts used. It was noted that many concepts seem to have no defining features. Does this mean that such terms never undergo such a shift? Consider, for example, natural kind terms such as "tiger" or "gold" (Putnam, 1975), where no one feature seems absolutely essential for meaning. While space prevents a detailed exposition here, an analogous shift does seem to occur for natural kind terms. The shift, however, is not from characteristic to defining features but from characteristic-based representations to those recognizing the fallibility of characteristic features (cf. Boyd, 1979). What may be typical properties can be completely undermined by a deeper, more principled aspect of meaning. The principle may either be a brief definition, as with the terms in this study, or perhaps a detailed scientific theory about speciation, chemical structure, or physiology. A research project in progress on the development of artifacts and natural kind terms is supporting such an analysis.

REFERENCES

Allwood, J., Andersson, L., & Dahl, O. (1977). *Logic in linguistics.* Cambridge: Cambridge Univ. Press.

Anderson, J. R., & Bower, G. H. (1973). *Human associative memory.* Washington, DC: Winston.

Anglin, J. M. (1977). *Word, object, and conceptual development.* New York: Norton.

Armstrong, S., Gleitman, L. R., & Gleitman, H. (1983). What some concepts might not be. *Cognition, 13,* 263–308.

Bever, T. G., & Rosenbaum, P. S. (1971). Some lexical structures and their empirical validity. In D. D. Steinberg & L. A. Jakobovits (Eds.), *Semantics.* Cambridge: Cambridge Univ. Press.

Bolinger, D. L. (1965). The atomization of meaning. *Language, 41,* 555–573.

Boyd, R. (1979). Metaphor and theory change: What is "metaphor" a metaphor for? In A. Ortony (Ed.), *Metaphor and thought.* Cambridge: Cambridge Univ. Press.

Brown, A. L. (1976). Semantic integration in children's reconstruction of logical narrative sequences. *Cognitive Psychology, 8,* 247–262.

Bruner, J. S., Olver, R. R., Greenfield, P. M., et al. (1966). *Studies in cognitive growth.* New York: Wiley.

Carey, S. (1978). The child as a word learner. In M. Halle, J. Bresnan, & G. Miller (Eds.), *Linguistic theory and psychological reality.* Cambridge, MA: MIT Press.

Carey, S. (1982). Semantic development: The state of the art. In E. Wanner & L. R. Gleitman (Eds.), *Language acquisition: The state of the art.* Cambridge: Cambridge Univ. Press.

Chi, M. T. H. (in press). Interactive roles of knowledge and strategies in development. In S. Chipman, J. Segal, & R. Glaser (Eds.), *Thinking and learning skills: Current research and open questions* (Vol. 2). Hillsdale, NJ: Erlbaum.

Chi, M. T. H., Feltovich, P. J., & Glaser, R. (1981). Categorization and representation of physics problems by experts and novices. *Cognitive Science, 5,* 121–152.

Clark, E. V. (1973). What's in a word? On the child's acquisition of semantics in his first language. In T. E. Moore (Ed.), *Cognitive development and the acquisition of language.* New York: Academic Press.

Fodor, J. A., Garrett, M. F., Walker, E. C. T., & Parkes, C. H. (1980). Against definitions. *Cognition, 8,* 263–367.

Garner, W. R. (1974). *The processing of information and structure.* Potomoc, MD: Erlbaum.

Gibson, E. J. (1969). *Principles of perceptual and cognitive development.* New York: Appleton-Century-Crofts.

Glass, A., & Holyoak, K. J. (1975). Alternative conceptions of semantic theory. *Cognition, 3,* 313–339.

Katz, J. J. (1972). *Semantic theory.* New York: Harper & Row.

Keil, F. C. (1979). *Semantic and conceptual development: An ontological perspective.* Cambridge, MA: Harvard Univ. Press.

Keil, F. C., & Carroll, J. J. (1980). The child's conception of "tall": Implications for an alternative view of semantic development. *Papers and Reports on Child Language Development, 19,* 21–28.

Kemler, D. G. (1983a). Exploring and reexploring issues of integrality, perceptual sensitivity, and dimensional salience. *Journal of Experimental Child Psychology, 36,* 365–379.

Kemler, D. G. (1983b). Holistic and analytic modes in perceptual and cognitive development. In T. Tighe & B. E. Shepp (Eds.), *Perception, cognition, & development: Interactional analyses.* Hillsdale, NJ: Erlbaum.

Kemler, D. G., & Smith, L. B. (1978). Is there a developmental trend from integrality to separability in perception? *Journal of Experimental Child Psychology, 26,* 498-507.

Kossan, N. E., (1978). *Structure and strategy in concept acquisition.* Ph.D. dissertation, Stanford University, Palo Alto, CA.

Kripke, S. (1972). Naming and necessity. In D. Davidson & G. Harmon (Eds.), *Semantics of natural language.* Boston: Reidel.

Kun, A., Parsons, J., & Ruble, D. (1974). Development of integration processes using ability and effort information to predict outcome. *Developmental Psychology, 10,* 721-732.

Landau, B. (1982). Will the real grandmother please stand up? The psychological reality of dual meaning representations. *Journal of Psycholinguistic Research, 11* (1), 47-62.

MacNamara, J. (1971). Parsimony of the lexicon. *Language, 47,* 359-374.

Putnam, H. (1975). The meaning of meaning. In H. Putnam (Ed.), *Mind, language, and reality* (Vol. 2). London: Cambridge Univ. Press.

Rosch, E. (1978). Principles of categorization. In E. Rosch & B. B. Lloyd (Eds.), *Cognition and categorization.* Hillsdale, NJ: Erlbaum.

Rosch, E., & Mervis, C. (1975). Family resemblances: Studies in the internal structure of categories. *Cognitive Psychology, 7,* 573-605.

Russell, B. (1924). Logical atomism. In J. H. Muirhead (Ed.), *Contemporary British philosophy, 1st series.* London: Allyn and Unwin.

Ryle, G. (1938). Categories. *Proceedings of the Aristotelian Society, 38,* 189-206.

Smith, E. E. (1978). Theories of semantic memory. In W. K. Estes (Ed.), *Handbook of learning and cognitive processes: Vol. 6. Linguistic functions in cognitive theory.* Hillsdale, NJ: Erlbaum.

Smith, E. E., & Medin, D. L. (1981). *Categorization and concepts.* Cambridge, MA: Harvard Univ. Press.

Smith, L. B. (1981). Importance of the overall similarity of objects for adults' and children's classifications. *Journal of Experimental Psychology: Human Perception and Performance, 7,* 811-824.

Sommers, F. (1963). Types and ontology. *Philosophical Review, 72,* 327-363.

Vygotsky, L. S. (1962). *Thought and language.* (E. Hartmann and G. Vakar, trans.) Cambridge, MA: MIT Press. (Original work published 1934.)

Werner, H. (1948). *Comparative psychology of mental development.* New York: International Univ. Press.

QUESTIONS FOR FURTHER THOUGHT

1. How are defining and characteristic features similar to one another? How do they differ?

2. Why might children rely more on characteristic features than adults do?

3. What is the essence of the developmental shift as described by Keil and Batterman?

4. Might the task that children are given influence the children's use of defining versus characteristic features? How?

5. Might the type of representation children use to represent word meanings vary for different words?

11

INTELLIGENCE

INTELLIGENCE: KNOWNS AND UNKNOWNS

*Ulric Neisser, Gwyneth Boodoo, Thomas Bouchard, Jr.,
A. Wade Boykin, Nathan Brody, Stephen Ceci,
Diane Halpern, John Loeblin, Robert
Perloff, Robert Sternberg, and
Susana Urbina*

INTELLIGENCE: KNOWNS AND UNKNOWNS

Ulric Neisser et al.

INTRODUCTION

The publication of *The Bell Curve* (Herrnstein & Murray, 1994) created an uproar among psychologists and laypeople alike regarding what scientists know and do not know about intelligence. In the book, Richard Herrnstein and Charles Murray argued that the creation of a meritocracy on the basis of intellectual ability in the United States has resulted in the formation of a cognitive elite. In other words, people with high IQs have risen to the top of the society, socioeconomically, whereas those with low IQs have dropped to the bottom. According to Herrnstein and Murray, this trend is likely to continue.

Partially as a result of this book, and partially as the result of a generalized perceived need, the American Psychological Association created a task force to study what is known and what is unknown about intelligence. The committee was unusual not so much for its distinguished membership, but for the diversity of points of view it encompassed. Members represented all scientifically responsible positions from one end of the spectrum of opinion to the other. Despite these differences, the committee was able to reach a consensus, and produced the document that you are about to read.

This article has already become a classic, because it represents a consensus view of experts regarding both what is known and what is not known about intelligence. It covers a wide variety of topics regarding intelligence, and deals evenhandedly with each. Reading the article will give you a good idea of the current state of the field.

———

In the fall of 1994, the publication of Herrnstein and Murray's book The Bell Curve *sparked a new round of debate about the meaning of intelligence test scores and the nature of intelligence. The debate was characterized by strong assertions as well as by strong feelings. Unfortunately, those assertions often revealed serious misunderstandings of what has (and has not) been demonstrated by scientific research in this field. Although a great deal is now known, the issues remain complex and in many cases still unresolved. Another unfortunate aspect of the debate was that many participants made little effort to*

Source: From Neisser, U., Boodoo, G., Bouchard, T. J., Boykin, A. W., Brody, N., Ceci, S. J., Halpern, D. F., Loehlin, J. C., Perloff, R., Sternberg, R. J., & Urbina, S. (1996). Intelligence: Knowns and unknowns. *American Psychologist, 51* (2), 77–101. Copyright © 1996 by the American Psychological Association. Reprinted with permission.

distinguish scientific issues from political ones. Research findings were often assessed not so much on their merits or their scientific standing as on their supposed political implications. In such a climate, individuals who wish to make their own judgments find it hard to know what to believe.

Reviewing the intelligence debate at its meeting of November 1994, the Board of Scientific Affairs (BSA) of the American Psychological Association (APA) concluded that there was urgent need for an authoritative report on these issues—one that all sides could use as a basis for discussion. Acting by unanimous vote, BSA established a Task Force charged with preparing such a report. Ulric Neisser, Professor of Psychology at Emory University and a member of BSA, was appointed chair. The APA Board on the Advancement of Psychology in the Public Interest, which was consulted extensively during this process, nominated one member of the Task Force; the Committee on Psychological Tests and Assessment nominated another; a third was nominated by the Council of Representatives. Other members were chosen by an extended consultative process, with the aim of representing a broad range of expertise and opinion.

The Task Force met twice, in January and March of 1995. Between and after these meetings, drafts of the various sections were circulated, revised, and revised yet again. Disputes were resolved by discussion. As a result, the report presented here has the unanimous support of the entire task force. ∎

1. CONCEPTS OF INTELLIGENCE

Individuals differ from one another in their ability to understand complex ideas, to adapt effectively to the environment, to learn from experience, to engage in various forms of reasoning, to overcome obstacles by taking thought. Although these individual differences can be substantial, they are never entirely consistent: A given person's intellectual performance will vary on different occasions, in different domains, as judged by different criteria. Concepts of "intelligence" are attempts to clarify and organize this complex set of phenomena. Although considerable clarity has been achieved in some areas, no such conceptualization has yet answered all the important questions and none commands universal assent. Indeed, when two dozen prominent theorists were recently asked to define intelligence, they gave two dozen somewhat different definitions (Sternberg & Detterman, 1986). Such disagreements are not cause for dismay. Scientific research rarely begins with fully agreed definitions, though it may eventually lead to them.

This first section of our report reviews the approaches to intelligence that are currently influential, or that seem to be becoming so. Here (as in later sections) much of our discussion is devoted to the dominant *psychometric* approach, which has not only inspired the most research and attracted the most attention (up to this time) but is by far the most widely used in practical settings. Nevertheless, other points of view deserve serious consideration. Several current theorists argue that there are many different "intelligences" (systems of abilities), only a few of which can be captured by standard psychometric tests. Others emphasize the role of culture, both in establishing different conceptions of intelligence and in influencing the acquisition of intellectual skills. Developmental psychologists, taking yet another direction, often focus more on the processes by which all children come to think intelligently than on measuring individual differences among them. There is also a new interest in the neural and biological bases of intelligence, a field of research that seems certain to expand in the next few years.

In this brief report, we cannot do full justice to even one such approach. Rather than trying to do so, we focus here on a limited and rather specific set of questions:

- What are the significant conceptualizations of intelligence at this time? (Section 1)
- What do intelligence test scores mean, what do they predict, and how well do they predict it? (Section 2)
- Why do individuals differ in intelligence, and especially in their scores on intelligence tests? Our discussion of these questions implicates both genetic factors (Section 3) and environmental factors (Section 4)
- Do various ethnic groups display different patterns of performance on intelligence tests, and if so what might explain those differences? (Section 5)
- What significant scientific issues are presently unresolved? (Section 6)

Public discussion of these issues has been especially vigorous since the 1994 publication of Herrnstein and Murray's *The Bell Curve,* a controversial volume which stimulated many equally controversial reviews and replies. Nevertheless, we do not directly enter that debate. Herrnstein and Murray (and many of their critics) have gone well beyond the scientific findings, making explicit recommendations on various aspects of public policy. Our concern here, however, is with science rather than policy. The charge to our task force was to prepare a dispassionate survey of the state of the art: to make clear what has been scientifically established, what is presently in dispute, and what is still unknown. In fulfilling that charge, the only recommendations we shall make are for further research and calmer debate.

THE PSYCHOMETRIC APPROACH

Ever since Alfred Binet's great success in devising tests to distinguish mentally retarded children from those with behavior problems, psychometric instruments have played an important part in European and American life. Tests are used for many purposes, such as selection, diagnosis, and evaluation. Many of the most widely used tests are not intended to measure intelligence itself but some closely related construct: scholastic aptitude, school achievement, specific abilities, etc. Such tests are especially important for selection purposes. For preparatory school, it's the SSAT; for college, the SAT or ACT; for graduate school, the GRE; for medical school, the MCAT; for law school, the LSAT; for business school, the GMAT. Scores on intelligence-related tests matter, and the stakes can be high.

Intelligence Tests. Tests of intelligence itself (in the psychometric sense) come in many forms. Some use only a single type of item or question; examples include the

Peabody Picture Vocabulary Test (a measure of children's verbal intelligence) and Raven's Progressive Matrices (a nonverbal, untimed test that requires inductive reasoning about perceptual patterns). Although such instruments are useful for specific purposes, the more familiar measures of general intelligence—such as the Wechsler tests and the Stanford-Binet—include many different types of items, both verbal and nonverbal. Test-takers may be asked to give the meanings of words, to complete a series of pictures, to indicate which of several words does not belong with the others, and the like. Their performance can then be scored to yield several subscores as well as an overall score.

By convention, overall intelligence test scores are usually converted to a scale in which the mean is 100 and the standard deviation is 15. (The standard deviation is a measure of the variability of the distribution scores.) Approximately 95% of the population has scores within two standard deviations of the mean, i.e., between 70 and 130. For historical reasons, the term "IQ" is often used to describe scores on tests of intelligence. It originally referred to an "Intelligence Quotient" that was formed by dividing a so-called *mental age* by a chronological age, but this procedure is no longer used.

Intercorrelations Among Tests. Individuals rarely perform equally well on all the different kinds of items included in a test of intelligence. One person may do relatively better on verbal than on spatial items, for example, while another may show the opposite pattern. Nevertheless, subtests measuring different abilities tend to be positively correlated: People who score high on one such subtest are likely to be above average on others, as well. These complex patterns of correlation can be clarified by factor analysis, but the results of such analyses are often controversial themselves. Some theorists (e.g., Spearman, 1927) have emphasized the importance of a general factor, *g,* which represents what all the tests have in common; others (e.g., Thurstone, 1938) focus on more specific group factors such as memory, verbal comprehension, or number facility. As we shall see in Section 2, one common view today envisages something like a hierarchy of factors with g at the apex. But there is no full agreement on what g actually means: it has been described as a mere statistical regularity (Thomson, 1939), a kind of mental energy (Spearman, 1927), a generalized abstract reasoning ability (Gustafsson, 1984), or an index measure of neural processing speed (Reed & Jensen, 1992).

There have been many disputes over the utility of IQ and g. Some theorists are critical of the entire psychometric approach (e.g., Ceci, 1990; Gardner, 1983; Gould, 1978), while others regard it as firmly established (e.g., Carroll, 1993; Eysenck, 1973; Herrnstein & Murray, 1994; Jensen, 1972). The critics do not dispute the stability of test scores, nor the fact that they predict certain forms of achievement—especially school achievement—rather effectively (see Section 2). They do argue, however, that to base a concept of intelligence on test scores alone is to ignore many important aspects of mental ability. Some of those aspects are emphasized in other approaches reviewed below.

MULTIPLE FORMS OF INTELLIGENCE

Gardner's Theory. A relatively new approach is the theory of "multiple intelligences" proposed by Howard Gardner in his book *Frames of Mind* (1983). Gardner argues that our conceptions of intelligence should be informed not only by work with "normal" children and adults but also by studies of gifted persons (including so-called *savants*), of virtuosos and experts in various domains, of valued abilities in diverse cultures, and of individuals who have suffered selective forms of brain damage. These considerations have led him to include musical, bodily–kinesthetic, and various forms of personal intelligence in the scope of his theory along with more familiar linguistic, logical–mathematical, and spatial abilities. (Critics of the theory argue, however, that some of these are more appropriately described as special talents than as forms of "intelligence.")

In Gardner's view, the scope of psychometric tests includes only linguistic, logical, and some aspects of spatial intelligence; other forms have been almost entirely ignored. Even in the domains on which they are ostensibly focused, the paper-and-pencil format of most tests rules out many kinds of intelligent performance that matter a great deal in everyday life, such as giving an extemporaneous talk (linguistic) or being able to find one's way in a new town (spatial). While the stability and validity of performance tests in these new domains are not yet clear, Gardner's argument has attracted considerable interest among educators as well as psychologists.

Sternberg's Theory. Robert Sternberg's (1985) triarchic theory proposes three fundamental aspects of intelligence—analytic, creative, and practical—of which only the first is measured to any significant extent by mainstream tests. His investigations suggest the need for a balance between analytic intelligence, on the one hand, and creative and especially practical intelligence on the other. The distinction between analytic (or "academic") and practical intelligence has also been made by others (e.g., Neisser, 1976). Analytic problems, of the type suitable for test construction, tend to (a) have been formulated by other people, (b) be clearly defined, (c) come with all the information needed to solve them, (d) have only a single right answer, which can be reached by only a single method, (e) be disembedded from ordinary experience, and (f) have little or no intrinsic interest. Practical problems, in contrast, tend to (a) require problem recognition and formulation, (b) be poorly defined, (c) require information seeking, (d) have various acceptable solutions, (e) be embedded in and require prior everyday experience, and (f) require motivation and personal involvement.

One important form of practical intelligence is *tacit knowledge,* defined by Sternberg and his collaborators as "action-oriented knowledge, acquired without direct help from others, that allows individuals to achieve goals they personally value" (Sternberg, Wagner, Williams, & Horvath, 1995, p. 916). Questionnaires designed to measure tacit knowledge have been developed for various domains, especially business management. In these questionnaires, the individual is presented with written descriptions of various work-related situations and asked to rank a number of options for dealing with each of them. Measured in this way, tacit knowledge is relatively independent of scores on intelligence tests; nevertheless it correlates significantly with various indices of job performance (Sternberg & Wagner, 1993; Sternberg et al., 1995). Although this work is not without its critics (Jensen, 1993; Schmidt & Hunter, 1993), the results to this point tend to support the distinction between analytic and practical intelligence.

Related Findings. Other investigators have also demonstrated that practical intelligence can be relatively independent of school performance or scores on psychometric tests. Brazilian street children, for example, are quite capable of doing the math required for survival in their street business even though they have failed mathematics in school (Carraher, Carraher, & Schliemann, 1985). Similarly, women shoppers in California who had no difficulty in comparing product values at the supermarket were unable to carry out the same mathematical operations in paper-and-pencil tests (Lave, 1988). In a study of expertise in wagering on harness races, Ceci and Liker (1986) found that the reasoning of the most skilled handicappers was implicitly based on a complex interactive model with as many as seven variables. Nevertheless, individual handicappers' levels of performance were not correlated with their IQ scores. This means, as Ceci has put it, that "the assessment of the experts' intelligence on a standard IQ test was irrelevant in predicting the complexity of their thinking at the racetrack" (1990, p. 43).

CULTURAL VARIATION

It is very difficult to compare concepts of intelligence across cultures. English is not alone in having many words for different aspects of intellectual power and cognitive skill (*wise, sensible, smart, bright, clever, cunning . . .*); if another language has just as many, which of them shall we say corresponds to its speakers' "concept of intelligence"? The few attempts to examine this issue directly have typically found that, even within a given society, different cognitive characteristics are emphasized from one situation to another and from one subculture to another (Serpell, 1974; Super, 1983; Wober, 1974). These differences extend not just to conceptions of intelligence but also to what is considered adaptive or appropriate in a broader sense.

These issues have occasionally been addressed across subcultures and ethnic groups in America. In a study conducted in San Jose, California, Okagaki and Sternberg (1993) asked immigrant parents from Cambodia, Mexico, the Philippines, and Vietnam—as well as native-born Anglo-Americans and Mexican Americans—about their conceptions of child-rearing, appropriate teaching, and children's intelligence. Parents from all groups except Anglo-Americans indicated that such characteristics as motivation, social skills, and practical school skills were as or more important than cognitive characteristics for their conceptions of an intelligent first-grade child.

Heath (1983) found that different ethnic groups in North Carolina have different conceptions of intelligence. To be considered as intelligent or adaptive, one must excel in the skills valued by one's own group. One particularly interesting contrast was in the importance ascribed to verbal versus nonverbal communication skills—to saying things explicitly as opposed to using and understanding gestures and facial expressions. Note that while both these forms of communicative skill have their uses, they are not equally well represented in psychometric tests.

How testing is done can have different effects in different cultural groups. This can happen for many reasons. In one study, Serpell (1979) asked Zambian and English children to reproduce patterns in three different media: wire models, pencil and paper, or clay. The Zambian children excelled in the wire medium to which they were most accustomed, while the English children were best with pencil and paper.

Both groups performed equally well with clay. As this example shows, differences in familiarity with test materials can produce marked differences in test results.

DEVELOPMENTAL PROGRESSIONS

Piaget's Theory. The best-known developmentally based conception of intelligence is certainly that of the Swiss psychologist Jean Piaget (1972). Unlike most of the theorists considered here, Piaget had relatively little interest in individual differences. Intelligence develops—in all children—through the continually shifting balance between the assimilation of new information into existing cognitive structures and the accommodation of those structures themselves to the new information. To index the development of intelligence in this sense, Piaget devised methods that are rather different from conventional tests. To assess the understanding of "conservation," for example (roughly, the principle that material quantity is not affected by mere changes of shape), children who have watched water being poured from a shallow to a tall beaker may be asked if there is now more water than before. (A positive answer would suggest that the child has not yet mastered the principle of conservation.) Piaget's tasks can be modified to serve as measures of individual differences; when this is done, they correlate fairly well with standard psychometric tests (for a review see Jensen, 1980).

Vygotsky's Theory. The Russian psychologist Lev Vygotsky (1978) argued that all intellectual abilities are social in origin. Language and thought first appear in early interactions with parents, and continue to develop through contact with teachers and others. Traditional intelligence tests ignore what Vygotsky called the "zone of proximal development," i.e., the level of performance that a child might reach with appropriate help from a supportive adult. Such tests are "static," measuring only the intelligence that is already fully developed. "Dynamic" testing, in which the examiner provides guided and graded feedback, can go further to give some indication of the child's latent potential. These ideas are being developed and extended by a number of contemporary psychologists (Brown & French, 1979; Feuerstein, 1980; Pascual-Leone & Ijaz, 1989).

BIOLOGICAL APPROACHES

Some investigators have recently turned to the study of the brain as a basis for new ideas about what intelligence is and how to measure it. Many aspects of brain anatomy and physiology have been suggested as potentially relevant to intelligence: the arborization of cortical neurons (Ceci, 1990), cerebral glucose metabolism (Haier, 1993), evoked potentials (Caryl, 1994), nerve conduction velocity (Reed & Jensen, 1992), sex hormones (see Section 4), and still others (cf. Vernon, 1993). Advances in research methods, including new forms of brain imaging such as PET and MRI scans, will surely add to this list. In the not-too-distant future it may be possible to relate some aspects of test performance to specific characteristics of brain function.

   This brief survey has revealed a wide range of contemporary conceptions of intelligence and of how it should be measured. The psychometric approach is the oldest and best established, but others also have much to contribute. We should be open to the possibility that our understanding of intelligence in the future will be rather different from what it is today.

2. INTELLIGENCE TESTS AND THEIR CORRELATES

The correlation coefficient, r, can be computed whenever the scores in a sample are paired in some way. Typically, this is because each individual is measured twice; he or she takes the same test on two occasions, or takes two different tests, or has both a test score and some criterion measure such as grade point average or job performance. (In Section 3, we consider cases where the paired scores are those of two different individuals, such as twins or parent and child.) The value of r measures the degree of relationship between the two sets of scores in a convenient way, by assessing how well one of them (computationally, it doesn't matter which one) could be used to predict the value of the other. Its sign indicates the direction of relationship: When r is negative, high scores on one measure predict low scores on the other. Its magnitude indicates the strength of the relationship. If $r = 0$, there is no relation at all; if r is 1 (or -1), one score can be used to predict the other score perfectly. Moreover, the square of r has particular meaning in cases where we are concerned with predicting one variable from another. When $r = .50$, for example, r^2 is $.25$: this means (given certain linear assumptions) that 25% of the variance in one set of scores is predictable from the correlated values of the other set, while the remaining 75% is not.

BASIC CHARACTERISTICS OF TEST SCORES

Stability. Intelligence test scores are fairly stable during development. When Jones and Bayley (1941) tested a sample of children annually throughout childhood and adolescence, for example, scores obtained at age 18 were correlated $r = .77$ with scores that had been obtained at age 6 and $r = .89$ with scores from age 12. When scores were averaged across several successive tests to remove short-term fluctuations, the correlations were even higher. The mean for ages 17 and 18 was correlated $r = .86$ with the mean for ages 5, 6, and 7, and $r = .96$ with the mean for ages 11, 12, and 13. (For comparable findings in a more recent study, see Moffitt, Caspi, Harkness, & Silva, 1993.) Nevertheless, IQ scores do change over time. In the same study (Jones & Bayley, 1941), the average change between age 12 and age 17 was 7.1 IQ points; some individuals changed as much as 18 points.

Is it possible to measure the intelligence of young infants in a similar way? Conventional tests of "infant intelligence" do not predict later test scores very well, but certain experimental measures of infant attention and memory—originally developed for other purposes—have turned out to be more successful. In the most common procedure, a particular visual pattern is shown to a baby over and over again. The experimenter records how long the infant subject looks at the pattern on each trial; these looks get shorter and shorter as the baby becomes "habituated" to it. The time required to reach a certain level of habituation, or the extent to which the baby now "prefers" (looks longer at) a new pattern, is regarded as a measure of some aspect of his or her information-processing capability.

These habituation-based measures, obtained from babies at ages ranging from 3 months to 1 year, are significantly correlated with the intelligence test scores of the same children when they get to be 2 or 4 or 6 years old (for reviews see Bornstein, 1989; Columbo, 1993; McCall & Garriger, 1993). A few studies have found such correlations even at ages 8 or 11 (Rose & Feldman, 1995). A recent meta-analysis, based on 31 different samples, estimates the average magnitude of the correlations at about $r = .36$ (McCall & Garriger, 1993). (The largest rs often appear in samples that include "at risk" infants.) It is possible that these habituation scores (and other similar measures of infant cognition) do indeed reflect real cognitive differences, perhaps in "speed of information processing" (Columbo, 1993). It is also possible, however, that—to a presently unknown extent—they reflect early differences in temperament or inhibition.

It is important to understand what remains stable and what changes in the development of intelligence. A child whose IQ score remains the same from age 6 to age 18 does not exhibit the same performance throughout that period. On the contrary, steady gains in general knowledge, vocabulary, reasoning ability, etc. will be apparent. What does *not* change is his or her score in comparison to that of other individuals of the same age. A 6-year-old with an IQ of 100 is at the mean of 6-year-olds; an 18-year-old with that score is at the mean of 18-year-olds.

Factors and g. As noted in Section 1, the patterns of intercorrelation among tests (i.e., among different kinds of items) are complex. Some pairs of tests are much more closely related than others, but all such correlations are typically positive and form what is called a "positive manifold." Spearman (1927) showed that in any such manifold, some portion of the variance of scores on each test can be mathematically attributed to a "general factor," or g. Given this analysis, the overall pattern of correlations can be roughly described as produced by individual differences in g plus differences in the specific abilities sampled by particular tests. In addition, however, there are usually patterns of intercorrelation among groups of tests. These commonalties, which played only a small role in Spearman's analysis, were emphasized by other theorists. Thurstone (1938), for example, proposed an analysis based primarily on the concept of group factors.

While some psychologists today still regard g as the most fundamental measure of intelligence (e.g., Jensen, 1980), others prefer to emphasize the distinctive profile of strengths and weaknesses present in each person's performance. A recently published review identifies over 70 different abilities that can be distinguished by currently available tests (Carroll, 1993). One way to represent this structure is in terms of a hierarchical arrangement with a general intelligence factor at the apex and various more specialized abilities arrayed below it. Such a summary merely acknowledges that performance levels on different tests are correlated; it is consistent with, but does not prove, the hypothesis that a common factor such as g underlies those correlations. Different specialized abilities might also be correlated for other reasons, such as the effects of education. Thus while the g-based factor hierarchy is the most widely accepted current view of the structure of abilities, some theorists regard it as misleading (Ceci, 1990). Moreover, as noted in Section 1, a wide range of human abilities—including many that seem to have intellectual components—are outside the domain of standard psychometric tests.

TESTS AS PREDICTORS

School Performance. Intelligence tests were originally devised by Alfred Binet to measure children's ability to succeed in school. They do in fact predict school performance fairly well: the correlation between IQ scores and grades is about .50. They also predict scores on school achievement tests, designed to measure knowledge of the curriculum. Note, however, that correlations of this magnitude account for only about 25% of the overall variance. Successful school learning depends on many personal characteristics other than intelligence, such as persistence, interest in school, and willingness to study. The encouragement for academic achievement that is received from peers, family, and teachers may also be important, together with more general cultural factors (see Section 5).

The relationship between test scores and school performance seems to be ubiquitous. Wherever it has been studied, children with high scores on tests of intelligence tend to learn more of what is taught in school than their lower-scoring peers. There may be styles of teaching and methods of instruction that will decrease or increase this correlation, but none that consistently eliminates it has yet been found (Cronbach & Snow, 1977).

What children learn in school depends not only on their individual abilities but also on teaching practices and on what is actually taught. Recent comparisons among pupils attending school in different countries have made this especially obvious. Children in Japan and China, for example, know a great deal more math than American children even though their intelligence test scores are quite similar (see Section 5). This difference may result from many factors, including cultural attitudes toward schooling as well as the sheer amount of time devoted to the study of mathematics and how that study is organized (Stevenson & Stigler, 1992). In principle it is quite possible to improve the school learning of American children—even very substantially—without changing their intelligence test scores at all.

Years of Education. Some children stay in school longer than others; many go on to college and perhaps beyond. Two variables that can be measured as early as elementary school correlate with the total amount of education individuals will obtain: test scores and social class background. Correlations between IQ scores and total years of education are about .55, implying that differences in psychometric intelligence account for about 30% of the outcome variance. The correlations of years of education with social class background (as indexed by the occupation/education of a child's parents) are also positive, but somewhat lower.

There are a number of reasons why children with higher test scores tend to get more education. They are likely to get good grades, and to be encouraged by teachers and counselors; often they are placed in "college preparatory" classes, where they make friends who may also encourage them. In general, they are likely to find the process of education rewarding in a way that many low-scoring children do not (Rehberg & Rosenthal, 1978). These influences are not omnipotent: Some high scoring children do drop out of school. Many personal and social characteristics other than psychometric intelligence determine academic success and interest, and social privilege may also play a role. Nevertheless, test scores are the best single predictor of an individual's years of education.

In contemporary American society, the amount of schooling that adults complete is also somewhat predictive of their social status. Occupations considered high in prestige (e.g., law, medicine, even corporate business) usually require at least a college degree—16 or more years of education—as a condition of entry. It is partly because intelligence test scores predict years of education so well that they also predict occupational status—and, to a smaller extent, even income (Herrnstein & Murray, 1994; Jencks, 1979). Moreover, many occupations can only be entered through professional schools which base their admissions at least partly on test scores: the MCAT, the GMAT, the LSAT, etc. Individual scores on admission-related tests such as these are certainly correlated with scores on tests of intelligence.

Social Status and Income. How well do IQ scores (which can be obtained before individuals enter the labor force) predict such outcome measures as the social status or income of adults? This question is complex, in part because another variable also predicts such outcomes: namely, the socioeconomic status (SES) of one's parents. Unsurprisingly, children of privileged families are more likely to attain high social status than those whose parents are poor and less educated. These two predictors (IQ and parental SES) are by no means independent of one another; the correlation between them is around .33 (White, 1982).

One way to look at these relationships is to begin with SES. According to Jencks (1979), measures of parental SES predict about one third of the variance in young adults' social status and about one fifth of the variance in their income. About half of this predictive effectiveness depends on the fact that the SES of parents also predicts children's intelligence test scores, which have their own predictive value for social outcomes; the other half comes about in other ways.

We can also begin with IQ scores, which by themselves account for about one fourth of the social status variance and one sixth of the income variance. Statistical controls for parental SES eliminate only about a quarter of this predictive power. One way to conceptualize this effect is by comparing the occupational status (or income) of adult brothers who grew up in the same family and hence have the same parental SES. In such cases, the brother with the higher adolescent IQ score is likely to have the higher adult social status and income (Jencks, 1979). This effect, in turn, is substantially mediated by education: The brother with the higher test scores is likely to get more schooling, and hence to be better credentialed as he enters the workplace.

Do these data imply that psychometric intelligence is a major determinant of social status or income? That depends on what one means by *major*. In fact, individuals who have the same test scores may differ widely in occupational status and even more widely in income. Consider for a moment the distribution of occupational status scores for all individuals in a population, and then consider the conditional distribution of such scores for just those individuals who test at some given IQ. Jencks (1979) notes that the standard deviation of the latter distribution may still be quite large; in some cases it amounts to about 88% of the standard deviation for the entire population. Viewed from this perspective, psychometric intelligence appears as only one of a great many factors that influence social outcomes.

Job Performance. Scores on intelligence tests predict various measures of job performance: supervisor ratings, work samples, etc. Such correlations, which typically lie between $r = .30$ and $r = .50$, are partly restricted by the limited reliability of those measures themselves. They become higher when r is statistically corrected for this unreliability: In one survey of relevant studies (Hunter, 1983), the mean of the corrected correlations was .54. This implies that, across a wide range of occupations, intelligence test performance accounts for some 29% of the variance in job performance.

Although these correlations can sometimes be modified by changing methods of training or aspects of the job itself, intelligence test scores are at least weakly related to job performance in most settings. Sometimes IQ scores are described as the "best available predictor" of that performance. It is worth noting, however, that such tests predict considerably less than half the variance of job-related measures. Other individual characteristics—interpersonal skills, aspects of personality, etc.—are probably of equal or greater importance, but at this point, we do not have equally reliable instruments to measure them.

Social Outcomes. Psychometric intelligence is negatively correlated with certain socially undesirable outcomes. For example, children with high test scores are less likely than lower-scoring children to engage in juvenile crime. In one study, Moffitt, Gabrielli, Mednick, and Schulsinger (1981) found a correlation of −.19 between IQ scores and number of juvenile offenses in a large Danish sample: With social class controlled, the correlation dropped to −.17. The correlations for most "negative outcome" variables are typically smaller than .20, which means that test scores are associated with less than 4% of their total variance. It is important to realize that the causal links between psychometric ability and social outcomes may be indirect. Children who are unsuccessful in—and hence alienated from—school may be more likely to engage in delinquent behaviors for that very reason, compared to other children who enjoy school and are doing well.

In summary, intelligence test scores predict a wide range of social outcomes with varying degrees of success. Correlations are highest for school achievement, where they account for about a quarter of the variance. They are somewhat lower for job performance, and very low for negatively valued outcomes such as criminality. In general, intelligence tests measure only some of the many personal characteristics that are relevant to life in contemporary America. Those characteristics are never the only influence on outcomes, though in the case of school performance they may well be the strongest.

TEST SCORES AND MEASURES OF PROCESSING SPEED

Many recent studies show that the speeds with which people perform very simple perceptual and cognitive tasks are correlated with psychometric intelligence (for reviews see Ceci, 1990; Deary, 1995; Vernon, 1987). In general, people with higher intelligence test scores tend to apprehend, scan, retrieve, and respond to stimuli more quickly than those who score lower.

Cognitive Correlates. The modern study of these relations began in the 1970s, as part of the general growth of interest in response time and other chronometric measures of cognition. Many of the new cognitive paradigms required subjects to make same/different judgments or other speeded responses to visual displays. Although those paradigms had not been devised with individual differences in mind, they could be interpreted as providing measures of the speed of certain information processes. Those speeds turned out to correlate with psychometrically measured verbal ability (Hunt, 1978; Jackson & McClelland, 1979). In some problem-solving tasks, it was possible to analyze the subjects' overall response times into theoretically motivated "cognitive components" (Sternberg, 1977); component times could then be correlated with test scores in their own right.

Although the size of these correlations is modest (seldom accounting for more than 10% of the variance), they do increase as the basic tasks were made more complex by requiring increased memory or attentional capacity. For instance, the correlation between paired associate learning and intelligence increases as the pairs are presented at faster rates (Christal, Tirre, & Kyllonen, 1984).

Choice Reaction Time. In another popular cognitive paradigm, the subject simply moves his or her finger from a "home" button to one of eight other buttons arranged in a semicircle around it; these are marked by small lights that indicate which one is the target on a given trial (Jensen, 1987). Various aspects of the choice reaction times obtained in this paradigm are correlated with scores on intelligence tests, sometimes with values of r as high as $-.30$ or $-.40$ (r is negative because higher test scores go with shorter times). Nevertheless, it has proved difficult to make theoretical sense of the overall pattern of correlations, and the results are still hard to interpret (cf. Brody, 1992; Longstreth, 1984).

Somewhat stronger results have been obtained in a variant of Jensen's paradigm devised by Frearson and Eysenck (1986). In this "odd-man-out" procedure, three of the eight lights are illuminated on each trial. Two of these are relatively close to each other while the third is more distant; the subject must press the button corresponding to the more isolated stimulus. Response times in this task show higher correlations with IQ scores than those in Jensen's original procedure, perhaps because it requires more complex forms of spatial judgment.

Inspection Time. Another paradigm for measuring processing speed, devised to be relatively independent of response factors, is the method of "inspection time" (IT). In the standard version of this paradigm (Nettelbeck, 1987; Vickers, Nettelbeck, & Wilson, 1972), two vertical lines are shown very briefly on each trial, followed by a pattern mask; the subject must judge which line was shorter. For a given subject, IT is defined as the minimum exposure duration (up to the onset of the mask) for which the lines must be displayed if he or she is to meet a pre-established criterion of accuracy—e.g., nine correct trials out of ten.

Inspection times defined in this way are consistently correlated with measures of psychometric intelligence. In a recent meta-analysis, Kranzler and Jensen (1989) reported an overall correlation of $-.30$ between IQ scores and IT; this rose to $-.55$ when corrected for measurement error and attenuation. More recent findings confirm this general result (e.g., Bates & Eysenck, 1993; Deary, 1993). IT usually correlates best with performance subtests of intelligence; its correlation with verbal intelligence is usually weaker and sometimes zero.

One apparent advantage of IT over other chronometric methods is that the task itself seems particularly simple. At first glance, it is hard to imagine that any differences in response strategies or stimulus familiarity could affect the outcome. Nevertheless, it seems that they do. Brian Mackenzie and his colleagues (e.g., Mackenzie, Molloy, Martin, Lovegrove, & McNicol, 1991) discovered that some subjects use apparent-movement cues in the basic IT task while others do not; only in the latter group is IT correlated with intelligence test scores. Moreover, standard IT paradigms require an essentially spatial judgment; it is not surprising, then, that they correlate with intelligence tests which emphasize spatial ability. With this in mind, Mackenzie et al. (1991) devised a *verbal* inspection-time task based on Posner's classical same-letter/different-letter paradigm (Posner, Boies, Eichelman, & Taylor, 1969). As predicted, the resulting ITs correlated with verbal but not with spatial intelligence. It is clear that the apparently simple IT task actually involves complex modes of information processing (cf. Chaiken, 1993) that are as yet poorly understood.

Neurological Measures. Recent research has begun to explore what seem to be still more direct indices of neural processing. Reed and Jensen (1992) have used measures based on visual evoked potentials (VEP) to assess what they call "nerve conduction velocity" (NCV). To estimate that velocity, distance is divided by time: each subject's head length (a rough measure of the distance from the eye to the primary visual cortex) is divided by the latency of an early component (N70 or P100) of his or her evoked potential pattern. In a study with 147 college-student subjects, these NCVs correlated $r = .26$ with scores on an unspeeded test of intelligence. (A statistical correction for the restricted range of subjects raised the correlation to .37.) Other researchers have also reported correlations between VEP parameters and intelligence test scores (Caryl, 1994). Interestingly, however, Reed and Jensen (1993) reported that their estimates of "nerve conduction velocity" were *not* correlated with the same subjects' choice reaction times. Thus while we do not yet understand the basis of the correlation between NCV and psychometric intelligence, it is apparently not just a matter of overall speed.

Problems of Interpretation. Some researchers believe that psychometric intelligence, especially g, depends directly on what may be called the "neural efficiency" of the brain (Eysenck, 1986; Vernon, 1987). They regard the observed correlations between test scores and measures of processing speed as evidence for their view. If choice reaction times, inspection times, and VEP latencies actually do reflect the speed of basic neural processes, such correlations are only to be expected. In fact, however, the observed patterns of correlations are rarely as simple as this hypothesis would predict. Moreover, it is quite possible that high- and low-IQ individuals differ in other ways that affect speeded performance (cf. Ceci, 1990). Those variables include motivation, response criteria (emphasis on speed versus accuracy), perceptual strategies (cf. Mackenzie et al., 1991), attentional strategies, and—in some cases—differential familiarity with the material itself. Finally, we do not yet know the direction of causation that underlies such correlations. Do high levels of "neural efficiency" promote the development of intelligence, or do more intelligent people simply find faster ways to carry out perceptual tasks? Or both? These questions are still open.

3. THE GENES AND INTELLIGENCE

In this section of the report, we first discuss individual differences generally, without reference to any particular trait. We then focus on intelligence, as measured by conventional IQ tests or other tests intended to measure general cognitive ability. The different and more controversial topic of group differences will be considered in Section 5.

We focus here on the relative contributions of genes and environments to individual differences in particular traits. To avoid misunderstanding, it must be emphasized from the outset that gene action always involves an environment—at least a biochemical environment, and often an ecological one. (For humans, that ecology is usually interpersonal or cultural.) Thus all genetic effects on the development of observable traits are potentially modifiable by environmental input, though the practicability of making such modifications may be another matter. Conversely, all environmental effects on trait development involve the genes or structures to which the genes have contributed. Thus there is always a genetic aspect to the effects of the environment (cf. Plomin & Bergeman, 1991).

SOURCES OF INDIVIDUAL DIFFERENCES

Partitioning the Variation. Individuals differ from one another on a wide variety of traits: familiar examples include height, intelligence, and aspects of personality. Those differences are often of considerable social importance. Many interesting questions can be asked about their nature and origins. One such question is the extent to which they reflect differences among the genes of the individuals involved, as distinguished from differences among the environments to which those individuals have been exposed. The issue here is not whether genes and environments are both essential for the development of a given trait (this is always the case), and it is not about the genes or environment of any particular person. We are concerned only with the observed variation of the trait across individuals in a given population. A figure called the "heritability" (h^2) of the trait represents the proportion of that variation that is associated with genetic differences among the individuals. The remaining variation ($1 - h^2$) is associated with environmental differences and with errors of measurement. These proportions can be estimated by various methods described below.

Sometimes special interest attaches to those aspects of environments that family members have in common (for example, characteristics of the home). The part of the variation that derives from this source, called *shared variation* or c^2, can also be estimated. Still more refined estimates can be made: c^2 is sometimes subdivided into several kinds of shared variation; h^2 is sometimes subdivided into so-called *additive* and *nonadditive* portions (the part that is transmissible from parent to child versus the part expressed anew in each generation by a unique patterning of genes). Variation associated with correlations and statistical interactions between genes and environments may also be identifiable. In theory, any of the above estimates may vary with the age of the individuals involved.

A high heritability does not mean that the environment has no impact on the development of a trait, or that learning is not involved. Vocabulary size, for example, is very substantially heritable (and highly correlated with general psychometric intelligence) although every word in an individual's vocabulary is learned. In a society in which plenty of words are available in everyone's environment—especially for individuals who are motivated to seek them out—the number of words that individuals actually learn depends to a considerable extent on their genetic predispositions.

Behavior geneticists have often emphasized the fact that individuals can be active in creating or selecting their own environments. Some describe this process as active or reactive genotype–environment correlation (Plomin, DeFries, & Loehlin, 1977). (The distinction is between the action of the organism in selecting its own environment and the reaction of others to its gene-based traits.) Others suggest that these forms of gene-environment relationship are typical of the way that genes are normally expressed, and simply include them as part of the genetic effect (Roberts, 1967). This is a matter of terminological preference, not a dispute about facts.

How Genetic Estimates Are Made. Estimates of the magnitudes of these sources of individual differences are made by exploiting natural and social "experiments" that combine genotypes and environments in informative ways. Monozygotic (MZ) and dizygotic (DZ) twins, for example, can be regarded as experiments of nature. MZ twins are paired individuals of the same age growing up in the same family who have all their genes in common; DZ twins are otherwise similar pairs who have only half their genes in common. Adoptions, in contrast, are experiments of society. They allow one to compare genetically unrelated persons who are growing up in the same family as well as genetically related persons who are growing up in different families. They can also provide information about genotype-environment correlations: In ordinary families, genes and environments are correlated because the same parents provide both, whereas in adoptive families one set of parents provides the genes and another the environment. An experiment involving both nature and society is the study of monozygotic twins who have been reared apart (Bouchard, Lykken, McGue, Segal, & Tellegen, 1990; Pedersen, Plomin, Nesselroade, & McClearn, 1992). Relationships in the families of monozygotic twins also offer unique possibilities for analysis (e.g., R. J. Rose, Harris, Christian, & Nance, 1979). Because these comparisons are subject to different sources of potential error, the results of studies involving several kinds of kinship are often analyzed together to arrive at robust overall conclusions. (For general discussions of behavior genetic methods, see Plomin, DeFries, & McClearn, 1990, or Hay, 1985.)

RESULTS FOR IQ SCORES

Parameter Estimates. Across the ordinary range of environments in modern Western societies, a sizable part of the variation in intelligence test scores is associated with genetic differences among individuals. Quantitative estimates vary from one study to another, because many are based on small or selective samples. If one simply combines all available correlations in a single analysis, the heritability (h^2) works out to about .50 and the between-family variance (c^2) to about .25 (e.g., Chipuer, Rovine, & Plomin, 1990; Loehlin, 1989). These overall figures are misleading, however, because most of the relevant studies have been done with children. We now know that the heritability of IQ changes with age: h^2 goes up and c^2 goes down from infancy to adulthood (McCartney, Harris, & Bernieri, 1990; McGue, Bouchard, Iacono, & Lykken, 1993). In childhood h^2 and c^2 for IQ are of the order of .45 and .35; by late adolescence h^2 is around .75 and c^2 is quite low (zero in some studies). Substantial environmental variance remains, but it primarily reflects within-family rather than between-family differences.

These adult parameter estimates are based on a number of independent studies. The correlation between MZ twins reared apart, which directly estimates h^2, ranged from .68 to .78 in five studies involving adult samples from Europe and the United States (McGue et al., 1993). The correlation between unrelated children reared together in adoptive families, which directly estimates c^2, was approximately zero for adolescents in two adoption studies (Loehlin, Horn, & Willerman, 1989; Scarr & Weinberg, 1978) and .19 in a third (the Minnesota transracial adoption study: Scarr, Weinberg, & Waldman, 1993).

These particular estimates derive from samples in which the lowest socioeconomic levels were underrepresented (i.e., there were few very poor families), so the range of between-family differences was smaller than in the population as a whole. This means that we should be cautious in generalizing the findings for between-family effects across the entire social spectrum. The samples were also mostly White, but available data suggest that twin and sibling correlations in African American and similarly selected White samples are more often comparable than not (Loehlin, Lindzey, & Spuhler, 1975).

Why should individual differences in intelligence (as measured by test scores) reflect genetic differences more strongly in adults than they do in children? One possibility is that as individuals grow older, their transactions with their environments are increasingly influenced by the characteristics that they bring to those environments themselves, decreasingly by the conditions imposed by family life and social origins. Older persons are in a better position to select their own effective environments, a form of genotype–environment correlation. In any case the popular view that genetic influences on the development of a trait are essentially frozen at conception while the effects of the early environment cumulate inexorably is quite misleading, at least for the trait of psychometric intelligence.

Implications. Estimates of h^2 and c^2 for IQ (or any other trait) are descriptive statistics for the populations studied. (In this respect, they are like means and standard deviations.) They are outcome measures, summarizing the results of a great many diverse, intricate, individually variable events and processes, but they can nevertheless be quite useful. They can tell us how much of the variation in a given trait the genes and family environments explain, and changes in them place some constraints on theories of how this occurs. On the other hand, they have little to say about specific mechanisms, that is, about how genetic and environmental differences get translated into individual physiological and psychological differences. Many psychologists and neuroscientists are actively studying such processes; data on heritabilities may give them ideas about what to look for and where or when to look for it.

A common error is to assume that because something is heritable, it is necessarily unchangeable. This is wrong. Heritability does not imply immutability. As previously noted, heritable traits can depend on learning, and they may be subject to other environmental effects, as well. The value of h^2 can change if the distribution of environments (or genes) in the population is substantially altered. On the other hand, there can be effective environmental changes that do not change heritability at all. If the environment relevant to a given trait improves in a way that affects all members of the population equally, the mean value of the trait will rise without any change in its heritability (because the differences among individuals in the population will stay the same). This has evidently happened for height: the heritability of stature is high, but average heights continue to increase (Olivier, 1980). Something of the sort may also be taking place for IQ scores—the so-called "Flynn effect" discussed in Section 4.

In theory, different subgroups of a population might have different distributions of environments or genes and hence different values of h^2. This seems not to be the case for high and low IQ levels, for which adult heritabilities appear to be much the same (Saudino, Plomin, Pedersen, & McClearn, 1994). It is also possible that an impoverished or suppressive environment could fail to support the development of a trait, and hence restrict individual variation. This could affect estimates of h^2, c^2, or both, depending on the details of the process. Again (as in the case of whole populations), an environmental factor that affected every member of a subgroup equally might alter the group's mean without affecting heritabilities at all.

Where the heritability of IQ is concerned, it has sometimes seemed as if the findings based on differences between group means were in contradiction with those based on correlations. For example, children adopted in infancy into advantaged families tend to have higher IQs in childhood than would have been expected if they had been reared by their birth mothers; this is a mean difference implicating the environment. Yet at the same time, their individual resemblance to their birth mothers persists, and this correlation is most plausibly interpreted in genetic terms. There is no real contradiction; the two findings simply call attention to different aspects of the same phenomenon. A sensible account must include both aspects; there is only a single developmental process, and it occurs in individuals. By looking at means or correlations one learns somewhat different but compatible things about the genetic and environmental contributions to that process (Turkheimer, 1991).

As far as behavior genetic methods are concerned, there is nothing unique about psychometric intelligence relative to other traits or abilities. Any reliably measured trait can be analyzed by these methods, and many traits including personality and attitudes have been. The methods are neutral with regard to genetic and environmental sources of variance; if individual differences on a trait are entirely due to environmental factors, the analysis will reveal this. These methods have shown that genes contribute substantially to individual differences in intelligence test performance, and that their role seems to increase from infancy to adulthood. They have also shown that variations in the unique environments of individuals are important, and that between-family variation contributes significantly to observed differences in IQ scores in childhood although this effect diminishes later on. All these conclusions are wholly consistent with the notion that both genes and environment, in complex interplay, are essential to the development of intellectual competence.

4. ENVIRONMENTAL EFFECTS ON INTELLIGENCE

The "environment" includes a wide range of influences on intelligence. Some of those variables affect whole populations, while others contribute to individual differences within a given group. Some of them are social, some are biological; at this point, some are still mysterious. It may also happen that the proper interpretation of an environmental variable requires the simultaneous consideration of genetic effects. Nevertheless, a good deal of solid information is available.

SOCIAL VARIABLES

It is obvious that the cultural environment—how people live, what they value, what they do—has a significant effect on the intellectual skills developed by individuals. Rice farmers in Liberia are good at estimating quantities of rice (Gay & Cole, 1967); children in Botswana, accustomed to story-telling, have excellent memories for stories (Dube, 1982). Both these groups were far ahead of American controls on the tasks in question. On the other hand, Americans and other Westernized groups typically outperform members of traditional societies on psychometric tests, even those designed to be "culture-fair."

Cultures typically differ from one another in so many ways that particular differences can rarely be ascribed to single causes. Even comparisons between subpopulations can be difficult to interpret. If we find that middle-class and poor Americans differ in their scores on intelligence tests, it is easy to suppose that the environmental difference has caused the IQ difference (i.e., that growing up in the middle class produces higher psychometric intelligence than growing up poor). But there may also be an opposite direction of causation; individuals can come to be in one environment or another because of differences in their own abilities. Waller (1971) has shown, for example, that adult sons whose IQ scores are above those of their fathers tend to have higher social-class status than those fathers; conversely, sons with IQ scores below their fathers' tend to have lower social-class status. Since all the subjects grew up with their fathers, the IQ differences in this study cannot have resulted from class-related differences in childhood experience. Rather, those differences (or other factors correlated with them) seem to have had an influence on the status that they achieved. Such a result is not surprising, given the relation between test scores and years of education reviewed in Section 2.

Occupation. In Section 2, we noted that intelligence test scores predict occupational level, not only because some occupations require more intelligence than others but also because admission to many professions depends on test scores in the first place. There can also be an effect in the opposite direction, i.e., workplaces may affect the intelligence of those who work in them. Kohn and Schooler (1973), who interviewed some 3,000 men in various occupations (farmers, managers, machinists, porters, etc.), argued that more "complex" jobs produce more "intellectual flexibility" in the individuals who hold them. Although the issue of direction of effects was not fully resolved in their study—and perhaps not even in its longitudinal follow-up (Kohn & Schooler, 1983)—this remains a plausible suggestion.

Among other things, Kohn and Schooler's hypothesis may help us understand urban/rural differences. A generation ago, these were substantial in the United States, averaging about 6 IQ points or 0.4 standard deviations (Terman & Merrill, 1937; Seashore, Wesman, & Doppelt, 1950). In recent years the difference has declined to about 2 points (Kaufman & Doppelt, 1976; Reynolds, Chastain, Kaufman, & McLean, 1987). In all likelihood this urban/rural convergence primarily reflects environmental changes: a decrease in rural isolation (due to increased travel and mass communications), an improvement in rural schools, the greater use of technology on farms. All these changes can be regarded as increasing the "complexity" of the rural environment in general or of farm work in particular. (However, processes with a genetic component—e.g., changes in the selectivity of migration from farm to city—cannot be completely excluded as contributing factors.)

Schooling. Attendance at school is both a dependent and an independent variable in relation to intelligence. On the one hand, children with higher test scores are less likely to drop out and more likely to be promoted from grade to grade and then to attend college. Thus the number of years of education that adults complete is roughly predictable from their childhood scores on intelligence tests. On the other hand, schooling itself changes mental abilities, including those abilities measured on psychometric tests. This is obvious for tests like the SAT that are explicitly designed to assess school learning, but it is almost equally true of intelligence tests themselves.

The evidence for the effect of schooling on intelligence test scores takes many forms (Ceci, 1991). When children of nearly the same age go through school a year apart (because of birthday-related admission criteria), those who have been in school longer have higher mean scores. Children who attend school intermittently score below those who go regularly, and test performance tends to drop over the summer vacation. A striking demonstration of this effect appeared when the schools in one Virginia county closed for several years in the 1960s to avoid integration, leaving most Black children with no formal education at all. Compared to controls, the intelligence-test scores of these children dropped by about 0.4 standard deviations (6 points) per missed year of school (Green, Hoffman, Morse, Hayes, & Morgan, 1964).

Schools affect intelligence in several ways, most obviously by transmitting information. The answers to questions like "Who wrote Hamlet?" and "What is the boiling point of water?" are typically learned in school, where some pupils learn them more easily and thoroughly than others. Perhaps at least as important are certain general skills and attitudes: systematic problem-solving, abstract thinking, categorization, sustained attention to material of little intrinsic interest, and repeated manipulation of basic symbols and operations. There is no doubt that schools promote and permit the development of significant intellectual skills, which develop to different extents in different children. It is because tests of intelligence draw on many of those same skills that they predict school achievement as well as they do.

To achieve these results, the school experience must meet at least some minimum standard of quality. In very poor schools, children may learn so little that they fall farther behind the national IQ norms for every year of attendance. When this happens, older siblings have systematically lower scores than their younger counterparts. This pattern of scores appeared in at least one rural Georgia school system in the 1970s (Jensen, 1977). Before desegregation, it must have been characteristic of many of the schools attended by Black pupils in the South. In a study based on Black children who had moved to Philadelphia at various ages during this period, Lee (1951) found that their IQ scores went up more than half a point for each year that they were enrolled in the Philadelphia system.

Interventions. Intelligence test scores reflect a child's standing relative to others in his or her age cohort. Very poor or interrupted schooling can lower that standing substantially; are there also ways to raise it? In fact many interventions have been shown to raise test scores and mental ability "in the short run" (i.e., while the program itself was in progress), but long-run gains have proved more elusive. One noteworthy example of (at least short-run) success was the Venezuelan Intelligence Project (Herrnstein, Nickerson, de Sanchez, & Swets, 1986), in which hundreds of seventh-grade children from underprivileged backgrounds in that country were exposed to an extensive, theoretically based curriculum focused on thinking skills. The intervention produced substantial gains on a wide range of tests, but there has been no follow-up.

Children who participate in Head Start and similar programs are exposed to various school-related materials and experiences for 1 or 2 years. Their test scores often go up during the course of the program, but these gains fade with time. By the end of elementary school, there are usually no significant IQ or achievement-test differences between children who have been in such programs and controls who have not. There may, however, be other differences. Follow-up studies suggest that children who participated in such programs as preschoolers are less likely to be assigned to special education, less likely to be held back in grade, and more likely to finish high school than matched controls (Consortium for Longitudinal Studies, 1983; Darlington, 1986; but see Locurto, 1991).

More extensive interventions might be expected to produce larger and more lasting effects, but few such programs have been evaluated systematically. One of the more successful is the Carolina Abecedarian Project (Campbell & Ramey, 1994), which provided a group of children with enriched environments from early infancy through preschool and also maintained appropriate controls. The test scores of the enrichment-group children were already higher than those of controls at age 2; they were still some 5 points higher at age 12, 7 years after the end of the intervention. Importantly, the enrichment group also outperformed the controls in academic achievement.

Family Environment. No one doubts that normal child development requires a certain minimum level of responsible care. Severely deprived, neglectful, or abusive environments must have negative effects on a great many aspects—including intellectual aspects—of development. Beyond that minimum, however, the role of family experience is now in serious dispute (Baumrind, 1993; Jackson, 1993; Scarr, 1992, 1993). Psychometric intelligence is a case in point. Do differences between children's family environments (within the normal range) produce differences in their intelligence test performance? The problem here is to disentangle causation from correlation. There is no doubt that such variables as resources of the home (Gottfried, 1984) and parents' use of language (Hart & Risley, 1992, in press) are correlated with children's IQ scores, but such correlations may be mediated by genetics as well as (or instead of) environmental factors.

Behavior geneticists frame such issues in quantitative terms. As noted in Section 3, environmental factors certainly contribute to the overall variance of psychometric intelligence. But how much of that variance results from differences between families, as contrasted with the varying experiences of different children in the same family? Between-family differences create what is called *shared variance* or c^2 (all children in a family share the same home and the same parents). Recent twin and adoption studies suggest that while the value of c^2 (for IQ scores) is substantial in early childhood, it becomes quite small by late adolescence.

These findings suggest that differences in the life styles of families—whatever their importance may be for many aspects of children's lives—make little long-term difference for the skills measured by intelligence tests. We should note, however, that low-income and non-White families are poorly represented in existing adoption studies as well as in most twin samples. Thus, it is not yet clear whether these surprisingly small values of (adolescent) c^2 apply to the population as a whole. It remains possible that, across the full range of income and ethnicity, between-family differences have more lasting consequences for psychometric intelligence.

BIOLOGICAL VARIABLES

Every individual has a biological as well as a social environment, one that begins in the womb and extends throughout life. Many aspects of that environment can affect intellectual development. We now know that a number of biological factors—malnutrition, exposure to toxic substances, various prenatal and perinatal stressors—result in lowered psychometric intelligence under at least some conditions.

Nutrition. There has been only one major study of the effects of prenatal malnutrition (i.e., malnutrition of the mother during pregnancy) on long-term intellectual development. Stein, Susser, Saenger, and Marolla (1975) analyzed the test scores of Dutch 19-year-old males in relation to a wartime famine that had occurred in the winter of 1944–1945, just before their birth. In this very large sample (made possible by a universal military induction requirement), exposure to the famine had no effect on adult intelligence. Note, however, that the famine itself lasted only a few months; the subjects were exposed to it prenatally but not after birth.

In contrast, prolonged malnutrition during childhood does have long-term intellectual effects. These have not been easy to establish, in part because many other unfavorable socioeconomic conditions are often associated with chronic malnutrition (Ricciuti, 1993; but cf. Sigman, 1995). In one intervention study, however, preschoolers in two Guatemalan villages (where undernourishment is common) were given ad lib access to a protein dietary supplement for several years. A decade later, many of these children (namely, those from the poorest socioeconomic levels) scored significantly higher on school-related achievement tests than comparable controls (Pollitt, Gorman, Engle, Martorell, & Rivera, 1993). It is worth noting that the effects of poor nutrition on intelligence may well be indirect. Malnourished children are typically less responsive to adults, less motivated to learn, and less active in exploration than their more adequately nourished counterparts.

Although the degree of malnutrition prevalent in these villages rarely occurs in the United States, there may still be nutritional influences on intelligence. In studies of so-called *micro-nutrients,* experimental groups of children have been given vitamin/mineral supplements while controls got placebos. In many of these studies (e.g., Schoenthaler, Amos, Eysenck, Peritz, & Yudkin, 1991), the experimental children showed test-score gains that significantly exceeded the controls. In a somewhat different design, Rush, Stein, Susser, and Brody (1980) gave dietary supplements of liquid protein to pregnant women who were thought to be at risk for delivering low-birth-weight babies. At 1 year of age, the babies born to these mothers showed faster habituation to visual patterns than did control infants. (Other research has shown that infant habituation rates are positively correlated with later psychometric test scores: Columbo, 1993.) Although these results are encouraging, there has been no long-term follow-up of such gains.

Lead. Certain toxins have well-established negative effects on intelligence. Exposure to lead is one such factor. In one long-term study (Baghurst et al., 1992; McMichael et al., 1988), the blood lead levels of children growing up near a lead smelting plant were substantially and negatively correlated with intelligence test scores throughout childhood. No "threshold dose" for the effect of lead appears in such studies. Although ambient lead levels in the United States have been reduced in recent years, there is reason to believe that some American children—especially those in inner cities—may still be at risk from this source (cf. Needleman, Geiger, & Frank, 1985).

Alcohol. Extensive prenatal exposure to alcohol (which occurs if the mother drinks heavily during pregnancy) can give rise to fetal alcohol syndrome, which includes mental retardation as well as a range of physical symptoms. Smaller "doses" of prenatal alcohol may have negative effects on intelligence even when the full syndrome does not appear. Streissguth, Barr, Sampson, Darby, and Martin (1989) found that mothers who reported consuming more than 1.5 oz. of alcohol daily during pregnancy had children who scored some 5 points below controls at age 4. Prenatal exposure to aspirin and antibiotics had similar negative effects in this study.

Perinatal Factors. Complications at delivery and other negative perinatal factors may have serious consequences for development. Nevertheless, because they occur only rarely, they contribute relatively little to the population variance of intelligence (Broman, Nichols, & Kennedy, 1975). Down syndrome, a chromosomal abnormality that produces serious mental retardation, is also rare enough to have little impact on the overall distribution of test scores.

The correlation between birth weight and later intelligence deserves particular discussion. In some cases, low birth weight simply reflects premature delivery; in others, the infant's size is below normal for its gestational age. Both factors apparently contribute to the tendency of low-birth-weight infants to have lower test scores in later childhood (Lubchenko, 1976). These correlations are small, ranging from .05 to .13 in different groups (Broman et al., 1975). The effects of low birth weight are substantial only when it is very low indeed (less than 1,500 gm). Premature babies born at these very low birth weights are behind controls on most developmental measures; they often have severe or permanent intellectual deficits (Rosetti, 1986).

CONTINUOUSLY RISING TEST SCORES

Perhaps the most striking of all environmental effects is the steady worldwide rise in intelligence test performance. Although many psychometricians had noted these gains, it was James Flynn (1984, 1987) who first described them systematically. His analysis shows that performance has been going up ever since testing began. The "Flynn effect" is now very well-documented, not only in the United States but in many other technologically advanced countries. The average gain is about 3 IQ points per decade—more than a full standard deviation since, say, 1940.

Although it is simplest to describe the gains as increases in population IQ, this is not exactly what happens. Most intelligence tests are "restandardized" from time to time, in part to keep up with these very gains. As part of this process the mean score of the new standardization sample is typically set to 100 again, so the increase more or less disappears from view. In this context, the Flynn effect means that if 20 years have passed since the last time the test was standardized, people who now score 100 on the new version would probably average about 106 on the old one.

The sheer extent of these increases is remarkable, and the rate of gain may even be increasing. The scores of 19-year-olds in the Netherlands, for example, went up more than 8 points—over half a standard deviation—between 1972 and 1982. What's more, the largest gains appear on the types of tests that were specifically designed to be free of cultural influence (Flynn, 1987). One of these is Raven's Progressive Matrices, an untimed, nonverbal test that many psychometricians regard as a good measure of g.

These steady gains in intelligence test performance have not always been accompanied by corresponding gains in school achievement. Indeed, the relation between intelligence and achievement test scores can be complex. This is especially true for the Scholastic Aptitude Test (SAT), in part because the ability range of the students who take the SAT has broadened over time. That change explains some portion—not all—of the prolonged decline in SAT scores that took place from the mid-1960s to the early 1980s, even as IQ scores were continuing to rise (Flynn, 1984). Meanwhile, however, other more representative measures show that school achievement levels have held steady or in some cases actually increased (Herrnstein & Murray, 1994). The National Assessment of Educational Progress (NAEP), for example, shows that the average reading and math achievement of American 13- and 17-year-olds improved somewhat from the early 1970s to 1990 (Grissmer, Kirby, Berends, & Williamson, 1994). An analysis of these data by ethnic group, reported in Section 5, shows that this small overall increase actually reflects very substantial gains by Blacks and Latinos combined with little or no gain by Whites.

The consistent IQ gains documented by Flynn seem much too large to result from simple increases in test sophistication. Their cause is presently unknown, but three interpretations deserve our consideration. Perhaps the most plausible of these is based on the striking cultural differences between successive generations. Daily life and occupational experience both seem more "complex" (Kohn & Schooler, 1973) today than in the time of our parents and grandparents. The population is increasingly urbanized; television exposes us to more information and more perspectives on more topics than ever before; children stay in school longer; and almost everyone seems to be encountering new forms of experience. These changes in the complexity of life may have produced corresponding changes in complexity of mind, and hence in certain psychometric abilities.

A different hypothesis attributes the gains to modern improvements in nutrition. Lynn (1990) points out that large, nutritionally based increases in height have occurred during the same period as the IQ gains; perhaps there have been increases in brain size, as well. As we have seen, however, the effects of nutrition on intelligence are themselves not firmly established.

The third interpretation addresses the very definition of intelligence. Flynn himself believes that real intelligence—whatever it may be—cannot have increased as much as these data would suggest. Consider, for example, the number of individuals who have IQ scores of 140 or more. (This is slightly above the cutoff used by L. M. Terman [1925] in his famous longitudinal study of "genius.") In 1952, only 0.38% of Dutch test-takers had IQs over 140; in 1982, scored by the same norms, 9.12% exceeded this figure! Judging by these criteria, the Netherlands should now be experiencing "a cultural renaissance too great to be overlooked" (Flynn, 1987, p. 187). So too should France, Norway, the United States, and many other countries. Because Flynn (1987) finds this conclusion implausible or absurd, he argues that what has risen cannot be intelligence itself but only a minor sort of "abstract problem solving ability." The issue remains unresolved.

INDIVIDUAL LIFE EXPERIENCES

Although the environmental variables that produce large differences in intelligence are not yet well-understood, genetic studies assure us that they exist. With a heritability well below 1.00, IQ must be subject to substantial environmental influences. Moreover, available heritability estimates apply only within the range of environments that are well-represented in the present population. We already know that some relatively rare conditions, like those reviewed earlier, have large negative effects on intelligence. Whether there are (now equally rare) conditions that have large positive effects is not known.

As we have seen, there is both a biological and a social environment. For any given child, the social factors include not only an overall cultural/social/school setting and a particular family but also a unique "micro-environment" of experiences that are shared with no one else. The adoption studies reviewed in Section 3 show that family variables—differences in parenting style, in the resources of the home, etc.— have smaller long-term effects than we once supposed. At least among people who share a given SES level and a given culture, it seems to be unique individual experience that makes the largest environmental contribution to adult IQ differences.

We do not yet know what the key features of those micro-environments may be. Are they biological? Social? Chronic? Acute? Is there something especially important in the earliest relations between the infant and its caretakers? Whatever the critical variables may be, do they interact with other aspects of family life? Of culture? At this point we cannot say, but these questions offer a fertile area for further research.

5. GROUP DIFFERENCES

Group means have no direct implications for individuals. What matters for the next person you meet (to the extent that test scores matter at all) is that person's own particular score, not the mean of some reference group to which he or she happens to belong. The commitment to evaluate people on their own individual merit is central to a democratic society. It also makes quantitative sense. The distributions of different groups inevitably overlap, with the range of scores within any one group always wider than the mean differences between any two groups. In the case of intelligence test scores, the variance attributable to individual differences far exceeds the variance related to group membership (Jensen, 1980).

Because claims about ethnic differences have often been used to rationalize racial discrimination in the past, all such claims must be subjected to very careful scrutiny. Nevertheless, group differences continue to be the subject of intense interest and debate. There are many reasons for this interest; some are legal and political, some social and psychological. Among other things, facts about group differences may be relevant to the need for (and the effectiveness of) affirmative action programs. But while some recent discussions of intelligence and ethnic differences (e.g., Herrnstein & Murray, 1994) have made specific policy recommendations in this area, we will not do so here. Such recommendations are necessarily based on political as well as scientific considerations, and so fall outside the scope of this report.

Besides European Americans ("Whites"), the ethnic groups to be considered are Chinese and Japanese Americans, Hispanic Americans ("Latinos"), Native Americans ("Indians"), and African Americans ("Blacks"). These groups (we avoid the term *race*) are defined and self-defined by social conventions based on ethnic origin as well as on observable physical characteristics such as skin color. None of them are internally homogeneous. Asian Americans, for example, may have roots in many different cultures: not only China and Japan but also Korea, Laos, Vietnam, the Philippines, India, and Pakistan. Hispanic Americans, who share a common linguistic tradition, actually differ along many cultural dimensions. In their own minds they may be less "Latinos" than Puerto Ricans, Mexican Americans, Cuban Americans, or representatives of other Latin cultures. "Native American" is an even more diverse category, including a great many culturally distinct tribes living in a wide range of environments.

Although males and females are not ethnic or cultural groups, possible sex differences in cognitive ability have also been the subject of widespread interest and discussion. For this reason, the evidence relevant to such differences is briefly reviewed in the next section.

SEX DIFFERENCES

Most standard tests of intelligence have been constructed so that there are no overall score differences between females and males. Some recent studies do report sex differences in IQ, but the direction is variable and the effects are small (Held, Alderton, Foley, & Segall, 1993; Lynn, 1994). This overall equivalence does not imply equal performance on every individual ability. While some tasks show no sex differences, there are others where small differences appear and a few where they are large and consistent.

Spatial and Quantitative Abilities. Large differences favoring males appear on visual–spatial tasks like mental rotation and spatiotemporal tasks like tracking a moving object through space (Law, Pellegrino, & Hunt, 1993; Linn & Petersen, 1985). The sex difference on mental rotation tasks is substantial: a recent meta-analysis (Masters & Sanders, 1993) puts the effect size at $d = 0.9$. (Effect sizes are measured in standard deviation units. Here, the mean of the male distribution is nearly 1 standard deviation above that for females.) Males' achievement levels on movement-related and visual–spatial tests are relevant to their generally better performance in tasks that involve aiming and throwing (Jardine & Martin, 1983).

Some quantitative abilities also show consistent differences. Females have a clear advantage on quantitative tasks in the early years of school (Hyde, Fennema, & Lamon, 1990), but this reverses sometime before puberty; males then maintain their superior performance into old age. The math portion of the Scholastic Aptitude Test shows a substantial advantage for males ($d = 0.33$ to 0.50), with many more males scoring in the highest ranges (Benbow, 1988; Halpern, 1992). Males also score consistently higher on tests of proportional and mechanical reasoning (Meehan, 1984; Stanley, Benbow, Brody, Dauber, & Lupkowski, 1992).

Verbal Abilities. Some verbal tasks show substantial mean differences favoring females. These include synonym generation and verbal fluency (e.g., naming words that start with a given letter), with effect sizes ranging from $d = 0.5$ to 1.2 (Gordon & Lee, 1986; Hines, 1990). On average females score higher on college achievement tests in literature, English composition, and Spanish (Stanley, 1993); they also excel at reading and spelling. Many more males than females are diagnosed with dyslexia and other reading disabilities (Sutaria, 1985), and there are many more male stutterers (Yairi & Ambrose, 1992). Some memory tasks also show better performance by females, but the size (and perhaps even the direction) of the effect varies with the type of memory being assessed.

Causal Factors. There are both social and biological reasons for these differences. At the social level, there are both subtle and overt differences between the experiences, expectations, and gender roles of females and males. Relevant environmental differences appear soon after birth. They range from the gender-differentiated toys that children regularly receive to the expectations of adult life with which they are presented, from gender-differentiated household and leisure activities to assumptions about differences in basic ability. Models that include many of these psychosocial variables have been successful in predicting academic achievement (Eccles, 1987).

Many biological variables are also relevant. One focus of current research is on differences in the sizes or shapes of particular neural structures. Numerous sexually dimorphic brain structures have now been identified, and they may well have implications for cognition. There are, for example, sex-related differences in the sizes of some portions of the corpus callosum; these differences are correlated with verbal fluency (Hines, Chiu, McAdams, Bentler, & Lipcamon, 1992). Recent brain imaging studies have found what may be differences in the lateralization of language (Shaywitz et al., 1995). Note that such differences in neural structure could result from differences in patterns of life experience as well as from genetically driven mechanisms of brain development; moreover, brain development and experience may have bidirectional effects on each other. This research area is still in a largely exploratory phase.

Hormonal Influences. The importance of prenatal exposure to sex hormones is well-established. Hormones influence not only the developing genitalia but also the brain and certain immune system structures (Geschwind & Galaburda, 1987; Halpern & Cass, 1994). Several studies have tested individuals who were exposed to abnormally high androgen levels in utero, due to a condition known as congenital adrenal hyperplasia (CAH). Adult CAH females score significantly higher than controls on tests of spatial ability (Resnick, Berenbaum, Gottesman, & Bouchard, 1986); CAH girls play more with "boys' toys" and less with "girls' toys" than controls (Berenbaum & Hines, 1992).

Other experimental paradigms confirm the relevance of sex hormones for performance levels in certain skills. Christiansen and Knussmann (1987) found testosterone levels in normal males to be correlated positively (about .20) with some measures of spatial ability and negatively (about −.20) with some measures of verbal ability. Older males given testosterone show improved performance on visual–spatial tests (Janowsky, Oviatt, & Orwoll, 1994). Many similar findings have been reported, though the effects are often nonlinear and complex (Gouchie & Kimura, 1991; Nyborg, 1984). It is clear that any adequate model of sex differences in cognition will have to take both biological and psychological variables (and their interactions) into account.

MEAN SCORES OF DIFFERENT ETHNIC GROUPS

Asian Americans. In the years since the Second World War, Asian Americans—especially those of Chinese and Japanese extraction—have compiled an outstanding record of academic and professional achievement. This record is reflected in school grades, in scores on content-oriented achievement tests like the SAT and GRE, and especially in the disproportionate representation of Asian Americans in many sciences and professions. Although it is often supposed that these achievements reflect correspondingly high intelligence test scores, this is not the case. In more than a dozen studies from the 1960s and 1970s analyzed by Flynn (1991), the mean IQs of Japanese and Chinese American children were always around 97 or 98; none was over 100. Even Lynn (1993), who argues for a slightly higher figure, concedes that the achievements of these Asian Americans far outstrip what might have been expected on the basis of their test scores.

It may be worth noting that the interpretation of test scores obtained by Asians in Asia has been controversial in its own right. Lynn (1982) reported a mean Japanese IQ of 111 while Flynn (1991) estimated it to be between 101 and 105. Stevenson et al. (1985), comparing the intelligence-test performance of children in Japan, Taiwan, and the United States, found no substantive differences at all. Given the general problems of cross-cultural comparison, there is no reason to expect precision or stability in such estimates. Nevertheless, some interest attaches to these particular comparisons; they show that the well-established differences in school achievement among the same three groups (Chinese and Japanese children are much better at math than American children) do not simply reflect differences in psychometric intelligence. Stevenson, Lee, and Stigler (1986) suggest that they result from structural differences in the schools of the three nations as well as from varying cultural attitudes toward learning itself. It is also possible that spatial ability—in which Japanese and Chinese obtain somewhat higher scores than Americans—plays a particular role in the learning of mathematics.

One interesting way to assess the achievements of Chinese and Japanese Americans is to reverse the usual direction of prediction. Data from the 1980 census show that the proportion of Chinese Americans employed in managerial, professional, or technical occupations was 55% and that of Japanese was 46%. (For Whites, the corresponding figure was 34%.) Using the well-established correlation between intelligence test scores and occupational level, Flynn (1991, p. 99) calculated the mean IQ that a hypothetical White group "would have to have" to predict the same proportions of upper-level employment. He found that the occupational success of these Chinese Americans—whose mean IQ was in fact slightly below 100—was what would be expected of a White group with an IQ of almost 120! A similar calculation for Japanese Americans shows that their level of achievement matched that of Whites averaging 110. These "overachievements" serve as sharp reminders of the limitations of IQ-based prediction. Various aspects of Chinese American and Japanese American culture surely contribute to them (Schneider, Hieshima, Lee, & Plank, 1994); gene-based temperamental factors could conceivably be playing a role, as well (Freedman & Freedman, 1969).

Hispanic Americans. Hispanic immigrants have come to America from many countries. In 1993, the largest Latino groups in the continental United States were Mexican Americans (64%), Puerto Ricans (11%), Central and South Americans (13%), and Cubans (5%) (U. S. Bureau of the Census, 1994). There are very substantial cultural differences among these nationality groups, as well as differences in academic achievement (Duran, 1983: United States National Commission for Employment Policy, 1982). Taken together, Latinos make up the second largest and the fastest-growing minority group in America (Davis, Haub, & Willette, 1983; Eyde, 1992).

In the United States, the mean intelligence test scores of Hispanics typically lie between those of Blacks and Whites. There are also differences in the patterning of scores across different abilities and subtests (Hennessy & Merrifield, 1978; Lesser, Fifer, & Clark, 1965). Linguistic factors play a particularly important role for Hispanic Americans, who may know relatively little English. (By one estimate, 25% of Puerto Ricans and Mexican Americans and at least 40% of Cubans speak English "not well" or "not at all" [Rodriguez, 1992]). Even those who describe themselves as bilingual may be at a disadvantage if Spanish was their first and best-learned language. It is not surprising that Latino children typically score higher on the performance than on the verbal subtests of the English-based Wechsler Intelligence Scale for Children—Revised (WISC–R: Kaufman, 1994). Nevertheless, the predictive validity of Latino test scores is not negligible. In young children, the WISC–R has reasonably high correlations with school achievement measures (McShane & Cook, 1985). For high school students of moderate to high English proficiency, standard aptitude tests predict first-year college grades about as well as they do for non-Hispanic Whites (Pennock-Roman, 1992).

Native Americans. There are a great many culturally distinct North American Indian tribes (Driver, 1969), speaking some 200 different languages (Leap, 1981). Many Native Americans live on reservations, which themselves represent a great variety of ecological and cultural settings. Many others presently live in metropolitan areas (Brandt, 1984). Although few generalizations can be appropriate across so wide a range, two or three points seem fairly well-established. The first is a specific relation between ecology and cognition: The Inuit (Eskimo) and other groups that live in the arctic tend to have particularly high visual–spatial skills. (For a review see McShane & Berry, 1988.) Moreover, there seem to be no substantial sex differences in those skills (Berry, 1974). It seems likely that this represents an adaptation—genetic or learned or both—to the difficult hunting, traveling, and living conditions that characterize the arctic environment.

On the average, Indian children obtain relatively low scores on tests of verbal intelligence, which are often administered in school settings. The result is a performance-test/verbal-test discrepancy similar to that exhibited by Hispanic Americans and other groups whose first language is generally not English. Moreover, many Indian children suffer from chronic middle-ear infection (otitis media), which is "the leading identifiable disease among Indians since record-keeping began in 1962" (McShane & Plas, 1984a, p. 84). Hearing loss can have marked negative effects on verbal test performance (McShane & Plas, 1984b).

African Americans. The relatively low mean of the distribution of African American intelligence test scores has been discussed for many years. Although studies using different tests and samples yield a range of results, the Black mean is typically about one standard deviation (about 15 points) below that of Whites (Jensen, 1980; Loehlin et al., 1975; Reynolds et al., 1987). The difference is largest on those tests (verbal or nonverbal) that best represent the general intelligence factor g (Jensen, 1985). It is possible, however, that this differential is diminishing. In the most recent restandardization of the Stanford-Binet test, the Black/White differential was 13 points for younger children and 10 points for older children (Thorndike, Hagen, & Sattler, 1986). In several other studies of children since 1980, the Black mean has consistently been over 90 and the differential has been in single digits (Vincent, 1991). Larger and more definitive studies are needed before this trend can be regarded as established.

Another reason to think the IQ mean might be changing is that the Black/White differential in *achievement* scores has diminished substantially in the last few years.

Consider, for example, the mathematics achievement of 17-year-olds as measured by the National Assessment of Educational Progress (NAEP). The differential between Black and White scores, about 1.1 standard deviations as recently as 1978, had shrunk to .65 *SD* by 1990 (Grissmer et al., 1994) because of Black gains. Hispanics showed similar but smaller gains; there was little change in the scores of Whites. Other assessments of school achievement also show substantial recent gains in the performance of minority children.

In their own analysis of these gains, Grissmer et al. (1994) cite both demographic factors and the effects of public policy. They found the level of parents' education to be a particularly good predictor of children's school achievement; that level increased for all groups between 1970 and 1990, but most sharply for Blacks. Family size was another good predictor (children from smaller families tend to achieve higher scores); here too, the largest change over time was among Blacks. Above and beyond these demographic effects, Grissmer et al. believe that some of the gains can be attributed to the many specific programs, geared to the education of minority children, that were implemented during that period.

Test Bias. It is often argued that the lower mean scores of African Americans reflect a bias in the intelligence tests themselves. This argument is right in one sense of *bias* but wrong in another. To see the first of these, consider how the term is used in probability theory. When a coin comes up heads consistently for any reason, it is said to be "biased," regardless of any consequences that the outcome may or may not have. In this sense the Black/White score differential is *ipso facto* evidence of what may be called *outcome bias.* African Americans are subject to outcome bias not only with respect to tests but along many dimensions of American life. They have the short end of nearly every stick: average income, representation in high-level occupations, health and health care, death rate, confrontations with the legal system, and so on. With this situation in mind, some critics regard the test score differential as just another example of a pervasive outcome bias that characterizes our society as a whole (Jackson, 1975; Mercer, 1984). Although there is a sense in which they are right, this critique ignores the particular social purpose that tests are designed to serve.

From an educational point of view, the chief function of mental tests is as *predictors* (Section 2). Intelligence tests predict school performance fairly well, at least in American schools as they are now constituted. Similarly, achievement tests are fairly good predictors of performance in college and postgraduate settings. Considered in this light, the relevant question is whether the tests have a "predictive bias" against Blacks. Such a bias would exist if African American performance on the criterion variables (school achievement, college GPA, etc.) were systematically higher than the same subjects' test scores would predict. This is not the case. The actual regression lines (which show the mean criterion performance for individuals who got various scores on the predictor) for Blacks do not lie above those for Whites; there is even a slight tendency in the other direction (Jensen, 1980; Reynolds & Brown, 1984). Considered as predictors of future performance, the tests do not seem to be biased against African Americans.

Characteristics of Tests. It has been suggested that various aspects of the way tests are formulated and administered may put African Americans at a disadvantage. The language of testing is a standard form of English with which some Blacks may not be familiar; specific vocabulary items are often unfamiliar to Black children; the tests are often given by White examiners rather than by more familiar Black teachers; African Americans may not be motivated to work hard on tests that so clearly reflect White values; the time demands of some tests may be alien to Black culture. (Similar suggestions have been made in connection with the test performance of Hispanic Americans, e.g., Rodriguez, 1992.) Many of these suggestions are plausible, and such mechanisms may play a role in particular cases. Controlled studies have shown, however, that none of them contributes substantially to the Black/White differential under discussion here (Jensen, 1980; Reynolds & Brown, 1984; for a different view see Helms, 1992). Moreover, efforts to devise reliable and valid tests that would minimize disadvantages of this kind have been unsuccessful.

INTERPRETING GROUP DIFFERENCES

If group differences in test performance do not result from the simple forms of bias reviewed above, what is responsible for them? The fact is that we do not know. Various explanations have been proposed, but none is generally accepted. It is clear, however, that these differences—whatever their origin—are well within the range of effect sizes that can be produced by environmental factors. The Black/White differential amounts to 1 standard deviation or less, and we know that environmental factors have recently raised mean test scores in many populations by at least that much (Flynn, 1987; see Section 4). To be sure, the "Flynn effect" is itself poorly understood. It may reflect generational changes in culture, improved nutrition, or other factors as yet unknown. Whatever may be responsible for it, we cannot exclude the possibility that the same factors play a role in contemporary group differences.

Socioeconomic Factors. Several specific environmental/cultural explanations of those differences have been proposed. All of them refer to the general life situation in which contemporary African Americans find themselves, but that situation can be described in several different ways. The simplest such hypothesis can be framed in economic terms. On the average, Blacks have lower incomes than Whites; a much higher proportion of them are poor. It is plausible to suppose that many inevitable aspects of poverty—poor nutrition, frequently inadequate prenatal care, lack of intellectual resources—have negative effects on children's developing intelligence. Indeed, the correlation between "socioeconomic status" (SES) and scores on intelligence tests is well-known (White, 1982).

Several considerations suggest that this cannot be the whole explanation. For one thing, the Black/White differential in test scores is not eliminated when groups or individuals are matched for SES (Loehlin et al., 1975). Moreover, the data reviewed in Section 4 suggest that—if we exclude extreme conditions—nutrition and other biological factors that may vary with SES account for relatively little of the variance in such scores. Finally, the (relatively weak) relationship between test scores and income is much more complex than a simple SES hypothesis would suggest. The living conditions of children result in part from the accomplishments of their parents: If the skills measured by psychometric tests actually matter for those accomplishments, intelligence is affecting SES rather than the other way around. We do not know the magnitude of these various effects in various populations, but it is clear that no model in which SES directly determines IQ will do.

A more fundamental difficulty with explanations based on economics alone appears from a different perspective. To imagine that any simple income- and education-based index can adequately describe the situation of African Americans is to ignore important categories of experience. The sense of belonging to a group with a distinctive culture—one that has long been the target of oppression—and the awareness or anticipation of racial discrimination are profound personal experiences, not just aspects of socioeconomic status. Some of these more deeply rooted differences are addressed by other hypotheses, based on caste and culture.

Caste-Like Minorities. Most discussions of this issue treat Black/White differences as aspects of a uniquely "American dilemma" (Myrdal, 1944). The fact is, however, that comparably disadvantaged groups exist in many countries: the Maori in New Zealand, scheduled castes ("untouchables") in India, non-European Jews in Israel, the Burakumin in Japan. All these are "caste-like" (Ogbu, 1978) or "involuntary" (Ogbu, 1994) minorities. John Ogbu distinguishes this status from that of "autonomous" minorities who are not politically or economically subordinated (like Amish or Mormons in the United States), and from that of "immigrant" or "voluntary" minorities who initially came to their new homes with positive expectations. Immigrant minorities expect their situations to improve; they tend to compare themselves favorably with peers in the old country, not unfavorably with members of the dominant majority. In contrast, to be born into a caste-like minority is to grow up firmly convinced that one's life will eventually be restricted to a small and poorly rewarded set of social roles.

Distinctions of caste are not always linked to perceptions of race. In some countries, lower and upper caste groups differ by appearance and are assumed to be racially distinct; in others they are not. The social and educational consequences are the same in both cases. All over the world, the children of caste-like minorities do less well in school than upper-caste children and drop out sooner. Where there are data, they have usually been found to have lower test scores, as well.

In explaining these findings, Ogbu (1978) argues that the children of caste-like minorities do not have "effort optimism," that is, the conviction that hard work (especially hard schoolwork) and serious commitment on their part will actually be rewarded. As a result, they ignore or reject the forms of learning that are offered in school. Indeed, they may practice a sort of cultural inversion, deliberately rejecting certain behaviors (such as academic achievement or other forms of "acting White") that are seen as characteristic of the dominant group. While the extent to which the attitudes described by Ogbu (1978, 1994) are responsible for African American test scores and school achievement has not been empirically established, it does seem that familiar problems can take on quite a different look when they are viewed from an international perspective.

African American Culture. According to Boykin (1986, 1994), there is a fundamental conflict between certain aspects of African American culture on the one hand and the implicit cultural commitments of most American schools on the other. "When children are ordered to do their own work, arrive at their own individual answers, work only with their own materials, they are being sent cultural messages. When children come to believe that getting up and moving about the classroom is inappropriate, they are being sent powerful cultural messages. When children come to confine their 'learning' to consistently bracketed time periods, when they are consistently prompted to tell what they know and not how they feel, when they are led to believe that they are completely responsible for their own success and failure, when they are required to consistently put forth considerable effort for effort's sake on tedious and personally irrelevant tasks . . . then they are pervasively having cultural lessons imposed on them" (1994, p. 125).

In Boykin's view, the combination of constriction and competition that most American schools demand of their pupils conflicts with certain themes in the "deep structure" of African American culture. That culture includes an emphasis on such aspects of experience as spirituality, harmony, movement, verve, affect, expressive individualism, communalism, orality, and a socially defined time perspective (Boykin, 1986, 1994). While it is not shared by all African Americans to the same degree, its accessibility and familiarity give it a profound influence.

The result of this cultural conflict, in Boykin's view, is that many Black children become alienated from both the process and the products of the education to which they are exposed. One aspect of that process, now an intrinsic aspect of the culture of most American schools, is the psychometric enterprise itself. He argues (Boykin, 1994) that the successful education of African American children will require an approach that is less concerned with talent sorting and assessment, more concerned with talent development.

One further factor should not be overlooked. Only a single generation has passed since the Civil Rights movement opened new doors for African Americans, and many forms of discrimination are still all too familiar in their experience today. Hard enough to bear in its own right, discrimination is also a sharp reminder of a still more intolerable past. It would be rash indeed to assume that those experiences, and that historical legacy, have no impact on intellectual development.

The Genetic Hypothesis. It is sometimes suggested that the Black/White differential in psychometric intelligence is partly due to genetic differences (Jensen, 1972). There is not much direct evidence on this point, but what little there is fails to support the genetic hypothesis. One piece of evidence comes from a study of the children of American soldiers stationed in Germany after the Second World War (Eyferth, 1961): There was no mean difference between the test scores of those children whose fathers were White and those whose fathers were Black. (For a discussion of possible confounds in this study, see Flynn, 1980.) Moreover, several studies have used blood-group methods to estimate the degree of African ancestry of American Blacks; there were no significant correlations between those estimates and IQ scores (Loehlin, Vandenberg, & Osborne, 1973; Scarr, Pakstis, Katz, & Barker, 1977).

It is clear (Section 3) that genes make a substantial contribution to individual differences in intelligence test scores, at least in the White population. The fact is, however, that the high heritability of a trait within a given group has no necessary implications for the source of a difference between groups (Loehlin et al., 1975). This is now generally understood (e.g., Herrnstein & Murray, 1994). But even though no such implication is *necessary,* some have argued that a high value of h^2 makes a genetic contribution to group differences more *plausible*. Does it?

That depends on one's assessment of the actual difference between the two environments. Consider Lewontin's (1970) well-known example of seeds from the same genetically variable stock that are planted in two different fields. If the plants in field X are fertilized appropriately while key nutrients are withheld from those in field Y, we have produced an entirely environmental group difference. This example works (i.e., h^2 is genuinely irrelevant to the differential between the fields) because the differences between the effective environments of X and Y are both large and consistent. Are the environmental and cultural situations of American Blacks and Whites also substantially and consistently different—different enough to make this a good analogy? If so, the within-group heritability of IQ scores is irrelevant to the issue. Or are those situations similar enough to suggest that the analogy is inappropriate, and that one can plausibly generalize from within-group heritabilities? Thus the issue ultimately comes down to a personal judgment: How different are the relevant life experiences of Whites and Blacks in the United States today? At present, this question has no scientific answer.

6. Summary and Conclusions

Because there are many ways to be intelligent, there are also many conceptualizations of intelligence. The most influential approach, and the one that has generated the most systematic research, is based on psychometric testing. This tradition has produced a substantial body of knowledge, though many questions remain unanswered. We know much less about the forms of intelligence that tests do not easily assess: wisdom, creativity, practical knowledge, social skill, and the like.

Psychometricians have successfully measured a wide range of abilities, distinct from one another and yet intercorrelated. The complex relations among those abilities can be described in many ways. Some theorists focus on the variance that all such abilities have in common, which Spearman termed g ("general intelligence"); others prefer to describe the same manifold with a set of partially independent factors; still others opt for a multifactorial description with factors hierarchically arranged and something like g at the top. Standardized intelligence test scores ("IQs"), which reflect a person's standing in relation to his or her age cohort, are based on tests that tap a number of different abilities. Recent studies have found that these scores are also correlated with information processing speed in certain experimental paradigms (choice reaction time, inspection time, evoked brain potentials, etc.), but the meaning of those correlations is far from clear.

Intelligence test scores predict individual differences in school achievement moderately well, correlating about .50 with grade point average and .55 with the number of years of education that individuals complete. In this context, the skills measured by tests are clearly important. Nevertheless, population levels of school achievement are not determined solely or even primarily by intelligence or any other individual-difference variable. The fact that children in Japan and Taiwan learn much more mathematics than their peers in America, for example, can be attributed primarily to differences in culture and schooling rather than in abilities measured by intelligence tests.

Test scores also correlate with measures of accomplishment outside of school, e.g., with adult occupational status. To some extent those correlations result directly from the tests' link with school achievement and from their roles as "gatekeepers." In the United States today, high test scores and grades are prerequisites for entry into many careers and professions. This is not quite the whole story, however; a significant correlation between psychometric intelligence and occupational status remains, even when measures of education and family background have been statistically controlled. There are also modest (negative) correlations between intelligence test scores and certain undesirable behaviors such as juvenile crime. Those correlations are necessarily low; all social outcomes result from complex causal webs in which psychometric skills are only one factor.

Like every trait, intelligence is the joint product of genetic and environmental variables. Gene action always involves a (biochemical or social) environment; environments always act via structures to which genes have contributed. Given a trait on which individuals vary, however, one can ask what fraction of that variation is associated with differences in their genotypes (this is the *heritability* of the trait) as well as what fraction is associated with differences in environmental experience. So defined, heritability (h^2) can and does vary from one population to another. In the case of IQ, h^2 is markedly lower for children (about .45) than for adults (about .75). This means that as children grow up, differences in test scores tend increasingly to reflect differences in genotype and in individual life experience rather than differences among the families in which they were raised.

The factors underlying that shift—and more generally the pathways by which genes make their undoubted contributions to individual differences in intelligence—are largely unknown. Moreover, the environmental contributions to those differences are almost equally mysterious. We know that both biological and social aspects of the environment are important for intelligence, but we are a long way from understanding how they exert their effects.

One environmental variable with clear-cut importance is the presence of formal schooling. Schools affect intelligence in many ways, not only by transmitting specific information but by developing certain intellectual skills and attitudes. Failure to attend school (or attendance at very poor schools) has a clear negative effect on intelligence test scores. Preschool programs and similar interventions often have positive effects, but in most cases the gains fade when the program is over.

A number of conditions in the biological environment have clear negative consequences for intellectual development. Some of these—very important when they occur—nevertheless do not contribute much to the population variance of IQ scores because they are relatively rare. (Perinatal complications are one such factor.) Exposure to environmental lead has well-documented negative effects; so too does prenatal exposure to high blood levels of alcohol. Malnutrition in childhood is another negative factor for intelligence, but the level at which its effects become significant has not been clearly established. Some studies suggest that dietary supplements of certain micro-nutrients can produce gains, even in otherwise well-nourished individuals, but the effects are still controversial, and there has been no long-term follow-up.

One of the most striking phenomena in this field is the steady worldwide rise in test scores, now often called the "Flynn effect." Mean IQs have increased more than 15 points—a full standard deviation—in the last 50 years, and the rate of gain may be increasing. These gains may result from improved nutrition, cultural changes, experience with testing, shifts in schooling or child-rearing practices, or some other factor as yet unknown.

Although there are no important sex differences in overall intelligence test scores, substantial differences do appear for specific abilities. Males typically score higher on visual–spatial and (beginning in middle childhood) mathematical skills; females excel on a number of verbal measures. Sex hormone levels are clearly related to some of these differences, but social factors presumably play a role, as well. As for all the group differences reviewed here, the range of performance within each group is much larger than the mean difference between groups.

Because ethnic differences in intelligence reflect complex patterns, no overall generalization about them is appropriate. The mean IQ scores of Chinese and Japanese Americans, for example, differ little from those of Whites though their spatial ability scores tend to be somewhat higher. The outstanding record of these groups in terms of school achievement and occupational status evidently reflects cultural factors. The mean intelligence test scores of Hispanic Americans are somewhat lower than those of Whites, in part because Hispanics are often less familiar with English. Nevertheless, their test scores, like those of African Americans, are reasonably good predictors of school and college achievement.

African American IQ scores have long averaged about 15 points below those of Whites, with correspondingly lower scores on academic achievement tests. In recent years, the achievement-test gap has narrowed appreciably. It is possible that the IQ-score differential is narrowing, as well, but this has not been clearly established. The cause of that differential is not known; it is apparently not due to any simple form of bias in the content or administration of the tests themselves. The Flynn effect shows that environmental factors can produce differences of at least this magnitude, but that effect is mysterious in its own right. Several culturally based explanations of the Black/White IQ differential have been proposed; some are plausible, but so far none has been conclusively supported. There is even less empirical support for a genetic interpretation. In short, no adequate explanation of the differential between the IQ means of Blacks and Whites is presently available.

It is customary to conclude surveys like this one with a summary of what has been established. Indeed, much is now known about intelligence. A near-century of research, most of it based on psychometric methods, has produced an impressive body of findings. Although we have tried to do justice to those findings in this report, it seems appropriate to conclude on a different note. In this contentious arena, our most useful role may be to remind our readers that many of the critical questions about intelligence are still unanswered. Here are a few of those questions.

1. Differences in genetic endowment contribute substantially to individual differences in (psychometric) intelligence, but the pathway by which genes produce

their effects is still unknown. The impact of genetic differences appears to increase with age, but we do not know why.

2. Environmental factors also contribute substantially to the development of intelligence, but we do not clearly understand what those factors are or how they work. Attendance at school is certainly important, for example, but we do not know what aspects of schooling are critical.

3. The role of nutrition in intelligence remains obscure. Severe childhood malnutrition has clear negative effects, but the hypothesis that particular "micro-nutrients" may affect intelligence in otherwise adequately fed populations has not yet been convincingly demonstrated.

4. There are significant correlations between measures of information-processing speed and psychometric intelligence, but the overall pattern of these findings yields no easy theoretical interpretation.

5. Mean scores on intelligence tests are rising steadily. They have gone up a full standard deviation in the last 50 years or so, and the rate of gain may be increasing. No one is sure why these gains are happening or what they mean.

6. The differential between the mean intelligence test scores of Blacks and Whites (about 1 standard deviation, although it may be diminishing) does not result from any obvious biases in test construction and administration, nor does it simply reflect differences in socioeconomic status. Explanations based on factors of caste and culture may be appropriate, but so far have little direct empirical support. There is certainly no such support for a genetic interpretation. At present, no one knows what causes this differential.

7. It is widely agreed that standardized tests do not sample all forms of intelligence. Obvious examples include creativity, wisdom, practical sense, and social sensitivity; there are surely others. Despite the importance of these abilities, we know very little about them: how they develop, what factors influence that development, how they are related to more traditional measures.

In a field where so many issues are unresolved and so many questions unanswered, the confident tone that has characterized most of the debate on these topics is clearly out of place. The study of intelligence does not need politicized assertions and recriminations; it needs self-restraint, reflection, and a great deal more research. The questions that remain are socially as well as scientifically important. There is no reason to think them unanswerable, but finding the answers will require a shared and sustained effort as well as the commitment of substantial scientific resources. Just such a commitment is what we strongly recommend.

REFERENCES

Baghurst, P. A., McMichael, A. J., Wigg, N. R., Vimpani, G. V., Robertson, E. F., Roberts, R. J., & Tong, S.-L. (1992). Environmental exposure to lead and children's intelligence at the age of seven years: The Port Pirie cohort study. *New England Journal of Medicine, 327,* 1279-1284.

Bates, T. C., & Eysenck, H. J. (1993). Intelligence, inspection time, and decision time. *Intelligence, 17,* 523-531.

Baumrind, D. (1993). The average expectable environment is not good enough: A response to Scarr. *Child Development, 64*, 1299–1317.

Benbow, C. P. (1988). Sex differences in mathematical reasoning ability in intellectually talented preadolescents: Their nature, effects, and possible causes. *Behavioral and Brain Sciences, 11*, 169–232.

Berenbaum, S. A., & Hines, M. (1992). Early androgens are related to childhood sex-typed toy preferences. *Psychological Science, 3*, 203–206.

Berry, J. W. (1974). Ecological and cultural factors in spatial perceptual development. In J. W. Berry & P. R. Dasen (Eds.), *Culture and cognition: Readings in cross-cultural psychology* (pp. 129–140). London: Methuen.

Bornstein, M. H. (1989). Stability in early mental development: From attention and information processing in infancy to language and cognition in childhood. In M. H. Bornstein & N. A. Krasnegor (Eds.), *Stability and continuity in mental development* (pp. 147–170). Hillsdale, NJ: Erlbaum.

Bouchard, T. J., Jr., Lykken, D. T., McGue, M., Segal, N. L., & Tellegen, A. (1990). Sources of human psychological differences: The Minnesota study of twins reared apart. *Science, 250*, 223–228.

Boykin, A. W. (1986). The triple quandary and the schooling of Afro-American children. In U. Neisser (Ed.), *The school achievement of minority children* (pp. 57–92). Hillsdale, NJ: Erlbaum.

Boykin, A. W. (1994). Harvesting talent and culture: African-American children and educational reform. In R. Rossi (Ed.), *Schools and students at risk* (pp. 116–138). New York: Teachers College Press.

Brandt, E. A. (1984). The cognitive functioning of American Indian children: A critique of McShane and Plas. *School Psychology Review, 13*, 74–82.

Brody, N. (1992). *Intelligence* (2nd ed.). San Diego, CA: Academic Press.

Broman, S. H., Nichols, P. L., & Kennedy, W. A. (1975). *Preschool IQ: Prenatal and early developmental correlates.* Hillsdale, NJ: Erlbaum.

Brown, A. L., & French, A. L. (1979). The zone of potential development: Implications for intelligence testing in the year 2000. In R. J. Sternberg & D. K. Detterman (Eds.), *Human intelligence: Perspectives on its theory and measurement* (pp. 217–235). Norwood, NJ: Ablex.

Campbell, F. A., & Ramey, C. T. (1994). Effects of early intervention on intellectual and academic achievement: A follow-up study of children from low-income families. *Child Development, 65*, 684–698.

Carraher, T. N., Carraher, D., & Schliemann, A. D. (1985). Mathematics in the streets and in schools. *British Journal of Developmental Psychology, 3*, 21–29.

Carroll, J. B. (1993). *Human cognitive abilities: A survey of factor-analytic studies.* Cambridge, England: University of Cambridge Press.

Caryl, P. G. (1994). Early event-related potentials correlate with inspection time and intelligence. *Intelligence, 18*, 15–46.

Ceci, S. J. (1990). *On intelligence … more or less: A biochemical treatise on intellectual development.* Englewood Cliffs, NJ: Prentice-Hall.

Ceci, S. J. (1991). How much does schooling influence general intelligence and its cognitive components? A reassessment of the evidence. *Developmental Psychology, 27*, 703–722.

Ceci, S. J., & Liker, J. (1986). A day at the races: A study of IQ, expertise, and cognitive complexity. *Journal of Experimental Psychology: General, 115*, 255–266.

Chaiken, S. R. (1993). Two models for an inspection time paradigm: Processing distraction and processing speed versus processing speed and asymptotic strength. *Intelligence, 17*, 257–283.

Chipuer, H. M., Rovine, M., & Plomin, R. (1990). LISREL modelling: Genetic and environmental influences on IQ revisited. *Intelligence, 14*, 11–29.

Christal, R. E., Tirre, W., & Kyllonen, P. (1984). Two for the money: Speed and level scores from a computerized vocabulary test. In G. Lee & T. Ulrich (Eds.), *Proceedings, Psychology in the Department of Defense, Ninth Annual Symposium* (USAFA TR 8-2). Colorado Springs, CO: U.S. Air Force Academy.

Christiansen, K., & Knussmann, R. (1987). Sex hormones and cognitive functioning in men. *Neuropsychobiology, 18,* 27–36.

Columbo, J. (1993). *Infant cognition: Predicting later intellectual functioning.* Newbury Park, CA: Sage.

Consortium for Longitudinal Studies. (1983). *As the twig is bent . . . lasting effects of preschool programs.* Hillsdale, NJ: Erlbaum.

Cronbach, L. J., & Snow, R. E. (1977). *Aptitudes and instructional methods.* New York: Irvington.

Darlington, R. B. (1986). Long-term effects of preschool programs. In U. Neisser (Ed.), *The school achievement of minority children* (pp. 159–167). Hillsdale, NJ: Erlbaum.

Davis, C., Haub, C., & Willette, J. (1983). U. S. Hispanics: Changing the face of America. *Population Bulletin, 38* (No. 3).

Deary, I. J. (1993). Inspection time and WAIS-R IQ subtypes: A confirmatory factor analysis study. *Intelligence, 17,* 223–236.

Deary, I. J. (1995). Auditory inspection time and intelligence: What is the causal direction? *Developmental Psychology, 31,* 237–250.

Driver, H. E. (1969). *Indians of North America.* Chicago: University of Chicago Press.

Dube, E. F. (1982). Literacy, cultural familiarity, and "intelligence" as determinants of story recall. In U. Neisser (Ed.), *Memory observed: Remembering in natural contexts* (pp. 274–292). New York: Freeman.

Duran, R. P. (1983). *Hispanics' education and background: Prediction of college achievement.* New York: College Entrance Examination Board.

Eccles, J. S. (1987). Gender roles and women's achievement-related decisions. *Psychology of Women Quarterly, 11,* 135–172.

Eyde, L. D. (1992). Introduction to the testing of Hispanics in industry and research. In K. F. Geisinger (Ed.), *Psychological testing of Hispanics* (pp. 167–172). Washington, DC: American Psychological Association.

Eyferth, K. (1961). Leistungen verchiedener Gruppen von Besatzungskindern im Hamburg-Wechsler Intelligentztest fur Kinder (HAWIK) [The performance of different groups of occupation children in the Hamburg-Wechsler Intelligence Test for Children]. *Archive fur die gesamte Psychologie, 113,* 222–241.

Eysenck, H. (1973). *The measurement of intelligence.* Baltimore: Williams & Wilkins.

Eysenck, H. J. (1986). Inspection time and intelligence: A historical introduction. *Personality and Individual Differences, 7,* 603–607.

Feuerstein, R. (1980). *Instrumental enrichment: An intervention program for cognitive modifiability.* Baltimore: University Park Press.

Flynn, J. R. (1980). *Race, IQ, and Jensen.* London: Routledge & Kegan Paul.

Flynn, J. R. (1984). The mean IQ of Americans: Massive gains 1932 to 1978. *Psychological Bulletin, 95,* 29–51.

Flynn, J. R. (1987). Massive IQ gains in 14 nations: What IQ tests really measure. *Psychological Bulletin, 101,* 171–191.

Flynn, J. R. (1991). *Asian-Americans: Achievement beyond IQ.* Hillsdale, NJ: Erlbaum.

Frearson, W. M., & Eysenck, H. J. (1986). Intelligence, reaction time [RT], and a new "odd-man-out" RT paradigm. *Personality and Individual Differences, 7,* 807–817.

Freedman, D. G., & Freedman, N. C. (1969). Behavioral differences between Chinese-American and European-American newborns. *Nature, 224,* 1227.

Gardner, H. (1983). *Frames of mind: The theory of multiple intelligences.* New York: Basic Books.

Gay, J., & Cole, M. (1967). *The new mathematics and an old culture: A study of learning among the Kpelle of Liberia.* New York: Holt, Rhinehart & Winston.

Geschwind, N., & Galaburda, A. M. (1987). *Cerebral lateralization: Biological mechanisms, associations, and pathology.* Cambridge, MA: MIT Press.

Gordon, H. W., & Lee, P. (1986). A relationship between gonadotropins and visuospatial function. *Neuropsychologia, 24,* 563-576.

Gottfried, A. W. (Ed.). (1984). *Home environment and early cognitive development: Longitudinal research.* New York: Academic Press.

Gouchie, C., & Kimura, D. (1991). The relationship between testosterone levels and cognitive ability patterns. *Psychoneuroendocrinology, 16,* 323-334.

Gould, S. J. (1978). Morton's ranking of races by cranial capacity: Unconscious manipulation of data may be a scientific norm. *Science, 200,* 503-509.

Green, R. L., Hoffman, L. T., Morse, R., Hayes, M. E., & Morgan, R. F. (1964). *The educational status of children in a district without public schools* (Cooperative Research Project No. 2321). Washington, DC: Office of Education, U.S. Department of Health, Education, and Welfare.

Grissmer, D. W., Kirby, S. N., Berends, M., & Williamson, S. (1994). *Student achievement and the changing American family.* Santa Monica, CA: RAND Corporation.

Gustafsson, J.-E. (1984). A unifying model for the structure of the intellectual abilities. *Intelligence, 8,* 179-203.

Haier, R. J. (1993). Cerebral glucose metabolism and intelligence. In P. A. Vernon (Ed.), *Biological approaches to the study of human intelligence* (pp. 317-332). Norwood, NJ: Ablex.

Halpern, D. (1992). *Sex differences in cognitive abilities* (2nd ed.). Hillsdale, NJ: Erlbaum.

Halpern, D. F., & Cass, M. (1994). Laterality, sexual orientation, and immune system functioning: Is there a relationship? *International Journal of Neuroscience, 77,* 167-180.

Hart, B., & Risley, T. R. (1992). American parenting of language-learning children: Persisting differences in family-child interactions observed in natural home environments. *Developmental Psychology, 28,* 1096-1105.

Hart, B., & Risley, T. R. (in press). *Meaningful differences in the everyday experience of young American children.* Baltimore: P. H. Brookes.

Hay, D. A. (1985). *Essentials of behavior genetics.* Melbourne, Australia: Blackwell.

Health, S. B. (1983). *Ways with words.* New York: Cambridge University Press.

Held, J. D., Alderton, D. E., Foley, P. P., & Segall, D. O. (1993). Arithmetic reasoning gender differences: Explanations found in the Armed Services Vocational Aptitude Battery (ASVAB). *Learning and Individual Differences, 5,* 171-186.

Helms, J. E. (1992). Why is there no study of cultural equivalence in standardized cognitive ability testing? *American Psychologist, 47,* 1083-1101.

Hennessy, J. J., & Merrifield, P. R. (1978). Ethnicity and sex distinctions in patterns of aptitude factor scores in a sample of urban high school seniors. *American Educational Research Journal, 15,* 385-389.

Herrnstein, R. J., & Murray, C. (1994). *The bell curve: Intelligence and class structure in American life.* New York: Free Press.

Herrnstein, R. J., Nickerson R. S., de Sanchez, M., & Swets, J. A. (1986). Teaching thinking skills. *American Psychologist, 41,* 1279-1289.

Hines, M. (1990). Gonadal hormones and human cognitive development. In J. Balthazart (Ed.), *Hormones, brains, and behaviors in vertebrates: 1. Sexual differentiation, neuroanatomical aspects, neurotransmitters, and neuropeptides* (pp. 51-63). Basel: Karger.

Hines, M., Chiu, L., McAdams, L. A., Bentler, M. P., & Lipcamon, J. (1992). Cognition and the corpus callosum: Verbal fluency, visuospatial ability, language lateralization related to midsagittal surface areas of the corpus callosum. *Behavioral Neuroscience, 106,* 3-14.

Hunt, E. (1978). Mechanics of verbal ability. *Psychological Review, 85,* 109–130.

Hunter, J. E. (1983). A causal analysis of cognitive ability, job knowledge, job performance, and supervisor ratings. In F. Landy, S. Zedeck, & J. Cleveland (Eds.), *Performance measurement and theory* (pp. 257–266). Hillsdale, NJ: Erlbaum.

Hyde, J., Fennema, E., & Lamon, S. J. (1990). Gender differences in mathematics performance: A meta-analysis. *Psychological Bulletin, 107,* 139–155.

Jackson, G. D. (1975). On the report of the Ad Hoc Committee on Educational Uses of Tests with Disadvantaged Students: Another psychological view from the Association of Black Psychologists. *American Psychologist, 30,* 88–93.

Jackson, M., & McClelland, J. (1979). Processing determinants of reading speed. *Journal of Experimental Psychology: General, 108,* 151–181.

Janowsky, J. S., Oviatt, S. K., & Orwoll, E. S. (1994). Testosterone influences spatial cognition in older men. *Behavioral Neuroscience, 108,* 325–332.

Jardine, R., & Martin, N. G. (1983). Spatial ability and throwing accuracy. *Behavior Genetics, 13,* 331–340.

Jencks, C. (1979). *Who gets ahead? The determinants of economic success in America.* New York: Basic Books.

Jensen, A. R. (1972). *Genetics and education.* New York: Harper & Row.

Jensen, A. R. (1977). Cumulative deficit in IQ of Blacks in the rural South. *Developmental Psychology, 13,* 184–191.

Jensen, A. R. (1980). *Bias in mental testing.* New York: Free Press.

Jensen, A. R. (1985). The nature of the black–white difference on various psychometric tests: Spearman's hypothesis. *Behavioral and Brain Sciences, 8,* 193–263.

Jensen, A. R. (1987). Individual differences in the Hick paradigm. In P. A. Vernon (Ed.), *Speed of information processing and intelligence* (pp. 101–175). Norwood, NJ: Ablex.

Jensen, A. R. (1993). Test validity: *g* vs. "tacit knowledge." *Current Directions in Psychological Science, 2,* 9–10.

Jones, H. E., and Bayley, N. (1941). The Berkeley Growth Study. *Child Development, 12,* 167–173.

Kaufman, A. S. (1994). *Intelligent testing with the WISC-III,* New York: Wiley.

Kaufman, A. S., & Doppelt, J. E. (1976). Analysis of WISC-R standardization data in terms of the stratification variables. *Child Development, 47,* 165–171.

Kohn, M. L., & Schooler, C. (1973). Occupational experience and psychological functioning: An assessment of reciprocal effects. *American Sociological Review, 38,* 97–118.

Kohn, M. L., & Schooler, C. (1983). *Work and personality: An inquiry into the impact of social stratification.* Norwood, NJ: Ablex.

Kranzler, J., & Jensen, A. R. (1989). Inspection time and intelligence: A meta-analysis. *Intelligence, 13,* 329–347.

Lave, J. (1988). *Cognition in practice.* New York: Cambridge University Press.

Law, D. J., Pellegrino, J. W., & Hunt, E. B. (1993). Comparing the tortoise and the hare: Gender differences and experience in dynamic spatial reasoning tasks. *Psychological Science, 4,* 35–40.

Leap, W. L. (1981). American Indian languages. In C. Ferguson & S. B. Heath (Eds.), *Language in the USA.* Cambridge, England: Cambridge University Press.

Lee, E. S. (1951). Negro intelligence and selective migration: A Philadelphia test of the Klineberg hypothesis. *American Sociological Review, 16,* 227–232.

Lesser, G. S., Fifer, G., & Clark, D. H. (1965). Mental abilities of children from different social-class and cultural groups. *Monographs of the Society for Research in Child Development, 30* (Whole No. 102).

Lewontin, R. (1970). Race and intelligence. *Bulletin of the Atomic Scientists, 26,* 2–8.

Linn, M. C., & Petersen, A. C. (1985). Emergence and characterization of sex differences in spatial ability: A meta-analysis. *Child Development, 56,* 1479–1498.

Locurto, C. (1991). Beyond IQ in preschool programs? *Intelligence, 15,* 295–312.

Loehlin, J. C. (1989). Partitioning environmental and genetic contributions to behavioral development. *American Psychologist, 10,* 1285–1292.

Loehlin, J. C., Horn, J. M., & Willerman, L. (1989). Modeling IQ change: Evidence from the Texas Adoption Project. *Child Development, 60,* 993–1004.

Loehlin, J. C., Lindzey, G., & Spuhler, J. N. (1975). *Race differences in intelligence.* New York: Freeman.

Loehlin, J. C., Vandenberg, S. G., & Osborne, R. T. (1973). Blood group genes and Negro–White ability differences. *Behavior Genetics, 3,* 263–270.

Longstreth, L. E. (1984). Jensen's reaction-time investigations of intelligence: A critique. *Intelligence, 8,* 139–160.

Lubchenko, L. O. (1976). *The high-risk infant.* Philadelphia: Saunders.

Lynn, R. (1982). IQ in Japan and the United States shows a growing disparity. *Nature, 297,* 222–223.

Lynn, R. (1990). The role of nutrition in secular increases in intelligence. *Personality and Individual Differences, 11,* 273–285.

Lynn, R. (1993). Oriental Americans: Their IQ, educational attainment, and socio-economic status. *Personality and Individual Differences, 15,* 237–242.

Lynn, R. (1994). Sex differences in intelligence and brain size: A paradox resolved. *Personality and Individual Differences, 17,* 257–271.

Mackenzie, B., Molloy, E., Martin, F., Lovegrove, W., & McNicol, D. (1991). Inspection time and the content of simple tasks: A framework for research on speed of information processing. *Australian Journal of Psychology, 43,* 37–43.

Masters, M. S., & Sanders, B. (1993). Is the gender difference in mental rotation disappearing? *Behavior Genetics, 23,* 337–341.

McCall, R. B., & Garriger, M. S. (1993). A meta-analysis of infant habituation and recognition memory performance as predictors of later IQ. *Child Development, 64,* 57–79.

McCartney, K., Harris, M. J., & Bernieri, F. (1990). Growing up and growing apart: A developmental meta-analysis of twin studies. *Psychological Bulletin, 107,* 226–237.

McGue, M., Bouchard, T. J., Jr., Iacono, W. G., & Lykken, D. T. (1993). Behavioral genetics of cognitive ability: A life-span perspective. In R. Plomin & G. E. McClearn (Eds.), *Nature, nurture, & psychology* (pp. 59–76). Washington, DC: American Psychological Association.

McMichael, A. J., Baghurst, P. A., Wigg, N. R., Vimpani, G. V., Robertson, E. F., & Roberts, R. J. (1988). Port Pirie cohort study: Environmental exposure to lead and children's abilities at the age of four years. *New England Journal of Medicine, 319,* 468–475.

McShane, D. A., & Berry, J. W. (1988). Native North Americans: Indian and Inuit abilities. In S. H. Irvine & J. W. Berry (Eds.), *Human abilities in cultural context* (pp. 385–426). New York: Cambridge University Press.

McShane, D. A., & Cook, V. J. (1985). Transcultural intellectual assessment: Performance by Hispanics on the Wechsler Scales. In B. B. Wolman (Ed.), *Handbook of intelligence: Theories, measurements, and applications.* New York: Wiley.

McShane, D. A., & Plas, J. M. (1984a). Response to a critique of the McShane & Plas review of American Indian performance on the Wechsler Intelligence Scales. *School Psychology Review, 13,* 83–88.

McShane, D. A., & Plas, J. M. (1984b). The cognitive functioning of American Indian children: Moving from the WISC to the WISC-R. *School Psychology Review, 13,* 61–73.

Meehan, A. M. (1984). A meta-analysis of sex differences in formal operational thought. *Child Development, 55,* 1110–1124.

Mercer, J. R. (1984). What is a racially and culturally nondiscriminatory test? A sociological and pluralistic perspective. In C. R. Reynolds & R. T. Brown (Eds.), *Perspectives on bias in mental testing.* New York: Plenum Press.

Moffitt, T. E., Caspi, A., Harkness, A. R., & Silva, P. A. (1993). The natural history of change in intellectual performance: Who changes? How much? Is it meaningful? *Journal of Child Psychology and Psychiatry, 34,* 455-506.

Moffitt, T. E., Gabrielli, W. F., Mednick, S. A., & Schulsinger, F. (1981). Socioeconomic status, IQ, and delinquency. *Journal of Abnormal Psychology, 90,* 152-156.

Mydral, G. (1944). *An American dilemma: The Negro problem and modern democracy.* New York: Harper.

Needleman, H. L., Geiger, S. K., & Frank, R. (1985). Lead and IQ scores: A reanalysis. *Science, 227,* 701-704.

Neisser, U. (1976). General, academic, and artificial intelligence. In L. B. Resnick (Ed.), *The nature of intelligence* (pp. 135-144). Hillsdale, NJ: Erlbaum.

Nettelbeck, T. (1987). Inspection time and intelligence. In P. A. Vernon (Ed.), *Speed of information-processing and intelligence* (pp. 295-346). Norwood, NJ: Ablex.

Nyborg, H. (1984). Performance and intelligence in hormonally different groups. In G. J. DeVries, J. DeBruin, H. Uylings, & M. Cormer (Eds.), *Progress in brain research* (Vol. 61, pp. 491-508). Amsterdam: Elsevier Science.

Ogbu, J. U. (1978). *Minority education and caste: The American system in cross-cultural perspective.* New York: Academic Press.

Ogbu, J. U. (1994). From cultural differences to differences in cultural frames of reference. In P. M. Greenfield & R. R. Cocking (Eds.), *Cross-cultural roots of minority child development* (pp. 365-391). Hillsdale, NJ: Erlbaum.

Okagaki, L., & Sternberg, R. J. (1993). Parental beliefs and children's school performance. *Child Development, 64,* 36-56.

Olivier, G. (1980). The increase of stature in France. *Journal of Human Evolution, 9,* 645-649.

Pascual-Leone, J., & Ijaz, H. (1989). Mental capacity testing as form of intellectual-developmental assessment. In R. J. Samuda, S. L. Kong, et al. (Eds.), *Assessment and placement of minority students.* Toronto: Hogrefe & Huber.

Pedersen, N. L., Plomin, R., Nesselroade, J. R., & McClearn, G. E. (1992). A quantitative genetic analysis of cognitive abilities during the second half of the life span. *Psychological Science, 3,* 346-353.

Pennock-Roman, M. (1992). Interpreting test performance in selective admissions for Hispanic students. In K. F. Geisinger (Ed.), *Psychological testing of Hispanics* (pp. 95-135). Washington, DC: American Psychological Association.

Piaget, J. (1972). *The psychology of intelligence.* Totowa, NJ: Littlefield Adams.

Plomin, R., & Bergeman, C. S. (1991). The nature of nurture: Genetic influence on "environmental" measures. *Behavioral and Brain Sciences, 14,* 373-427.

Plomin, R., DeFries, J. C., & Loehlin, J. C. (1977). Genotype-environment interaction and correlation in the analysis of human behavior. *Psychological Bulletin, 84,* 309-322.

Plomin, R., DeFries, J. C., & McClearn, G. E. (1990). *Behavioral genetics: A primer* (2nd ed.). New York: Freeman.

Pollitt, E., Gorman, K. S., Engle, P. L., Martorell, R., & Rivera, J. (1993). Early supplementary feeding and cognition. *Monographs of the Society for Research in Child Development, 58* (Serial No. 235).

Posner, M. I., Boies, S. J., Eichelman, W. H., & Taylor, R. L. (1969). Retention of visual and name codes of single letters. *Journal of Experimental Psychology, 79,* 1-16.

Reed, T. E., & Jensen, A. R. (1992). Conduction velocity in a brain nerve pathway of normal adults correlates with intelligence level. *Intelligence, 16,* 259-272.

Reed, T. E., & Jensen, A. R. (1993). Choice reaction time and visual pathway conduction velocity both correlate with intelligence but appear not to correlate with each other: Implications for information processing. *Intelligence, 17,* 191–203.

Rehberg, R. A., & Rosenthal, E. R. (1978). *Class and merit in the American high school.* New York: Longman.

Resnick, S. M., Berenbaum, S. A., Gottesman, I. I., & Bouchard, T. J., Jr. (1986). Early hormonal influences on cognitive functioning in congenital adrenal hyperplasia. *Developmental Psychology, 22,* 191–198.

Reynolds, C. R., & Brown, R. T. (1984). Bias in mental testing. An introduction to the issues. In C. R. Reynolds & R. T. Brown (Eds.), *Perspectives on bias in mental testing* (pp. 1–39). New York: Plenum Press.

Reynolds, C. R., Chastain, R. L., Kaufman, A. S., & McLean, J. E. (1987). Demographic characteristics and IQ among adults: Analysis of the WAIS-R standardization sample as a function of the stratification variables. *Journal of School Psychology, 25,* 323–342.

Ricciuti, H. N. (1993). Nutrition and mental development. *Current Directions in Psychological Science, 2,* 43–46.

Roberts, R. C. (1967). Some concepts and methods in quantitative genetics. In J. Hirsch (Ed.), *Behavior-genetic analysis* (pp. 214–257). New York: McGraw-Hill.

Rodriguez, O. (1992). Introduction to technical and societal issues in the psychological testing of Hispanics. In K. F. Geisinger (Ed.), *Psychological testing of Hispanics* (pp. 11–15). Washington, DC: American Psychological Association.

Rose, R. J., Harris, E. L., Christian, J. C., & Nance, W. E. (1979). Genetic variance in non-verbal intelligence: Data from the kinships of identical twins. *Science, 205,* 1153–1155.

Rose, S. A., & Feldman, J. (1995). The prediction of IQ and specific cognitive abilities at 11 years from infancy measures. *Developmental Psychology, 31,* 685–696.

Rosetti, L. (1986). *High risk infants: Identification, assessment, and intervention.* Boston: Little, Brown.

Rush, D., Stein, Z., Susser, M., & Brody, N. (1980). Outcome at one year of age: Effects on somatic and psychological measures. In D. Rush, Z. Stein, & M. Susser (Eds.), *Diet in pregnancy: A randomized controlled trial of nutritional supplements.* New York: Liss.

Saudino, K. J., Plomin, R., Pedersen, N. L., & McClearn, G. E. (1994). The etiology of high and low cognitive ability during the second half of the life span. *Intelligence, 19,* 359–371.

Scarr, S. (1992). Developmental theories for the 1990s: Development and individual differences. *Child Development, 63,* 1–19.

Scarr, S. (1993). Biological and cultural diversity: The legacy of Darwin for development. *Child Development, 64,* 1333–1353.

Scarr, S., Pakstis, A. J., Katz, S. H., & Barker, W. B. (1977). Absence of a relationship between degree of White ancestry and intellectual skills within a Black population. *Human Genetics, 39,* 69–86.

Scarr, S., & Weinberg, R. A. (1978). The influence of "family background" on intellectual attainment. *American Sociological Review, 43,* 674–692.

Scarr, S., Weinberg, R. A., & Waldman, I. D. (1993). IQ correlations in transracial adoptive families. *Intelligence, 17,* 541–555.

Schmidt, F. L., & Hunter, J. E. (1993). Tacit knowledge, practical intelligence, and job knowledge. *Current Directions in Psychological Science, 2,* 8–9.

Schneider, B., Hieshima, J. A., Lee, S., & Plank, S. (1994). East-Asian academic success in the United States: Family, school, and cultural explanations. In P. M. Greenfield & R. R. Cocking (Eds.), *Cross-cultural roots of minority child development* (pp. 332–350). Hillsdale, NJ: Erlbaum.

Schoenthaler, S. J., Amos, S. P., Eysenck, H. J., Peritz, E., & Yudkin, J. (1991). Controlled trial of vitamin-mineral supplementation: Effects on intelligence and performance. *Personality and Individual Differences, 12,* 351–362.

Seashore, H., Wesman, A., & Doppelt, J. (1950). The standardization of the Wechsler Intelligence Scale for Children. *Journal of Consulting Psychology, 14,* 99–110.

Serpell, R. (1974). *Estimates of intelligence in a rural community of Eastern Zambia: Human Development Research Unit Reports, 25,* Mimeo, Lusaka: University of Zambia.

Serpell, R. (1979). How specific are perceptual skills? A cross-cultural study of pattern reproduction. *British Journal of Psychology, 70,* 365–380.

Shaywitz, B. A., Shaywitz, S. E., Pugh, K. R., Constable, R. T., Skudlarski, P., Fulbright, R. K., Bronen, R. A., Fletcher, J. M., Shankweiler, D. P., Katz, L., & Gore, J. C. (1995). Sex differences in the functional organization of the brain for language. *Nature, 373,* 607–609.

Sigman, M. (1995). Nutrition and child development: More food for thought. *Current Directions in Psychological Science, 4,* 52–55.

Spearman, C. (1927). *The abilities of man.* New York: Macmillan.

Stanley, J. (1993). Boys and girls who reason well mathematically. In G. R. Bock and K. Ackrill (Eds.), *The origins and development of high ability.* Chichester, England: Wiley.

Stanley, J. C., Benbow, C. P., Brody, L. E., Dauber, S., & Lupkowski, A. (1992). Gender differences on eighty-six nationally standardized aptitude and achievement tests. In N. Colangelo, S. G. Assouline, & D. L. Ambroson (Eds.), *Talent development, Vol. 1: Proceedings from the 1991 Henry B. and Jocelyn Wallace National Research Symposium on Talent Development.* Unionville, NY: Trillium Press.

Stein, Z., Susser, M., Saenger, G., & Marolla, F. (1975). *Famine and human development: The Dutch hunger winter of 1944–45.* New York: Oxford University Press.

Sternberg, R. J. (1977). *Intelligence, information processing, and analogical reasoning: The componential analysis of human abilities.* Hillsdale, NJ: Erlbaum.

Sternberg, R. J. (1985). *Beyond IQ: A triarchic theory of human intelligence.* New York: Cambridge University Press.

Sternberg, R. J., & Detterman, D. K. (Eds.), (1986). *What is intelligence? Contemporary viewpoints on its nature and definition.* Norwood, NJ: Ablex.

Sternberg, R. J., & Wagner, R. K. (1993). The geocentric view of intelligence and job performance is wrong. *Current Directions in Psychological Science, 2,* 1–4.

Sternberg, R. J., Wagner, R. K., Williams, W. M., & Horvath, J. A. (1995). Testing common sense. *American Psychologist, 50,* 912–927.

Stevenson, H. W., Lee, S. Y., & Stigler, J. W. (1986). Mathematics achievement of Chinese, Japanese, and American children. *Science 231,* 693–699.

Stevenson, H. W., & Stigler, J. W. (1992). *The learning gap.* New York: Summit Books.

Stevenson, H. W., Stigler, J. W., Lee, S. Y., Lucker, G. W., Kitamura, S., & Hsu, C. C. (1985). Cognitive performance and academic achievement of Japanese, Chinese, and American children. *Child Development, 56,* 718–734.

Streissguth, A. P., Barr, H. M., Sampson, P. D., Darby, B. L., & Martin, D. C. (1989). IQ at age 4 in relation to maternal alcohol use and smoking during pregnancy. *Developmental Psychology, 25,* 3–11.

Super, C. M. (1983). Cultural variation in the meaning and uses of children's "intelligence." In J. B. Deregowski, S. Dziurawiec, & R. C. Annis (Eds.), *Explorations in cross-cultural psychology.* Lisse, Netherlands: Swets & Zeitlinger.

Sutaria, S. D. (1985). *Specific learning disabilities: Nature and needs.* Springfield, IL: Charles C. Thomas.

Terman, L. M. (1925). *Genetic studies of genius: Mental and physical traits of a thousand gifted children.* Palo Alto, CA: Stanford University Press.

Terman, L. M., & Merrill, M. A. (1937). *Measuring intelligence: A guide to the administration of the new revised Stanford-Binet tests of intelligence.* Boston: Houghton Mifflin.

Thomson, G. H. (1939). *The factorial analysis of human ability.* Boston: Houghton Mifflin.

Thorndike, R. L., Hagen, E. P., & Sattler, J. M. (1986). *Stanford-Binet intelligence scale: Fourth edition (Technical Manual).* Chicago: Riverside.

Thurstone, L. L. (1938). *Primary mental abilities.* Chicago: University of Chicago Press.

Turkheimer, E. (1991). Individual and group differences in adoption studies of IQ. *Psychological Bulletin, 110,* 392–405.

United States Bureau of the Census. (1994). *The Hispanic population of the United States: March 1993* (Current Population Reports, Series P20-475). Washington, DC: Author.

United States National Commission for Employment Policy (1982). *Hispanics and jobs: Barriers to progress* (Report No. 14). Washington, DC: Author.

Vernon, P. A. (1987). *Speed of information processing and intelligence.* Norwood, NJ: Ablex.

Vernon, P. A. (1993). *Biological approaches to the study of human intelligence.* Norwood, NJ: Ablex.

Vickers, D., Nettelbeck, T., & Wilson, R. J. (1972) Perceptual indices of performance: The measurement of "inspection time" and "noise" in the visual system. *Perception, 1,* 263–295.

Vincent, K. R. (1991). Black/White IQ differences: Does age make the difference? *Journal of Clinical Psychology, 47,* 266–270.

Vygotsky, L. S. (1978). *Mind in society: The development of higher psychological processes.* Cambridge, MA: Harvard University Press.

Waller, J. H. (1971). Achievement and social mobility: Relationships among IQ score, education, and occupation in two generations. *Social Biology, 18,* 252–259.

White, K. R. (1982). The relation between socioeconomic status and academic achievement. *Psychological Bulletin, 91,* 461–481.

Wober, M. (1974). Towards an understanding of the Kiganda concept of intelligence. In J. W. Berry & P. R. Dasen (Eds.), *Culture and cognition: Readings in cross-cultural psychology* (pp. 261–280). London: Methuen.

Yairi, E., & Ambrose, N. (1992). Onset of stuttering in preschool children: Selected factors. *Journal of Speech and Hearing Research, 35,* 782–788.

QUESTIONS FOR FURTHER THOUGHT

1. What are some of the main conceptions of the nature of intelligence?

2. What is the best available evidence regarding the degree of heritability of intelligence?

3. What are some alternative explanations of why group differences in intelligence are found on conventional intelligence tests?

4. What is the Flynn effect, and what might explain it?

5. What prompted the origin and publication of this report? Is this appropriate?